To

Amy Meeper

Enjoy!

Dennis Erdey

1997

KERMIT EDNEY
REMEMBERS

Where Fitz Left Off

Kermit Edney

Publisher: Ralph Roberts

Vice President/Publishing: Pat Roberts

Dust Jacket Design: Gayle Graham

Editors: Barbara Blood, Susan Parker

Interior Design and Electronic Page Assembly: **WorldComm**®

Printed in the United States of America

10 9 8 7 6 5 4 3 2 1

Library of Congress Cataloging-in-Publication

Edney, Kermit.   1924-
    Kermit Edney remembers where Fitz left off / Kermit Edney.
       p.   cm.
    Includes index.
    ISBN 1-56664-126-8 (hc : alk. paper)
    1. Hendersonville (N.C.)--History.   2. Hendersonville (N.C.)--Social life and customs.   3. Hendersonville (N.C.)--Biography.
    4. Edney, Kermit, 1924- . I. Title.
    F264.H49E35   1997
    975.6'92--dc21
                                                  97-42207
                                                     CIP

WorldComm®—a division of Creativity, Inc.–is a full-service publisher located at 65 Macedonia Road, Alexander NC 28701. Phone (704) 252-9515 or (704) 255-8719 fax.

WorldComm® is distributed to the trade by **Alexander Distributing**™, 65 Macedonia Road, Alexander NC 28701. Phone (704) 252-9515 or (704) 255-8719 fax. For orders only: 1-800-472-0438. Visa and MasterCard accepted.

This book is also available on the internet in the **Publishers CyberMall**™. Set your browser to http://www.abooks.com and enjoy the many fine values available there.

Table of Contents

Dedicated to
Dr. Kenneth Cosgrove

Preface
by Jody Barber

Everyone about my age growing up near Hendersonville knew Oscar Meyer, the local pioneer of aviation. While I was still in high school, I was privileged on Sunday afternoon to work at the airport concession stand and during the week would trade those hours in on flying lessons from Oscar. Through those early years and still today I have a profound respect for that man and his ability as a pilot. It is flattering when someone talks about the old grass strip airport and associates my name with Oscar Meyer as Kermit has done in this book.

As Kermit and I were growing, we probably nodded to each other while walking barefoot along Main Street but our friendship started after World War II. For more than fifty years I have watched, listened to and worked with Kermit Edney. With profound respect, the children and grandchildren of this community should know about Kermit, his visions, his accomplishments and the impact he has had on our town.

Kermit was born in Hendersonville, attended Rosa Edwards and while in the fourth grade, transferred to Edneyville. His military service during World War II was with the 12th Armored Division in Europe. After the war but before leaving, he wrote a history of the 152nd Armored Signal Company reflecting every station and bivouac of the Company during the entire war, along with the name and home address (at the time of enlistment) of every member of the Company, a priceless document these fifty years later to some 200 survivors.

Influenced by his brother Grady, whom he idolized, Kermit chose to enter the field of broadcasting so he changed his major at the University of North Carolina to the field of Radio, TV, and Motion Pictures. When his father was totally disabled by a stroke, he returned home to care for the family and found a job with the newly licensed local station WHKP.

Having our own local radio station opened up a whole new world of local news. The *Times-News* was an afternoon newspaper. Most of us had changed our radios from WWNC in Asheville to WHKP and the dial was never moved off 1450. Kermit extended the number of hours in his day and it seemed that no matter what time of the morning, he was there. His Good Morning Man theme song was "On The Sunny Side Of The Street," and he used a two-tone door chime to punctuate his announcing the correct time. Kermit again extended his work day, getting up an extra hour early in the morning to have breakfast at the Hot Spot so he would know what the average man on the street was talking about. It was not uncommon to see Kermit with mismatched socks . . . he dressed in the dark to avoid waking his "child bride."

After Jimmy Fain retired as editor of the *Times-News* we spent many hours together discussing what he found in the basement of the Courthouse (number two, built in 1904 on Main Street). There were handwritten minutes of town meetings and other records which were the history of our community. A name which we already knew appeared in document after document. That of William A. Smith.

W.A. Smith, an attorney/businessman, was elected mayor of Hendersonville in 1880. He resigned so that he could become the town attorney, and wrote the charter for the town and many ordinances, after which he was re-elected mayor. With offices at 4th and Main he also founded the Oklawaha Land Company, the W.A. Smith Estates, the Florida Carolina Estates, the Laurel Park Estates and even started the Town of Laurel Park. He built lakes, canals, observation towers, dance pavilions, club houses and the Laurel Park Railway System. He built an inn on the top of Sugar Loaf Mountain. He headed banks, saving and loan groups and even edited a local newspaper.

Jimmy Fain had a well grounded respect for Kermit. They worked together creating a local power of the press. Neither had the desire for a political office but their written/spoken word has made the difference in more than one election. Having a few more years in age, Jimmy would allow his mind to wander about our town, wondering about how about how various problems could be solved. We both realized that in Kermit Edney, we had another W.A. Smith.

The green pea and roast beef circuit added still more hours to Kermit's day. Every Chamber of Commerce annual meeting, and Merchants Association, and Kiwanis Ladies' Night. . .and every other club or group had to have Kermit. The Apple Festival fell on its face when Kermit wasn't available and they brought in a high priced TV star from Charlotte.

Katherine and Kermit have two children, Kerry (Kermit Edney, Jr.) and Katina. Their pets had names starting with the letter K, and now their grandchildren's names start with K.

One simple reason why Kermit is so well known and loved: Up until a few years ago we had two school systems. If the weather was just threatening, the city would have school but with school busses on back roads, the county would not. Children, my daughter included, thought of Kermit as their personal friend, so if there was a skim of snow when they woke up in the morning, they called Kermit and asked "Is there any school today?" Remember, over a period of fifty years those kids have grown up to be the mainstay of our community.

During large public meeting as well as many, many sessions in the "smoke filled rooms" it was fascinating to watch Kermit and see his frustration with all the ranting and raving over nit-picky issues. I knew his patience and learned to wait for him to condense all that had been argued for hours into the fewest possible word and suggest a game plan to solve the problem.

Two years before Will Smith died, the whole town turned out in his honor and presented him with a loving cup inscribed "To the Famed William A. Smith-Best Loved Citizen and Builder of Our Town."

Kermit Edney has become Will Smith's successor. What would we have done without him? As you read chapter after chapter, you will begin to see his total involvement in most thing that are of benefit to the general public. His creative talent is like magic. For over fifty years I have been privileged on many occasions to stand by his side. With these pages you have the opportunity to walk along with Kermit and let him tell you what happened.

–Jody Barber
September, 1997

A Word From The Author

When Art Cooley asked me to do a radio series to mark WHKP's 50th Anniversary, there was no question about the format. Frank L. FitzSimons for twenty-five years had mastered the art of radio storytelling with his "From The Banks Of The Oklawaha" series which he then edited into a three-volume set of books he liked to call "his trilogy."

I knew that I could try to emulate, but there was no way I could duplicate the magnetism of his voice, nor continuously conjure up the precise words which made his tale worth telling.

His closings were all original masterpieces, "when I speak to you again from the banks of the cool, rippling waters of the Oklawaha" (Indian for Mud Creek). Every ending was different, ranging from "the ice-covered, snowy banks," to "warm, sunny banks." If I could just dream up an imaginative ending, maybe the listeners would forgive me for having the impudence to call the program "Where Fitz Left Off."

When I was very young, my dad used to rub my head and say, "You have much to accomplish. You have a very broad forehead, and you're the seventh son of a seventh son." That was not exactly true, but I was the seventh child of a seventh child, and my forehead would become more expansive as the years went by.

In January of 1966, I received a letter from my old and dear friend Senator Jesse Helms in which he used a closing: Sursume corda. My curiosity got the best of me, and I finally found the words in my Webster's unabridged dictionary. In the Anglican Church, the Latin phrase means "lift up your hearts," addressed by the celebrant to the congregation.

I queried Senator Helms about his use of Sursume Corda to close his letters, and he responded:

"I am intrigued with the reaction you've had to 'sursume corda.' I began using it in private correspondence with special friends sometime back after I ran across it in the dictionary. If I remember correctly, my high school principal used it in a letter, so he and I began using it instead of 'Sincerely' or 'Yours truly.' I think its meaning is far more meaningful than either of those."

This, then explains the closing I devised which concluded each of the 260 programs broadcast:

"Another thought from this seventh child of a seventh child, lucky enough to have been born here, the good sense never to leave and with a job he's loved all his life, Sursume Corda (Lift up your hearts) as we approach the next fifty years."

I am told by my Catholic friends that the phrase is used as part of a belief response before the preface of the Mass.

I felt that I had been successful in devising a closing memorable enough to make listeners want to tune in again, when I discovered that most people were more concerned with the meaning of 'Sursume Corda' than anything else I had said.

Thanks: To Art Cooley who convinced me that is was my duty to do the radio series which required all the research. To my child-bride, Katherine, who has tolerated books, notes, pads, typewriters, word processors, copy machines, and a total preoccupation with this project for two years. To Oma Edney who typed the manuscript, and to my daughter Katina Hampton who prepared the Appendix. To Jody and Mary Barber for help beyond definition.

And finally, the encouragement of friends, (whether sincere or not) who insisted that it was my duty to preserve my experiences and observations for reference by future generations.

> –Kermit Edney
> Hendersonville, N.C.
> 1997

Tricks Memory Will Play

I was born and raised in Hendersonville and having been a part of the staff of WHKP for most all of the past 50 years, I figured I could put together a radio series of local vignettes from memory. For years, I had enjoyed regaling newcomers with stories of either the way the town used to be, or describing the antics or adventures of some of the unusual characters who had not only lived here but left their mark on the community. After sharing with an unusually appreciative audience some of the antics or eccentric ways of such people as Walter B. Smith ("B" as in bull–"S" as in sunshine); the late and great S.T. "Smiley" McCall; Phil Kelly, who founded the Second Wind Hall of Fame; or Milas Case, who Kelly says was the world's greatest salesman, invariably, folks would insist, "You ought to write a book. The stories are priceless, and once you're gone, there'll be no one to remember them."

It dawned on me during the very first week of the radio series– "Kermit, you've bitten off a challenge that's going to be hard to chew." When you're sitting around after dinner, in a totally informal atmosphere, you're entitled to use generalities; and if you don't remember exact names or dates, it doesn't dull the story you're telling. And, if your memory gets a bit clouded, you can just brush over the blank and no one knows the difference.

As I started to put together the series, I thought it appropriate to recall the way Main Street was when WHKP signed on the air on October 24, 1946. I thought I could remember every crack in the sidewalks from 1st to 7th Avenue. I was in for a quick and startling discovery. My mind quickly produced an indelible picture of Skin Drake's Store and the A&P Food Store across 1st Avenue on Main. I could remember Carl Brown's O.K. Store and Hayes Market and even Walker Hardware Company. But what other businesses were on that very first block? I pulled a total blank.

To my rescue came Harold Huggins, who worked most of his life for Shepherd's Funeral Home. Harold knew the locations of every cemetery (public and private) and in many cases who was buried where. But Harold, bless his heart, was what my mama would have called a pack rat. Any time he ran across anything old or memorable, he'd save it, and I knew he had in his possession a 1946 City Directory of Hendersonville. The back had long since been torn off, it was yellowed with age and utmost care was required to leaf through the pages without them falling loose from the binding. A similar directory, in very good condition, is also in the local history section of the library, but it cannot be checked out. I knew that as the year went by, this directory (along with a 1946 phone book loaned to me by Gordon Carpenter) would be in constant use, and Harold and Gordon were kind enough to loan me their directories.

The city directory reminded me that just above Walker Hardware was the City Cafe, which I did remember— and then there was the Dixie Home Store at 126 N. Main and The Food Store on the corner of 2nd and Main. Neither business rang a bell of any sort. Fred Pressley was manager of the Dixie Store on Main, and the larger Dixie Store on 5th Ave. was managed by Maurice Owens. The Food Store was owned and operated by Roy and Marvin Taylor. I don't remember the Food Store at all. And yet, a picture in the chapter dealing with the dedication of the Woodmen of the World water fountain clearly shows The Food Store on the corner diagonally across from the stump-shaped fountain that stands on the northwest corner of 2nd and Main. Paul Garner was manager of the A&P Store across from Skin Drake's historic establishment, and Carroll Presson was manager of the A&P at the corner of 6th and Main.

Those first "chain stores" were not supermarkets as we know them today. They looked just like any other grocery store except they sold only for cash, and did not carry hardware, cloth, sewing thread or other items carried by many of the general food stores. A&P did offer (in the beginning) their famous 8 O'Clock Coffee freshly ground. And both the A&P and the Dixie Home Stores were able to get volume discounts which allowed them to sell at lower prices, and they advertised heavily in the *Times-News.* Jimmy Fain, the *T-N* Editor, once told me that during the days of the Depression, chain store grocery ads made the payroll for the newspaper.

The Times-News was an afternoon daily published except on Sunday in a part of the old Henderson County Bank Building, which is now occupied by Scotties. The old hotel first built as the Ripley House (and variously known as the Globe, the Gates, the St. John) burned in 1915 leaving a littered eyesore for some 25 years. The newspaper carrier boys would play on the red clay bank of the burned-out hole until the papers were ready for delivery. The paper moved to 6th Avenue on September 28, 1941.

Mr. Hugh A. Nuckolls bought the corner lot at 2nd and Main and erected a two-story brick building which housed Nu-Better Foods. For years, this building was known as Nuckoll's Building until its name was changed to the Toms Building after being bought by Jim Toms. Just up the street was

Cowan's Grocery, run by Ellis Cowan, and on the other side of the street was Carolina Fruit Co. run by Fay Hall and Gardner Shipman. I discovered that instead of three or four grocery stores near the Court House (as I had first remembered), there were actually eight grocery stores within a block and a half of the old Jockey Lot. Frank FitzSimons recalls the glory days of the Jockey Lot in Vol. I, "From the Banks of the Oklawaha."

In the earlier days of Hendersonville, farmers would load their wagons with produce, and hitch all day at the Jockey Lot where animals had access to fresh running water, which ran in a continuous stream through a cement trough in the middle of the lot. From this location, farmers could peddle their goods or barter with the various food merchants, all located nearby. Back then even the chain stores had authority to barter and trade goods with the farmer. One business that still operates on Main Street (though it's on the other side of the street) is McFarlan's Bake Shop, which was operated in 1946 by Earl McFarlan. Wayne Cole worked for Earl McFarlan, and his son Mike runs the bake shop today. And it's only the old timers like Jody Barber, Johnny McLeod, Larry Feagin and other locals who grew up here that remember "Dad" Croasdale's Florida Fruit Market. "Dad" not only had specimen fancy fruits but an elaborate line of penny candies. "Dad" sold peppermint patties for a penny; and if you happened to get one with a pink center, you got a nickel candy bar free. I never saw a pink center in all the years he ran the fruit stand. F.W. Woolworth and McLellans both had very successful 5 and 10 cent stores in the '40s. Between 4th and 5th Avenues, sandwiched in between Woolworth's and O.E. Bass Jewelers, was City Meat Market and Dorn's Grocery. This was the building in which Japan Art & Gift Shop operated prior to World War II. I worked for the Japanese owner (Kantaro Endo) as a high school student, and I never knew a finer American. He is buried at Refuge Cemetery. Finally, in food stores, there was the A&P mentioned earlier (at the corner of 6th and Main). It was the most like a supermarket of any of the food stores of the '40s; and across Main Street was John Ellison's Market and Johnson's Stop & Shop run by Manual Johnson.

In addition to McFarlan's, there was one other bakery on Main when WHKP signed on the air. It was Quality Bakery run by Sam Hottel at 524 North Main near the Skyland Hotel. Just one of the new mega-markets today would probably have an inventory that would equal the total stock of all the independently owned food stores and markets doing business in the 1940s. And yet this awesome selection of merchandise can be a nuisance. Want to buy a Coke? Should you choose classic or new? Or maybe Diet Coke, or Diet Coke without caffeine—each in a multitude of sizes in cans or plastic, glass or bottles; and they've got a new contoured plastic bottle for Coke, bringing a new wave of packaging of the same basic products that were displayed on a single counter in the 1940s. You could also see with your own eyes the rich cream at the top of every quart of milk. Back then you had a choice of whole or skimmed (called Blue John). Today, you have whole, 2%,

The candy counter and record racks in the McLellan's 5 & 10 ¢ Store on Main between 3rd and 4th. The Hallmark Shop is in one of the buildings today. Note the patriotic World War II decorations.

1%, ½% or skimmed—and all selling at about the same price. The biggest headache for the modern food shopper, however, is the total emphasis on pre-packaging. Whether it's meat, cheese, coffee (usually ground and pre-packaged), crackers, chips or even raisins or dates – everything is packed or blister-packed. Beware to the shopper who in haste simply picks up an item near the front of a display without checking expiration dates for freshness. I had to return raisins to a local superstore because their freshness had expired more than a year earlier. The little independent operator of yesteryears knew every item in the store. You could be sure he personally supervised rotation of stock, and he was always on hand to be sure you were pleased with the goods he sold to you. In produce he was Walter.

Not a Store—An Institution

As I grew up in Hendersonville, I simply took for granted "Skin" Drake's store on the corner of 1st and Main. Although the building was old and weather-beaten as far back as I can remember, I never realized that it was the first store that was built in the town of Hendersonville. It was constructed up off the ground and you had to climb several steps to get inside. It was a store that appealed to farmers, hunters, traders and "tellers of tall tales." Mountain men would bring the biggest rattlesnake they could catch into the store and Mr. Drake would always offer to add it to those he already had in cages. As a youngster, I always feared one of the snakes had gotten out of its cage and was wriggling around under the floor of the store; and so I ran past the store as fast as I could. I was never concerned with "Skin" Drake's real name. I knew his initials were H.E. because painted on the windows facing Main Street was "H.E. Drake Groceries."

My brother, the late Grady Edney, who was the really professional broadcaster in our family, was always fascinated with the unusual nicknames tagged onto people here. "Damon Runyon would have a field day," he laughed and recalled sobriquets such as "Pretty Daddy" Gibbs, "Polka Dot" Anders, "Strawberry" Brock, "Rosebud" Nelson, "Greasy" Barnett, "Dump" Stepp, "Bully" Waldrop, "Sleepy" Brookshire or "Pappy" Lampley. I didn't know until I was doing the radio series "Where Fitz Left Off" that "Skin" Drake's real name was H. Elezar Drake, probably a slight misspelling of the biblical Eleazer. His daughter (Kay Drake Miller) told me how he had come by the nickname "Skin." "Well," she said, "Daddy was always so skinny, I guess they just shortened it down to 'Skin.'"

That old building which served as Hendersonville's first post office was acquired by Mr. Flave Hart who Mrs. H. Patterson would always smile and say, "The cabbage king!" With the coming of the railroad, Mr. Hart became the first major produce broker of the area. He used the big wooden store building and the vacant lot behind the store which would become the Jockey Lot. Mr. Hart would weigh and purchase produce both there and also at the railroad siding at the depot. Flave Hart was grandfather to Louise Howe Bailey.

The famous Florida Fruit Market operated by Dad Croasdale on the East Side of Main Street between 3rd and 4th. A Collins-McCord Department Store was built here in the '50s, and later became the Home Food Shop.

The building was later acquired from Hart by M.M. Shepherd, who ran a general store in that location until he had built a new building in the block between 2nd and 3rd Avenues. The upstairs of the old building was leased by Jody Barber's "Uncle Baker," who remodeled the building for a portrait studio (adding a huge skylight in the roof) and made it the photographic center of the entire county. Later, Baker would build his own building at the corner of 4th and Main and still later another building, which was demolished to make way for the new First Federal Building, now First Citizens Bank. When Baker vacated the old wooden building across from the court house, it was acquired by H.E. Drake and made into a general store complete with a big pot-bellied stove, around which customers and just plain loafers would stand and warm themselves on the cold days of winter.

Working with "Skin" in the store was his brother Robert, who thought the sun rose and set on a little boy named Jeff Miller. Jeff's mother (Kay) was Robert's niece; and anything that Jeff Miller wanted, you could be sure would be provided by Great Uncle Robert. When I was doing the radio series, I asked Jeff if he remembered the rattlesnakes in his grandfather's store. "No, but I remember throwin' and bustin' eggs!"

"Bustin' eggs???"

"Yeah," he said, "my Uncle Robert spoiled me and he'd say, 'Jeff, you want to bust some eggs?' And I'd just stand there and throw and bust egg after egg."

I asked his mother (Kay Drake Miller) about this. "Did your Uncle Robert really let Jeff throw eggs inside the store building?"

"He sure did," she answered. "What did Robert do, keep track of the eggs figuring how long it had been from the cackle, and just let Jeff get rid of the older eggs?"

"Nooo," she said, "he would let him throw eggs Dad had just traded for."

"But where did he throw them?"

"On the floor," she said. "You've never seen such a mess he'd make, and then I'd have to clean it up."

Jeff Miller today owns and operates Miller's Laundry and Cleaners, founded by his grandfather, and in which his own dad (Bert) and uncles Norman, Ted and Winfield all grew up working. Jeff admits he still likes to bust eggs!

"Skin" had another brother, Albert W. Drake, who was an outstanding builder and also mayor of Laurel Park. Not only did "Skin" have the unusual name of Elezar, but his wife's name was Armilda, which Kay says everyone shortened down to "Mildy." "Skin" and "Mildy" had four children: H.B., Orlette (who married Preston Lane), Everette, and, as mentioned, Katherine (or Kay), who married Bert Miller. The Drake family was raised in a big house which stood on the corner of Barnwell and Church, just three and a half blocks from his famous store. This property was sold in December 1954 to Hunter Atha, and today the main office of Wachovia Bank covers the entire block.

What's in a Name?

In 1946, when WHKP first signed on, Hendersonville could boast of a Ft. Sumter Cannon, a walking and talking X Ray, as well as J. Fenimore Cooper, H.G. Wells and Ulysses S. Grant.

Ft. Sumter Cannon was born into the Cannon family of Tembroke, Ga. I knew Ft. Sumter quite well—a bright and pleasant personality, which you had to have if your daddy (in a light-hearted moment) named you Ft. Sumter. He had taught school and engaged in truck farming in the Charleston area. Later he became involved in the hotel business in South Carolina and Florida, and finally became connected with Metropolitan Life Insurance Company. He spent his summers in Hendersonville, and from time to time bought real estate in this area, including the tract of land and a house on which radio station WHKP now stands. He died in 1954.

The elder Mr. Cannon was not the only father with a sense of humor. A Walter Lenoir Ray worked for the *Asheville Citizen* and elected to name his first son simply "X." The young man would have probably taken less ribbing if he had been named Roentgen. Mr. Ray named his third son Horace Greeley Ray, and his fourth son Theodore Roosevelt Ray (although he later changed his name simply to Ted R. Ray and made quite a reputation for himself as one of the top executives of Harcourt Brace Jovanovich, publishers). Not only did the father, Walter Lenoir Ray, work for the post office, but the son he named "X" also became a postal employee; and X's son, Charles Lenoir Ray, became Postmaster at Flat Rock. Charles Lenoir Ray was fascinated by the evolution of postal service in the Western Carolina mountains, and authored a book titled "Postmarks," which is now out of print and a collector's item. It not only identified all of the small post offices which at one time or another served neighborhoods in Henderson County, but Lenoir was able to research the names of the many families who operated these post offices. It established a whole new resource for genealogists tracing local family histories. Lenoir was very active in veterans and civic affairs. He

Walter Lenoir Ray, who worked for the Asheville Citizen, named his first son X Ray, his third son Horace Greeley Ray, and his fourth son Theodore Roosevelt Ray (pictured).

married Lucille Stepp Ray, who worked for many years with Noah Hollowell in the *Western Carolina Tribune* and also at the *Times-News*. Lenoir died at the age of 48 in 1971.

The J. Fenimore Cooper who lived here in 1946 did not write "The Deerslayer" or "The Pathfinder" but worked as freight agent for Southern Railroad.

Our H.G. Wells had nothing to do with "The War of the Worlds" or any other book as far as I know. He was a realtor with offices in the Hunter Building on Main Street. Back in 1946, his office phone number was 27 and his home phone was 29J.

And our Ulysses S. Grant did not gain fame as a general nor as the 18th president of the United States. Instead he became well known by the molasses he sells in the fall of the year; and at the time the radio program was broadcast covering this material, he was the only one still living with one of these unusual names. He is a son of John Vernon Grant of Fruitland.

By the way, Kermit Edney was around a long time before Miss Piggy and her frog friend appeared. I was supposed to have been named for my grandfather, the Rev. Thomas Jefferson Waters. Dad didn't like the name Thomas, and he had about made up his mind to name me Kermit Jefferson Edney. On the way to the Register of Deeds office, he ran into his sister, Aunt Sally Kate Pace, who convinced him that "it would be a travesty to hang the name Jefferson on that child." When he filled out the birth certificate, it was simply Kermit Edney—no middle name. And in the military, at all formations when your last name is called, you answer with your first name and middle initial. Thus throughout World War II, every time my name was called . . . "EDNEY". . .I'd yell back, "Kermit N M I" (no middle initial). After treating my son Kerry with the same thing (only adding Junior) when his son was born, he (being in the military) revolted:

"There ain't no way I'm going to name a child without a middle name."

Very few people realized that Berry was his middle name for he was widely known in Henderson County by his first and middle names, Green Berry. Green Berry Hill lived on Chimney Rock Road on the first plateau below Edneyville headed toward Reedy Patch. When all the banks closed during the Depression, he became one of the wealthier men in the county. He had invested only in Canadian bonds. He not only farmed but was active in politics. Dad used to say that in the olden days, Green Berry could take fifty dollars and make Edneyville precinct vote either way.

Robert McCall, who everyone knew only as "Fats," for obvious reasons. Shown here at a sports event, Fats was an avid fan whose greatest joy was heckling the officials.

Few people would recognize the name Robert McCall, but every sports fan in those early WHKP years would be familiar with "Fats" McCall. "Fats" drove a delivery truck for Gossett Furniture Company, and although overload springs had been installed on the driver's side, when "Fats" plopped his weight in the cab, the entire truck would tilt. He was a diehard sports fan, and along with an entourage of fans who constantly egged him on, he was a mortal terror, especially at basketball games when he tried to find a seat on the front row near the centerline and started working on the officials even before the game began.

I always thought "Greasy" Barnette got his nickname for driving a Thomas Shepherd ambulance as fast as greased lightning. It was only in the last year that I was told that when he was a baby (after baths) his mother would put so much baby oil on he and his sister that his Uncle Gus Johnson nicknamed him "Greasy" and his sister "Shiny."

I have no idea as to why Mr. Grey Newman named his son Brown.

And for cruelty in naming a child, the distinction would go without question to James Stephen Hogg, who was governor of Texas. Governor Hogg named his daughter "Ima."

When You Throw Away the Mold

In small towns across America, you could almost always find a "Shine," a "Slim" or even a "Smiley." But only in Hendersonville would you ever find a person like Smiley McCall. Smiley was not a nickname, he actually was

Smiley T. McCall. And few of the thousands of people who heard him speak at giant rallies across the South never knew his name because he was an Anonymous: a member and sought-after speaker in Alcoholics Anonymous.

In those early days of WHKP, you never culled a prospect for advertising. There just weren't that many businesses in the area. I had routinely pitched ads to Blythe's Grocery and Osteen's Market at the corner of 7th Avenue and Maple Street, but I don't remember ever selling them any sort of campaign. But one day someone in the store said, "The McCalls are opening a new business in the back. You might want to talk to them."

I entered through a door on Maple Street and met a lady sitting on a stool next to a Number 10 washtub, dipping and rising cans of food stuff from some 20 or 25 cases of "bents and dents" canned goods stacked nearby. I learned she was called "Sonny" and she and her husband, Smiley, had gone into the salvage business. Smiley had purchased the merchandise as salvage goods from Southern Railroad. The cases had apparently been pretty well banged up in shipping, and the railroad had to dispose of the goods at salvage prices. Smiley at one time had been a top salesman for General Foods. He had traveled in the fast lane when he was brokering food; and, as he said, "I finally hit bottom, bounced, joined AA and started all over again."

While some of the cans were dented so bad they had to be discarded, most of the stock could be cleaned up and sold and even at discount prices would turn a nice profit. Sonny said, "You may want to come back and talk to Smiley. We're just getting started and he may want to buy some advertising."

Thus began a relationship that continued 'til Smiley's death in 1976. Smiley was not only a super salesman, he was a real entrepreneur. His enthusiasm was contagious. When he purchased an entire freight carload of telephone poles that had been singed by a fire near the railroad siding, he saw them as supporting beams for small bridges or corner posts for farm buildings. We promoted them on a program called the Trading Post, and Smiley sold 'em. He bought an entire freight carload of pink bathtubs. It took a while, but in the end, he sold every one.

The business was an instant success and grew larger and moved to larger facilities up and down 7th Avenue four times. His fame as a salvage agent spread beyond Southern to other railroads. He began working large whole-sale firms for goods damaged in their warehouses which he could buy from them at deep discount. His business grew to the point that he was forced to buy an 18-wheel tractor-trailer to handle the claims.

And throughout the years, annually he would add a new chip for sobriety. He gave an enormous amount of time to Alcoholics Anonymous. I learned a lot about AA and life in general from old Smiley. Some nine years ago when I quit a 4-and-a-half-pack a day smoking habit, I followed the fundamental which had given Smiley success in giving up alcohol. "You never say you've quit, or you're going to quit," Smiley would say. "That's too big a sacrifice. Just tell yourself that I'm a strong enough person to give it up just for today.

The great Smiley T. McCall, behind the wheel of the 18-wheeler he used to bring salvage merchandise to Depot Salvage Company on 7th Avenue East. It started on Maple Street, and moved all up and down 7th Avenue, each time seeking bigger quarters. Its final location was next to the M & M Freezer Locker plant.

I'll worry about tomorrow when it comes." And Smiley would emphasize, "and you can't run from a bad habit. You have to face it down every day." On one occasion when WHKP was celebrating one of its bigger anniversaries, Smiley's name was on the invitation list for a non-alcoholic reception. Smiley was obviously quite irritated with me. "You had me on the wrong list. I'd have loved to have been at the event where drinks were served. I could have sipped on my ginger ale and had a marvelous time, knowing how good I was going to feel the next morning."

As the years went by, he gave more and more time to AA. He was also very active in the First Baptist Church, but always stayed in the back row because as Smiley said, "Nobody in church wants to hear from a reformed drunk."

He became active in the Merchant's Association, and especially with 7th Avenue Merchants. Glenn Thompson and the Thompson family were active in the chicken business on 7th; and Smiley used to say, "In the Depression, Glenn made more money selling feathers and chicken guts on 7th Avenue than most merchants did on Main Street."

Smiley had grown up in Hendersonville. In fact, Frank FitzSimons in Vol. III of "From the Banks of the Oklawaha" had a chapter on "hacking"– young men who drove buggies or hanks from the railroad depot around to the various hotels. Smiley started as a hacker, and in Fitz's book you'll see a full-length picture of a young and handsome Smiley McCall. In his "fast lane" days with General Foods, Smiley drove convertibles with running boards and played golf on the more sumptuous layouts of that time. He was at home with the rich and famous. As was with so many successful entrepreneurs, only Smiley knew what Smiley was planning or doing.

Several years before Smiley died, he was taken to Pardee Hospital with a mysterious ailment. Everything that could make a man miserable afflicted Smiley. His close friend and physician, Dr. Nick Fortescue, ordered him admitted and started a mass of tests which he hoped would help identify Smiley's problem. Smiley said, "I could hear Nick talking in whispered voice to other doctors, and I could tell that they viewed whatever I had as being serious. Kermit, you know me—nobody knows what I'm doing except me; and if anything should happen, Sonny and the girls would be in a big mess." I nodded and waited for him to continue. "Finally," he said, "I turned over and prayed, 'Lord, you know old Smiley. If you'll let me have just a few days on my feet to straighten everything out, then if you want me, take me.'" Smiley said he immediately dozed off into a deep and restful sleep—the first in many days. He said when he awoke, he remembered the prayer and it deeply troubled him. He said, "I prayed again and this time I said, 'Lord, you do know Smiley, and you know if you gave me those few extra days, I'd be in no better shape than I am now. So if you want me, go ahead and take me.'" He said within the hour, the fever broke, his appetite returned and he felt like a new man. He said Dr. Fortescue told him, "Well, I guess one of us finally hit on the right medicine for you." Smiley smiled real big and said, "What Nick didn't know was that not one of the doctors had prescribed anything, not even an aspirin. I guess the Lord simply rewarded me for my honesty."

By the way, "Sonny" was a nickname. Her real name was Mary.

Shave and a Haircut

One thing common to all barber shops in America back in the '40s was the array of colorful, aromatic and exciting bottles that were spread across the back bar behind every barber chair. Lucky Tiger hair tonic and Fitch and Pine Oil Tar shampoo were there for the deluxe treatment. All barber shops were full-service, offering not only haircuts and shaves, but also most of them featured elevated shoeshine stands and shower baths in the back or in the basement.

When WHKP signed on the air, hair cuts were 25 cents and shaves 20 cents, although it took as long or longer to shave a man as it did to cut his hair. Shaving required generous lathering of the face from the old-timey barber's mug, covering the face with a steaming hot towel to soften the whiskers, a thorough stropping of the razor, the shaving time itself, and then the application of the after-shave lotion. In Dad's shop, the old Palace, every barber knew which customer would want a shave; and if they could spot one of them coming toward the shop, you'd hear, "I ain't gonna shave that squirrel today," and one or more barbers would dash out the back door.

Fifty years ago, virtually all barber shops were on Main Street—there were only a couple on 7th Avenue. The Model Barber Shop was perhaps the most elaborate in town in that it sported a full-fledged smoke shop with tobaccos and cigars next to the front window. It was located in the building where Mac's Mens' Wear is today. It was owned and operated by J. Louis Albea, who also dealt in real estate on the side. Among the barbers at the Model were Bill Bomar and Merity Lyda.

Across the street was Tom's Barber Shop, which had operated at one time in the basement under the old State Trust Company. There was a big stairway going down from the sidewalk which looked very much like the entrance to a New York subway; there were glass bricks in the sidewalk to provide light for the barber shop. This shop was operated by Murph Elliot, grandfather of

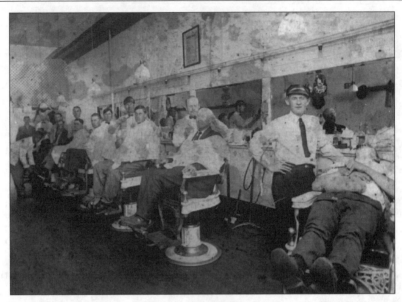

The old Palace Barber Shop, which operated at 238 North Main Street. The barber/owner on the first chair is H. Grady Edney, and on the second chair is Phydell Orr. The customer in the second chair is L. Trade Dermid, a hardwareman who lived to be 105.

the great Bob Elliot who was a star fullback for the University of North Carolina and, at one time, secretary of the local YMCA. Along with Murph were two other colorful characters: Tynch Godshaw and "Polka Dot" Anders. My own father barbered from time to time. "Polka Dot" Anders was related to Art and Dave Cooley; and Mr. Albea's family turned to golf—with Phyllis Albea marrying Hendersonville's Country Club pro, Cliff Collins, and Hays Albea becoming the professional at Etowah Valley Country Club.

There was a big shop in the Skyland Hotel which was owned in whole or in part from time to time by D.C. and Pete Orr, and Kenneth Reid. Troy's Barber Shop was manned by Troy and Carl Justus. Across the street from the Court House was appropriately the Court House Barber Shop, where you'd find George Drake and Frank Orr, the father of Boyce Orr, who was comptroller at WHKP until he retired.

At the Palace was Eldon Leland "Smokey" Levi Jr.; he worked the first chair after returning from making airplanes in Seattle during WWII. Phydell Orr was on the second chair, Ross Parlier was on the third, and my dad handled the last chair across from the shoeshine stand. (Later, Smokey operated his own shop on 4th Avenue at the corner of Wall Street, and still later a shop on Church Street above Freeman's News Stand, owned today by Kimberly Carling.)

Down on 7th, there was the famous Crystal Barber Shop operated by my uncle James J. Pace, who was also chairman of the local Republican Party. Working with him was a diehard Democrat, Charlie Lowrance. The shop was not only a hotbed of political discussion, but was headquarters for all the better checker players of the county. Near the big pot-bellied stove in the rear was a professional checker table either in use or set up and ready to go. Donald "Red" and Joan Price run this shop today.

Over across the railroad tracks was the Carolina Barber Shop, which was operated by James H. Dorn and J.R. Neill. The Dorn family would later operate a grocery store, and still later a menswear shop. Zeb Brookshire started in the barber trade and later became a minister. And one of the most colorful of all local barbers was the late Clint Redden, who could blow a harmonica through his nose. There was a black barber shop back then operated by Lomax Foster on Ashe Street. Later H.H. Young would operate a shop.

While the days of barber shops with showers and shoeshine stands are no more, there are still a few shops that have come into being in recent years, such as the Mug and Brush, owned by Virgil Kepner on the busy bend of Kanuga. Working with Virgil is Jerry Boyer on the front chair, along with Doug Singleton. From time to time, Kenneth Reid has filled in for one of the other barbers. Kenneth Reid, Smokey Levi and Carl Justus are about the only surviving barbers of those golden years of Lucky Tiger Tonic and Fitch Shampoo.

It's a Different Crowd Doing It

Dan Waddell loves to recall the conversation between O.E. Hedge and Worth Lyerly when one said to the other, "I don't believe there's as much sex going on now as there used to be."

"Oh yes . . . it's just a different crowd doing it."

You don't hear of too many people today playing practical jokes as was common back in the less hectic days when there were only two traffic signals on Church Street. My dad, back then, ran the Ames Hotel Barber Shop on 4th Avenue West, and his associate, Bob Case, was on the first chair. Bob was a fairly big man and had spent his life standing behind a barber chair. Bob was a dyed-in-the-wool New York Yankee fan, and throughout the baseball season, you'd have to tolerate his observations about every Yankee player as if he knew them personally.

Bob was also what we called in the Bible Belt a "closet drinker." Publicly he was opposed to demon rum or the fruit of the grape, but surreptitiously he nipped a little all day. At Bob Freeman's News Stand (around the corner) you could buy a standard Dixie cup of Old Maude wine for a dime; the large cup was 15 cents. From so much standing behind the barber chair, Bob had suffered foot trouble through most of his adult life and gingerly walked on

*Originally built as the Hodgewell Hotel, this building was also called
the Ames and Bowen. Freeman's News Stand is on the Church Street
side of the building. The property is now a downtown parking lot.*

the balls of his feet. Several times a day, he would make his way (tiptoeing)
around to the news stand for a little "pick me up."

One of Bob's regular customers was the great William B. "Bill" Hodges,
who after the banks busted in the Depression, restored financial stability to
the community with the esteemed State Trust Company. Bill was a regular
in Bob's chair; and though partially concealed by the strong fragrances of
after-shave lotions, Bill was aware of the smell of wine always on Bob's breath.

Hodges learned that Bob was about to have a birthday, so he arranged with
Bob Freeman at the news stand that a gallon of Old Maude wine be given to
Bob with the stipulation that it not be covered or placed in a bag. Bill then
waited on the corner next to the post office and watched for Case to make his
first trip to the news stand. True to schedule, he didn't have to wait long. As
he spied the barber sheepishly come out of the news stand carrying the gallon
jug of wine, Hodges started yelling at the top of his voice, "Thief! Thief! Stop
that man. He's stolen that wine." The natural reaction of Case was to run—
and around the corner went Case, being chased by Banker Hodges still
yelling "thief" almost to the First Baptist Church. For days, Case would
glower at his barber chair as he stropped his razor. "When he comes back in
here, I'm going to cut him from ear to ear." This just egged Hodges on.

He later learned that Case had been bumped and knocked down by a car
while trying to cross 7th Avenue. Hodges, a man of great influence,
persuaded Mayor Al Edwards (who also served as Judge of City Court) to

have Bob "picked up" and charged with "running into a car." The mayor went along with the joke, and at the hearing, urged Case to be more careful to avoid a more serious charge of damaging a motor vehicle.

And Case stropped his razor even more forcefully.

Dad used to say, "The most unpredictable people on earth are barbers, screamin' preachers and guitar pickers." An old story passed down through the years was about one certain barber (who liked to preach on the side) who had a customer lying on his back (lathered and ready to shave). As the barber finished stropping his razor, he asked the customer, "Are you ready to meet your maker?" The customer eyed the barber as he continued poppin' his razor up and down that leatherstrop, and suddenly decided the best thing he could do was get out of there fast—and that he did, running down Main Street with the barber's cloak flying in the breeze behind him.

The Burger Wars

A check today of current classified listings for restaurants in the Hendersonville area shows 78 different eating places. Some of these offer only sandwiches or a very limited menu; but the bulk of them are fast-food franchises. In the city directory of 1946, there are only nine restaurants listed, along with ten lunchrooms. The lunchrooms were basically places that sold hamburgers, hot dogs and beer.

The most popular eating place at the time of WHKP's sign-on was the Home Food Shop Cafeteria operated by Carl Morris and his mother Charm Keeter. In those years, beer and wine could be served in eating places, but no mixed drinks. Neither the Home Food Shop nor the Skyland Coffee Shop served alcohol of any sort. Listed as "restaurants" back then were the Blue Grill between 3rd and 4th Avenues on Main; the City Cafe across from the Court House (which probably should have been listed as a lunchroom); Rhody's Coffee Shop, located between 6th and 7th on Main; and the Marmack Grill on 7th. The lunchroom category included the Hot Spot and Blue Bird, the Brunswick, the Pastime, the Pickwick and Tracy's at the Union Bus Terminal.

Up through the '50s and '60s, drive-in eateries became very popular. Two of the most famous were operated by the Brock family: Strawberry's and Johnny's. One of the most popular drive-ins was known as Shorty's and was operated by the Kilpatrick family until it was acquired by Jim Franklin, who renamed it Jody's Drive-in. Also on the southside was the Skyline Drive-in, operated by Mr. and Mrs. J.A. Banks. Some of the folks who worked on the southside now work for Jilly's on Spartanburg Road. Pat's Jiffy Burgers was operated by W.J. Paterson; and then there was the Rebel Restaurant, operated by M.A. Bullman. Farther out on Spartanburg Road, Charley Worley ran the Tasty Treat.

As in most other small towns of America, "cruisin'" the drive-ins each night was the number one recreation. And it appeared back then that this "way of life" was destined to be successful forever. That is, until December 14, 1971, when Spartan Food System of Spartanburg announced they would open a new fast food restaurant named Hardee's, which would be in operation by March 1972. Most people simply jeered at the announcement—"some out o' town burger place thinks they can come in here and compete against our big drive-ins—they won't last a month."

While the Hardees's chain was based in Rocky Mount, N.C., Spartan held the franchise rights in certain areas of North and South Carolina, all of Tennessee, Alabama and Mississippi and parts of Louisiana. The company president was Jerome Richardson. The Richardson family has been responsible for the phenomenal success of the Charlotte Panthers pro football team.

The Hendersonville Hardee's (the first fast-food franchise locally), on the corner of Greenville Highway and White Street, quickly became the most successful operation in the entire Hardee's chain.

The Blue Grill at 315 North Main was one of the few restaurants on Main Street. Most other eateries were hot dog and hamburger places, many with a pool room in back.

The most successful local food merchant was Clifton Shipman. Cliff always had a variety of diversified interests, ranging from horses and a dance pavilion known as the Saddle Club to the leased operation of Boyd Park during the summer months. Cliff's first move in the food business was the operation of a restaurant at the corner of 3rd and Church. He then established a new edge in the competition for the hamburger and hot dog business with the opening of Hasty Tasty at the corner of Oakland Street and the Asheville Highway, where you could buy either sandwich for 19 cents. The success of this operation resulted in building the rock buildings and moving the operation to the corner of 8th Avenue and Church. Even though at one time or another he's owned and operated the Chicken Shack, car washes and sporting goods stores, his pride and joy has been his Clifton's Cafeteria and associated catering business featuring the facilities of the Cedars.

If I remember correctly, Jimmy Dement operated the Blue Grill until he built his Royal Steak House in Fletcher. Jimmy introduced Greek salad and the genuine "Sirloin for Two" to most locals. He loved to waddle among his customers and pass out free cigars.

One of the most colorful of all restaurant owners was Dan Justice, who, along with his wife Reba, had taken over what once had been the Marmack Grill on 7th. I was fascinated with Dan. He had retired from Kress 5 and 10 as company head of their candy department, and he ran the restaurant as he would have managed a dime store. The day after New Year's, he would decorate for Valentine's Day. On February 15, the Easter decorations came out. He catered to rural church goers, and virtually every wall had pictures of the crucifixion or of Mary and Jesus. He installed a decorative water fountain near the front window, which subconsciously gave one the urge constantly to go to the bathroom. I was usually the first customer to come in, and would always be treated to the first cup of coffee from the steaming urn behind the counter. The second customer was usually Bert Cantrell, one of the truly great movers and shakers in the community who, in his twilight years, could never reset his biological clock.

Bert owned one of the first major beer and wine distributorships in Western North Carolina, and became one of the largest produce growers in the South. He was a dynamic person. He knew what he wanted and he expected every one of his employees to do exactly what he said with no argument. One day, as he sipped on his coffee, I could tell he was deeply troubled. Responding to my questions he finally said, "Ah, it's that young smartass I have working with me at the farm. He needed his butt whipped this morning in the worst kind of way and I've gotten so damned old I can't do it anymore."

Runt Robertson, a well-known cattle trader, was also an early customer, and he and Bert would invariably get to the bet-making stage over some ball game. I'd hear them argue over point spread, the "spot" and who would give the other what—and was shocked one morning when I discovered all their argument was over a one-dollar bill.

Bert was never happy with Dan's coffee—it wasn't strong enough or wasn't hot enough. One morning, out of the corner of my eye, I noticed Dan had put Bert's cup directly on top of the hot stove back in the kitchen. I kept watching, and in a few minutes Dan walks triumphantly up to Bert carrying the red-hot cup in a saucer, sets the coffee in front of Bert and says sarcastically, "See if that's hot enough for you." Bert barely got the smoking hot cup off the saucer when he quickly let go and unleashed an oath buried deep within. "I guess that's hot enough for you," Dan harumphed as he headed back to the kitchen. Another morning, he served Bert a cup of steaming hot water to which had been added only food coloring and was brilliantly red.

Bert Cantrell was one of those people who had never been sick a day in his life, and when he was sent to Duke Hospital for a series of tests, he was convinced that he was approaching the very end. He and Nell boarded the train at Biltmore bound for Durham and had made their way back to the lounge car. In a matter of minutes (by sheer coincidence) the noted undertaker W.M "Bill" Shepherd came into the lounge car also. He had that aloofness and carriage that signified reverence and silence for the dearly departed. When Bill came through the door, Bert jumped from his seat and said, "My God, what chance do I have, they've even sent the undertaker to bring me back." Bob Freeman shared that story with me, and before I used it on the radio series, I checked with Bert's widow, Nell, about the truth of it. She laughed heartily and said, "Those may not have been his exact words but that's pretty much how it happened."

In later years, Dan and Miss Reba sold the restaurant and moved to California along with their poodles, where he could be near his two sons. Without Dan Justice, the restaurant on 7th Avenue was short-lived. With Dan gone, I discovered that Frank Edney also opened the Hot Spot at about 3:30 each morning, so I then regularly joined Frank and his assistant Rex Rhodes. Rex has worked with Cliff Shipman at Clifton's Cafeteria since Frank retired from the Hot Spot.

The Breakfast Club

I discovered that there was a much larger and more diverse group of people gathered each day for breakfast at the Hot Spot. Tom Collins, Frank Stepp and Bill Brookshire were on the opening shift at the post office; and occasionally another of their cohorts, Sonny Hamilton, would be there also. Leroy Dill drove a Coca-Cola truck; Robin Clayton was one of the best carpenters in town and occasionally did small contracting jobs. F.C. Justus was a carrier for the *Asheville Citizen*; and Clayton Drake and John Pittman were both retired but enjoyed the bantering and cajoleries that went on at the early hour. Calvin King delivered Biltmore Dairy products to supermarkets, and

Don Hill was the best-known surveyor in the county. The dean of the group (which was nicknamed "The Breakfast Club") was Ruppert Jackson, who along with his wife, operated Jackson Flower Shop. Ruppert knew every person who was sick, and checked the obits in the morning paper to see who had died. It would be many years before the custom of making memorial gifts (instead of flowers) took hold locally, and the popularity of any person could be judged by how many arrangements of flowers were displayed at the funeral.

Ruppert was another individualist who thoroughly enjoyed the practical joke. When Worth Lyerly bought the first Volkswagen beetle and started bragging about the fantastic gas mileage he was getting, Ruppert's ears pricked up and he could quickly see the fun he was going to have at the expense of Worth. Ruppert observed Lyerly's comings and goings in his beetle, and any time he could find the car unattended, Ruppert would add gasoline to the tank. Worth Lylerly became the local champion of the beetle, announcing during the first week that he was "getting 35 to 40 miles to the gallon." Ruppert kept adding more gas. "Now that the car's broken in," Lyerly would say, "it's nothing for me to get 88 miles to the gallon." By this time, word had leaked around as to what Ruppert was doing; and as the beetle continued to improve its unbelievable performance, raised eyebrows were replaced by restrained snickers.

Then Ruppert struck the telling blow. He continued to watch for the beetle to be left unattended, but this time, he would siphon gas from the car. At first small amounts, and as each week went by, larger quantities. Lyerly's car was no longer getting 80 or more miles per gallon. In fact, it was now getting less than five. Worth took it to every garage in town for tune-ups and diagnoses. Finally, someone couldn't hold back the truth and Lyerly discovered Ruppert had pulled one of his all-time best practical jokes.

One of the leading doctors of that era was Dr. Robert C. Sample, who was in Ruppert's flower shop every day to pick up a red carnation which he always wore as his boutonniere. When the survey crew establishing rights-of-way for the new I-26 had finished staking in the vicinity of Dr. Sample's home, Ruppert (under the cover of darkness) slipped out and moved the stakes so that the road would come right across Dr. Sample's front porch. The next morning, the irate doctor was on the phone to DOT in Raleigh; and within an hour, the highway people saw what had been done and quickly traced the handiwork to Ruppert. The DOT didn't think this Jackson joke was funny, and with their severe admonition, Ruppert slowed his practical jokes for a while.

After Frank and Alice Edney retired, the Hot Spot/Blue Bird was operated by Frank's brother Willie and his wife Elsie for a short time before the building was acquired for the Habitat Real Estate office. In the meantime, the "Breakfast Club" had moved to the Home Food Shop, where it thrived until fire gutted the interior of the building. The cafeteria was moved to the

The old Justus Pharmacy, which opened in its present location in 1882, was acquired by Kathy and Bill Danielson, who have restored the old building to its original grandeur and now operate a museum, antique and soda and sandwich shop at 303 North Main St.

old Collins-McCord Building across from where the Hot Spot had been.

Very few of the original organization are still alive, but a successor group of retirees has taken the place of the old "club" and now gathers in the shank of the morning at "Days Gone By," which is located at the corner of 3rd and Main in the old Justus Pharmacy Building (the oldest drug store in town). They now serve food and refreshments in a solid nostalgic environment. However, the conversation now is more limited to memories of "back when"—with tales of the battles of Kasserine Pass, big dances put on by the VFW 50 years ago, and a sincere concern as to whether William E. Jamison's foot will still be asleep when it's time to go.

Days Gone By

There's only one left: The old marble soda fountain that was the hallmark of every drug store in town. Bill Danielson and his wife, Kathy, acquired the old Justus Pharmacy several years ago and have successfully restored the old facility to its original grandeur, including the bright metal ceiling of the original building. Most of what you see on the shelves is not for sale. The myriads of museum-quality apothecary bottles and precious stock of old-timey herbs and drugs displayed provide the atmosphere for the pleasure of old-fashioned soda fountain treats still served at the marble counter, or complete meal service using the authentic conversational sized drug store tables throughout. The 3rd Avenue outside wall of the old building sports a freshly painted Coca-Cola sign with the wording exactly the same as it was 50 years ago:

"Relieves Fatigue & Exhaustion Drink Coca-Cola"

When WHKP first signed on the air, there were seven drug stores in the downtown area, and every one of them featured a solid marble soda fountain. In addition to the Justus Pharmacy, there was Speight's Cut-Rate Drug Store on South Main Street. Archer Speight was the owner, and it had all the appearance of a drug store. In the summer months, the paddle fans over the open front door would waft the drug store aroma onto the sidewalk, but I never saw a customer in there. Rose Pharmacy was a block north of the Justus Drug Store (at the corner of 4th and Main), run by Dr. Billy Harper and his family. Yet another block north was the Economy Drug Store, owned and operated by Dr. W.B. Wilson. He had earlier sold his old drug store (Wilson Drug) on 7th Avenue (along with the family name) to Jack Lovingood. Up in the middle of the block next to the Carolina Theatre was Freeze Drug Store, run by Dr. Wiltshire Grifith and his son Buddy. It had the most elaborate cosmetics department of any store in the area and Annie Lou Heaton, who managed that department, was known as the only cosmetologist in the entire area.

All of the drug stores back then were family-owned and at least one member of the family was a college graduate and licensed pharmacist. On the corner of 4th and Church Street was Jackson Pharmacy, operated by the Feagin family, Dr. Eugene and his sons, Gene and Larry. Jackson's was the only drug store in town that had an ice "shaving" machine which permitted them to offer a cherry ice in a paper cone.

Fifty years ago, you could tell if you were in a drug store with your eyes closed. There was an aroma, an ambience that set it apart from any other business. And at Christmas, with the elaborate displays of the cobalt blue bottles of "Evening in Paris" cosmetics, it's where Christmas dreams were made. Today, most drug stores look like supermarkets and vice versa. Seventy-five percent of the products available in drug stores today had not even been discovered fifty years ago. The biggest category of patent medicines offered in 1946 dealt with cough and cold products. Each drug store had its own formula cough syrup, as well as other brands. And a company had to be pretty shrewd just to get a drug store to stock its product.

I remember a man coming into our WHKP office one day and introduced himself as the owner of the B&B Cough Syrup Company. He wanted to buy a saturation campaign of spot announcements for two weeks. I offered to escort him around to several of the local drug stores where I personally knew the owners. "Oh no!" he said. "I don't plan to try to sell the first bottle until I've created a demand." He then explained he had done a study and found if you heavily promote a product and create a desire to purchase on the part of the customer, the customer will make three and a half calls trying to find the product before they give up. "This exaggerates demand by 350 percent."

His psychology worked. After the campaign had been running for about three days, we started getting calls from local drug stores. "You guys are advertising B&B Cough Syrup?"

"Yes, we are."

"Well, where do you get it? My customers are asking for it and I've never heard of it." At the end of the second week, the B&B salesman simply went from store to store taking orders.

Tonics were also big sellers, especially if they were advertised as herbal, with the secret recipe having been handed down by Indians. Repeat business for Scalf's Indian River Medicine or Hadacol was guaranteed also by the eighteen percent alcohol base of the tonic. The brewers of the formula also saw to it that the tonic had a horrible taste because many people were want to say, "Anything that tastes that bad is bound to be good for you."

The miracle drug when I was growing up was castor oil. If cocoa quinine or syrup of pepsin didn't cure you, it was time for castor oil. I am a witness that psychogenics does work. I could mentally will my fever down to avoid having to take castor oil.

Laxatives were widely promoted on radio, and the most famous was Krazy Water Krystals, hawked by an Arkansas patent medicine pitchman, Dr. Brinkley. It was nothing more than epson salts in a fancy package. Take it a week and you were addicted.

How Business Has Changed

Every little town had at least one ice plant 50 years ago. Usually it was an "ice and coal" company because in winter months the firm would sell coal for heating, and in the summer, blocks of ice up to a hundred pounds. There were seven different firms advertising coal, wood and fuel for sale in 1946: Fisher's Coal Yard on East Caswell Street; Hendersonville Supply & Coal Company (operated by the Latt family on Whitted); Spurgeon Hyder Coal Yard on 7th; Orr's Coal Yard on Kanuga; Richardson's on 5th Avenue; and Star Dray & Cash Coal Company on 7th Avenue East (operated by the Patty family). There was only one City Ice and Coal Company. It was owned by Fred Suddeth and was also on Whitted Street.

When you planned a party or were going on a picnic, you had to "go by the ice plant," where they'd chop one of the massive ice blocks down to the exact weight and size you wanted. There was a touch of magic to buying ice. You'd tell the man on the loading dock how much you wanted and he would mash a button on the wall. You'd hear loud machinery running inside the building, and finally a block of ice would come out on the conveyor belt, pushing aside leather flaps which covered the opening. Block ice is available today only in Asheville.

Fred Suddeth

Most homes and businesses in the city then heated with coal. Fifty years ago, coal smoke was hardly an environmental problem. Out in the country, they burned wood "cut off the place." In school, you could identify the girls who lived in a house with only fireplace heat (and no stove) because they'd have red lines on their legs during the wintertime. All the coal yards were located adjacent to the railroad—either the main line through town or on the Toxaway line, such as Richardson's on 5th Avenue West. Retailers would buy coal by the freight carload and coal cars would be switched onto their railroad siding where the hoppers would be emptied, creating large mounds of coal on the coal yard.

In 1946, only Richardson's was advertising heating oil for sale. Oil heaters (manufactured to look like a piece of living room furniture) finally replaced the big cast-iron coal stoves; and gradually, most of the dealers who sold fuel made the switch from coal to heating oil. Most businesses, hotels and even large boarding houses had installed central heat, although it would be another decade or so before air conditioning became common.

Nineteen boarding houses were listed in the 1946 city directory. Only one (the Bonnie Haven on Hyman Avenue) is still in operation. Some of the better-known boarding houses were the Jackson House and the Jackson House Annex on King Street. These facilities were operated by Mrs. Rose Jackson and her son Leon (Ruppert's mother and brother). The Hunthurst on South Main was also known as the Bonner House. The Waverly was run by Mrs. Helen Harrison. It would later be operated by Ed and Dot McCurry, and today is one of the leading bed and breakfast facilities. My grandmother ("Granny" Waters) used to operate a large boarding house at 319 Washington Street called "The Washington." In addition to the main house, there were several cottages in the rear which were reserved for specific times each year for the entire Jimmy Livingston Orchestra, which would rest there between college tours. Woe be to anyone who would make any noise before lunch that would wake up the band.

Across the street was the famed Weeping Willow Swimming Pool. It was not only the public swimming pool, it was the only pool in the county back

The famed Laurel Park Beach. The water slide was removed in later years. Fire destroyed the old dancing pavilion, one of the largest in the area, which extended out over the lake.

then. It was an elaborate facility for that era, complete with showers and dressing rooms. The only other swimming facility during this time was Laurel Park Beach, operated by John and Lucille Prescott. At one time, the Laurel Park Dance Pavilion extended out over the lake and featured the second largest dance floor in the entire region. The dance pavilion burned in 1930 and was never replaced. There was a small recreation building and concession stand at the lake where you could take shelter during a storm. Laurel Park Lake boasted a diving tower and two other surface diving platforms closer to the beach. In its heyday, the sandy beach was raked to be without blemish at the start of every day.

I was told that one year the Prescotts drained the lake when they closed Laurel Park Inn for the summer just to spite neighbors around the lake. Muskrats followed the water level down and dug holes in the earthen dam during the winter. To repair the damages required building a totally new dam and, as a result, the Rhododendron Lake ceased to exist. It was at one time a showplace of Laurel Park.

Life Below the "Grits" Line

I have heard it argued that there is a more definitive line than the Mason-Dixon, which establishes whether you get grits or hash browns at breakfast. Of course, in Charleston and the "low country" of South Carolina, loosely ground corn is called hominy instead of grits. Folks who move into communities in the South also find it strange to season greens and green beans with pork side meat. They're more accustomed to the quick-cooked green beans which squeak when you chew them.

It takes a spell for newcomers to understand the customs of the native Southerner, and especially politically correct burial. Neither Tom Shepherd nor Fred Jackson have any idea of how the custom was established, and admittedly it is not as rigidly followed today as in the days of my parents. But if you were a Democrat, it was ordained that Shepherd's would handle your funeral. If you were a Republican, you'd be buried by Walter Stepp Funeral Home up through the '40s and by Jackson Funeral Home since then. There was one major exception and that involved former Mayor Boyce Whitmire. Boyce was a loyal and lifelong Democrat, but his daughter Patricia (who everyone called Sis) married Fred Jackson, the owner of the Republican funeral home. The family developed a compromise, which called for both funeral homes to handle the service—the only time in history that has happened.

In the earliest days of funeral homes, they also sold furniture. Young Tom Shepherd recalls his grandfather saying, "We probably would have been better off if I'd stayed in the furniture business." There were also no funeral chapels. The body of the deceased was embalmed and taken to the home where it would lie in state in the parlor for at least a couple of days before the funeral.

Back then, memorial gifts were unheard of—everyone sent flowers. You judged a person's standing in the community by simply looking at the elaborateness of the floral arrangements surrounding the coffin.

The wake (or watch over the dead body) required someone to sit in the same room with the deceased until burial had taken place. Visitation was always at the home, and continued around the clock 'til time for the service. The service was not only elaborate, it was exhausting. In rural areas, it was common to have at least two (and sometimes three) preachers, as well as several vocal groups to sing hymns. In addition, you had "flower girls" or "flower boys," who would assist the mortuary in carrying out the service. As soon as the funeral service had ended and the motorcade of mourners began slowly moving toward the cemetery, the flower children would carry all the sprays and other arrangements from within the home and place them in a truck. They would ride with the truck, which would speed to the cemetery, where they would unload the cargo, covering all the freshly dug dirt with the floral display, completing the work before the motorcade arrived. I was six years old when my Grandma Edney died and I served as a flower boy.

Thomas Shepherd & Son Funeral Home was founded by M.M. Shepherd and Flave Hart in 1899. In November 1903, M.M.'s brother, Tom, joined the firm and within a short time became general manager. Tom was succeeded in the business by his only son, William "Bill" Shepherd. Bill had four sisters: Mrs. Nana West, Mrs. Ridley Kessler, Mrs. "Tommy" Fain (wife of J.T. Fain, editor of the *Times-News*) and Martha Shepherd. Bill's son Tom is now the third generation of Shepherd ownership and management. The original Thomas Shepherd Home forms the nucleus of today's modern mortuary.

The Walter Stepp Funeral Home was located on King Street across from present-day Miller's Laundry. It advertised as "The successor of J.M. Stepp & Son." Walter Stepp was the son of Thomas Jones Stepp. His brother was named Bynam. Walter had risen to the rank of corporal in the Old 6th Company, which was also called "the lost squadron" during World War I. I also found where Walter had been a contributor to that infamous Firemens' Convention held here in 1929 when the drunken conventioneers disrupted the city for three days, wrought thousands of dollars in damage to the brand new Skyland Hotel, and resulted in a resolution passed by City Council that firemen should never be asked to return to the city. The event ran from July 15 to 18, and climaxed with "Reel Races" and "Firetruck Races" on 8th Avenue, and a Firemens' Ball on Thursday night.

In the Depression years, Stepp Funeral Home had experienced particularly hard times. I was told that the decision to sell was made when their hearse had a flat tire on the way to the cemetery and the cortege had to wait for the tire to be repaired before proceeding to the burial plot. The business was sold to the Shepherds, but the days without competition were few when a new business (Jackson-Thompson Funeral Home) was organized by Clyde Jackson, Jim Thompson and Jack Lovingood (who owned Wilson Drug Store on 7th Avenue). Clyde had a beautiful tenor voice, and was always asked to sing the hymn "Sunrise Tomorrow" at each service they conducted. One Democratic politician complained to me once, "There ain't no way we can beat Clyde Jackson as long as he keeps singing 'Sunrise Tomorrow.'"

Clyde had become active in politics when he alleged he found the county-owned hospital was routinely transferring the deceased to Shepherd's following the death of any patient at Pardee. He had argued that the patient's family should be consulted before the body was sent to either funeral home; and he vowed that if elected to the County Commission, he would see that the policy was carried out. He won by an enormous majority, and served as a most capable chairman of county government for many years.

Thomas Shepherd & Son had already built a lovely funeral chapel on Church Street adjacent to the funeral home. And, following the opening of Jackson-Thompson Funeral Home, Clyde completed theirs, which was called Chapel in the Pines. Shepherd's had also developed Shepherd Memorial Gardens, a large perpetual care cemetery on the Asheville Highway near Naples. Meanwhile, Clyde Jackson, Homer Hobbs, Herbert Fields and Ray Farmer established Grand View Gardens (now known as Forest Lawn and under different ownership). Clyde had earlier bought out Jim Thompson and Jack Lovingood and it became Jackson Funeral Home. He sold his interest to a holding company in Oregon; but it was later reacquired by the Jackson family and is now operated by Fred Jackson, Clyde's son.

Prior to 1941, Hendersonville had no black funeral home. A few black funerals were handled by Shepherd's, and a young man (James Pilgrim) had been hired to develop a liaison between the black community and the funeral home. Most black funerals were handled then by Jesse Ray in Asheville. On July 2, 1941, James Pilgrim made a courageous move. He decided to leave Shepherd's and form his own Pilgrim Funeral Home. He acquired a house at the corner of 3rd Avenue and Whitted Street, which became primary offices for the funeral home on the ground floor and living quarters for the family on the second floor.

In the late '40s, I emceed a program sponsored by Pilgrim's and featuring singers from the Star of Bethel Church, which was across Whitted Street from the funeral home. James did his own commercial and would always conclude, "It is better to know us and not need us than to need us and not know us." I've never forgotten that slogan. James, his wife and family became the heart of the leadership of the black community.

I vividly remember when Mrs. Pilgrim died. About thirty minutes prior to the time for the service, I went to the Star of Bethel Church, knowing there would be a large crowd. When I arrived, there was an enormous crowd already, spilling out of the jammed and packed sanctuary into the yards and streets. Police simply closed Whitted Street, and a loudspeaker system was put to use so that those outside could hear the service. As owners of black funeral homes converged on Hendersonville for the service, I can truthfully

James Pilgrim opened a black funeral home on July 2, 1941, in Hendersonville. The firm operates in the same location, 836 Third Avenue West. When James acquired a modern hearse and family car for large funerals, he had the cooperation of local black taxi operators. James and his son Sonny stand on the sidewalk in front of the home.

say I have never seen so many funeral limousines in all my life as were at Mrs. James Pilgrim's funeral.

In the stormy years following the Warren Supreme Court decision, James Pilgrim (along with Sam Mills) provided solid leadership with calm deliberations and exercised moderation. The community, with the leadership of these two men, weathered minor racial unrest while turmoil occured in many other communities.

Recently I was chatting with James R. Marable, who was principal of the old 9th Avenue black high school. Marable is probably the oldest of the pioneer black educators who have been part of the total remake of the public school system. James and I shared bits of nostalgia about the old days, and the Pilgrim family. He told me that James Pilgrim Jr. was a colonel and was stationed at Ft. Bragg, and for over a year had planned to return home to take over the family business. The military, however, kept persuading him to extend his service "just for one more year." Obviously, James Jr. will be back someday to operate the business his father established. Tom Shepherd is very much still the owner/operator of Shepherd's, and Fred Jackson still carries on where his father left off. It's one of the few industries that has survived the years with succession in ownership from generation to generation.

Like Father—Like Son

Businesses that operated here in 1946 and are still in operation by the same family generally fall into categories, such as automobile sales and service. Being awarded a local dealership by any of the well-known automakers is not an everyday occurrence, and not just anybody can offer a net worth statement acceptable for a local dealership. Also, there are obviously huge tax advantages when a dealership simply stays in the family.

Boyd Pontiac was established more than 50 years ago by Cam "Bubba" Boyd on 4th Avenue at Church Street. He was to later add the Cadillac line and, following the death of Gus Thomas, he acquired the Buick dealership. His son (L. Cam Boyd Jr.) has modernized and vastly expanded the dealership and added the Izusu line at Five Points.

Hunter Chevrolet operated in 1946 on South Main Street. Back then, in addition to Chevrolet, the firm sold Allis Chalmers farm equipment. It was established by T.D. "Tom" Hunter Jr. Now his two sons (Hal and Bud) operate from two locations, Hunter Chevrolet-Volvo-Suburu-GEO-Honda on the Asheville Highway, and Hunter Nissan-Lincoln-Mercury on the Spartanburg Highway.

Fletcher Motor Company in 1946 was also a Chevrolet dealer and was operated by Pete Youngblood. His son, Joe, is now the dealer and also handles BMWs. While W.F. "Pete" Folsom was the Chrysler-Plymouth-Dodge dealer

Hunter Chevrolet in its original location, South Main Street. Back then their only other product was Allis Chalmers Tractors. Now Bud and Hal (sons of T.D) own Hunter Chevrolet, Suburu, Volvo on Asheville Highway, and Hunter Lincoln, Mercury, Nissan on Spartanburg Road.

back in the '40s, that dealership was acquired by Bud Egolf and is now operated by his son, Jeff, who moved the operation from S. Main Street to a beautiful new building on Duncan Hill Road. Cecil Garrett became the Ford dealer after it passed through the hands of Ming Shipman and Grady Rankin. Garrett sold to Bryan Easler, who also added (at another location) the Toyota dealership. This second dealership is now being managed by his son, Steve, and son-in-law, Ken Feagin. T. Lee Osborne Oldsmobile-GMC Trucks (which was founded by T. Lee), operated then by T. Lee Jr. (whom we call Tom) and now by T. Lee III (who is called Lee).

Insurance businesses also have a reasonable expectation of perpetuating through family ownership. It is not easy to become an agent of a well-known and established company. There are also residuals usually which have developed into substantial assets in later years; and again, the capital requirements are demanding. Ewbank & Ewbank dates back to the turn of the century and is still operated by Frank A.W. Ewbank II. The Ewbank name has been associated also in banking, real estate, newspaper publishing, politics, and government service.

The Morrow Insurance Agency was established by J.C. Morrow, Jr. When his son (Charles Morrow) chose to stay at the University of North Carolina and pursue a career in higher education, the business was sold to William F. Stokes Jr., who still operates it, using the same mission statement. The Penny Insurance Agency was organized by Earl Penny and is operated today by his nephew Bill Penny. The Sutherland Agency was founded by Edward R.

The original King Hardware Company, located on 7th Avenue East, was operated by Joseph and Myrtle King. The store was later moved to the corner of 7th and Grove Street, its present location.

Sutherland, inherited by his nephew Marvin, and then spun off to a lifetime employee of the firm, Ed Jones.

One of the remarkable success stories of business survival and perpetuation within families lies in hardware. In spite of Lowe's, Wal-Mart, K-Mart and all the other alphabet discounters, Walker Hardware, King Hardware and Louis Williams & Sons are still very healthy businesses and are being operated by second and third generation members of those families. When a "Mr. Fixit" shops for hardware items, he wants to talk to someone who can share with him helpful advice on what he needs for his project and how to go about the job.

King Hardware was established seventy-five years ago by the father and mother of the late Lt. Col. and Mrs. J.D. King. Now, J.D.'s wife (Wilma), who retired from teaching in public schools, gives a greeting and smile to everyone who comes in the store, and tries to help her son, Joe, and staff find exactly what each person is looking for. Prior to J.D.'s death, Joe was also a professional educator at Appalachian State University. J.D.'s sister (Mrs. Sam Bryson) handles the accounting operation for the store.

Walker Hardware Company was established by Marion Walker, who had his business so well organized that he could take whatever time was necessary to manage the county government as chairman of the commissioners. He was also a giant in the Baptist church. His son Ed followed in his footsteps, and now grandson Phillip is the third generation to operate the business.

Another remarkable and highly successful business now being run by the third generation is Louis Williams & Sons. Sons Jake and Sammy were already active in the business when Morris Kaplan married their sister, Anne, and became a part of the family management team. Now, all the older ones have retired and grandson Danny, who had advanced to professional status in show business, did an about-face and returned to the store, immediately expanding and enlarging it to cover about a city block.

On Main Street, the Western Auto Store was established by an ex-school teacher (Dan Barber Jr.). Today the store covers twice the space and double the merchandise and service and is run by his son, Dan Barber III. Of all the locally owned and operated drug store, only Southcenter Pharmacy is still being operated by the same Ponder family who built the store.

Oil distributorships also involve valuable franchises. Long before 1946, there was a J.H. Reaben Oil Company operated by Hall Reaben; and there was a Youngblood Amoco Oil Company owned by Pete Youngblood and managed for years by Vic Jones. Reaben had the Texaco franchise for several counties in Western North Carolina. In 1946 the business was listed as "The Texaco Company–J. Hall Reaben, consignee." It was located then where it is today, at 751 Ashe Street. The phone number is different–it was "3" in 1946. Hall Reaben ran the firm for 42 years. Dan Waddell had married one of the Reaben girls (Claire), and he joined the Reaben business in 1960 and purchased controlling stock. Today, he and his son (Hall Waddell) operate under the same name, Reaben Oil Company. Mr. Reaben, Dan Waddell and now the grandson, Hall, have all been active in civic, fraternal, commercial and religious activities.

I did not know until 1973 (two years after Mr. Reaben's death) that he was a second generation immigrant from Switzerland, the son of Alexis and Naomi Buckner Rieben, who had left the Rougemont area in the Alps and migrated to Asheville. I learned this when the child bride and I (along with Dan and Claire) took a three-week tour of Europe together from mid-may to June 1973. The timing was perfect because my son and his family lived at a military kaserne in Kitzingen just outside Wurzburg, Germany. They were our hosts while in Bavaria, and we reloaded on cigarettes and other supplies at the Post Exchange while with them. Claire still had relatives living in Switzerland, so that our second stop for provisions and freeloading was when we visited her Aunt Blanche and cousins Maurice Mayor and Georges Dubois. When we arrived at the Hotel Carlton in Lausanne, there was a neon sign near the entrance

Dan Waddell

which read "Cafe Richelieu." Back in the '30s, our family had lived in a giant, rambling old wooden tourist hotel at the depot known as Hotel Richelieu, located on Harris Street . . . and that old hotel was exactly three blocks from J.H. Reaben Oil Company. From Lausanne we met other kith and kin even in Rougemont, a tiny Alpine village where the Rieben family cemetery was located. Then we caught the Trans-European Express to Rome, where we next freeloaded with Paul Rappaport and his wife. They were related to my daughter's husband (Steve Hampton). Paul was with the American Embassy. We had an insider's tour of Rome . . . the statues, the fountains, the American tourist traps. It was truly a memorable experience–the longest period of time I had ever taken away from WHKP. Many years later, Maurice Mayor and his daughter came to America and we had the chance to be co-hosts with the Waddells in a reciprocation of the most fantastic period of my life.

J.H. Reaben would be extremely proud of what's happened to the business he established 70 years ago. Reaben now operates 16 convenience centers in Henderson, Polk and Transylvania counties, along with four stores in Greenville and Spartanburg. The firm specializes in industrial lubricants with more than 300 different products offered at their plant, still located at 751 Ashe Street. A companion business (Southern Alarm) is operated by Dan's son-in-law (Steve Johnson).

The other oil jobber mentioned (Youngblood Amoco Oil Company) is operated today by Joe Youngblood, a son of Pete and brother of attorney Kenneth Youngblood.

Only one laundry in town is still operated by the same family who built the firm more than 65 years ago, and that's Miller's on King Street with additional facilities in the Laurel Park Village. First there was Norman Sr. and then sons Winfield, Norman Jr., Ted and Bert joined the firm. Now it's Bert and Katherine Drake Miller's son, Jeff, that carries on.

In my mind, I can still see Lou Sherman (with a George Burns-type cigar in his mouth) swaggering up and down Main Street in front of the old Sherman's Sporting Goods and Jewelry Store. Lou's store on Main Street has now expanded into a number of malls in Western North Carolina. Kalman and his brother-in-law Walter Gaeser have been succeeded by the third generation, Becky Sherman Banadyga and her husband.

The Star Dray & Cash Coal Company still operates in the same location on 7th at the railroad, but it no longer is in either the dray or coal business— the specialty of founder Elijah (or Lige Patty) and perpetuated by his son Tottsie. Today, a third generation of Pattys (Tommy) runs an auto sales and service center there.

McFarlan's was originally a bake shop and deli, and was operated by Earl H. McFarlan. Wayne Cole worked for McFarlan for years, bought the bakery, then sold it to the late Arthur Rubin; following Art's death, he reacquired it for his son, Mike, who operates it today. It's been on one side or the other of Main Street in the same block for more than 60 years.

In 1946, at the same location as today was the Quality Tire Company, which was operated by Pete Youngblood. Allen Freeman (brother of Bob at the News Stand) bought the operation, and then later sold it to the Charlie Murphy family, who runs it today.

Flanagan Printing was started by Noah Hollowell, using the same old equipment from the old *Hendersonville News* after he had sold that newspaper to the *Hendersonville Times* back in the '20s. The print shop was acquired by the Flanagans (George and Harold) and operated under their ownership until one of their employees (Harry Clark) purchased the firm, and his family operates the shop today. Fred Higgins worked for many years with Leonard Hesterly, who owned the Quality Press. In the '40s, it was located on 4th Avenue East, but today it is on Main between 6th and 7th, and Fred's son (Rob) has joined him in the operation of the business.

There's the modern Martin Heating Company (organized by the late Bill Martin) and operating today in their own plant on Berkeley Road with ownership of Jud Ammons, a long-time Martin associate. The old Byers Sheet Metal Company (organized by Paul Byers) is now the large and elaborate Precision Fabricators, fronting on the interstate and operated by his son Roger. B&A Hyder Truck Lines, an offshoot of old man Clay Hyder's "Hyder Truck Lines" is operated by Clay's grandson Bub. Pace Heating & Plumbing (founded by Finlay Pace) is now operated by Fin Jr. and "Pooch." Rosenberg's (established by Jake Rosenberg) is today Mac's Mens Wear, run by his son-in-law Max Provda. Morris Kalin still runs Kalin Furniture; Bill Deaver has

Deaver's Taxi; and though "Bo" passed away, J.R. Thomas Produce is still in the same family ownership; Ed Diem operates the firm founded by his father (Hans Diem), Southern Agricultural Insecticides; and there's Arnold Kemp at Diamond Brand.

Over three dozen businesses still operate locally that were established 50 years or more ago and still owned by the same family.

The Food Chain and How It Changed

Every retail business today operates with logistics totally different from the systems used 50 years ago. In 1946, there were three thriving, bustling wholesale grocery companies in this area: the American Drug Company, Byers Brothers Wholesale Grocers and Overton's Wholesale Grocery Company. All three firms had similar operations. Their salesmen would make calls on all grocery stores, general merchandise stores, and even service stations to take orders for goods. These orders would be processed and grouped for delivery later in the week. These wholesalers, some canneries (or food processors) would employ what were called manufacturers reps that did store-to-store calls, pitching the brands they personally represented. Many of the reps would put together special deals for the retailer.

The coast-to-coast chain stores (such as A&P, along with the smaller regional operations such as Dixie Home Stores) found that by pooling their buying power, they could go directly to the manufacturer and cut their own deals—which they could then use to offer lower prices. The independent stores fought back by organizing such groups as IGA (Independent Growers' Association); of MDI (Merchants' Distributing Inc.). By banding together they also could demand and get the same kind of volume discount as a group—which could then be shared with each store.

The three local wholesalers were catching it from all sides. The first to discontinue operations was Byer Brothers. A.J. Overton fought back. He arranged exclusive rights for the sale of Kansas Maid Flour in this area, and would buy (to protect his exclusivity) freight carloads of 25-pound sacks of flour.

WHKP developed for him one of the most successful grocery promotions ever undertaken. We originated every day "The Kansas Maid Quizmaster"; all you had to do to win substantial prizes would be to correctly answer questions based on information clearly printed on every bag of Kansas Maid Flour. We emphasized that you didn't have to buy the product, that you could copy all the wording on the sack and be able to answer our questions. Most listeners preferred simply to buy a sack of Kansas Maid Flour.

It was always a sheer pleasure for me to visit with Mr. Overton. I had gone to school with his son (A.J. "Buddy" Overton Jr.) who is now the host of the nationwide radio series "Message to Israel." I enjoyed the aroma of coffees and soaps, and all the odors associated with the goods in the Overton warehouses on 7th Avenue East. Mr. Overton was quite a student in Bible prophecy, and an interesting man with whom to converse. He loved azaleas and rhododendrons, and his private gardens on Kanuga Street highlighted exotic varieties he had imported from China. He always welcomed the public to visit those gardens during the springtime when blooms (spread over a couple of acres) were of every vivid color.

Jesse Jenkins

While his unique radio program had sold a lot of flour, he had to face the inevitable: Local food stores no longer needed a wholesale grocer. With his son (the Rev. A.J. Jr) traveling widely in Russia, Poland and the Middle East (and operating from New York), there was no successor to take his place. Mr. Overton quietly liquidated his inventory and closed the operation.

That left only the smallest of the three, the American Drug Company, still in business. This past April 1996, I stopped in for a visit with the man who operated the company for 75 years, Jesse Jenkins. He celebrated his 96th birthday in 1996, and even to the time of his death, he made up the daily bank deposit and was overseer of all operations. He had outlived his son, Lawrence, who had been in business with his father until his death. But working alongside him was his daughter, Betty Jenkins May, and a supremely loyal staff who now concentrated not on trying to sell goods to large food stores but catered to the smaller country stores at Gerton, small cafes in Bat Cave, and service stations throughout the area. There has been only one man who was active in business for a longer period than Jesse Jenkins, and that was L. Trader Dermid, who ran a hardware store and lived to be 105.

A Rose is Like a Rose

I remember vividly Mr. Louis Williams seated in that old beat-up swivel chair in a cubicle he called his office at his junkyard on 7th Avenue East. Mr. Frank FitzSimons in Volume III of "From the Banks of the Oklawaha" told how Mr. Williams lost everything he owned with the crash of the land boom here in the late '20s, and how he was able to raise $200 and go into the junk and metal salvage business on 7th. In the '30s, young men would scrounge around trying to find discarded copper or brass pipes or hardware which could be sold to Louis Williams to provide spending money. In those hard years of the Great Depression, for some that scrap metal meant food on the table. Then, after World War II (when new cars were still scarce and hard to come by), many vets would buy old used cars and then scavenge through the junkyard at Louis Williams hoping to find parts to fix them up.

The Williams family consisted of three kids: Anne, Jake and Sammy. After the war, Sam and I had a common bond in that we had both served in

Louis Williams started a junk and metal salvage business in the late 1920s. It quickly became a family affair.

the Signal Corps. And in dull moments, we'd chew the fat about equipment that we operated and experiences each of us had had. That's when I discovered that Sam was given a special assignment to Paris and was billeted just a few blocks down the street from Gertrude Stein, whose writings included "Novel of Thank You –Vol. 8" and "How Writing is Written." I don't remember the grade in school when I was forced to read Gertrude Stein's "A Rose is Like a Rose that Grows Like a Rose," but when Sam mentioned her name, I remembered and was impressed. She (along with many other "free spirits") were drawn together in Paris during and at the end of the war, and I can only gather that Gertrude found Sam (smiling and nattily dressed in his Signal Corps uniform) a delightful addition to the intellectual elite who gathered at her home for regular soirees. Any time Sam and I would be involved in a nostalgia session, if I boasted that I was once billeted in the Messerschmidt house in Bavaria and met Mrs. Messerschmidt, Sam would casually toss in his Gertrude Stein experiences, which quickly put me in my place.

Another man who served in the Signal Corps was Morris Kaplan. He and Sam did their basic training together at Miami Beach. All summer in Florida, their outfit wore woolen ODs, and at the end of their training, they were finally issued summer cottons. That's when they were shipped to radio school in frigid Madison, Wisconsin—where Morris came down with the flu. Sammy, a good ole boy from the South, was helpful and sympathetic to Morris as he recuperated. Sammy was also a prolific letter writer, and one day shared with Morris a picture of his sister Anne, a beautiful girl. Morris was immediately smitten and asked Sam if he could add a few lines to Anne in one of Sam's letters. It ended in an idyllic romance, and Morris, a Scranton, Pennsylvania boy who had graduated from St. Thomas of Aquinas (now University of Scranton), had come straight to Hendersonville to marry Anne and join the Louis Williams family and business.

Morris became active in about every civic function in the community and served as president of most of the organizations of which he was a member. He took a strong leadership role in the Agudas Israel Synagogue. In 1968 he was asked by County Commissioner Gene Staton to serve on the County Library Board of Trustees. He not only went through the chairs, but still serves on the Library Board twenty-eight years later. His first experience in the little library building on King Street was to observe librarian Elizabeth Marshall resting her feet on a fruit box because water covered the basement floor. Morris watched the construction of the new building on the Freeze property on Washington Street, and twenty years later would oversee the multi-million dollar expansion which would make any community five times the size of our town swell with pride. He remembered to me the day he was handed a check from Russell Caywood; and he said when he looked at the number, he almost keeled over–a sum involving seven digits. Mr. Caywood retired here from a career in utilities. Morris also remembers a special gift from M/M Richard Sauer. He said they chatted for a few minutes, and Mrs. Sauer just sat down and wrote him a check for $50,000. Morris said he could mention Donald Stuart Atkins or Dudley Courtenay–but then he'd be bound to leave out some very important person. Next time you enter the library from the parking entrance, glance to your right. You'll see the Morris Kaplan Auditorium – the same Morris Kaplan who was nursed back from the flu by his would-be brother-in-law (Sam Williams) while serving in WWII in Madison, Wis.

I asked Morris to recall folks who were most helpful to him at the library over the past nearly thirty years; and he quickly recalled, "Oh, Louise Bailey–what a dear person, and what an asset to have her on the Board. And J.M. Foster–with his background in the public schools, he was a godsend. The FitzSimons family–that's both Frank Sr. and Young Frank." Morris paused and said, "I am making a mistake giving any names because I'll leave out so many who were vital to us." After a pause he said, "Sophie Davis could be difficult to get along with, but she was a brilliant person and she made a generous contribution to all our efforts."

Morris and Anne's son, David, and my son, Kermit Jr., had almost parallel careers in the military. David elected to leave the military and is now a research fellow at Logistics Management Institute in the D.C. area. Morris' daughter, Eileen, is married to a Dr. Stang and they live in Pikesville.

"And how did it feel, Morris," I asked, "to move to Hendersonville and be in business with the Williams family?"

"Oh," Morris said, "Sammy was already my best friend, and Jake (Sammy's older brother) was the smartest guy I ever met. Valedictorian in high school, 4.0 in college, Jake graduated in chemistry at Carolina." I nodded and recalled the many times I'd asked Jake a question about some paint, and he'd be standing there when I left, still spieling off every chemical and its characteristic that was in that paint bucket.

I always worked with Morris or Sammy, even when Mr. Williams was alive. I was in awe of Mr. Williams, though he was always smiling and was a very friendly individual. I was more comfortable with "the young bucks." They were anxious to change the emphasis of their business to hardware, plumbing supplies and structural steel. But "the old man" had started the business in junk and scrap metal, it had carried him through the Depression, and he would tolerate no thought of giving up that phase of the business—though it was nothing but hard work, dirt, and nickels and dimes. But the two boys never argued with this.

Mr. Louis Williams died in June 1971. On October 27, 1971, there was an ad in the *Times-News* which read:

NOTE: LOUIS WILLIAMS & SONS, INC., 701 7TH AVENUE EAST IS NO LONGER BUYING SCRAP METAL, AS THIS DIVISION OF OUR BUSINESS HAS BEEN DISCONTINUED.

Sam and I were active together in many community activities but most all in the Hendersonville Merchants' Association. Sam served as president of HMA, and his son, Danny, also has served as president of the organization. The highlight of the year for the Merchants' Board of Directors was a summertime "cookout" in what Sam and his wife, Flossie, called their "little shack out back." This screened-in pavillion was equipped with huge grills, refrigerators, tables—everything for a great social gathering. Flossie and the child bride had worked together on projects of the Junior Women's Club and the Possum Hollow Women's Club. Even now at Christmas, it takes a total family effort to make chicken liver pate from Flossie's famous recipe.

I knew their son, Sidney. He reminded me of myself at times because he was so hooked on broadcasting and show business. Sidney went to a broadcast school in Atlanta, then became involved with television, doing freelance work for WBTV and other stations for a number of years. In 1995 he traveled over Europe as stage and sound manager of the touring North Carolina School of the Arts. The daughter of Sam and Flossie, Sharon, is married to Kyle Wooten, who is a graduate speech therapist. And then we come to Danny. He got hooked watching Edgar Bergen and Charlie McCarthy, and at age eleven (as a ventriloquist), entered the local Rotary Club's Talent Hunt and insisted on competing in the Adult Division, which he won. Danny went on to become a professional magician which gave him a double whammy appeal in show business.

But Sammy said, "When Danny went to N.C. State and graduated in mechanical engineering, all of the sudden he could see the real potential of operating a business such as Dad had started and which we had kept alive." Sam said, "He's a real businessman. He could see what we needed to do now for the future. He had the courage to make the big investments and add services which no one else offers. As long as you have a guy with the talents of Danny," Sam proudly said, "you don't need to worry about a Lowe's or Wal-Mart–they'll send customers to you."

Jake Williams was valedictorian–though Sammy didn't do bad. He was salutatorian, and if Jake were around, he too would look with pride on his nephew Danny who started as a ventriloquist and magician at the age of eleven...but today serves on the board of First Union Bank, is a leader in the east side area, as well as serving as head of the Merchants. He is a pilot, a scuba diver, a mountain climber, a motorcycle rider; and above all else, carries the Williamosky banner proudly in today's business world. Yes, "the old man" (Grandpa Louis Williamosky) would be proud.

Not One—But Two

It is unusual for a town the size of Hendersonville to sprout and nurture not one but two ventriloquists, Danny Williams and Alex Houston. Back in 1948, WHKP was trying to establish itself in a field of competition that was fierce. We started with the old Mutual Broadcasting System which had a couple of great daytime ladies' audience participation shows: "Heart's Desire" and "Queen for a Day" with host Jack Bailey. Mutual did have the greatest kids' lineup in the afternoon with Tom Mix, Hop Harrigan and the Lone Ranger. But Mutual simply was not in the running in the evening prime-time hours. And with television first coming into the market with WBTV-Charlotte, and then Channel 4 Greenville, WHKP was forced to be innovative. We sponsored a 13-week-long Talent Hunt–a live stage show from the stage of the old State Theatre (a movie house that featured Grade B movies and westerns). The so-called stage facilities were virtually non-existent, and for a young man cutting his teeth in show business before a rude and unruly audience, it became a great learning experience for me. The talent show was a weekly elimination affair that lasted thirteen weeks and ended with the really big show with each of the thirteen winners and presentation of the grand prize in a winner-take-all competition.

That night we really packed 'em in, and they came ready to boo and hoot and hiss–the audience hit a new peak in being difficult to handle. But for some reason, the recalcitrant tolerated Alex. He had withstood the hoots and hollers and the catcalls and finally, as it became obvious he was to be the winner, the crowd started cheering Alex. Half-heartedly at first, but then in total conversion, they began to roar their approval at everything Alex said and did, and he was the stand-apart winner.

His grand prize was an all-expense-paid trip to New York for him and his parents (Mr. and Mrs. John Bell Houston) and also a guest appearance on the Lanny Ross Show on the Mutual Broadcasting System.

I included the following clip on the radio show of April 18, 1996, which is part of the cassette collection at the Henderson County Public Library and can be monitored along with any of the other excerpts included and referred to in this book.

(Alex has already completed about two minutes of his routine.)

Alex: Why, you're just plain stupid, Elmer. I'll bet you don't even know where Washington is.

Elmer: Washington, why he's dead.

Alex: No, no, Elmer. I mean the capital of the United States.

Elmer: Oh! They've loaned it all to Europe.

Lanny: (interrupting) Say, this

Alex Houston entered show business as a ventriloquist with his dummy Elmer, given to him by a show business personality from High Point.

fella's not so dumb after all. Alex, I want to congratulate you on winning those wonderful prizes down there. Tell me, is Elmer playing hookie from school today?

Alex: Yes sir, I'm afraid he is.

Lanny: I hope he'll learn his lessons. Does he know how to sing?

Alex: Well, he tries a little bit.

Lanny: Well, there's a new song—the one I opened with this morning, called "Zing, Zing, Zoom, Zoom." Suppose Elmer and I warm up our pipes and sing a little duet together.

Alex: How do you like that, Elmer?

Elmer: Sounds fine to me.

Lanny: Elmer, all you have to do is sing "Zing, Zing, Zoom, Zoom" every time it comes up.

Elmer: Zing, Zing, Zoom, Zoom—oh, that's easy!

(A reprise of the chorus with both singing)

Lanny: The song is over, Elmer, but you are very good.

Net Ancr: No wonder he won all those prizes down South.

Alex Houston did acts with Elmer whenever he could to help pay his way through Brevard College. Meanwhile, he and his brother (John Bell Houston Jr.) clog danced with the North Carolina Cloggers, managed by their mom and dad. Alex then got a chance to do a USO Show in Korea. From that work, he was signed by Agent Promoter Connie B. Gay, who ran a huge country dance hall and radio show outside of Washington D.C. starring Jimmy Dean. Alex worked this variety show up through the summer of 1958 when Dean was given an opportunity on a new CBS-TV show. Alex took on a much more important role with the Connie B. Gay troupe, he became a writer—not just for his own part of the show, but for the show itself, which had such guest stars as Ronnie Milsap, Dolly Parton and others.

Alex received a recording contract and dubbed a few records including a comedy parody, "Here Comes Peter Cotton Klaus." Over the years, Alex worked on the Charley Pride Show while making appearances in Miami and Las Vegas. In one summer, Alex worked nineteen state fairs. Alex has reached the "greying age," but could write a book about his experiences in show business, a career that started on the stage of the old State Theatre in 1949.

Hilde – Who?

In February of 1997, I was visiting with Jody Barber. It was one of our regular get-togethers to associate memories with pictures, and he was bubbling with excitement. He discovered a picture of Jan Garber different from any others known to exist. Just then, Jeff Michels, an RN at Pardee Hospital Home Health Care, walked in with an associate he was training. Jeff has monitored Jody's health for many months and has experienced similar excitement of Jody's before. Jody excitedly greeted him with, "Jeff, here's a picture of Jan Garber you haven't seen before." The first reaction he got from Jeff was exactly the same as the reaction the whole staff at the radio station gave to me when I proudly announced that Hildegarde was coming to town and would entertain at one of the art galleries each day before the auction of some of her jewelry. In unison, "Who is Hildegarde?" Jeff's facial expression said the same, "Who is Jan Garber?"

At times, it is difficult for our generation to understand that most of the people we see and talk to today were not even born when Jan Garber's big band played all summer at the Laurel Park Pavilion (the South's second largest dance floor); or Hal Kemp, whose band played all summer at the Carolina Pavillion. And even folks who have retired here from metro areas in the East and Midwest are surprised to learn that Hendersonville was a mecca for big bands. . .in large part due to the J.K. Livingston family. "Jake" was almost 40 years old when he moved his family from Charleston to Hendersonville. He and his wife, Maude, had five children, the oldest boy was named Cyral Earl (who everyone knew as "Buster") and another son was named "Jimmie" (who organized his own big band while going to school at Belmont Abbey). The three girls were Virginia (who married W.H. Kriedler and lived in Cincinnati), Lutrell (who married Sam Fortson and lived in Augusta), and Millicent (who married John T. Wilkins Jr., the son of a former mayor).

J.K.'s first business was the Cinderella Shoe Store. The very name of the store reflected the imaginative flair of the old man. He also operated a summer hotel in Edneyville and an emporium on 4th Avenue that he called "The Bandbox," which became a number one hangout for teens. With the help of his son "Buster" (his son Jimmie already headed his own big band), J.K. Livingston became the promoter of big-name bands booked for Hendersonville for one-night stands. Most of these big band dances were held in the old Hendersonville High School gymnasium (a huge, old wooden building which stood on the north end of Dietz Field, next to Boyd Pontiac-Cadillac).

Meanwhile, his son Jimmie's band was signed by MCA (Music Corporation of America), which is still today one of the largest show business management firms. He dubbed one record for Victor, "I Can Dream, Can't I?" and "Don't Cry Joe, Let Her Go." Jimmie played primarily the college circuit in those years. They would do a one-night stand, and then back into the big old touring cars or a second-hand bus to drive all night to the next stop. Jimmie Livingston was seriously injured in a wreck and never regained his full health. He moved to Daytona Beach where he sold real estate when he felt up to it. He died at age 44. Hal Kemp was killed in a car crash at Madera, Calif. He was only 36. "Buster" followed in the footsteps of his father, booking into Hendersonville such big names as Guy Lombardo and the Royal Canadians, and Cab Calloway and his 15-piece Cotton Club Orchestra. Calloway was known as "His Royal Highness of Hi-De-Ho." Later, "Buster" brought to town the famous Dorsey Brothers band, Bob Crosby and the Bobcats, and even Johnny Long's Orchestra, which had dubbed the famous song about Charlie Justice, "All the Way, Choo Choo," on the King label.

The last time Jan Garber appeared in Hendersonville, Walter B. Smith gave him a lot in Laurel Park on which to build a house and retire. He didn't retire here, but in retirement, Jan was featured in ads appearing in veterans and fraternal magazines endorsing a product to get rid of grey hair.

"Buster" Livingston is the one person in Hendersonville you would describe as avant-garde. If Buster walked into a room (and you didn't know him), you'd make it a point to find out who he was before he left. He wore mens' fashions at least two years ahead of what was being worn in this area at that time. He stood erect, with a carriage that quickly identified him as being "somebody." And yet, if you were fortunate enough to find yourself in conversation with him, he gave to you the feeling that he thoroughly enjoyed seeing you, and that he was listening to every word you had to say. He spoke with the opposite of a drawl–his words were clipped, thoroughly enunciated, and whatever he had to say, you had the feeling you'd just heard something profound.

Buster promoted big bands on the side. His livelihood came from food, fun, and people businesses. After he had acquired the franchise to operate a union bus terminal, he built a brand new building at 7th and Main which gave

Tracy's Place was opened by Buster Livingston, named after basic training buddy Tracy Oelkers.

Greyhound, Trailways, and Queen City much more elaborate and complete facilities. Next door, he added a large restaurant called Tracy's Place.

The mark of a smart and successful man is one who can lure other smart men to align themselves with him and devote their entire career to managing his business interests. He hired Oden Morris to run the bus station; and even today, I would match Oden's memory against any computer in any travel agency. I used to watch Oden at work—talking on two telephones with a customer in front of him at the counter—quoting exact times of departure and rates all at the same time. And he always wore a broad smile. I never saw Oden lose his patience or his temper. I don't know the arrangement Buster had with the manager of the restaurant, or lunchroom. It was called Tracy's Place, named for a fella from Murphy by the name of Tracy Oelkers.

Young people today react with incredulousness when you mention that you took your basic training in Florida and your quarters were in one of the hotels. America's buildup for entry into World War II moved so fast it almost bankrupted the tourist business in Florida and elsewhere. I suppose it was old Sen-a-tuh Claude Pep-puh (persimmon mouth trough feeder) who dreamed up the scheme of having the government lease all the empty hotels and use them to billet troops while they were given training. It would also inspire patriotism among the locals and the few tourists who were there. They watched the recruits marching through the streets, observed their calisthenics on high school athletic fields and in parks, and sat in the grandstands and watched retreat formations. The GI's stood at attention (under a blistering sun) so long on the hot asphalt, their combat boots would gradually sink into the tar surface.

Tracy Oelkers and I were assigned to the Huntington Hotel in St. Petersburg. Please bear in mind that Tracy's life to this point had been in the cafe where he either watched over the food operation at night or searched for a cockfight that was being held somewhere in the mountains. Tracy was a man who had rarely seen the light of day. In our first weeks at the Huntington, Tracy would sit in the bathroom (it was the only room with a light on at night) and he would ready funny books. Just before dawn, he'd make it to his bunk and sack out. When the roll was called at reveille, Tracy was nowhere to be seen. As the drill sergeant worked his way down the alphabetical roll, his shout of each last name would get a response from the troops:

Drill Sgt.: "EDNEY"

Me: "Kermit (NMI)"

When he would get to Tracy's name, his struggle with Oelkers was so great that he never noticed that I was yelling back "Tracy M" and Tracy would sleep on until time for drill formation. As we'd fall out for training, we were supposed to add one salt tablet to our canteen as it was filled each morning. This was to make up for perspiration which came from the blazing heat on the drill fields and parade grounds. Instead of salt, Tracy would fill his canteen with whiskey "for a little pick-me-up later in the morning." This worked fine until one day the drill sergeant ordered all the non-coms to test the water in each man's canteen to be sure salt had been added. The non-com took one swig of Tracy's firewater, and all hell broke loose. The entire battalion spent the rest of the afternoon double-timing around the track, and Tracy had threats on his life.

I discovered that a couple of civilians sitting near the pay telephone were undercover police who were trying to catch the guy who was putting slugs in the coin slot of the telephone. It was Tracy. While the rest of us struggled with full packs on forced marches, Tracy was as fresh as a daisy–his pack was stuffed with the pillow from his bunk. He went AWOL just to get a beer. Tracy Oelkers (who had run Tracy's Place at the bus station) was given the perfect assignment for his qualifications: He ran a beer PX in California for the rest of the war.

A Hole in the Head

For many of the older, dilapidated hotels in Florida, World War II was a godsend. If you were not able to lease the building to the Army, Air Force, or Navy, the rooms in the hotels (not leased by the military) were suddenly in great demand by the sweethearts and/or families of the servicemen training in that area. The more enterprising hotel owners even developed a specialty service–"rooms by the hour." Space in the busier training centers was at such a premium, smart hotel operators figured out that with quick maid service early in the morning, the room used the night before could be rented again for the daytime customers.

A young fellow by the name of Arnold Schulman was growing up in Miami Beach during the war, and his father ran such a hotel. In the late '50s Arnold got the urge to write about these experiences and called the book "A

Hole in the Head." In 1957 it was staged on Broadway, and in 1959 was made into a movie starring Frank Sinatra, Eleanor Parker, Edward G. Robinson, Carolyn Jones, and Keenan Wynn. It was directed by Frank Capra. James Van Heusen and Sammy Cahn's song "High Hopes" won the Oscar that year. This was the springboard which would, in 1963, see Arnold Schulman do the screenplay of "Love With the Proper Stranger," starring Natalie Wood. And in 1969 Arnold did the screenplay for "Goodbye Columbus," starring Ali McGraw.

At the time, I was ignorant of the fact that the famed playwright Arnold Schulman was the nephew of Hendersonville's Jack Schulman, who ran a clothing store on Main Street. Jack had earlier come to me and asked if I would consider running a "speakeasy" for those people who had difficulty in public speaking. I was familiar with the Toastmaster's Club, but there was not one in operation here. Jack insisted that he would help recruit members who would be willing to pay a tuition which would provide for me a reasonable stipend for leading the group, moderating, teaching, and critiquing. Part of my study at UNC had been in speech and these classes would deal with confidence, self-assurance, some voice techniques, breath control, lack of phonation, and exercises to increase vocabulary. I remember Morris Kaplan also became interested and was a big help in recruiting members. We met weekly in the basement of Jack Shulman's store.

Morris remembered the classes as being fun, and how well most of the participants did. But Jack Shulman's fear of speaking in front of an audience was a long way from being conquered. At Kiwanis, when he was asked to introduce the speaker at the weekly meeting, he quickly caught a plane for New York and called back to tell them he was out of town and unable to make the meeting.

Jack and I worked together in the Henderson County Industrial Development Corporation, and I was very proud of the progress he had made. He presided over the meetings and keep the direction of the discussion focused. One day, General Manager Art Cooley of WHKP came in and said, "Jack Schulman wants to do a daily talk show with you every morning."

"What kind of talk show?"

"I don't know. As you know, he watches Johnny Carson and all those public affairs discussion programs. He feels that the two or you could take ten or fifteen minutes

Caricature of Jack Schulman promoted his radio series "Talk About Talk."

every morning and talk about anything from mish mash to hodge podge."

I had great trepidations over such a series. We never had time to rehearse, certainly no time to write anything special, and in fact, in all the years we did the program, the only words spoken before the show began were "Good morning." The shows were taped. After all, we were not only "winging it," we were "flying blind." But in all the years the program was on the air, we only had to redub once.

Jack dearly loved catching me off guard. He would spend endless time reading through trivia books, or finding words such as "ampersand" and would open with something like, "O.K., let's talk about the old ampersand this morning." If I was really lucky and knew the word, I could respond with something like, "And what else would you like to talk about other than the symbol for 'and'?"

Each day was tougher than before . . . he'd challenge me with "obsequious" or "stertorously" or "suspiration." Sometimes a root word would give me a clue, but when I pulled a total blank, it made his day. I discovered that Jack Schulman was not only a lover of, but a learned student of history. He had read and re-read Will and Muriel Durant's multi-volume History of Civilization.

Perhaps it came from his nephew Arnold, but his love for the theater was unmatched. He kept the playbills from every Broadway show he and his wife, Evelyn, attended. Before they retired and moved to Atlanta, he brought a huge box down to the radio station filled with over a thousand playbills. When his nephew Arnold was just getting started in show business, he roomed with Paddy Cheyefsky. Jack became their patron sponsor. He helped pay rent, buy groceries and take care of their cost of living in New York as they worked their apprenticeships. And he lived for those brief periods each year when he and Evelyn would go on a buying trip to New York and he'd get to see all that was new on Broadway.

Jack Schulman's store, located on Main Street, operated as a typical small-town department store with clothing for all ages. Later, it became a discount store specializing in overcuts.

Every day I learned more and more about Jack Schulman. At the end of each show, I'd say, "Come in and sit a spell with me." Jack's father brought his fairly large family south from New York City after their mother became institutionalized. His father's trade was tailoring. The family rented a building in a small Southern town, opened a tailor shop downstairs and the family lived upstairs. Jack had a very heavy accent and quickly became the target of school bullies, "Who gets to beat up the little Jew boy today?" Jack confided that the only time he felt safe was when he was in his garret room upstairs with the shades pulled. He could not think of one happy memory from childhood.

One morning, Jack shared with me one of the most poignant, touching experiences I'd ever heard. In school (very much like Charlie Brown in the comic strip "Peanuts") there was one little girl in his class that Jack absolutely worshipped, but he could never gain enough confidence to speak to her. In his senior year, out of the blue, she came up to Jack and asked if he'd like to drive her to the Jewish Debutante Ball in Raleigh the following month. Jack was delirious. He had no car and he didn't know how to drive, but he took driving lessons and was able to borrow a car. On the assigned day, he picked up "his dream" and they headed for the Sir Walter Hotel. As he pulled up to the curb in front of the hotel in Raleigh, a handsome Beau Brummel stepped up, opened the passenger door and helped the girl out of the car. She turned and said, "Thanks for bringing me to Raleigh, Jack, I have a ride home." In all my life, I had never heard of a more perfidious performance. When he finished the story, I felt like crying on Jack's behalf. He quickly retorted, "It's good that it happened that way. She grew up to be fat and ugly. I'm glad I didn't get stuck with her." When I got to know Jack, I could understand how he had erected this crusty shell around himself. He was protecting an innocent little New York boy forced into being an object of hate and ridicule, and he had drawn a line to stand for no further abuse from his peers or even would-be friends.

Being the avid reader that he was, Jack was familiar with the writings of Mark Twain, who had been born in 1835, and who said his life was based on the orbit of Halley's comet and it would end when the comet reappeared in 1910. Sure enough, Halley's comet appeared on schedule in April 1910, and Mark Twain died. Jack was born in 1910 and he feared when the comet reappeared in 1986 that would also be the end for him. But April in 1986, the comet came and went—Jack lived on and on. He was still doing "Talk About Talk" when he became an octogenarian.

After First Federal purchased the buildings he owned on Main Street, he decided it was time to dispose of his business and move closer to his daughter Toni in Atlanta. After they had already sold or given away most of their furnishings, he and I did a last walk through their house, which he insisted should be built with no interior doors. He spotted a gallon jug of Borghini Chianti (with a decorative spout standing one full meter above the colorful straw casing which encased the bottle). He said, "Take this." Then he spotted a watercolor of the Cote d'Azur and said, "And this too. Maybe Katherine can use it in her new sunroom." And believe it or not, the pastel pinks and blues in the framed watercolor were the exact color tones that predominated the new sunroom. There was not much conversation on this last visit between us. It was obvious he dreaded leaving Hendersonville. But he occasionally would say, "They do have great libraries in Atlanta, and I hear there are frequent seminars I'll be able to attend."

His only complaint here: "All the men want to talk about is business and sports. I care nothing for either. It's such a thrill when someone wants to talk about history, the arts, even movies." There was only one Jack Schulman.

Carl Sandburg

O f all the writers who were born (or had roots) in Hendersonville, the most famous was the biographer of Lincoln, Carl Sandburg. I was still in Europe in 1945 when Sandburg bought the Memminger place in Flat Rock which originally had been named Rock Hill. When Capt. W.A. Smyth bought the place, he changed the name to Connemara. As I remember, my dad (in one of his infrequent letters to me overseas) told me that Carl Sandburg bought the home, but was more impressed that his first cousin, K.G. "King" Morris, had handled the sale and pocketed a nice commission. The name "King" came from his mother, Amanda King (dad's aunt, who had married William Brownlow Gunaway Morris, one of the early educators of the county). King Morris' nephews included: Richard Morris, who worked for the *Asheville Citizen*; Carl Morris, who ran the Home Food Shop; Jim Morris, who worked for the *Durham Morning Sun*; and Frank Van der Linden, who was a Washington correspondent and confidante of Cordell Hull.

In an interview with WHKP's Larry Freeman, Mrs. Lillian Steichen Sandburg (wife of Carl) described how the Sandburg family ended up buying a home and moving to Western North Carolina (an audio cassette of the following is in the Henderson County Public Library):

"We made the trip toward Cincinnati, and then came on toward Blue Ridge and Virginia; and as we traveled along that way, it was very pleasant. It was a little warmer and up North there'd been some ice and snow when we left there. But it was when we came near Asheville that we said, 'The air is different, there's a taste about this air that's just wonderful. This is where we're going to want to live whenever the time comes when we can move.' We also went across the Smoky Mountains, too, and made the tour of the Smokies. And then we traveled further south and we said, 'It's all very nice down here, but in this part of the world the trees were sort of like what we were used to. We didn't want to get to living way down in Florida. There was beautiful scenery and everything here, this would be the place.' That made up our minds to it. But then we had to wait until the war was over."

Mrs. Sandburg had grown weary of the hustle and bustle of big city life in the Chicago area, and yearned for "a place in the country" where Carl could shut himself off from the world and meditate and create, and where Mrs. Sandburg could raise her beloved goats. Mrs. Sandburg was the business manager for the Sandburg family. If one went directly to the famous poet with a request for an appearance or some-

The Sandburgs at Connemara.

thing he had written, it wouldn't be long before they'd hear from Mrs. Sandburg—"that if Carl were to appear, there would be an honorarium amounting to several hundred dollars."

Mrs. Sandburg enjoyed being the herdsperson for her prize-winning goats, she also found buyers willing to pay premium prices for the goat milk produced at Connemara. Carl's favorite beverage was his own homemade rhubarb wine (which he would occasionally share with visitors); he also enjoyed an occasional malt beverage. A number of convenience stores remember Mrs. Sandburg making her selection from the cooler but insisting on paying the lower price charged for beer on the shelf.

Carl Sandburg not only experienced very productive years at Connemara, they were happy years. The community afforded the Sandburgs as much privacy as they desired, but Carl also enjoyed the role of a world-class celebrity when he ventured into the community to share of himself with young and old alike. Sandburg had already passed his 75th birthday when Lt. Gov. Luther Hodges became governor on the death of William B. Umstead on Nov. 7, 1954. Hodges was one of the very few governors to come from the field of business or commerce. He earned a special niche in history for developing the concept and building the now famous Research Triangle Park. Following his term as governor, he was appointed Secretary of Commerce by President John Kennedy. Governor Hodges was always credited with being glib of tongue, being suave, and being a smooth talker. He quickly saw the merit of honoring Carl Sandburg to draw favorable national publicity for North Carolina, the state Sandburg had chosen for retirement. So Gov. Hodges (after a lengthy accolade and flattering remarks) named Carl Sandburg, quote: NORTH CAROLINA'S AMBASSADOR OF GOOD WILL! Sandburg was most gracious in accepting the high honor but managed a bit of chivalrous wit in his acceptance (cassette in library):

"Course I could say I falter for words, that wouldn't be strictly accurate. It's all been so warm-hearted here, and these two friends of mine, they have the words. I have a right to ask it. Did you write that yourself?

He mentioned novelties or human performance—at once it made me think of that six-volume biography of Lincoln. It was written by a man whose father could not sign his name. He made his mark on documents. And it was written—the whole million and a half words—written by a man whose mother could not write her name. She made the mark!"

Carl Sandburg was not only a world-renowned writer and poet, he was also known for his songbooks and Rutabaga stories; and with his guitar, he could charm the stripes off a zebra. One talent he possessed but never heralded was his acting ability. There was a certain presence about Sandburg. At a cocktail party, if it appeared the great man was about to speak, the room would (with prompting from no one) become hushed and attentive.

Sandburg was born Jan. 6, 1878, in Galesburg, Ill., and on Jan. 5, 1953, he left by train for Chicago, where he would be guest of honor at a birthday celebration marking his 75th birthday. WHKP broadcast that program from 9:30 to 10 a.m. on Jan. 6, 1953, but we have no recording of it. We were still dependent on wire recorders, which were totally undependable.

For his 75th birthday, BMI shipped to WHKP one of the first magnetic tape recorders. The station was asked to transport and present it to Mr. Sandburg with appropriate greetings. It was a large and heavy machine in a wooden case, and because there was a handle on the case, it was called portable. Our chief engineer, Charlie Renfrow, discovered that if you fed a portion of the output of the machine back into the input, you could create electronic reverberation. Prior to this time, to get an echo, you had to build an "echo chamber" which only the networks could afford. And now this miracle—an electronic echo (either quick or sustained), depending on the speed of the tape.

Sandburg knew nothing about tape recorders, and it fell to me to deliver the machine to him and orient him as to its operation. He was delighted, and planned to immediately record some songs for his grandchildren.

I crossed the front porch and was in the process of taking my leave when he issued the equivalent of what we in the mountains would equate to, "Why not take time to sit a spell?" For me, it was an invitation which I quickly accepted. But having been taught respect for my elders ("not to speak unless spoken to"), I waited for Mr. Sandburg to open the conversation. It was a warm, still summer afternoon, and we sat silent for some time before he began talking about the history of Connemara. Not so much about Connemara itself, but the fact that Christopher Memminger, treasurer of the Confederacy, had built and lived on this place.

On this occasion, as I sat alone on the porch with the great author, I really was dealt first-hand an example of his ability to make the uttering of mere words a tremendously dramatic experience. Sandburg gazed out across the terraced front yard—in those days populated by a goat herd—it WAS more of a yard than a lawn—and he said, "In the evening hours, when the air is very still, if you listen carefully, you can hear the ghost of Memminger." Hearing him speak those words so eloquently was awesome. I stayed only a short while, not wanting to wear out my welcome.

Several months went by and a call came in that Mr. Sandburg's tape machine was not working—could we have someone check on it. Hoping to maintain the cordial relationship we had established with the poet, I went to Connemara, struggled with that heavy machine, manhandling it down those steep front steps, and on back to the radio station where it was placed on the work bench.

Charlie Renfrow examined the machine, made repairs and said it could be returned. When I had brought the machine into the station, there was a tape on it with Carl and his grandchildren cavorting through songs and jokes. Before returning it to Sandburg, I flipped the machine on to be sure it was working; and all that I heard was "HELLO THERE, HELLO THERE," in full echo. One of the station employees (fascinated with the electronic reverb) had played around and erased Sandburg's tape.

You cannot imagine the panic that hit me. How could this goof-up be explained to the great Carl Sandburg... the Sandburg who was always treated to the great watering holes of New York by Edward R. Murrow (who worshipped at his feet). I was able to get the phone number of Sandburg's daughter, Helga, in Alexandria, Va., and chatting with her for the first time on the phone, explained my horrible predicament. I said, "If I can contract with a radio station there in Alexandria to bring a tape recorder to your home, would you be kind enough to have your children do an oral 'letter to Grandpa'?" She laughed and then said with sincere tenderness, "Mr. Edney, we'll be delighted to cooperate, and I'm sure that my father will be most understanding."

I don't remember the charges billed, but it did wipe out our meager profit for that month. When the tape came in, I knew at once we had scored big. The two kids, coaxed by a quality radio personality in Alexandria, had done a "spirited letter to Grandpa" which was delightful and very touching.

With great trepidation, I manhandled that voluminous machine up those front steps again and was encouraged, "Just bring it on in the office." I remember Carl's "office" back then was a large room, perhaps ten times as big but just as chaotic as Kenneth Youngblood's office. He and I pushed aside old stacks of newspapers, magazines, and books and made room for the recorder.

As I punched the start button, I watched the expression on his face. He absolutely was glowing with excitement and enthusiasm. As the grandchildren went through their routine, he would clap his hands and sing along with them, thoroughly enjoying every minute. When the tape ended, I then explained to him what had happened. He leaned back in his chair and rolled with laughter. "That's the greatest gift I've ever been given. How soon can

I get you to pick this thing up again for service and be sure to have the same fellow do the same thing again. This is marvelous." After that, he would call about every three or four months and inquire, "How are things? Is there anything in the community I should know about?"

The simple greatness of Carl Sandburg might be illustrated from an experience dating back to May 3, 1956. I was told that a member of the faculty, the Rev. Earl Kilpatrick (now with Missionary Frontier Baptist Church in Harlingen, Texas) had suggested to the senior class that they dedicate their yearbook, "The Parade," to their most distinguished neighbor, Carl Sandburg. When Sandburg learned of this, he insisted on coming to the school to receive his personal copy, which was presented to him by the editor, Wilma Hill (now Mrs. Bob Dermid, owner of Dermid's Exxon). After receiving the book, Carl brought forth his guitar, sang songs, read poetry, and simply shared his thoughts with the students.

The Sandburgs listen to the replacement tape made by their grandchildren after WHKP accidentally erased the original.

Every high school student had to memorize Sandburg's descriptive "Fog like cat feet descending on Chicago." But for this group he chose: "Let the nanny goats and billy goats of the shanty people eat the clover over my grave, and if any yellow hair or any blue smoke of flowers is good enough to grow over me, let the dirty fisted children of the shanty people pick the flowers."

Most great writers are avaricious readers. And Carl Sandburg had an awesome collection of books. It was not a library of handsomely bound classics nor collector quality heritage books nor first editions. Instead there were paperbacks and old tattered books. He would take a single line some author had penned and would ruminate at length over the author's intent. One of his favorite authors was Ralph Waldo Emerson. Here is Sandburg critiquing an Emerson line (cassette in library):

"One day in the month of March, the entry in his journal was not a complete sentence at all. He wrote, quote: 'Bad to see a row of children looking old.' BAD

TO SEE A ROW OF CHILDREN LOOKING OLD. I can think of writers nowadays in the fields of both fiction and poetry, some in the realm of history, and as I read them I have the feeling–'You were born old. You never had a childhood. You never knew what it was to have the follies of healthy children.'"

Down through the years, it has been a truly rare occasion when anyone is asked to address a joint session of the North Carolina House and Senate. Sandburg was given that honor and distinction and he thoroughly enjoyed the experience.

Carl Sandburg enjoyed a remarkably long life. I would recommend Mead Parce's book "Twice Told True Tales of the Blue Ridge and Great Smokies" to digest over again the details of the quiet funeral held at St. John in the Wilderness Church, which made national and international news wires for twenty-four hours.

Shortly after Sandburg died in 1967, the Chamber of Commerce and media began pressuring Congressman Roy Taylor to secure Congressional authorization for the U.S. Department of the Interior to purchase the Sandburg home and establish it as a national historic park. In 1968, Congressman Taylor spoke to the Thanksgiving joint session of the Rotary and Kiwanis Clubs in Hendersonville (tape in library):

"I've introduced a bill authorizing the acquiring by the government of the Carl Sandburg home property at Flat Rock as a national historic site. Carl Sandburg was one of America's greatest writers and great citizens of all time. Mrs. Sandburg favors this legislation that I have introduced, and she thinks the home in Flat Rock is the most appropriate place in the nation to develop an historic shrine or site honoring Carl Sandburg. Mrs. Sandburg stated to me that they had lived in Flat Rock longer than any other place in the nation and that beautiful home and grounds there can be left intact along with the furnishings, the books, and momentoes which reflect the life and personality of the great Carl Sandburg."

At the time Taylor introduced the resolution, there was only one other historic site in North Carolina at Ft. Raleigh. The National Military Park at Guilford Court House, the National Battlefield at Moore's Creek, part of the Blue Ridge Parkway, and the Appalachian Trail existed; but this would be the first time a staffed national historic site would be located in this region, and it was a major first. The legislation was signed by Richard M. Nixon, and Ronald G. Thoman was appointed the first superintendent. The dedication and first tours took place on May 11, 1974. Congressman Taylor was the featured speaker (cassette in library):

"Mrs. Sandburg donated the personal effects in the building which are valuable, and much of her husband's literary effects–a gift to the nation. Now this home and this farm are in keeping with the genuine rugged personality of Carl Sandburg, and constitute a fitting tribute to his memory."

Mrs. Connie Hudson Backlund served as superintendent in 1997. She told me that in an average year, 65,000 people tour the grounds and go through the historic mansion. She said that at least that number simply walk the trails, visit the grounds and barnyard, or attend programs in the amphitheater, which would boost total attendance to 130,000 each year. The busiest time of the year is, of course, the summer months, with another peak in the leaf color season of autumn.

In recent years, the budget remained flat—a total of only $500,000 for year-round operation of this 258-acre site. Ms. Backlund said the Sandburg site depends heavily on VIPs (Volunteers in the Park). Of only seventeen positions on the federal payroll, four are seasonal rangers who work only six months during the busier months; three are part-time employees; and four others are furloughed two months out of the year. She has logged more than 11,000 volunteer hours at the Sandburg place.

In the future, there are plans to use the park as a classroom with the goal of improving the experience of school groups visiting the Sandburg home, creating lesson plans and activities which will provide an exceptional learning experience. Cooperating in this effort are UNC-Asheville, UNC-Charlotte, the University of South Carolina, Blue Ridge Community College, and Eastern National Park & Monument Association. The Vagabond Workshop Theatre will continue both "World of Carl Sandburg" and "Rutabaga Stories" under the trees during the summer months each year.

Sandburg used to say he could hear "the ghosts of Memminger". This past summer as I walked back down the drive from the old Sandburg home, I felt I could hear Sandburg laughing when I told him how badly we had goofed up at WHKP.

Before the Face of God

C arl Sandburg was part of this community for more than twenty years, and now the Sandburg home is the number one tourist destination in the community. But the area can also boast of its connection with F. Scott Fitzgerald, Sidney Lanier and Dubose Heyward.

Fitzgerald spent several months writing in his room in the Skyland Hotel, while his wife was hospitalized in Asheville. When asked why he chose Hendersonville, he said, "I didn't know anybody there and wouldn't be bothered."

Sidney Lanier lived in Lynn, in Polk County. He was a close personal friend and often a guest at George Gustav Westfeldt's home, a portion of which you can still see from I-26 as you pass the Rockwell plant. In one of Lanier's memorials he wrote:

"Night slipped to dawn and pain merged into beauty,
　　　Bright grew the road his weary feet had trod.
He gave his salutation to the morning
　　　And found himself before the face of God."

On January 28, 1986, when the spacecraft Challenger exploded (killing the crew of seven), President Ronald Reagan, in a eulogy to the space crew, concluded with the final line of the above memorial written by Sidney Lanier.

Dubose Heyward lived at Dawn Hill at the corner of old Kanuga and Price Roads. It was in a cottage adjacent to the main house that he and George Gershwin wrote the bulk of "Porgy and Bess." Heyward did the libretto for Gershwin, which was based on his play "Porgy."

The most prolific writer to have lived here was Glenn Tucker, the famed Civil War writer. Among his books available in the public library are: "High Tide at Gettysburg"; "Tecumseh, Vision of Glory"; "Chickamaugua, Bloody Battle of the West"; "Barbary Pirates–Dawn Like Thunder"; "Lee and Longstreet"; "Mad Anthony Wayne"; and "Zeb Vance, Champion of Personal Freedom." Tucker was a native of Indiana and a writer for the *New*

York World newspaper. He covered the White House under Presidents Wilson, Harding and Coolidge. After being involved for a while in ad agency work, he and his wife Dorothy (influenced by his old friend E.E. McBride) decided to move here and bought the house next door to the McBrides. Tucker was also a student of the War of 1812, and wrote a two-volume set titled "Poultroons and Patriots." His "Tecumseh, Vision of Glory," written in 1956, won him the coveted Mayflower Award. After he had written "High Tide of Gettysburg," which was looked upon as a masterpiece of literature, he gave great credit to Mr. Frank L. FitzSimons for assist-

Glenn Tucker

ing him with first-hand knowledge he was able to incorporate in his writing.

In 1963, Tucker changed directions totally with the book on the "Barbary Pirates–Dawn Like Thunder." This is a period of history usually covered with a few brief paragraphs in school textbooks. Most Americans do not know that for more than 20 years (beginning with the administration of George Washington and continuing through James Madison), the U.S., along with all other nations, followed a policy of paying tribute in money, ships, and goods to a collection of pirates who did not have the force to exact such a policy. Tucker impacts fully in this book that it was the Barbary wars with the pirates that really gave birth to the U.S. Navy and Marine Corps. And for the second time, Tucker (with this book) was given the Mayflower Award.

After Ernest McBride and his wife moved from Crest Road at Upward, N.C., Tucker and his wife, Dorothy, also moved over to Fairview to be near another old friend, Joe McKinnon. Joe had been in the circus business and wrote a book about circus life called "Horse Dung Trail." Glenn Tucker received an honorary Doctor of Letters degree from the University of North Carolina. He also won the Mayflower Award for an unprecedented third time for his book on Zeb Vance.

Glenn Tucker, Carl Sandburg, Dubose Heyward and F. Scott Fitzgerald are only four of more than a dozen individuals who wrote of the history of the county, or wrote while living here.

One of the earliest books published was by Henry Grady Edney, my father, written in 1928. It was the life story of the famous black boxing champion, Theodore "Tiger" Flowers. The book, available at the Henderson County Public Library, was published by the Country Club Publishing Company of Biltmore. This particular "Country Club" was also known as "The Green House." It was a large green building with a porch virtually surrounding the structure and was located on Brookside Camp Road at the

Asheville Highway across from Grimesdale. It had a reputation of being home to high-stakes card games, and I was told that several entrepreneurs of the time felt that a book about "Tiger" Flowers (the first black to win a major title in boxing) would experience strong sales throughout the black communities in the South. This group hired Dad to write the book. By the time it was published, the boom was nearing its end, the gaunt days of the Depression were just around the corner, and Dad's share of the profits turned out to be thousands of unsold books. I can remember every time we moved (which was often in my youth), those hundreds of boxes of books would have to be carried along. Blessed mildew finally got into the boxes and all had to be disposed of as garbage. Other than the copy in the Henderson County Library, only a few copies held by collectors are available today.

The first book dealing with the history of the county was written by Sadie Patton and was published in 1947. It immediately created a furor between the mountain natives and the aristocracy of Flat Rock. The natives felt she had given far too much credit to Flat Rock people for their role in establishing the county. Both Sadie Smathers and Preston Fidelia Patton were of the landed gentry. In the Register of Deeds office in the Henderson County Court House (both in Grantee and Grantor Indexes from 1900 to 1967) hundreds and hundreds of documents are registered involving Sadie and Pres Patton. But even today, Sadie is still controversial. Many people raise their eyebrows when Sadie Patton is referred to as the county's first historian. I tend to take sides with Sadie. She did make the start, gave the beginning to historical writing about this area. Virtually every local writer since she was first published has used Sadie's book as a benchmark for testing further research. Plus, Sadie was most generous in

Sadie Patton

seeing that her husband, Preston, was properly memorialized through major gifts of land for Blue Ridge College and Patton Park.

Sadie used to josh me, saying mischieviously that all Edneys were really the bastard children of another writer, old man Bill Nye (the folklorist and newspaper editor who moved here and built an elaborate home overlooking Buck Shoals). She would laugh and say, "Your real name is spelled Ed-Nye." Just for the record, in the State Genealogical Library in Raleigh, Edney is spelled a variety of ways, including Ednye. But to have the last word, I'd always retort, "The Edneys were here long before Bill Nye was ever born."

Miss Sadie wrote in her introduction:

"Memories grow hazy and recollections differ, but a determined effort has been made to bind together in these pages such facts as to be accurate, lest for want of recording, these sink into oblivion."

As a testimonial to her work, the book (after being out of print for more than 20 years) was reprinted in 1976 and is available at Mountain Lore Bookstore.

I'm sorry to say I never knew Lila Ripley Barnwell. Of course I, along with everyone else who lived here, knew *of* her. She was the daughter of Col. and Mrs. Valentine Ripley. He operated the stagecoach line from Greenville, S.C., to Greenville, Tenn. He also built and operated the famous Ripley Hotel, which was later known under many different names, including the Globe. Lila Ripley Barnwell spanned the period from the Civil War 'til her death March 15, 1961. She was within one month of her 99th birthday. Lila Ripley Barnwell knew, from personal experience, virtually the entire history of Hendersonville and the county. She wrote widely about our mountain people, whom she loved dearly. I still treasure a clipping of an article by her, "Few Changes in Mountain Customs." It was published in the summer of the early '50s. She opened by writing of her resentment at tourists and visitors coming to this area and vilifying local people as being ignorant, shuffling mountaineers. She wrote: "Until quite recently, our people have been so far removed from the great centers of the outer world, they had no admixture brought to them." In the article she wrote: "Scores of Shakespearean words

Lila Ripley Barnwell

are still in use in this community. Many of these words are also from Chaucer, Gower, Bacon and Philip Sidney." She cites as examples, mountain folk saying "nestes," "ghostes," "beasties" used by both Sidney and Lord Bacon.

My grandfather used the word "fetch" (old English). Mrs. Barnwell pointed out that words like "drug" for dragged, "clum" for climbed, "wropt" for wrapped are all old English. Mountain folks say, "I allow hit'll be a good crop" that's old English for assuming the crop will be good. From Shakespeare, a small bag is a "poke"; mountain folks say "stair steps"; "church house"; "biscuit bread"; "ham meat"; and instead of a stake, he drives a "staub" in the ground. A mountain man may say, "She holped me a right smart" again old English.

She concluded by writing: "The language of the mountaineers is often original, picturesque, and perhaps incorrect; but the great part of it is a survival of English literature and shows the influence of Shakespeare, Chaucer, Milton, and others, and cannot be considered a low form if the literature of a few centuries ago is to be respected."

Mrs. Barnwell used her writing ability to pester the politicians in the legislature into passing laws protecting songbirds and other wildlife. In 1957 (she was 94), she published a book of her poems. Barber's Studio dedicated their front window display to the book, and to pictures covering most of her life. One picture made in 1901 shows Mrs. Barnwell and Dr. Morey (who built the Morey Building on Main Street) in a lively game of tennis.

On her 90th birthday, Lila Ripley Barnwell wrote this poem:

> "Our hope is a wonderful treasure
> > Belonging to mortals alone.
> We share many things with the creatures
> > but hope, blessed hope, is our own.
> Sometimes you'll hear life is hopeless,
> > Yet we know that cannot be true
> As long as we live hope is with us
> > To help and to comfort us, too.
> Perhaps you will hear I have lost it,
> > Yet hope, is of each life a part;
> So long as life lasts it is with us
> > It will always be in our heart.
> There are times of sorrows and trouble,
> > Days seem like the darkness of night.
> Whatever the gloom and the shadows
> > Hope gives us a glimmer of light.
> How barren would life be without it,
> > So cheerless, so dreary, and then
> Hope brings us new strength and fresh courage
> > And life is worth living again.
> 'ere long we will go over yonder,
> > When time here has ended our days.
> There—hope will have reached its fulfillment
> > And changed into prayer and praise.

She was officially given the title of "Poet Laureate of Hendersonville." In 1953, the Blue Ridge Bird Club paid homage to her on her 90th birthday. Mrs. Hilliard Maxwell presented her with a gorgeous birthday cake, served to those gathered by Mrs. A.H. Houston, Miss Bertha Lemort and Mrs. D.R. Justus. R.C. McCaw recited a poem, Mayor Al Edwards lauded her life and achievements. Other sponsors included Mrs. J.S. Brown, Mrs. W.S. Lockman and Mrs. J.E. Shaw. Miss Lila, Hendersonville's celebrated dowager poet "changed her hope into prayer and praise" on May 15, 1961.

The book on "Tiger" Flowers was a speculation investment by high rollers at the "Green House." The printing costs of Sadie Patton's book were subsidized by pledges of 326 "pre-publication subscribers." The list included

Carl and Helga Sandburg. These subscribers were asked to commit by members of the Womens' Club, friends or by Sadie herself. The publication of the little book of poems by Lila Ripley Barnwell was paid for from her own resources.

In 1970, a "first" in local publishing occurred. Lenoir Ray published his book "Postmarks" with no advance sales, no guarantee of any sort. He advanced the money for publishing out of his own pocket with faith that enough people would buy the book to enable him to recover the costs. It was a trying period for both Lenoir and his wife Lucille (who worked first at the *Tribune* and then the *Times-News*). Geneaology had not yet caught on with any great enthusiasm. In fact, Lenoir's book probably did more to stimulate interest in genealogy than any other publication; but in that first year, sales were slow. Genealogical research was just beginning here, and his book concentrated on the history of small post offices in the county that were established and existed, some for only a short time.

Lenior was Postmaster at Flat Rock, and over a ten-year period was able to secure from the U.S. Postal Service an abundance of historical material on the earliest forms of postal delivery and on the small post offices. At one time, there were seventeen post offices in this county most of them serving little more than the nearby neighborhood. At one time, letters emanating from the county bore such postmarks as "Love," "Money," "Rump," "Gypsy," "Lead," or even "Goodluck." Most of these post offices were organized or passed from one member of a family to another. Lenoir's book contains the names of more than 2,000 early settlers here, with a bit about their occupation and what they did in the community. It was a pure gold mine for genealogy buffs. It has been out of print for twenty-seven years, and if you're lucky enough to find a copy in a flea market or used book store, prepare to pay big bucks.

At about the time Lenoir was beginning his research into local post offices, another Henderson County man had already begun writing his first novel. Ernie Frankel had met, courted and married Louise Lazarus of Hendersonville; and after leaving the University of North Carolina, moved to Hendersonville to take over the mens' store operated by Louise's father, George. Ernie had served as a captain in the Marines during the Korean War, and had been chosen each year to produce the fabled Army/Navy show for the services. Ernie had no interest in becoming a master merchandiser; his heart was in the arts, writing, directing or producing. While he was doing one of the Army/Navy shows, he met Leon Uris (who wrote "Battle Cry"). He chatted with Uris about the plot of a book he was thinking of writing. Uris's advice: "Sit down and write it." After returning home, he and Louise decided the time had come for him to make his move. Ed and Doris Patterson became their patron saints, providing a job for Louise at Williams Jewelers, and gave Ernie part-time work with Walter Drake in the Mens' Store any time he was not writing.

Uris had taken the first three chapters of the book to Putnam Publishers and they agreed to publish the book, which would be titled "Tongue of Fire."

The plot revolved around a congressman who was the epitome of Senator Joe McCarthy. Ernie had already lined up an impressive schedule of guest appearances on talk shows to promote the book when he received a terse message from Putnam..."This book is too hot to handle." Senator McCarthy had died in 1957, after having been condemned by the U.S. Senate for certain actions. But there were strong sentiments across the nation that rather than being a fanatical witch hunter, McCarthy had saved the nation by exposing Communist infiltration of the government.

Unfazed, Frankel dug right in and wrote a second novel, "Band of Brothers," depicting that nightmarish and heroic period of the Korean War during which U.N. troops were forced to retreat from the Yalu. It is the story of a company of Marines and its commanding officer, who in two weeks was transformed from an insecure, inexperienced and distrusted leader into a battle-hardened, respected veteran. This book was published by McMillan & Company and went on sale Oct. 28, 1958. The next year, the book was awarded one of the top literary honors in the state, the Sir Walter Raleigh Award.

He, Louise and their two daughters decided their future was in the Hollywood area. He joined North American Aviation in Los Angeles as a writer-director of public relations material. In his spare time, he rewrote the first book, "Tongue of Fire," deleting certain parts that had been considered inflammatory. It was published by Dial Press and released May 16, 1960. Folks in Hendersonville rushed to buy "Tongue of Fire" because (though fictional) Ernie had patterned "Manton, N.C." as a carbon copy of Hendersonville. Locals could find sharp resemblance in some of the characters in the book to local people living in Hendersonville. The most notable example was the character of Ed Patterson, owner of Patterson's Mens' Shop, where Ernie had worked while writing the book. Manton even had a gold-domed court house.

At one time in that court house, the Office of the Register of Deeds was occupied by Frank L. FitzSimons. He resigned that office to become vice president and director of the State Trust Company (which later merged with Northwestern Bank of North Wilkesboro). He served both on the local and general board of that bank during his long banking career. William B. "Bill" Hodges sensed early on that FitzSimons would be (by virtue of his enormous popularity) a great asset to the bank as a radio personality, and Frank was then given the freedom to develop a daily program based on the history of Henderson County and its people.

The program ran daily for 25 years, and FitzSimons had kept his handwritten scripts of every one of those thousands of programs. Young Frank and I had fretted at length that the FitzSimons work should be preserved, that the priceless material he had gathered should be put into book form. It took years of cajolery. Frank Sr. always retorted to the two of us, "Ain't nobody gonna spend good money to read anything written by a fool like me." In 1976, "the book" finally made it into print, and 3,000 copies were sold in less than 60 days.

Young Frank ordered a reprint and we started pressuring Frank to do a second volume, and finally a third. He called the books "his trilogy." The title of each was the same as that of his radio program, "From the Banks of the Oklawaha." Some of the great memories of my life were those gatherings when my brother Grady (who edited all three volumes) would come up from Florida and we'd have a "family conference" of the two Franks (occasionally Maggie), Grady, and myself. Wonderful memories.

The bronze plaque (placed in the library at the dedication of the FitzSimons local history section) refers to Frank (among many other things) as a raconteur. For many, many years Mr. Fitz and I worked together, I was the emcee and he was the featured speaker at about every program, every dedication, every pig giveaway that took place. One of his greatest stories was called "The Arabella Shuffle." Fitz was the first coach at Hendersonville High whose team won a football game. In addition to teaching and coaching, Frank owned a farm on Howard Gap Road. As a football coach, he worried about his small team having to play the mighty Asheville High team. Back then, they didn't have helmets; they wore what were called aviator caps, had no padding, and not every player had a uniform. As he was milking a cow named Arabella early one morning, he dreamed up a formation where his team simply scattered all over the field. (Tom Landry later used a variation of this in his shotgun formation.) Fitz called the play "the Arabella shuffle." The Asheville team had no idea of how to defend this oddball formation and the Bearcats won the game.

Frank was awarded the coveted Navy Cross in World War I, but he never shared the details of the military action which led to this award.

Fitz lived among a people and in a time when the worst thing that could be said about you was "he got above his raisin'." He would go out of his way to maintain his accessibility and his humility. He was almost eighty years old, but still agreed to speak to the English class at Flat Rock Junior High School. He shared with them how "the old man on the mountain" could forecast the weather of a winter to come. He passed along to them old folk sayings, such as:

"Moles on the neck mean money by the peck."

"Bite a mule's ear to tame him."

"If you take the last piece of cake, you'll be an old maid."

He made very few appearances in his final years. He said, "I want folks to remember me as a person with reasonable intelligence, not some doddering old fool wandering around not knowing what day it is." Fitz continued, "The sad thing is that neither your family nor your friends will tell you when you're senile. So I just play it safe, I stay at home and if my mind is wandering, I'll not be out in public where everybody can see it."

Frank L. FitzSimons died January 29, 1980, but the great man lives on in his son, Frank Jr. He not only bears a strong resemblance to his father, he served aboard a PT boat in the Navy, he farmed all his life, then had a career in banking with the same bank his father served, and has been engaged in civic activities and farm organizations like his father. He is not just custodian of his father's historical papers, but is familiar with local people and history based on information in these notes and in his personal experiences.

Frank FitzSimons Sr. married Margarita Kershaw. Her father built a house on Barnwell Street which became known as the Kershaw house. The great coincidence was that this seventh child of a seventh child was born in 1924 in the Kershaw house. The FitzSimons family was one of the few who were looked upon as "local folks" and were also accepted in the Flat Rock community. Mr. Fitz used to say, "Flat Rock is not a place, it's a state of mind."

Frank FitzSimons Sr.

Another family with the same distinction would be the family of Dr. William B.W. Howe. His son is a distinguished attorney here, and a daughter, Louise, is the widow of Dr. Joseph P. Bailey. Louise said she grew up on what was called a farm in Flat Rock in those days. She said, "Until Carl Sandburg and the Flat Rock Playhouse came into our midst, Flat Rock (though well known across South Carolina) had hardly been heard of beyond Asheville or as far away as Charlotte." Though she was educated at Fassifern School and Winthrop College, she was a graduate of library science at Columbia University and held positions at Edgefield Public Schools and Winthrop College. Having heard her father ("Old Doc Howe") tell a multitude of stories about people and places in Flat Rock and the county, Louise always had a hankering to write. In 1967, the *Times-News* asked her to write a column, which she called "Along the Ridges."

Now, 1,500 newspaper columns and four books later, she has to her credit: "Go Home With Me"; "From Rock Hill to Connemara: The Story Before Sandburg"; "Draw Up a Chair"; and "St. John in the Wilderness: 1836." She co-authored with Jody Barber "Hendersonville-Henderson County, a Pictorial History," which has been reprinted and is available at Mountain Lore. In 1996, she wrote "50 Years with the Vagabonds," and has been commissioned to write the history of health in the community and the Pardee Hospital story. Louise and "Dr. Joe" raised three sons, including Joe (a local school teacher); Bob (a local physician); and the late Bill, who was a camp director. They were raised on Little River Road in a home built many, many years ago by Miss Chary Morton of Kentucky. She had named the place Laurelhurst, but the young Bailey boys always called it Liverwurst. "The Pictorial History" was commissioned and underwritten by First Federal to coincide with the opening of their new office building in 1988 at the corner of 6th and Main (now First Citizen). I have no idea of how much time Jody spent selecting more than 325 pictures from the Baker-Barber collection; but for months, each time I'd drop in at Barber's, Jody would be back in his office (aided by a green shaded desk lamp) pouring over negatives or glass plates that would make local history come alive again.

Jody has dipped into the Baker-Barber collection for the FitzSimons books, "50 Years with the Vagabonds," and selected pictures are highlighted in the new Henderson County Court House. The basic Baker-Barber collection was given to the Henderson County Community Foundation to be housed in the Henderson County Public Library. Pictures used in this volume and the "Weather Book" were also personally selected and provided by Jody Barber.

The "Weather Book" was published in 1986. I had no illusions that it would be considered of literary substance, nor a bestseller. I published the book purely to preserve some forty years of weather observations and a hundred years of local weather records. Perhaps one hundred copies of an initial publication of 3,000 books are still available in 1997 at the Henderson County Historical and Genealogical Society on Main Street.

The Society published "Heritage of Henderson County - Vol. 1" in 1985 and Vol. 2 in 1988. Though the books contain contributions from hundreds of Henderson County people, the publication became a reality primarily because of the work of Dr. George Alexander Jones and his wife, Evelyn. The two of them have provided intransigent leadership to this organization, which is now housed in the county-owned building originally built as First Citizens Bank at Main and 4th. The most voluminous task undertaken by the Society, however, was "Henderson County, North Carolina Cemeteries," published in 1995.

Without hesitation, when anybody asks me for the most definitive history of this area, I always say, "A Partial History of Henderson County" by James T. Fain Jr. In 1925, J.T. Fain Sr. (nicknamed "Old Marblehead" by a former disgruntled employee) moved his family to Hendersonville and purchased the *Hendersonville Times*. At that time, there was another daily newspaper in town called *The Hendersonville News*, published by Mr. Noah Hollowell. In 1927, Mr. Fain took as a partner C.M. "Mike" Ogle. The newspaper expanded and he bought *The Times*, combined it with his paper and began publishing the *Times-News*. Mr. Hollowell later began a weekly newspaper known as the *Western Carolina Tribune*, but the *Times-News* has been the only daily paper published here for the past seventy years.

Except for a brief period in World War II when young Jimmy served as a lieutenant colonel in the Army, he was with the paper until 1975, when he retired as editor but took on a weekly historical column about local people and their works. From these historicals came Jimmy's book, "A Partial History of Henderson County." Jim wrote on the dust cover of his book:

"Two hundred and eighty-seven weeks after its beginning, the work was discontinued...not because it had been finished but primarily because it was felt that the columns should be collected in one entity. This book is the result."

Jim and I epitomized the total cooperation that can exist between the fourth and fifth estate. He and I joked with each other that as boss, we each did whatever no one else wanted to do. We covered news and sports together; and in the press box, we always tried to keep our mikes as far away from Jimmy as possible because he was famous for shouting epithets and strong four-letter words at officials or players. The former TV anchorman and author, Bob Inman, writes a Sunday column in the *Charlotte Observer*. I kept the column of March 2, 1997, because he was chastising ABC and the Food Lion story; and the Peter Jennings costly blunder for his comment on NBC about Richard Jewell's role in the Olympic bombing in Atlanta. Bob Inman's comments could have been a description of Jim Fain's ethics and integrity in covering news. Over the years, I learned that if a column written by Jimmy Fain appeared to be even slightly biased, he was writing as the "devil's advocate," and probably personally disagreed with what he had written.

Jim married Thomasina Shepherd (an aunt of today's Tom Shepherd at the funeral home). He and "Tommy" were active in every aspect of community life. He was named VFW Man of the Year in 1966. Their oldest son (Jim III) is a regional executive with First Union National Bank in Raleigh; the second (Mike) was associated with Duke Power; and the youngest (Robert) is an Episcopal priest.

While Tommy nursed Jim through many years of health problems, it was she who died first in 1977. To fill the huge void without her, Jim plunged into his research for daily newspaper columns. His nearly 600-page book was published in 1980. It is the only true and accurate resource book on the specifics of the history of Hendersonville and the county. It is still available at Mountain Lore.

Another *Times-News* writer and editor (Mead Parce) has published the first volume of a book, "Twice Told True Tales of the Blue Ridge and Great Smokies."

Also, a number of paperbacks have been written by Roy Bush Laughter, George Wilkins, Evelyn Haynes and others.

The Fourth Estate

When power was wrested from the monarchies in Europe, there came into common expression "the three estates" – the first being the king, queen, president, or emperor. The second estate referred to the House of Lords or Nobles; and the third estate was the House of Commons. Historians added a fourth estate, newspapers, to keep a watchful eye on the first three. And finally, with the advent of radio and TV, we had the fifth estate.

The early staff of the Times-News. Old-timers can easily recognize Mike Ogle, young Jimmy and George Fain, J.B. Creech and Clayton Vandiver. At this time, the paper was located in part of an old bank building between Second and Third avenues on Main Street.

The fourth estate fifty years ago consisted locally of the *Times-News* and the *Western Carolina Tribune*. When J.T. Fain Sr. brought his family to Hendersonville in 1925 and purchased the *Hendersonville Times*, he also brought along two trusted associates: J.B. Creech (who had the title of mechanical superintendent) and W.L. "Bill" Burrell (who was listed as pressman).

In 1946 there was no photo offset printing. The columns of type came from linotype machines; headlines and ads were handset from various fonts of type; pictures or drawings were made from matrixes or zinc plates. The paper was put together in the composing room and the presses started to roll about 3 p.m.–just in time for the carrier boys to start delivering the paper after they got out of school. Back then, Joe Freeman and Clayton Vandiver operated the linotypes and Carl Blythe was second only to Bill Burrell in the press room.

Mr. Fain's two sons (George and Jimmy) worked at the paper, George in advertising and Jimmy in news. George died very young in 1947. His son later became publisher of the paper when it was purchased by the New York Times Company. The city editor was Leo Hummel Wise, who would stop by WHKP every afternoon and kibitz over the affairs of the day. Bob Lindsay and Leonard Terry were in advertising. Mrs. C.R. McManaway was society editor.

Jimmy Fain experienced serious health problems in the early '60s and C.M. Ogle in 1963 also experienced serious heart problems; he died in 1968. Mike then sold his interest to Lawson Braswell, a Tennessean who had operated a number of small-town newspapers in that state. After buying Ogle's interest, Lawson became vice president and general manager. Jim Fain continued to serve as editor until his retirement in 1971. He was succeeded as editor by Mead Parce. The paper moved to a new building on Four Seasons Boulevard in 1973.

As the newspaper and the radio stations continued to grow with ever-larger staffs, the close comradeship that had existed in those first thirty years began to fade. The old *Western Carolina Tribune* (a weekly) had been purchased by Lawson Braswell in the mid '60s. This paper had been started by Mr. Noah Hollowell, who had originally owned and published the *Hendersonville News*, which became part of the *Times-News* in 1927. After Noah sold the newspaper, he kept the equipment and operated a job printing company for a number of years.

But newspapering was in his blood and he ultimately started publishing a weekly paper which leaned heavily to agricultural and religious news (particularly in the county). He had already sold his printing equipment, so he arranged with Curtis Russ (who published the semi-weekly *Waynesville Mountaineer*) to publish the *Hollowell Mountain Farmer*, which in 1936 became the weekly *Tribune*. Hollowell ran the weekly paper for thirty-three years, selling it in 1962 to John Sholar.

Sholar was a maverick, a non-conformer. He reached the absolute crown of his career on April 1, 1965. On that day, the 4,400 subscribers went into shock after absorbing just a few paragraphs from what he called "an April Fool edition." Yes, it was All Fool's Day 1965, but no one had ever seen an entire newspaper published as an April Fool's prank. Many readers turned back to the front page to check the masthead, it had been changed to read "The Coonskin Crusader," and in very small type, "Special edition of the Western Carolina Tribune."

On the front page there was a banner headline concerning a huge cotillion to be staged May 1. The article read (and I'm only quoting excerpts here, and I'll not attempt to write the pig Latin French that John had attempted):

"The Grand Dame of Zirconia Society will be Geneva Bowden, who will lead the first dance of the evening wearing a Paris original croaker sack, adorned with Swift and Armours configurations."

Another excerpt:

"The limelight was then focused on Madame Gertrude Arledge. Her Dior gown was a flowing Poi de Soir caught at the plunging neckline by a red cabbage rose."

The article continued:

"The event was held at the Terrace Hill Roller Rink, which was beautifully decorated with Heineken beer cans and La Boheme sherry bottles with cornstalks and chigger weeds by Tony Lefeber."

Another excerpt:

"The beautiful affair was climaxed with the guests adjoining for the midnight nuptials (and I'm going to omit the name of the very lovely lady in this community whom Sholar chose to vilify) of she and Don Gilmore, Esquire (who worked for WHKP and was executive director of United Way). She would wear an imported seaweed skirt for the gown, she chose a barrel of cyprus. Mr. Frank FitzSimons sang with deep feeling, "Parlex Vous Francais" and the "Marine Hymn."

The further you read, the worse it got:

"William V. Powers, chief of police, said he would propose to eliminate all signs on one-way streets. This would help to eliminate many citizens who have complained about the new traffic patterns."

Other excerpts:

"Eleanor Cosgrove was hostess for the ten-year Natives' Club. She served pinto beans a la fatback, cracklin' bread and sweet potato souffle."

"The children of this area will be happy to know that the Ray Chamberlains will open an alligator and reptile farm on Laurel Drive, and that Smiley McCall was planning a 4th of July Possum Bar-B-Que for city officials."

After you read through this April 1, 1965 edition of the *Western Tribune*, the feeling experienced by everyone was incredulity. Never in the history of journalism has any newspaper anywhere been known to attack virtually every leader and well-known person in the community and justify the slanderous columns as being "just in fun." Poor Mr. Hollowell (who was still writing a column for his old paper) had to suffer enormous humiliation after this paper was published. He discontinued his column in 1970 and moved to be with his daughter in Mars Hill. He died in 1973 at age 87. Lawson Braswell bought out Sholar after Mr. Hollowell had left, and simply put the paper out of business in 1971.

Radio—The Fifth Estate

When I first joined radio station WHKP, it had been on the air for a bit more than two months. It had been built in late 1946 by a partnership known as Redege Broadcasting Company, owned by Monroe M. Redden Sr. and W.A. "Bill" Egerton. Monroe Redden had been elected to Congress in November of 1946, and felt there might be some conflict of interest in being a partner in the only radio station in his home town. A new company was formed, called Radio Hendersonville Inc., and Mr. Redden sold his interest to L.B. Prince and R.L. Whitmire.

The station had been planned, built and was being managed by Ed Leach. Virtually no professional planning had gone into the original station. The transmitter was a tiny concrete block building next to the tower on Devil's Fork Creek. Back then, the FCC required a first-class engineer to be on duty at any time the transmitter was on. The station rented a two-room office suite on the second floor of the Staton Building, which also required a staff. In still a third location, a tiny studio and control room was built where the old bus station had been located in the Bowen Hotel (also known as the Hodgewell and Ames at other times). The control room was so small, one had to climb over the turntables to get behind "the board" or control console. There were no windows, no air-conditioning, only a wall heater.

In those early days of broadcasting, we had a marvelous local program (produced by Paul Perry) called "The Christian Youth Hour." At times, the number of participants would be equal to a full choir. Plus, our "rinky-dink" studio was dominated by a baby grand piano. The twenty or so people on that broadcast would jam against each other just to get in. One summer afternoon, one of the singers simply keeled over from the heat and lack of oxygen.

It became obvious to Egerton, Prince and Whitmire that the station desperately needed added capital and experienced management. Clarence E. Morgan (mayor of Asheville and part-owner of Morgan Candy Company) was sold majority interest in WHKP. He also purchased a minority interest for his son-in-law (Bob Amos), who was an announcer then with WNCA in Asheville. Amos was made manager of the station. Bob recruited me from the Department of Radio, TV, and Motion Pictures at UNC-Chapel Hill, and I came to work for WHKP on Jan. 10, 1947.

I had no carpentry experience, but was able to tear out a partition in back of the control room, eliminate a non-vital storage area which gave us room to get to "the board" without climbing over turntables. As for lack of oxygen, I simply knocked a hole through the wall and ran a stove pipe to the outside, with a small fan mounted in the pipe to force air into the studio. There were no restroom facilities, and there was nothing I could do about that. When the spirit called, you'd try to find a 10-inch 78 RPM record (LPs had not yet been developed). When the record started, you'd run as fast as you could down Church Street and up the steps into the Bowen Hotel lobby, use the restroom and dash back to the control room before it ended. Bob McGarrity, Bill Reilly and I could make it, but Tom Egerton (Bill's brother) was too old. He simply used a jar he brought with him to work.

When Mr. Morgan acquired control of the station in 1947, he set up a fund to build a new building to house the entire operation; but Amos could not get expenses under control and the building fund was eaten up in 1947 by operating losses.

Another active investor (Beverly "Bevo" M. Middleton) was enticed to become part-owner by the end of that year. Bevo's uncle Henry owned one of the ante-bellum estates in Flat Rock, which was known as "Piedmont." Bevo had spent his life in broadcasting, and though he had an excellent voice (with a touch of the old Charleston accent), he was involved in sales. He was sales manager for Colonel Wilder's group of stations in New York and New England, and it was while in this job that he became associated with Edwin S. "Eddie" Lowe.

Eddie Lowe invented Bingo in 1929, and though his income from Bingo royalties made him a very wealthy man, Eddie was always on the lookout for

Carl Sandburg does radio show on WHKP with Bevo Middleton.

innovations to Bingo which would make even more money. Bevo dreamed up Radio Bingo that could be played on the radio. Paper cards were distributed by the sponsor (the Grand Union Stores) and numbers were called over their Wilder stations. Eddie and Bevo became fast friends. Eddie and his wife came down to visit the Middletons, and at their pool, Eddie's wife suddenly appeared in one of those transparent-when-wet swimsuits. When she first climbed out of Bevo's pool, "My eyeballs almost popped out, but then, being a good ole Southern moralist, I tried not to look her way again the rest of the afternoon." Eddie was the kind of buddy that hired John Horton (our sales manager) away from WHKP to head up a new sports division Eddie was establishing.

Bevo was a thoroughbred Charlestonian. His aunt, Mrs. Robert E. Lee III, also had a home at Flat Rock. When President Eisenhower ordered federal marshalls into Little Rock, Bevo's Aunt Mary sent Ike a tersely worded telegram: "Abe Lincoln got his. You'll get yours. Signed Mrs. Robert E. Lee III"

Bevo (having worked and lived in the "big time" most of his life) was accustomed to the "liquid lunch" circuit, taking the noon break at bars on Madison Avenue. He continued to enjoy "the fruit of the grape" in Hendersonville. But his wife, Eve (Evelyn Howe Middleton) kept the booze in a cabinet in the dining room at Piedmont which she called "the caboose." Bevo would slip into the caboose and fill numerous small bottles with "hootch," which he then placed in his own medicine cabinet for "emergency purposes."

One morning he came in to the radio station and kept taking real deep breaths and exhaling fully. It was so obvious, I finally inquired, "What's wrong with you this morning?" "Oh," he answered, "I reached into my medicine cabinet and pulled down one of my bottles and guzzled the whole thing down before I discovered that the little medicine bottle did contain medicine—nose drops. Even my toes are breathing this morning."

Bevo and Eve's marriage failed in 1959, and he left here to work in Alexandria, Va. Months after he had gone, ladies would say to me, "Oh, how I miss Bevo. He always told me how lovely I was." Following his divorce, complications arose between Bevo and Eve, so to make peace he deeded to her his burial plot in St. John's Churchyard, where she was later buried. Bevo (when he died in 1973) was buried in Gettysburg National Cemetery in Pennsylvania.

When Bevo "bought into WHKP," it appeared we had a perfect team. Bevo's strength was sales and marketing, Bob Amos's background was news and announcing. While I had no experience, I inadvertently became an untitled business manager. One afternoon the engineer called me from the transmitter and said, "There's a Duke Power man out here and he says he's gonna cut our power because we ain't paid our bill." I couldn't believe it—a radio station goes off the air because their power is cut off?? I begged the Duke Power man to give me just thirty minutes. I raced around town and collected enough money to appease the Duke Power man and avoid the disconnect. After that, as friction grew between Bob and Bevo, I had to act as their go-between and was entrusted with the checkbook.

Finally, Bevo challenged Mr. Morgan. He alleged that he couldn't work with Amos and would buy or sell. Amos left WHKP in 1951 to join Kenyon and Eckhart Ad Agency in New York. I worked with Bevo for eleven years. We secured a license for a TV station in Hendersonville, but returned the permit without prejudice when the FCC changed grant rules which doomed the station to failure at that time. It now operates as WHNS Fox 21. We added an FM station which, in the beginning, merely duplicated the WHKP program schedule. We built, operated and sold WWIT-Canton.

After Bevo left, Art Cooley purchased the remainder of stock held by C.E. Morgan. In the '60s, we added twenty local businessmen as stockholders to raise capital for the construction of the cable television system for Hendersonville, which was ultimately sold to a company owned by the TV star Ed Sullivan, and was operated by his son-in-law, Bob Precht. It has been sold several times since then.

Art and I then revamped the FM station entirely, increased the power to 100,000 watts, and introduced into Western North Carolina the Great American Country format, one of the great success stories of that decade. In 1986, KIT was sold to George Francis and the station was moved to Greenville, S.C., with call letters WMYI. It is now owned by WSFX. The stock of the twenty local businessmen was repurchased, and the station formed an ESOP (Employee Stock Option Plan). When I retired in 1991, Art became the majority stockholder, with the remainder of the stock held by the employees. Art has since brought his daughters (Karen Cooley Gibson and Kim Cooley Morin) into the ownership of the station. WHKP is now in its 51st year of being locally owned and operated.

A Few Words on Behalf of

Coo Coo Enterprises in 1996 published a 96-page history (written by Louise Bailey) called "50 Years with the Vagabonds." On the final page, you'll learn that Coo Coo Enterprises is a partnership between Dave and Art Cooley. Anyone who has lived here over the past 40 years would say, "Well, I know Art, but who is Dave Cooley?" For your information, he is the older brother who, in 1948, succeeded P.M. Camak as secretary of the Hendersonville Chamber of Commerce. I worked with Dave at the Chamber, in fairs and in festivals. The two of us dreamed up the slogan "The City of Four Seasons."

When Dave left Hendersonville to take a bigger job in Jacksonville, Fla., he committed himself from that day forward to be willing to move wherever necessary for bigger opportunities and enhanced position. He would manage Chambers in Memphis, Tenn. He became head of the largest in the country in Dallas/Fort Worth. He even became head of the Chamber Executives Association in Washington. He and his wife, Beth, retired to Hendersonville and now live in Chateloupe.

While going to school at UNC-Chapel Hill, Art worked during the summer months at the Hendersonville Chamber, and he obviously was tempted to follow in his older brother's footsteps. But at every opportunity, I tried to plant the seed that his future was in radio. In 1957 (following his graduation from college), he still was hesitant to leave the Chamber and enter the broadcast field. One day I simply told him, "Art, you've wasted enough time. It's now time for you to get on with your career. Be at work at the station Monday morning." He came to work that Monday morning, and today he and his daughters own and operate WHKP.

I have always marveled at the rigid discipline with which Art has managed his time. He followed a schedule every day that would have exhausted even the far above average executive. On Dec. 12, 1972, at a special meeting of the Board of Directors), a resolution was adopted promoting Art to general manager. William F. Edmundson would succeed him as sales manager. Art worked his way through the chairs at both the Chamber of Commerce and the Lions Club. He has served on the boards of the United Way and was co-chairman of a capital fundraising campaign for the American Red Cross. He has served on the Planning and Zoning Board and after many, many years, still serves on the Board of Carolina Village. He has also served on the board of the North Carolina Broadcasters Association. Phil Kelly, who conceived and promoted the "Second Wind Hall of Fame," called himself "the world's greatest salesman." That was before he met Art Cooley.

In thinking back over the past 50 years, I want to pay credit to Bevo Middleton, who was vital to the success of WHKP. For that matter, every person who has been a part of our staff carved their own niche in the station's climb to success, starting with early morning personalities–beginning with Tom Egerton. Most of our local young people grew up listening every morning to Charley Renfrow. He was succeeded by "Chuck" Gaines (who came out of retirement to lend a seasoned hand when Renfrow was going through his terminal illness). Then there's the incorrigible Al Hope, who still sips on a giant cup of tepid coffee as he expresses his dry wit and sometimes caustic or impious comments.

Fifty years ago, we couldn't afford a "women's program," so we called on our secretary at the time (Janet O'Neill) to come into the studios and read features that had moved on the United or Associated Press wire that appealed to women. She thoroughly detested this extra chore. We then persuaded Mary Barber to do a full-blown women's program on a daily basis. I acted as producer and the show was a big success–until her husband, Jody, realized she was putting in those hours for about $4.50 a week. Our sales staff argued that it was difficult to sell advertising on a women's program, so this was just a personnel expense; and considering that I worked full-time for only $35 bucks, we simply couldn't afford more.

The next commitment in women's programming was made as a decision "of the heart." Both our children had begun their education at Immaculata School, and we personally knew the Mother Superior, Mother O'Brien. She walked in one day (not dressed in her habit) and said she was looking for work. I discovered that she and Father Lane (the parish priest) had come to a parting

Remembering early days of WHKP, from left: Mary Barber; Irvin Price, the Grand Ole Man of the Mountains; Jo Kuykendall, WHKP's first full-time Women's Director; and Frank Hawkins.

of the ways and he had dismissed her. We had no budget which would support her, but I felt compelled to do something for this inspiring and salubrious person. So we put her on the air with a program to mothers on "raising children." She even tried to help us sell the program, but it was ahead of its time.

It would be 1957 before we found ourselves truly involved in a women's programming effort, and that was when we hired Jo Kuykendall. Jo was a graduate of Queen's College and had completed special courses in radio and theater at Fagan School in New York. Her husband, Cal, was owner and operator of a home and auto store (he would ultimately become the executive director of the Merchants' Association). Jo's first guests were Mary Barber and Ernie Frankel. She said she was so scared, she wrote out a script for everything that would be said. On a broadcast marking her 15th anniversary on WHKP, Mary Barber was again her special guest and Ernie Frankel called her from Hollywood.

In those early years, Jo used a lot of wire service filler material, recipes, book reviews, comments on Broadway shows and the movies. As she developed a strong personality, the show featured topical interviews with guests from all walks of life. She was active not only in civic activities, but as her personality grew, she was pressed to emcee every fashion show or benefit aimed at the fairer sex. After retiring from broadcasting, she later became active in coordinating social activities at Carolina Village.

WHKP's first full-time newsman was a professional accordion player from London, England, by the name of Frank Hawkins. Back in the '60s, his parents had passed away and his only close relative was a sister who had married a U.S. pilot in World War II and was then living in Indiana (headquarters for the famed Hohner Music Company). Frank Hawkins had worked most of his life for Hohner as an in-store accordion demonstrator and appeared as a professional musician on the BBC radio network. His sister felt that Frank should "come to the states" to be near her, and thought it would be easy for him to find an opportunity with Hohner.

On the plane (flying from London) Frank learned that his sister's husband had been transferred by his company to a plant near Asheville. In New York he changed destinations and found himself in Western North Carolina, where he quickly discovered there was virtually no demand for any professional accordion player. Frank pleaded with me for a job of any kind. I mused, "To have local news with a British accent deserved creation of a new job," so Frank joined our staff as news director.

It took patience to educate Frank. He had to learn that in football it was a "game," not a "match." In covering city council meetings, he had to learn that a loud complaint from a resident about a stopped-up sewer was not as important as a resolution quietly approving a multi-million dollar bond issue. In fact, for the first few years, Frank would tape record the entire council meeting and I would come in early enough to monitor what had taken place and edit clips for the news.

But Frank was a superb interviewer—especially with people in the music and show business. On March 30, 1981, the famed Liberace arrived at the airport and agreed to meet with the media prior to moving on to a concert that night in Asheville. Frank was always super punctual, and he had a choice position with our mikes before the famed pianist:

Frank: (After referring to Liberace's classic performance of two songs) "Regarding those two particular items, which incidentally were both in the key of C sharp minor, 'Prelude to C Sharp Minor' by Rachmaninoff; the other was 'Sonata Una Quasi Fantasia' by Beethoven."

Liberace: "Yes, uh huh."

Frank: "Because of the way that you've constructed that synthesis, do you feel that this proved to be the cornerstone of your inimitable and highly successful career?"

Hawkins continued this sophisticated questioning of Liberace—asking about his other performing name (William Buster Keys), about his father being a professional horn player, about the influence of Paderewski on his life; and during this time, all the other reporters (radio, TV, and newspaper) sat there completely buffaloed by this character with an English accent who was probably asking Liberace questions he'd never been confronted with before.

The only complaint we ever had about Frank was during the Piedmont Airlines disaster in 1967. We broke that story less than ten minutes after the crash occurred. From then (about 12:10 p.m.) until about midnight that night, we had all four phone lines in constant use feeding stories to networks, metro stations, even overseas broadcasts. Frank was one of the four of us manning a phone line. Occasionally, a station would call back and say, "Hey, give me another feed on that story by anybody other than that guy with the English accent. Our listeners want to hear from somebody that sounds like North Carolina—not the BBC."

Frank took time off in 1984 for a long-anticipated return to London. He had looked forward for months to the return to the England of his youth. It wasn't there. He found very few friends and the change was so great he did not recognize even his own neighborhood. I still have a copy of the *Illustrated London News* he brought back for me.

Out of all the people listed as staff members in the appendix, Emilie Swearingen stands out as having the greatest political savvy; and Jennie Irvin for dedication in the round-the-clock coverage of the manhunt that started on Sugar Loaf Mountain.

As I was putting together this chapter, I took the time just to lean back and try to recall the people who were part of the staff at one time or another over the past 50 years. I thought of the late Marty Morgan. He and I were working on a special project together at the time of his untimely death. As I sat daydreaming, I could see in my mind Reg Hill, whose deep bass voice rivaled Big Jim Weatherington. And Jim Northington (who I had nicknamed J.

Worthington Northington)–back in those years, Jim could smoke two cigarettes at one time. I thought of Bob McGarrity, who lives now in Lawrenceville, Ga. When Bob worked at WHKP (with all the goof ups) you would have thought it was WKRP. Doug Brooks had perhaps the greatest God-given voice of anyone who ever worked at WHKP. "Cactus Pete" Wilson had worked at more radio stations and knew more people than anyone I ever met. There was Dave Brown, who handled the night shift after the retirement of Irv Price (the Grand Ole Man of the Mountains). Irv had more popular albums of his own

Marty Morgan

than we had in the WHKP library. I mused over the artificial snowstorm that Nancy McKinley created on 1st Avenue between Main and Church, just to prove that we could accurately forecast a local snowfall. (She arranged snow blowing machines to lay down a one-block sled run when there was no snow elsewhere within 200 miles.)

People ask me how has radio changed over the past 50 years. I should refer them to Mary Barnette Ashe or Marge Duncan. From old-fashioned manual typewriters to the latest in desktop and mainframe computers and terminals, they have made the transition in the office. As for our broadcast capability, chief engineer Norman Lyda has taken the station from 78 RPM acetate records to laser discs, digital sound, and music programmed from satellites.

Marge Duncan

Fifty years ago we were not only much younger, but in such great shape we could run from the cubbyhole studios to the second floor of the Ames Hotel to go to the bathroom while an old 78 record played. The old timers are grateful for the changes that have occurred. Today, when broadcast professionals or celebrities walk into Broadcast House for the first time, they stand agape that the little town of Hendersonville has one of the finest facilities in the state. It is not operated by employees, but members of our broadcast staff who are now the owners.

L.B. Prince — Surrogate father

While attorneys L.B. Prince, R. Lee Whitmire and Bill Egerton had sold their interest in WHKP to Clarence E. Morgan, mayor of Asheville, Prince continued to represent our station as its attorney.

When I joined the station, our offices in the Staton Building were directly across the hall from the law offices of Ben Prince. In my going and coming from the WHKP offices to the studios, I could not help but notice that Mr. Prince's outer office was always full of people. While my family had been active in the Republican Party, at that time my primary concern was to make a success of WHKP, and I had no reason to be aware of the fact that Ben Price was chairman of the Democratic Executive Committee, and that the bulk of the people waiting to see him were there on political matters or wanted political patronage of some sort.

My first interest in anything political occurred in 1948 when Prince asked me to come into his office. He told me that he was aware of the fact that my family members were Republican, but that he wanted to hire me as professional ghost writer for the Democratic Party. At that time, anything to augment $35 a week merited serious consideration. Thus began a close association that continued throughout his years as chairman, through 1952. He permitted me the freedom of being able to decline any assignment that violated my personal principles.

In those years, the Democratic Party was far more conservative in Henderson County than the Republican Party is today, so I rarely had difficulty in carrying out my end of the agreement. Being a "ghost writer" to me (back then) was similar to the role of a professional soap salesman. This experience allowed me to develop not just a closeness to Ben Prince, but after the death of my own father in 1958, Ben became my surrogate father. I sought his advice on virtually all important matters. It was in later years that I discovered Ben Prince must have had a couple of dozen surrogate sons just like me.

Over the years I discovered that Ben Prince had served as chairman of the State Highway Commission and Public Works Commission in 1941 and 1942 before resigning to go on active duty as lieutenant colonel in the Pacific Theater during World War II. He also served in France during World War I. When Prince served as chairman of the Highway Commission, he was also head of the North Carolina Highway Patrol, and was assigned a patrol car and drivers for his use in conducting state business. He was second in power only to the governor. Today, the responsibilities he shouldered are assigned to three different men. When he was appointed chairman of the Highway Commission by Gov. J.M. Broughton, he was responsible for more than 76,000 miles of highway, the largest road system of any state in the union.

Ben was a native of Laurinburg, and had graduated at the Citadel before attending law school at the University of Virginia. He moved to Hendersonville in 1926 and married Louise Bly (daughter of Mr. and Mrs. C.H.T. Bly). Ben never discussed any past accomplishments with me. He was always more concerned and outspoken on problems he was facing in the community, which happened to fall under any one of a dozen hats of leadership he wore.

Luther Hodges campaigned that if he was elected, he would bring a businessman's training and efficiency to the office of governor. Shortly after his election he announced he would appoint a professional engineer to head the Highway Commission. I remarked to Ben, "I think that's a good idea." Ben reacted with a wrath he reserved only when confronted with a statement from someone he thought should have better sense. "I believe that's the dumbest opinion you've ever expressed, and I believe it's the dumbest thing I ever heard Luther Hodges say!" I was dumbfounded. "Why would a professional engineer not be good for the Highway Commission?" I asked. Ben was obviously pretty worked up by this time. "Because a professional is going to build every road on a straight line. He will not be concerned with the people who live in an area. If his road is not convenient to one single soul" (and by this time his voice had raised slightly and he was rolling rubber bands furiously around his fingers), "he couldn't care less because as a professional engineer his job is simply to build a straight road from Point A to Point B. Any good politician can hire all the fancy engineers he wants–but it is the job of the politician to serve the people!" He paused for a minute, then gave that quick smile he was famous for, and said, "I thought you had better sense."

When I was appointed in 1992 to the Board of the Department of Transportation (the old State Highway Commission), the first time I walked into the board room in the Highway Building in Raleigh, I noticed hanging on the wall pictures of former chairmen and spotted Ben's picture. I arranged with the department photographer to make a print of that picture for me. I then created a montage, using a photo of the board room and a blowup of Ben's picture in its proper place on the wall. I had it framed and gave it to Kenneth Youngblood to hang in Ben's former law office at Prince, Youngblood & Massagee.

Photo of L.B. Prince which hangs in N.C. DOT Board Room

In the years we worked together, once in a while Ben would ask me to write material and I would volunteer, "Sir, that's going to create controversy." He would laugh and say, "You forget that controversy is a lawyer's business."

When Frank FitzSimons resigned as Register of Deeds, the Party (headed by Ben Prince) appointed Larry Burgin to succeed Fitz. When the next election came up, Larry announced his intention to run for re-election; but Fitz's former assistant (Marshall Watterson) announced that he also would run for the office. Ben felt this was a breach of party discipline because the Party had already endorsed Burgin. Ben then asked me to prepare a campaign critical of Watterson. This was one of the few times I exercised my independence. "Ben," I said, "I don't agree with what you're proposing. I don't want to criticize Marshall and I think what you're proposing will also hurt Larry." Quickly he responded, "Thank you very much. I'll do it myself." Marshall's friends ("out on the Ridge") were so angered by the ads Ben wrote, that voters in record numbers changed their registration from Republican to Democrat so they could vote in the Democratic primary for "little Marshall." Marshall won in the primary and in the general election. Ben said later, in retrospect, "Marshall Watterson was perhaps the best Register of Deeds this county ever had."

Ben was well-known across the state. He had served in the State Senate in 1939; he was a member of the North Carolina Medical Care Commission; the North Carolina Textbook Commission; the State Board of Elections and the Confederate Pension Board. In Henderson County he served as president of the Chamber of Commerce, the Kiwanis Club and Pardee Memorial Hospital, and was head of the Masons and a strong leader in the Presbyterian church.

When he was chairman of the Hendersonville School Board, he called me one day and asked me to stop by his office. I assumed that this was another occasion to serve as the devil's advocate. I had learned that when Ben was in the process of making up his mind on an issue, he would call on a number of his "surrogate sons" and present to them a position opposite to that which he favored, and would then seek to draw them into a debate on the matter.

But when I arrived, I learned that he had just been advised that Rosa Edwards School building would have to be closed unless certain major repairs and improvements could be made immediately. He said, "You're a Republican. How about you going down and talking to Clyde Jackson (Republican chairman of the Board of County Commissioners) and see if the county can come up with some money for emergency repairs." I didn't hesitate. "Your honor, you don't need for me to talk to Clyde. You're chairman of the School Board, and this is not a political matter and will not be viewed as such by Clyde Jackson." I got his usual, "Thank you very much."

Several days later I stopped in for a visit. "How did it go?" Ben sat twirling several key chains between his hands and said, "I told him the problems we faced, and he asked me two questions. He asked how much money we needed and how quick did we want it." He sat silent for a couple of minutes and said, "I wouldn't want this to get out, but I was so favorably impressed by Clyde Jackson, if he runs again, I'll vote for him."

Clyde Jackson

Ben was voted "Man of the Year" by the VFW in 1960.

One day we were chatting about nothing in particular when he suddenly laughed heartily and said, "Do you know what Virginia (his daughter) said to me the other day? She said, 'I realize it's not easy for you to write personal letters, but would it be too hard if after you put down Dear Virginia, you eliminate the colon and just put in a comma?'" He chuckled heartedly. All the time Virginia was courting Jim Creekman, he merely called him "that boy."

The morning after the Warren decision of the Supreme Court, Ben called me to his office and announced very simply, "It makes no difference how I feel about this Warren decision; but I will tell you now that it is the law of the land, and our school system will obey the law. We will not seek any sort of token integration. Our school people will begin working on plans today, and as quickly as possible, we will institute full integration as dictated by this Court decision." The announcement came as no surprise. Had Ben been around, Nixon would not have had a Watergate and Clinton no Whitewater. Ben didn't need a rule book to tell him what was right and wrong. He knew it from his raisin'.

Massive changes in education

A t the time of the Warren decision (May 17, 1954), there were eight high schools in Hendersonville and Henderson County. Two of the schools (Hendersonville High and Ninth Avenue High) operated under the authority of the City School Board, appointed by City Council. The six schools in the county operated under a three-man appointed County School Board. Most of the schools were "union" with each school building providing classes from the first grade to the senior class (all in the same building). Every one of the buildings were occupied to or near capacity. Superintendent Hugh Randall of the city system said, "It's easy for me to make room for the 56 black students at Ninth Avenue who are residents of the city, but what will happen to the other 200 students at that school who are being bussed into town from Henderson, Polk and Transylvania counties?"

Superintendent J.M. Foster and his assistant, Glenn Marlowe, were already involved in planning for massive changes and improvements to the county system. Two new consolidated high schools were to be built: one to be called East Henderson (and educate students from Dana and Flat Rock); the other would be called West Henderson (and would provide for high school students from Etowah, Fletcher and Mills River). In that Edneyville (though also a "union" school) had already been consolidated from elementary students at Bat Cave, Ebenezer and Fruitland, the county board recommended no changes in that school. There was still unrest in the Edneyville community over the first consolidation; and Foster and Marlowe were anxious to avoid organized opposition to the $2.7 million bond issue which was necessary for the proposed reorganization. The bond issue passed 2,849 for and 2,131 against. Eleven of the twenty precincts favored the issue in the 1957 vote.

At Ninth Avenue, John R. Marble had come to the school in 1940 and became principal in 1946. Marble was a native of Vance County and received his master's degree in school administration from the University of Pennsylvania. He had worked with Randall in the city and Marlowe in the county to develop a plan of integration. In 1959 he received an offer he couldn't turn down from the Anson County School System, so he left Hendersonville and served there until his retirement in 1978. With the public aware that Ninth Avenue School was to be phased out, the City Board had difficulty retaining a principal over the next five years (with Cedric Jones succeeding Marble, followed by Mr. Anderson and Mr. Wright).

In 1962, federal district courts ruled that students could not be bussed across county lines; therefore, the black students from Polk and Transylvania counties at Ninth Avenue were transferred back to their home counties.

In 1963, an Education Committee was appointed from the black Community Council to press for speedier integration. That committee consisted of the Rev. H.L. Marsh, the Rev. J.D. Ellis, Mrs. Alberta Floyd and Mrs. Kathleen Williams. However, most of the planning had already been completed and in May 1964, it was announced that total integration of all schools in the city and county would take place at the start of the 1965 school year. Fifty-six black students would be transferred to their appropriate schools in the city; West High would receive 31 (mostly from the Brickton area); Etowah would have 15; Mills River, 19; Fletcher, 54 (again, mostly from the Brickton area); Balfour would have 28; East High, 11; East Flat Rock, 8; Hilldale, 3; Flat Rock Junior High, 5; Edneyville High, 7; and Edneyville Elementary would add 15. With the high schools consolidating into two huge new campuses (and by achieving total integration), local schools would survive the greatest upheaval in the field of education in its history—all in a ten-year period.

Fifty years ago when WHKP first signed on the air, the venerable R.G. Anders was in his 25th year as superintendent of county schools and would serve until 1953, when he would be succeeded by J.M. Foster. For a consummate history of the transition from 53 one-room schools to only seven school districts during Anders' reign, read Jimmy Fain's "A Partial History of Henderson County."

R.G. Anders

As former superintendent Glenn Marlowe and I were reminiscing over his twenty years as head of the county school system, we both got a kick out of Fain's description of "Professor Anders" as a "Lincolnesque figure whose features were as rugged as the mountains of his native Buncombe." He could qualify as the original ecologist, loving boys and girls and trees in that order; and when not speaking on education, was deploring the wide cutting of trees solely to obtain the bark which was used in the early tanning process. To pick Glenn's memory, I invited him to lunch at Binions. As we sat cracking peanuts and throwing the hulls on the floor, I asked Glenn for memories of when he served as Foster's assistant superintendent. "Let me correct you," he said. "I was associate superintendent back then."

In 1953 (when Eisenhower was inaugurated president and J.M. Foster moved from principal ofBalfour School to become superintendent of county schools), he not only had a three-man school board and the County Commissioners to report to, he also had 23 school committeemen to deal with in the seven school districts of the county. At the time, the County School Board consisted of B.B. Massagee (who had succeeded Floyd Osborne) as chairman. (Osborne had served on the board for 28 years, as chairman for 16.) Also on the board were W.O. Waters of Tuxedo and L.C. "Pete" Youngblood.

In 1953, the committeemen in each district were:

Balfour: W.E. Hammond, M.C. Allen, Robert Johnson

Mills River: S.R. Cathey, T.S. Nichols, L.L. Burgin

Fletcher: James L. Cunningham, Dan Smith, George Fowler

Edneyville: Tom Oates (father of Lemuel Oates, who owns and operates "A Day in the Country & Craft Manufacturing Plants"), William Wilson, Fred Lyda

Dana: Mrs. Ray Lamb (the only woman to serve as committeeman), V.C. Orr, W.R. Staton

Flat Rock: T.B. Lockaby, Norman Jones, F.D. Bell, Charles Painter and P.J. Surrett (Flat Rock had five because of a greater number of schools in the district)

At the time, J.M. Foster was promoted from principal at Balfour to county school superintendent, his twin brother, A.M. was principal of Mills River School. This may have been the only time in history that twin brothers were principals of two different public schools in the same county. At Balfour, Glenn Marlowe became principal; at Dana, C.F. Jervis; at Edneyville, W.J. Nesbitt; at East Flat Rock, Ralph Jones; at Etowah, Howard "Buck" Sitton; at Flat Rock, Ernest L. Justus; at Fletcher, Albert Hill; at Fruitland, Aletta Plank; at Tuxedo, Dean Ward; and at Valley Hill, Clara Babb. A.D. Kornegay was superintendent of city schools. At Hendersonville High, Henry Davis was principal; at Rosa Edwards was Mrs. Almonte Jones; and at Ninth Avenue was Spencer Durante.

Very rarely during the Anders' years were schools ever closed because of the weather. Back then the law provided that busses were required to come only within two and a half miles of a student's home; and most of the busses traveled only primary roads. As Glenn and I continued lunch at Binions, I asked, "When did the state reduce the distance from two and a half miles?" "They never did," he replied. "When Foster and then later I had the responsibility of transporting kindergartners (little 5-year-olds) to school, we ignored the state law on mileages. There was no way J.M. or I (or any other superintendent) was going to require a little 5-year-old to walk more than a mile in the dark to catch a school bus. We ignored the rule and simply added more busses. It was done all over the state. The state told us that if we would buy a bus outright with local monies, they'd replace that bus whenever needed. So while Anders was only running about 50 busses, quickly J.M. and I added to that number; and when I retired, we were running 103 or 104 busses–a few making more than one run a day.

I said, "Glenn, the first school bus I ever remember riding was hardly more than a flatbed truck with a wooden body and benches bolted to the floor, running lengthways." He laughed, "When schools first started using busses, you had to make your own or take what you could get. Even in J.M.'s time, he just bought 'em. There was no maintenance program, nor did we even have a place to store them when school was not in session."

You could tell he was reliving the past as he took another bite of his sandwich. "Nobody in this county will ever know our good fortune in having Pete Youngblood on the school board. He owned an auto dealership out in Fletcher. When he discovered the total lack of organization and maintenance for the school bus fleet, he, on his own, persuaded the county commissioners to give us four acres of land in the old County Home property and authorization of a small fund to build a garage, buy tools, hire and train mechanics, and set up a routine maintenance program. As he sipped his coffee, he said, "Pete did all that on his own. Didn't charge the county a penny for all the work he did."

After a pause, I inquired, "I know you don't want to mention any names because you're bound to leave out people who were vital to you in your years with the school system." With no hesitation, he replied, "Oh, there's one name I will recollect and that's Pete's son, Kenneth Youngblood. Ken served as our attorney through all J.M.'s years and my years, too, and he never charged a penny. I knew of all the other community work he was doing–like organizing all the volunteer fire departments, and doing all that legal work without charge. He was one of a kind."

By this time, Glenn was watching as they poured his fourth cup of coffee. I observed, "They just don't make coffee anymore with that delicious nutlike flavor I used to make for you on those snowy mornings when you'd arrive at WHKP." He looked up and spoke contemptuously, "In spite of all Renfrow's teaching, you never did learn to make a decent cup o' coffee . . . now Renfrow knew how to make coffee." I didn't answer. I could see in my mind, Renfrow pouring full a 30-cup urn of coffee at around 3 a.m. It gradually reduced itself into a thick syrup–this was the coffee Glenn was remembering.

Glenn suddenly asked, "How long was the school year when you graduated at Edneyville?"

"I think it was eight months – but back then, we only had a two-day Thanksgiving holiday, and from Christmas to New Year's." (Later I checked the official record and found that the law called for a 160-day school year.)

Glenn mused a minute or two and said, "I think the school year changed to nine months when the state added the 12th grade. The extra grade was optional for the class of 1942. You could go ahead and graduate or come back for another year. That's when the number of teaching days was increased to 180, and it's been 180 ever since."

I don't know why, but Edneyville didn't add a 12th grade until the 1945-46 school year, and there were only three graduates that year: Gordon Collins, Alice Hill and Loula Powell.

Back in 1961, Senator Boyce Whitmire secured approval of the Legislature to increase the size of the school board from three to seven members. The enlarged board included: Bill McKay, Mrs. J.O. Bell Jr. (the first woman to serve on the Board of Education), L.L. Burgin Sr., Harvey Gale (from Bat Cave) and Robert Greer, along with carryovers from the earlier board, Jimmy Fain and Pete Youngblood.

Nine years later (in 1970), the Legislature kept the number of board members at seven, but provided that they should be popularly elected. The only member of the existing board who chose to run was Bill McKay (who became chairman), with a new board that included: E.L. Justus, Wade W. Worley, John H. Love, C.M. King, Alex Booth Jr., and Mrs. Frank (Virginia) Drake. That same year (1970) J.M. Foster retired and Glenn Marlowe became superintendent; so we called the next 20 years the Marlowe/McKay years (although McKay stepped down prior to Marlowe's retirement and was succeeded by Hardy Caldwell).

Glenn recalled that when he took office, he and the county commissioners were in the same building. He said that J.M. Foster used to laugh and say, "When I'd get the budget completed, I'd slip it under the door of the County Commission and run before the explosion would occur." He once said he happened to cross paths with Chairman Clyde Jackson and said to him, "Mr. Jackson, I'd like to sit down with you one of these days and discuss our proposed budget." He said Clyde looked a bit surprised and said, "That'll be fine. I'll get in touch with you. About a week later, he said he was advised that a meeting had been set. Glenn said, "I made it a point to arrive precisely on time and was ushered into the boardroom and seated at a table across from Clyde, Gene Staton and M.K. Sinclair—the full board. He said Clyde leaned back and as much as said, "We're listening. . . prove your case."

Glenn opened by saying, "This is not MY budget—this is what we see as OUR budget. Our system is not now accredited with the Southern Association; and unless we can increase our funding, we will not be accredited. He said that for more than an hour, he went over proposed expenditures line by line, explaining what was necessary if the county was to be accredited. At the end of the meeting, he said Clyde merely said, "Thank you. We'll get back in touch with you."

Glenn said, "We didn't get everything we asked for but he said the county was the most generous with funding in history." He said every year until he retired in 1990, he followed the same pattern: Get approval of all your principals, your assistants, associate superintendent Sam Reese and assistant superintendent Bill Barnwell. Examine every proposed expenditure, put it in open and understandable language and then take it personally to the County Board of Commissioners.

By the time we were getting up from the table, having spent most of the afternoon in Binions, Glenn said, "The results speak for themselves. The county kept increasing funding for us, our scholastic ratings improved every year, and we finally became accredited in 1975."

As we walked across the parking lot, I asked, "Glenn, where did you grow up?" "Wilkes County," he drawled. "Actually it was in Moravian Falls." I knew better than that—you grow up on the edge of Moravian Falls like you live on the edge of Polk County; but I did learn he was a product of Lenoir Rhyne and ASU, and gained a master's degree before he applied for his first teaching job.

County and Then City; Public and Then Private

The county school system should be dated from 1921 forward because that was the year R.G. Anders became superintendent, and devoted his full energies into eliminating one-room schools and developing larger schools in each district. From 1921 to 1990, only three men headed the county system: J.M. Foster succeeded Anders and Glenn Marlowe served as superintendent from 1970 til 1990.

The city system was created by the state Legislature in 1901 but for practical purposes, only temporary facilities were used until Rosa Edwards School was built in 1912. Professor T.W. Valentine never served as superintendent, but is better remembered than any of the five men who served from 1901. A.W. Honeycutt was hired as superintendent by the City Board in 1919 and served until 1932. Only the real old timers remember either Valentine or Honeycutt. Most local residents recall Fred Waters as their first superintendent. (His son, Fred Jr., married Joyce Withers, whose family owned and operated the Dude Ranch on Sugar Loaf Mountain.) Waters served until 1946 and was succeeded by A.D. Kornegay. Kornegay had just moved to Hendersonville, and took part in the initial WHKP sign-on ceremony on the stage of the Carolina Theatre. Kornegay was serving as head of the city system in 1950 when voters approved a bond issue providing for a new building for black students on 9th Avenue to replace the old wooden structure on 6th Avenue. Also added was the new bathroom at HHS, and an auditorium, cafeteria and firewalls at Rosa Edwards School.

With the large new building on 9th Avenue, the city system began permitting the bussing of black students from Transylvania and Polk counties. The enhanced enrollment at 9th Avenue, with the importation of these out-of-county students, provided the numbers needed to field competitive basketball and football teams and an outstanding 9th Avenue band. In the early years, the "9th Avenue Tigers" played in a black league.

Kornegay's reputation as a strong manager of an educational system created a number of attractive offers for him to move to larger systems. He obviously was looking for a successor when he recruited Hugh Randall to Hendersonville in 1953. The very next year, Kornegay moved on to Statesville and Randall became superintendent.

Randall laughed and said, "I not only remember Kornegay, but Fred Waters. He said after Fred's wife had died, Waters came back to Hendersonville and married his secretary (Helen McKinney) and took her away from the superintendent's office and Hendersonville. Helen was a member of the large Bly family, which had five girls and three boys. Helen's sister Linda was the wife of Mayor A.V. Edwards. Another sister married Ben Prince. Grace had married Bob Severy, and Mary Bly married a Dellinger. Gardiner Bly (one of three boys) was not only still living but attended the VFW's 50th anniversary celebration in 1996. The other brothers were Dan and Lawrence.

In my long years of association both with Glenn Marlowe and Hugh Randall, our conversations always revolved around public schools and their needs and problems. I finally conned Hugh to reminisce over his youth. I was surprised to learn that he had been raised in the Muddy Fork-Buffalo neighborhood in Cleveland and Gaston counties. Hugh had attended Mars Hill College before World War II, serving with the 1st Marine Division in the Pacific. After separation, he received his B.S. and Masters degrees from Wake Forest University.

Hugh said, "Before I was named superintendent, the office was next door to the principal's office at Hendersonville High. I quickly learned that you might as well not have a principal if people can see the superintendent next door. So I got approval from our board to move our offices to the upstairs of the Hartnett Electric Building on 5th Avenue (now a part of the First Citizens Bank complex).

"Hugh," I said, "tell me about your Board."

"That first year," Hugh said, "I had a fantastic board. Bruce Drysdale was chairman and board members included Bill Shepherd, Dr. J.D. Lutz, Roy Johnson and C.E. "Buster" Livingston. I had many great board members serve with me over the next twenty-four years; but I especially remember that first board because it was so thoroughly experienced, and gave me such help and guidance during my first years here."

According to Jimmy Fain in his "Partial History of Henderson County," a total of more than sixty Hendersonville leaders served on the City School Board from 1901 (and with more members since that publication). Only five superintendents served from the days of the one school system of Rosa Edwards: A.H. Honeycutt, Fred Waters, A.D. Kornegay, Hugh Randall, Bill Bates (for only one term) and Charles Byrd.

During those critical years of preparation for total integration, Ben Prince served as chairman of the board. He called me to his office one day, opening the conversation with, "You're chairman of the Planning & Zoning Board, aren't you?"

"Yes sir."

"Well, if we're going to have equal school facilities, then we ought to have equal housing facilities and clean up those slums down on 7th Avenue East and elsewhere in the city. And we need to do it now! Thank you very much." (Ben always signaled the conversation was over when he'd say "Thank you very much.")

The Planning & Zoning Board (working with the city) went through required procedures and filed all documents calling for the establishment of a Hendersonville Housing Authority in 1964. Its first chairman was T.B. Meadows, and A.S. "Bert" Browning Jr. became executive director. A very wise decision was made by the Housing Authority to scatter public housing into small developments throughout the community. This permitted "public housing" to blend in with surrounding neighborhoods, and avoided the problems experienced in larger cities where housing was concentrated in one large sprawling area which would be referred to in the future as "the public housing area." Construction was made possible by government guaranteed 40-year bonds issued by the Housing Authority.

On the snowy mornings, I used to say on the "Good Morning Man" program, "Schools closed today—that's city and county, public and private." That eliminated the need for delineation of all the various schools that were closed.

Private schools (including Fassifern and Blue Ridge School for Boys) were successfully operating here before the new public high school building was constructed in the '20s.

The Blue Ridge School for Boys, shown above, was torn down to make way for the new Blue Ridge Mall; the Fassifern School for Girls was demolished to make way for an Ingle's supermarket.

Both Fassifern and Blue Ridge begun operations here in 1914. Fassifern moved to Hendersonville from the Lincolnton area by the owners, the Shipp sisters. A committee of E.W. Ewbank, W.A. Smith and R.M. Oates had recruited Miss Kate Shipp and her sister to move their school and offered to assist them in acquiring the Caldwell Robertson place at the corner of Fleming and the Asheville Highway. In 1925, the school was acquired by the Rev. Joseph L. Sevier (who also owned and operated Camp Greystone which he had moved from Tennessee to Lake Summit.) Sevier added major expansion to the various buildings and a brick gymnasium on the northwest side of the campus. The gym is the only building still standing after the other buildings were razed to make way for the present Ingle's supermarket in 1968. Fassifern was a quality "finishing school" and was attended by local girls such as Louise Howe Bailey and Frances Peebles Barber and out-of-town girls such as Mary and Martha Douglass (twin daughters of Judge Douglass of Dayton, Ohio. Mary married Jody Barber.

One wedding on June 6, 1953, that attracted a good deal of local attention was when Mary Pat, the daughter of Dr. John J. Anthony of radio's "Dr. I.Q." fame, married Daniel Case who lived on Barker Street. Anthony also had hosted "Stop the Music," "Can You Top This." "The $64,000 Challenge" and "Inner Sanctum." Mary Pat Anthony and Dan Case are parents of two sons and a daughter and now live in Spring, Texas. Don Michalove and T. Lee Osborne Jr. participated in that wedding.

Blue Ridge School for Boys was established in 1914 by Professor Joseph R. Sandifer—known as "Sandy Joe" by local students and boys from forty other states and fifteen foreign countries during the school's fifty-three years of operation. It was looked upon as one of the finest quality schools for young men in the South. Mrs. Sandifer operated the school for a few years after the professor died; but at the end of 1968 school year, she sold the school to a group from Wofford College. The school was empty for a number of years, and finally sold to a local group who recruited an investment firm to build the Blue Ridge Mall on the old school site.

A goodly number of school yearbooks from both Fassifern School and Blue Ridge School for Boys are available in the Genealogy and Historic Room at the Henderson County Public Library.

In the meantime (more than 50 years ago), both the Catholic Church and the Seventh Day Adventist Church would build parochial schools, primarily to educate the youth of their faiths.

The Immaculata Parochial School (Sisters of Christian Education in Charge) was operating in 1946 in a house located at 1133 Oakland Street. The Rev. Mother Landry was Superior Principal. Later the church would build a modern building which stands today facing Buncombe Street.

Meanwhile, the three Seventh Day Adventist churches in the county elected to build their own parochial school at Mountain Sanitarium. In 1950, Navy Captain W.W. Gilmer had retired and settled into that community. He was so concerned over the children being crowded into a single room with only an outside privy, he donated $2,000 (a nice sum back in 1950) to buy materials to add another classroom and construct both a boy's and girl's bathroom. The people of the community provided the labor and the additions were made.

Who was Captain Gilmer??? I discovered (in talking to Ferdi Wuttke, principal of the school in 1996) that Gilmer was one of thirty-six to graduate from the Naval Academy in 1884. He spent three years in the Philippines, serving as commandant of the 12th Naval District up and down the West Coast. He commanded the Battleship USS South Carolina and after World War I was named Naval Governor of Guam.

Capt. Gilmer

Wuttke said, "At the end of this school year, I'm planning to retire."

"My goodness," I said. "How long have you been here?"

"Thirty-nine years. I came to the school in 1957." He told me that Capt. Gilmer died in January of 1955–just shy of his 92nd birthday, the oldest living officer in the United States Navy.

Following the Warren decision of the Supreme Court in 1954, the Federal Judiciary across the land began issuing decisions which would cumulatively lower educational standards, have the effect of destroying morals, and damage morale throughout the public school systems across America.

In 1961, a large group of parents met and discussed the need to establish a privately operated school that would still emphasize religious beliefs and teach character and morals. The consensus at the meeting was the faculty should consist of dedicated teachers of the highest quality. This group then formed the Henderson County Faith Christian Day School Association, applied for a charter from the Secretary of State and hired the Rev. Earl Kilpatrick as the first principal. Kilpatrick was not only an eminently qualified teacher in the public schools but was also pastor of the Grace Baptist Church at East Flat Rock. The Rev. Maynard Nutting (pastor of the Mountain Home Bible Church) was elected president of the association. Some six months later, the association announced it had purchased 13 acres of land from Mrs. John Randall and Mrs. Joseph Hannah (the old Tom Pace homeplace) for the new campus. In a statement at that time, the association said: "The teachers of the Christian School must have training that would qualify them to teach in the public schools, plus the spiritual and moral standards that other schools do not often require. Bible study and a prayer period are a part of the day's schedule."

The school began classes in August of 1962. In the first year, classes were offered only from kindergarten through the third grade, and thirty-seven pupils were enrolled. By 1965, the enrollment had grown to 132.

On November 18, 1965, Principal Kilpatrick announced that a fund drive would be launched to build a brand new brick fireproof classroom building which would be named for the Rev. W.F. Sinclair, who had just passed away. The Rev. Sinclair had been active as a charter enthusiast, had served on all committees and was serving as vice president of the board at the time of his death. The building was occupied in the fall term of the following year. Since then, a gymnasium has been added, as well as other utility buildings and a large playground is now fully equipped.

In July 1996, spokesperson Sandra Landreth told me that for the fall term of 1996, they expected to have 250 students. It is no longer called a "day" school. It's simply Faith Christian School. Ms. Landreth advised me that their faculty included some thirty-five fully accredited teachers, and that the school itself is also fully accredited. Graduates of Faith Christian School are qualified for entrance to any college in the country on the same basis as any student from any public school. The principal today is Don Schearer. He's been at Faith for only the past five years but he has thirty years of experience in school administration.

Ms. Landreth told me that a full program of healthy extra-curricular activities is offered, and their teams compete in statewide Christian Leagues—with the high school team known as the Mustangs and the grade students play as the Mavericks. The school now operates from kindergarten 4 (that's 4-year-olds) through the 12th grade. In addition to income received from fees paid by students and their families, funds are also raised to support the school by the Henderson County Christian Day School Association. The school operates on a non-profit basis, and all contributions are fully tax deductible. They're listed in the phone book as Faith Christian School, dial 692-0556. This is the 35th year Faith has been teaching education courses, blended with character, morals and Christianity.

A Step to Higher Learning

Back in the early '60s, I was asked to attend a meeting in the Skyland Hotel having to do with the possibility that Henderson County might be chosen by the Legislature as the site for one of the new technical schools.

In World War II, the Army had sent me to Dodge Radio and TV School in Valparaiso, Indiana (now Valparaiso Tech), and this is the kind of school I thought was to be discussed. The presentation and discussion leader at the time was Harry Buchanan. Harry had not only served in the State Senate, but he was a full-time lobbyist for the Willoughby-Kinsey chain of motion picture theaters in North Carolina. Henderson County was fortunate to have Harry "Buck" in Raleigh. He was aware of every move pending in the Legislature and could give Henderson County a jump on its neighbors in any new opportunity created by the state.

We learned that day that the state was on the verge of enacting legislation in 1963 providing for community colleges and technical schools in about half the counties in the state. Buchanan was anxious to see Henderson County make the first move necessary to ensure that one of the schools would be placed in Henderson County. Generally, the response from those at the meeting was enthusiastic but reservations were expressed by J.M. Foster and Hugh Randall (superintendents of the county and city schools). They feared that placing a new vocational-type school in this county would simply take away vocational programs in the high schools and also funds which might otherwise go to local public schools.

Committees were appointed and planning was instigated to bring one of the schools to Henderson County—providing that the public school systems would appoint one-fourth of the board to monitor its own vested interests. The school would be called Henderson County Tech Institute. A most timely gift by Mrs. Sadie Smathers Patton of 148 acres of land on which to build the new school played a strong role in persuading the Legislature to make Henderson a recipient county for one of the schools.

To secure the endorsement of the city and country school systems, the Founding Committee had already asked that four appointments to the 12-man board be made by the public school systems: two appointed by the city systems and two by the county. The required legislation that called for the governor to appoint one-third of the board and the county commissioners to also appoint one-third. Terms of the enabling legislation called for the county to provide funds to build and maintain all buildings and the campus itself. Similar to public school funding, the state then would provide funds for teachers and administrative personnel based on a formula developed by the new Board of Community Colleges and the General Assembly.

At the time the Organizing Committee was exploring how best to raise the capital funds that would be needed for the first building, Pardee Hospital and the public school systems let it be known that they also had urgent needs that had to be met with issuance of bonds. A meeting was held under the trees on the lawn of Bill Prim's house of Chimney Rock Road to discuss strategy and planning to help the passage of all the bonds. Perhaps forty or fifty people sat there on a warm summer night offering their input on how to go about getting voter approval. A plan was adopted and enabling bond legislation was approved by the General Assembly, and the bond issue was approved by voters on May 21, 1960.

The original Board of the Institute included John Gregory (of Cranston Print Works), named chairman. The remainder of the board included William McKay, Hugh D. Randall and J.M. Foster. Also, F.G. Schnatz (of DuPont), James T. Mayfield (of GE), Reginald Hill, Bob Wick (of Berkeley), Frank W. Ewbank, Edmond M. Walker, Pat Whitmire and Frank L. FitzSimons Jr.

The Trustees immediately secured the services of William D. Killian (a native of Lincolnton) to become president. He was serving as evening director of Catawba College Valley Technical Institute in Hickory. Killian settled into two small offices only recently vacated by the County Board of

Blue Ridge Community College, with 10 buildings constructed in 23 years, has a full-time enrollment of 1,602 and 3,200 enrolled in continuing education courses.

Education in the Court House (they had moved to the Wetmur Motor Building on Barnwell Street).

Killian negotiated a short-term lease for the old Thomas Motor Company building on Church Street which would be used for classes while the new buildings on the campus were being built between East High and Myers Airport. The three new buildings on Airport Road were completed in the summer of 1973, and a dedication and Open House was held November 18, 1973. While the buildings just completed could house 500 students, during the school's first enrollment period in September of 1973, 363 students had registered.

This school was one of 58 community colleges or technical schools approved in North Carolina. Here in Western Carolina, no facilities were authorized for Clay, Graham, Macon, Swain, Polk, Transylvania or Yancey counties. Although Brevard College did serve the Transylvania area, leaders in that county quickly brought pressure to the Technical School in Hendersonville to make it a two-county school, and it was agreed. In October of 1970, the name was changed to Blue Ridge Technical Institute.

When the Legislature was drawing plans for a statewide system of technical schools, no one had the vision to see that these campuses being built would also be in great demand for a continuing education program and also an expansion into the arts. In the fall session of 1996, 48 curriculum programs were offered, but 250 continuing education courses were offered. There were five times as many courses in continuing education as were being offered in the technical curricula. Though regular full-time students at Blue Ridge now numbered 1,602, adults seeking enhancement of their general education now numbered 3,200 students. An earlier decision by the Trustees to again change the name of the school was proven wise. It is now Blue Ridge Community College.

When the first president, Bill Killian, first unlocked the doors of that temporary facility on Church Street, there was no way he could envision that the tiny temporary facility being used for the first time would grow (over a period of just twenty-three years) to ten new buildings, plus others under construction or in use at the Brevard campus.

From the tiny staff Bill Killian had back in 1973, David Sink now manages 377 full- and part-time faculty members. If a new manufacturing plant moves into the area (or if an existing plant is projecting an expansion—either of which would require specialized training for workers hired), the industry only needs to show that enough new jobs would be created to pay for the teaching program. Boosted by the demands of one of the largest retirement communities in the state, the college offers one of the most elaborate and diversified continuing education programs available anywhere. The 260 part-time faculty members who teach these classes are recruited from retirees who offer superlative credentials.

Some of the graduates at Blue Ridge have achieved unique honor and distinction: Robbie Kirtly, named by USA Today to All USA two-year college student first team; Judi Sloan, an Ada Comstock scholar and Phi Beta Kappa at Smith; Theresa Dixon Metcalfe, one of the top five graduates at WCU and now with National Climatic Data Center; Kathy Stevens Young and Helen Owen, both named Henderson County Teachers of the Year; and Rebecca McCall, specialist in International Pricing & Customer Service at General Electric.

As for pulchritude, there's Jessica McMinn (Miss North Carolina USA). And Carol Edwards won a national modeling contest while at Blue Ridge, and pursues her career as Carol Edwards Boissier, living in New York City.

I like to toss out this little thought provoker to the unsuspecting. When I first enrolled at the University of North Carolina in 1942, there were fewer students on the Chapel Hill campus than the 4,802 full- and part-time students who in 1997 attend our local Blue Ridge Community College.

Education with Honors

What a coincidence! In April of 1992, I was in Raleigh to attend a two-day meeting of the Department of Transportation. Though I had given up the every-day morning show almost five years earlier, I had been totally unsuccessful in being able to reset my biological clock. I'd be wide awake at 3:30 a.m., rarin' to go for another day. On Friday morning, April 2, 1992, at 4 a.m., I was sitting in the lobby of the Radisson Hotel waiting for the dining room to open and glancing through the pages of the *Raleigh News and Observer*. Suddenly I noted a headline on the front page of the second section:

PIONEER OF UNC SYSTEM DIES
ARNOLD K. KING, HELPED UNITE CAMPUSES!

It rang a bell. In Volume II of the Genealogical Society Heritage Book,

I remembered reading about Arnold Kimsey King. The name had stuck because after Dad died, I found in his memorabilia an old tintype, and on the back in Dad's beautiful Spencerian script was written "Uncle Dr. Benjamin King." I knew that this Arnold Kimsey King I was reading about in the *Raleigh News and Observer* had to be Dr. Benjamin King's grandson. He was. He was the son of William Fanning Pinckney King and Julia Anderson King. He was Dr. Benjamin King's grandson; and the reason Dad had written "Uncle Dr." on the back of that tintype was because Dr. Benjamin King was the uncle of Grandma Juno King Edney.

The *News and Observer* story referred to Arnold K. King as "an institution"; the famed Bill Friday referred to him as "a walking encyclopedia"; and co-workers dubbed their deeply religious friend as "the Bishop." Arnold King served as a UNC professor or administrator for a record sixty-one years. The *News and Observer* said, "He lived and wrote the history of UNC; he held nearly every job the university had to offer . . ."

Arnold Kimsey King didn't retire until he was eighty-four, and then sat down and wrote a 379-page history of the UNC system. Bill Friday freely credits Arnold Kimsey King with bringing the Asheville, Wilmington, and Charlotte campuses into the UNC system in the 1960s.

I had finally bummed a cup of coffee from the desk clerk and mused over the fact that "Perhaps this is the first time in history a Henderson County man ever received accolades and headlines in the *Raleigh News and Observer*. I then flipped over to the editorial page and the lead editorial that morning was

Arnold King served as a UNC-Chapel Hill professor and administrator for a record sixty-one years.

"THE KING OF THE HILL." And when I read that first paragraph, it so vividly expressed the tribute: "The blue in Carolina blue is a little paler this day. Arnold King has died after a rich 90 years, and few have added more color to the Chapel Hill landscape than he did in a 61-year career." The editorial detailed how King had served as troubleshooter, friend, and confidante of UNC presidents from Frank Graham to Bill Friday and C.D. Spangler. Remember, this editorial was published in the prestigious *Raleigh News and Observer.*

Arnold's parents are buried in Refuge Baptist Church Cemetery. His great-grandfather (Hiram King) is buried in the King's Grove Cemetery on Pace Road. Hiram's tombstone has chiseled into the rough stone "Lived 98 years 7 months and 8 days." Arnold, who lived to be 90, descended from a family which had experienced extensive life.

There were several others who contributed mightily to the Carolina scene, not the least of which would be Leonard Victor Huggins. "Vic" was also raised "out on the ridge" and made his way to UNC in the early '20s. "Vic" became head cheerleader in 1924-25; he wrote the song "Here Comes Carolina" (which you'll still hear sung at every ball game); and he selected the "ram" as the school mascot and named him Ramses. He left Chapel Hill for a while but UNC was in his blood, and he returned to own and operate Huggins Hardware on downtown Franklin Street. He became very active in the Rotary Club; and in 1981, he dug out all his old jokes he'd used in speeches to other Rotary Clubs on the "green pea circuit" and put them into a book form, utilizing Henderson County names as the featured characters of each story. He called the book "Anecdotes."

Some of the stories in the book are not anecdotes—they are true stories. One involved a church organist who was pregnant out of wedlock at the old Advent Church in Dana. The church was forced to decide between adhering to the strict admonition against sin or permit the evermore pregnant organist to provide music for the worship services. The organist was a relative of mine (and Vic had made minor changes to her name) but the person would be immediately recognized by anyone familiar with the story.

Vic was a mentor to Deacon Andy Griffith. In a foreword to Vic's book, Andy Griffith wrote, "I did a show over at Carolina Inn for a civic group of which Vic was a member. I did a monologue on 'Hamlet' which Vic didn't think was too funny; and to tell the truth, it hadn't gone over well that day. After lunch, Vic got me out on the sidewalk and told me a story that had to do with a football game. I believe it was in Tennessee because I seem to recall the word 'volunteer' in it." Andy Griffith concluded, "About a year later, I needed an extra monologue for a show I was doing and Vic's joke sprang to mind. As a result, I wrote a monologue called "What It Was, Was Football." You know the rest of the story.

Vic came to Hendersonville to autograph his book for his old friends "out on the ridge," and in a letter to me confessed he'd sold more books that day at Carolyn's Book Store than at any other autograph party.

There are many other university ties. Chapel Hill was also the ultimate home of J. Charles Morrow III. I believe he had the title of provost when I bumped into him at a retirement dinner for Earl Wynn and his wife, Rhoda (who had established and managed the Department of Radio, TV, and Motion Pictures during the time I was a student there). Clifford Pace (son of James J. and Sallie Kate Pace of Hendersonville) was assistant to Albert Coats and helped found the Institute of Government at UNC. He later served as city manager of Asheboro. Jeff Shealy (son of R.B. and Inga) is a

Dr. John Charles Morrow III

consultant and professor at Cornell University. He holds a variety of patents on gold transistor chips. Bob Morgan was also on the faculty of Cornell. I beleive he is the son of Fannie Morgan. Old-timers will all remember "Pop" Lance, who left his mark in the hallowed halls of Mars Hill College. Dr. George Jones was a professor of religion at the University of South Carolina, and played a major role in developing the Southern Baptist Theological Seminary at Louisville, Kentucky. Also at Louisville is Dr. Bill Waddell (brother of Dan Waddell), who is chairman of the Audio Radiology Department of Pharmacology and Toxicology at the University of Louisville. As I recall, Willett Bennett and Billy Nesbitt both taught at State. Willett was the son of Willett Sr.; and Billy, the son of W.F. Nesbitt, former principal at Edneyville High School. Joe King, who now runs King Hardware (with his mother, Wilma, and Aunt Lucille), left a career of teaching at Appalachian State University to return home to take over the family business following the death of his father, J.D. Joe, by the way, is a cousin of the fabled Arnold Kimsey King of UNC fame. David Kaplan (son of Morris and Anne) was on the faculty at West Point until he resigned to become associated with Logistics Management Institute in McLean, Va. Jack Reese (son of Alyce and W.J. Reese) headed up the prestigious University of Tennessee at Knoxville. Jack's nephew (Allen) worked at WHKP in news in the early '90s and now owns WPNF-Brevard. He was a son of Tommy Reese, an old classmate of mine. The father of the late of great Bob Edwards was also a chancellor at Clemson University.

Other names have been given to me. Richard Pierce (who also worked for HKP back in the '40s) received a law degree at Rollins in Florida, and either taught or became an administrative executive at Rollins. Ann Cathey (daughter of T.A. Cathey, former principal at Edneyville) was an exchange professor at the University of Oxford and later taught at UNCA and UNCC. Mary Duncan was on the faculty of the University of Buffalo. Jack Hill Jr. of Etowah was teaching at a branch of the University of South Carolina. Myra Middleton Brown, I was told, teaches medical records at East Carolina

University. Dr. John Potts grew up in Flat Rock, taught at Avery Institute in Charleston, S.C., and also at Voorhees College. He has been awarded honorary doctoral degrees from Morris College, Benedict College and Virginia Theological Institute. He has served as a consultant to fifteen colleges in areas of program evaluation.

It Ran in Families

I earlier mentioned that A.M. and J.M. Foster were probably the only twins ever to have served (each as a principal of a school) in the same county. Teaching also seemed to run in families. I can think of the Griffins. The oldest (Woody) would become principal of Asheville High School and later Asheville City School Superintendent. His brother (Odell, who played professional baseball) returned to become principal of Flat Rock High School and, later, West Henderson. A younger brother (Brown) was principal of Clyde High School when I was managing WWIT in Canton.

The Whitmires would be the all-time champion "family in education" locally. Mayor Boyce's son ("Blondie") was principal at Flat Rock and spent his entire life in education. His older brother, Pat, would coach a year or so at Edneyville; but Pat's wife (the former Shirley Ray) taught school for thirty-one years. Then there was Bill Whitmire. He was at Edneyville and East Henderson and retired after thirty-two years. John Whitmire has spent more than twenty years in education at Edneyville and Hendersonville Junior High; in 1996, he helped manage the school bus transportation program.

The Pryors? Tom was active for years in teaching and coaching, and in 1996 was elected to the school board. Harris was principal at the giant Tuscola High School in Haywood County.

There are numerous examples of fathers succeeded by sons in teaching. Billy Nesbitt (son of W.J. Nesbitt, principal at Edneyville) was on the faculty at N.C. State.

And many, many teachers or principals married other teachers or principals. Howard "Buck" Sitton (principal of Etowah) married Lucy Gilliam (teacher at Edneyville). At Edneyville High School, teacher John D. Moore would marry the sixth grade teacher, Elva Schreyer.

The Whitmires and the Elks Camp for Boys

Recently I was loaned a copy of the BPOE (the Elks Club Magazine) published back in 1947; and on page 9, there is a large picture of a very handsome young man, and above the picture in bold letters:

NORTH CAROLINA PRESIDENT

and beneath the picture:

Boyce A. Whitmire, Hendersonville

Not only did Boyce believe in young people, he and Patricia produced quite a good crop of 'em on their own: Pat, Boyce Jr., Blondie, Bill, John (ready-made basketball team) along with their own cheerleader, "Sis' (now Mrs. Fred Jackson). At the time Boyce was going through the chairs in the Elks organization, he was also the family attorney for the J.Z. Cleveland family. The Clevelands were part of the old aristocracy, and owned huge acreages of land, among which was one 300-acre tract near U.S. 25 on the North and South Carolina line. Boyce suggested to the Clevelands that this site would be a wonderful place to build a camp for "deserving boys selected by the Order of the Elks." The Clevelands agreed and said they would contribute 7/8th interest in the land if the Benevolent and Protective Order of the Elks would pay 1/8th of the value of the place. That 1/8th amounted to about $9,000. Whittler put the proposal before the NC Elks Convention in Charlotte on Sept. 22, 1944, and the Elks Camp for Boys became a reality.

Boyce Whitmire

In the first year about 300 boys from across the state came in 75 camper segments—each for a two-week stay at the camp. Cottages, swimming pools, gymnasium, craft shops—all were constructed from contributions from the Elks organization and individual members of the Elks. Boyce Whitmire was so wrapped up in this fantastic project, he took a virtual hiatus from his law practice in the summer to "be at the camp." By now, 600 boys were coming and going during a season.

Boyce's young sons gave him the nucleus of a staff but other full-time workers at the camp numbered twenty-two by the year 1954. In that year, Secretary of State Thad Eure was on the Elks Board; and it was only natural

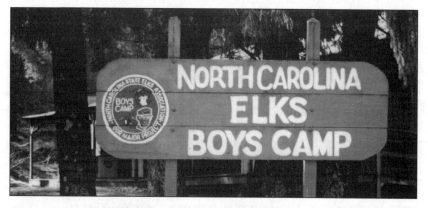

Entrance to the Elks Camp for Boys on old U.S. 25, this side of the Greenville watershed.

that his son, Thad Eure Jr., would become a staff member. Boyce's long association with that beloved educator, Ernest L. Justus, led to his appointment as assistant administrator of the camp.

As Boyce directed activities at the camp, he was also moving through the chairs in the National Elks organization and served as the Knight directly under the Grand Exalted Ruler of Elkdom. With this position, he was able to persuade the Elks Grand Board of Governors to hold their annual meeting at the camp. In 1955, Grand Exalted Ruler, John Walker of Roanoke, Va., was the principal speaker at the annual retreat. One of the "Whitmire 5" (Pat) recalls with no fond memories the 10-day period before this meeting and others that would be held at the camp. The camp was put through an inspection which would have rivaled that at the Citadel or even West Point prior to a visit by the Commander-in-Chief.

In those early '50s, many young high school students and graduates would work at the camp during the summer. Three former Bearcats who played basketball for Clemson were Ed Morgan, John McGraw, and Tommy McCullough. They were joined by such folks as Glenn Marlowe and Woody Griffin, and college stars such as Furman's Frank Selvy. This inspired Whitmire to strike an alliance with HHS's coach, Ted Carter, to stage an annual basketball clinic at the camp. Carter had coached an HHS team to state championships in 1948, '49, and '53. The basketball clinic was a huge success from the start with such famous guest coaches as Everette Case (coach at N.C. State) and who introduced the "fast break" to the A.C.C. There were also Hall of Famers Frank McGuire (then coach at UNC) and Bones McKinney (coach at Wake Forest).

In 1956, in the very heyday of the Elks Camp, the City of Greenville, S.C., announced that they were purchasing 1,639 acres of land for a watershed for the city, and it would require the taking of 175 of the Elks Camp's original 300 acres. Whitmire was able to negotiate with the City of Greenville to take primarily the undeveloped land and leave the camp with the lake and as many buildings as possible; and pay the camp $80,000, which could be used for the construction of new facilities. At the same time, the DOTs of both North and South Carolina announced that U.S. 25 would be relocated on a more westerly route, and the existing roadway would be used for local traffic only. When the project was completed, you no longer "passed by the Elks Camp." It had to be your destination.

By the '60s, Boyce no longer had this family cadre to be the nucleus of his staff—they'd grown up and gone their own ways. Boyce had also become much more actively involved in politics, serving in the Legislature and then winning a bitterly fought battle for the N.C. Senate against the late Bobby Redden. He had now become so involved in state politics, he had to step down at the camp and turn over the reins to Ernest L. Justus. While in the Senate, he was able to pass legislation enlarging and then another law electing the County School Board; and he persuaded the state

Mayor Boyce Whitmire, in his dedication remarks, said: "This is a wonderful and momentous occasion for the City of Hendersonville for it is the first time that we have opened a municipally owned park." He named it Patton Park, on behalf of Sadie Patton, who had donated about 20 acres of land in memory of her husband, Preston.

to name the Flat Rock Playhouse "The State Theatre of North Carolina."

In the meantime, a movement to establish a YMCA had begun in Hendersonville and Boyce became one of the most active charter leaders. So, here's a man who had served in the Legislature; in the N.C. Senate; had been second only to the Grand Exalted Ruler of the Elks; had founded, organized and operated the highly successful Elks Camp for Boys for close to fifteen years; who was a driving force in building the first YMCA here . . . and then???

Boyce Whitmire runs for and is elected mayor. During Whitmire's tenure as head of the city, he led the City Council into building an Olympic-size swimming pool, support buildings, outdoor basketball court, tennis courts and picnic areas in Patton Park. He named it Patton Park on behalf of Sadie Patton, who had donated twenty acres of land in memory of her husband, Preston. The park does not operate today as it did in the beginning, nor as Boyce envisioned it to be run. I suppose, however, if "Bot" Whitmire was still around today, he'd be doing a little politickin' to make the Patton Park Dream still a reality for the kids of this community.

From Hendersonville to Fame and Fortune

Henderson County has had its share of stellar athletes in the past. My own memory goes back to the years when Mitch Taylor and Ed Shytle were on the Edneyville Yellowjacket basketball team. Odell Griffin (who would later play professional baseball) was also on that team of 1937-38. Ed Shytle made the starting lineup for the UNC Tar Heels, and was nominated for All-American. Ed died in a field hospital on an island in the Pacific one week before his son was born.

Bill Wilson was also an Edneyville graduate. He played in the industrial leagues, which had teams such as the Champion YMCA. Bill would have loved the 3-point rule, because he could hit fifty percent of shots attempted from the center line. Other Edneyville stand-outs included Harris Pryor and Donald Dalton, who both played for Western Carolina.

The most amazing group of local athletes were members of the '48-'49 Hendersonville Bearcats Basketball Team. This team won consecutive state championships in both 1948 and 1949. That team consisted of Boyce "Blondie" Whitmire (who would later play for Western Carolina), John McGraw and Tommy McCullough (who were in the starting lineup at Clemson), Ed Morgan (started in basketball for the University of Tennessee, but also won a scholarship in football as a wingback for the "Vols". Tommy Osborne was a member of the 1953 Bearcat team which also won the state championship.

Other Hendersonville athletes: Bud Hunter played basketball and football for Davidson. Sandy Kinney was quarterback for the UNC Tar Heels and then later joined UNC as assistant coach. The great Bob Elliot (captain of the 1956 Bearcats) was a star fullback at Carolina. His dad, Charlie, played for Western Carolina. Willett Bennett Jr. played basketball for N.C. State. Sam Galloway was in the Auburn starting football lineup in the '50s, and Donnie Heilig played quarterback for the Clemson Tigers. Yogi Poteet, starting his first game for Carolina in 1961, scored 14 points and was the standout in a

62-56 upset over N.C. State. Another of the Whitmire boys, Pat, played for Wake Forest when it was located in the little town of Wake Forest outside of Raleigh. Tommy Williams (who would later coach at East) was a starter for Western Carolina; and Dan Waddell was star quarterback for Eastern Carolina University.

Ronald Wagner played basketball at Furman, and Freddie Streetman was a starter for Davidson.

And while Asheville might object, I'm sure Charlie (and particularly Sarah) won't mind if I include the Justices as a part of the Henderson County heritage. Charlie "Choo Choo" Justice was born in Asheville or to be more specific, Shiloh; but for the greater part of his adult years, he's been a part of Henderson County. In fact, Sarah says she feels more at home here than any place they have lived in their 50-plus years of marriage.

After "Choo Choo" had completed his football years with the Tar Heels and the Red Skins, he and Sarah bought a home in 1956 in Sylvan Heights and moved here to go into partnership with Joel Wright in what was then Justice & Wright Oil Company. Joel ("the little old oil man") had been quarterback in the single wing formation during Justice's first two years at Carolina. Both men had been raised in the Asheville area and were close personal friends.

Later Charlie left the partnership and went into the insurance business in Greensboro. He ultimately established the Charlie Justice Insurance Agency in Cherryville and handled all insurance underwriting for Carolina Motor Freight. More and more he turned the business over to his son in law (Billy Crews) and he and Sarah began the search for a place to return to their beloved North Carolina mountains. They found it at Kenmure.

Charlie "Choo Choo" Justice and his wife, Sarah, at Keenan Stadium for the NC vs. NC State game in 1996.

After World War II (when Charlie and other servicemen returned to college campuses across the land), on Franklin Street you could buy a Coke or an ice cream cone for a nickel, a hot dog for a dime. Most vets, after having spent three years in service, suddenly found it a bit difficult being a college boy again. They had lost their war hero (Gen. George S. Patton) in December of 1945. He died from injuries in a jeep truck collision in Germany. The vets (maybe the entire country) were looking for another hero, and then there appeared Charlie "Choo Choo" Justice. He was all humility until he stepped out on the football field. While at Carolina he broke two dozen records, fifteen of which still stand. He led the Tar Heels to three major bowl games in four years; and his picture was on the cover of *Life*, *Look*, *Colliers*, and the *Saturday Evening Post*.

Even today, Charlie is just as emotional about victory for the Tar Heels as he was from 1946 to '49. Sitting with him in the stands as the play develops on the field, he'll suddenly leap to his feet and shout, "Cut, cut, cut, you fool!" Sitting back down he'd grumble, "He could have had another 20 yards if he'd just cut back."

After 50 years, the younger generation may not know him, but they know of him. At the Carolina-State game in 1996, loads of young people came to him in the stands and asked for his autograph. The other day, I had just read the latest episode of a certain so-called professional basketball player who kicks a photographer, elbows another player in the groin, and goes "drag" just for kicks and the dozens and dozens of his ilk who are paid millions of bucks to scratch their crotch or, without their nanny-chauffeur to drive them, couldn't find their way home. And the thought struck me: How sad that the young people today have virtually no professional athlete to set examples, to establish goals, to be one whom they can look up to. How sad that the Charlie Justices no longer exist in this world.

Why Did They Do That?

Several years ago, I was on a committee to stage a benefit dinner-dance at Kenmure for the benefit of the Four Seasons Arts Council. A number of us were involved in running light stringers around the perimeter of the giant tent; and I asked Sherman Morse (one of the group), "What did you do before you retired to Kenmure?" Without hesitation, "Punched holes in Life Savers" was his immediate response. I did a double take. He smiled. Sherman A. Morse Jr. was working for Beechnut Foods, and he and two associates were given an opportunity to acquire the Life Saver Division which was being spun off. "Sherm" became director and chief operating officer of Beechnut Life Savers Inc. "When you were young, would you ever have dreamed that some day you'd be an owner or manager of Life Savers?" He smiled and we let the matter drop.

I suppose I would also have let the matter drop if young Donald H. Keith had told me, "I'm building and preserving replicas of the Christopher Columbus fleet." In fact, the more I learned about the unique qualifications of this son of D.B. and Dean Keith (who had grown up in Hendersonville), the more I was amazed. Don has been a guest on the most prestigious network news specials and features; and he's had articles published by *Reader's Digest*, *National Geographic*, *National Geographic Research*, *Antiquity* and a host of other professional archaeological magazines. In fact, Donald said while he had written articles of far greater significance, it was his first article in *National Geographic* about a shipwreck he had worked on in Korea that meant the most to his long-suffering parents who, up until this point, had always hoped that "I would grow tired of larking about and find a real job."

Now he was immersed (literally) in a new career of underwater archaeology. After working on sunken wrecks on sites in Jamaica, Korea, Italy, Turkey and Mexico with the American Institute of Nautical Archaeology, and after two years researching the Chinese Age of Exploration and Discovery, his big opportunity came. He was recruited to lead an exploration team to study a shipwreck on the Molasses Reef (a part of the British Crown Colony of Turks and Ki-Kos) about ninety miles north of Haiti. Their work was given the total blessing of the Crown Colony; and, in addition, the government allowed them to take with them better than ten tons of artifacts back to Texas A & M for cleaning, conserving, analyzing, and cataloging. He (and other "Aggies" under his leadership) built a conservation lab at Texas A & M and spent the next eight years in the tedious work of restoring these artifacts which had been beneath the sea since 1520 to 1530.

Donald said that as he commuted back and forth between College Station and the Crown Colony of the Turks and Ki-Kos, he made up his mind that some day there should be a museum set up on the island which would be used to display these priceless artifacts when totally restored. In 1990, a group of influential citizens pooled resources and formed the Turks and Ki-Kos Museum. They converted one of the oldest stone buildings on the island and devoted the entire ground floor to the artifacts from the Molasses Reef Wreck.

The museum had been opened about a year when Prince Philip (Duke of Edinburgh) directed the Royal Brittania to make port at Turk and Ki-Kos Island. And it was the pleasure of this Hendersonville young man (Donald H. Keith) to serve as the Duke's private escort and guide. Don was at the end of the receiving line of all the high muckity mucks on the island, and the Duke said nothing just smiled at each as he slowly made his way down the line. When he reached Keith, he asked, "Where are you from?"

Being a Navy man, the Prince (the Duke of Edinburgh) was truly interested in all the artifacts in the museum. As he started to leave, he asked Don, "Have you ever had contact with the British Maritime Museum or the British Science Museum?"

"Both, sir," Don answered.

The Prince then pointed out that he had served on the Board of Directors for both organizations for many years, "and if you ever need anything, give me a call." But Don said he didn't bother to leave his phone number.

That night there was a gala dinner aboard the Royal Britannia. Don received a personal invitation from the Duke to attend the reception. Perhaps Donald H. Keith of Hendersonville is the only American ever to have spent the evening being entertained aboard the Royal Britannia.

Don reminisced of the years growing up, being with, and then being apart from his family; and how often his mom and dad didn't agree with his plans for the future. But once he had made up his mind, they gave him their full support. He remembered how his dad, Donald B. Keith, used to enjoy remembering poetry he had been required to memorize in high school, and young Donald shared a few lines from Robert Frost's "The Road Not Taken": "Two roads diverged in a wood and I took the one less traveled by, and that has made all the difference." He then observed, "I'm still not sure where that road leads."

The senior Keith (down through the years) has answered to Donald, D.B., or, as I always called him, "Doing Business" because regardless of where he was, he always had a handful of yellow pads or file folders and Xerox copies by the handsful—always planning a new promotion or new twist in marketing.

D.B. graduated from Hendersonville High at age fifteen. He majored in Business Administration at the University of North Carolina; and joined J.N. Brunson in his furniture store as business manager at the age of twenty-three. Mr. Brunson protected his job with the firm as Keith served in World War II. Immediately following his discharge, Keith returned to the business and purchased part ownership. When Mr. Brunson died in 1954, D.B. continued to manage the store for Mrs. Brunson until he and Bill Watts purchased her interests and became sole owners. Later Bill Prim (brother-in-law of Watts) joined the film and became store manager of the Fashion Furniture House. As the firm continued to grow, still other stores were opened: a discount furniture outlet and a patio store. Richard Nix then joined the firm. For some 50 years, D.B. Keith remained at the helm of leadership of the Brunson operation.

Though Keith was a merchant first and foremost, he was another native of Hendersonville who was always searching for ways to make the community, and especially downtown, a place people could enjoy. When the water fountain in front of Brunson's operated only about half the time, he demanded that the city either fix it or take it away. (They took it away.) From my earliest association with D.B. Keith, he was always concerned with the dearth of restrooms in the downtown area.

As did all dedicated natives, he went through the chairs at the Chamber of Commerce and the Merchants Division; and when the future of downtown began to come into question with the development of malls and strips, he established a Parking Corporation and constantly scouted for lots or tracts of land that could be acquired for parking. He was a leader in establishing the Special Tax District, which would provide funds needed for the Central Business District Improvement. He recruited guarantors of the note and sold stock in the industrial corporation.

D.B. had always dreamed of the day when young Donald would take over the furniture complex he had built. Dad's dreams of Don's being a part of his business did not come true, but he and Dean can take deep pride in the international accomplishments in underwater archaeology achieved by their son, Donald H. Keith.

Local Boy was First

Everybody in Boston knew him as Bill, but when he was going to school at Dana, he was known as Fays. Nobody in Boston had ever heard of Fays Brown. In fact, when we were in Boston a few years ago (on a fall trek for leaf watching in New England), we had not yet met Fays–nor Bill Brown.

Boston is not just an historic city, it's a year 'round tourist destination. Everyone has to see the U.S.S. Constitution (better known as "Old Ironsides") and there's Ben Franklin's statue in front of the old City Hall. Every tourist has to go to Quincy's Market and Faneuil Hall.

When Fays Brown arrived in Boston, there was a pub on Beacon Street known then only as the Bull and Finch, and it was known on a local basis only. Long after Fays Brown got to Boston did the TV producers select the Bull and Finch as the perfect setting for a new TV show, "Cheers." The programs weren't filmed there, they just constructed (on a set) a recreation of the Bull and Finch. Today, at almost any hour, a line winds around the block with "Cheers" fans waiting their chance to get inside and quaff at least one brew and relive "Cheers."

Fays Brown was born William Lafayette Brown to Mr. and Mrs. William W. Brown. He went to Dana School under Principal C.F. Jervis, just like his brother, Garland (who for years was Sheriff Ab Jackson's top

The Brown brothers, William Lafayette (left) and his brother, Garland. William today is the only non-New Englander to ever head the Bank of Boston. Garland was Sheriff Albert Jackson's chief investigator.

detective) and like Laberta Lamb and Mrs. Willie B. Marshall, all of Henderson County. After Dana High School, Brown attended Mars Hill College and then Newberry in South Carolina. He had toyed with the idea of the Naval Academy, but instead graduated from Harvard University and served in the Navy. While on that tour of duty, he became assistant manager of the Bank of Guam. That apparently got him started in banking. In 1949, having outgrown the nickname Fays, he was known as Bill Brown. After mustering out of the Navy, he landed a job as a trainee of the First National Bank of Boston.

If C.F. Jervis (the crusty old principal of Dana School) was alive today, he probably would tell you that he expected nothing less than Brown being quickly promoted to loan officer and in just ten years to become a vice president of the Bank of Boston. In his early years in banking, he concentrated on credit and lending – especially to small denovo loan companies that were springing up along Route 123. These small firms were supplying capital for small firms on the Eastern shore specializing in research and development. By 1966, Bill Brown had become an executive vice president, and three years later would be named to the Board of Directors. He was assigned Planning & Control activities, supervision of mutual funds, stock transfers and custody.

In the summer of 1971, William Lafayette Brown of Dana, N.C., was elected president of the First National Bank of Boston (at the time, New England's largest bank). Brown would be the first Southerner to hold that position in the history of the bank. There is a certain contagion about serving on a large corporate board. You rub elbows with other corporate leaders, and then you're invited to serve on boards of companies they control. At one time, Bill Brown served on such boards as Stone & Webster, First Capital Corporation of Boston, First Bank Financial, Boston Overseas Financial, Overseas Trade Development Corp. and Standard International. Among his eleemosynary leadership roles in Boston, he was president of Children's Hospital Medical Center.

In talking to Velda Brown (Garland's wife), I learned that Bill Lafayette Brown is retired but still has access to the corporate limousine. The family home is in Weston, Mass., although they do have a place on Cape Cod and a wintertime watering hole in Naples, Fla. Bill married Helen Presbrey and they have two daughters and two sons.

I first met Bill out at Jack Ward's Tractor in Dana. Jack was throwing a big political barbecue, and Bill Brown and I happened to bump into each other. He told me they come back to the mountains about once a year, and always keep their eyes peeled for a place of their own, just to prove Thomas Wolfe wrong–"you can go home again."

The Golden Bear

When I was actually broadcasting the series "Where Fitz Left Off," I thought it appropriate to salute former staff members during the week of the station's 50th anniversary. Strictly from memories that quickly popped into my mind, I did five programs and mentioned a dozen or so people who had worked with us from time to time down through the years.

About a week after those programs aired, I started getting phone calls: "You left out 'so-and-so' and he was one of my favorites." To avoid slighting anyone (knowing that recalling names is not a strength in the twilight of one's years), I spent the better part of a day going through old bits of memorabilia, pictures taken down through the years; and then posted a master list of names on the bulletin board at the radio station with a request that if any of the old times could recall other names of people I'd left out, please add to the list. A week later I was floored when I checked the list and found that better than twenty-five names had been added, and the list now numbers more than one hundred people. I suppose with a staff of some fifteen to twenty people over fifty years, a turnover of one hundred people is remarkably low.

We had young people who worked during summer vacation and young women who were married while working at the station and simply left the business world to raise a family. Others got valuable experience in our smaller station before moving on to bigger markets. And, of course, some who were not "radio addicts" found more satisfying or more profitable work. I have included in the appendix section of this book a list of every person who ever worked at WHKP at some time or another over the past fifty years.

You'll find the name "Robert F. Orr" included. He was a son of Kay and Minnie Sue Orr. Bobby worked in sales during the summers when he was attending the University of North Carolina. One summer Jack Nicklaus and Gary Player were booked for an exhibition round at the Asheville County Club. Bobby was an avid golfer, and he pestered Art Cooley for weeks to let him have time off to go to the match, even promising to get a personal interview for WHKP with Nicklaus. To attest to the tenacity of young Bobby Orr, he did get the interview and he still has the original recording in his personal memorabilia.

He remembers the experience vividly. "To begin with, there was a press conference with both golfers, but I think I failed, in my nervousness, to push the "Record" button, so nothing was on the tape. At the end of the press conference, both Player and Nicklaus went to the practice range and as Jack was hitting practice balls, I told him my sad story. Nicklaus promised to meet me after the exhibition and we'd do a one-on-one interview. I sweated the entire match, thinking that Jack, once the round was finished, would just get in his car and drive away. But he was true to his word, and we did a great interview together. It was one of the proudest moments of my life." When Bobby sent me the letter with his recollections of that day, I thought, "I should send this to Jack Nicklaus." I doubt if even the Golden Bear has ever been interviewed by a young college student who today sits on the North Carolina Supreme Court. The guys around the Pro Shop kidded me, "Nicklaus will just throw that letter in the trash. With his success and fame, no way he'll even acknowledge receiving the letter." On page XX I have included a copy of the letter Jack Nicklaus wrote to Judge Robert Orr. It simply proves once again, the most successful people on earth are also the nicest.

The Department of Justice Building in Raleigh is across the corner from the Department of Transportation Building. Whenever there is a need for someone to be sworn in or an oath to be administered, usually someone in DOT will simply call over to the Justice Building and ask one of the judges to assist. One day I noticed Bobby coming into the DOT Board meeting. We exchanged warm greetings and shared a few memories; and when it came time for Judge Orr to administer the oath, he said: "I am delighted to see my old boss Kermit Edney sitting here. He gave me the first job I ever had, and it was in the field of broadcasting." I sat there proud and as puffed up as a Mr. Toad in Toad Hall.

Judge Orr was the first Republican to be elected to the Court of Appeals since Reconstruction days. He also became the first Republican to sit on the North Carolina Supreme Court. I think of how proud old man H.M. Flynn would have been of his grandson, and the adoration of all the beautiful Flynn girls of their nephew Bobby.

Greener Pastures

WHKP has been a stepping stone for a number of individuals who found greater opportunities in larger markets. Bob McGarity managed a station his family owned in Georgia; Les Grattick owned several stations, also in Georgia. Kenneth Blackwell has worked for stations in a variety of metro markets in Virginia. Jerry King and Bill Christie moved into the advertising agency field, producing custom commercials for a variety of regional and national advertisers. Cathy Hunnicutt worked in radio sales in the Charlotte area; Cliff Inman was an engineer with the "Voice of America"; and Bob Marlowe was running his own station in Kissimmee, Fla., when he was killed in an auto accident.

A number of other locals did not begin their careers with WHKP but experienced notable careers in broadcasting, folks like my brother Grady Edney, Reginald Wilcox, Roone Arledge, Jim Lampley, my nephew Ron Kershaw and Bob Wisnewski, who became an executive of the Cox Broadcasting Group.

I never had the pleasure of meeting Reginald Wilcox. On one trip to New York, I asked if he was in his office and was told that as vice president in charge of facilities, he was rarely in the office. I did know his mother, Mrs. Alice Fuller, who was not only executor of the Fuller Estates but also trustee in bankruptcy for the W.A. Smith Estates, the Florida/Carolina Estates, and the Rhododendron Estates. When the land boom turned to bust, these three corporations were carrying enormous amounts of paper on many, many lots in Laurel Park. I remember in 1962, just before she died, I paid her the usual fee; and she, acting as trustee in bankruptcy, issued a quit claim deed for the corporation's interest in the property.

Reginald Wilcox's mother, Mrs. Alice Fuller, had married H. Walter Fuller, president of Laurel Park Estates, and Reginald became sales manager of the corporation. After the bust, Reginald used his real estate experience in Laurel Park to land the job of handling facilities for ABC. Wilcox had kept (at his Long Island home) enormous quantities of memorabilia about the town of Laurel Park; and even had in his possession the professional motion picture made in the mid-'20s as a selling tool for Laurel Park properties. Reginald gave this to Jim Toms, his attorney, for safekeeping. It has been refurbished by Bob Jones University and is priceless memorabilia.

My brother Grady started with WSJS in Winston-Salem. After VE Day, he joined AFN Paris (the American Forces Network) and did the live worldwide coverage of the Nuremberg War Crimes Trials. Later he worked with stations in Philadelphia, Boston and San Diego before becoming a vice president of Storer Broadcasting in Miami. He served on Mrs. Lyndon Johnson's committee working for highway beautification.

Jim Lampley worked with Jim Heavner at WCHL Chapel Hill while a student at UNC, and then was selected by ABC Sports to do live broadcasts on the field or in the stands during football games. He later was a part of the ABC Sports golf team working with Johnny Miller. Jim Lampley was speaker at the 1982 annual dinner meeting of the Chamber of Commerce. He drew hearty laughter when he shared with them his first day experience at ABC. He was getting off the elevator at ABC in New York and came face to face with Howard Cossell. Jim said, "Mr. Cossell, it is a real thrill to meet you. I'm Jim Lampley and I've just been hired by ABC Sports." He said Cossell eyed him with reservation and then said, "It is not just a thrill to meet Howard Cossell. This could be the most memorable day of your life." Jim Lampley is a grandson of Pappy Lampley and the son of James and Peggy Lampley.

Jim Lampley

Roone Arledge applied for the job with ABC with no broadcast experience. Some have said that not being encumbered with previous "bad luggage" gave him the freedom to be totally creative in bringing sports on an around-the-clock basis to the network. In 1961 he secured a 20-week commitment for ABC's "Wide World of Sports" to orient viewers with sporting events most people had only read about. He insisted that every program be done live

Ron Kershaw (left), a nephew of Kermit Edney, became romantically involved with Jessica Savitch as they both rose in the ranks of TV news. She died in an auto accident in 1983; he of cancer in 1988.

(no tape delays). He added Monday night football, the first time ever a sporting event had a regular slot in prime time. He developed instant replay and slow-motion action. He produced ten Olympic games, became president of ABC News Division, and introduced "Nightline", the first late-night news presentation. Roone premiered "20/20," "This Week With David Brinkley" and "Prime Time Live."

In 1991, he was named by the national trade magazine of the industry, *Broadcasting Magazine* to the 60-year Hall of Fame–graced by such luminaries as David Brinkley, Johnny Carson, Arthur Godfrey, Bob Hope, Edward R. Murrow, Ted Turner and Lucille Ball. Because Roone's last name begins with an "A," his biography appeared third, right before Lucille Ball.

In that special edition of "Broadcasting" of 1991 (honoring the top 60 people in the 60 years of Broadcasting Magazine), directly across from the article on Roone Arledge, there is a clever ad for the USA Network. "60 is too cold for sunbathing, 60 is too fast for a school zone, 60 is too big a drop in the Dow, 60 is a terrible day on the back nine, 60 is too many floors to walk up, 60 is too many housecats, but 60 sure looks good on you."

I mentioned Ron Kershaw. He was the oldest son of my sister June; but he and his brother, Dale, lived a good part of their young years here in this area, attending Dana School and living with my mother, Minnie Lee Waters Edney. Ron served in the Air Force and after service, took a job with the *Washington Post*. But having two uncles in broadcasting drew him like a magnetic force to go into television in Houston, Texas. Ron went to work for KTRK and met a vivacious and attractive reporter from another station in Houston (KHOQ) by the name of Jessica Savitch. There is no doubt that Jessica and Ron's commonality of interest in television stoked the fires of the love/hate relationship that obsessed the two of them for the rest of their lives. I will not attempt to rehash Jessica's glory days with KYW Philadelphia, or the years she spent with NBC. Nor will I go into Ron's challenges and successes with news operations in Baltimore and New York (which included heading up the ABC weekend news operation). He was serving as news director of WBBM-TV Chicago 'til he died.

Jane Rouse (a graduate of the UNC School of Journalism) had shared with me her copy of the summer edition of the school newspaper which included an article by Jeni Cook reviewing the new movie "Up Close and Personal." Jane felt that the article should be of interest because of the Hendersonville connection with Jessica Savitch and my family. This had been earlier covered in an article written for the *Times-News* on Oct. 16, 1988, by James Woolridge, staff writer.

Jessica Savitch first wrote her own book, "Autobiography of an Anchor Woman." Then immediately after her death, Gwenda Blair wrote "Almost Golden–Jessica Savitch and the Selling of Television News."

This third book ("Up Close and Personal") was written to give Robert Redford and Michelle Pfeiffer a chance to again resurrect and rebury Jessica. On Sept. 4, 1995, "Almost Golden" had been made into a film with Sela Ward playing the role of Jessica and Ron Silver playing Ron Kershaw. The movie was followed immediately by a documentary, "Intimate Portrait," which gave a much superior depiction of both Ron and Jess. Still another book was written by Alanna Nash, titled "Golden Girl." The name "Golden Girl" had been pinned onto Jessica in a 1979 *Newsweek* magazine.

In James Woolridge's review in the *Times-News*, excerpted from the Nash book, "Jessica's longtime boyfriend–the most influential and important man in her life–was Ron Kershaw, a brilliant TV news director who grew up in Hendersonville. Mr. Kershaw died this past July at the age of 44 of cancer." Mr. Woolridge wrote, "Mrs. Nash said, 'In August I visited his grave at the King's Grove Cemetery. Alas, my book identifies Ron as being from Asheville. I have sent a correction to the publisher for future editions.'"

On Oct. 3, 1983, Jessica and a companion (Martin Fishbein) both died when blinded by rain and fog, their car drove through a parking lot at Chez Odette Restaurant and into a drainage ditch of the Delaware Canal.

Jessica died at age 36 on Oct. 3, 1983. Ron died at 44 of cancer on July 3, 1988. He is buried near his grandmother in King's Grove Cemetery.

Churchmen Who Left Their Mark

Two Hendersonville men are well-known radio personalities, though neither was ever an announcer, and their programs were never broadcast on WHKP.

Back in the winter of 1996, I was doing a little radio "surfin'" and dialed up WAGI in Gaffney, S.C. They have a very unusual format: gospel and religion at night, and country music by day. Having been unable to reset my biological clock, it's quite common for me to dial across radio and TV anywhere between two and four in the morning. And lo and behold on this particular morning, I heard the voice of the Rev. Maze Jackson. Maze grew up in Hendersonville. He chose to be evangelistic in his career, and is heard on an impressive lineup of stations. Maze has always been an old-time fundamentalist and still resorts to fervent exhortations in his delivery. That morning, as I listened to Maze, I suddenly discovered that what I was hearing was a taped portion of one of his live evangelistic meetings.

And then, immediately following Maze, WAGI broadcasts a program by the Rev. J. Harold Smith. My memory of Harold Smith went back to a giant tent on Church Street across from the jail. He conducted a revival that ran all summer long. In fact, he even bought a home on Allen Road, and the 1946 phone directory listed his number as 494-W.

J. Harold Smith had all sorts of gimmicks to solicit donations from the folks packed into that tent every night. Ushers would walk down the aisles holding a clothesline with loads of clothespins attached, and this would be suspended two or three feet above the sitting congregation. As the clothesline passed overhead, worshippers were urged to stand and pin a dollar bill (or even bigger paper money) to the clothesline. He would then ask people sitting in their cars to blow their horns and they'd send an usher out to each car to pick up the donation. Finally, he'd laugh and say, "All right, pass the plates," and folks would snicker and say, "That's for the chicken feed."

Since World War I, the Chamber of Commerce and the city had sponsored Monday night street dances on Main Street between 3rd and 4th Avenues. The Rev. J. Harold Smith (always the showman) asked for permission to move his revival meetings on Monday to Main Street. The city approved the request but specified that there be at least one block of separation between the dancing and the revival meeting. Those first few weeks, most of the crowd stayed on the move, walking down to the Court House to see what sort of crowd the revival was drawing, and then back up to watch the dancing.

In those years, unrest with Sunday blue laws was being evidenced more and more. When the local theaters announced that they would show movies on Sunday, J. Harold Smith sensed this was his great opportunity for massive action. He exhorted all his followers to join him in a march down Main Street to the City Hall and demand that the city forbid "these movie houses, these dens of sin" to open on the Sabbath. The giant crowd weaved and surged down Main and then down 5th in front of the entrance to City Hall. Smith preached a while to get his followers really worked up and then demanded assurance from Mayor Al Edwards that he would stop this unrestrained orgy into sin. Mayor Al had been standing on the very top step at the doors to City Hall while all this screaming and foment was going on. Suddenly, the mayor raised his arms and the crowd became silent. He motioned to Fire Chief Ed Edney "to have your boys get ready." The crowd watched as city firemen carried from each side of the building high-velocity fire hoses around City Hall and had now aimed them at the crowd. The mayor said, "I have listened patiently to everything you've had to say. It is my duty to uphold the law. What the theaters are proposing is within the law, and your mass demonstration and misbehavior here today is not within the law. I'm going to count to ten, and then our city firemen will turn on their hoses and point to any of you who still chooses to remain." The crowd had dispersed by the time Mayor Al got to eight.

Harold later broadcast over the super power "X" stations in Mexico, whose signals were beamed at the Ozark Mountains. These were the stations used by Dr. Brinkley for his great success in selling Krazy Water Krystals (which were noting but Epsom salts, and after you'd taken salts for a week, you were laxative addicted). Dr. Brinkley struck out when he started peddling goat glands to restore virility to old men.

At one time on the Canton station WKIT, we had a program by the Rev. Preston Garrett, who had followed in Harold's footsteps on the Mexican stations. He complained that if you had an 18-wheel truck of mail come in with offerings every day, by the time the Mexican bureaucracy got its cut, you had nothing left.

The record for greatest tent revival would be held by the Rev. Hyman Appleman (a converted Jew), a Christian evangelist who would stage a two-week meeting under the biggest tent ever seen in Hendersonville. It was set up on the north end of Dietz Field and could seat 2,500 people. It was just after

World War II and, being without a job and as a member of the 52/20 club that went along with your ruptured duck discharge pin, I agreed to donate time to the sponsoring organization in promotion, public relations, and general pitchman.

After working with Hyman Appleman every day, I became enormously impressed with this man. He was brilliant yet the epitome of sincerity, humility and dedication. The meeting was interdenominationally sponsored. A committee was responsible for accepting and auditing all income and expenses. Appleman received only a love offering at the end of the two-week revival. There was a huge choir and more flowers on stage than Jimmy Swaggart or Oral Roberts had ever seen. It was a memorable experience for me, getting to know Hyman Appleman and being involved with a tremendously successful effort that had all the integrity of a Billy Graham crusade.

However impressed I was with Hyman Appleman, I do remember once someone asking me, "What Christian person has made the greatest impression on you in your entire career?" With no hesitation I answered, "Actually, two people: Father Patrick Peyton (who produced Family Theatre on network radio for the Catholic Church) and the Rev. W.F. Sinclair (pastor of the local Calvary Baptist Church).

Father Peyton, I believe, is the man responsible for the slogan used on Family Theatre: "The family that prays together—stays together." In both men there was absolute love of Christ and Christians everywhere. Just in talking to them, you could feel total devotion to their life's work.

In reading over the UNC Journalism School's publication loaned to me by Jane Rouse, I ran across an article on the future of the media by the former Dean Wayne Danielson. He wrote: "Will there be any need for newspapers, post offices, libraries, television, radio? Journalism is becoming more diffused, it's becoming more participatory.

I mused over this line at length. It brought back memories of some twenty-five years ago of a meeting I attended as a board member of the Protestant Radio & Television Commission in Atlanta, Ga. The board back then consisted of 42 individuals. Most were ministers or laity with wealth. There were only two broadcasters on that board (myself and Bob Covington of WBTV Charlotte). The board included a bishop, business executives, a college president and faculty members, and denominational executives and pastors. I remember vividly an impassioned speech made by a very young Episcopal priest from New York City deriding the very proceedings then taking place and emphasizing: "All this is a waste of time. In the future, we won't need to do these Protestant Hour Radio programs, nor TV features. We won't even need this building. And in fact, church sanctuaries themselves will be a waste of money because religion will consist entirely of thought transfer."

I had earlier met a very quiet, unassuming man who reminded me very much of my friend, the Rev. W. F. Sinclair. When the young Episcopal priest finally finished his tirade about the backwardness of present-day tools of religion, the old man simply asked everyone to bow their head for a word of prayer. As I recall, he said something like: "Lord, we thank you for the dynamic vision of this young man, and I'm certainly happy he is on our side in your work. But Lord, do give us the patience and guide us to use what tools we have in our hands this very day. We remember, Lord, that Christ served the multitudes without even a P.A. system. Amen."

The meeting had started on a contentious note. Dr. Ernest Arnold (president) and Bill Horlock (executive vice president) were desperate for operating funds. In order to develop vital cash flow, they had agreed to lease the beautiful studios at the center (which featured the world's largest pipe organ) to gospel music groups for taping of TV shows—groups like the Speer Family, the Statemen, the Happy Goodmans, etc. This had angered some denominational members because they felt such uses cheapened the center.

Folks who know me probably recall how adverse I am to engaging in public debate; but after listening to the derision voiced by those elite of religious academia, I hit the floor in defense of Dr. Arnold and Bill Horlock. Before I finished, I called for a total reorganization of the PRTVC, which would guarantee staff, sufficient cash flow to carry on the work of the center for generations to come.

I have no idea of what I said that afternoon, but a few days later I received a letter from Bill Horlock saying: "Really there is no way of expressing the feeling I personally have concerning the words of wisdom you gave to all of us in the meetings this week. They were words of strength, truth and courage. Hopefully this will be the turning point for this center." Almost every Sunday morning, I listen to the Protestant Hour. Because of health reasons, I resigned from the board shortly after the reorganization had been effected; but something worked because twenty-five years later, I'm still hearing those great broadcasts recorded in the beautiful studios on Clifton Road in northeast Atlanta.

Churchmen Who've Left Their Mark

I never knew the man's name was Charles Mortimer—I (as most others) simply called him Ted, although I learned recently his nickname was actually Tad. I can't recall the occasion on which we first met; but even after fifty years, he's a person I'll never forget. If you had not formally met him, you had the feeling that you did know him because of a picture Don Barber had made—obviously one he was most fond of because it was displayed in the window of Barber's Studio more than any other. The picture showed Tad to be a natty dresser, wearing a hat with a sassy brim and an ascot that leaped from the picture. I'm referring, of course, to the Rev. Tad Heymann. Though he had studied at the Moody Bible Institute in Chicago, Tad had moved to Beverly Hills, Calif., where he was very successful in the real estate business. Tad had to have been successful because he retired to Hendersonville in about 1935. In 1940, he was persuaded to be ordained as a Baptist minister and was elected pastor of the French Broad Baptist Church.

Some seven years later, Tad was asked to speak periodically to a small group of worshipers who were meeting in various homes. The group then began regularly scheduled worship services in Rosa Edwards School. However, the seats were a bit uncomfortable for the older worshipers since they were designed for elementary grade students. The group then began services in the American Legion building until a small church could be built on the corner of 5th Avenue West and White Pine Drive. The total dedication of this small band of worshipers so impressed Tad Heymann, he resigned his pastorate at French Broad Baptist and became the unpaid pastor of this new church, which did not even have funds to buy pews for their most unpretentious new church building. That first winter, the congregation borrowed from the city the green benches which were used in the summer on Main Street.

Jody Barber recalls the congregation did not even have a collection plate. At first, a man's felt hat was passed. Then one of the congregation made by hand a wooden collection plate. Finally, through a donation, they were able to acquire a sterling silver offering receptacle. That winter, even with only the green benches from Main Street, each service was "standing room only."

I remember how excited Tad was when he told me that they had raised enough money to put "drive-in type speakers" in the church parking lot—and if anyone wanted to attend church and not have to get dressed up (or if they had difficulty getting into or out of a car), they could simply drive up, park and join the worshipers inside via the parking lot speakers.

After some six years (operating purely as a community non-denominational church), the church elected to become a part of the

The Rev. Tad Heymann

Congregational Christian Church. The action was taken at a meeting Aug. 13, 1953. In the first two years of worshipping together in 1947 and 1948, young John Daniel Hart would come from his class in the Sunday School of the First Baptist Church and play the piano for the congregation at the morning worship service. Mrs. Lenoir Johnson Dixon took over the role as pianist in 1948 and served the church until 1969. In later years, the church acquired an organ which was used by Mrs. Dixon.

In addition to his very active role in the religious life of the community, Tad was active in civic work. He was very active in the Lion's Club. He helped generate interest in establishing a chaplaincy program at Pardee Hospital; and served (again unpaid) as the hospital's first chaplain, offering himself on call at any hour day or night. Tad Heymann served as organizer, patron, friend, co-worshipper and pastor of the Congregational Church until ill health forced him to resign July 23, 1967. He died at St. Augustine, Fla., a year and nine months later.

I have driven past the Congregational Church on a daily basis for more than thirty years. I watched as major additions were added, providing for the enlargement of the chancel—also, the addition of a pastor's study and church office. The continuing beautification program (even this year) filled an unsightly ditch in front of the church, and new trees and shrubs are constantly added. If Tad were riding along with me, wearing his sassy fedora and his colorful ascot, I could imagine that smile of his that stretched entirely across his face as he would say, "Isn't it wonderful what they have done?" And I never knew until I did the radio series that this affable, amicable, gentle man once was a Golden Gloves boxer and won a major championship fighting in Madison Square Garden.

Back in the '50s, the First Presbyterian Church stood on the corner opposite its present location, the sanctuary was at the corner of 7th and King Street. In March of 1953, the church purchased the two houses near the corner of Grove and 7th. This was known as the P.K. Braswell place. The property was purchased from Mrs. J.R. Sandifer of Hendersonville and Mrs. J.P. Rogers of Florence, S.C. The two houses were appraised for $15,900 and the church was able to buy them both for $15,000. To put the purchase price in proper perspective, the congregation (at the same meeting which approved the land purchase) adopted a nine-month operating budget to change the accounting of the church from a fiscal year to a calendar year; and the nine-month operating budget amounted to only $16,430—which was to cover all church expenses, including the salary of the pastor, Warren Thuston.

The house which stood on the corner of 7th and Grove had been rented by Jane and Brownlow Merrell; and they, in turn, rented rooms and apartments in the large, rambling structure. Brownlow was freight agent for Southern Railroad. I knew the house very well because my brother (Grady and his first wife, Katherine Stepp) had rented their first apartment in that house from the Merrells.

Four years later, on July 22, 1957, officers of the church announced that a brand new church building would be built on the site and the old church sanctuary would be razed. The new church building would seat 650 people on the main floor, and another 100 in the balcony. Among those participating in the signing were L.K. Singley, L. B. Prince, T.D. Hunter Jr., Fred Streetman, John Hurley and George Stowell. Others (not including contractors) who were included in the picture of that historic signing were John Price and E. E. Fies.

The honor for the official groundbreaking went to Lila Ripley Barnwell (94 years old) and a member of the church for 80 years. She was assisted by the pastor, Warren Thuston. John Hurley and George Stowell became an oversight committee, and one or both of these men would be on the site at any time any kind of work was taking place.

There was no problem in the razing of the two large frame houses, but there was a very small cemetery in the churchyard which brought about considerable study and research. It was found that when the new Methodist church had been built, there was also a small cemetery section where it was proposed to build the church. As the Methodists had done, the congregation approved relocating the remains and the stones to Oakdale Cemetery. At the time I was preparing this material, I asked Professor George Jones (of the Henderson County Historical & Genealogical Society, publishers of the Cemetery Book) is there was any indication on these relocated graves that they once had been located elsewhere. "To my knowledge, no. The graves and stones are there and over the years they have been weathered in and appear the same as any other grave in Oakdale."

This was one of two major church buildings to be built here in my personal memory, and I found it convenient to periodically check in on the progress of both as an unofficial Sidewalk Superintendent. I would always have a chance to visit with John Hurley or George Stowell (who, now retired, could put their engineering and industrial background to excellent use in their role as Volunteer Overseers).

They both lived in the same neighborhood of Oak Terrace. Oak Terrace was made up of lots of interesting people back then: Betty Ann and Aiken Pace (Pace was a pharmacist and one time ran Pace's Drug Store on 7th Avenue East). Living there also was Colonel Bob and Peggy Fox. Bob had operated the Packard Agency here for a number of years. He was very active in Kiwanis (serving even as lieutenant governor), plus he was the perfect Santa Claus for every community Christmas event. Also living on Oak Terrace were Helen and Monroe Redden Jr. (of the Redden, Redden & Redden law firm). There was Bob and Esther Wilson (Bob owned Economy Drug Store); and at one time, Cecil and Grace Garrett lived there.

The congregation of the First Presbyterian Church owed their gratitude to John Hurley and George Stowell, who took charge and maintained oversight on every penny spent in that beautiful place of worship.

Think of all the people who come to mind when you start reminiscing over friends you've known who retired to Hendersonville, and then recall their major contributions. How lucky we were to have Jack Peck, who single-handedly was responsible for the successful beginning of the American Red Cross Bloodmobile. There was Phil Kelly, who dreamed up the Second Wind Hall of Fame, and 13ert A. 13oyd, who gave us a park and celebrated his birthday every Friday the 13th. And certainly Phil Green and his wife, Elsa, left their mark. Even after he retired, he personally raised enough money in the community to air condition the Hendersonville High auditorium. Phil brought his whole family here, including the late Jean Pearce, Barbara Stricker, and his son, P.T. "Pete" Green Jr., who has built more houses, business buildings, civic structures, and created more top-quality developments than any other man in the history of the community. Pete has certainly left his mark.

There are a couple of parallels to the construction of the First Baptist Church, and the First Presbyterian Church here. The First Baptist approved their new construction in 1956. The Presbyterians made their move just a year later. But for awhile, there were two major church buildings under construction in Hendersonville.

The old Presbyterian Church stood on the corner of 7th and King and the new sanctuary was built on the opposite corner at 7th and Grove. Likewise, the old First Baptist Church (which was the second building constructed by that congregation) stood on the corner of 4th and Washington, facing 4th Avenue. The new church (approved in 1956) would face 5th Avenue and run along Washington Street.

The long-range plans for the Baptist congregation called for the construction of an educational building first; then the fellowship hall in this new building could be used for worship services while the old church building was torn down to make room for the much larger church, which would be dedicated on Easter Sunday 1958. Mack Goss would take as his subject, "The Past is Prologue." A special program by the church's 90-voice youth and adult choirs would be featured at the evening services, and 60 people would be baptized.

This day had to be one of the two most memorable days in the life of W.W. "Bill" Martin, Jr. In 1943, Bill had opened a heating, roofing, and guttering operation at 211 North Main. As the years went by, Bill became dedicated to the "total comfort" concept of heating and air conditioning businesses and homes as well. He spun off the roofing portion of his business and it became known as Carolina Roofing & Sheet Metal Construction.

Architects in the area were particularly pleased to have Bill Martin's firm in business here because with his education and professional training, architects would simply provide space layouts to Bill, and he would engineer the entire system for heating and air conditioning for them. He was a true professional. Although he was on every job his firm had under contract, instead of tin snips, he carried a slide rule. And though being "in the trenches" with his workmen, he was always neatly dressed and could step off a job and into an owner's and/or architect's conference with no extra preparation.

Once he had established a table of organization of professionally trained men, Bill had more "walk away" time available; and he accepted any challenge which would make Hendersonville a better place to live. He advanced through the chairs of the Chamber of Commerce, the Rotary Club; and in the year he served as president, established the Fabulous 4th of July

Observance staged for many years by the club. He served on Board of Pardee Hospital and was vice president in 1955. He was on the Board of the YMCA, and served as chairman of the Urban Renewal Project for Hendersonville.

But his greatest love of all was his beloved First Baptist Church, where he not only was a deacon, but was automatically accepted as general overseer of every building project. He was named by the VFW for their prestigious "Man of the Year" honor, and he accepted it with his usual humility.

You can only imagine the pride Bill felt that Easter Sunday morning in 1958, as he sat and marveled at this beautiful sanctuary being used for the first time, a structure he had watched over from the time the foundation was poured. Bill was only thirty-five years old. At age forty-three, Bill Martin could hardly restrain himself when he heard and felt the music pouring forth from the largest pipe organ in the mountains. . .all 2,390 pipes.

Bill Martin's magnificent management ability was obvious. His Lennox dealership was growing by leaps and bounds, and he was ever more involved in activities to better the community. At age 50, Bill saw the necessity of bringing into the firm with him another top professional and he recruited Jud Ammons, who joined the firm in June 1973. That decision was the most fortuitous of his life. Jud Ammons had been working with Bill a little less than a year when terminal illness struck Bill and he was taken from us at the untimely age of 52.

Today, Martin Heating & Air Conditioning occupies a spacious, new manufacturing/sales center on Berkeley Road with loads of parking and adequate space for storage of raw materials. Around Hendersonville, you can see the modern fleet of Martin Heating & Air Conditioning service trucks. If we could pull a Thornton Wilder and have Bill Martin get one last look at "our town," I can almost hear him say, "I picked a good man in Jud Ammons. He's done a terrific job."

Church Buildings

A distinguishing characteristic of the countryside in the "Bible Belt" is the proliferation of churches, many of them small and some located in areas where there is no visible sign of neighborhood or community of people. Doctrinal differences, personality conflicts, and dissatisfaction with pastors have all been causes for splits to occur within churches; and the dissidents then usually move to form their own church, a totally new church in the community.

Also, in some denominations when churches have grown exceedingly large, members are encouraged to "mother a new church," which is designed to accelerate growth in that denomination. The best example of this is the Main Street Baptist Church, which was started as a mission church of Hendersonville's First Baptist, with their new building completed in September of 1968.

Today, a "quick" check of the Hendersonville phone book will identify 165 churches of various denominations here in Henderson County. Within the city you have, of course, all new sanctuaries built by the First Baptist, First Presbyterian, Grace Lutheran, Church of the Nazarene, Main Street Baptist, Calvary Baptist (with a new sanctuary in a totally new location on Haywood Road), the Union Grove Church in Green Meadows, and the St. Paul's Tabernacle on 6th Avenue West. Within the next two years, the Immaculate Conception Catholic Church will build an all new two-level building with the worship sanctuary seating 750 people.

Also, major expansions of facilities have taken place at other city churches, such as an educational building and new chapel at the First United Methodist Church; the expansion and final completion of the original plan of the St. James Episcopal Church. First United Methodist will build a Christian Life Center in 1998. In addition to these churches named, I would estimate that twenty-five additional church buildings have been completed in the county in the past fifty years.

The champion builder of churches would be the congregation of Mud Creek Baptist Church on Rutledge Drive. Just in the last thirty-five years, two magnificent sanctuaries have been completed. It is one of the oldest churches in the county (founded in 1804) and today boasts a membership of some 3,000 members. A new sanctuary was built in 1963, but by 1990 it was obvious that a larger facility would be needed. The new imposing edifice is complemented

Mud Creek Baptist Church, founded in 1804, keeps on building.

by a worship service that features a choir and orchestra numbering more than 200. The pastor (the Rev. M. Gregory Mathis), in addition to shepherding this huge flock of worshippers, has also found time to serve two terms as head of the North Carolina State Baptist Convention.

While inside the city the new First Presbyterian Church has been built, outside in the suburbs were new worship centers for the Covenant Presbyterian, the Pinecrest and the Trinity Presbyterian churches.

The Jehovah Witnesses built a Worship Center on North Justice Street, and have acquired property on 5th Avenue West for a new and larger Kingdom Hall.

In 1970, the Tuxedo Baptist Church began worshipping in a new auditorium; Ebenezer Baptist built an interim sanctuary with the understanding that once a new worship center was completed, the interim building would be made into Sunday School classrooms. Also in 1970, the Rev. L. K. "Chick" Holbert was pastor of the new Fellowship Baptist Church out in Druid Hills and then built a large new building on Howard Gap Road which would seat 300. The membership doubled in its first year.

Out on U.S. 64 East beyond Ebenezer, trees have matured and now block the view of the St. Mary's Chapel of the Pisgah Lutheran Church. The building is on the left side of the road going toward Edneyville. It was built by the Seagle family in 1957 as a family chapel, and later was dedicated as a church parish.

Also in 1957, the Bethel Wesleyan Methodist Church was completed on Tracey Grove Road. In 1958, the Horse Shoe Methodist Church underwent several changes. It became the Cummings Memorial Methodist Church, acknowledging a large gift for the new building made by Dr. James H. Cummings. The new sanctuary would seat 200, and would also provide space for a fellowship hall, kitchen and five classrooms. In 1959, the Horse Shoe Methodist Church dedicated a new building with services conducted by the Rev. Robert Tuttle, superintendent of the Asheville District. First services at the Balfour Methodist Church were held on Sunday, Oct. 25, 1964. The Rev. Bud Ellington was pastor then.

A congregation that started with six worshippers in 1955 blossomed into a full-fledged church with dedication address given in 1961 by Dr. Bob Jones, head of Bob Jones University. This was the Mountain Home Bible Church, and when completed, had an auditorium that would seat 200, along with nine classrooms.

On Feb. 11, 1968, dedication services for the new nave at St. James Episcopal Church were held. This finished nave completed the St. James Church as it was envisioned in the first decade of this century. The first part of the church was built of cut granite. The final construction utilized stone taken from the old Judson College, one of Hendersonville's great landmarks which stood for decades at the corner of 3rd Avenue West and Fleming Street. Also in 1968, the Etowah Baptist Church dedicated a new

The nave at St. James Episcopal Church was completed in 1968 to specifications made around the turn of the century; stone from the old Judson College was used.

building which would house all departments of the Sunday School, provide for a pastor's study, office and major new sanctuary. This was the third building program for this church in ten years.

Though absolutely unintentional, I realize I may have left out the names of a number of brand new churches or churches that have been substantially enlarged and remodeled.

I am fascinated when I drive down roads I have not been on in eight or ten years. I am amazed not just at the number of new homes built but always at the new church buildings that have come into being.

I grew up going to Vacation Bible School at the Edith Grove Chapel at King's Cemetery. One day I was in that vicinity and noticed that there was no longer an Edith Grove Chapel. It had been torn down and a brand new church (King's Grove Baptist Church) was built across the road.

I will make no attempt, either, to try to update the modernization and expansion of the various religious denominational retreats and conference center—such as Kanuga and Bonclarken.

Many, many people across the nation relate to Hendersonville by virtue of a summer spent here, a retreat attended, or special study at a seminar conducted in one of the denomination-owned religious assembly areas.

If you'd like to look at one of the oldest churches in the county that still stands pretty much as it did close to 100 years ago, drive out to Dana, turn to the left and a few hundred yards down the road on the right, you'll see the Christian Advent Church—a tiny little white building sitting up on a bank. A handful of members still worship there, though the weekly offerings barely pays for the urgently needed upkeep and maintenance. This was the denomination my grandfather (the Rev. Thomas Jefferson Waters) headed and the church he pastored in his lifetime. The membership has almost died out. Only the older ones still come and remember the days when the Christian Advent Church played a dynamic role in the religious life "along the ridge."

Keeping Christ in a Christmas Parade

You'd have to be 50 years old to remember the "Keeping Christ in Christmas Parade."

You'd have to be even older if you can recall when each elementary class in the city schools would practice singing carols in their classroom (directed by Mrs. Charles Morrow). Just before Christmas, all the classes would march to the First Methodist Church (this was long before it became United) and the balconies would be filled to the rafters with children singing their annual Christmas concert. The main floor was reserved for the mamas and papas and other adults.

In those years, Christmas had not yet been degraded by "Mama Got Run Over By a Reindeer" or "Daddy Got Drunk and Fell Into the Christmas Tree." There was not even a Frosty the Snowman or Rudolph the Red-Nosed Reindeer" or even "White Christmas." Most of the Christmas songs were the sacred carols, although we did have "Santa Claus is Coming to Town" and "Jingle Bells" and "Up on the Housetop." If you remember, "White Christmas" was the first really big new Christmas pop song and it was not introduced until 1942 in the movie "Holiday Inn."

Even in the early years of WHKP, you would be reminded constantly of the number of shopping days left before Christmas. Prior to World War II, stores didn't decorate until around the first of December (or at least not until after Thanksgiving). But as returning GIs began building their families, December became one of the biggest shopping months of the year, and still is by far the biggest month for jewelry stores.

Even small towns began staging Christmas parades and the parades kept getting bigger. Santa began arriving not on sleighs but in helicopters or on fire trucks and the cash registers sang an ever merrier song.

In 1952, and I don't know who or even what organization to credit, but someone said, "Enough is enough!! It's time to put Christ back into Christmas."

A delegation of religious leaders met with merchants in the Chamber of Commerce office and asked that the 1952 Christmas parade be totally religious. All the floats would be built and provided by individual churches in the community. The merchants reacted positively and thought the concept was great. However, a concern was expressed: Could just a loosely coordinated group of churches (with virtually no budget) really put together a quality and meaningful parade? The religious leaders had no qualms, no misgivings of any kind.

The merchants did request that Santa Claus, so important to children at Christmas, be included. The religious leaders agreed. They proposed that after the religious parade had passed through, there would be a block separation and Santa (preceded by a band) would arrive on his float, thereby separating the religious parade from the secular Santa Claus.

The parade was staged on the night of Dec. 1, 1952 and in spite of sub-freezing weather, a crowd gathered which was estimated to be larger than the downtown crowd for the 1952 Apple Parade.

So much work had gone into the construction of the floats, and with so many volunteers involved, officials wanted as many people to see the parade as possible; so the parade not only followed the usual parade route from Five Points down Main but this time it turned back up Church Street and returned to Five Points.

A color guard, led by the church flag, and the Rev. Allard Garren, bearing an open Bible, headed the parade. The theme was established by the leading float. An altar and an open Bible bore the inscription, "The Greatest Story Ever Told." Following were floats in tableaux design telling the Christmas story from the prophecy of the coming of Christ to the accomplishment of the prophecy through the birth of the Savior in the Bethlehem manger. Included were floats depicting the decree of Augustus Caesar, the journey of Mary and Joseph to Bethlehem, the refusal of room at the inn, the manger scene, the vision of the shepherds, the appearance of the three kings, the visit of the shepherds, and finally the worldwide spread of Christianity as exhibited in a float with children dressed in costumes of all nations.

The realism was awesome. Live sheep were used, actual campfires burned on floats, traditional Christmas hymns were sung by marching choirs, and songs played by four bands, Ecusta, Hendersonville High, Ninth Avenue

Putting Christ back into the Christmas parade: This float depicted the Littlest Angel. The girl at right is the late Betty Rogers Lee.

High, and the Junior High. At the very end (after the religious parade had passed) there was Santa Claus in a 46-foot long float, with mechanized reindeer. It was simply spectacular. While several attempts were made to recreate the parade, it was never done. That parade in 1952 still stands as the greatest parade every produced entirely by Christian laymen.

Oberammergau—1958

Back in the '20s, Hendersonville had been caught up in a frenzy of excitement with the construction of the 15-story Fleetwood Hotel at the very top of Echo Mountain. A cement highway, adorned with electric street lights, had already been completed. The local population was convinced that there were no limits to the growth and prosperity that lay ahead for this area. And then the Florida land boom collapsed, and the entire Fleetwood project went belly-up. The unfinished hotel stood as a ghost for close to fifteen years before the structure was sold for salvage and the steel in the building was used to build bridges in Georgia in World War II.

So Hendersonville was not overly excited when at a news conference it was announced that a spectacular amphitheater would be built here for the staging of the famous Oberammergau Passion Play. Hendersonville had not only become callused to big deals of outside promoters, but in the spring of 1958, few people locally had ever heard of the Oberammergau Passion Play.

The Consolidated Concerts Corp. at the news conference revealed that Val Balfour (the fourth generation Balfour to have the lead role) would star in the Hendersonville production. In 1958 we had no travel and tourism agency supported by accommodations tax monies, but there was a Hendersonville Tourist Development Company, operated only by volunteers. This group did assist the Balfour group in negotiating an agreement with the Hendersonville City School Board for the lease of the high school auditorium for the entire summer. The auditorium had been used as a movie theater after the Carolina Theater fire. The agreement called for the Balfour group to provide new stage curtains and rewiring of the entire stage.

The original Passion Play (presented in Oberammergau) runs all day, with time out for meals, and is presented only every ten years. The local production would be a two to three hour condensation of the original, which Balfour described as a compromise between Shakespearean and real drama.

The Passion Play opened here on Sunday, June 29 and ran through August. Attendance during July was only spotty but had begun to pick up during August after word of mouth brought visitors here from surrounding states to see the production.

The play had a substantial cast, including Balfour (who played Christus) and his wife (from Albany, N.Y.), who played Mary Magdalene. The average attendance of 260 per performance during the entire summer resulted in heavy losses for Passion Play Tours Inc. of New York City and Charles E. Green of New York, their agent.

In a final report to the Tourist Development Co. on Sept. 8, the group sought to save face and said they were very optimistic about returning to Hendersonville in 1959, but nothing was ever heard further from Val Balfour or Consolidated Concerts Association.

It was a mystery to me at the time why Hendersonville was chosen for this summer-long production. It became an even deeper mystery some fifteen years later when the child bride, our son Kerry, and his wife, plus Dan and Claire Waddell made a pilgrimage to the village of Oberammergau in Germany. It is an absolutely breathtakingly beautiful little village on the Upper Ammer River located near Garmisch Partenkirchen (site of the 1936 Winter Olympics).

In 1634 when the black plague swept over Europe, for some reason the village was spared, and the inhabitants vowed to pay homage to Christ through the staging of the Passion Play at least one year in every decade.

In addition to the baroque church steeples, the walls of every building in the village feature full-color, painted religious murals. The little town is located forty-five miles southwest of Munich in the picturesque Ammer Valley in the Bavarian Alps.

There is absolutely nothing of resemblance between Hendersonville and the little village in the Ammer Valley nor even in the terrain is there any similarity. Why Passion Play Tours Inc. and Consolidated Concerts Association would make a summer-long commitment of this most unusual stage extravaganza to our little town of Hendersonville, no one understands to this day. This group did have contracts to stage this play at several other locations that summer because in August a Victor Sprouse brought a $150,000 lawsuit against the principals for failing to live up to performance contracts which had been negotiated for the 1958 season.

Interesting neighbors

According to my notes, it was the third week in January of 1963 when I received a phone call from Mayor Al Edwards asking if I would agree to serve as the chairman of the Planning & Zoning Board. Harry Buchanan had been the chairman, but when he was appointed to the chair of the ABC Board, he had to resign from the Zoning Board. Others serving on that board then were I.E. Johnson, Albert Dixon, Bill Stokes, and Marvin Sutherland. At that time, the board was involved with aerial mapping, land use study and developing a thoroughfare plan (which I believe is not a heckuva lot further along now, thirty-four years later).

One morning I received an urgent call from Dr. Kenneth Cosgrove, who wanted to discuss with me a major project under consideration for Hendersonville that would require a totally new zoning designation (which we would later call M.I.C.–Medical, Institutional, & Cultural). I hurried down to Dr. Cosgrove's office, and for the first time met Mrs. Mignon Sullivan, a native New Yorker. She and her husband had been professionally involved in Washington for most of their life with the FHA, the Federal Housing Authority.

She had come to Western North Carolina with a dream–"a self-contained retirement community." Back in 1963, no one around here had even heard of the term "cradle to grave" living accommodations. Her dream was that once you became a resident of a retirement community, you could stay there (even in infirmary facilities at the center) for the rest of your life.

Mrs. Sullivan was represented by attorney Bruce Elmore of Asheville, and though she had made brief pitches to Elmore and to Northwestern Bank executive Stanley Wright to consider building her center in Asheville, she really felt it better suited Hendersonville. She was a patient of Dr. Cosgrove and felt that he would be a perfect intermediary for her project in this area. Mrs. Sullivan had already achieved major success in her project by having the famous architect Edward Durrell Stone do the conceptual designs. When

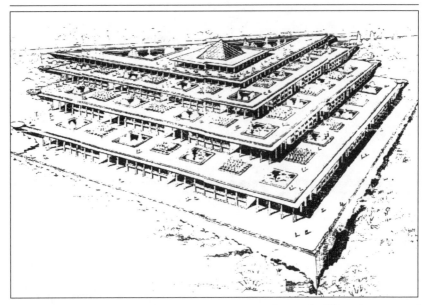

Architect Edward Durrell Stone's drawing of Mrs. Sullivan's proposed retirement community, Robin Hood Lodge.

Dr. Cosgrove unrolled before me those architectural plans for the project which Mrs. Sullivan called "Robin Hood Lodge," I blurted out without thinking, "Lodge? That's the Babylonian Hanging Gardens!"

Edward Stone's plan called for a mammoth structure, with footings plunged deep into the earth to hold the multi-level tiers of developments that soared high into the sky. I was flabbergasted. As Mrs. Sullivan talked (which was incessantly), I scanned the specs: "515 apartments requiring 300,000 square feet of air-conditioned living area. Each apartment would open onto a promenade measuring 120 x 150 feet. That was 54,000 square feet of promenade, with trees, shrubs and miniature arboretums on each of the five levels. On the second level, there would be an auditorium, boutique shops, a coffee shop, a clinic, and barber and beauty shops.

Each floor would feature a nurses' station, a lounge, sewing and craft rooms, as well as laundry facilities.

On the top floor, there would be a lounge, a large dining room, recreation room, and library each at least 50 x 70 feet in size."

Suggestions had been made that the project be located on such sites as the F.R. Houston property, the Frank Bly property, the Bennett property (where The Oaks is located today), on the Johnson Farm, or perhaps the Jesse Cleveland place. All these locations had been ruled out. The owners simply did not want to sell. It was now felt by those leading the project that an entire city block be acquired specifically bounded by 5th Avenue, 6th Avenue,

Buncombe, and Fleming streets. (This is the block where the post office is located today.) All this property was then zoned as residential and a change in zoning acceptable to the surrounding neighborhood would be necessary. This is where the planners dreamed up the M.I.C.

I took the Edward Durrell Stone drawings with me to a specially called meeting of the Planning & Zoning Board. Now I'll admit, being a little country boy who had grown up walking barefoot through sweet briars and sassafras, it was understandable that I would get a little pop-eyed looking at these drawings which probably were even more elaborate than the Babylonian Hanging Gardens. But the same kind of shock appeared on the faces of I.E. Johnson, Albert Dixon, Marvin Sutherland and Bill Stokes. Here was a dream that might even have been a bit pretentious for the pharaohs.

But the board got hold of Dan Vismore (our professional planner) and with his expertise, we dreamed up the new Medical, Institutional, & Cultural zone—the M.I.C. The boutique shops and other specialty stores were designed to serve only the residents of these 515 apartments, the board felt that it would not adversely affect the existing zoning of any adjacent property.

While Hendersonville has always been known for fostering dreams, the magnitude of this project was totally overwhelming. The consensus was "this will never be built"; but we learned through Mr. and Mrs. Sullivan's inside contacts in "Beltway politics" that this project had already been given approval in Washington and was already being reviewed by the Greensboro office of FHA. In fact, the legitimacy of the project was attested to by the fact that honest money to further develop site plans had been advanced by Daniel's Construction Co. of Greenville. Through my association with Northwestern Bank, I had developed a friendship with one of the executives of Carolina Mortgage Company, and was asked if I could persuade him to come to Hendersonville to examine the plans and take an overview of the project to determine its feasibility, and if they would put up additional "up front money."

Now, here's a story within a story! My friend from Carolina Mortgage justified his trip to Hendersonville by arranging an appointment with two brothers who had retired here and were interested in discounting to Carolina some of the "paper" the two of them held. At lunch, he shared with Dr. Cosgrove and me his experience with these two men. (He never would identify them in any way.) He said they lived in an inauspicious home, one wearing khaki pants, the other jeans. He said when he asked to see some of the mortgages they wanted to sell, they started pulling down cigar box after cigar box off the shelves, handing him what obviously was Grade A "paper." He said he quickly offered to buy about a quarter of a million dollars of the mortgages (which had hardly made a dent in the boxes on the shelf) when one said abruptly, "I guess that's enough for today." He said as he had approached the house earlier, he noticed some goats and a few little kid goats in the yard, and asked the brothers about the animals. They told him about their love for animals, and especially little goats. Further, they said they had been reading about the Eliada Home for Children and were considering some sort of bequest to it; but before making a final decision, they thought they'd drive over and have a look at the place and maybe take a couple of their little kid goats along for the children to play with. He said they were astonished when they were told abruptly by one of the attendants at Eliada, "We don't have any place here for goats." So they turned around and brought the goats back home. One made the comment to the other, "Anybody that doesn't like baby goats is not a friend of ours." Even though my friend steadfastly refused to give us even a slight inkling as to the identity of those two men, I made up my mind right then: "If anybody ever offers me a couple of little goats, you can bet I'm gonna take 'em."

My friend's conversation to this point had been confined totally to the purchases of the mortgages. He then unrolled the elaborate plans of Edward Durrell Stone and studied them briefly; and as he started rolling them up again, he said simply, "This project is bigger than we are."

It was made quite clear in Mrs. Sullivan's incessant monologue that the building would be constructed, adhering religiously to the plans. There would be no changes.

In reading over the yellowed minutes of this committee recently, I noticed that references were now being made about Mrs. Sullivan's "militant manner." Mrs. Sullivan was grating to the nerves, plus she had a very bad habit of popping her girdle. She used this physical act to punctuate an important point she was trying to make. "When I say no changes, I mean no changes!" POP went the girdle. Since my dealings with Mrs. Sullivan, I have never trusted a lady who pops her girdle to accent her vocabulary.

Shortly after our meeting with the mortgage people, I received notice that a "call meeting" would be held in the offices of Bruce Elmore in Asheville, at which time Daniel's Construction would have an important announcement to make. This was in 1966. The meeting opened with a fierce scolding of the committee by Mrs. Mignon Sullivan. She heaped derision on those present for not fully sharing her dream, and then launched into a tirade about the wording that should go on the dedication plaque inside the elevators. (That really caught my attention. She's in a harangue over the wording on a dedication plaque, and the project does not yet own one foot of ground.)

It was then that the spokesman from Daniel's Construction announced that they were simply pulling the plug. They planned to write off all monies which they had advanced on the project, but emphasized very strongly that they were contributing to the committee all their work, their drawings, and wished us well.

The committee minutes read, and I quote: "She (referring to Mrs. Sullivan) actually self-destructed the project because she was unwilling to forfeit any control to objective business people who would underwrite and direct the program."

All of my association with this project came through Dr. Kenneth Cosgrove. I had been acquainted with Ken and his lovely wife, Eleanor, ever since they had moved to Hendersonville; but through Mignon Sullivan, I really got to know Ken Cosgrove. His infinite patience in dealing with this irascible woman never ceased to amaze me. At times when tempers would flair and Mrs. Sullivan would be on the verge of another tantrum, he'd say, "We've come too far to let this slip away from us." Mrs. Sullivan intransigent??? That's putting it mildly.

Actually, Ken Cosgrove was a visionary back in the '60s when he kept projecting the need for elder care in the future. At that time, there was not one single rest home or nursing home in the community.

In the minutes of Nov. 9, 1964, Cosgrove had inserted: "Robin Hood should now be deleted from our thinking. Certainly we wish to point out, however, that we definitely believe that the Hendersonville area is an ideal place for the location of an apartment complex designed primarily for use by older people." By this time, Dr. Cosgrove had been able to persuade the Chamber of Commerce that strong priority be given to establishing a facility such as what we now call Carolina Village.

That first chamber committee consisted of Ray Ireland (chairman), W.B.W. Howe, Larry Butler, Jack Freeman, the Rev. John Hawn and, of course, Dr. Cosgrove. It would be impractical to try to credit all the many individuals who devoted so much time to accomplishing completion of what has been referred to at various times as Four Seasons Village, Skytown, Carolina Town, Henderson House, Henderson Village, and as late as 1972 as Western Carolina Retirement Village. There would be Dr. Richard Porter, the Rev. Walter Roberts, attorney Kenneth Youngblood and, by all means, Dan Gibson. In fact, it has been said that THE most dedicated people in establishing Carolina Village were Larry Butler, Dan Gibson and Kenneth Youngblood.

There were times in the late '60s when only the most faithful believed Carolina Village would ever become a reality. The minutes show that the most productive guidance came from a group known as Christian Home Service, who not only acted as consultants but, through a subsidiary, the Weitz Company, arranged for construction. The formal signing of the construction agreement was announced Aug. 2, 1972; and Dan Gibson told the board on Aug. 22, 1972, that the Prudential Insurance Co. had approved a loan of $2,400,000. The entire project was to cost some eight million dollars, with one-half of the capital coming from residents' endowments. Folks began moving into the Village in June of 1974. The formal dedication took place in October 1974.

When I think of what Carolina Village has meant to this area, it would be impossible to define the asset that has been both the Village property and the people who are the Village. The Milo Oliphants from the Midwest had heard about a "proposed" village, and that's really all it was at that time–a proposal,

Carolina Village was formally dedicated in October 1974.

an idea, no buildings, just drawings and lots of dreams. But Milo and Virginia Oliphant were so impressed with Larry Butler and his obvious faith in the great future that was ahead for the Village, they became one of the first buyers to retire to Carolina Village. In addition, they each made a contribution of $50,000 to help assure future maintenance, monies for additional sidewalks and to add more windows to the proposed structure. Before coming here, Milo had established the Oliphant Eye Clinic at the University of Michigan. After they moved to Hendersonville, they became one of the area's most generous benefactors.

I recall one Christmas when an envelope was slipped under the door to the conference room at Pardee Hospital, and inside was a stock certificate from Rockwell International worth some $50,000 (given by Milo and Virginia Oliphant entirely unsolicited). They also provided start-up funds for the Virginia Oliphant School of Nursing at Blue Ridge College. It's hard to believe that when the Oliphants committed to retiring at Carolina Village, it was then only a dream, evidenced only by architects' drawings shown to them by Larry Butler.

One of the early residents of the Village was my personal friend, Evelyn Haynes, who attested to the conceptual success of the Village in a letter she called her Happy New Year's Letter. Evelyn wrote: "I take one meal a day in the dining room, and 350 interesting men and women are as one order, one big family all over sixty years old, and living in their adjoining apartments. There is so much talent to share." Evelyn loved Carolina Village, and the Village was good to her. She lived to be ninety-six. In fact, living at Carolina Village was so good for so many people that the center almost fell on hard times simply because so many were living much longer than expected.

In all the advance planning for the operation of Carolina Village, roughly one-half of the eight million dollar cost of building and operating the facility, would come from residents' endowments. Based on actuarial tables, these endowments would also provide the subsidy needed for the day-to-day cost of operation. But in the late '80s, residents were confounding the actuarial tables, a testimony that happy, secure people do live longer. I was told that the board was reanalyzing the projections and were considering various contingencies when the reality of the actuarial tables was born out and the administration could go back to the original plans.

Huckleberry—A State of Mind

Evelyn Haynes was by no means a wealthy person, but she was truly a free spirit. She took a pine thicket out toward Fruitland and turned it into what *Life Magazine* called "one of the top five cultural centers in the entire United States." "My mind was filled with plans and ideas that kept me enthused," she wrote. Her niece, Val LeVander, quotes Evelyn in that comment made in 1940 while recuperating from surgery. It appears in a little booklet called "True Adventures in Florida Days and Mountain Country" which was written about Evelyn by her niece.

When Evelyn Haynes became one of the first residents of Carolina Village, she could envision activities by the residents the likes of which no social planner ever dreamed. She was able to persuade management to assign a small plot in a communal garden area to each resident so they could grow their own flowers or fresh vegetables. She donated to the Village the park shelter now known as the Sanctuary.

Evelyn was the eternal optimist. She was always a witness to the beauty surrounding her. She was a defender of the innate goodness of her fellow man. Perhaps it was because of the ruggedness and harshness of her upbringing, living in exiguous circumstances on Merritt Island, Fla. and then to the wilds of Hickory Nut Gorge, that caused Evelyn to treasure everything around her. Hence, she gave exotic names to all of the places and things around her.

Evelyn Haynes

On my first visit to Huckleberry Mountain Artists' Colony, she talked of "Logs of Contentment." I found she was referring to a two-story plain old log cabin. What she called "Hideaway" was a cabin so small that double doors formed the entire wall. "Meditation Walk" looked to me very much like the path that led to Grandpa Edney's spring. I discovered "Meditation Bench" was a rough-hewn board resting on the top of two stumps. What Evelyn Haynes called the "Dining Hall" was a large room in the main log cabin with a tree growing right through the roof.

In 1996, I watched the Anthony Hopkins movie, "Road to Wellville," which was a depiction of life of one of the Kelloggs of Battle Creek. This

A discussion group held in the main building and dining hall. Life Magazine rated Huckleberry Mountain Artists' Colony as one of the top 10 summer centers of art and academia.

brother established a sanitarium to promote healthful living, which included such rituals as massive and frequent purgatives, a vegetarian diet heavy on bulk and fiber. Evelyn had similar sentiments. A typical breakfast at Huckleberry consisted first of a spoonful of sulfur and molasses to ward off chiggers and ticks, and every diner was served first a dish of stewed prunes to promote regularity.

And yet, I was amazed at the almost faddish devotion of the artists who came to Huckleberry. On the faculty was Dr. Edwin Grover, vice president of Rollins College; Dr. Harold Blodgett, professor from Cornell University; Vivian Laramore, poet laureate of Florida; and Carola Bell Williams, nationally known playwright. I don't remember his name, but the assistant director of the FBI under J. Edgar Hoover spent a month at Huckleberry.

After several visits to the Artists' Colony, I was deeply impressed with what Evelyn had been doing and had already done on her own. I suggested she change the operation from a proprietorship to a corporation, which would allow her to parade all these well-known names on her letterheads as members of a board or committee. I suppose it was so obvious to all the rest that I was NO artist of any kind, the artists developed a sympathy for me and asked that I serve on their board. We would have our meetings in Log Staff House, and at lunch break each of us were given a small recycled paper poke, inside of which was a peanut butter sandwich, a piece of fruit and a tea bag for our beverage. Having been brought up on pinto beans seasoned with a bit of side meat and a pone of cornbread, I felt the rations were a bit skimpy, but those poets, fiction writers, painters and artists all treated these lunch breaks as receiving manna from on high.

Very few local people ever knew the many things Evelyn Haynes had done for the community, apart from single-handedly making the Artists' Colony work. Before anyone ever dreamed of a bookmobile, Evelyn had gathered donations of books from all her friends and associates around the country, and arranged with general stores in Bat Cave, Edneyville, Fruitland, Lake Lure and Gerton to accept cardboard boxes (each with some 50 books) which would be loaned to local people who came in and out of the stores. Also, she was able to persuade the Sheriff's Department to periodically rotate the boxes among the stores. She opened a Community Store, which operated much like a "next-to-new" shop except she kept her prices at rummage sale levels. In this experiment, Evelyn (in a period of just three weeks) had found clothing in some forty-six boxes to fit members of seventy-six local families. Without credentials of any kind, Evelyn had met with the dean of the School of Architecture at N.C. State University and sold him on the idea of having a senior class project: student designs for a civic auditorium for Hendersonville. Each student would familiarize himself with the little town of Hendersonville and then, on his own, would draw his concept of a multi-purpose auditorium-community building. What excitement as we unrolled dozens and dozens

Evelyn Haynes gathered donations and ran a thrift shop to help support Huckleberry, as well as the community

of conceptual drawings of these N.C. State seniors explaining the justification and reasoning for each design. No one knows what happened to all those volumes of drawings which Evelyn had at Huckleberry.

At the end of the 1959 season, we had a real shock. Evelyn was diagnosed as having Addison's disease. I vaguely remember offering a motion approved by the board "recognizing that without the dynamic energies of Evelyn Haynes (who was the heart and soul of Huckleberry), the Artists' Colony should be closed and all assets deeded back to Evelyn Haynes personally." While Evelyn did live for an amazing twenty-five additional years, she did not have the health or stamina which would have permitted her to carry on her work at Huckleberry. She died at age ninety-six in 1994, but not before she had deeded the last vestige of her beloved Huckleberry to Wycliff Bible Translators for use by workers home on furlough.

Changing Face of Industry

T he vital ingredient to the formula for bringing industry and business to Hendersonville in boom years was the plentiful supply of dependable electric power. Jim Fain covers the very early history of electric power in the county when the primary concern was to generate enough power to supply electric light bulbs, and little else. In 1916, Oscar A. Meyer was hired to manage the old Blue Ridge Power Company. The very first thing he did was construct Lake Summit, which would provide the hydroelectric energy to turn the massive generators at Pot Shoals Generating Station, which would feed electricity to the town.

The 1946 telephone directory (thirty years later) still lists only three numbers for Duke Power: the main office downtown, the New Hope substation, and the Pot Shoals Generating Plant. Meyer had leased a building on Main Street for a period of fifty years and Duke Power occupied that building until the lease expired in June 1965. By then Duke had built their own building on Church Street. When Duke vacated the Main Street building, it was quickly leased by McFarlan's Bakery, which had been operating across Main Street since the '30s.

Later Mr. Meyer was joined by W.P. "Wick" Andrews in 1919, and in 1925 C.C. Oates ("Uncle Charlie") would become part of the Duke management team. All three of these men would play a strong role in civic, religious and fraternal affairs of the community for thirty to forty years. Mr. Meyer also changed the name of the firm to Broad River Power Company before it was acquired by Duke Power and added its power grid through the Carolinas. Meyer continued to manage until about 1940, when he retired.

Jim Sloan became the "Duke Power Man" for this district until a 1954 promotion transferred him to Duke's headquarters in Charlotte. Mr. J. M. Gaines served as manager for a short period, being borrowed from the Brevard office until 1959 when Keith Arledge moved in to become district manager in 1959. He served until Duke's CEO (Bill Lee) decided they needed

Upon taking control of the old Blue Ridge Power Company, Oscar A. Meyer's first project was to build a dam, creating Lake Summit, which would provide constant power to turn generators at Pot Shoals.

Keith in Hickory and he would be promoted to vice president of Duke for that region. Keith said, "I guess the most emotional thing I ever had to do was to turn my keys to the Hendersonville office over to Sam McGuirt. Hendersonville was my home, and I had loved every minute of being here." McGuirt was a native of Monroe (home of country singer Randy Travis and Senator Jesse Helms). McGuirt had worked in Burlington and in North Wilkesboro before coming to Hendersonville.

At about the time Sloan was brought up from Spartanburg, a husky young engineer (Claude Miller) was brought in from Rutherfordton. After service in World War II, Claude returned and became superintendent.

Claude was one of the greatest assets Duke Power ever had. He did so many favors for people all over the county, he could usually get needed right-of-way for Duke at no charge. I remember when WHKP owned some land on top of Jump Off, and Claude called one day and started explaining his need to run a new line to a development across the road from our property and I interrupted, "Claude, do whatever you want to do and send me the papers to sign."

Beginning on New Year's Eve and continuing through New Year's Day in 1964, Western Carolina was hit by one of those "once every fifty years" ice storms. Everywhere the ice was built up several inches thick, and even heavier toward Polk and Transylvania counties. Keith Arledge told me, "I'd never seen as heavy accumulation of ice on our lines as we had that day. Just the weight of the ice on the lines was actually causing the heavy utility poles to snap at the base." The storm knocked out power that fed the WSPA Channel 7 mountain transmitter. Keith said, "I personally received a call from Mr. Walter Brown (the owner) . . . I interrupted, "I'm very familiar with Mr. Brown, Keith, we've had our distasteful relationships with him, also."

Keith continued, "I listened to Mr. Brown through one of the most abusive phone calls I have ever had to endure in my entire career." Keith said, "I immediately called Charlotte and shared with them Mr. Brown's conversation."

Charlotte was familiar with Hogback Mountain and the hairpin turns all the way to the top. Keith said, "It was obvious if we were going to get new poles to the site, we'd have to have bulldozers, which Charlotte said they would dispatch." He said that Tryon had one Diamond T line truck with a small bore, short piston engine which they had hooked to a trailerload of creosote poles. That truck almost got to the top of the mountain when it stalled out. Earlier, Claude Miller was in touch with a friend who had loaned to him a lighter-weight dozer and he had already taken that dozer to the top to survey the total damage that would have to be repaired. When he heard that the truck had stalled, he said, "You all stay put. I'll bring the dozer down and pull the poles on up."

Claude Miller

On the way down off the peak, as the dozer tried to round a precarious bobby pin curve, its cleats simply could not break through the ice, which was now five to six inches thick. As it became obvious Claude was losing control of the dozer, everyone yelled, "Jump!" ... and Claude did. But he jumped to the right and the dozer slid off on top of him, less than 200 yards from where Keith and his support crew were standing. He died instantly.

Pioneer in Power—First in Flight

When Oscar Meyer took over management of the old Blue Ridge Power Company and moved his family to Hendersonville, he was still in his 30s. His son, Oscar Jr., exhibited no interest in following in his father's footsteps. He was totally dedicated to unraveling the mystery of man's ability to fly.

His interest had probably been whetted by an event that took place in 1921. That summer, the famed daredevil stuntman of the air, Roscoe Tanner, came to Hendersonville. He advertised that he would fly in an airplane, traveling over 100 miles an hour, and would jump out of that plane and land in Kanuga Lake.

The flight was postponed because of bad weather, but several days later, an enormous crowd gathered again around the lake to watch this death-defying feat. There was a great disappointment when only a handful of people were witnesses to his actual landing in a heavily wooded area on Echo Mountain. He had miscalculated and missed Kanuga Lake by half a mile.

When Oscar decided he should take up flying, it was something that had to be self-taught. There were no airports, no civilian schools, and very few books on flying. As he continued to learn more about aeronautics, he would build wings and strap them to his arms, which helped him to understand the

Oscar Meyer, self-taught pilot, stands in front of one of the planes he personally built. Once Oscar taught himself to fly, he taught many others in the county to do the same.

basic aspects of flight. He would put on a pair of roller skates, strap the wings to his arms and have someone tow him with a car down First Avenue West fast enough to actually cause him to lift off the ground. First Avenue was a neighborhood street with no through-traffic, and was one of the widest residential streets in Hendersonville. At the time, our family lived at the corner of First and Rhodes Street. When it became known that Oscar was going to practice, you could be sure of a total turnout of all the kids in that section to watch. In the fall of 1996, to refresh my memory I drove down First Avenue through the old neighborhood and it's amazing how little it has changed. There's a huge parking lot now where the old Horowitz Inn stood. As a young man, I'll never forget watching the kosher preparation of chickens for guests at the Horowitz. Also I found there's a church on First Avenue where the Gibbs family used to live. There was a huge old catalpa tree about a block away next to the old lily pond which grew what the kids called Indian cigars. The lily pond has long been filled in for shuffleboarders.

On top of Tom's Hill was where the Toms home (Oklawaha) had stood before it burned. Back then, you could find hundreds of shards of brilliantly colored glass from the stained glass windows that had been in the olds Toms mansion.

I pulled along the curb in front of "our old house" which still stands today, and reached back in my mind to remember the ice wagon coming down First Avenue. The wagon was always pulled by a very large horse and was driven by a man wearing a full-length leather apron that covered his entire front. He could chip off ten, twenty, fifty or even one hundred pound blocks of ice from within the wagon, and carry it against the leather apron without getting himself wet. Icemen were always kind and gentle (as I remember them). They'd let you jump on the back of the wagon for a ride of a few feet, and you were welcome to chunks of ice that had scattered in the wagon as he cut specific size blocks from the huge masses that had come from within the ice house.

Oscar taught himself to fly, and ended up teaching about every other young man in the county to fly, either before the war or at least to solo before he went into service. Oscar had bought some bottom land off Shepherd Street, where he kept his aircraft, and almost every weekend, Oscar and all his young flying fans would be "out at the airport" just hanging around, hoping someone would fly and maybe they could bum a ride.

Oscar enjoyed doing a "drunk flying act" where, as he took off, he would cause the plane to weave and swerve all over the field until just before he ran out of pasture, and then the plane would miraculously soar into the air. This was always a big crowd pleaser. Once in the air, he would continue to maneuver erratically, finally unfurling a roll of toilet tissue and then, in graceful sweeps, proceeding to shred the entire roll before it hit the ground.

I doubt if Oscar remembers how many young Henderson County men he trained to fly, and who became leading pilots in World War II. I ran across a picture and story about a Jack Edney, a carrier for the *Times-News*, who was commissioned in the U.S. Air Corps at Kelly Field. His career started under the tutelage of Oscar Meyer. Jack would later command Bartow Air Base in Winter Haven, Fla., and would ultimately serve as air attaché to Ireland. He was the son of Mr. and Mrs. Fred Edney, who moved from Hendersonville to Chapel Hill so all of their boys could live at home and go to the university.

When I was doing the radio show in 1996, I was sharing these discoveries with Jody Barber and young Frank FitzSimons; and when I say "young" Frank FitzSimons, you have a good indication of my advanced years.

Meyer stands in front of yet another of his "home made" airplanes.

Unidentified skater throws rope around the tail wheel of Oscar Meyer's tail wheel; soon others joined in for a virtual snake dance of ice skaters.

Jody interrupted and asked, "Are you going to tell them how Oscar would land on Highland Lake and tow ice skaters around the lake with his airplane?" When I looked with askance at Jody, he adamantly said, "Yes, he did that and I have a picture to prove it."

It is fairly common for lakes and ponds to freeze over in winter. The landed gentry could afford to build ice ponds and "deep in the ground" ice houses to store the ice until it was needed during the hot days of summer. Back then, there was no refrigeration equipment in the mountains. My uncle Crate Thomas had built the dam for the ice pond at Kenmure, and had constructed a very deep well into the ground, topped by a small building and wench in the roof. Big chunks of ice would be lowered in the winter, layered with straw, and more layers added until the ice house was filled. In the summer, you'd climb down the ladder, attach the wench to a block of ice and hoist it up for use in the kitchens and dining rooms of Kenmure. The ice house was covered over years ago.

Whenever the ice on the ponds would become strong enough, young people would don ice skates. Oscar Meyer heard that a large crowd had gathered at Highland Lake for skating, so he flew one of his lightweight planes over to the lake, landed, tossed out a tow rope and yelled, "Hang on!"

He then pulled the procession in sort of a snake dance around and around Highland Lake.

Before World War II, Oscar Meyer was given approval by the government for primary flight training, a program called CTTA. The "book learning" of aviation was taught at Brevard College, and flight training was conducted at Meyer's Airport. On Sept. 30, 1941, he announced the start of his next training class, and that there was now available at the airport a newly purchased Culver Dart for advanced students (along with seven other training planes). The announcement also noted that Tommy Stocks (who had learned to fly with Oscar) was returning from Winston-Salem to assist in the program, along with Kenneth Arnett, another long-time professional associated with Meyer.

There was another Oscar who was a well-known flyer and who had a long association with Oscar Meyer. This was Oscar Case, one of the best crop dusters in the area during the truck farming years. Once I asked Oscar Case, "Oscar, as you come to the end of a beanfield (flying at maybe fifty feet off the ground) and pull back the stick to bring the plane above the trees at the end of the beanfield, do you ever worry about what would happen if you pulled on that stick and nothing happened?" Without a second's hesitation, he answered, "Nope, if I ever even thought that might happen, I wouldn't even get in the plane. See, I always did my own maintenance so I knew that plane was going to do exactly what I told it to do."

I have to admit that I had really expected Oscar to answer me with something like, "I'll be OK because I know the Lord is flying with me" because Oscar Case was a very religious man. He wrote a number of gospel songs recorded by nationally known gospel singers. In fact, at one time he owned the Professional Diplomats Quartet, with his own fancy bus for road trips and singing engagements. Two of Oscar's great songs were "Oh, What a Mountain" and "I Found a Place to Hide." Oscar Case flew as a crop duster for twenty-eight years. He had three sons: Kenny, Gary, and Wally Case.

The first commercial and passenger service by air did not come until Oct. 12, 1937, when Eastern Airlines delivered the first shipment of airmail to the old Asheville-Hendersonville Airport (now an industrial park) in Fletcher. The delivery was tied into a Postmasters Association Convention in Asheville. The plane was a Stenson Reliant and the shipment included some 4,000 pieces of mail. The plane also picked up sacks of outgoing mail which were also given the distinctive "franking" honoring the historic flight. Mrs. H.M. "Flo" Flack wrote a letter to her mother (Mrs. A.G. Williams in Washington D.C.) which received that historic "franking" stamp. That letter is now in the possession of Flo's granddaughter, Susan Flack Wright.

Covering the entire left side of the envelope is an imprint made by a large rubber stamp with the wording, "First ALL N.C. AIRMAIL FLIGHT." Beneath that, the date: Oct. 11-16, 1937. Then there is a round seal depicting the Wright Memorial, on the left is worded Wright Memorial, and on the

A copy of the envelope used to mail the first air mail letter from the Asheville-Hendersonville Airport on Oct. 12, 1937. The letter was written by Mrs. Flo Flack to her mother, Mrs. A.G. Williams.

right, Kitty Hawk, N.C. And across the bottom of this historic "franking" is written—HENDERSONVILLE, THE GEM CITY." This is the only time I have ever seen Hendersonville referred to as "the Gem City." In the 1880s, Thomas Edison made two trips to Hendersonville investigating the feasibility of using zirconium in the filaments of his new electric light bulbs. Captain Toms leased all the land and little mines in the Tuxedo area and allowed local people to mine zirconium on their own; he would then broker it to the Edison Company. The railroad and postal service were trying to find an appropriate name for the little village, and someone suggestion Zirconia, which was quickly adopted and made official. Apparently, someone in the group planning for the first historic pickup of mail had remembered the area being known for zirconium mining, and quickly created a logo ("the Gem City"). The slogan was used only on that one occasion.

It would be another four years before commercial aviation arrived. A Penn Central Airlines eastbound ship arrived at the port at 1:40 o'clock and was christened "Miss Asheville-Hendersonville" by Miss Pauline Bourne (1941 Queen of the Rhododendron Festival). Then it flew on to Norfolk, Va. That evening a dinner was held at the old George Vanderbilt Hotel in Asheville. At the head table were Don Elias and C. Mike Ogle (both publishers of newspapers and both presidents of their Chambers of Commerce). Others attending from Hendersonville were Harry Buchanan and Monroe M. Redden.

As late as October 1949, the old Asheville-Hendersonville Airport was owned jointly by the two cities and Henderson County. The old airport was expected to continue on a long-range basis because during World War II the federal government approved a grant of $26,700 for improvements to the port to provide for a control tower, medium intensity lights for night flying, and for paving an access road.

However, pilots objected to a couple of fairly steep mountains along the northern approach. Also, the City of Asheville was never comfortable having Hendersonville share control of the official name of their airport. So less than ten years later, a movement was afoot to move the port to another location and, at the same time, eliminate Hendersonville and Henderson County from the operating authority.

After a number of stormy meetings with the three different governmental agencies, a compromise was finally reached buying out Hendersonville's ownership. Henderson County would trade sovereignty over Henderson County land on which the new port would be built to the City of Asheville. The City of Asheville would trade to Henderson County all its interests in the old A&H Airport, which would then become an industrial park operating within the tax base of Henderson County.

The new Asheville Regional Airport has been served by such airlines as Penn Central, Capitol, United, Delta, and especially by Piedmont, which would become U.S. Airways. In recent years, the massive changes following deregulation of the airline industry has seen Asheville lose all the major carriers except U.S. Airways. It continues to be served by a number of small feeder airlines, connecting to the hubs of Delta and American. Recently some of the feeder lines announced they would be replacing their small commuter planes with larger and more comfortable jets. Asheville, over the past several years, has totally remodeled and enlarged the airport facility. They have just completed improvements which will facilitate the handling of planes as large as 757s. Runways have been extended from the old 4,000-foot length at A&H to 8,000-feet-plus at the Asheville Regional Airport. Total repaving of the runways was accomplished in 1997. Asheville Regional Airport can park 879 cars, offering long-term and handicapped storage.

As a result of the trade, Henderson County established an industrial park on the site of the old A&H Airport and today:

• Steelcase operates a manufacturing center for wooden office furniture in the park. The building covers 800,000 square feet.

• Ralph Wilson Art has a manufacturing plant that covers 300,000 square feet.

• The Eaton Corporation plant covers 100,000 square feet.

• White Industries and other storage facilities complete the development of the park.

That's almost 27 acres of finished manufacturing facilities under roof, with between 1,900 and 2,000 full-time employees with jobs where the old A&H Airport used to be. All this property is taxable to Henderson County.

I'd say, offhand, when cooler heads prevailed in Raleigh in June 1959, and a little horsetrading took place between Henderson County and the City of Asheville, both sides came out smelling like a rose.

Back in 1946, when WHKP first signed on the air, if you wanted a job in an industrial plant in the county, chances are you would work in textiles. We did not have the diversified industrial family of today and even what there was, there wasn't much of it.

In 1946, only seven of what we could call substantial manufacturing plants were located in the entire county.

Of the seven, five of them were textile plants. In addition, there was the Moland Drysdale plant, which manufactured brick, and Wing Paper Box Company, which made cardboard boxes. George Wing later sold the plant to Federal Paper Board Company.

Of the five textile plants, three of them are no longer in existence: Chipman LaCrosse Hosiery Mills (operated by the Katzenmoyer family) at East Flat Rock; Green River Mills (operated by the Boys family and later sold to J.P. Stevens, now used primarily as a distribution center); and Grey Hosiery Mills (operated by Charley and James P. Grey), the building of which was bought by the city. The city is now trying to sell it to a group promoting a civic center. One of the two other textile plants back when WHKP signed on the air was Balfour Mills (operated by the Smyth family and managed by E. A. Smyth III). It would later be sold to Kimberly Clark and is known by most folks today as Berkeley Mills, one of the largest industrial operations in the entire county. The other plant was operated by Dave Kemp and most folks knew it as Diamond Brand Canvas Co., although it also operated under another name, the New York Drop Cloth Company. Today, it still manufactures canvas products, but is best known for the huge camping store

Balfour Mills at the time of purchase by Kimberly Clark. The purchase price was said to be $3 million for the 189-acre plant site and facilities.

that draws thousands of people to this area who are searching for the exact camping item they need.

Back in 1946, Forrest Gardiner ran a very small operation of Ashe Street known as Advance Thread Company. On Locust Street, George Fullerton ran Blue Ridge Cord Company, which would later become part of Wellington Puritan.

Jim Duff managed the Burroughs Manufacturing Company on 3rd Avenue, which made bedspreads. Mrs. Anne Fullwood had the Colonial Spin Braid firm on 7th Avenue East. Right across the street from City Hall, Charlie Elliot ran Coronet Manufacturing, which made yarn. Frank Adcox worked with him as plant manager.

It's important that I tell you more about Coronet Imports because (from that Lilliputian operation) came the establishment of Hendersonville's famed Michaelian & Kohlberg Co., which manufactures custom-made wool rugs for virtually every U.S. Embassy around the world. The plant is better known locally as Spinning Wheel Rugs, and among its unique products was carpet for the aircraft carrier USS Independence in 1959. Before old carrier hands rise to argue about carpet in an aircraft carrier, the carpet made by Spinning Wheel Rugs was installed only in the captain's quarters, quarters of the chief of staff, the flag officers' cabins, and the ship's staterooms. There was 2,026 feet of loomed carpet: grey and beige for the flag officers' quarters; blue, black, beige and natural for the chief of staff; and light and dark tan for the captain's area.

Michaelian & Kohlberg began operations here in 1941 out on the Asheville Highway with twenty-five employees. In the beginning, the workers actually "hooked rugs", exactly the same as some mountain women still do, selling these products at the Curb Market. Later, the principal in the firm Frank Michaelian was able to develop machinery which would do the same kind of quality handwork that his custom rug operation demanded. Mr. Michaelian was a graduate of Columbia University and minored in agriculture. When he bought their home from Bobby Jones in Haywood Forest, he put in an elaborate grape vineyard as a hobby. Frank married the very lovely Lorna (the ex-wife of William Randolph Hearst). I remember they had what may have been a multiple garage converted into an outdoor recreation and barbecue center. One wall was covered with photographs of Lorna (who had appeared in a number of motion pictures), along with famous movie stars from Clark Gable to Gary Cooper. Another wall featured pictures of Frank he with heads of state like Nehru of India or foreign ministers of most of the great countries of the world, especially in the Orient.

When the Downtown Parking Corporation was seeking to acquire added lots for parking, Frank's two sisters still owned the old Coronet Manufacturing building across from the City Hall. They were not interested in selling but were anxious to lease the property for a number of years for income and then it would be transferred to the city for "other valuable considerations." City Attorney Frank Coiner developed a lease plan agreeable to the two.

After Michaelian had built the main plant on North King Street, he needed more storage and acquired property on 7th Avenue (where, at that time, King Street dead-ended). There he built a building. When King Street became the northbound leg of U.S. 25 through downtown, it was necessary to curve King Street to the left to connect into Main Street to avoid having to buy and demolish that brand new Spinning Wheel Storage building. Spinning Wheel Rugs (or Michaelian & Kohlberg) came to Hendersonville in 1941. It was managed for a time by Charlie Elliot, later by Grover Peace, and is now operated by descendents of the family. It still supplies exclusive custom carpets for the most prestigious buildings around the globe.

Balfour—Smyth—Kimberly Clark

Back in 1924, Captain Ellison Adger Smyth retired from a variety of executive positions and moved, at age seventy-eight, to his home in Flat Rock, which had been known as Rock Hill. Captain Smyth changed the name to Connemara, which is now a national historic site as the home of Carl Sandburg. At the peak of his activities, Frank FitzSimons said Smyth served on the board of directors of thirty-six different corporations and twelve banks. In his retirement, Mr. Smyth saw the acute need for jobs for local people, and then organized a brand new textile plant called Balfour Mills. Back in the '30s and '40s, the tiny railroad station at Balfour was named Smyth. Though "the Captain" (as he was known) lived just shy of his 95th birthday, the mill was managed in later years by E.A. Smyth III.

The Kimberly Clark Corporation negotiated the purchase of the mill and took over its operation on Oct. 1, 1946 just twenty-four days before WHKP signed on the air. Taking over as manager of the plant was H.T. Rindal, whom everyone knew only as "Luke." The "H" stands for his Swedish first name, Hjalmer. Luke managed the plant from 1946 to 1958, then was transferred to the home office in Neenah, Wisconsin. He later was transferred to New York for an experimental partnership with the J.P. Stevens Company.

When Luke left Hendersonville, he was succeeded by Bob Toms. Bob's specialty when he and Liz lived in Neenah, Wis., was personnel relations and his work involved traveling to the various Kimberly Clark plants around the world. He was known as the chief bargainer. After managing the Hendersonville plant, Bob moved to a plant operated in Niagra, Wis. Luke Rindal returned for a second tour before he was made director of manufacturing for Kimberly Clark, with his office in Neenah. He retired in 1971, and he and his wife, Nat, first moved to Cashiers until the lure of Hendersonville drew them back here in 1983.

After Luke left the second time, Don Gladieaux was brought in to become plant manager, serving until 1972 when he was succeeded by Bob Wick, who had been head of marketing for Kimberly Clark in Neenah. Earlier, Bob had been production manager at their plant in Memphis. Bob and Maree were here with the Berkeley operation for ten years until 1982, when he retired. In 1984, Kimberly Clark built a new plant in Lexington, N.C. The company learned of a totally new manufacturing concept Wick had developed and they prevailed upon him to come out of retirement only long enough to oversee the building of the new plant and the implementation of the new "team concept" in manufacturing. In the early days of American manufacturing, mass production methods had been devised where workers stood at a single work station and performed the same duty over and over again. (I'm sure you remember in the "I Love Lucy" series the routine where Lucy and Ethel are on the chocolate candy production line). Bob Wick was a pioneer in the concept that workers be formed into teams and that everyone on the team be qualified to do any chore of any other worker. He theorized that individuals working together would be more apt to improve quality and production and would be rewarded as a team on an improved performance basis. He also theorized that this would eliminate the boredom of doing the same thing over and over day after day. Wick put this innovative management concept into action in Lexington. It is now in place in virtually the entire Kimberly Clark operation.

Then there was Dick Kimberly. He was the son of the chairman of the board of the corporation (which is to say, whatever he wanted to do was looked upon with favor from Neenah). He worked out of Atlanta for a while (I remember him calling me once from there about a PR problem) and I understand he's still active as a lobbyist for the company in Washington.

But the most important aspect of the Berkeley story is that every one of these executives were active in all community activities. Luke helped organize the United Way and was its first president. Bob Toms, Bob Wick, Bill Benoit and Don Gladieaux were all active; and, as far back as I can remember, there was a Berkeley man serving on the Board of Trustees of Pardee Hospital–right now it's Bill Altman. When you call the roll of these men (all of whom were at one time or another general manager out at Balfour), they all (Luke, Bob Toms, Bob Wick, Bill Benoit), all of them (after serving elsewhere around the world with Kimberly Clark), all of them returned to spend their retirement years in Hendersonville. I didn't mention Don Gladieaux because he did not leave Hendersonville to retire.

Industry Recruitment—Breaking New Ground

With thousands of veterans returning home after World War II, they had no job opportunity if they wanted to stay in Henderson County. The handful of mostly textile plants had an obligation to protect the job of any of their employees who had been away in service. In the mid-'40s, the various states had devoted only a token effort, if any, toward encouraging economic growth. The only industry recruiter at that time was Southern Railroad, and they basically had their sights set only on industry that required huge tonnage access for both raw materials and finished products. The Chamber of Commerce had made a lot of noise about getting new plants to move here, but it had no budget with which to operate. It did have one volunteer worker, Jim Duff, who just for the excitement devoted his full time to trying to snag a new plant. Duff spent so much time in his volunteer work as industrial hunter that it impacted his little Pure Oil Distributorship.

In 1949 (the year Jimmy Fain became head of the Chamber), the rumor circulated throughout the county that Jim Duff had hit the jackpot. A brand new, major industrial plant had bought land and would build a new plant out toward Fletcher. It was to be the third major plant of Cranston Print Works, a firm that specialized in taking plain cloth and printing colorful patterns onto the material. Cranston's largest operation was in Cranston, R.I., but they also had a major plant in Massachusetts. John Gregory had been plant superintendent at the plant in Rhode Island and was transferred here to become general manager of the North Carolina operation at Fletcher.

While there had been some test runs from time to time in late 1949, John says they look upon Jan. 1, 1950 as the actual start of regular production at the plant. They started with sixty employees and by May the number had more than doubled to 125. Because of modernization and the coming of the computer, unskilled positions had been eliminated, but the plant still has increased the number of employees to some 300 people.

If someone in 1950 would ask, "Who owns Cranston?," the response would have been "the Rockefellers." But as John Gregory was always quick to point out: There was the enormously wealthy John D. Rockefeller but he had a brother (William) who was innovative and entrepreneurial but always had to get capital from John D. before he could undertake a venture. It was William's family who was responsible for all the Cranston operation.

Gregory said that by mid-April (in 1950), the plant had operated long enough to get the kinks out, and he decided it would be of interest to the people of the county to come inside and see how the plant worked. So an "Open House" was scheduled for Friday and Sunday, May 3 and 5. There was a tremendous turnout both days.

Cranston believed in training local men to move into executive positions in the plant. Among them were guys like Kay Orr, who today would work in something called logistics, he controlled when raw materials arrived and when the finished product would be shipped. Kay and Minnie Sue Orr were the parents of young Robert Orr, who moved up from a judge on the Court of Appeals to the North Carolina Supreme Court.

There was Rick Orr, who was head of personnel and only recently retired. There was also William C. "Bill" Parker, who became plant superintendent. These men (and many others of the Cranston family) were local and were

An open house was held in May 1950 for the new Cranston Print Works factory. A mass of colorful designs were created by Cranston artists and then printed on white cloth.

always heavily involved in community activities. Bill served not only as a county commissioner, but was active until his death on the Pardee Memorial Hospital Board.

I don't know when it started, but during the twelve years that I was active at Pardee Hospital, every single year we'd receive (unsolicited) a contribution of $5,000 from Cranston Print Works "to help maintain excellence in service in the field of health for the people of this county."

A number of years ago, William Rockefeller created an ESOP, that's an acronym for Employee Stock Option Plan. Each year funds which came from the operation of plant were placed in a tax-free ESOP account. Over the years, these contributions (and the return on these invested funds) grew to the point where the employees (using these monies as guarantee) simply bought out the plant. Now the employees own Cranston Print Works. It's exactly the same plan followed at WHKP.

Cranston was indeed a great breakthrough, the first major manufacturing plant to open in Henderson County denovo. The year was 1950, and while there was no celebrating in the streets, there was a new optimism that the area could attract new industry and jobs could be created so that our young people did not have to leave the county just to make a living. The year 1950 was the year Jim Duff and Dave Cooley were reported to be able to walk on water.

Jim's GreatestVictory

While Jim Duff and the Chamber had experienced a few minor successes in luring small industrial plants to relocate to the area after 1950, nothing rivaled the coming of Cranston until 1955. Rumors had been circulating during the autumn of 1954 that something really big was in the works,–a major new "name" plant that might employ a thousand new workers. As the rumor mill hummed, Duff and Cooley became even more close-mouthed:

"At this time, the plant demands total anonymity"–even after the Chamber found it necessary to raise local monies to offset an exorbitant price that had been placed on one small tract, which happened to be smack dab in the middle of the overall site which by now was under option to third parties.

The first official word that the new plant would be owned by the General Electric Company came during a luncheon (called hastily) and held with a "standing room only" crowd in the Skyland Hotel ballroom. The announcement made by then General Manager Byron Cherry said that GE's Outdoor Lighting and GE Traffic Control Departments would be relocated from Lynn, Massachusetts to Hendersonville.

The formal groundbreaking of the new plant took place on Feb. 4, 1955. Richard Crowe (Cherokee Indian) would light a torch from the Cherokee Eternal Flame and run on foot from Cherokee to the plant site at East Flat Rock, where the flame would activate a photoelectric cell that would signal groundbreaking machinery to begin operations. Cherry said General Electric anticipated that it would take twenty months to complete the facility and move the manufacturing plant from Lynn to Hendersonville. On Feb. 4, 1955, the old A&H Airport was hectic with activity. U.S. Senator Sam Erwin and Congressman George Shuford flew in from Washington, and Philip D. Reed, chairman of GE's board, came in from New York.

In the greatest triumph of Dave Cooley's young career, the interior of the old rock gymnasium at Hendersonville High School had been transformed into a mighty convention hall with flags, bunting, huge signs, and banners and a seating arrangement for more than 750 people. The dais rose three levels up from the main floor. The top level was for outgoing Chamber president I.E. Johnson and incoming president Bevo Middleton along with Senator Erwin and Chairman of the Board Reed. In studying pictures Jody Barber made of the event, the second level was for top state officials and the level just off the floor was for state senators and members of the legislature.

Until I saw this picture, I had forgotten that for this pretentious event, there was a small table, seating only three people placed on floor level to the right as you faced the speaker's platform. At this table were places for Katherine (the child bride), Diane Cooley (Dave's wife) and myself. Dave was too busy with his master production to even think of having a place reserved for himself. As I studied the picture, it suddenly dawned on me that for the only time in my life, when emceeing a program, I had not sat at the head table. There simply wasn't room up there for me to sit. So each time the emcee was to be heard from, I had to climb a ladder up three tiers, step onto the dais and suddenly my smiling face would appear from nowhere.

Mrs. Calhoun Hipp of Greenville, S.C. (the former Miss Jean Jones of Hendersonville who had appeared in a number of Broadway shows) provided special musical entertainment, accompanied by Miss Kate Dotson on the piano. I had prepared all my humor anticipating that the 750 people in the crowd would be very urbane and would best appreciate

Dave Cooley's triumph: The transformation of an old high school gym into a convention hall for the announcement of GE's groundbreaking. Bevo Middleton and his wife are at top table; Kermit and the child bride sit at lower table, far right and left respectively, with Diane Cooley between them.

cunning little one-liners the likes of which Bob Newhart made famous. Boy, was that a mistake! After I had dropped a half dozen of those carefully prepared ingenious bits of humor, I was greeted only by thunderous silence. It was panic time. I had nothing else prepared. So, as Minnie Pearl would have done, I went back to pure corn from memory and was greeted by guffaws and leg-slapping laughter. That night I learned never, never try to evaluate an audience in advance.

Twenty months went by (from February 1955 to Nov. 2, 1956) as contractors worked at a heated pace trying to get the construction finished before winter closed in. Perhaps sixty families had sought out houses as they were transferred here with GE from the outdoor lighting department in Lynn, Mass. I certainly wouldn't hazard trying to remember the names of all those sixty families we gained as new Hendersonville citizens made their way here to establish new homes, new neighbors and friends, and a new future. I do remember the Schwalbachs were in the first cadre, along with the Jim Thorndikes and Art and Haddie Harrington (Art would later become mayor of Laurel Park). The sudden chaos in house hunting and new families getting settled into their new home communities made it like an enormous number of people who moved here from Lynn with the GE plant. Looking at hard numbers though, for every person transferred as cadre to the new plant, nine local workers were hired and trained for employment in the new operation.

Another insight into the GE move: A number of years ago, Buck Fraley (who was CEO of Carolina Motor Freight) told me that the GE move to North Carolina provided their trucking company with a new springboard of opportunity which they were able to exploit, and enabled them to become one of the top ten motor carriers in the entire nation. Buck Fraley dreamed up something called "portal to portal" and entered bids to move the GE plant by truck. While the railroad cost (purely from Lynn, Mass., to Hendersonville) was much less than Carolina was able to offer, Carolina factored in having their trucks actually back into the Lynn plant, load the machinery onto their trucks, and then upon arriving in Hendersonville, would back the trucks to the proper sites on the plant floor and unload. This savings on local dray charges gave the edge to Carolina, and GE was the first plant in the country moved entirely by truck. Unfortunately, Carolina experienced major problems recently and was bought out by ABF (Arkansas Best Freight). Should you see a Carolina Freight logo, it's because ABF just hasn't gotten around to painting it out.

Through most of the years, the GE plant has been operating under a general manager with five sections (engineering, manufacturing, etc.) each with its own manager reporting to the general manager. The plant's name was changed many years ago to GE Lighting Systems with the proliferation of many other products other than outdoor lighting itself; but in the beginning it was called the Outdoor Lighting Department and originally consisted of 184,000 square feet of manufacturing area and a 11,000 square foot laboratory wing. In addition to the executive office section, the plant also offered a cafeteria for staff members, later enlarged to serve the whole workforce.

GE's new plant here was the first totally self-contained industrial branch of a major corporation to operate here. The engineering for everything manufactured here was invented, devised, and lab-tested by in-house engineers. Worldwide sales and marketing of all GE's outdoor lighting products was also headquartered here. One of the first spectacular tools for selling GE's products was Lamplighter's Hall, to which customers were brought to see products. After this, customers were taken outdoors to the "Crossroads of Light," where all products could be switched on and off to demonstrate their usage on dark city streets, etc.

Shortly after GE located here, the local plant even established its own legal department, headed by Dwight Carhart. In four years the plant had achieved such success, Ronald Reagan (who was at that time associated with GE in the production of GE Theater) was assigned time to do a PR visit in 1960.

General Electric had an enormous impact on this area through hundreds of jobs offered locally, but equally as important, wages paid by General Electric to employees whether on assembly line, in die casting, or clerical impacted the pay levels of every business in the county. From the very beginning with the Byron Cherrys, the Joe Baileys, the Stan Smiths, the

"Chuck" Melons, the Phil Milroys, and the Bill Vineyards, these general managers set the example for more than a thousand other GE people to become committed to the neighborhood and community needs.

What about Jim Duff and Dave Cooley, who walked on water after they brought Cranston to Hendersonville??? From contributions in the community, Duff was given a brand new car and named the first VFW "Man of the Year." Cooley gained the savvy to take on Chambers of Commerce in the largest cities in the country, including the mighty Fort Worth/Dallas chamber.

Dupont to Buy 10,500 Acres of WNC Land

In July 1956, one company purchased 10,500 acres of land in Henderson and Transylvania counties. It was the largest land transaction since the days of the Speculation Land Company. Let me recommend strongly that you read the first five chapters in Volume III of the Frank FitzSimons trilogy, "From the Banks of the Oklawaha," because once you've absorbed the saga of the Speculation Land Company, you'll be able to understand how one man had a 5,000 acre tract to sell in 1956 adjacent to another tract of some 5,400 acres held by another man.

When the announcement of the land purchase was made by the Dupont Company, the firm said they would build a new manufacturing plant on this site to make hyper-pure silicon. (The press release educated me to the fact that hyper-pure is a hyphenated word.) The manufacturing process would require virtually a wilderness-type environment, and the land they found was in the ownership of the Frank Coxe family of Asheville and the A.H. Guion family of Henderson County. Mr. FitzSimons describes in detail how a handful of families were able to acquire millions of acres of Western North Carolina land at a price of about ten cents per acre. One of those families was the Tench Coxe family, with Frank Coxe a direct descendent. In addition to the Coxe and Guion lands, there was a small tract of 139 acres owned by Donald Rhoads which was also purchased.

This purchase was discussed on many occasions by a group of men who gathered daily for coffee and breakfast at the old Hot Spot on Main Street. Frank Edney owned the eatery and every morning at 3:30, he would be assisted by Rex Rhodes in opening up the place and getting the giant urn of coffee going for "the regulars" one of whom nicknamed the group "The Breakfast Club." Those men who gathered every morning provided a real cross-section of the local population. I could eat breakfast each morning and simply listen to the conversations among the group and get a good idea of major concerns in the community.

There were among the dependable regulars such folks as Tom Collins, Bill Brookshire, and Frank Stepp (all who worked the early shift at the post office). Tom Collins' brother Richard ran one of the finest cabinet shops in the area (and still does in 1997), and Tom moonlighted on the side in painting and refurbishing automobiles. Bill Brookshire was a descendent of the famous Brookshire families who operated the stables and livestock market in the town's early years. LeRoy Dill was a Coke man who delivered Cokes for better than forty years all over WNC, including handling the dreaded "Highlands Run." Another man was Calvin King, who drove a Biltmore Dairy run, which required him to be ready for pickup before 5 a.m. John "Jack" Pittman and Clayton Drake were both retired, but Clayton was old enough to have helped build the dam for Lake Lure. Robin "Bob" Clayton was a finish carpenter who had worked with Albert Drake and other top builders in his early years but, by this time, he contracted only his own specialty projects. One of the real characters in the group was Ruppert Jackson (owner of Jackson Flower Shop). Ruppert had strong opinions on virtually every subject and was anxious to debate anyone at any time.

One other regular was a very quiet, soft-spoken native who was one of the best-known surveyors in the area, Donald Hill. The reason there was so much conversation about the Dupont deal among these "breakfast clubbers" was, before any purchase could be finalized, all 10,539 acres had to be surveyed and both the buyers and sellers had specified that Hill do the surveying. Hill had simply said, "Not now. There's no way I'm going to walk that snake country 'til there's freezing weather." Please remember most of this property was virtual wilderness. So, all summer long in 1956 (as the world waited for the Dupont deal to close and the buyers and sellers waited for Don Hill), he'd be greeted with a jovial, "Been up on the mountain yet?"

Back in 1956, you'd drive out Kanuga through the Crab Creek area (which had been nicknamed "Cat Head" because of all the liquor made back in the coves in that section of the county in the early years). There was a big dairy on the left (owned by the Kemps) known as Shoals Falls. A winding two-lane road led up the side of the mountain to the top of the ridge, where the 10,539 acres sprawled across the ridges. Today, a modern paved road runs to the top of the ridge and across the Dupont property to U.S. 276 at Cedar Mountain. It is a magnificent highway and because Dupont has maintained a virtual wilderness environment, it is not uncommon to spot animals along the road that you may have thought were extinct.

Dupont not only invested huge sums of money to build their plant and manufacture hyper-pure silicon, but they brought to this area another great asset—people. People like Steve Thomas, Bill Morrill, and George Hembree, all of whom volunteered their abilities to make the area a better place to live.

I don't know whether or not Dupont is still in the X-Ray field at their Transylvania, plant; but for all those years that the breakfast group gathered at the Hot Spot, any time a hospital, a clinic, or any user of Dupont X-Ray medium would let their inventory get too low, a local cab driver would race up to Dupont, then drive the film straight to the Greenville/Spartanburg

Airport and personally place it on the next plane out. He would then return to Hendersonville and join the rest of us at the Hot Spot for his breakfast. I always thought this sort of service on the part of Dupont was far above the normal call.

An Industrial Park without Local Tax Money

Back in the early '60s, the old Wing Paper Box Company in Lennox Park was sold to the Federal Paper Board Company. Federal was anxious to purchase additional land for a plant expansion and installation of new equipment. A local Realtor helped them acquire a site on U.S. 176 near the railroad overpass, and everything seemed copacetic.

In 1961, I had succeeded Jim Duff as chairman of the Industrial Committee, and was notified by Federal that a new piece of equipment purchased for this plant would require greater load bearings than were available at the Spartanburg Road site. Hendersonville had fought a valiant battle with a town in Georgia over getting this plant to come to Hendersonville—the Georgia offer even included free land on which Federal could build. The message I received from the Federal people basically was either buy this site, which we cannot use, and help us find another site, or we'll move the plant to Georgia. At that time, there were no buyers for the Spartanburg Road site at the price Federal had paid; but it was felt that if given a couple of years, a buyer could be found.

So, the Chamber of Commerce called an urgent meeting of the "doers" we had back then. We could always count on fifty to seventy-five people to respond without question when the community faced a problem and needed assistance and these people did respond with their time and with their money. In the Skyland Hotel ballroom the problem of Federal Paper Board was simply presented with a proposed solution being the organization of an Industrial Development Corporation would raise from stockholders enough money to buy the aborted site on U.S. 176 and help locate a suitable site which would be found on Tabor Road near GE.

Some seventy-five community "doers" present at the meeting that night bought stock in the Industrial Development Corp., in increments of $1,000 and within an hour, we had sufficient capital to buy the aborted site on 176 and counter the Georgia offer of a denovo site. Jack Schulman was elected president of what we now called the Henderson County Industrial Development Corporation. The organization papers had hardly been made official when a request was received from Youngstown Aluminum (now the Selee Corp.) for the new Industrial Development Corp. to help them secure an SBA loan, which was approved in a matter of weeks in 1962 to the tune of $211,300. So even before the arrangements with Federal could be consummated, the newly formed corporation had secured yet another industry.

In was June 1962 before the final agreement was worked out with Federal Paper Board to close the deal on the two sites. The Tabor Road site is still being used by this expanded company (which doubled in size in eight years). The Industrial Development Corp. was later able to sell the old site on Spartanburg Highway to Francis & Wright, where a new retail store was built for the firm.

That Industrial Corporation was first headed by Jack Schulman with a board consisting of Jim Barrett, John Holley, Bleecker Morse, R.B. Shealy, Hank Sinclair, Joe Wright, Bill Howe, Bud Hunter, Charles Metzger and Gene Staton. Jack Schulman would later be succeeded by R.B. Shealy as president, who would lead the corporation into buying acreage at Mountain Home for a totally new industrial park.

Industrial Park After Site was Purchased

The first order of business was to persuade government officials to pay for the cost of extending water three miles from the city mains to the site at Mountain Home. At a joint meeting of city and county officials, a good deal of discussion concentrated on the size of the water line that would be needed to serve the industrial park and all the area out on the Asheville Highway to the site. Manager Bill Stokes said a 12-inch line might be too small, but that a 14-inch line would cost too much. I'll not mention the name of the city commissioner who made a motion that a 13-inch line be built. Stokes quickly pointed out that 13-inch lines would have to be custom made and would be three times the cost of a 14-inch line. The commissioner withdrew the motion. The city and county finally decided to spend $205,000 on the line, the city would pay half and the county would pay the other half. The county would be reimbursed from tap charges and the city would own outright the line.

The first plant recruited for the park was Textile Paper Products Inc., which would employ forty people to make paper tubes and cores. Over the years,

Sign at entrace to Mountain Home Industrial Park.

American Cyanamid (which would become Kyosera Ceramics); Jefferson Smurfit; Brandford Wire; Printpack Inc.; Quality Rubber Manufacturing; Seneca Foods and Mini-Storage all moved in, utilizing all 165 acres in the park. Shortly thereafter, with no more land to sell, the corporation was liquidated and every stockholder received his money back, plus enhancement. No ad valorem tax money was used, and the government had put up no monies except for self-refunding water lines.

This was an example of free enterprise at its best: Local people putting their money where their mouth was and doing what was needed on their own without government subsidy. Next time you drive past the Mountain Home Industrial Park (throbbing with activity and employing hundreds of local people), remember it was made possible by volunteers and private capital.

Farming, the Way it Was

When WHKP first went on the air (and into the '50s), spring was the time of year when everybody was up to their ears in activity. The tourist industry was in the midst of their cleaning and getting things ready for another season. This was when perhaps a thousand farm families here in the county were putting final touches to gardens, truck crops, flocks of chickens, pigs, and calves. This took place in spite of the fact that many people who owned and operated a family farm also found a regular job in one of the industrial operations in the county.

In late April, all the doors were open at Francis & Wright on Railroad Avenue and large trucks, as well as pick-em up trucks, were parked everywhere. The same was true at Hatch Feed Store on South Main Street and out in the county at such huge general stores as Arthur Turner at Edneyville and J.H. Stepp out on the ridge.

We still have Valley Ag where Davenport's Store operated out on Mills River. There's Fletcher Feeding Service and Southern States; but with the number of what you could describe as "farming families" now down to less than half of what it used to be, you just don't have the numbers that used to be involved in family farming.

Melvin S. Hatch operated first as the Houston Feed Store, which he later renamed M.S. Hatch Feed Store. Melvin was the Purina dealer and he cooperated fully with the Purina Beautena and Mike and Ike programs. In January Melvin would purchase a newborn Holstein calf. He had a pen made for it in the store and he fed it only the proper Purina feeds for five months. In June he'd give the calf away, along with $300 in other cash prizes.

Bill Francis (not to be outdone) would install a huge barrel made out of hog wire and have it up near the cash register. For every payment made on account, the customer was given coupons on which he'd print his name and address and drop 'em in the barrel. Francis & Wright would have a giveaway of all sorts of major appliances and cash. Then as a double whammy, Hatch would build two hog pens, and in one would place a pig called Ike (which would be fed only shorts and corn) and in the other pen would be placed a pig called Mike (which would be fed Purina's balanced hog feed). The pigs would graphically show the advantage of feeding Purina as Mike would weigh at least a third more than Ike by Thanksgiving, when both pigs would be given away.

These events were tremendous crowd pullers. On the day of the give-aways, folks would start arriving in mid-morning, although the drawings would not be held until around high noon. Always, Mr. FitzSimons (the Genial Squire of the Gold Glow Farm) would join me for our "Mutt and Jeff" or "dog and pony show." I would be the emcee and Mr. Fitz (the Raconteur of hilarious tall tales) would take over. He was a master at telling those old yarns where all along the way in the story there was humor which called for ever heftier laughs until finally when he would come to the punch line. He'd have everybody slapping their legs and bent double with laughter. (In Cincinnati, they call those "Shaggy Dog Stories.")

Back then, folks took their politics a lot more seriously than they do today. In 1952, Melvin Hatch told me that several Democrats kept coming in wanting him to change the name of the pigs to Adelai and Ike instead of Mike and Ike. He replied, "I can't do that. Ike is sure to get beat he's already thirteen pounds behind." Besides, Melvin said, "There are a lot of Democrats who don't want to have their man's name put on a pig. I'll shore be glad when this election is over." In that same year, feelings got so spirited that D.E. Patty (the "E" was for Elijah and they called him "Lige") and J.N. Albritton made a bet: The loser would roll the winner in a wheelbarrow from the Southern depot up 7th and down Main Street. Eisenhower beat Stevenson and it was "Lige" pushing J.N. Albritton one mile up 7th and down Main. In farming or in politics, folks really got a lot out of life back then.

The Glad Era

Today folks take pride in local floral industries such as Carolina Roses and Van Wingerdens, all out in the Mills River area. The entire operation of each is in climate-controlled hot houses. It may surprise you to know that back in the 1940s and 1950s you could drive through the Mills River Valley and see hundreds of acres of gladioli in full bloom, right out in the open field.

The man who started the gladioli business in Henderson County was Howard C. Tate. Mr. Tate lived out on 6th Avenue West near an old road then named Gaillimore. Today it would be in the vicinity of Glasgow Lane. At first, he rented limited acreage of the dark, rich bottomland from some Mills River people and planted his first glad bulbs. As the bulbs began breaking through the ground, Mr. Tate was busy contacting florists and securing orders for his first flower shipments. During the peak season, it took around twenty-five additional hands to cultivate, harvest, grade, and package

Freshly harvested gladiolas were kept in garbage cans full of water until they were transfered to special cartons to be shipped to florists.

for shipment the harvested glads.

In the early and mid'50s, he rented land along N.C. 191 just beyond the old Davenport's Store (now Valley Ag). Words simply can't describe the breathtaking beauty of seeing acres and acres of brilliantly colored glads budding to almost full bloom. WHKP was operating a sister station in Canton (WWIT) back in those years, and it was necessary for me to commute back and forth two or three times a week and always a highlight of those boring drives to Haywood County was to watch the progress of the glads in their spring to fall growing season. Glads, like other farm crops, must be rotated annually with other crops to restore certain vital nutrients to the soil. So one year, they'd be on the right side of the highway and the next year on the left.

Mr. Tate, in his start-up years, would add labor to cut the flowers. They would then bring them to a wooden shed behind the Tate house, where they'd be graded and bunched and placed in huge garbage cans half full of water. The next step would be to place them in boxes which Tate had personally designed to give the flowers the ultimate protection during shipment and at the same time keep the stems moist to preserve the flowers. At first, shipments would be made via Railway Express in these boxes, directed to individual florists' shops throughout the South. As business grew, Tate was able to ship in carload lots to one city such as Atlanta or Birmingham, resulting in substantial savings.

Howard C. Tate built a reputation not just for his glads, but for his superior quality of glads. Other glads were now beginning to be produced by other growers in Henderson County. In 1948, the City Directory shows there were only two firms growing and selling wholesale galioli: Howard C. Tate and Caroline's Flower Farm (which operated in the rear of Bert Cantrell's Produce Warehouse on King Street). In a matter of a few years, the LeFevre family would move here and go into the business. By 1952, the number had grown to twelve growers, shipping 250 Railway Express carloads of gladioli from here in one summer. John Waddell (the father of Dan Waddell of Reaben Oil Company), who was the manager of

Railway Express, reported that express charges alone for the shipment of these glads totaled $104,802.

The early to mid-'50s was a time that folks could drive out through the Mills River Valley and see a blooming spectacle that would have equaled tulip growth in Holland. Up to 350 acres of glads were farmed each year by the twelve growers. A phenomena began to emerge and be noticed by many of the more entrepreneurial glad growers. There were more homeowners who wanted to grow their own glads than there were florists wanting to buy the blooming flowers. So these growers began to grow glads only to produce bulbs to sell to homeowners and garden shops. They wanted any revenue they could gain from the sale of the flowers, but income from the sale of flowers was secondary to the sale of bulbs and the quality of the flowers declined. These promotional growers, to spur sales, began to ship on consignment. The market became even more glutted and the price of glads dropped even further. Mr. Tate, to survive, kept trying to find ways to lower his costs. He was, as president of the Hendersonville Gladiolus Growers Association, able to wring concessions from Railway Express, which lowered the cost of shipping to match the lowest shipping charge anywhere in America. But the glutted market began taking its toll. In 1956 in a speech to the Rotary Club, Gary Harthcock said there was only nine growers.

But the mad hunger for the big bucks in selling bulbs became prevalent all over the country and some high-flying growers in other states became totally dishonest in their quest for the fast buck. Here at WHKP we received an order from an advertising agency in Los Angeles for a gladioli bulb firm in Oregon. The copy advertised 100 glad bulbs for something like $6.95. In those years, local stations rarely received orders for campaigns from agencies. If you did get an order, it was a plum prize because even with agency discounts, the rate was higher and it was fresh money coming into the market. We didn't bother to check the reputation of this agency and ran the spots. (Plus, we didn't even reason on the preposterous offer this was: 100 bulbs for $6.95.) About a week later, the industry's trade magazine, *Broadcasting*, ran a feature story exposing the agency as a fraud and the glad growers as con artists. We tried everything we knew to catch and corral all the orders that had been mailed from this area. Someone, someday may want to write a book on how difficult it is to get the post office to stop delivery of mail once it is posted.

Something the average person doesn't know is that no newspaper or periodical can be held responsible for the truth of any advertisement it runs. I discovered this when I answered a scam ad in the *National Observer* newspaper. They didn't deny the ad was false; they merely relied on the defense that it was not their responsibility to check the veracity of any advertisement before it was printed. The same, of course, would apply to radio advertising. But to satisfy our friends and listeners who had been "took," we saturated the air with announcements that "if you were a victim of this scam advertising and had ordered the 100 glad bulbs for $6.95 merely bring to us a copy of your check or postal receipt and we would refund every penny out of our own pockets." This little experience cost us dearly, but we did retain our integrity.

Farming and the Africa Corps

Today the apple industry is the dominant crop in local agriculture. In the early 1940s, the major growers were truck farmers: beans, potatoes, squash. Truck crop harvesting is even more labor intensive than the harvest of apples. At a meeting in April 1943, farm agent G.D. White was told that if the big growers could be assured of adequate labor for harvest, instead of planting 3,500 acres in truck crops (as they had the year before in 1942), the would plant not just 10,000 acres but 12,000 acres.

This was in 1943 and World War II was demanding ever increasing food production. Even the average civilian was urged to plant victory gardens; but with the country drained of enormous numbers of young men in the service (and men and women who had taken defense jobs away from this area), the labor for harvest was critical. In 1942, with only 3,500 acres in truck crops, the shortage of harvest labor brought the importation of 600 workers who were housed in a labor camp at what was then called "the fairgrounds" (near where East High is now). That was the first year migrant labor was imported into Henderson County. The big growers were assured by Harry B. Caldwell (master of the State Grange and director of the N.C. Farm Labor Commission) that there would be an adequate supply of labor if they'd plant the crops. There was talk of bringing in 1,800 workers to the labor camp at the fairgrounds and also talk of another labor camp to be built in the Mills River area. The growers moved ahead with their enormous plantings.

By the time the beans were ready to pick in mid-June of 1943, there were not 1,800 farm workers nor were there even 600 (the same number they'd had in 1942). There was a total of 70 workers at the labor camp. County agent G.D. White said if drastic action was not taken immediately, between 5,000 and 10,000 bushels of beans would rot on the vines. Mayor Al Edwards declared a state of emergency and Police Chief Clarence Edney and Sheriff Bill Dalton announced that any vagrant not working would be arrested and would stay in jail until he did work. Merchants voted to close their stores at noon on Tuesdays and Wednesdays so that everyone working in the retail field (as well as would-be shoppers) could go and pick beans. Local theaters though continuing to show matinees, asked that able-bodied citizens not go to the movies, but head to the bean fields.

The big growers sent trucks to Florida in hope of recruiting farm labor. Only fifty workers were rounded up to pick beans on Sunday, June 27, 1943. Boy Scouts circularized the town asking for everyone's help in saving the crops. By the 3rd of July, there were 200 workers at the fairgrounds and Carl Buchanan of the local employment office said they'd have another 200 workers within the week. It was reported that 350 Bahamians were on their way, and the growers asked the workers to pick beans on Sunday.

W.H. Stallworth, county agent in Spartanburg County, said that he would start trying to recruit surplus labor in that area that had been idled by the failure of the S.C. peach crop. He said in the past, folks from Henderson County had come down and helped pick peaches and felt there were lots of farm folks in South Carolina who would now respond by helping to save the truck crops here. But a major hitch developed, seventy-five percent of the labor in South Carolina was white and the migrant labor camp had facilities only for blacks. In 1943, they could not be co-mingled. By July 19, 1943, 297 Bahamian blacks arrived and the total number of migrants now reached 725 at the labor camp at the fairgrounds. Also, 251 of famed German General Erwin Rommel's Africa Corps (now prisoners of war) had been shipped into the county to aid in the harvest.

Nazi Germany's Reich Marshall Hermann Goering joked on many occasions: "If you have one German, you have a fine man. But if you have two Germans, they form a Bund. . .and if you have three Germans, they start a war." Goering also said, "If you have one Englishman, you have an idiot; two Englishmen immediately form a club; and three Englishmen create an Empire." He laughed and said, "Now, one Italian is always a tenor; two Italians make a duet; with three Italians you have total retreat."

Mussolini pulled one of the greatest blunders of World War II. Without consulting Hitler, Il Duce ordered his Italian military forces to invade Ethiopia in North Africa , a tiny country that was so backward, their army fought only with sticks and stones. And yet, in short order their leader, Emperor Haile Selassi and the Ethiopians had the Italians in full retreat and Hitler, though engaged in a massive war effort in Russia had to transfer vital troops to North Africa to save the Italians. The Allied Forces chose to make North Africa the first arena where the British, Americans, and French would fight side by side against the Nazi forces, led by Field Marshall Erwin Rommel. For sheer panache, the Allies only had one general who could stand equal with Rommel and that was General George S. Patton.

Rommel reversed the course of war in North Africa and on one day (Feb. 25, 1943) had inflicted 65,000 casualties on green, inexperienced American soldiers in the Kasserine Pass area. But by March 6, General George S. Patton took command of the II Corps, and in one battle, Patton destroyed fifty of Rommel's tanks. At Rommel's own request, he was removed from command and returned to Germany for R&R. Command was given to General Jurgin Von Arnin. It didn't take Patton long. In two months, on May 12, General Von Arnim surrendered, along with 238,243 German troops.

The Geneva Conference established rules for the treatment of prisoners of war. One of the most important is that every prisoner must be removed from risks of battle as quickly as possible. So as thousands of American troops aboard ships steamed from the U.S. to Europe during the war, after the ships had been unloaded, they were immediately filled with prisoners of war in North Africa to be taken to camps in the United States. Let me repeat: They were 238,243 soldiers captured from Rommel's Africa Corps alone. Most of them were sent to giant compounds in Southern states, such as Alabama, where temporary structures needing no heat would be used for housing.

Then the U.S. government developed a plan where small contingents of German POWs could be sent to meet specific smaller-area needs. After these needs had been met, they then could be returned to the larger holding centers for continued incarceration. And so on July 1, 1943, that contingent of 251 Germans (under the watchful eyes of a military police detachment headed by Capt. W.C. Boyce) arrived and set up camp out on N.C. 191 toward Mills River. Of the 251, one was a German officer who maintained military command even though a POW. There are very few living today who remember the POW camp. Bob Freeman remembered that he drove past it every morning. He thought it had a fence around it, but had no recollection of the kind of fence. He didn't remember any sign nor did he recall whether or not there were even temporary buildings. One old timer told me he used to go out there and hire one of them once in a while; but his memory was faulty because in order to have MPs with the POWs, you had to hire at least ten at a time. You couldn't hire one or two.

One morning in May 1996, after I had sat in with Al Hope on the Morning Show, I was seeking commiseration from some of the staff over my frustration in not being able to locate people who had any contact with the German POWs. Suddenly Mary Ashe, a career employee of WHKP spoke up and said, "I remember some of them coming to our house, wanting a drink of water." Mary (before her marriage to Roy Ashe) was a Barnett and had grown up in the Boyleston section. She said once in a while you could see the Germans working in the fields of adjacent farms. She said on one hot day, several of the POWs came to their house and it was obvious by their demeanor they meant no harm. She said that as they spoke words in German, they would use sign language and it suddenly dawned on her they were thirsty and were asking for a drink of "wasser, wasser." (That's the German word for water.) She said her mother brought some glasses out and drew a bucket of water from the well and they all drank very heartily from the cold well water. Mary said she noticed one in particular because he had such blond hair and blue eyes. I interjected "the perfect Aryan."

As these German POWs headed back to the fields, one of them came over and took a gold ring from his finger and gave it to Mary. It looked like a wedding ring, she said. It could have been that he'd gotten a "Dear John" letter from his wife back in Germany but it could have also been a "pinkie" type ring. She said the ring had some sort of etching she couldn't read. When she showed it to her mother, Mrs. Barnett said, "You can't wear that! It was owned by a Nazi!" But Mary says, as a little girl, she'd occasionally sneak and wear it. She thinks the ring is still somewhere in the Barnett house and I have a feeling that refreshing Mary's memory about the events of 1943 might just be the catalyst for her doing a thorough search now for that little ring, given to Mary Ashe for a drink of water.

The German POWs (who did not speak English) had the same difficulties as we Americans who tried to converse with Germans after the war in Germany, using sign language. There are so many sound-alike or look-alike words in German, that with a bit of sign language, you could converse better than you expected. As examples: I was 18 years old—that was "achtzehn." If you were cold, it was "kalt." Hot was "heiss." Good was easy: "Gut!" If you saw any of those war movies, the Germans were always yelling "schnell," which meant fast, "macht schnell" was mighty fast. If you were called a pig,

As a girl, WHKP employee Mary Barnette Ashe was given a ring (worn on pinkie) by a German POW in the Afrika Corps after she gave the men some water.

you were a "schwein." You also learned the idiomatic expressions such as "Wie Geht's?" (How are you?) The biggest problem in trying to carry on a conversation with any German is their guttural accent, which we Americans don't make just as we do not duplicate the French nasal sound. Also the Germans have a penchant for taking a whole group of little words and putting them all together to make one big word such as, "the little pub in the Wurzburger Hof in Kitzingen." I finally wrote the name of the place down and then, using a German dictionary, discovered that the bar was Goat's Head Bar, "Little Bar of the Head of a Goat."

The commanding officer of the MP detachment was Capt. W.C. Boyce, assisted by Lt. John Partridge.

I talked at length with Patsy Pryor. Mrs. Pryor was a niece of Miss Jennie Bowen, and she remembers vividly that the POW camp was located on the south side of the Bowen Farm where Coach Rob Brown and his family lived. This would have it at the bottom of the hill at Middleton Place. There is no lease on record between the Bowen family and the U.S. government. Apparently, this was such a short-term arrangement, the family did not see any necessity in recording the lease. The users of the POW labor apparently paid minimum wages to the MPs for the government and of that, $1,20 per day went to the prisoner. The rest was used to defray the cost of food and lodging of the prisoners.

In a speech to Kiwanis, Captain Boyce said most of the prisoners were still convinced that Germany would win the war, and their ambition was to visit New York and Chicago to see how badly the American metropolitan areas had been bombed. Users of the labor were high in their praise of the German workers. Mr. H.E. Hyder said it had been the best labor he'd had. Same report from Mr. H.H. Young in Mills River. John Holloman (who was county agent in 1944) said all arrangements for the labor had to go through his office. T. D. Hunter used some for clearing a pasture; Gay Lyda and Mrs. Dawson for ditching banks; the Hooper brothers for harvesting potatoes; Jim Duff and Vance Gilbert for work in bean fields. Very few remember it today, but from July to October in 1943 and 1944, Erwin Rommel's Africa Corps did work in the fields of Henderson County, housed in tents at the Bowen Farm on Mills River Road.

Farming and Dwight Bennett

In the last year of World War II, the truck farming business in Henderson County had grown to enormous proportions. In July of 1944 alone, J. Fenimore Cooper (the freight agent for Southern Railroad) reported that ninety-four freight carloads of fruits and vegetables had been shipped from Hendersonville that month alone. If it had not been for wet weather interfering with the harvest on the last two days of that month, more than one hundred freight cars of truck crops would have left Hendersonville. Mr. Cooper was quick to emphasize that this did not include any produce transported from here by refrigerated trucks. Of even greater interest in the changing face of local agriculture in 1944, out of ninety-four carloads of fruits and vegetables, only one car contained apples. There were forty-six freight carloads of beans, thirty-five freight cars of cabbage and twelve cars of cucumbers. Back then some of our big growers were Cantrell Produce Company, Cornelius & Johnson, and J.R. Thomas Produce. Smaller operators included Dokhorn at 1302 North Main out near Ray Avenue, and Butler & Seyler on 6th Avenue East.

I remember in the golden years of truck farming in Henderson County, Bert Cantrell used to plant 2,000 acres of potatoes. In fact, when the fairgrounds property was acquired for the construction of East Henderson High School, Bert was able to acquire all the migrant labor buildings that had been in use of the fairgrounds and moved them out on Clear Creek Road in order to have facilities to house workers in the future. In those days, there were very few Mexicans involved in the harvesting of crops. Most of the labor was provided by black migrant crews who were transported and supervised directly by a crew chief. After he had taken his cut, the migrant laborers were paid. The crews would begin work in the Florida fields and as warm weather moved north, so would the migrants. In those years, the migrants were virtually indentured servants to the crew chiefs or labor bosses. The grower dealt only with the crew chief or boss man, and most of the laborers had no place to go but to the labor camps as they worked their way north.

In later years, as the huge growers of truck crops found access blocked to the big canneries in Tennessee by various forms of Tennessee State embargoes (sponsored by Tennessee farmers and politicians), our growers, after working the fresh market, had no large processor or canner who could take the overflow and gradually our big growers simply stopped planting. There was still good harvests of truck crops locally, particularly with the Johnson farms; but not on the scale it could boast of in the late '40s and early '50s. Today, the big money crop is apples.

Harvest labor has evolved from the huge former migrant camps to individual quarters local apple growers build for their own workers. While the apple crop certainly is perishable, the harvest of apples does not have the urgency of a field full of beans ready to pick. The grower does have some breathing room from the time the apples begin to ripen to the time they become too ripe to pack and ship. It is true that many of the Mexicans who come to the area to assist in the apple harvest elect to remain here and find other employment. This has led to a substantial increase in the Mexican population in Henderson County in the past two decades.

In Bert Cantrell's twilight years, he (like many of us) was never able to reset his biological clock. So I had the good fortune of sharing his company (and that of "Runt" Robertson and other growers) while having breakfast at Dan's Restaurant in the '60s and early '70s. Bert used to say that a fellow ought not to be in farming unless he's a gambler at heart. You have to be able to survive when you see a crop go out the window with one big thunderstorm or you may experience the loss of a thousand acres of potatoes because there was not enough rain. Bert used to say if a grower can "make it" three years in a row, he can retire. If his crop fails three years in a row, he's busted, bankrupt, he can't come back again. He said ninety-nine percent of all farmers usually win some and lose some, and don't have the guts to quit and get out.

Rummaging through personal notes and bits of memorabilia associated with agriculture, I ran across a eulogy I'd written for my friend D. W. Bennett. I'd received a call from Dwight and Pat's son, Ray, telling me of Dwight's death. Knowing the long years of great friendship, of heckling and general horseplay between Dwight and I, Ray asked if I'd do the eulogy for Dwight. I told him that I would consider it a personal honor to write the eulogy and that I would be there to hear it. "But," I said, "Ray, old men should never be asked to say anything emotional for the simple reason that old men tend to lose composure with the passing years." I have been super impressed with Steve Scoggins (Dwight's pastor) and it was my hope that Steve would agree to deliver the eulogy at the memorial service (which he did, beautifully).

County Agent Dwight Bennett (left) with another soil lover, poet Carl Sandburg of Flat Rock.

As I was glancing over this material to write this chapter, an error suddenly shouted from the page. The article said Dwight had served as county agent twenty-four years after taking the job in 1945. The official record shows that D.W. Bennett officially succeeded John S. Holloman on Aug. 1, 1944 (not 1945). When Bennett retired in 1969, he had served continuously twenty-five years not twenty-four.

When Dwight graduated at North Carolina State, he knew that his life's work would be to serve as county agent. The state dreamed up all this "extension service" and "chairman of extension" stuff later. Dwight was first hired here as assistant county farm agent under G.D. White. He became county farm agent on Aug. 1, 1944, succeeding John Holloman (who had succeeded White but in less than a year had taken the job as farm manager of Dave Kemp's Shoals Creek Farm). In the interim, Dwight had served two years as county agent over in Graham County in the far remote mountains of Western Carolina where the only town is Robbinsville and where most of the land is either Joyce Kilmer National Forest or land covered by the waters of Fontana Lake.

One can only imagine how excited both Dwight and Pat were to be able to return to this growth county and the City of Hendersonville.

When Dwight first came here as assistant county agent, growers only hoped they'd harvest 200,000 bushels of apples annually. When Dwight retired, the county expected a minimal harvest of six million bushels.

He was involved in a leadership role in every organization that involved farming, from apples to eggs, from the dairy industry to trellis tomatoes. For the endless hours he so freely gave to farming and to farmers, Dwight did receive just praise and honor. The very greatest (to him) was presented to him just months before he died when he was named to the Western North Carolina Agriculture Hall of Fame. Occasionally I would be invited back to the Kiwanis Club where Dwight's perfect attendance record was awesome. If I had a part on the program, I'd always look for Dwight because I knew that we would have a ball heckling each other.

Dwight lived to be eighty-seven. I have a long way to go to get to that point, but I already recognize the unpleasant side of passing years, unable to remember names like I used to, daydreaming, and absent-mindedness. Just a month or so before he died, Dwight brought a sack of apples to me at the radio station. We chatted, shared memories, and enjoyed each other's company. Then Dwight got up, picked up the sack of apples he'd brought, and left. I glanced at my watch. In less than three minutes, he walked sheepishly back into the office and said, "Don't that beat all. I brought you these apples, and then took 'em with me." We laughed uproariously.

In that his wife and lifelong helpmate, Pat, spent her life in public education, it was only natural that Dwight would give more free time in retirement by offering himself to the County School Board, on which he served with distinction for sixteen years. His perfect attendance record at the Kiwanis Club was without blemish. In the Hendersonville First Baptist Church, he was *NOT* just a trustee, a deacon, a Sunday School teacher, and even superintendent of the Sunday School Department. The church gave him a *LIFE* Deacon Award.

William Thackery once wrote, "The world is a looking glass—and gives back to every man the reflections in his own face." The face of this county, as it has blossomed and become ever so much more beautiful since Dwight Bennett came here in 1936 this will be our looking glass, and in it we'll see Dwight's image.

Farming & the Kiwanis Club

Kiwanis Club was only one of the many non-farm organizations in which Dwight Bennett was active. But many other farm leaders were also members and served as president of the Kiwanis Club: J. Loren Brown, Frank FitzSimons, Harley Blackwell, Hardy Caldwell, and Dwight's son, Ray.

While I came in contact with Truman Westmoreland in his work with the Farmer's Home Administration here, I really got to know Truman and his attractive wife, "Chic," through our association in the Kiwanis Club. Back in the '50s (maybe still so), if you were a member of the Kiwanis Board of Directors, once a year you were host to the other members of the board for a meeting at your house, where you'd serve everyone dinner. Some wives objected to these added chores and once in a while, a member would simply take the board to a local restaurant and pick up the tab. "Chic" Westmoreland never objected, though, because her old man Truman billed himself as the "master of the country ham, red eye gravy, and grits." As such, he reigned over the kitchen on Kiwanis night.

I never did really ask Truman but I always thought he came from the great Westmoreland family over around Marion. He used to tell some pretty tall tales about herding fifty head of cattle eighty miles through Asheville to McDowell County. I later learned he was born in Haywood

County. Truman's job was more than just lending money to help farmers get going or to modernize and improve. He also had the responsibility to advise farmers in business practices to help them make money. Truman first started working for the FmHA back in the '30s. (That little "m" is to clarify the distinction that it's Farmer's Home Administration.) In the beginning, the agency made only one kind of loan. When Truman retired, they were making twenty-three different kinds of loans.

When Westmoreland first came to Hendersonville, the FmHA had a policy (this was in 1946) of having a cap (a maximum of $5,000) that could be loaned on a farm, regardless of size. At the time Truman retired in 1975, you might find one acre of land priced at $5,000. Today it would more likely be twice that amount.

Truman recalled that when he first started, you could help a fellow acquire ten to fifteen cows and operate a profitable dairy farm. The number now required is more like 100 to 150 cows and the hazards of failing are even greater than back in the '40s. Farming is now high tech, capital-demanding agribusiness. A bad freeze, a hailstorm, an infestation of bugs or fungus, or the influx of one of the dread diseases can literally wipe out the average family farm.

There is another local man who has spent his life working in research to give support to family farms, and that is Harley Blackwell, who recently retired as director of the North Carolina Agricultural Experiment Station near the Asheville Airport. I grew up knowing the Blackwell family. There were the parents, Blanch and Otho Blackwell, and one of their sons, Kenneth, worked for us here at WHKP for a number of years. The last I heard, Kenneth was in broadcasting in the Richmond area. There were sisters, Blanch M. Blackwell, Pearl B. Laughter, Nora, who married Paul Green, and Laura, who became a highly skilled registered nurse. Then there was Harley. He started in 1963 and spent most of the years of his life up to retirement as superintendent at the Experiment Station.

I'm glad I didn't have to interview one of Harley's mentors when he came to the Experiment Station to announce a comprehensive study of apple diseases. The man who announced this program was the assistant head of the State Agricultural Experiment Stations, and his name was Lawrence Apple. I had, in earlier days of my career, interviewed a State College professor of horticulture at the Western Carolina Fair, and when he told me his name was George Turnipseed, I laughed and said, "You're putting me on, what's your real name?" Being wet behind the ears, I didn't know there was a large prominent family of Turnipseeds in Eastern North Carolina.

Harley (being another boy locally born and bred) fit the typical mold. He couldn't say no to anything that bettered the area. He took an active role in civic affairs of all kinds. Among many distinctive positions Harley held was president of the North Carolina Society of Farm Manager and Rural Appraisers.

I have a feeling our agricultural community would still be way back down the road had it not been for people like Truman Westmoreland and Harley Blackwell. And I wouldn't dare mention the name Westmoreland without including Chicora, who spent her entire life teaching our kids in the city school system. "Chic" practiced back then what is frequently absent in today's teaching profession. She was so concerned about every child that she didn't mind giving the parents a few pointers on what help the child needed.

Leaders of the community

When Truman Westmoreland came to Hendersonville and began making loans for FmHA, there were only two other sources of money in the area: the State Trust Company and First Federal Savings & Loan Association. Bruce Drysdale was president of the "Building & Loan" and D.H. Lee and son managed and operated it. D.H. Lee was listed as executive vice president and treasurer; his son Robert was secretary and assistant treasurer. The Lees also operated D.H. Lee & Son Insurance, in the same building as First Federal.

The State Trust Company (headed by William B. Hodges) had acquired the old Citizens National Bank building on the northeast corner of 4th and Main, then also acquired the First National Bank building across the street. From 1941 to the late '50s, the State Trust was headquartered on the east side of Main and across the street, it operated the Westside Branch of the State Trust Company. While much has been written about Bill Hodges' leadership in the community and his brilliance in the field of finance, let me tell you of one thing Bill did which illustrates the rather casual way banks operated back then. When war clouds gathered, Bill Hodges purchased cases of golf balls, stored them in the basement and carried them on the books as collateral, quite an asset when (during World War II) State Trust had the only golf balls in town.

Bill Hodges ran a good bank, and he surrounded himself with good people. Bill found the time to become engaged in politics and represented our local Senatorial District on several occasions. When Bill Hodges was involved in promoting the annual Horse Show, he knew everybody's net worth and would decide for them how much they should give as their support for this worthwhile community event. In those early years, Hodges was surrounded by such competent and popular bankers as F. V. "Foffy" Hunter (who became Chairman of the Board when Bill died). There was also Roy Williams, who was always the top vote-getter in elections for City

Interior of the State Trust Company, located in the old First Citizens Bank on the corner of 4th and Main.

Council. Donald Jones served as cashier (Bill's right-hand man); and Francis Drake established the first auto loan department in local banking.

For some 25 years Hodges ran the State Trust Company without competition; but when rumors circulated that outside banks were casting an eye toward Hendersonville, Hodges quickly decided to build branches in local neighborhoods around the county. When he decided to open a branch on the southside, he shrewdly picked Myrtle Greenwood (one of the original employees) to manage the new branch. He also named her assistant cashier. She became, in 1959, the first woman to serve as an officer of a bank in Hendersonville.

Bill Hodges (being an old-line banker) never liked to tie up too much money in "bricks and mortar", so he inveigled Fred Reid into designing a prototype of a branch bank building that could be built quickly and at the least cost. While Fred (a theater manager) was not an architect, he had worked with Bill helping to manage and promote horse shows, fairs and other community events. Fred came up with a simple design using concrete blocks, perma-stone and wood. The only expensive item in each building was the vault. In 1997, the Southside Branch of First Union National Bank is one of the few remaining structures that Fred Reid designed.

The State Trust, to fend off competition, opened branches at Southside, on 7th Avenue East, Fletcher and Etowah. Hodges then made another bold move; he recruited Frank L. FitzSimons Sr. as a loan officer and public relations specialist. He had won the election to be Register of Deeds by such a wide margin, no one would even run against him. After Mr. FitzSimons had resigned as Register of Deeds and joined the State Trust, it was decided that he would do a daily radio program dealing with the history of this area and its people. It quickly became the most popular broadcast on WHKP, and continued for twenty-five years. From these more than 5,000 programs came the publication of "From the Banks of the Oklawaha"—three volumes, which Fitz called his trilogy. It is still the most popular set of local books ever published here.

Hodges fell victim to ill health in 1958 and felt the time had come to arrange the future. He had developed a longstanding friendship with Edwin Duncan Sr. at the Northwestern Bank in North Wilkesboro. The two agreed to a friendly merger (although the succeeding operation was more like an association than a consolidation). Hodges continued as executive in charge, and Hendersonville's old State Trust Company (though now known as Northwestern Bank) operated almost autonomously until shortly before Northwestern's merger with First Union. Bill Hodges—a man of great local power, but always insisted that his desk be situated next to the front door of the bank.

When We Still had Time for Humor

Fred Reid proved that you could be a dynamic community leader and still have a great sense of humor. It was always a pleasure for me to make a sales call on Fred at the Carolina Theatre. He was in that cadre in the '40s and '50s who laid the foundation to build Hendersonville into the community we love today. Fred Reid came to Hendersonville from the Spartanburg area in 1938 and moved into the Willoughby Kinsey Chain of Theatres. He became active in the Lions Club, was director of the Western Carolina Fair Association, and a director and business manager for the Hendersonville Horse Show. He served as president of the Apple Festival.

As we indicated, when people in authority wanted favors done and Fred could not fit it into his schedule, he just added hours onto his day, such as when Bill Hodges wanting branch banks and Fred found time to design the prototype. Or, if B.P. Justice (who was a constable and owned a private patrol service), promoted a stock car race at the old fairgrounds, he'd arrange with Fred to handle it. Fred would schedule all the advertising, arrange for staff to handle the race, sell the tickets, and on Monday morning, would settle up with Pierce and tell him how much, if any, money he'd made. Fred got a simple fee for this.

It was a real shocker to the whole community that September day in 1956 when word passed quickly in the business community. "Fred Reid has had a heart attack." In such circumstances, you only get sketchy details,

The late Fred Reid, manager of Carolina Theatre and much more.

and everyone hopes the reality is nowhere as serious as the rumor being circulated. Fred was Chamber of Commerce president when the massive heart attack hit him. He had written a letter to me a few months before that, dated March 11, 1956, in which he said, and I quote:

"Dear Kermit,

I intended to write you and congratulate you when the VFW honored you by unanimously electing you as "Man of the Year"; but I found out that the Jaycees were going to do the same. In line with our new economy drive at the Chamber this year, only one letter to a customer."

That was typical Fred Reid humor. This letter is now forty years old, and I cherish it as if it had come in the morning mail.

At the annual dinner meeting of the Chamber of Commerce, president W. W. "Bill" Martin presented an impressive eulogy to Fred Reid. And just a few weeks later, the Hedrick Rhodes Post of the VFW bestowed posthumously on Fred Reid the "Man of the Year" Award, the very same award he had so kindly complimented me on receiving. On Feb. 21, 1957, it was announced that the award would be made posthumously in Fred Reid's honor and would be given to his widow, Ethelyn, and his son, William, on April 4.

In just the period from 1946 to his death in 1956, Fred had already "made it through the chairs," so to speak. He had headed up the Chamber, the Merchants, the Fair, the Horse Show, the Apple Festival, the United Fund, the Community Concert Association, and still had time to run two theaters and do odd freelance jobs, like designing bank buildings for his old friend, Bill Hodges.

Parallel Careers

It is indeed rare when two young men from different parts of the world end up in the same town, spend a great part of their life as total competitors and then find themselves as compatriots (and a part of the same company) before they retire. Such is the experience of Dan Gibson and Bill McGee.

Up through the '40s, the old State Trust Company had a total monopoly on all banking in the county and when the First National Bank of Asheville persuaded Jonathan Woody of Waynesville to merge his First National into their bank, they then set their sights on Henderson County.

Bill Hodges at State Trust tried every gimmick to block their move into Hendersonville but when H.B. "Mike" Kelly resigned his position at First Federal and joined the First National Bank, it sort of marked the end of Bill's fight to stay competition free. Mike Kelly was not only a most honorable man but a gentleman by carriage. When he opened the First National Bank office at the corner of Main and Third, there was no doubt that Asheville's First National had established a successful bridgehead in Henderson County.

With braggin' rights to the three most important counties in Western Carolina, First National of Asheville suddenly became a number one acquisition priority for the Union National Bank in Charlotte. And thus began merger mania, which would see the establishment of First Union National Bank, merged with Union Bank of Charlotte and First National Bank of Asheville, and the arrival of Dan Gibson here in 1953 to succeed Mike Kelly. The merger of State Trust and Northwestern Bank would bring the retirement of Bill Hodges, and the arrival of Bill McGee, who would ultimately succeed F.V. "Foffy" Hunter.

Though competitors (with offices just a block from one other), Dan Gibson and Bill McGee worked together in the community. They were both active in the Chamber of Commerce, the United Way, civic clubs, the Country Club, and even in the Grace Lutheran Church.

McGee took an active role in the Merchants' Association, the Flat Rock Playhouse, and was treasurer of the Second Wind Hall of Fame. He also served as president of the Western N.C. Chapter of the North Carolina Bankers Association. McGee was on the Advisory Board of the Daniel Boone Council of the Boy Scouts, active in the Executives Club, Henderson County Concert Association, the Red Cross and was on the Advisory Board of Brevard College. McGee married Christine Sigmon (a big name in Burke, Catawba, and foothills counties).

Dan Gibson married "Happy" Lentz, an employee of the bank and whose family had been prominent in the wholesale grocery business. Dan was co-founder of Carolina Village, serving as president for nine years, and currently is serving as treasurer. Dan was active as a trustee and treasurer at Flat Rock Playhouse, the Apple Festival, and many other civic and community activities.

The two men were friends and associates but competitors for some 30 years, when, with no choice of their own, they became co-workers of the same bank with the merger of Northwestern and First Union. When that merger occurred, Henderson County, by far, experienced the greatest negative impact of any county in the state. Northwestern and First Union banks were number one and two in the market. The Federal Trade Commission simply ruled that the joint banks bordered on being monopolistic and as a condition to the merger ordered a divestiture of a percentage of the assets which resulted in the sale of several branches of both banks. The loyal customers of each bank simply could not understand why

*William E. McGee (left photo) and Dan Gibson
(above) worked together after bank merger.*

overnight their account had been transferred to another bank and they were no longer doing business with the old bank they'd traded with most of their lives.

This became the single biggest headache of both Bill McGee and Dan Gibson for the next several years.

They're both retired now (as is their successor, H.L. "Jack" Ruth), but all three continue to maintain active presences in the community.

Bruce Drysdale - A Man to Emulate

Very little has been written of the success in completing the Skyland Hotel at the very time that virtually all hope was gone for the famous skyscraper "Fleetwood" on Echo Mountain. Bruce Drysdale should be given the lion's share of credit for having the faith and the stamina to see the Skyland successfully completed. Originally, both the Skyland in Hendersonville and the Selwyn Hotel in Charlotte were to be built by the J.A. Jones Construction Company, and when completed, would be acquired by a hotel-operating corporation. During construction, the operating concern went belly-up, and the Jones family elected to complete both hotels and operate both of them until they could be sold to an operating company.

Bruce Drysdale was president of the Chamber of Commerce in 1929 during the negotiations with the Jones family and during construction. Drysdale and ten other men put up $10,000 to help purchase furnishings for the hotel, a stipulation made by the Jones firm. When completed in 1929, Hendersonville had its first modern fireproof hotel, and the Chamber immediately began to recruit for conventions. You can imagine the excitement when it was announced that the North Carolina Firemens' Convention would be coming here July 15-18, 1929, and that more than a thousand firemen would attend from across the state. Let me recommend strongly that you read about what took place at this convention as described by Frank FitzSimons in Vol. II of "From the Banks of the Oklawaha."

I happen to have in my possession one of the original programs handed out during that convention. On the inside cover, Otis Powers is listed as fire chief; A.D. Hill, assistant chief. Four "nozzle men" are listed, including W.H. Bangs, J.B. Raines, C.H. Edney and Carl Bly. Fifteen other men are listed as part of the Fire Department in 1929. In the 1929 official program, events included on July 18 were Reel Races on 8th Avenue, and at 2:30 fire truck races. These events had to be anti-climatic to the wild shenanigans that had been going on for three days, already involving 1,000 drunken firemen driving fire trucks wildly on the streets of the city, with sirens going full blast. Firemen would tie sheets together and repel down the walls of the hotel and then climb back up the wall and back into the windows. It was not safe to be near the hotel because of glass bottles and jars being thrown from the windows above. When the convention ended, the Chamber of Commerce adopted a resolution to drop any further recruitment of conventions. Bruce Drysdale (instead of throwing his hands up in defeat) quietly put up his own money and raised the funds necessary to repair the thousands of dollars in damages done to Hendersonville's beautiful new hotel.

Bruce Drysdale first served on the City School Board in 1925. For most of the period from 1945 to 1959, he was chairman of that board. He was president of the United Fund, and had a leadership role in the Kiwanis Club, Junior Achievement, Flat Rock Playhouse, and is the only Hendersonville man to serve both as chairman of the Savings & Loan and, at the same time, director of the Northwestern Bank in North Wilkesboro. It won't happen

Bruce Drysdale

again because today's banking laws do not permit it. Back when the Cadillac automobile was such a status symbol, I used to say that the only man in Hendersonville who can ride in a Cadillac and not make others jealous is Bruce Drysdale. He was named "Man of the Year" by the VFW in 1959.

But to show you the true greatness of Bruce Drysdale, let me (as Paul Harvey would say) tell you "the rest of the story." When Bruce Drysdale came to Hendersonville in 1918, he and George Moland formed the Moland-Drysdale Brick Corporation. Mr. Moland was almost thirty years older than Mr. Drysdale, and in 1936 at the age of seventy-seven, Mr. Moland died. Mr. Drysdale made a very generous settlement with his widow, Jean Williamson Moland, for her husband's interest. It is a matter of common knowledge that when a wife becomes a wealthy widow, charities and benevolences quickly find a path to her door. Mrs. Moland was such a caring and generous person, she could not say "no" to anyone, and within a few short years, she had given away all her money and was penniless. Mr. Drysdale had observed her experiences and quietly and with no fanfare stepped in and provided her income for a comfortable living for the rest of his life. The practice was continued by his son-in-law, Frank Todd, until Mrs. Moland died at age eighty-nine.

Long before recycling and the environment were hot topics, Frank Todd had developed an idea to convert the old clay pits used for brickmaking at Etowah into a showplace golf community. Drysdale was enthusiastic but insisted that all the land which surrounded the course (then owned by former employees) would be left with the employees, and that each of them would be advised of the company's plan so they could also benefit from the profits of the long-range investment of the company. Bruce Drysdale—a man to emulate!

Frank Todd—In His Footsteps

Growing up, one of the more popular expressions was, "I'm just a country boy." That was supposed to cause folks to accept the fact that you weren't too educated maybe not too smart. In the early days of radio, federal regulations were so intense, even tiny stations like WHKP were almost required to be represented by a Washington law firm. I used that old expression to our Washington lawyer (Lee Lovett), "Remember Lee, I'm just a country boy." He quickly responded, "Great, because I can now bill you double the normal fee. Most country boys I've met are in reality exceedingly shrewd." I never used that line again.

But Frank Todd was that sort of self-deprecating person. He was always

Frank Todd

playing down his skills, his formidable talents, and he used to always joke that the easiest way to get to the top was to marry the boss' daughter. Frank did marry Elizabeth Ann Drysdale. Most folks know her not as Elizabeth Ann, but Betty Ann.

Frank Todd was the son of John Haywood Todd and Lenora Jane Todd. After graduation from Hendersonville High School, he interrupted his college career and did a stint in the Navy during World War II. He returned home to add a degree in law at Wake Forest University and was admitted to the local bar. He shared an office with Frank Coiner in the Staton Building and began practicing law in the late '40s. For a time, they were joined by R.L. Whitmire, Jr.

Frank hardly had the time to hang out his shingle before he first started feeling the pressure from his father-in-law, Bruce Drysdale, to come into the brick business (Moland-Drysdale Corporation).

Drysdale wanted Frank particularly to develop a pension and retirement program for his employees. Once Frank joined the company, he spent all his time for the better part of two years honing and fine-tuning the pension document which was ultimately approved by the various federal agencies. Frank had drawn the plan to permit pension funds to be used to buy assets of the brick company. Frank used to joke, "One of these days, the pension plan will actually own the company." Frank and I talked on many occasions about various pension plans, and our radio staff can be thankful to Frank for instilling the desire in me to create an ESOP plan for WHKP employees. The ESOP program was later used by the employees to buy the radio station.

If I remember correctly, Frank was elected to the general board of Northwestern Bank in 1965 and I took office in 1967. Frank and I took turns doing the driving on those seventy-five or eighty mile round trips we made to North Wilkesboro for board meetings. On our very first trip, we had gone down I-40 to the Jamestown Road exit and had by-passed Morganton, cutting through Lenoir, crossing U.S. 421 to hit N.C. 18 from Lenoir to Wilkesboro. That's a tortuous twenty-six mile stretch of two-lane road which was primarily residential except for an occasional broiler house. Wilkesboro at that time was known not only for Northwestern Bank, but Lowe's, Holly Farms Poultry (now Tyson Foods), and Carolina and Gardner Mirror Companies (the two largest in the world) and yet it was accessible only by two-lane roads.

As Frank took the short cuts through Lenoir, at the very edge of town (where we hit N.C. 18), he wheeled into a convenience store, went inside and ordered two King Edward cigars then wrote a check to pay for them. "Do you always write checks for as little as $1.00?"

He answered, "No need to carry large sums of money around with you." This conservative attitude toward cash would come back to haunt us sooner than expected.

That day it was his turn to drive and he wheeled up in the fanciest Cadillac I'd ever seen. "It was a wedding anniversary gift from our kids," he volunteered. I knew no better until I was doing this article and had shared this information with their son, Frank Jr. He laughed heartily "It wasn't really an anniversary gift." He and Ralph Jones (down at Boyd's) had been arguing for months over a trade and they were fifty bucks apart. Both were so stubborn that neither would give in so the kids decided to force the issue and we put up the fifty dollars to make the trade. Now this new Cadillac (back in the 1980s) was luxurious beyond belief. The entire interior was done in deep blue velour. I settled back in the passenger's seat and said, "It make you sort of feel like you're riding in a coffin, doesn't it?"

Now we come to where his habit of cashing checks for a dollar got him in a bind. As we made the turn at Moravian Falls to get on N.C. 18 to travel the twenty-six miles back to Lenior, I glanced at the instrument panel and observed, "Frank, you're almost out of gas." Now remember, it's twenty-six miles back to Lenior and there's only one country grocery store/filling station in between. Powered now only by fumes, Frank wheeled into this country store, pulled out his credit card and said, "Fill 'er up."

The seasoned old merchant observed as to how, "We don't take no credit cards."

Unfazed, Frank reached for his trusty checkbook.

The old man then said, "And we don't take no checks, either."

Frank looked at me and said, "How much money you got?"

"Oh, maybe $2.00," knowing there was one bill and some change. "$1.75 to be exact."

Without hesitation, Frank said, "Give us $1.75 worth."

The old man dutifully filled the order, and as we started to drive away, he observed, "I don't know what this world is comin' to. You fellers driving an expensive car like that and you can't raise but $1.75 between the two of you."

I don't think it impacted Frank's habit, but I personally tried to be sure of carrying a little more money in the future.

Frank and I made those trips together for almost eighteen years. Marvelous memories especially of the fact the Lord seemed to shield us from being put on the spot during board meetings by the chairman, Edwin Duncan, Sr. Mr. Duncan had a computer mind, and he could calculate fractions against decimal points in his head. It was not uncommon for Mr. Duncan to be discussing a loan and suddenly say, "Mr. Collier, if we were to lower that rate by an eighth on this $75,000 twenty-year loan, what impact would it have on his monthly payments?"

I'll never forget Mr. Duncan saying over and over again, "Remember, a man's success is determined by his footings." I have never subscribed to that philosophy.

The Ewbanks, A Clock, and U.S. Currency

It was big news (March 11, 1927) and the talk of the town. The new downtown clock on the Citizens National Bank building. It had four faces and it chimed on the quarter hour. At a quarter past the hour, it would give the four-stroke Westminster peal. At half past the hour, the eight-stroke peal. At 45 minutes past the hour, what was called the 12-stroke reveille; and at each full hour, the 16-stroke Westminster chime, followed by the striking of the hour.

This clock was built by the O.B. McClintock Clock Company, which was sold in 1945 to the old Diebold Corporation, which promptly discontinued manufacture of all street clocks. When it was installed at the corner of the Citizens National Bank building, Mr. E. W. Ewbank was president of the bank. He said, "The clock is being installed to indicate the bank's faith in the

The famed Ewbank Clock, mounted on the corner of the First Citizens Bank building on March 11, 1927, showed bank's faith in future growth of the city.

future growth of Hendersonville into a major city of the South." You remember, I earlier told you that it was the E.W. Ewbank Estate which provided the substantial land for Jackson Park at a fraction of its value. When all the banks failed in 1930, Citizens Bank also went under.

In 1936, the bankruptcy courts ordered the sale of all assets of the failed banks to be sold at an auction. Bill Hodges (president of State Trust Company) was at that sale and bought the Citizens National Bank building (including the famous Ewbank Westminster clock) for $16,000. I don't know what Mr. Ewbank had paid for the clock in 1927, but the building alone cost $125,000 to build. The State Trust Company moved their headquarters to that building and the great old clock kept ticking and chiming along. The clock stopped running sometime between 1965 and 1968, and just hung there waiting for some bold person to consign it to the scrap heap.

But Betty Ingersoll (wife of Clyde Ingersoll), one of Troy Justus' very attractive daughters, had grown up hearing the chiming of that clock, and in 1988 launched an effort to save it. She enlisted the help of the local chapter of the National Association of Watch and Clock Collectors and the restoration was assured. Phil Gilbert, John Saby, Charles Graf, Verge Kenerson and Vic Johannsen all played a strong role in the restoration. Edison Capps and Bill Powers worked the cherry picker to gain access into the bronze cabinet. It had a copper hood at the top and bottom. Jim Crafton rebuilt the interior of the clock, which required replacing much of the rusted framework. Dick Bowen restored the four dials, and the electrical work was done by R.B. Shealy. A new control cabinet became necessary for the clock's operation and Fred Collier supplied that.

Earlier efforts to repair the clock had damaged the chime hammer system and all five chimes were now gone. The clockmakers decided that with no hope of finding replacement parts, they would develop an electronic chime and strike system which would be amplified electrically to the same levels as produced by the original chime tubes. When the work was completed in April 1989, Phil Gilbert explained that within the new control cabinet, buttons could be pushed which would reset the clock, vital to this era of Daylight Savings Time. When Betty Ingersoll began her campaign to restore the Ewbank clock on the old First Citizens Bank building, she nor anyone else realized the monumental task at hand which, with the heroic volunteer efforts, has brought again the sound of the chimes throughout the downtown area.

The Ewbank family (sired by Ernest Lucas and Virginia Amelia Ewbank) consisted of four sons and two daughters. Perhaps their son (Ernest W. "Whit" Ewbank) was most visible. He was an attorney that had practiced with Lee Whitmire. He was active in politics, having chaired the Democratic Party here for 15 years. He and his family owned, at one time, the *Hendersonville Times* and sold it to the Sargeant family, who hired John Temple Graves to be editor. But the Ewbanks had to repossess after the Sargeant effort failed. The Ewbanks then sold the paper in 1925 to the J. T. Fain family.

Ernest W. "Whit" had organized the Citizen's National Bank with his brother (Frank A.) as second vice president. In addition to gaining notoriety with the installation of the Westminster clock, Ewbank also arranged with the Federal Reserve for Citizen's Bank in Hendersonville to print U.S. currency in denominations of $10 and $20. It was quite a feat for a little town bank like Hendersonville to have U.S. currency with a local bank's name printed as the issuer. These bills are major collector's items today and bring well over a thousand dollars apiece. The Rainbow Coin Shop on Fourth Avenue has two of these bills for sale.

In 1996, I received a call from Stan Shelley at Shelley's Jewelry advising that in their auction operation they had received on consignment for sale several of the First Citizen bills bearing the signature of Ernest W. Ewbank.

Twenty-dollar bill printed by Treasury for Citizens Bank. It's still legal tender, but is much more valuable as a collectors item.

It was legitimate U.S. currency. The bank had agreed to transfer certain sound assets to the Federal Reserve in exchange for the privilege of the bank securing authority to print an equal amount of its own currency, valid and guaranteed anywhere in the United States.

"Whit" Ewbank served as Hendersonville Postmaster from 1935 'til his death in 1945. Ernest W. Ewbank and his wife, Florence, lived in the old Ewbank Estate (which is now the headquarters building of Jackson Park). There was brother Frank A., who (with his son) founded the Ewbank Insurance Agency. There was also H.H. and John and daughters Aline and Amelia. At one time, the Ewbank family owned a tremendous block of land fronting Tracey Grove Road. The residue of that property is the land which was sold at a fraction of its value to Henderson County for the establishment of Jackson Park. Frank W. Ewbank, who devoted his life in the service of the public school system and Blue Ridge College, was a son of Frank A. and a grandson of Ernest Lucas Ewbank.

Public Parks, a Product of Porter Persistence

It's hard to believe that in 1973 Henderson County had no park facilities, and no budget for recreation. The City of Hendersonville operated several small parks, but the large park in the county would come from the acquisition by the county of the remainder of the Florence and Ernest W. Ewbank Estate. This large tract of more than 100 acres (including the Ewbank home) would ultimately become Jackson Park, and that would be the catalyst for the first recreation budget of $150,000 approved by the County Commission for the fiscal year 1973-74.

Alice Porter served as chairman of the Henderson County Recreation Advisory Council, but at the December 1973 meeting of the County Commission, a new County Recreation Commission was created with five members each serving five years on a staggered basis. The County Commission authorized this new recreation commission to spend on its "own initiative" funds budgeted by the County Commission. The budget for the initial fiscal year was $150,000 of which Mrs. Porter recommended $120,000 be used to develop facilities on the Ewbank property and $30,000 be spent on a recreation director and staff.

Mrs. Porter said the development would take place in four phases. Phase One would include remodeling of the Ewbank home to serve as a community center and offices for the recreation staff. Phase Two would include as many as three or four athletic fields to provide for softball and baseball as well as concession stands.

Phase Three would include children's play area, multi-purpose activity court, shuffleboard courts, horseshoe pits and later, tennis courts. Phase Four would include nature trails, a possible fishing area, and proposed equestrian trails. The hope expressed by Mrs. Porter (the chairman of the new commission) was to retain as much of the natural surroundings as possible.

The members of the predecessor advisory committee (before it officially became the Recreation Commission) had visited facilities in a number of other counties in the state and it was felt that this new park would rival the size and quality of facilities ultimately to compare favorably with any they had visited.

The "Ernest Ewbank place" had originally consisted of a mile of frontage on Tracey Grove Road, along with the homeplace. The land along Tracey Grove Road had already been sold. The land which remained would be acquired

The Richard A. Porter family individually and collectively have made Hendersonville a better place to live. The mother, Alice Porter, led the first recreation advisory council.

by the county on a gift/purchase formula. The county only paid $100,000 for the home and surveys revealed the tract contained 100 acres.

As the county park began to develop, Commissioner Bill Prim made a motion that it be named Jackson Park in honor of Clyde Jackson, the longtime chairman of the County Commission, which had moved to include recreation as a county function and responsibility. The budget called for hiring a recreation director with a salary of $6,400 approved for the five months remaining in the 1974 fiscal year. This left slightly more than $23,000 for all other expenses to support recreation for the remainder of that first fiscal year.

The current budget (23 years later) is $1,103,000, which covers the cost of recreation director Larry Harmon's salary, along with the salaries of twelve full-time year-round employees and 360 "temporaries." This is a word used by Larry to describe any and everyone who has been paid fees for supervising games and activities, maintenance and other chores that hit their peak during the summer months. This budget not only includes operating Jackson Park, but also the county-owned park at Edneyville, the park at Dana (which was the community center), the recreation facilities at Stoney Mountain (built originally as the "County Home"), and the Westfelt Park (which was made possible with the gift of part of the famed Westfelt Estate at Fletcher by Mesa Westfelt Eschelman). There is also the recreation facility at Etowah donated by the Etowah Lions Club, and the facility proposed for the old East Flat Rock Elementary School.

The Westfelt Park was given to the county in 1993, and will be the only park that offers boating access to the French Broad River. By the way, the historic Westfelt home (which can be seen from I-26 at the Rockwell plant) is still owned by the Westfelt family. I'm told that George Gustav Westfelt's great-great granddaughter (Kay Rapier) spends part of the summer living in the cottage on the Westfelt place, known originally as the Rugby Grange.

The famed poet Sidney Lanier, on a visit to the Westfelt's a week or two before his death said,

"All my life I have searched for the father of my spirit, but never have I found him until now, when I greet him in the person of George Gustav Westfelt."

Lanier died at Lynn in Polk County on Sept. 7, 1881.

So, Alice Porter, James Mayfield, Joe Tolbert, Glenn Marlowe and Harley Blackwell persisted back in the late '60s and early '70s and ultimately there are seven county-owned parks, and a budget for recreation of $1,103,000.

Frank Lipp and Paul Jones: Two for the Birds

Someone commented to me the other day, "Kermit, it is amazing how many interesting people have lived in Hendersonville over the years." One that would certainly fit that category would be Frank Lipp, who lived here for twelve years and operated a motor court on the Greenville Highway until he sold it in 1954 and moved to Florida. Mr. Lipp had been born in Germany and in early manhood had come to this country and settled in the Toledo, Ohio area. He quickly gained fame nationally as a naturalist and ornithologist. It was the only natural thing to do to name his motor court "Bird Haven."

Not only could Frank Lipp identify every kind of bird that frequented this area, he also organized the Blue Ridge Bird Club. At one of their meetings, I noted that the beloved Lila Ripley Barnwell gave a most interesting nature lesson. Mrs. Barnwell was widely accepted as Hendersonville's Poet Laureate, and the Bird Club called her its greatest bird lover and lecturer. The report on that meeting said music for the meeting was provided by the Ralph Mott family pet, a yellow head Costa Rican parrot. Other individuals active in the Bird Club were Miss Marian Schmerber, Mrs. J.H. Maxwell, Miss Edith

Braine, Mrs. John Williams and many others. Mr. Lipp wrote regular columns for the *Times-News*. One written in 1953 talked about a huge flock of wild canaries and pine siskins stopping here on their way north. He said the air around his motor court was filled with warbling song concert as they feasted on patches of chickweed and dandelion blossoms. Mr. Lipp said all the birds were females and that the males would come along in about ten days.

When Mrs. Z.Z. Blythe (who lived near Myers Airport) reported seeing an albino robin, Mr. Lipp became very excited. He said the frequency of an albino occurring within the various bird families is about as rare as it occurs among humans.

The famous Oak Hall Hotel in Tryon was anxious to provide year-round music in their huge dining room, and contacted Mr. Lipp to request that he assist them in choosing the proper birds to add music for the diners to enjoy. Mr. Lipp created a bird orchestra consisting of deep orange singer canaries, which were crossed with the precious blackhooded South American red siskin finches. It was not exactly New Orleans' "The Court of Two Sisters" but it is said the music delighted the guests. Back during World War II, there was a cafeteria on downtown Hill Street in Los Angeles called "The Cliffs" which couldn't arrange birds for their facility but they featured an organist who whistled like canaries as he played the organ.

My ability to identify birds is limited perhaps to robins, crows, cardinals, wrens and maybe even towhees and nuthatches. Members of the Bird Club knew that solitary birds are the most gifted singers such as the hermit and wood thrush. Night singers are the mocking bird, catbird, wren, and white throat. At early morning and in the early evening, bird clubbers knew the times you'd hear the wood thrush, robins, and brown thrashers tune up with the catbirds and others. I knew that for most birds, the male is more vividly colored and I suppose that helps to perpetuate the species. The female is not nearly as visible and camouflages more easily than the male. I was not aware (until Mr. Lipp came along) that the males are always the singers and when the females do sing, the sound is more subdued.

Frank Lipp was not only a nationally known ornithologist and had articles published in many national magazines, he was very active in civic affairs including the Chamber of Commerce and some service groups active in promoting tourism. He served as director of a tourist travel club in Toledo and was widely experienced in travels to Europe.

There have been others, many others, including Paul Jones, who promoted and organized "birders" in the community. A "birder" (according to Paul Jones) is a person who loves and watches the antics, the feeding, and the general habits of all birds.

Paul came to Hendersonville, as I remember, from the National Safety Council, and immediately upon meeting him, you could understand why he was the perfect man for handling public relations for the council. He was very outgoing, very animated and a man who could sell and excite Eskimos to buy refrigerators. He loved music and played in that Joe Falvo and Frank Hawkins combo I mentioned earlier, which I always called the "Rinky Dink Band."

Paul did regular columns for the *Times-News,* and even special features when appropriate. One such feature back in 1974 reported on the annual bird count which took place here. This was not just "a" bird count. The Carolina Bird Club (which was recognizing Hendersonville's extraordinary interest in birds) held its spring meeting here and was attended by more than 100 experienced "birders" from the two Carolinas, Georgia and Alabama. A major feature was a "field trip bird count" and another count carried out by volunteers just sitting in their easy chairs on the porch or in the yard. Several hundred members of the Henderson County Bird & Nature Club comprised this second group.

Now the much more experienced group (the professional "birders" on their field trip through the woods and across the mountains) sighted 110 species of birds, while the backyarders in their easy chairs were able to sight 93 species. Each of the two groups saw birds the others didn't see, which gave each group "braggin'" rights about their methodology. The most common bird sighted was the rufus sided towhee, and I'll go along with that because my yard is full of them all winter. In order of most frequent sightings were the cardinal, blue jay, mourning dove, tufted titmouse (and I have a bundle of that variety, also), the brown thrasher, robin (this was in July, bear that in mind), the song sparrow, the little black capped chickadee, and the tenth most sighted was the white breasted nuthatch. Half of the top ten birds are also called darters, based on their roller coaster movement in flight.

Would you believe the 15th most commonly sighted bird in this area is my arch enemy, the downy woodpecker. Unlike their much larger cousins, who bore into wood for insects, the downy woodpecker hunts out houses with soft pine siding from the Northwestern states because it's easy to bore into. They are not looking for food, they're building nests in the wall of the house. In a single afternoon, a family of downys can bore several holes some three inches in diameter in a house sided with soft pine imported from Washington and Oregon. On one occasion, I even resorted to calling the North Carolina Commissioner of Agriculture (James Graham) for advice, hoping he would provide some brilliant solution to the woodpecker problem. The word sent back (attributed to Jim) was "coat your house with wood preservative about every six months." Graham said, "There is a chemical in wood preservative that makes the woodpeckers' peckers sore." I can attest that it does work. After the first coating, the downy woodpeckers moved to another house. But six months later, the chemical was apparently transitory and was no longer effective. That's when I heard about owls, mounted on lazy susans which rotate in the slightest breeze. That, and a peregrine falcon (also rigged to assure some animation) has given me blessed relief for several years.

In addition to the downy woodpecker, we do have the red-bellied woodpecker, the hairy woodpecker, the pileated peckerwood, the yellow-bellied woodpecker, and down at Fort Bragg, the red-cockaded woodpecker. It has made the endangered species list and has literally caused a great part of that giant military base to simply close down and cease operations.

I was surprised to learn that the crow was 27th on the list. The gang of crows who nest in the pines behind my house hold a war conference each day about that owl and falcon in my yard. They go through their vociferations until it reaches a mad cacophony and then leave for the day.

Thomas Wolfe was a bird watcher. When he couldn't find the appropriate word in his thesaurus, he'd create a word, such as "She had wrenny-legs." It took me quite a while (after finding no such word in the dictionary) to realize Tom Wolfe was saying she had legs like a wren. With ninety-three species, he could have a whole new vocabulary of adjectives just to describe a woman's legs—junco, flycatcher, growback or grackle.

Turkeys Can't Fly

One of the most popular episodes in the TV sitcom series "WKRP in Cincinnati" involved a promotion dreamed up by the station's sales manager (Herb Terlock) which called for the dropping of turkeys in Cincinnati from an aircraft. If you remember the episode, the news director (Les Nesman) was on the ground to describe the tremendous excitement when the turkeys were dropped from the plane. The turkeys couldn't fly! It was hilarious—and an unforgettable episode in the WKRP series.

Perhaps the writers of that chapter were around Hendersonville in 1939, or maybe knew someone who was, because the Merchants Association ran that same promotion here. It was announced in mid-November that throughout the holiday season, turkeys would be released from the top of the Skyland Hotel, to become the property of the successful captor. The first of the turkeys was released on Nov. 25, 1939, and it was said that the turkey dropped almost straight down, made a perfect landing and was captured by Grady Maxwell of Brightwater Farms—without damage to the turkey or Mr. Maxwell.

The release had been widely publicized in the *Times-News.* Press releases said that periodically a live turkey gobbler would be released from the top of a downtown building, and the slogan was adopted: "To the captor belongs the gobbler." Wiseacres in the community were quick to point out that "turkeys can't fly—the best they can do is simply spread their wings, which slows their descent." One turkey raiser called in to offer turkeys to the merchants at half price. He said he'd bred his turkeys with homing pigeons and when you turn 'em loose, they'd just fly right back home. Another of the turkeys was caught by Jane Turner Childs. It was said that old-time hunters were doing a brisk business selling homemade turkey callers. One person purchased a sack of corn and built a trail of kernels from Main Street to the parking lot behind the Skyland Hotel where it ended in a little pile of corn on top of a chopping block beside which a new axe had been placed.

In a 1939 show of women's liberation, the ladies demanded that a Ladies Day be observed. One lady complained that releasing the turkey from the top of a building automatically gave all the tall men the break. So, merchants agreed that a Ladies Only turkey release would be held on Saturday, Dec. 2, and only women would be allowed to participate.

While in the early days of the promotion, turkeys had only been released one day a week, starting Saturday, Dec. 9, and until Christmas, the re-

One of the turkeys tossed from the top of the Skyland Hotel managed to crash land in the stairwell directly behind the Barber's stores on 6th Avenue West. Jane Turner Childs was the lucky catcher.

lease of a turkey would be held every day (that is, except Sundays–the blue laws were still in effect in 1939).

While not as hybrid and broad-breasted a fowl as today's turkeys, those released back in 1939 were like all varieties of turkeys even today, direct descendants of the North American wild turkey.

As the "flying turkey" event continued on toward Christmas, it continued to gain in popularity and was the talk of the town. A rumor was circulated that *Life* magazine would send a crew here to film the "turkey fly" and arrangements were quickly made that if a major news magazine did decide to come to Hendersonville, instead of just releasing a single turkey, they'd turn loose twenty-five turkeys. Chamber officials now estimate that 3,000 people had turned out for the Flying Turkey event.

Other gimmicks were added. Certain turkeys would have a dollar bill wrapped around each leg. And Saturday, Dec. 11, was to be known as "Wings Against the Sky" which would demonstrate the fortunate difference in living in America in 1939 rather than in Europe, where pursuit planes and bombers were flying instead of turkeys. One person even quipped, "We ought to turn loose a few guineas, who would be the pursuit planes and the lumbering turkeys would be the heavy bombers." The final day of the "Flying Turkeys" was Saturday, Dec. 23, and Main Street was jam packed for the occasion. Fortunately, the only casualties in the entire promotion were the birds.

In 1955, the merchants of the city had forgotten the chaos and confusion of dropping turkeys from the top of the Skyland Hotel and were searching for a brand new idea to boost spring business.

In those years, it was traditional for the Chamber of Commerce (and later the Merchants Association) to stage cooperative trade events known as "citywide events." There were usually four, one in early springtime to get people in the mood to shop for Easter, gardening, and clean-up-fix-up projects. In addition, there was always a mid-summer event, plus a big autumn event timed for back to school, storing up for the winter and harvest time, canning, etc. And then, of course, there was the big Christmas promotion and the arrival of a community Santa Claus. I suppose most small towns in the United States followed that same pattern. These cooperative citywide events would be planned in January, and every merchant in town would agree to participate.

In 1955, the spring event was to feature free baby chicks for every customer at forty-nine participating stores. In 1955, the Holly Farms and the Purdues had not started chicken "manufacturing." Back then, chicken sold for even more money than fryers do today. All of the "cockeral" (or "he") chickens were sold at a give-away price, just to get rid of them. They kept only the females to sell to local growers, first as laying hens and then as "bakers." At that January meeting in 1955, Melvin Spofford Hatch (who bought out Houston's Feed Store and was running it as M.S. Hatch Feed Store) announced that he could get us all the day-old chicks we could use for a nickel apiece and we ought to have every store in town give every customer a free day-old chick. All right!!! The little yellow chicks would add color and they would add the sounds of spring chirping in every store.

On Friday, March 18, 1955, downtown Hendersonville was packed with baby chicks. We had devised little cardboard cartons (complete with breathing holes and handles) for folks to use when they carried the little chicks home. I thought it was one of the greatest ideas that had ever been promoted in this area.

Until the local Humane Society reacted the following week. The Merchants Association went through the appropriate apologies and hung our heads in shame; but the truth of the matter was that these day-old chicks never had it so good. Our son Kerry was only about seven years old, and his sister Katina was going on three. That day-old cockeral we took home lived in the kitchen, had its own box and special roost. It was fed the finest start feed. That chicken lived the life of Reilly. The kids played with it and petted it until (as it matured) that rooster became an unholy monster. He would flare his wings and charge anybody that moved (except for the kids). We finally had to take the rooster to the larger confines of the child bride's family farm, where it immediately took over. It was great fun to watch because, by now, this big old rooster would charge any and everybody that came near. One day Katherine's Aunt Estelle was visiting, and when she walked across the back yard, here came that rooster. That evening, Paw Rhymer provided the ingredients for a meal of chicken and dumplings (which, by the way, was passed up by the two kids who had raised that rooster from the time it was a day old).

Ed Patterson: A Pacesetter in Retailing

The baby chick the kids carried to our home on Chimney Rock Road that spring day in 1955 came from Patterson's store. Though Harry Patterson (everyone knew him as "H") had died in 1956, the Patterson family would celebrate their 50th anniversary in business in Hendersonville.

Minnie Patterson (widow of "H" and mother of Ed) chatted with me at length in a special broadcast for the event. She remembered arriving with "H" in 1906 with their one-and-a-half year old son, Ed, at the train depot. They carried their luggage up 7th Avenue and all the way down Main Street to the old Blue Ridge Inn on the corner of 3rd and Main, where they spent their first night.

Mrs. Minnie Patterson had had health problems in Kentucky and their doctor in Somerset had told them she would not live more than a year if she didn't move to a climate with good clean mountain air. He had referred them to Hendersonville's Dr. Redin Kirk. Dr. Kirk met them at the Blue Ridge Inn the next morning and had them move to the Kentucky Home (at the corner of 4th and Washington) and stay there until they could find a house. Their first cottage was on 3rd Avenue East.

"H" Patterson moved his mercantile business from Kentucky to Hendersonville and opened a store at 306 N. Main Street. While everyone remembers the stock market crash of 1929, there was also a severe recession in 1907 which wiped out the infant business of "H" Patterson. He then went to Cincinnati and learned the cleaning business. By selling some of their furniture, he was able to return to Hendersonville and open a small cleaning and pressing business on Main Street between 2nd and 3rd Avenues. This business grew rapidly and Mr. "H" then re-entered the mercantile business, opening a store on the east side of Main Street between 3rd and 4th. This business also grew and J.M. Emmet Gudger (a Buncombe County man who had defeated John Grant for Congress in 1910) agreed to build a large building for Patterson on the corner of Main and 4th Avenue (a location which later became Efird's Department Store, and then later was Jack Schulman's "Can Do-Will Do" Store).

The first Pattersons store was opened in 1906, run by "H" Patterson.

Then 1929! The stock market crashed and a year later all banks in town were closed. In the dark days of the Depression, "H" would acquire the building at 327 N. Main Street, which would later become Charlie French Jewelers. This was the first Patterson's store I remember. Suits, coats, and dresses hung on homemade racks along each wall. With barely room to move among them, there were tables throughout the store on which were piled shirts, blouses, sweaters, underwear, and even hats. Hanging from the ceiling were strings and strings of socks, stockings, and other miscellaneous merchandise. For a little kid from out in the country, it was awesome. Later, Mr. H's son (Ed) was able to acquire the building in the next block at 415 N. Main, a much better location. In the meantime, Mr. H had leased and moved to the building next to Rose Pharmacy. For a brief period of time, you had one store being operated by Mr. H. Patterson, and the bigger store operated by his son, Ed, and his wife, Doris.

In May and June of 1943, Mr. H closed out his entire inventory and announced his retirement. In his announcement, he said simply that he had been experiencing declining health and his doctor and his family advised that he should give up his role as an active merchant, although he said he would assist his son, Ed, in an advisory capacity. Ed and Doris (in their new store) had already begun to change the entire concept of fashion merchandising. They had studied the marketing techniques being used in the more exclusive boutique shops, as well as in the large stores such as Bon Marche. They also had committed to carrying only brand-name merchandise, such as London Fog, Bass Weejun, and all the top names in mens' and womens' fashions.

Ed recalled that in those early years when he and Doris would make a buying trip to New York, it would cost them $11.95 to ride the day coach on

Ed (son of H) and Doris Patterson operated four different stores at the time of their retirement.

the train; and their double room at the Edison Hotel in New York was $4 per night.

Ed and Doris were the first merchants in the area to market only feminine styles in a ladies' shop, with a totally separate mens' store. The Mens' Shop was first opened across and up the street from the ladies store at 442 N. Main. The Pattersons later were able to acquire the adjacent building at 419 N. Main, which had been occupied by the Lord's chain.

On a day in February 1960, I dropped into Patterson's Mens' Shop strictly for a public relations visit with manager Walter Drake. I knew there was little likelihood of his buying any advertising because it was too late for winter sales and too early for spring promotion. We had visited for a few minutes and Walter wandered into the back of the store, and suddenly I heard him say, "There's a fire back here." I quickly spotted the smoke, turned around, picked up the phone and dialed the police department. I knew the number because I called it every morning. In nothing flat, the fire truck was in the alley behind the store but the blaze was in a trash bin between the interior of the store and the back door, and Walter couldn't get to the door to unlock it, so the firemen had to break down the door.

Even with the speed in answering the call, by the time the fire was out, the total interior of the store and all the contents had suffered extensive smoke damage. Ed and Doris did not have any sort of fire sale or smoke damage sale. They simply disposed of the entire inventory to a salvage dealer and immediately started the cleanup so that refitting and remodeling could begin at once. In what had to be some sort of record, the Mens' Shop had a grand reopening exactly eight weeks to the day from the date of the fire. For the remodeled building, the recessed front featured glass and rubbed cypress. The interior featured walnut paneling, with white, gold, and beige coloring in the fixtures and furnishings.

It truly had the elegance of a mall-type store—before malls were even in existence. Less than two years later, the new Patterson's Ladies' Fashion Center was refurbished and reopened on Feb. 23, 1962, with departments highlighting accessories, foundation garments, and even cosmetics to totally serve the fashion-conscious woman. The new Patterson's featured the "casual nook," an "Ivy League Section," and dressier lines grouped separately. A new dropped ceiling created a warmer interior. Utilities, heating and air-conditioning, were totally concealed. The one thing the Pattersons decided not to change was the original oak flooring in the building. It was sanded and finished as new, with strip carpeting here and there to highlight the beauty of the floors.

The boundless energies of Ed and Doris Patterson can also be reflected with the opening of a store in Greenville, S.C. An opportunity for this expansion came when a developer opened a neighborhood elite shopping center off Augusta Road. Taking advantage of their long association with America's leading fashion labels, they were able to enter the Greenville market with a most impressive array of name brands. Securing as their store manager a person widely known in Greenville for her fashion expertise, the store was an immediate success.

In 1952 after the death of Mrs. Leona Allen Young, Ed and Doris acquired the fixtures of her jewelry business, leased the building adjacent to the Main store, and opened Williams Jewelers. William Cohen had joined the Patterson's operations after his marriage to their daughter, Betty Ann, and Bill was made the manager of the jewelry store.So, in 1962 (fifty-six years after the doors had opened on the first Patterson's store on Main Street), Ed and Doris Patterson and members of their family would be operating a ladies' fashion store, a mens' store and a jewelry store, all in Hendersonville, and a boutique in Greenville, S.C.

In the fifty years Ed had personally been in business in Hendersonville, he had changed the very nature of retail selling. Legitimate sales were held only twice a year. Patterson's ads were known for their elegance and white space. Ed was named "North Carolina Merchant of the Year" by the North Carolina Merchants' Association.

A Mind for Retail

The business people and community leaders of the 1950s and '60s were unique. Many of them had been yanked from their education or jobs or businesses to serve in World War II. Their vistas, their perspectives were not confined now to the small area in which they'd grown up. They'd been there. They'd done that. They had been given responsibility and authority over airplanes, tanks, and naval vessels. They had sprouted wings. In the short years of war, they had become men. They were no longer willing to stand in the shadow of their fathers. And, to those on the home front, the metamorphosis was the same. They, too, were anxious to stand and be counted when the community needed them.

When the war ended, not enough cars could be built to satisfy America—not enough roads could be constructed. Instead of green benches, the town had to have loads of new parking. It was obvious that the downtowns of America were in deep trouble. As the effort began to locate new parking and to launch the downtown revitalization program, Ed Patterson was in the forefront—along with people like John Holly, D.B. Keith, Smiley McCall, Hank Sinclair, Bob Wilson, Buddy Richardson, Bob McCormick, Bob Linder, Winfield Miller, and Sam Williams. There are a dozen or so additional names I'll get to later.

During this period, there were no malls or WalMarts. The feeling existed that if Hendersonville moved fast enough and got the jump, the downtown could be saved. There were efforts on many fronts on behalf of downtown, with the Hendersonville Merchants' Association acting as a catalyst for the multi-faceted moves to save the business district. Those tremendous efforts did succeed! But perhaps not in maintaining a status quo of the old business section that we all knew. The department stores left and have not returned in Hendersonville. The central business district now offers unique shops and specialty stores with goods that are not available in malls and mass merchandise stores. The next time you wheel into any of the parking lots on Church Street or King Street (directly behind the stores on Main) just remember it was guys like Ed Patterson and Donald B. Keith who devoted their total energies toward saving their hometown's business district.

Ed served on the Board of Directors of the Chamber of Commerce. Doris was on the board of Pardee Hospital. Ed was a major driving force behind not only the organization of the Sheltered Workshop but also the committee to raise funds to acquire and remodel the Workshop's permanent home. In those years when Bobby, Betty Ann, Larry and Alan Patterson were attending Hendersonville schools, Doris found whatever time was necessary for activity in schools' parent groups.

Then there's one other Patterson most newcomers have never heard of, Ed's brother, Dr. Joe Patterson.

Joe Patterson was about eight years younger than Ed, but that still puts Joe in his 80s. He retired ten years ago. Folks locally hardly know Joe because after he graduated from Hendersonville High School, he went to the University of North Carolina, was Phi Beta Kappa, and then graduated from Vanderbilt Medical School. In World War II, he was in the Army Medical Corp, where he was assistant chief of medical services and later consultant to the Third Army. He served as chief physician of Egleston Hospital for Children, which is a teaching hospital for Emory University in Atlanta. In the 1960s, Dr. Joe Patterson received national media attention for research work he engaged in at Grady Hospital. He also served as chief of pediatric services at Crawford W. Long Memorial Hospital in Atlanta.

When Ed Patterson's memorial service was held on May 29, 1996, his lifelong friend Ernie Frankel delivered an impressive eulogy. Ernie included in his remarks: "Ed loved his brother Joe with uncommon devotion, admiring him as a human being, trumpeting his great achievements and honors. And over all the years, there was never a tinge of envy, only pride, never a scintilla of conflict, only unreserved and absolute respect and affection for the young brother who was his idol, his hero, his friend, his confidante, his adviser, and his strong right arm."

I can certainly agree. During the year I was doing the historical series on WHKP, Ed and I had many, many long discussions reminiscing over events that had occurred in Hendersonville over the past 50 years. And, invariably he would find reason to bring up specific accomplishments of his brother Joe. "I was just a merchant; Joe had control over life and death." And he always was more concerned over Joe's health than his own. Can you imagine how proud Mr. H. and Mrs. Minnie would be of both their sons, Ed and Joe! They both left their mark!

Hendersonville and the arts

Ernie Frankel, a former Marine officer (who would later become an author, a TV producer, and a film director, arrived in Hendersonville shortly after World War II to take over his father-in-law's store, Lazarus & Company. He was lured to Hendersonville by the lovely Louise Lazarus, daughter of George and Ellen Lazarus. George was a successful clothier, having operated Lazarus & Co. for a number of years. When Ernie moved into the family, he took over management of the store and changed the name to Ernie Frankel's. While Ernie was not a big advertiser, there was much in common between the two of us, and I'd always find time for a visit to kibitz with the former Marine Corps officer, who always would argue with this old 12th Armored Division "tanker" that there was only one direction–"FORWARD!" I nicknamed him "Always Forward Frankel."

In his military years, he not only was an instructor in amphibious warfare but, from his days at the University of North Carolina, he had writing and show business in his blood. Somehow he hectored and finagled his way into producing the annual Army-Navy Show, quite an honor for an apprentice in show business.

He and Louise were very fond of the Lake Summit Playhouse and especially the producer, Robroy Farquhar. In those early years (before the playhouse had developed into a year-round operation) it was feast or famine. The money rolled in during the summer months, but the long days of winter were difficult even for survival. Ernie had made plans with Robbie to set up a purely amateur "Little Theatre" company to operate during the winter of 1949-50, which would provide at least a stipend for Robbie. Frankel had even chaired a campaign and had sold out the house with season tickets for all performances.

Suddenly, Robbie was given an offer to bring the Vagabonds to Florida for the winter on terms that Robbie couldn't turn down. Then suddenly

A scene from Ernie Frankel's comedy "Two Blind Mice," performed in 1948 at the Little Theatre. From left, Carl Williams as Ensign Jamison, Francis Drake as Senator Kruge and Kermit Edney as Tommy Thurston.

Ernie was in a position to have to deliver four plays to local "Little Theatre" patrons who had already plunked down their money for the shows. Ernie opened the season with "January Thaw" and was blessed by the talents of a number of semi-pros. There was some concern as to whether this young director (in his first year) could maintain the same superb quality throughout the season. His second show, "Two Blind Mice," gave a clear-cut answer. Ernie had coerced 22 of his friends into taking part in this production. The cast included his wife, Louise, myself, Dave Cooley, Eddie Rogers, Bill Pearce, and even Francis Drake and Ed Patterson. This cast was the largest yet used by Ernie and rehearsal time was the shortest. Eleven of the twenty-two players were making their first-ever appearances on stage.

I definitely recall the late Carol Bird, who carried a major role in the play. Carol was in reality Hendersonville's Norma Desmond (played by Gloria Swanson in "Sunset Boulevard"). Carol was incensed at the opening-night review of her performance in the *Times-News*, feeling it was insufficient for the talent she had displayed. She demanded that Ernie go to the *Times-News* and demand an apology or she would not appear the second night. Ernie chose to walk away from her without giving an answer of any sort. She kept shouting, "You come back here and you do what I say!" Ernie called for an early cast meeting and arranged for the beloved Jo Kuykendall to read the lines from Carol's part for the performance that night. The cast did a walk-through with Jo for the evening performance. Ernie gave a brief explanation to the audience that Joe would be taking the role played by Carol Bird the night before. We hit the boards with everything we had, and at the end of the show the SRO crowd gave Jo Kuykendall a standing ovation.

This was my only experience in little theater. The role of Tommy Thurston required me to be onstage constantly, except for three very brief periods. The part had no less than 487 lines, of which 188 are in the second act. The small roles handled by Francis Drake (as Senator Kruger) and Ed Patterson (as Luigi, the tailor) were high spots of the show. Hubert Harrelson, Frank Reid, Carl Williams, and Julienne Carter rounded out the huge cast. The review read, "The show is the second directed by Ernie Frankel. Only the participants know how much work and effort went into the production. He has given Hendersonville two outstanding shows, and the term amateur director applies only insofar as there is no monetary compensation for his work."

The season would set the stage for a collaboration in writing with Ernie and Robroy that would lead to a first prize award for playwriting for their "Harp for Tomorrow," seen on the playhouse stage in 1951. From time to time in the late '40s, Ernie Frankel and Robroy Farquhar worked together on this play. During the winter of 1950, he and Robbie put their heads together for a final rewrite of "Harp for Tomorrow" and Robbie scheduled it for production during the summer of 1951.

With Ernie on active duty in the Marines, the major responsibilities as producer fell on Robbie. He lined up John Farrow as the director. The all-star cast was headed by Lew Gallo, along with veteran Dodee Wick, local favorite Pat Orr, and Don Dubbins, who already had five major films to his credit, starring in them with Paul Newman, Jack Webb, Dana Andrews, Vince Edwards, Edward G. Robinson, Elke Sommers and Leo Carroll (among others). Also in the cast were Bill Vance, Robert Matheo, Dan Hogan, and the ubiquitous George Spelvin. Please remember that in 1951, the Vagabonds were still at the Lake Summit Playhouse. The production was greeted with audience enthusiasm and rave reviews from area critics. In fact, the *Greenville News* predicted "It should surprise no one if this play is eventually produced on Broadway."

The drama concerns the affairs of the Giovanni family (mother, father, two sons, and a daughter). The youngest son is a musical prodigy, and to develop his talent, he must have a piano. The mother holds out for a delay in buying the piano until the family has the money to pay for it. The father wants a piano *now*, not a *harp* later—thus the title. The basic conflict (which later spreads to the children) is between the mother and father. The mother (whose comfort comes from her religion) feels the next life will be better and

The all-star cast for "Harp for Tomorrow," the Farquar/Frankel play that was named Most Outstanding New Play by the University of Nebraska. Seated at right is Hendersonville's Pat Orr.

this one is not too important. The father, an opportunist, doesn't want his children to undergo the hardships he faced and feels the end justifies the means, especially when he comes into possession of a sum of money—not his. This conflict is resolved in a surprise climax by a theatric device more in keeping with tragedy than drama, for it only removes the problem and does not solve it.

The reviews raved over the performance of the cast: "Probably the best performance of any cast in the history of the playhouse." A varied audience reaction was shown from what was written on the comment cards left after each performance: "not enough plot," "less Italian accent, please"; but most comments ended in saying, "I really believe you have something good here."

Robbie and Ernie felt enough enthusiasm from the reaction of the newly written play to enter it in the University of Nebraska's National Play Contest. On Feb. 22, 1952, Robbie received from Lincoln, Neb., the following correspondence:

Dear Mr. Farquhar,

I am pleased to be able to inform you that "Harp for Tomorrow" is one of three finalists in the Masquer's Play Contest. The three plays are now on the way to the National Judges, where they will receive helpful criticism and the winning manuscript will be selected. I am unable to predict just how long it will take our judges, but we will notify the contestants as soon as we are advised ourselves.

/s/ Marjorie Miller

Contest Chairman

One week later, the Flat Rock Playhouse was advised that "Harp for Tomorrow" had been chosen as the winning script. The distinguished judges included Margo Jones, managing director of Dallas Theatre Inc.; John Gassner of the New York Dramatic Critics Circle, and E.P. Conckle, professor of playwriting at the University of Texas and author of "Prologue to Glory."

Elise Pinckney wrote in the *Times-News*, "A very playable drama, 'Harp for Tomorrow' is the happy creation of Robroy Farquhar of the Flat Rock Playhouse and Ernest Frankel of Hendersonville. It seems made to be acted, and is well supplied with emotional tenseness and exciting action. But it is also thoughtful, and remains always true to its own composite personality. A sense of good theater and good taste have developed a top-notch plot into a drama that even with premiere peccadilloes is more than promising."

Ed Patterson—The Poor Man's Medici

Ed Patterson, in the spirit of the famous Florentine Medicis, volunteered to give Louise a job in Williams' Jewelers and Ernie could work part-time with Walter Drake in the Mens' Shop. This would keep the Frankels eating and a roof over their heads while he dove wholeheartedly into writing. In January 1960, Frankel (with two books now under his belt), his wife and their two daughters loaded up their belongings and left Hendersonville for the West Coast, where he would become associated with North American Aviation in Los Angeles as a writer-director and public relations motion picture specialist.

Both of his books have been out of print for some time. I found neither listed in the R.R. Bowker Company publication "Books in Print" 1976 edition. So to read either "Tongue of Fire" or "Band of Brothers," put your name on the waiting list at the Henderson County Public Library. They offer both books.

Once the Frankels arrived in Los Angeles and as Ernie became more immersed in his work, his wife, Louise, became ever more active in civic affairs in Los Angeles. She was elected to a fourth consecutive term as president of the Tarzana Property Owners' Association. She served on the Mayor's Community Advisory Committee and on the Board of the San Fernando Valley Young Women's Christian Association. She became a member of the Brandeis House of Books (a philanthropic society which provides scholarships for deserving youngsters).

So for Ernie Frankel of Charlotte and his bride, the little Louise Lazarus who grew up in Hendersonville: THEY'D DONE GOOD!

In July 1975, I received a letter dated July 14 and signed by Colonel Ernie Frankel, USMC Reserve. Now bear in mind, when Ernie came back from World War II, he was a lonely louie. At the end of the Korean War, he had advanced to captain (this was when he and Robbie Farquhar won the national award for the best stage play of the year). And now, the man I had jokingly referred to in Ernie Frankel's Mens' Shop as "always forward Frankel," signs the letter Colonel Ernie Frankel, USMC Reserve.

Ernie Frankel and Louise Lazarus

The letter was to inform me that he had finalized plans to bring the entire "Movin' On" Television Company to Hendersonville and would likely film four episodes of the series while here. In the letter, he said shooting would take place over a seven-day period from September 2nd through the 9th, 1975. Actually, they received such widespread cooperation while here, they extended their shooting schedule.

The greatest joy of having the "Movin' On" crew here was to get to know the great Claude Akins. Claude was a veteran of more than 20 films, this in addition to a variety of "made for TV specials" and TV series. His credits included "Rio Bravo" and "Inherit the Wind." But more than anything else, Claude Akins was a golfer. He certainly didn't look like a golfer, but he had grooved his swing to suit himself and he could repeat that same swing incessantly. I arranged for him to play as my guest at the Hendersonville Country Club. As we were having a sandwich before going on to the course, he talked about the difficulties of having time to play in L.A. and how courses there are so crowded. They make no starting time. On your arrival, you drop your ball into a shoot and when your ball finally comes out at the bottom, it's your turn to hit. He had never seen the Hendersonville County Club course in his life and he turned it in 78. Rather pleadingly, he asked if he might play it again. "Sure, hit away." This time he cut two shots off his round. In the summer of 1996 when Ernie and Louise were visiting in Hendersonville, we reminisced about Claude Akins. Ernie pointed out that it had been his signal honor to deliver the eulogy at Claude's funeral. I'm sure Ernie and Louise enjoyed the time they spent here filming "Movin' On" in 1973. While so many things have changed, more is still the same. Ernie especially wanted to do a scene in Smokey Levi's Barber Shop. He wanted a scene with Clint Redden blowing a harmonica (a French harp) through his nose.

I don't know how Thomas Wolfe got into the conversation that afternoon as Ernie and Louise and I reminisced, but suddenly Louise asked if I knew how to tell if a sculptured angel is the real Thomas Wolfe angel or a counterfeit. A number of major cities do claim to have the real angel, though theirs are counterfeit. Louise told me the story. She had bummed a trip to New York with Ed and Doris Patterson. Her Ernie had been so busy writing and producing, she came down with cabin fever. She traveled with Ed and Doris and managed to see five Broadway shows. This was in 1958 when "Look Homeward Angel" had just opened on Broadway. Louise said that she went backstage after the show just to get an autograph from Miriam Hopkins. She said the man handling security was a kindly old gentleman. After he learned she'd come from Tom Wolfe country, he insisted that she come into Mrs. Hopkins dressing room. In a few minutes, Ed Begley and the rest of the cast was jammed in, and all were asking questions about "Altamont" and about the identity of the woman buried under the angel.

When Louise returned home, she got in touch with Mrs. Sadie Patton, and together they went to Oakdale Cemetery. Mrs. Patton, she said, made it quite clear that those buried there are the ones supposed to be buried there (contrary to the Broadway version). Sadie Patton said the angel was authentic–it had phthisicy toes. You can look that up in Webster's unabridged or, as Mrs. Patton did, I'm sure, simply look for the word on page four in "Look Homeward Angel." It also appears several times in the book. Phthisicy merely means "toes that have begun to draw and become gnarled from the ravages of TB."

Famed Thomas Wolfe angel in Oakdale Cemetery; it has genuine phthisicy toes.

It was a pleasant afternoon I spent with Louise and Ernie, here to see the Pattersons on a visit from their lavish home on Promontory Road in Los Angeles.

The Cover Paintings of Time Magazine

Broadcasting is one of those occupations that bind one broadcaster to another because of a commonality of interest in the profession, though they may never have met. I suppose that's the way the child bride and I came to know one of the most delightful and courageous couples ever to live here–Ernest and Ernestine Baker. Ernestine did radio work for a number of years in Putnam County, N.Y. She was a solidly interesting person to be around, with her interest in crafts and her magazine experience with *Harper's Bazaar*.

You may never have known Ernest Baker personally, but you certainly were exposed to his artistic efforts which graced the covers of *Time* magazine for hundreds of issues. These were not photographs, nor snapshots, nor sketches. These were what he called "journalistic portraits," as versus academic portraits. In a journalistic portrait, the view of the head and the facial expressions are candid, not posed. The background of a journalistic portrait reflects the subjects of interest and their position in public life.

Back in the early '50s, we were first invited for a visit to the Baker home on Brevard Road. Accenting the very warm and friendly living area were numerous of Ernest's paintings. There was a large portrait of a heavyset man with a scowl on his face and tousled red hair. The portrait had a mesmerizing quality. Your eyes were just naturally drawn to his glowering countenance.

Ernest noted my fascination and said, "They didn't buy it."

"Who didn't buy it?" I responded.

This Time *cover from May 21, 1956 is one of the many "journalistic portraits" done by Hendersonville's Ernest Baker.*

"Neither the Union nor his family." I continued to stare.

"You do recognize John L. Lewis of the United Mine Workers?"

"No," I answered. "I always thought he had coal black hair."

"Oh no, that's because the only pictures you've ever seen of him were in black and white." Ernest said that his major problem with the Lewis family was that they were provincial. His daughter insisted on having her dad slick his hair down with Brilliantine before he had his picture made. Ernest said he finally convinced her that his painting had to be natural and she ultimately cooperated.

Ernest Baker's contract with *Time Magazine* called for a number of journalistic portraits which would be used on the covers of the magazine, then the ownership of the painting reverted back to Ernest. Normally, the family and/or business associates viewed the original portrait as being priceless (regardless of price). Baker said that in the case of John L. Lewis, Mr. Lewis allowed as how he wasn't going to waste his family's hard-earned money by buying a picture of himself; and he said they weren't going to waste any Union money buying this picture to hang in the headquarters of the United Mine Workers either. As a result, Ernest Baker still had the John L. Lewis picture there at his home on Brevard Road.

The work of Ernest Hamlin Baker was on exhibit in the Skyland Hotel in the summer of 1955. Later, the pictures were featured in a traveling exhibition that toured the nation in 1957. Baker started doing the journalistic portraits for *Time* in 1939. Over the next two decades, Ernest would paint 390 portraits to be used on the covers of the magazine, most of them painted in his studio home on Brevard Road.

In the very early 1940s, he did one cover featuring the eccentric millionaire Howard Hughes. Then he did a second portrait of Hughes used on the *Time* cover July 19, 1948, which tied to the controversial story about Hughes and the now infamous book by Clifford Irving. But out of all the paintings done by Ernest Baker throughout his life, his pride and joy was a spectacular study featuring his wife, Ernestine, which he had worked on for years. Ernest had taken all the pictures of her at every age of her life. These miniatures provided the border of the featured portrait of Ernestine. The center painting was when he considered her to be most attractive. She would have been in her early to mid-40s and she was strikingly beautiful. As adornment, he had interlaced (between the miniatures) all of her favorite things: flowers, leaves, animals. And as each year went by, he would add still some extra little something symbolic of the year just past.

In their twilight years, they both suffered crippling arthritis and lived virtually twenty-four hours a day in specially built wheelchairs; but always (regardless of the pain you knew they were suffering) they were full of life and laughter. It was a sheer joy to visit them, even infrequently. Ernest and Ernestine Baker first moved to Hendersonville in 1951. They had twenty-one marvelous years living on Brevard Road. Ernestine was eighty-one when she died in early October of 1972.

Ernest Baker's paintings are located in the National Art Gallery and the Smithsonian Institution. Baker gave two paintings to Ernie and Louise Frankel. One was the Bernard Montgomery cover, the other, Joe McCarthy (as Ernie said was a tease to him about "Tongue of Fire"). Both were donated to the National Art Gallery. In the past, there has also been a traveling exhibition of Ernest's work. They're desperately trying to find more of Ernest's work. The bulk are still held by Ernest's daughter, who probably is not interested in parting with any of them at this time.

How-Dee — I'm Just So Glad to Be Here

Back on May 30, 1996, I just happened to catch a rerun of a TV special on the life of Minnie Pearl. Now any and everybody who lived anywhere in the range of WSM and the Grand Ole Opry back in the 1930s (and about anywhere in the country after that) was familiar with "Howdy" and the always smiling voice of Minnie Pearl. In fact, our high school class graduated the year that Minnie made the big, big breakthrough to the network portion of the Grand Ole Opry sponsored by Prince Albert tobaccos. One of the girls in our class could do a pretty good imitation of Minnie Pearl.

Minnie Pearl was a member of the Grand Ole Opry Hall of Fame, but she was always quick to point out that she actually got her start working up her act with the help of Sally Stokes (mother of Bill Stokes) in the Skyland Hotel in Hendersonville back in the '30s.

She was born Sarah Ophelia Colley, whose daddy ran a lumber mill in Centerville, Tenn. Little Sarah Ophelia learned to play the piano at the age of four; and dreamed of going to school at the American Academy of Dramatic Art. When the Depression hit, though, the most the family could afford was a school at nearby Ward Belmont Junior College.

There was virtually no support for a show business career in Centerville, so she took a job with the Wayne P. Sewell Co. of Augusta, Ga. She would

move from town to town, recruiting local talent, supplying the costumes, rehearsing the cast and staging a play in that town. It was a living, and Minnie always remembered Sally Stokes as helping her develop some of the music and skits.

In the early '80s when Minnie Pearl was at Carolyn's Book Shop for an autograph party, she was interviewed by Al Hope:

HOPE: Did you ever think many years ago that you'd be right back across the street?

MINNIE: No, I certainly didn't, because I did not have any idea of Minnie Pearl in my mind when staying over

Minnie Pearl at book signing at Carolyn's Book Shop in Hendersonville. The Grand Ole Opry legend died in 1995.

at that hotel in 1934. That's when it was. I was twenty-one years old. Can you imagine. Every time I come to Hendersonville to see Mary, my sister, I drive by that hotel and I thank the Lord in all reverence. I am not being flippant. I'm being serious, 'cause it was through that company that sent me her to Hendersonville to train, to go out and coach these plays that I found Minnie Pearl in Northern Alabama in 1936. You were not around anywhere!

HOPE: That's true.

(Readers can hear the full interview contained in the WHKP Sound Section of the Henderson County Public Library.)

This salute to Minnie Pearl I watched on May 30 on TNN was dubbed before Sarah Ophelia Colley Cannon died. It featured about everybody who was anybody in country music—all with testimonials to Minnie: Roy Clark, Little Jimmie Dickens, Charlie Pride, Boxcar Willie, Grandpa Jones, Pee Wee King and, of course, Roy Acuff. Roy and Minnie shared the honors for a number of years of being the senior performers on the Opry and they loved it. They loved working with each other on stage.

When Sarah Ophelia Colley came up with the idea of Minnie Pearl, she was afraid that if she used the name of Centerville (her hometown), her friends would think she was making fun of them. She remembered a railroad crossing just outside of town called Grinder's Switch, and forever and after, Minnie Pearl hailed from Grinder's Switch. Her outfit came from a rummage store and the price tag on the hat occurred by accident but drew such a response, she never took it off.

She was officially made a member of the Grand Ole Opry in 1940. She married Henry Cannon, a World War II Air Force pilot. The wedding was on Feb. 23, 1947, but Minnie had to wait almost thirty years before she was finally inducted into the Country Music Association's Hall of Fame.

Minnie Pearl's sister, Mary Kershaw, used to live on Kanuga Street. She lived into the ripe upper 80s and in 1996 still is in Hendersonville but lives in a rest home.

When Minnie had her autograph party at Carolyn's Book Shop back in the early '80s, it was bedlam. The crowds were enormous. But she always found time for Larry Justus at the House of Bibles & Books. In fact, if she was visiting "sister Mary" and didn't have time to get by the House of Bibles & Books, she'd always call Larry and visit with him on the phone.

I think the greatest tribute that can be paid to any person is for it to be said about them: "They never got above their raisin'." Minnie Pearl never did, up to her death in the autumn of 1995.

Unto These Hills

In recent years, most of the publicity coming out of Cherokee deals with legal gambling in that community (and on other Indian reservations around the country). Prior to 1950, Cherokee was a typical small Indian village with tourists jamming the one-way street town during a couple of months in the summer. They came to see a caged bear, an old Indian with extravagant headdress ready to pose for pictures with children, and a few shops selling beads and trinkets made in the Orient. A major undertaking was launched in 1950 which would change the very character of the community for generations to come. It was the opening of the outdoor drama, "Unto These Hills," which was a vision of a Hendersonville man, Harry Buchanan.

Harry had grown up in Sylva, and in his early years had operated a couple of small theaters in that community. He moved his family to Hendersonville in the '30s to become head of North Carolina Theatres, Inc. (which was a part of the Willoughby-Kinzey chain). He first ran the Rex Theatre and later would operate the Carolina and State theaters. Buchanan immediately plunged into every kind of community activity.

He was president of the Chamber of Commerce, headed the Rotary Club, was Ruler of the Elks Lodge and was elected to the State Senate. His support of the Democratic Party rewarded him in 1953 with an appointment to the powerful State Highway Commission by Governor Umstead, who had reorganized the commission and added the present 14th Division, which Harry would head. Buchanan was the second of only four men from Henderson County to be appointed to the powerful Transportation Department in the past sixty years.

Harry Buchanan

He established headquarters of the new 14th Division in Sylva (his hometown) and it still operates in that Jackson County town. He established District #1 Office in Hendersonville for Polk, Henderson, and Transylvania counties. District #2 in Bryson City serves the middle counties. District #3 in Andrews is for the far western section. With his jurisdiction covering the 10 westernmost counties, Harry Buchanan extended a leadership role throughout the area. He was one of the founders of the Cherokee Historical Association, and was its first chairman.

Being a theater operator, he had taken a keen interest in the beginning and success of the outdoor drama, "The Lost Colony," staged on the East Coast at Manteo, N.C. He felt that the story of the Cherokee Indian (in an outdoor presentation staged on the Indian reservation) would also be a huge success. The North Carolina Legislature advanced a loan of $25,000, which was later forgiven through action in the Legislature led by Lee Whitmire of Henderson, Frank Brown of Jackson, Ralph Fisher of Transylvania and Roy Taylor of Buncombe (who would later be elected to Congress).

The key to success or failure of the total venture would be in the selection of the general manager, who would be responsible for building the outdoor

Giant amphitheater was constructed for the "Unto These Hills" outdoor drama.

theater, contracting for the script, equipping for the stage presentation and casting the hundreds of roles in the spectacular. Buchanan "loaned" to the association his own house manager of the Carolina Theatre, Carroll White, who was one of the most brilliant theater people I've ever known.

The pageant opened in mid-June 1950 and through August played to over 107,000 people. The loan of Carroll thus became permanent. White went on to establish Oconoluftee Indian Village, which also operated only in the summer months; and then later, the Cherokee Historical Museum, which operated year-round. The museum consisted of a variety of exhibits and permanent displays. At each step, a visitor cold push a button and a recording would play, explaining that phase of the museum. Carroll asked me to do a recording for each of the "stations" throughout the building.

Throughout the 1950s, "Unto These Hills" was number one in attendance of any outdoor theater pageant. It played to an average of 130,000 each year. In 1954, Carroll set a new record with attendance of 150,900. Harry Buchanan was a great showman and had a fertile imagination, but even he would never have dreamed that since 1950, some six million people have attended the pageant, and literally remade the town of

Carroll White

Cherokee. "Unto These Hills" will celebrate its golden anniversary in the year 2000, and will show nightly except Sunday from mid-June to the end of August.

Mother Earth News

Folks in Hendersonville have some pretty heady memories of projects and dreams so grand as to intoxicate the mind of even the conservative. That is, if you have lived here long enough. I vividly remember seeing the Fleetwood Hotel before it was torn down during the World War II for scrap metal. It rose fourteen stories, right on top of Echo Mountain. (There was no 13th floor.) The brick had been finished up about eight or nine stories; and from there to the top, you could see the skeleton steel frame and even the bath tubs and plumbing were already in place and quite visible. We've had promoters of dreams of Babylonian Hanging Gardens to be built on 5th Avenue, and massive outdoor theaters to house "The Passion Play, as produced in Oberammergau, Germany." After Republican John Grant was elected to Congress from this area, the charge was made by the yellow dog Democratic newspaper (*The French Broad Hustler*) that Grant was going to get the Congress to approve building shipyards on the French Broad River.

Mother Earth News was full of practical information for do-it-yourselfers.

So in 1973, when it was announced that a nationally distributed magazine, *The Mother Earth News,* would be moving to Hendersonville, sirens didn't sound and church bells didn't ring. First of all, even though the magazine was printing 110,000 copies a month, it was virtually unheard of in this area. That's understandable because the first edition with a press run of only 10,000 copies had been published only a few years earlier in Madison, Ohio in 1970. Basically, the magazine was sold only through dealers at newsstands. It had a circulation of only 147 individuals when its first issue was published. The magazine had been started by Jane and John Shuttleworth. They had both quit their well-paid jobs and decided to "do something good for the planet," Shuttleworth said when he announced that headquarters for his publication would be coming to Hendersonville. He said, "I guess if we have to place ourselves in a category, we're ecologists."

They were both raised on farms; Jane on a farm in North Carolina, and John in Indiana. In Madison, Ohio (where they had been publishing since 1970), Shuttleworth said they had no space nor any pool for talent. He said, "Here we have more space, a greater pool of talent, and the people are much more pleasant."

While the first edition of the magazine only cost them $1,500 to publish, Mother Earth (according to Shuttleworth) had now become a multi-million dollar corporation. In the Henderson County Public Library you'll find editions Number 7 through 12 (published in 1971) with the publishing address given as Madison, Ohio. There are also copies of editions 13 and 14 in the library, and it is interesting to note that in edition 13 (published in 1972), the corporate address is given as P.O. Box 70, Hendersonville, N.C., which meant that though the magazine continued to be published in Ohio, the Shuttleworths had already made the decision and likely had moved to Hendersonville months before the official announcement was made.

At the time of the announcement, the Shuttleworths said that they were inviting all their present employees (sixty of them) to move with them to Hendersonville. Mrs. Shuttleworth said, "We don't know for sure who is moving and who isn't, at the moment. There are people who are considering moving but some of them may not find the kind of house they want or something after they get there." She said, "Most of the people on our editorial staff, as well as some of the layout staff, will be moving down." She said they were looking for a research site in the area. It would be one of four located at points around the world where experiments could be performed. The site they finally located was in the Penrose area.

Articles in the *Mother Earth News* might include: How to make a rag rug. How to build a house for $49. How to feast on $10 a month. How to produce your own gasoline. How to catch a water polluter for fun and profit.

The Mother Earth News Company (at the time the firm moved its headquarters to Hendersonville) was publishing the *Mother Earth News* with press runs of 110,000, published every other month. It also published "Lifestyle" for city dwellers who had yearnings for the farm, about 25,000 published bi-monthly. They also ran three bookstores and a print shop. Quickly, they got involved in a mail order catalog (similar to that published today by the Vermont Country Store).

Just a year after the move to Hendersonville, the Shuttleworths acquired a location on Church Street at 1st Avenue for the operation of their first "Mother's General Store." The location had earlier been used (when a vacant lot) as the site of the Rev. J. Harold Smith's tent revival meetings. It was then acquired by Gus Thomas and he built the big brick building which still stands there today to house his Buick dealership. Following this, it became the first home of the Blue Ridge College (known as Blue Ridge Tech back then). After the college moved (near the end of 1973), it was leased by Mother Earth News in April 1974; and after Mother's General Store closed, it became the Next to New Shop, which it is today.

When Mother's General Store opened in 1974, for most of us it was more like a museum, although everything in it was for sale. They had adzes for shaping wood, scythes, bottle cappers, even windmills. They offered clothing and candies somewhat similar to what you'll find today at Mast General Stores. Mother's General Store also offered organic food, such as gruel and soybeans, plus a book room offering titles on baking, crafts, organic farming and simple hobbies. They had saddles and harnesses, calico aprons, mechanical metal banks, and even cowbells.

I remember their selection of wood stoves imported from Sweden. The exterior of these stoves was fireproof baked-on enamel and they were super-efficient in function. One local quipped, "Them stoves are so efficient, you can heat your house and produce a good cord of wood a day doing it." I will say, though, seeing the price tag left me in shock. I could have installed a central heating plant for what one of those Swedish stoves sold for. In essence, Mother's General Store was a showcase of everything offered in the Mother Earth catalog; and during their heyday, they were by far the biggest mailer in the Hendersonville area – which included the mail-

Mother Earth News ceased publication in 1988; all assets, including old issues of the magazine, were auctioned off.

ing of magazines, catalogs and goods ordered. In addition to all the vintage and unique goods offered in the store, that location was also used to display some of Mother Earth News' original inventions. I well remember their first electric car, 20 years ago. As a publicity stunt, they arranged for "the little man" (Charlie Renfrow) to drive it around town and back and forth to the radio station. It was called a Shuttle Bug, named for the Shuttleworths.

By the mid-1980s, on the ownership masthead in the magazine, there was a listing of Jane and John Shuttleworth as founders, but the publisher then was listed as Owen J. Lipstein, the editor was Bruce Woods, and the national sales office was on 5th Avenue, New York. It still said, "Published at 105 Stoney Mountain Road, Hendersonville NC 28791. By 1988 it was obvious the *Mother Earth News* had become top-heavy in publishing expense, and prospects for a quick turnaround were dim. The decision was made to discontinue the Mother operation, which included closing the general store, ending publication of *Mother Earth News*, and liquidating the assets of the company. This was done by auction, which took place in the Mother Earth Printing Plant on the Asheville Highway, occupied now by Pardee's Home Health Division. In addition to all the furniture, printing equipment and research files, there were bales and bales of previous copies of Mother Earth News, which were sold by the bale. It was a heyday for flea market operators. Even by subscription, the magazine sold for $3 an issue. At the auction, bales of them were going for fifteen to twenty bucks. Plus, individual copies and printed materials were strewn everywhere throughout the building which were yours if you'd just bend over and pick them up.

They also brought in for the sale equipment and materials that had been used on their research farm at Penrose. I noticed they had developed a scarecrow consisting of a most life-like vinyl owl mounted on a lazy susan-type base, with a dowel rod running through the base and a wind fin on the end. The slightest breeze would case the owl to rotate and cast those fierce eyes toward you. I was under massive assault at the time by little downy woodpeckers (at least, I was told they were downy woodpeckers), which were boring holes and building nests in my house. I was further told that this contraption would scare them away. I bid almost ninety bucks for that rig (which I found later available in a catalog for about twenty-six dollars). But it's still standing guard, gently turning in the slightest breeze, and it works!

People and places

Triskadekaphobia. The word is spelled t-r-i-s-k-a-d-e-k-a-p-h-o-b-i-a but is not in most dictionaries. It means simply a fear of the number 13. The late Bert Boyd had no phobia about the number 13. He felt it was his lucky number. Bert Boyd had been a successful grain broker in Indianapolis. He once remarked that he had operated on a commission basis on the Indianapolis Board of Trade for 46 years and had never made a speculative trade nor owned a carload of grain, but he became a wealthy man.

In 1927, ill health at age 57 forced him to retire and on advice from his doctors he traveled to Europe and South America. This he did along with his wife. She died in 1934. In 1935, he moved from Florida to Hendersonville to live full time. You could have called Bert an eccentric or an individualist, but he was also a philanthropist. He fell in love with that little triangle of land between Church and Main which was named for him—Boyd Park. He put up money for tennis courts, concession facilities, restrooms and landscaping.

Starting at the age of 13, Bert Boyd got his first job with Western Union and was given Badge #13. He started work for the Indianapolis Board of Trade in 1885 – 8 plus 5 adds up to 13. He joined the Rotary Club in 1913, served on the Board of Directors of the Board of Trade and was treasurer of the Grain Association in Indianapolis for 26 years—that's twice 13.

It just goes on and on. His dog license was 13; he had locker #13 at the country club; he gave the city Boyd Park on Jan. 13, 1941. He called January the 13th month. The park opened on Friday the 13th. He even printed his name, separating the curlicues in the B from the upright part of the letter to form 13ert 13oyd. He pointed out that the Great Seal of the United States has 13 stars, 13 stripes, 13 arrows in the eagle's talons, 13 clouds in the glory, 13 letters in the motto, 13 laurel leaves, 13 berries on the branch and 13 feathers in each wing and in the tail. He also pointed out that Woodrow

Wilson was elected by California's 13 electoral votes in 1913; Joe Louis was born on the 13th and won the national championship on Friday the 13th, and sat in front of press box 13 during his trial. When Bert Boyd traveled, it was always in Pullman berth 13. He was also an amateur magician, holding membership number 13 in the International Brotherhood of Magicians.

Bert Boyd installed the first inclinator in Hendersonville. This machine was mounted on the wall of the staircase next to the banister and featured a monorail on which traveled a fold-down chair on which the occupant could ride up and down stairs to avoid the physi-

The late 13ert 13oyd

cal climb. This inclinator was installed in the Kirk Building at the corner of 5th and Main by the late Bert A. Boyd. In visiting him in his Apartment 13 in the Kirk Building (Main at 5th Avenue), I noticed he had a horseshoe hung the wrong side up so that all the good luck would run out over the door into his apartment. Another door to the apartment had a ladder painted over it, so to enter, you had to walk under the ladder. He always celebrated a birthday on Friday the 13th – there's always at least two in each year, and can be as many as four.

To justify changing the date of his birth, he wrote:

> Way back, ah many years ago
>> When things had found a level;
> Old Josh, he stopped the sun and so
>> With dates he played the devil.
> The Romans later then begun
>> to make each year to fit
> The steadfast orbit of the sun;
>> We thought that ended it.
> But now reform has laid us low,
>> And everything that is –
> Is wrong, for FDR says so
>> In this New Deal of his.
> Instead of our Thanksgiving date,
>> November twenty-seven

The twentieth we celebrate
      His order has been given.
A week before Thanksgiving day
      Was my first day on earth;
That makes the 13th my birthday –
      A week before my birth.
To stain my name with mystery
      I must somehow avoid;
I'll fix the date in history
      of the birth of Bert A. Boyd.
My proclamation all ye hear;
      Forever on this date,
November 13th of each year
      Is when I celebrate.

I was asked to emcee a birthday party on Friday the 13th in July of 1951. Mayor Al Edwards, "Unk" Barber and Pete Camak were on that program.

Bert Boyd spent 17 happy years in Hendersonville, living there on Main Street in the Kirk Apartments. When he died, he had specified that there be 13 honorary pallbearers representing the Rotary, Kiwanis, Lions Club, Kedron Lodge, the Elks Lodge, and the Chamber of Commerce. In his obituary in the *Indianapolis Star*, the editor, James A. Stuart, added "He was a grand fellow!"

The Two Greatest Salesmen

Phil Kelly didn't arrive in Hendersonville, he exploded. This dynamic person couldn't talk nearly as fast as his mind was working. He was always involved in something that he could make sound epochal. He dreamed up the Second Wind Hall of Fame, which even today delivers the same impact as he envisioned those many years ago.

My first encounter with Phil had to do with the publication of a little book he had written, "How to Grow Old Rebelliously." He had quickly prefaced discussion of his book by giving me a thumbnail sketch of his background: Advertising director of two of the major rubber companies; how he had introduced Chevis Regal to Scotch drinkers. I interrupted, "You introduced Chevis Regal?"

"Sure," he said, "Seagrams hired me. They had no Scotch to speak of in their product line, and they brought me on board to market their first major effort in this field."

"That was a pretty big order, wasn't it?" I asked.

"No," he said, "I only had enough money to budget one secretary —and me. That was it!"

"But now it is one of the major brands, and you did it with just your effort and that of one secretary?"

Kelly then explained that he had concluded that Scotch drinkers are really "snob" drinkers. So his first move was to price Chevis Regal above most all other Scotch whiskeys except Glen Fidditch and Glen Levitts. He said, "The price got their attention." He went on to explain that in the processing of the Scotch, the small Mom and Pop distillers in Scotland sell their product into a central marketing area. Unless the distributor adds other ingredients, the pure whiskeys brewed by the individual families are all poured together and basically are the same.

I remember my friend Phil Green, who brought his family including his children (Pete, Barbara Stricker, and the late Jean Pearce) to North Carolina when he decided to make the move. Phil used to offer to bet anyone that after they'd had their first drink of whatever Scotch they preferred, he could then take plain grain alcohol, cut it to about 80 proof, add a few drops of iodine and the drinker could not tell the difference in it and the other Scotch drinks placed before them. He alleged he'd never lost a bet.

So I believed what Phil was saying. He had come to me to ask that the radio station produce a speech to be made by him in our studios, and to make it sound like he was speaking to the National Marketing Association Convention. His idea was to just sit in our studios and make the speech. When he hit a point where there should be laughter or applause or cheering, I would introduce that sound effect, and cue him for the natural pause such reaction would demand. I tried to explain to him: "Look Phil, we're not New York. We don't have a lot of the fancy equipment they use up there, and not a lot of experience doing this type of thing." But he actually made me believe that I could do what he wanted. And, believe it or not, we did— and it worked. I don't know how many of those dubbed speeches he sold, but they sounded live to me.

One day, Phil came racing into my office and said, "OK, I know you won't believe it, but I have just discovered the world's greatest salesman and he lives out in the Dana community." I didn't say a word. Phil saw I was waiting for him to continue. Phil said he and his wife had just finished a lovely home on the point in Sky Village. He explained that this man named Milas Case had stopped by to try to sell some shrubbery. He said that he'd told the man that they might be interested later; but right now, they had no plan for the yard and they hoped to bring in a landscape architect to help them with the final design. Phil said, "The old man was very nice. He thanked me profusely for just letting him stop in my driveway." He said the man then turned and said, "Sir, I have one shrub up near the front of my truck that this lady on the next drive has ordered. Her yard is so small I don't have any place I can set off these other plants. Could I just set them off here for about thirty minutes, and I'll come right back and pick them up." Phil said, "I was a newcomer and he seemed to be such a nice man, I couldn't say no. So I said, 'Sure, set 'em off.'"

Phil said he went back in the house and about thirty minutes later his wife came rushing in and said, "Phil it's absolutely wonderful, I love it, I love it all." Phil said he went to the door and looked out. Milas Case had simply placed each shrub in a proper location and the total effect was impeccable. Kelly was yelling by this time. "I had to buy the whole damn load of shrubs! Now that's the world's greatest salesman."

I smiled. I had bought some shrubs from Milas back in 1963. Back then, Milas and I sat down and had drawn numbers in the sand, never saying a word. He would write one set of numbers. I'd sit and stare at the numbers and finally scratch out his numbers and write down my own. He would stare at my numbers for an interminable time. We must have sat scratching in that sand for an hour before he stood up and stuck out his hand, indicating a deal had been struck. Not a word was spoken. It was all written in sand.

Milas Case

The Way We Were

Hendersonville (and downtown business sections across America) was where you'd find intensive commercial development. In the downtown were the department stores and ladies' and mens' shops. Most drug stores were downtown, as were the furniture stores, hardware stores, and beauty and barber shops. Outside of the Central Business District were the great country stores out in the county. The wholesale, farm-related, salvage and service businesses were always in the depot section. Strip shopping centers and malls were nowhere to be seen.

Even my parents' generation grew up going to the "curb market" for not only everything sold there today; but back then at hog killin' time, there was always fresh pork. Most members of the market sold their own country hams and cured side meat.

I don't know whether it was the big wholesale ham packers or "do gooder" health specialists that persuaded the bureaucracy to stop farmers from selling their own hams and cured side meat. They used the guise that they were protecting the health of the public with such a ban. I have never seen a farm kitchen anywhere near as dirty as the average packing house, and I never heard of anyone getting sick from eating meat they'd bought directly from a farmer. The so-called country ham available today is nothing more than a ham off cold storage being hooked onto a conveyor belt and dragged through a huge trough of salt brine, with liquid smoke flavoring added. It's then packed in burlap and pitched as country cured ham. Old timers can remember when farmers could bring fruits and vegetables to town and do brisk trade, not just with the independent grocers but even managers of the small supermarkets back then had the authority to trade for locally grown products which they could sell in their stores.

Most small towns were "Friday and Saturday" towns. Folks got paid at the end of the week, and they'd go to the bank to cash their checks and then go shopping. More checks are now cashed in supermarkets than in commercial banks. Fridays and Saturdays were family days. As the shopping was done, many of the kids got a chance to go to the show. The Carolina Theatre featured John Wayne and Class A films. At the State Theatre, it was Lash Larue or Bob Steele. You could look up and down Main Street on the weekend and the sidewalks were full of people. The depot section bustled with business. The six or seven barber shops of Main Street did eighty percent of their business on Fridays and Saturdays, and normally didn't close 'til 11 p.m. on Saturday night. Most barber shops close today at noon on Saturdays.

In small towns across America (Hendersonville included) stores started closing at noon on Wednesdays to make the work week more manageable. Then the banks unloaded a bombshell. They proposed to give up closing for the many minor holidays if the public would allow them to close all day Saturday. Banks have awesome power! For a short period of time, the Fletcher branch of the State Trust Company continued to operate on Saturdays because they were not a part of the greater Hendersonville area. A constant stream of cars headed out U.S. 25 on Saturday mornings to get their checks cashed at the Fletcher branch. Then that branch was given permission to close. Then customer habits changed and the crowded Saturday sidewalks were no longer packed with people. You could drive a mule train down the sidewalks along Main Street.

In the winter of 1996, I heard the child bride chatting on the phone with our daughter, Katina Hampton, who lives in Greenville, S.C. I picked up an extension, and when an opportunity for me to say something occurred, I said, "Hey girl, what do you remember about Hendersonville when you were growing up here?" "What do you mean, 'what do I remember'?" Well, how many water fountains were there in town?" With no hesitation, she answered, "Two."

I was impressed. She's been only an occasional visitor to Hendersonville over the past twenty years, and the town has changed enormously—except for the water fountains. There used to be a fountain at the corner of 3rd and Main, in front of what was then Brunson's. But it was out of order most of the time, and was not a thing of beauty. D.B. Keith petitioned the city to either put a decent fountain in there or remove the one that was there. It was removed.

My memory may be misleading me, but I seem to remember a water fountain on 7th Avenue East back in the '40s and '50s. Today, we have two, and they're both very impressive. One was dedicated on June 1, 1947, and I do remember broadcasting the dedication. The program was held on the back of a flatbed truck, and one of the speakers, I remember, was particularly eloquent: A very dramatic lady wearing a huge wide-brimmed hat. Alas, she stepped too close to the edge and fell off the truck. This dedication was of an impressive white granite fountain shaped like a tree, located at the corner of 2nd and Main. The plaque on this fountain (across 2nd Avenue from the old Court House) reads: "Near this site, Joseph Cullen Root, founder of the Woodmen of the World, died December 24, 1913. Placed by local Camps of W.O.W."

In 1913, the local newspaper was published by the Mutual Printing Company, publishers of the *Western Carolina Democrat* and the *French Broad Hustler.* This paper had a lengthy story on Dec. 18, 1913, announcing that J.C. Root would be in Western Carolina for a district meeting of the Woodmen of the World. The local officials of the W.O.W. had received a telegram from Mr. Root in Omaha, Neb., announcing that he would be in Hendersonville for the initiation of some 200 candidates who will have degree work confirmed by the White Pine Camp of Hendersonville. The newspaper article said Mr. Root is regarded as one of the greatest fraternity men of the country; and in view of his prominence, the local camp is convinced that several thousand Woodmen from all over the Carolinas would be in Hendersonville.

John T. Wilkins was Sovereign Head of the W.O.W. at that time, and he said all the candidates will be paraded up and down the thoroughfares of

Woodmen of the World president Farrow Newberry (left) came from Omaha in 1947 for the dedication of a special water fountain dedicated to Joseph Cullen Root, a Grand Potentate who died in Hendersonville in 1913. At right, Kermit Edney records the program for broadcast to other area stations.

Hendersonville, to their mortification. (Woodmen took their initiations seriously.)

In the newspaper (published Christmas Day, 1913) it was reported that Mr. Root had been seriously ill in bed at the St. John Hotel ever since his arrival, suffering from bronchial irritation and fever. The Christmas Day newspaper was unaware at the time of printing that Mr. Root had actually died the day before, on Christmas Eve. On Jan. 1, 1914, the newspaper reported the death of Joseph Cullen Root, describing him as one of the truly great leaders of fraternal organizations in the United States; and that he (as Sovereign National Commander) had traveled extensively in most of the states of the nation. The article said in addition to his connection with the Woodmen, he was prominent in Masonic circles, being a 33rd degree Mason.

The other drinking fountain in the Central Business District is located at the corner of 4th and Main at First Union Bank. This fountain is of polished granite, and bears a plaque which reads: "In memory to our beloved citizen, Chief Otis V. Powers, who served this community for a long number of years in many useful ways, and was loved and respected by all. This fountain erected by grateful citizenship." As I read over that plaque back in the summer, I couldn't help but think: "That's also appropriate to his son, William V. Powers."

Later I was going over this chapter with Jody Barber, and he recalled a drinking fountain in front of the Court House that apparently was removed after the erection of the Woodmen fountain. That would have been appropriate to have had a drinking fountain in front of the Court House at that time because, even though there was water running twenty-four hours a day in the horse trough at the Jockey Lot just a half block away, it was illegal to drink from that source.

The Only Public Figure to Lie in State

I was a junior in high school when the news circulated through the community that Chief Powers was dead. He was the only police chief I had known. In fact, he had been police chief of Hendersonville for some fifteen years before I was born. Also, he was the first police chief to wear four hats: He was fire chief and chief of streets and sanitation. In those years, all policemen also served as firemen. Early in his administration, he established a policy that if the streets needed sweeping or sidewalks needed snow removed, he simply had his officers roust out everybody in jail and they would perform the work detail. Chief Powers also established a policy in the dead of winter and in the Depression years, if a transient appeared at the police department with nowhere to go, he could spend the night in the warmth of jail, and would be fed a hot meal along with the prisoners the next morning.

Powers was active in the community as well. He was a member of the

Presbyterian Church, a member of the Masons, Elks, Woodmen, and was vice chairman of the county Democratic Party for years. When J.M. Broughton ran for governor, Chief Otis Powers was his local campaign chairman. In fact, on a visit here, Broughton nicknamed Otis Powers the "wheel horse of democracy." In spite of the fact that his job required him to incarcerate individuals (and his preferences led him to be active politically in the Democratic Party), he was universally well-liked.

My father, H. Grady Edney, had taken me with him to the only political rally I ever attended. I must have been about ten or twelve years old. In those years, Mr. Joe Hollingsworth was what I'd call the "professional prayer" for the Republican Party. Mr. Hollingsworth could sometimes pray fifteen or twenty minutes, asking God's help from abominations being placed on us by the Democrats. I remember on this one occasion Mr. Hollingsworth prayed, "and God, you know that every Democrat is bound for hell (there was a pause) except for maybe 'Ote' Powers."

Upon Powers' death, Mayor Al Edwards and City Council announced that this man who had been Hendersonville's police chief for twenty-five years would be given the signal honor of having his body placed to lie in state in the great lobby of City Hall. Chief Powers' body lay in state from 10 a.m. to 2 p.m. when it was removed to the Presbyterian Church for the funeral. The *Times-News* reported in the edition of Oct. 8, 1940: "Hundreds of people, both white and colored, filed silently by the casket this morning and this afternoon, as the body lay in state at the City Hall."

Otis Powers was succeeded by one of his own officers, Clarence Edney. At his death, Edney would be succeeded by Everett Orr.

Clarence Edney also wore the same four hats that had been worn by Chief Powers, but only for five years. When Mayor A.V. Edwards reorganized the city, he created four different departments, each with its own head: police, fire, streets, and sanitation. Never again would any one man carry such a mantle of authority as Chief Powers during his twenty-five-year career, and during the brief career of Chief Edney.

Chief Powers had only one son, William "Bill" Powers, who attended school at Furman University. After military service in World War II, he entered a partnership for a brief period with his brother-in-law "B" Sims in the operation of the Jax Pax Grocery Store on 5th Avenue West. ("B" Sims had married Bill's twin sister, Betty). Bill sold his interest in the store to "B" when the opportunity arose for him to become chief of police, as his father had been. He also served some twenty-five years as police chief. Since 1915, it has been either Otis or Bill Powers serving as chief of police for Hendersonville for fifty of those years.

Bill later was promoted to wear other hats for the city. He played a critical role serving as a working superintendent of all other city employees in implementing the changes in streets, drainage, and general decor of the present unique downtown Hendersonville. Yes, it would be appropriate for

Police chief Otis V. Powers (left) and his son, police chief William V. Powers. Since 1915, the two men served as chief for a total of 50 years.

both Otis and his son Bill Powers to be honored on that water fountain at Main and 4th Avenue.

More Years Than Any Other Mayor

A.V. Edwards became mayor of Hendersonville in 1932 and served until he resigned in 1969. From the depths of the Depression through the industrialization of the area, from poverty to prosperity, Al Edwards ruled the city for thirty-seven years, said to be longer than any other mayor of any town. So with a precedent set for Chief Otis Powers, why did Mayor Al not lie in state in the lobby of City Hall when he died in 1971? No space! The bulk of the lobby of City Hall is now occupied with a plaster-of-paris mold of a giant bronze statue. "The real thing" stands on the grounds of the old capitol building in Raleigh.

How did this giant replica (featuring the life-size figures of three North Carolina-born presidents of the U.S. and a horse) find its way into the lobby of City Hall? It was purchased from the sculptor by genial Sam Siegal (proprietor of the Carolina Art Gallery), transported to Hendersonville, and crews reassembled it inside the lobby. It was Sam's gift to the city.

Sam Siegal jokingly called himself "an honest crook." He was proprietor of one of three art and auction galleries which operated through the summer in the downtown area. Sam originally worked with the originator of this auction concept (Herman Kimmel) but later opened his own gallery near the Skyland Hotel. The art galleries sold jewelry, fine china, sterling, crystal, Persian rugs and collectibles. Each of the galleries had small auditoriums for their patrons, and sales were held at 10:30 a.m. and 7:30 p.m. Some of the auctioneers had gained experience at "hole in the wall" actions on Times Square; others had worked the carnival and state fair circuit. This new concept introduced by Kimmel and Siegal featured genuine works of art and jewelry and show biz auctioneers with the ability to entertain a crowd and with the genius to make big buyers of jewelry by wealthy

This replica of a statue of the three North Carolina presidents takes up the entire lobby of City Hall, which made it impossible for Mayor Al Edwards or anyone else to lie in state there.

widows and the nouveau rich. Sam would sell a lace tablecloth and would cry as he described the nuns going blind while their fingers nimbly worked the intricate patterns of this priceless piece of art.

Sam was a #1 showman. He liked to pay the top dollar for the blue ribbon winner in the prize cattle show, and then donate the animal to a worthy cause. When Sam heard of this massive sculpture created for the state house lawn in Raleigh, he realized at once that the finished product would have to be cast from a mold. Sam reasoned, "Why not buy the mold and move it to Hendersonville, where folks can see what the real statue looks like that stands in Raleigh?" I doubt if Mayor Al or the City Council ever queried Sam on how big the mold would be. Their first reaction to receiving it had to be one of shock when the statue took virtually the entire lobby. Only in Hendersonville would one expect to see three life size presidents and a life-size horse standing outside the mayor's office.

One of Al's first acts as mayor was to become associated with the Salvation Army in distributing Christmas baskets to the needy in 1938. Between he and Captain George Gibbins (of the relief organization) there was created a Christmas basket containing one chicken, a can of milk, two pounds of dried beans, a can of corn and tomatoes, six pounds of flour, 10 pounds of cornmeal, 10 pounds of potatoes, one can of peaches, a dozen apples, six oranges, a loaf of bread, a pound of coffee, two pounds of sugar, five pounds of rice, a pound of lard, and a package each of Jello and raisins.

Otis Powers was chief of police when Al Edwards became mayor. The men who served under Chief Powers then were: S.E. "Seth" Edmundson (of Harley Davidson motorcycle fame), Gaston Freeman, W.C. Davis, G.T. Orr, Clarence J. Edney (who would succeed Chief Powers), J.A. Maxwell, Everett C. Orr (who would succeed Chief Edney) and L.E. Thompson. They were not only the police, they were also the fire department.

With federal funds, the old rock gymnasium at Hendersonville High School was built, and many people said, "The dang thing's so big it'll never be used." It has now been replaced by a new bigger brick gym. In the summer months and two weeks before Christmas, colored lights would be hung across Main Street to lend a festive air. The CCC boys came to town and built a new road from Green River to Cedar Mountain. Economists all agree: The one thing that broke the back of the Depression was World War II. And, there again, it was Mayor Al Edwards, attending every meeting to sell war bonds, to collect scrap metal, to assist local organizations in working with the USO. The old fighter of the 6th Company of WWI was always on hand to see the busloads of young men get coffee and doughnuts before boarding their buses to head off to World War II. When they returned, there stood Al, not only with his personal greetings but with his encouragement: "You've fought the war, now it's time to come home and we'll all work together to build on to this little town God has so richly blessed." And he meant every word of it.

Mayor Al first told me that I was to be a member of what was then called the Planning & Zoning Board; and then later, he said I would be chairman. We made trips together, one I mentioned earlier where the mayor, Dan Vismor, Melvin Hatch, Bill Powers and I drove to Raleigh to make a pitch for Four Seasons Boulevard. I remember when I emceed what was described as "Al Edwards Day." There was a regiment of the finest local speakers: Frank FitzSimons, Sr.; Dr. Ross Deeds; Wilshire Griffith; Dr. Sam Falvo; J.B. Maxwell; Joe Orr; William Ward; James Stephens; and Jim Fain. Mayor Al brought the house down when he looked wryly at the audience (after being told over and over again he was the all-time vote-getting champion in elections), and said, "If I had Jim Fain and Kermit Edney running my campaign, I'd run for president of France."

It fell to me occasionally to cover City Council meetings, and when I did, I always could find some amusement in the discussions between council members. Back when Melvin S. Hatch served on the council, he and fellow councilman Tom Clark were discussing how dry the weather had been. I believe it was Hatch who observed that the dry weather was even beginning to affect the ribbing of the leaves on certain trees. One of them observed, "When the weather gets really dry, it affects the sex life of trees." I sat quietly, choking back snickers. I never realized that trees had sex lives, but back then I was still wet behind the ears and had much to learn. And to show you how far back that meeting was, in April of 1997, Melvin Spofford Hatch passed away at Deerfield at age ninety-seven.

Al Edwards, who served as mayor for 37 years, was always available for ribbon-cuttings, such as this one, opening the valve which brought natural gas to Hendersonville. Looking on are Alvin Pressley and Maggie Good of Carolina Central Gas Co.

Those were totally different City Council meetings back then. The council took time for lengthy discussions of the birds and bees. Chief Bill Powers had received complaints of someone keeping a bee hive on 5th Avenue West, and he said the complaint alleged that people in the area were allergic to bee stings. The city attorney Francis Coiner observed, "This bee business is a hard thing to stop." Commissioner Frank Todd quickly agreed. He said the Grandfather Clause wouldn't stop the beekeeping. I sat there remembering when I grew up in Hendersonville, we had all kinds of animals on Jonas Street. In fact, one of us kids had to take the cow to pasture in the bottoms between Mud and Bat Fork creeks every morning and then bring her back to Jonas Street at night. The two hogs we raised each year stayed in their pens, which today would be almost in the middle of the Ashe Street intersection of Four Seasons Boulevard.

But this meeting of the City Council I'm referring to not only brought complaints about bees in hives on 5th Avenue West but also about chickens running loose in town. Remember, this was in 1970. The city attorney observed, "chickens may run loose at night under present law, while they must be penned during the day." Chief Bill Powers chuckled and said he'd never seen a chicken do the right thing on its own. Finally, Mayor Whitmire interrupted the discussion of fowl play and called on Mr. Coiner to draw up new regulations before the birds and bees got out of hand. Those were the days when it was fun to go to City Council meetings.

In October 1973, the council passed an ordinance which took a little of the spice out of Main Street life (especially on Saturdays) when they made it illegal to preach, exhort, give lectures or a discourse, or even give public demonstrations on the streets without the permission of the chief of police.

Frank Coiner said that by permitting the chief to give approval, he didn't feel the ban infringed on freedom of speech.

My cousin "Strawberry Bob" King had passed away about seven years before the City Council banned sidewalk preaching, and that was good, because Bob King (always with a very full, bushy and lengthy beard, somewhat like my friend Bush Laughter's today) felt his personal admonition in II Timothy: "Preach the word, be instant in season—out of season, reprove, rebuke, exhort with all long-suffering and doctrine."

Even as a little boy, I can remember when Bob, his brother Govan and other members of the Robert Jones King family (grandchildren of Hiram King) would come to town. Bob would peddle his strawberries, and from that was given his nickname "Strawberry Bob." He normally would preach on Main between 1st and 2nd Avenue in the Court House block; but at other times, he'd move on north on Main Street. It was colorful, and added real character: This man with the flowing beard, shouting and preaching, pounding his Bible and warning anyone who would listen of their sinful and wicked ways.

But this City Council was not reacting to my cousin Bob only. In later years, students from Bob Jones University would fan out into all the small towns within a radius of fifty miles or so from the Greenville campus. This was part of the school's missionary curricula: "street preaching." By this time, it was not just one, but there could be several different speakers in different blocks. I don't disagree with the ordinance drawn up by my friend Frank Coiner and passed by the City Council. I guess I just miss the color and excitement of seeing "Strawberry Bob" get out his Bible and begin to preach. I miss the small talk of foul play with chickens running loose and feigned deep concern over how to train bees not to leave their yard, or how dry weather affects the sex life of oak trees.

Making news

In May 1997, as I followed the progress of the battle between the Russian chess player and the computer, "Big Blue," I thought of the battle between John Henry and the steam drill. John Henry complained that the steam drill couldn't lay the track, couldn't do the other things a human hammer swinger had to do; and the Russian says it's no fun to compete against a machine because it has no personality, you can't read its expressions, and you can't psyche a machine.

That's what made the Southern Regional Checker Tournament in Hendersonville one of the greatest in history. No machines were used, just the best "woodpushers" (as checker players called themselves) in the South. The Southern Regional drew seventy-five top checker players from North and South Carolina, Virginia, Kentucky, Georgia, Alabama, Florida, Mississippi, and Tennessee; and it was the biggest show in checkers ever seen, either here or in North Carolina.

The practical headquarters for the local checkers organization was the Crystal Barber Shop of 7th Avenue East, where my Uncle Jim Pace not only handled the #1 chair but was also chairman of the Henderson County Republican Party. The other chair was handled by Charlie Lowrance, who was not only a cunning "woodpusher," he was always going for that spectacular play which would literally wipe out his opponent. Charlie also served as secretary-treasurer of the local Hendersonville Club, and the members were fondly called "woodpushers."

Throughout the year, checker players all kept pushing Lowrance to invite all the big boys to come here for a tournament. Charlie went to Fred Allen, Jr. (who was then secretary of the Chamber of Commerce) and asked him to make a pitch for the regional tournament to be played in Hendersonville. Fred took up the ball and promised the Southern Association that Hendersonville would raise more prize money than ever before offered by their association. That did it. The city was advised that the

Checker tournament of August 1940 brought best wood pushers to town.

tournament had been granted to Hendersonville, and the state tournament would have all the state champions and seventy-five of the best checker players in the world coming here in August 1940.

Now obviously, you couldn't stage a tournament with forty checker tables (and all the spectators they would draw) in the Crystal Barber Shop. So Charlie and Fred Allen were able to get approval of the City School Board to use the brand new rock gymnasium at Hendersonville High School, which had only opened a couple of years earlier. Charlie set to work and raised more than $200 in cash, which would enhance the cash prizes by the Southern Association.

And what a success! The tournament ran three days. It ran under what was called a "knockout" format: when a player lost any game, he was ousted from the tournament. Attorney General E.F. Hunt from Nashville, Tenn., came to serve as the official referee. Checker players from all the southern state quickly booked out the Skyland Hotel, the Bowen Hotel, along with Hendersonville Inn and all the tourist courts.

Heading the list of players was Basil Case, current Southern Champion from Russellville, Ala. Heading up the list of contenders were one former regional champ and the state champions from North and South Carolina, seventy-five "woodpushers" in all. With the "knockout" format, as each player was eliminated, the tables got fewer and fewer until on the last day, on the entire floor area of the gym, there was only one table. The finalists included Basil Case (the 32-year-old Alabama man who was defending his title) and Alex Cameron of St. Petersburg, Fla., and a native of Scotland.

The two players battled to a draw in the first game. Every move was as measured as in an international chess set. Word circulated through the community about this glare-off of the woodpushing gladiators in the gym, and the crowd grew. Game two ended in a draw. The tension was building to a peak when game three ended, also in a draw. Finally, the small, silent young man from Alabama outfoxed the Scot and established a clear-cut victory, giving him first prize of $100 and the cup. The Scot from Florida won runner-up of $50. Officials described the tournament as the most successful ever held. A total of fifty-three players had advanced to the second round in what turned out to be the largest field in Southern checkers tournament history. It was all planned out in great detail in the midst of the sound of hair clippers, the smell of Lucky Tiger and with the usual spirit that if anybody can do anything better, he's bound to be from Hendersonville.

Hendersonville's Famous Smelling Machine

In the olden days of barbering, unless your nose was totally stopped up with a cold, you could easily distinguish between the aroma of Lucky Tiger Hair Tonic and Pineoil Creosote Shampoo or Fitch's dusting powder. But a Hendersonville man suddenly surprised not just the local area, but one of three major broadcast networks of the country when he announced that he had invented a "smelling machine."

I will admit that I never knew Luther Shipman, but I did notice an obituary in the *Times-News* in 1959 which read: "Luther Shipman succumbs

Luther Shipman (left) explains how his Smelling Machine operates to Carol White, Don Barber, Fred Reid and others.

in VA Hospital." The story talked about his invention of the "smelling machine." I did not remember ever hearing about the "smelling machine" when I was going to high school at Edneyville. Much later, I ran across an article dated Jan. 2, 1940, which said, "Luther Shipman will be heard on 'We the People' program tonight at 9 o'clock, when he will be interviewed by Gabriel Heatter over the CBS System." If I had read that article in 1940, I didn't remember it. Of course, when you're still young and a bit wet behind the ears, you'll believe about anything. So the fact that a Henderson County man had invented a "smelling machine" didn't really impress me one way or the other.

But in 1975, when I was doing some research for the 33rd reunion of my old high school class at Edneyville, I happened to run across the story in the *Times-News* again. But this time, having been involved in radio broadcasting for some twenty-eight years, the article caught my attention. How did the program 'We the People' hear about this "smelling machine"? Even in this day of modern computer chips, I had not run across such a development. And then, for some reason, I thought Gabriel Heatter had always been on the Mutual Broadcasting System. I didn't remember him as being involved with "We the People." You remember Gabriel Heatter: "Ah, yes, folks, there's good news tonight." He was sponsored by Serutan (which, of course, is Natures spelled backwards).

The little article in the *Times-News* said that "the Hendersonville man will explain the mysterious workings of his odor machine." Then on Jan. 13, 1940, there was another article in the *Times-News* headlined, "Luther Shipman Deluged with Fan Correspondence." I'm quoting from the article now: "Luther Shipman, inventor of the 'smelling machine' who recently appeared on 'We the People' program in New York, had received numerous letters asking about his instrument, according to W.C. Mitcham, secretary of the Hendersonville Chamber of Commerce." The article goes on to say, "One hundred and forty-seven letters have been received by Mr. Shipman up to yesterday. These include inquiries from 12-year-old boys to an 80-year-old man. One doctor in Canada wanted information as to whether the machine could detect cancer in a patient, and a Boy Scout wanted a machine to use in tracking. A letter from Poteat, Oklahoma, addressed to the "Scientific Smelling Machine Man" wanted Mr. Shipman's cooperation in locating $90,000 in jewelry and money orders which he said were buried by train robbers who died before revealing the hiding place of their loot.

I made copies of those two stories from the *Times-News* and forgot about them. One day I inadvertently mentioned Luther Shipman's smelling machine and someone spoke up real quickly and said, "Ken Allen has the machine at Scotties." So I went by to see Ken and he confirmed that he did have the famous smelling machine in his possession but it was stored elsewhere. Well, my curiosity had my old forehead pounding. "You do have the smelling machine?"

The Smelling Machine, preserved at Scotties in Hendersonville.

"Oh yes, I have it."

"Could I see it?"

Ken indulgently went with me to another building where the machine was stored and we eyeballed, mused, wondered, speculated, and finally I concluded, "Ken, I don't really want to know if that machine works or not. It's enough for me to say I've seen it."

It has wires going into a little box and a sealed condenser, coils, resistors, tuning gauge and a little antenna. It fairly exudes mystery. Now here's the good news: This machine I've been telling you about (which was publicized in the *Times-News* on Jan. 2, 1940) is still in the possession of Ken Allen at Scotties. This machine was shown on the CBS Network show "We the People" and is still very real, the discussion of which brought to its inventor, Luther Shipman, 147 letters inquiring as to its availability. This machine which one man referred to as being made by the Scientific Smelling Machine Man is still in the possession of Ken Allen at Scotties in downtown Hendersonville.

Water Follies

Back in 1951, someone in the Chamber of Commerce dreamed up the staging of a Water Follies at Laurel Park Lake. That year, Ben Prince was president of the chamber, and it simply did not fit his honor's demeanor to take a keen interest in promoting any sort of entertainment, let along water follies here in the mountains. B.M. "Bevo" Middleton was chairman of the event, so I have a suspicion that "Bevo" is the one who dreamed up the idea. It would be held on the evenings of August 3 and 4 at Laurel Park Lake.

I had mentioned earlier that the two favorite places to swim in the summer were the Weeping Willow Swimming Pool and Laurel Park Lake. The lake was located directly in front of Laurel Park Inn, which was owned and operated by John and Lucille Prescott. While the lake was operated for guests of the inn, the general public was also encouraged to use the facilities.

For the staging of the follies, the committee would borrow bleachers from the athletic fields of the schools, and the State Highway Patrol and Sheriff's Department would not only assist with traffic but would keep cars moving around Lake Shore Drive so that freeloaders couldn't park and watch the show for nothing. The committee consisted of Bevo, Jimmy Fain, Don

Gilmore, Ed Smith, Hugh Eudy, Earl Martin, Bob Hunter and P.M. Camak. Earl Martin was conned into working with the committee because he was band director at Hendersonville High School and was the only one who knew anything about music. They also twisted the arm of high school coach Ted Carter to assist in the staging of the event.

Bevo Middleton, ever the entertainer, chaired the first and only Water Follies at Laurel Park Lake.

It was to be presented Friday and Saturday, Aug. 3 and 4, at 8:15 p.m., and there would also be a Sunday matinee at 3:30 p.m. Bevo Middleton proudly announced that the chamber had arranged for a special arc light to be transported from Knoxville, "so that every movement of the graceful ballet and precision diving may be seen." It was also announced that a professional diving board (purchased by the Chamber of Commerce) would be used for the first time in the Water Follies.

The diving pavilion at Laurel Park Lake got an additional professional board just for the Water Follies.

Full cooperation was assured by the Junior Chamber of Commerce. John Shipman (who was the president) said that advance tickets would be sold at the Jaycee Information Booth at the corner of 4th and Main. As part of the advance promotion, it was heralded that a professional diver would dive off the high diving board smoking a pipe. That guy was so good that when he came out of the water and climbed back up on the diving platform the pipe would still be lit, and he'd be puffing on it.

My memories of most of the follies was a bit hazy, but I do remember the high diver with the pipe-smoking routine. I remember he worked at Pete Folsom Motor Company. In mid-1996, I called Pete and asked, "Pete, do you remember when the Chamber of Commerce sponsored a Water Follies way back in the '50s; and there was a high diver who did a pipe smoking routine off the high board? I remember he worked for you. Do you remember his name?"

Pete didn't hesitate a second. "Oh, yes, that was Lewis Grant."

"Are you sure it was Lewis Grant?"

"Yes, I remember it well. He was the son of a former sheriff."

I knew that to be "Ec" or Sheriff Eccles Grant. I knew that Ec and V.E. Grant were brothers; so I called U.S. Grant, one of V.E.'s boys, and asked him if he remembered Lewis being a professional diver. "No, but he could have been. Why don't you call Rose Alice Dishner and ask her."

Lewis Grant married Marietta, Rose Alice's sister, who everyone called "Bittie." Rose Alice was the widow of that affable and "one and only" Jim Dishner. Rose Alice and "Bittie" were both Roziers before they married. In talking with Rose Alice I learned she was not aware of any professional diving background of Lewis Grant but said, "It could have been."

I remember the diving routine because when he hit the water with the pipe in his mouth, he may not have broken his teeth but it did require some major dental work.

The crowd was described as enthusiastic, but the number of people who turned out was only described as fair. No one ever knew the total attendance because, as I remember it, the guy who was in charge of the money simply disappeared on Monday morning, and it's my very good fortune to not be able to remember his name.

The professional diving board bought by the chamber stayed at Laurel Park Lake and was used until a few years later. The Prescotts got into a dispute with the other property owners around the lake; and before leaving for Florida, they simply drained Laurel Park Lake. The following spring, it was learned that muskrats always build their burrows near the surface of the water; and when the lake was drained down that winter, the muskrats went down with the water and bored holes in the base of the dam. The lake could not be refilled until the dam was totally rebuilt. It never has been. What at one time was the grand and glorious Laurel Park Lake is now just a small pool near the right side of the old dam. Once the Prescott property was sold and then sold again, it became part of the Laurel Park Villas, a condominium village where each property owner also owns a tiny fraction of what was once the lake; and the chance of ever rebuilding Laurel Park Lake is nil.

Skylarks

It would be an interesting experience to stand at the entrance to the Blue Ridge Mall and ask shoppers the question: "What comes to mind if I say skylark or skylarks?" I doubt if anyone would say: "Skylark was a movie which played at a local theater the day before Pearl Harbor. It starred Ray Milland and Claudette Colbert." There might be a few who would remember "The Skylarks" as being the only professional baseball team to play in Hendersonville.

Back in 1948, sports promoters from Marion, Forest City, Shelby, Lincolnton, and Newton-Conover were trying to put together a Western Carolina League of Class D baseball. Someone sold the pro-baseball idea to T. Lee Osborne (the father of Tom, grandfather of Lee and the founder of the Oldsmobile dealership here). There was no greater sports fan on earth than T. Lee Osborne. He quickly got hold of his friend Judson Miniard (another Olds dealer in Anderson, S.C.) and the Petersons in Asheville, who ran the Amy Store back then. They formed the Hendersonville Skylarks Inc. Play was to begin in April 1948. T. Lee became president and hired a man by the name of Charlie Munday as coach. The seven teams began sending out press releases for tryouts in this brand new minor league professional organization. Tom Osborne told me that back then North Carolina had more minor league teams operating than any other state in the union.

Just a short time later, players began arriving from all up and down the Eastern seaboard, and tryouts went on every day at the Hendersonville High School athletic field. While the formal season would not open 'til April 30, 1948, Munday and the other teams played exhibition games until the last week in April when the roster of each team had to be limited to fifteen players. Doesn't sound like a big deal until you start trying to meet a weekly payroll in a league which included the Marion Marauders, the Morganton Aggies, the Forest City (or Rutherfordton) Owls, the Shelby Farmers, the Lincolnton Cardinals, the Newton-Conover Twins, the Lenoir Red Sox, and the Hendersonville Skylarks.

I remember going to meetings to discuss radio play-by-play coverage of the league in the offices of WJIR, which stood for John I. Rabb, the owner of the station. For this seventh child, only in his second year of broadcasting, professional baseball play-by-play??? That was heady stuff!

The last week in April, Charlie Munday announced his lineup would include Big Jim Gudger from Candler (Jim had played earlier for Rocky Mount in another league). Among the fables and tall tales surrounding that

The Hendersonville Skylarks in May 1948. Second row at left is manager-catcher Charlie Munday.

old Skylark Team, it was known that Gudger could throw a ball like a bullet but was (from time to time) a bit on the wild side. In one instance, Jim had the ball in the dirt, the next pitch was over the catcher's head, he almost beaned several batters, and Coach Munday strolled out to the mound and said, "Big Jim, just settle down. I know you can hit that strike zone. I have all the confidence in the world in you." Coach Munday turned and started toward the dugout, stopped suddenly, turned and said, "Now Jim, I have confidence in your control, but if you don't mind, wait 'til I'm in the dugout before you throw that next pitch."

Most everyone who was around here for that 1948 season would remember Joe Plick. He played first base, was from Bound Book, N.J., and would later give up pro ball and concentrate on his career with Ecusta Paper Corp. He would raise a family here, including two sons who attended Hendersonville High. Verne "Dusty" Rhodes played with Rocky Mount before coming here. Ray Miller played second base. He had played in the Georgia-Florida League earlier. At third base was Tommy Holcombe from

First baseman Joe Plick.

Asheville. In the outfield were Les Bangs from Norfolk, Va., and Burr Head Whitten from Hot Springs. (Burr Head became one of the more active officials in football and basketball after his career with the Skylarks had ended.) Pete Hendershot from Somerville, N.J. (at twenty-seven, the oldest man in the club), Burl Gilbert of Cadillac, Mich., Norman Ayers of Swannanoa, and Fred Witek were other pitchers.

Try as he did, president T. Lee Osborne couldn't get the electric fixtures up at the fairgrounds in time for the opening of the first season, and only when they played on the road were they "under the lights."

Broadcasters interested in covering the Class D action met in the studios of WJIR in Lenior. Other meetings were held at WMNC in Morganton. When the season opened, we had a radio network where each station would originate all home games and the broadcasts would be carried also on the station of the visiting team. It certainly came into my juvenile thinking that soon my voice would be heard in Marion, Morganton, Forest City, Shelby, Lincolnton, Newton-Conover, and Lenior. Wow!

Everyone had faith and confidence in this new professional baseball team. The Hendersonville Skylarks would take the league title! Unfortunately, the team ended up in the cellar. Not just unfortunate, but tragic for T. Lee Osborne! His two partners, Judson Miniard from Anderson and the Petersons from Asheville) wanted out. The losses in 1948 were humongous. But T. Lee Osborne still believed the team could survive, so he bought out both partners and became the sole owner. He replaced Charlie Munday with Rube Wilson as manager. A few of the first year players returned, including Joe Plick and Burr Head Whitten. As the Skylarks began that second season, there was a sea of new faces: Mal Stevens, Tommy Bigby of Columbia, Gus Conegelakis (who in later years would play semi-pro softball), Roy Lamb, and Bruce Reynolds.

Though he didn't play for the Skylarks, there was a Henderson County boy who got his start in that old Class D league. He played for the Rutherfordton Owls, and his name was Odell Griffin, a left-hander, who had gone to school in Edneyville. Odell was good enough to advance out of the old Class D League and move on up to the majors. Odell's family were educators. Odell would become principal at West Henderson; a brother, Brown, was at Clyde (among other schools); and Woody was principal at Lee Edwards in Asheville and would become superintendent of Asheville City Schools.

Realistically, the odds were against the Skylarks ever succeeding. They played at the fairgrounds where the grandstands were designed for stock car racing. There were no stands along the baselines and the field was never in premium condition. In 1948 and 1949, television had exploded on the scene with reception from Channel 3 in Charlotte, and later, Channel 4 in Greenville. The Skylarks were competing against televised major league baseball.

In those years, the industrial plants of Western North Carolina had their own semi-pro softball league, and Berkeley's team was virtually professional. Plus Berkeley had a genuine, bona fide baseball park. Many of their players were actually better known to local sports fans than were the players for the Skylarks and the other teams in the Class D league. The Skylarks not only ended up in the cellar of the league in '48, but the new manager, Rube Wilson, didn't bring any miracles with him and the Skylarks fared no better in 1949.

I questioned, "Tom, didn't your dad lose a good deal of money on this baseball venture?"

"A ton of money!" He said, "I was just a school kid back then, but if there was ever any mention of the Skylarks or the money it was taking to keep the team afloat, mom would stop the conversation at once saying, 'I don't want to hear another word about it.'"

Somehow, T. Lee found a buyer in the Gastonia area and the team was moved there for the 1950 season. Things were not really rosy for any of the teams in that old Class D league. I don't know when it finally folded but it wasn't too long after the Skylarks left Hendersonville.

I always wondered if in any family there is a T. Lee, a T. Lee Jr. and a T. Lee III. What do you call each one? I challenged Tom with this as we were chatting about the old Skylarks. He said everyone had called his dad T. Lee and he had been called Tom or Tommy. He said when Red Reid (who, by the way, was from Portland, Ore., and came to WHKP in the late '40s as a sports announcer) kept referring to Tom or Tommy as T. Lee on the radio. He said folks really got confused, especially when those who had not grown up with him started calling him T. Lee). He said his dad was still alive when Tom's son was born, and to make Gramps happy, he and Jo Ann named their son T. Lee III, who is now called Lee. So the old man was T. Lee, the son, Tom, and now the grandson is Lee.

Sheriff W.G. "Ha Ha" McCall

No one has ever questioned that T. Lee Osborne was one of the greatest sports fans the area ever had, but there have been others, like Lum Morris. His son, Richard, was a sports writer for the *Asheville-Citizen*; and another son, Jim, wrote for the Durham paper. At football games, Lum was up and down the sidelines, berating the officials and shouting to the coach which play to run next. For a number of years, Lum rented a room in our house, and after football games, he could never go to sleep. You could hear him pacing up and down the halls all night, muttering his critique of the game.

"Fats" McCall (or Robert McCall) got as much pleasure in razzing the officials as in watching the game. And another McCall took sports quite seriously: W.G. "Bill" McCall. In the months that I did the Skylarks play-by-play, I was always looking for something to talk about to add excitement to the broadcast. Watching an average baseball game is about as emotion-filled as watching a cow ruminating. Bill McCall always had the seat directly behind home plate; and the home plate ump took a continuous tongue-lashing from Bill. At one game, I spotted the home plate ump jump up, yank off his mask and dart toward the grandstands where Bill was sitting. With no hesitation, Bill picked up a Coke bottle and bopped the ump on the head with it. He was out like a light. Man, this is the most excitement I had seen in weeks; but the sportscasters' protocol says you don't describe fist fights in the stands or fans cold-cocking officials. I tried to cover the activity, choosing my words very carefully. Apparently the listeners understood what had happened and Bill McCall was an instant folk hero. I don't know whether or not it helped his campaign, but he was elected sheriff of Henderson County the next year.

Shortly after Bill had been elected sheriff, the highly respected J. Hall Reaben came to see me and said, "Kermit, we need you to emcee the annual Horse Show for us." Hall was president of the Hendersonville Horse Show Association at that time. I did an instant recoil: "Not me, I know nothing about horses." Reid Wilson (the early morning man on WWNC for years) had developed an entire extra curricula career in emceeing horse shows, and though I never cared for Reid personally, he was the best emcee in the horse show field. Hall explained that for years, Reid Wilson had done a good job for the local show and at a reasonable fee–$100 per day and expenses. But for the preceding two years, the expenses had gotten out of hand. The year before, he had reserved the entire top floor of the Skyland Hotel for his cronies and had run up bills at Lawson's Stone Tavern in the hundreds of dollars.

I kept protesting. "I can truthfully say I can only identify the head and rear end of a horse and that exhausts my entire field of knowledge." Hall was quite a persuader. "We'll take you to a number of big horse shows where you can learn the ropes, IF you have to do any shows. But we're going to publicize the fact that we're training you and that you expect to compete with Reid Wilson for other shows in the area. What I'm saying is we'll help you with the training, but we're banking on you being our 'bluff card.' We think if Reid Wilson hears he has a competitor, he'll come to his senses."

How does this fit into my Bill McCall story? Well, Hall Reaben arranged for Bill McCall and Dr. Ross Deeds to be my mentors, and the four of us would travel together and they were to coach me on horse show lingo. Our first trip was to Galax, Va. All the way up, the sheriff and I listened to Dr. Deeds relive his days of glory when his family had lived in southern Virginia. Some of Ross Deed's relatives still live there in Galax but they only had one spare bedroom, so Hall Reaben and Ross bunked in the big house and Bill McCall and I bunked together in a little motel at the edge of town. You can imagine our amazement on Sunday morning when we discovered the *Charlotte Observer* had run a special edition of the little town of Galax.

As Bill and I sipped coffee, we memorized endless stories about "the big shoot-out in Galax near the Court House—you can still see the bullet holes." We committed to memory big land trades between prominent families, and endless trivia. We'd keep a solemn face as we were driving home, when Bill or I would recall the biggest real estate deal ever in Galax. I could see Doc's ears quiver and finally he turned in a burst of temper and said, "How the hell do you two lamebrains know anything about Galax?" Bill McCall and I rolled with laughter and handed him the Sunday edition of the *Charlotte Observer*. Hacked but happy, he'd found out how we'd learned so much about Galax. The rest of the trip home was in cordial conversation.

By the way, the bluff worked. Reid Wilson agreed to emcee the horse shows in the future with no expense allowance.

My memory of sheriffs goes back to Sheriff Will Garren, who served from 1928 to 1934. I remember even more vividly his famous Garren's Tonic, which Mr. Fitz told you about and wrote about in his "On the Banks of the Oklawaha" books. There was Morris Orr, who was sheriff for one two-year term, 1934-36. During his term, the state legislature increased the term of office for the sheriff from two to four years. There was Will Davis and the F.D. "Bill" Dalton, serving two terms from 1942 to 1950. Dalton is the only man to serve as sheriff and then later as chairman of the Board of Commissioners.

Then there was W.G. "Bill" McCall. We told you what a radical sports fan Sheriff McCall had always been. Bill also loved practical jokes and was beside himself when we pulled that prank on Dr. Ross Deeds (a proctologist who called himself "the Rear Admiral"). Bill McCall had a laugh that would bounce off canyon walls. Bob Freeman once told me about a visit Sheriff McCall had made to his friend and supporter, Dr. J.H. Cummings, who established the Cummings Foundation to benefit Hendersonville. When Sheriff McCall went to visit Dr. Cummings, the only person home was Dr. Cummings' Chinese houseboy. When Dr. Cummings returned, the houseboy said, "Man come to visit you. Don't know name but he constantly laughed ... ha ha ha ha." Dr. Cummings knew he was talking about Sheriff McCall, and Bob Freeman said folks started calling the sheriff "Ha Ha" McCall after that experience.

But Bill McCall could be tougher than nails when the occasion demanded it. Back in the '50s, a retired police officer bought a little house near the Flat Rock Playhouse. He made the preposterous statement that at the time of the purchase, he was not aware of the existence of the playhouse. He became very upset about all the cars (some parking in his driveway) and he objected to all the noise of the theater. In retribution, he bought his son an electric guitar and had him play it each night during the performance of the plays. Disruptive??? Totally. Managing director Robroy Farquhar went to my friend, L.B. Prince (who was a supporter of the playhouse) and related their problems. "Have you tried to reason with this man?" Ben asked. Robbie said, "We've tried everything but all he does is shout at us. He's insolent, insulting, and arbitrary in every way." Ben was aware that the man got his water from the source owned by the Flat Rock Playhouse and said, "All right, cut his water off." Robbie followed Ben's instructions. The next night, the man had bought a set of drums for his son and the disruption to the theater was total.

Ben then called Sheriff Bill McCall. "Sheriff, do you think you might be able to reason with this man at all?"

"I can try," Bill said. So he drove out, knocked on the door and started trying to reason with the man (a retired police executive from Detroit). Quickly McCall met violent and abusive language. This was the kind of guy that gives Yankees a bad name. The sheriff began seething inside and later told Ben Prince, "I thought the smart thing to do was just leave before I lost my temper with this idiot." But the guy followed the sheriff to the car, berating and ridiculing him all the way. When Bill had gotten into the sheriff's car, the fella even stuck his head in the window and yelled, "and what are you going to do about it?"

Sheriff W.G. "Bill" McCall

Bill said, "That did it." He calmly got back out of his car and beat the daylights out of the man. He really romped him in the dirt, and by the time McCall got back to town, the guy had already sworn a warrant charging the sheriff with assault and a variety of other things. The sheriff went back to Ben, told him what had happened and said, "Ben, he ain't got no right to treat the high sheriff of this county that a'way." Ben immediately swore a warrant for the man, charging him (among other things) "of approaching the high sheriff in a mean and truculent manner." The lawsuits flew right and left, and finally, the newcomer (facing the wrath of the entire community) agreed to sell the property to the playhouse.

On June 23, 1956, Sheriff McCall was riding with Deputy Carl Garrett on routine patrol on U.S. 176 near Shepherd Street when the patrol car was hit head-on by an automobile owned by Mrs. Lila Overby of Abbeville, S.C. Both she and the driver of the car were intoxicated, evidence showed, and hit head-on, though Garrett was about six feet totally off the highway on the right-hand side. The Overby car came across their lane and struck the patrol car head-on. Sheriff McCall battled for life for more than two weeks, suffering massive head and chest injuries; but finally succumbed on July 8, 1956, the only sheriff in the 159-year history of the county to be killed while serving in office.

Fruit of the Grape

No one living today remembers when Henderson County had legal distilleries operating here. My great-grandpa Samuel King operated one on the old Chimney Rock Road, just this side of Pace Road. It was in 1903 that the State of North Carolina first passed any law regulating the sale or manufacture of alcohol. The law was referred to as Chapter 233 of the public laws of that session; and basically is what we call today the "local option law." It provided that local governments had the right to determine for their own area whether or not whiskey would be made and sold.

In a matter of just a few months, a petition signed by one third of Hendersonville's voters asked for a vote on whether to outlaw the manufacture of whiskey, to ban barrooms and saloons, and whether dispensaries should be established, such as drug stores, which would be permitted to sell liquor "on prescription." Thirty days later, out went the manufacture and sale of whiskey in barrooms and salons, but it did permit drug stores to sell liquor on prescription.

Now, Frank Waldrop was a young man in his early 20s when that law was passed. Frank had a nickname, "Bully," although he was no bully but one of the most elegant gentlemen of his generation. Frank recalled that after the election, it was the fashionable thing for men to stop in at their favorite drug store and partake of a restorative before going on to work. The law did not provide for any oversight mechanism, so the druggist could be as generous in the sale of booze as their quest for profits would dictate. Frank Waldrop used to laugh and say, "The busiest part of the drug store was back in the prescription department, where, throughout the day, the druggists could

In front of Justus Pharmacy in 1880s: Frank "Bully Waldrop" is third from left; next is Tom Shepherd; boy on far right is Ed Patterson.

quench the thirsts of those willing to pay. It had gotten so bad by 1912 that the City Council passed an ordinance directing the chief of police to give to the newspapers the names of those who had purchased liquor on prescription during the preceding month. Prior to August 5, 1955, there was no law regulating the sale of beer and wine.

In 1946, there was a total of seventeen so-called eating places on Main Street, along with two newsstands and publication emporiums. Before the '50s would arrive, Johnny and "Strawberry" Brock's Drive-In on the south end of town, and the Atlantic Cafe on 7th Avenue would also open. The real eating places, or restaurants, back then were the Skyland Hotel Coffee Shop and the Home Food Shop Cafeteria.

But starting on the south end of Main, you had the Court House Cafe, the Nugget Cafe, the Blue Grill, the Hot Spot, the Brunswick Lunch and Billiard Parlor, the Pickwick, the Past Time Lunch and Billiard, and Tracy's Place, next to the bus station. On the south end of town, you had Jim's Drive-In, Shorty's Pig-N-Whistle, Dale's Drive-In, and the Snack Shack. On 7th Avenue East, there was the Marmack Grill; and also selling snacks, beer and wine were the Blue Ribbon Smoke Shop and Freeman's News Stand.

But the vast majority of these so-called eating places were really hot dog and hamburger stands that sold beer and wine. The more successful of them also offered pool tables—spelled, as Meredith Wilson wrote in "The Music Man," with a P which rhymes with T—and that spells trouble! The old Past Time, the Brunswick and the Pickwick were fairly quiet until Friday and Saturday came along. Then, all the "bubbas" would come to town and engage not just in quaffing a few, but partaking of a consummate ingestion of brews throughout the day. Some would consume a case of belch propellant. The old country music song "Girls Get Prettier at Closing Time" was certainly appropriate. Late in the evening on Friday and Saturday, great battles were waged by the inebriated walruses seeking to protect their beach.

Hendersonville did not have any serious zoning ordinance back then; and if you wanted to put in pool tables, you just bought them and put 'em in. Many of the other so-called eateries installed pinball machines. Slot machines were illegal but, with the same logic used with Indian reservation gambling, pinball machines supposedly required skill and therefore were legal. In the early days, the machines would actually dispense coins if you won, the same as slots. Then later, to stay within the law, the machines would only flash on the screen the number of games you'd won, and the owners could slip cash to you under the counter.

In the late '30s and '40s, punch boards came on the scene. At first, the winner would receive only merchandise—a plush teddy bear or a box of candy. Then, the smarter operators began paying off in cash. So next came baseball tip boards. Most of the boards had a twenty percent markup for the operator. You had 120 tips on a board, and say, if tips were sold for a dime, you'd take in $12 and pay out $10. Tip boards were available from a nickel to a quarter weekdays. On weekends, they'd add 50-cent and dollar boards. By the war years, they had proliferated all over town. It was wide open. The boards actually lay on the counter; put up your money and help yourself. Many of these places also began selling wine by the cup. A standard Dixie cup was 10 cents, a large Dixie cup was fifteen cents. Now these were not fermented wines, they were fortified—such brands as Old Maude, "the wine with a kick"!

By the war years, gambling had reached an all-time high. Someone (I never knew for sure who) rented the basement beneath the Pickwick Cafe (which is where Mac's Mens' Wear is today). You had access from the outside or you could walk downstairs from the Pickwick and inside was a small auditorium. There was a stage at one end. Behind the stage was a huge blackboard; and in the center of the stage was a baseball ticker. That was a machine you could lease from Western Union which would give you scores of every major league game every half inning. As the scores came in, they were posted on the big blackboard. The two teams listed on a ticket which scored the most runs established the winner, even if they played each other. If you had one team that was obviously going to win, and there were two other teams likely to score the same number of runs, it looked like there would be a split, and instead of winning $25, each ticket holder would win $12.50. However, if one of those two teams did score another run, that team paired with the top scoring team would be the winner; and the other team that had been likely to win was now out. So it became popular to do what was called "pool" your ticket. If you could find the holder of the other potential winning ticket, you would agree to split, regardless of the outcome. Pooling was highly popular; and you'd occasionally have runners who would go from place to place trying to find who had the ticket that could be pooled. If he found the guy, he'd get (on a $25 ticket) a buck, which was good money back in those years.

On Saturdays, especially, all the "bubbas" would come to town. By mid-afternoon, it began to get a bit rowdy (considering you had at least one beer parlor in every block on Main Street). On one Saturday afternoon, as I was walking down Main and approaching the Past Time Cafe – whammo! suddenly a body came hurtling through the window. We had a policeman back then who was calledBig Joe Hammack, and he was big. When the glass shattered and the man who had been thrown through the window found his only wound (other than a few small scratches) was his hurt pride, started to head back into the Past Time; but he hadn't seen Big Joe. Big Joe had been directing traffic on the corner of 5th and Main. He ambled over, snagged the "hurlee" by the collar, dragged him inside, and in a flash came back out with the "hurler" – and walked both of them down to the City Jail a block away. It was like living in the Old West.

I don't know if the movement was started by an individual or whether it was a spontaneous reaction in the community; but the County Commissioners were petitioned to call an election to consider outlawing sales of beer and wine in all of Henderson County. That election was held on Aug. 5, 1955, and the "drys" won in a smashing turnout. Beer was voted out by a vote of 5,976 to 1,499 (that's including all precincts except the tiny precinct of Raven Rock which always took an extra day to be heard from). In the Green River precinct, the vote was 15 to 1 against the sale of beer and the vote on wine was very similar. Dealers had sixty days to liquidate their stocks, so after Oct. 5, 1955, if you wanted a beer, you had to drive to the Buncombe County line where, overnight, an entire community of beer halls and convenience stores opened.

Henderson County would continue totally dry for the next five years. There is no official county available which would show the increase in traffic from Hendersonville to the Buncombe County line during that dry period. No one wanted to bring the beer joints back to Main Street but promoters felt being a totally dry county hurt the tourist business. So they called for a special election to seek approval of an ABC Store – just in Hendersonville. The group had no organization and the liquor store was voted down on Feb. 21, 1956, by a vote of 854 to 584.

The "wets" licked their wounds and gave up the ghost for four more years. In late 1959, a movement began again to vote (only in the city) on whether or not beer and wine could be sold in grocery stores only. This would guarantee that, though beer was available again, no beer joints could be opened anywhere in the city. Remembering the proliferation of beer joints up and down Main Street, the pro-beer and wine people had made it clear in the proposition that no one wanted to go back to the "way we were." Further, the pro-beer and wine forces contacted the national breweries trade group and they responded by sending James A. Stutts (an employee of the industry) to Hendersonville to aid the committee in the election.

In the meantime, the "dry" forces imported a firebrand evangelist from South Carolina to conduct meetings in churches throughout the community. The efforts of the "dry" forces came to a climax on the Saturday before the election when they staged a giant parade down Main Street, featuring automobiles in various stages of wreckage, covered with catsup. Inside the cars were people, also smeared with red liquids, and signs galore lambasting demon rum and the high cost paid by any community that allows it to be sold.

The "wets" were tutored by Jim Stutts (who, by the way, always wore the same James Bond-type trenchcoat, which caused him to be easily set apart as not being local). Stutts insisted on registering as many new voters as possible. According to the late Raymond English, who was named Registrar for the special election, some 800 new voters were registered.

The media was swamped with ads for both sides. The "dry" forces made the election a religious issue. The "wets" argued that nobody had stopped the sale of beer from neighboring counties and it was better to legally control the sale of beer and wine than to encourage locals to truck the products in from the county line. So the stage was set for the bitterest election ever to be held in Hendersonville.

When the polls opened at 6:30 a.m. on March 2, 1960, a heavy sleet was falling and the temperature was twenty-one degrees. When the weather warmed up a bit during the day, the sleet changed to snow. By the time the polls closed at 6:30 that night, twelve inches of sleet and snow had fallen, and side streets were virtually impassable. The roads south of the city (U.S. 25 and U.S. 176) were closed for awhile because of slides. But all day long, the voters came. Both sides had either four-wheel drive vehicles or tires with chains. As the voters came and went, tensions and feelings ran high in City Hall. An all-time record voter turnout had occurred: 1,720 had cast ballots in that election. Then the long count began.

Both sides had watchers gathered around the big table in the office, which was adjacent to the then-mayor's office. There were frequent challenges to ballots, and the election officials would need to make a ruling. Finally, the count was finished just after 9 p.m. The worst embarrassment WHKP ever suffered occurred on that night. Half of our staff was out with the flu, and the other half had served yeoman's time in keeping the news moving in such horrendous weather. Other than myself, we had only one young man still available whom we used once in a while for relief—a young apprentice with no training. My last instruction to him as I left the station was, "Wait for me to call you, and then simply switch to City Hall. You don't need to say anything!"

Meanwhile, out in Flat Rock, the noted attorney W.B.W. Howe was in bed with the flu, bored to death and fidgety to hear news on the outcome of the election. He picked up the phone and called our young man at the station. The next thing I knew is that I received a call at City Hall from Harold Worley, excitedly telling me that he had a pair of snowshoes and would loan them to me. "What for?" I asked, not knowing that our young man had bought Bill Howe's prank, hook, line and sinker, and had breathlessly announced on the air, "A man has broken into the counting room at City Hall and has stolen the ballot boxes and made off on a dog sled." I called the station and had our young man switch to me at City Hall, where I apologized profusely for the shenanigans—but to this day, we have never lived it down!

The "wets" won the election by almost a two-to-one margin, but the fight had only begun. I referred earlier to Mr. James A. Stutts, who was from Raleigh and a representative of the Brewers Foundation. He came here to assist in the planning for the "wet" forces and, in fact, stayed through the election. I mentioned how Mr. Stutts did not exactly blend in, always wearing a James Bond trenchcoat. On election day, Stutts was in and out of the voting place at City Hall on numerous occasions.

Both sides being suspect of the other were quick to spot this stranger and observe his every move. There were also allegations that some folks had been refused the right to vote, some had voted that shouldn't have, etc. So less than a week later, Superior Court Judge Willie McLean (responding to complaints brought by nine people on behalf of themselves and other citizens of the city) issued a restraining order forbidding the city from doing anything until the complaints (and, in fact, a legal case) could be heard.

The Superior Court assigned their "trouble shooting" specialist Judge George Fountain to hear the case, and after certain legal maneuvering, the case went to trial in late June. Some ten or fifteen witnesses were called on behalf of the "dry" forces. Some said they had seen money change hands between some "wet" workers and voters coming into City Hall. Others alleged that when one of the "wet" workers would talk to a voter and would help him mark the ballot, he would wink at Ben Israel (who ran a grocery store on 7th Avenue); and when the voter would start to leave, Israel would give the voter a slip of paper which entitled him to a free chicken. In fact, one of the "Get your hen from Ben" slips was brought into evidence; and the man was questioned as to how he had turned over the slip to the "dry" forces. He said he was threatened by them that they'd put him in jail if he didn't give them the slip. He also said when he handed over the slip, he was given $2. The testimony went on for the better part of two days; and when the plaintiffs rested, motion was made for a non-suit on the grounds that if every irregularity alleged could be proven, it would not have changed the outcome of the election. Judge Fountain immediately ordered the case non-suited and the restraining order dissolved. Plaintiffs then filed notice of appeal to the Supreme Court.

In the meantime, the "wet" forces decided that with such a lopsided victory in the beer and wine election, they should try for an ABC store. That election was held on Aug. 31 of the same year and voters approved the ABC store by 68 votes: 893 for, 825 against.

Meanwhile, the city had appointed I.T. Olsen as chairman, along with Melvin Hatch and John McLeod as the City Commission to receive applications for beer and wine licenses. They had adopted the ordinance establishing rules and regulations which went to City Council on July 7, 1960, but they could do nothing beyond that until the matter was resolved by the Supreme Court.

Also, the city appointed a commission to establish and oversee the ABC store, with Harry Buchanan as chairman and J. Steve Porter and Bob Quinn as members. This commission (being unfettered by legal action) moved quickly and the ABC store opened Nov. 19 in its present location. The Supreme Court threw out the appeal by the "dry" forces on the beer and wine election Nov. 10, but it would be some time before applications could be accepted and processed; and the incongruity became reality when the "dry" forces (who had fought beer and wine so hard) saw liquor being sold in the community while you still could not buy beer.

On August 28, 1980, a liquor-by-the-drink election was presented to the voters. It passed 1,016 to 810. Since then, the town of Laurel Park voted approval of an ABC store, liquor by the drink and off-premises sales of beer and wine. In both cases, no public money was used. Banks loaned initial funds for preparing a place of sale and for inventory, with loans repaid from proceeds.

In the city's ABC operation (since the store was first established), over six million dollars have been paid (up through mid-1996); 50 percent to the City of Hendersonville; 25 percent to Henderson County; 25 percent to schools and 1 percent for the library.

In the town of Laurel Park (since Jan. 17, 1983 through mid-1996) over $600,000 has been paid: 62 percent to the town, 25 percent to Henderson County, 12 percent to schools and 1 percent to the library.

But remembering what I said earlier, all the fights that raged for some 25 years were provoked by our "Wild West Days" back in the '30s and '40s.

Bob Freeman's News Stand

I visited Bob Freeman in 1996 and asked him about his very early days in the news stand. He said that when the Hodgewell Hotel was built (which would later become the Ames and then later the Bowen), a fellow by the name of Frank King operated a news stand on 4th Avenue in front of where Jackson Pharmacy was for years. This Frank King then opened the news stand and tobacco shop in the hotel, which became very successful. Later on, Bob said the news stand was purchased by a man from Greer, S.C., by the name of McLaughlin, who brought along with him an associate by the name of Bill Kendricks.

Bill would work the rest of his life in the news stand, even after Bob took it over. Kendricks (when he was in high school) was catcher on his high school baseball team. Wanting to impress the girls, he thought he was fast enough to reach out and grab the ball before the bat could be swung around by the batter. He wasn't as fast as he thought he was. The blow by the bat to the back of his head required a steel plate over a portion of his noggin for the rest of his life. The blow also caused Bill to lose most of his hearing.

I was working for Bob in the summer of 1941 when the Union Bus Terminal was in the north corner of the hotel. There were no restroom facilities in the bus station. One day a very attractive lady walked into the news stand and said quietly to Bill Kendricks, "Do you have a restroom?" Bill, not able to hear thunder at thirty paces, always wanting to accommodate a pretty lady, responded, "I beg your pardon?" In a louder voice she said, "Do you have a restroom?" Bill cupped his hand to his ear and said, "Lady, I didn't understand you." This time she bellowed out, "Do you have a restroom?" With this, it became so quiet in the news stand the only sounds to be heard came from the overhead paddle fan. Bill, not hesitating, climbed up on the magazine racks, looked behind several different magazines, climbed back down and said, "I'm sorry, lady, we just sold out." The entire news stand erupted into laughter; and the lady, her face beet red with embarrassment, stormed back out onto the sidewalk heading toward the bus station.

Bill Kendricks had an expression: "Have you been doing any huckle-de-buckin' lately?" It was such a euphonious saying, I "borrowed" it to use among all my friends at the University of North Carolina. A couple of years ago, I answered the phone and the voice on the other end asked, "Are you doin' any huckle-de-buckin' lately?" I quickly recognized the voice of Ben Cavin, who bunked with me a Carolina in 1942-43 (and who operates a large office equipment and computer firm in Fayetteville).

McLaughlin was the second owner of the news stand. Bob Freeman said that man was so full of hot air he could blow up a cabbage sack. He and the then-owner of the hotel, Alvin Ames, had a falling out over fifteen cents worth of kerosene, and Ames voided the lease and had him evicted.

J.K. Livingston then acquired the lease and Bob was able to get the lease from the Livingston estate in 1937. He celebrated a 60th anniversary in 1997. Bob had an older brother, Tom, who was an educator, and two younger brothers, Allen Ashworth (his grandmother's maiden name was Ashworth) and Albert "Bert" Shipman Freeman. Their mother's name was Shipman. There were also two sisters: Grace, who married Thomas Richard Vail, and Katherine, who married Joe Noffz. Bob Freeman's grandfather was Jerome Freeman, who owned all the land that is now Chimney Rock Park. As a publicity stunt, Jerome hired eight men to pull and carry a small mule to the top of the chimney, which later convinced the world it was safe to climb Chimney Rock. The Freemans later sold the property to the Morse family of St. Louis, Mo.

In the golden days when I was young (and before television had brought the multitudinous news channels), the well-rounded man always bought at least two or three newspapers every day. The visitors who were here for the summer simply had to have the *Miami Herald*, or their hometown newspaper from Jacksonville, Charleston or Savannah. Freeman's News Stand carried them all. Back then, it was truly a smoke shop. Freeman's offered every brand of cigarette you could think of, plus many which the younger generation had never heard of: Wings, Dominoes, Avalons, Spuds. Cigars?? Boxes and boxes of everything from Rum River Crooks to the most expensive Havana cigars on the market.

In the summer I worked for Bob, there was a huge man by the name of Edwards who always got his Copenhagen snuff at the news stand. Back then, the news stand not only sold beer, but fortified wine poured into Dixie cups out of a gallon jug kept in an iced-down cooler. Each morning, Mr. Edwards would take him a dip of Copenhagen, and then have a big cup of Old Maude for a little eye-opener. He would then step across the corner to the post office.

At left is Jimmy Freeman, who now operates the news stand and a catering service; with the coat and tie is young Bob Freeman, who was Jim Martin's congressional aide; the elder Bob Freeman; and Patricia Ann "Patsy" Freeman, who married Robert Clouse.

Shortly, he'd return and have another big cup of Old Maude, which would help him get home and face the cares of another day. Mr. Edwards, I believe, was a retired Naval officer, and had a brother in the Washington, D.C. area who owned a liquor store. When the brother died, Mr. Edwards was his only heir. He never thought of selling the store. He just rented a huge truck, drove to Washington and moved the entire inventory into his basement.

In the very back of Freeman's News Stand were the fabled leather chairs (actually, two chairs and a sofa that would seat two). They were never reserved but you could be sure that at least one (and likely all of the seats) would be occupied by local attorneys of the town. It was said (based on fact) that more court cases were decided in Freeman's News Stand than in the Court House. These leather seats sat up on a platform so that, though you were seated, you could look out over everybody coming and going in the news stand. There was a rail on which you put your feet.

It was after WWII (and after I had joined the staff of WHKP) that I innocently got myself into big trouble. The old wire recorders had just been invented and they were as much in vogue back then as lap tops are today. Someone goaded me into hiding one of these wire recorders under those leather chairs and recording the conversations that went on that morning before court. I turned the machine on and went back to my job at the radio station a few doors up the street. Around lunchtime, attorney Lee Whitmire (who would later become a Superior Court judge) came to the station and asked if I had put some sort of recording device under those chairs. Thinking he was anxious to hear the playback and get a hearty laugh on someone else, I said, "Yes, sir." Hell hath no fury like R. Lee Whitmire when he feels his privacy has been invaded. "Young man, you come with me right now and reveal that machine, and I want the contents destroyed!"

The wire spools were easy to destroy—just cut loose one end of the wire and, like a garage door spring, it would fly in all directions; I never met the man who could wind the wire back on the spool. That was just another of many lessons I learned at Freeman's News Stand, and should be taught by ABC and other TV networks: Never, even in fun, tape a person without his knowing it. I thought I would be the hero of comedy, but turned into a red-faced chump.

When the Downtown Parking Corporation acquired the old Ames Hotel (the Bowen or the Hodgewell), along with the Kentucky Home Hotel, which stood across Washington Street from the First Baptist Church, Bob Freeman had to find a new home for the news stand. O. Roy Keith owned the land and the house next door, which had been occupied by Bill Burrell, who was head pressman for the *Times-News*. Keith constructed a building on this property large enough to house the news stand and several other stores. Bob originally took the building where Coffee Lovers operates today, but quickly needed more space and moved to the next building farther north.

Bob married Elizabeth "Bess" Bryant, who died at the age of 66 in 1982. In December 1996, Bob was eighty-five years old and still working part-time in the news stand. Bob and Bess had a daughter, Patricia "Patsy" Ann, who married Robert Clouse. Bob's oldest son, Robert Jr., was an aide to Jim Martin when he served in Congress. He put on so many barbecues for Martin, he decided to get out of politics and into full-time catering. He has one of the largest catering services in Charlotte. Another brother, James "Jimmy" Weddington Freeman, saw a good thing and began his own catering service here, operating it in conjunction with the news stand. Jimmy's twin brother, John Bryant Freeman, died at an early age in 1972. He was only twenty-four.

Heinz Meets His Jim Farley

Back in the '50s, our firm was operating a sister station in Canton, WWIT, "Where the Wheels of Industry Turn." Suddenly there burst upon the political scene in Haywood County the owner of a shoe manufacturing plant in Waynesville, Heinz Rollman, on a much smaller scale than Malcolm Forbes, but he did spend his own money on his campaign. Western North Carolina had never seen a political campaign like Rollman's. His picture was on billboards everywhere. He handed out millions of matchbooks, nail files and ballpoint pens extolling the great leadership of Heinz Rollman, who (his ads said) would be the next congressman from the 11th district.

Mr. Rollman had sent word to our radio station in Canton that he wanted somebody from the station to come over and talk to him about a radio campaign. I made the trek over to his plant in Waynesville and met Heinz Rollman for the first time. He was a short, wiry, and fiery man with deep-set opinions on everything, but particularly about it being time for the average American to pull himself up by his own bootstraps. In our conversation, it was obvious that he was a total maverick in politics. He had immigrated to this country, had established a shoe manufacturing plant and had an enviable success record in his field. Out of the blue, he had decided it was time he shared his leadership skills, and decided he would run for Congress. He had met with no political leaders, he had no campaign organization, he had no copy or speechwriter. Heinz Rollman was simply an individual running for the GOP nomination for Congress. I gave him some names of people active in politics and suggested it might be wise if he at least became acquainted with some of them.

He called me back after a couple of weeks and was wildly enthusiastic. He said, "I have just met the Republican Jim Farley of North Carolina." Well, this was evidence that he'd taken my advice and done some home-work. He had learned that James Aloyisus Farley was not only the Democratic boss of New York, but was credited for having secured the presidential nomination for Franklin D. Roosevelt when he first ran for president in 1932. "And would you mind," I asked Mr. Rollman, "if I asked you who you are equating as the Republican Jim Farley of North Carolina?" Without hesitation he said, "Why, Bob Freeman, of course. That man knows more about politics than anybody else I've ever talked to."

This was no shock to me. I'd known Bob Freeman all my life, and had, in fact, worked for him at his celebrated news stand on Church Street, along with a number of other young men, including Ralph Jones and Grover Stepp. I had observed Bob as he raised money for candidates he supported, and he'd get substantial cash contributions from people (regardless of party) for whoever he was supporting. But Heinz Rollman paid little heed to the advice that Bob (or for that matter, anybody else) gave to him. Again, like Malcolm Forbes, it was *his* money and he didn't cow-tow to any so-called political boss. He ran his own campaign on his own platform.

The most unbelievable ending to this chapter: Heinz Rollman almost won the election! A total political unknown, running against an entrenched incumbent with unlimited resources. It had been close to fifty years since a Republican (John Grant) had represented this district in Congress, and Heinz Rollman (with very little support from his own party) had almost squeaked through to victory in one of the most bizarre debuts ever made in politics. However, after that defeat, Heinz Rollman never became involved in politics again, but the man he called "the Republican Jim Farley" continued his activity in behalf of the GOP. In fact, he was one of the first men named to the Republican Hall of Fame in Henderson County.

Bob Freeman started out working for the A&P but ultimately became a major political figure in the county. He was one of the very favorite people of Dottie Martin, the wife of Governor Jim Martin. It was only natural that Raymond Robert "Bob" Freeman would get involved in the grocery business as a young man. His father was Robert Patterson "R.P." Freeman (the Patterson stood for Elder Patterson, who was a preacher from the Flat Rock community). His father had run a grocery and general merchandise store on 7th Avenue East for many years; and in politics, Bob's dad had served a brief stint as sheriff.

Singular political honors

In the back of my mind I remembered that Brownlow Jackson was the first Henderson County man to serve as state chairman of the Republican Party and Monroe Redden the only local man to serve as state chairman of the Democratic Party. I also remembered that Don Garren was the only man from this county from either party to ever run for governor or lieutenant governor.

However, just as I was preparing to put together this material on politics, attorney Kenneth Youngblood shared with me an article he had acquired from the Sondley Collection in Asheville. In Ken's letter of transmittal, he said, "There was a fellow from Buncombe who had lived in Hendersonville for a short time (whose name he thought was Justice) who had run for Congress; but, instead, when he found the article it turned out to be a Jones." I'll quote from Ken's letter here (as I did to George Jones on the morning of June 26, 1996). Ken said, "I never checked with George Jones to see if he was one of his forebears but I doubt that George would acknowledge him, especially since he appeared (by his admission) to be 'rather successful.'" Reading this to George on the phone brought a hearty chuckle! This pamphlet is titled "Knocking on the Door–Alexander Hamilton Jones, Member-Elect to Congress, his course before the war (referring to the Civil War), during the war and after the war." George quickly recalled A.H. Jones and said that he'd received from an aide in Congressman Taylor's office, historical highlights confirming Mr. Jones' service. I was glad to have this confirmation from George because after having read this autobiographical piece Alexander Hamilton Jones wrote and had published by McGill & Witherow in 1866, I had concluded that he was one of the greater blowhards of the early history of the community.

In fact, my incredulity of the boasts and brags of Alexander Hamilton Jones had grown stronger when I read on page 192 of Jimmy Fain's book: "He (Monroe Redden Sr.) thus became Henderson County's first Democratic

Representative in Congress, although two others, Hamilton C. Ewart (1888-90) and John Grant (1908-10) had served as Republicans." Jimmy never referred to Alexander Hamilton Jones, who also alleged he was the editor of a local newspaper.

For a state to be readmitted to the Union, it had to frame a new constitution guaranteeing black suffrage and the 14th Amendment. This amendment denied suffrage for some who had served in the war. It said they could not hold public office and could be pardoned only by the Congress, not the President. North Carolina held a convention to adopt such a constitution in 1868. The delegates consisted of 13 conservatives, 108 Republicans and 18 carpetbaggers. By the way, that constitution drawn by such a motley assortment of post-Civil War political scurvy survives today with amendments ... but still no mention of Alexander Hamilton Jones.

I'll not continue the debate on the merits of Mr. A.H. Jones, who concludes this self-written puff piece with a postscript: "P.S. – January 5th, 1866, In pursuance of my duty to a loyal constituency, and in justice to myself, I am at the capital of the nation 'Knocking at the Door.'"

I will repeat the fact that Monroe Redden Sr. was the first Democrat ever to be elected for Congress from the 12th District. He served three terms (two of which were in the 11th Congressional District because we had lost a seat in the house by virtue of the count of the 1950 census). And I'll point out also, he took the oath of office as a freshman congressman with John F. Kennedy and Richard M. Nixon. He was chairman of the Democratic Party in this county for sixteen years, resulting in the clean sweep of 1932. He served six years as state party chief and managed the election to governor of J. Melville Broughton in 1940. That was when a Redden friend and associate (L. Ben Price) was made chairman of the Highway Commission.

Jimmy Fain credits Hamilton Glover Ewart as being the first congressman from the county, a Republican who had also served as judge and mayor of Hendersonville in 1878. He was a stepson of the famed Col. Valentine Ripley, who had served two terms in the state legislature and was appointed a federal judge by President McKinley after serving in Congress.

Everybody remembers the Man of the People (John Grant), another Republican elected to Congress to serve in 1908 through 1910. Mr. Fitz told you about him in Vol. 1 of "From the Banks of the Oklawaha." Son of William C. Grant, married his childhood sweetheart (Zuro Edney), taught himself to read and write and cipher (as math was called back then).

When Brownlow Jackson was state chairman, he was the first Henderson County man ever to serve in that capacity; and he, too, could revel in the huge success he experienced. He served in 1928, the year in which Herbert Hoover won a landslide victory over Al Smith, Democrat. Brownlow Jackson, after an illustrious career in community activities, passed away at the age of eighty-three in 1956. His son Brownlow, Jr. died two years later in 1958. Another son, Jonathan W. Jackson, served an illustrious career on the North Carolina Superior Court; and Jonathan's son Frank Jackson practices law in Hendersonville today.

Only Men to Run for or Win State Office

Don Garren is a person who has two "firsts" going for him. He was not only Minority Leader of the legislature, he was also the first man from Henderson County (of either party) to make a race out of the contest for lieutenant governor. The North Carolina Republican Party had only "existed" after the Roosevelt landslide in 1932. In 1968, Democrats had chosen Bob Scott over J. Melville Broughton, Jr. and Reginald Hawkins. The GOP had selected Jim Gardiner over Jack Stickley. When Don Garren was recruited to run for lieutenant governor, there was no apparent opposition, but a school teacher named Trosper Combs later announced he wanted to run. He passed out thousands of combs with the simple inscription "Combs for Combs." Pat Taylor, who was backed by the Democratic Party for lieutenant governor, also faced primary opposition.

After the May primary, the battle settled down between Bob Scott and Jim Gardiner, and between Pat Taylor and Henderson County's Don Garren. It did become a two-party race with Richard Nixon defeating Hubert Humphrey and carrying North Carolina. Bob Scott and Pat Taylor did win election for the Democrats; but Don Garren (totally unknown to any great degree except in Henderson County) polled 228,000 to Taylor's 284,000. In Henderson County, Garren won by almost 2 to 1, polling 9.805 votes to only 5,348 for Taylor. It was a big GOP year with Carroll Wilkie defeating Harry Buchanan for State Senate.

This set the stage for the elections of 1972 when the first Republican governor, Jim Holshouser, would be elected in this century. It was the Nixon landslide over George McGovern that swept into office the wife of Carroll Wilkie as state senator. She was nicknamed "Honey Bee" because of legislation she sponsored to make the honeybee the state insect.

I went to school with A.J. Overton, Jr. Years ago, when he would return to Hendersonville to visit his family, he would occasionally stop by and reminisce over school days at Rosa Edwards when we were in the same grade and over his years as pastor of Grace Baptist Church at East Flat Rock. His father, A.J. Overton, Sr. ran a business similar to Lawrence Jenkins', which we talked about earlier, that of a wholesale grocer. Mr. Overton, Sr. lived to be eighty-seven years old. His first interest was in his God and the study of prophecy; and his second love was growing azaleas or rhododendron. His garden on Kanuga Street was famous for varieties he had even imported from China. He was so proud of his son, the Rev. A.J., Jr., who left Grace Baptist Church for a totally new field dealing with Slavic Jews. The old man, though proud of the challenge his son was undertaking, hated to see him leave his beloved mountains.

There were three daughters: Lillian, Josephine and Martha. Virtually no one growing up with them realized that their mother's brother, Mitchell Lee Shipman, would be called today as a yellow, yellow dog, dog Democrat. In all the years I knew Mr. Overton, Sr. and in those years I was around A.J., Jr. (or "Buddy"), I never heard from either of them one word about politics. Yet Effie Shipman, who married Overton, Sr., was a sister to Mitchell Lee Shipman. He is the only man from either party from Henderson County to serve in what some would call "The Council of State"–Secretary of this or that. In North Carolina, these positions (unlike in the national government) are elected by the people. Mitchell Lee Shipman was (at one time or another) a schoolteacher, county superintendent of schools, secretary and treasurer of the Orphans' Association (whatever that was back then). He was also Clerk of the North Carolina Baptist Association, but first and foremost he was not just a politician, he was the epitome of a yellow dog Democrat.

Around the turn of the century, Mitchell Lee Shipman was editor of the *French Broad Hustler*, which was published here and distributed in Henderson and Transylvania counties. There never was a Republican who found mercy from the pen of M.L. Shipman. He wrote not just critical but nasty, vitriolic columns against the gentle and beloved Congressman John Grant. He accused him of planning pork barrel for naval shipbuilding operations on the French Broad River. Robert Byrd of West Virginia would have been an angel compared to Mitchell Lee Shipman. When C.F. Toms was elected to the legislature as a Democrat and then changed his registration to Republican, Shipman's pen pierced Mr. Toms in every issue with vindictive adjectives unknown to even the most literate of his readers. He found it a cause for rejoicing when a Democratic baby was born or a Republican died.

Several months ago, I pilfered through the old microfilm of many editions of the *French Broad Hustler*. I suppose Dot McDowell with her publication of "Gleanings from the *French Broad Hustler*" piqued my curiosity. As I read one of his editorials where Mr. Shipman would "let it all hang out," I enjoyed many a chuckle. He not only wrote about politics, he was chairman of the Henderson County Democratic Executive Committee, as well as the chairman of the 11th District Congressional Committee. In about 1912, he was appointed by Governor Glenn (and later Governor Kitchen) to be the Commissioner of Labor (and they also threw in Printing back in those years). From 1924 to 1930 he published another Democratic paper, *The Jeffersonian Weekly*. He was president of the North Carolina Press Association and held a host of other positions.

But above all else, he was the first person in Henderson County to hold a cabinet-level position in state government: Commissioner of Labor and Printing. A publication, "Shipman Family in America" by Rita Car et al, says he was also at one time named Secretary of State. He was married in 1896 to Lulu Osborne, daughter of W.K. Osborne of Transylvania County. He had two daughters: Mattie Josephine (who married a Hancock) and Dorothy Mae (who married a Pierce). There were two sons: William Franklin and Mitchell Lee Shipman, Jr. He was born out at Bowman's Bluff, and when he died at the age of 78 in 1944, he was buried in Raleigh.

Mitchell Lee Shipman, the only cabinet-level office holder in either party, a Democrat serving as both Commissioner of Labor and Printing, and Secretary of State, had organized and published the *French Broad Hustler* from the late 1880s into the late 1890s in Henderson County.

Jesse Helms' First Exposure to the Senate

Back in 1952, when Dwight Eisenhower succeeded Harry Truman and was inaugurated on Jan. 13, 1953, it had been 28 years since a Republican had occupied the White House. Quite a number of notable local Republicans made plans to go to the nation's capital to at least see the inaugural parade. Some of those who had announced making the trip included Sheriff W.G. McCall, Mr. and Mrs. Ash Houston, Frank "Bully" Waldrop, Miss Birdie West, M.D. McDaniel and many others.

Eisenhower had demanded that the parade be kept simple and dignified, but that phrase can mean one thing to one person and something totally different to another. One proposal turned down was to have each Republican ride his own elephant. That was vetoed because they couldn't find 269 elephants to ride. They finally settled on three, including an elephant named Miss Burma whose daily diet consisted of at least a quart of good bonded whiskey. Officials ruled she'd have to do her drinking in private. Florida citrus growers wanted to throw 60,000 tangerines into the crowd—nope, too dangerous—as was a proposal from the Clark County, Nevada's mounted sheriff's posse. They planned to throw ten thousand real silver dollars (I mean the real "cartwheels") into the stands. Safety officials said a flat "no" to that proposal.

Meanwhile, L.B. "Ben" Prince was saying without equivocation that the one many who should be credited with getting the Southern Democrats seated at the 1952 Democratic Convention was Senator Willis Smith. He had served as mediator to hold back the Southern hot heads and had secured concessions from the Northern liberals to try to hold to middle ground and keep peace at the 1952 convention.

Little did Mr. Prince (or anyone else) know that the solemn-faced, tall junior senator from North Carolina was anything but in the best of health. The 65-year-old Willis Smith was rushed to Bethesda Naval Hospital on Tuesday, June 23, after suffering a massive heart attack. He died on Thursday morning at 4:20 a.m.

There are many people today, especially worshippers of Frank Graham (liberal), who still hold a grudge against Willis Smith's campaign chairman and his administrative assistant, a man by the name of Jesse Helms. At the death of Gov. J. Melville Broughton in 1949, Frank Graham was appointed to serve out the term until the 1950 election could be held.

At first, it appeared that the soft-spoken, professorial-type UNC elite might go unchallenged; but suddenly formidable opposition appeared in the form of the famous Bob Reynolds, along with Willis Smith, who had served three terms in the House as well as Speaker of the House. They, along with the hog farmer, Olla Ray Boyd, would go against each other and Frank Graham for the remainder of the Broughton term. Graham had always been the darling of the liberal academia group and their full support was almost enough to carry the nomination. But, between the first and second primaries, the Supreme Court announced the end of Jim Crowism on railroad cars. A new emotional weapon was now turned loose on the quiet university president, who was being accused on a daily basis of harboring communists at UNC, allowing communist bookshops on campus and in Chapel Hill.

In fact, the first political ad I ever handled came from Richard Albritton. He had graduated from Hendersonville High, Wake Forest and the Wake Law School, and passed the bar, and practiced some law before resuming farming. He pulled out a checkbook and said, "Kermit, tell me how many spots I need to run to beat that commie Frank Graham, and tell me how much it'll cost." I wrote out some brief copy for him. He gave me a check for the proper amount and I placed the order in motion. Across the state, conservative and middle-of-the-roaders were reacting violently to having the liberal Frank Graham continue serving in the Senate. He had almost won it on the first ballot. The supporters of Reynolds and Boyd joined in with the Smith forces and soundly thrashed Graham in the runoff.

And who was in the midst of this battle, directing strategy and mustering forces? None other than Jesse Helms. Experience that came from the Smith campaign and guiding the Willis Smith program in the Senate gave Jesse Helms a graduate course of experience in Senate rules and how to manage that august body. He is perhaps the shrewdest player in the entire Senate, starting with Willis Smith in 1949 and 1950. There is irony in this victory, however, and that is though Smith won the runoff easily, he suffered a heart attack in his second year in the Senate, and was replaced by another liberal, Alton Lennon, who took the Smith seat July 11, 1953, appointed by William B. Umstead.

So when you hear folks criticize Jesse Helms, it may be because he was the strategist who helped elect Willis Smith over the liberal Frank Graham; or they may resent that when he was elected to the Senate as a freshman, he already knew more about the rules and how to get things done than seventy-five percent of the sitting senators. But more than anything else, Jesse helms is real to people. About two weeks after our house burned back in the 1980s, we had found a little house which would be acceptable for a temporary home while we rebuilt. About 11 o'clock one night, the phone rang and it was Jesse. He'd just heard about our losing the house, was most grieved over this misfortune and wanted to know, "What can I do to help you?"

Our friendship has blossomed through the years and today I'll occasionally write him a real "get it off your chest" letter; and he'll let it sit for maybe a week and the phone will start ringing. When I pick up the receiver, it's Jesse kidding me and laughing about a particular harsh or unkind

Kermit Edney emcees a Jesse Helms rally at Hillandale School in Hendersonville. At left is former senator and presidential candidate Bob Dole; at right is Senator Jesse Helms.

thing I've said about our mutual political enemies. If Jesse doesn't agree with you on any subject matter, he doesn't pussyfoot–he lets you know it. Sursume corda, Jesse!

Women on Juries

The noted columnist Sidney Harris used to regularly publish a column now and then he titled "Something I Ran Across While Looking for Something Else." This chapter is based on just such a finding. I was researching something that occurred in the late '40s and I noted in the *Times-News* (dated Sept. 13, 1947) a story headlined: WOMEN ON JURY LIST. The subhead read: Chosen for October term on Superior Court.

My mind quickly pounced on this. Did women not serve on the jury before 1947? For a number of years after that, each September 13th, I'd simply joke: "OK girls, this is the day you served on a jury for the first time." But I never dug into why women were not on the jury list earlier and what change came about as to permit them to serve for the first time in history in 1947.

In doing this series, when I ran across this note, I resolved to seek some answers. There was not a clue in reading the U.S. Constitution, nor was there anything in the encyclopedia. Not a clue in the Information Please Almanac. There was a reference to jury service in Section 26 of the North Carolina Constitution, but no clue as to when or why this section was adopted. It simply read: Article 1 - Section 26 "Jury Service: No person shall be excluded from jury service on account of sex, race, color, religion or national origin.

That's it. That's all I could find. So I turned for assistance once again to my friend, attorney Kenneth Youngblood, Esquire. In recent months, I have begun to think of Ken, Boyd Massagee and the other members of that law firm as being almost omnipotent because of all those new computers they have at their desks. As far as local history goes, they have quick and easy access to the information highways through their computers where, with the touch of a couple of keys, they can wander through the law library at Carolina (or any university, for that matter), gain access to periodical files, check on the codification of law. Some computer buffs even allege that the Internet in the future may be able to even sneak a peek at the Big Book minded over by St. Peter or the list of those poor souls consigned to Gehenna. I react to them with askance.

When I revealed to Ken my problem on the 4th of July, 1996, he turned quickly to the computer. In less than a minute he said, "Ah hah, here it is. It involves an associate justice of the Supreme Court from Henderson County, one Michael Schenck." As Ken scanned the screen, he shared with me the information that a man had appealed a conviction to the Supreme Court and the case had been assigned to Associate Justice Michael Schenck. The appeal argued that the man had been convicted by an all-male jury and that women were expressly eliminated from serving on juries in North Carolina, and this had violated the man's constitutional rights. When Judge Schenck issued his finding in 1938, he didn't pussyfoot around. He said the man's appeal was summarily denied because men should be tried by men for their crimes. There was no legal reason to bother the fairer sex with man's transgressions—it was up to men to decide the punishment of all men. And that's that – so sayeth Judge Michael Schenck, associate justice of the North Carolina Supreme Court, who lived in Hendersonville in 1938.

Ken said, "Boy, has he left the door open here. He's established, without saying it that women should also be tried by all-female juries. I don't believe this is going to fly. Give me another hour on this, if you would." An hour later he reported that Judge Schenck's unusual decision had caused foreheads to furrow in the State Legislature; and by 1946 a Constitutional amendment had been passed which became Article 1 - Section 26 of the N.C. Constitution, which I gave to you earlier: "No person shall be excluded from jury service on account of sex, race, color, religion or national origin."

So, by the autumn of the next year, the names of women were placed in the jury box. County Commission Chairman D.G. Wilkie said that the names, not only of women but of Negroes, had been obtained from tax records, from telephone directories and other sources as provided by the new law. Of the forty-two jurors drawn for the two-week October 1947 term of Superior Court, four were women. They were Mrs. Ruth Lee Harrell of Hendersonville, Mrs. Emma McCall Posey of Horse Shoe, Mrs. Margie Hamilton of Hendersonville, and Mrs. Mary H. Smyth of Hendersonville.

So these ladies (and all other females and blacks who have served on juries in North Carolina since 1947) can thank Judge Michael Schenck of Hendersonville for having issued such a strong denial of an appeal, stating without question that men should always be tried only by their peers (other men). That verdict directly led to the adopting of the 26th Amendment giving everyone the right to sit on juries.

Judge Schenck died in 1948 and is buried in Oakdale Cemetery. He would be amazed at how completely opposite the composite of the courts is today, compared to his vision in 1938. Not only have blacks and women served on hundreds of juries, in 1983, Mrs. Mary V. Mims, a teacher at

Mrs. Mary V. Mims

Hendersonville High School, was selected for Grand Jury duty; and on Jan. 1, 1984, she was named foreman of the Grand Jury. Mrs. Mary V. Mims is a black woman and she has a daughter, Yvonne Mims Evans, who serves as a district judge in Charlotte, N.C.

Paving the Way to the Future

In Volume 1 of "From the Banks of Oklawaha," Mr. Frank L. FitzSimons says (and I quote): "July 4, 1879 was undoubtedly the most momentous and important day in the entire history of Hendersonville and Henderson County in particular and all of Western North Carolina in general. On that day the first steam engine huffed and puffed up the Saluda grade, roared over the crest of the Blue Ridge Mountains, thundered down the long grade from Butte Mountain and East Flat Rock; and with screeching brakes and sparks flying from the wheels came to a stop at the new depot in Hendersonville."

Hendersonville had only become a county in 1838—so this huge development had occurred only forty-one years after the county came into being. It would take another eighty-eight years before the next truly major development in transportation would take place—the most important milestone for lifestyle enhancement and development opportunity in my entire lifetime and certainly the most important in the last fifty years.

The opening of I-26 took place with a ribbon cutting on Jan. 12, 1967. I-26 was first discussed as a part of the interstate system. That would have been in 1952. Eight years later (in 1960), public hearings were held in the counties which would be traversed by the new highway. The hearing in Buncombe County in 1959 suggested there would be greater input than the other public hearings because the State Highway Commission was considering two different locations for the huge intersection I-26 would make with the East/West I-40.

The hearing here in Henderson County was held on Jan. 26, 1960, and the locating of the new four-lane highway (which would be Henderson County's first such road) on its present site met no opposition. The crowd packed into the Court House was asked: "Is there any opposition to the location of this new road" Fifteen or twenty hands were raised, and it turned out that all of those people were from Polk County. Again, the question was

Seventh Avenue East at the time the state proposed making it the primary entrance into the city from the new interstate highway. Two-way traffic would have been continued, and there were no provisions for the surface crossing of railroad tracks.

then asked, "Is there any opposition from Henderson County residents?" Not a hand was raised.

The first sign of any construction took place on Feb. 19, 1963, when a small sign was erected on U.S. 25 near Rugby Road announcing the new I-26 highway would be constructed on this site. Rights-of-way were being acquired, however, as early as 1961. Some construction work had already begun on the four-lane highway when the State Highway Commission (on May 17, 1963) revealed its plans for the connector road from the highway into the city. Basically the proposed connector would simply follow the route of old U.S. 64 and 7th Avenue East. It would be widened into a four-lane highway from the interstate to the city limits at Mud Creek. West-bound traffic would simply continue up 7th Avenue which would continue to be a two-way street. Sixth Avenue would be extended from about Jonas Street (where it dead-ended) on down to Mud Creek, where it would tie into the widened old 64.

Well, the merchants and property owners on 7th Avenue East were jubilant. Just the announcement that the main connector to the new super highway would come in on Chimney Rock Road and boost traffic on 7th Avenue created a fever you could equate with the gold rush. The Exxon

Company raced in and purchased the Fred King house and land next to the old radio station at Devils Fork. They paid about twice what it was worth, even though there had been no firm decision on the location of the new connector. But when the specifics in fine print were analyzed, even the State Highway Commission admitted that present traffic flow on 7th Avenue (then just 9,400 vehicles a day) would within fifteen years reach a count of 17,800 vehicles a day.

The Highway Commission planned no improvements to the surface crossing of the Southern Railroad. There had been one death that had occurred the previous year when an ambulance could not come from the east side to the hospital because all crossings were blocked by a long freight train. I had made the comment that if Southern's trains get any longer, when the first engines come through Hendersonville, the caboose would not have left Cincinnati. The State Highway Commission made it abundantly clear that this was the plan, and that the commission would not entertain changes in any way.

I called a special meeting of the Planning Board and asked Dan Vismore (our professional planner from the WNC Regional Planning Commission) to examine in detail (in advance) what the state was proposing and the shortcomings he might find. At the meeting Dan said, "The enormous increase in traffic on both 6th and 7th avenues (neither to be improved) will be a major challenge to the city but the great weaknesses in the plan are the proposed surface crossings of the railroad on both 6th and 7th avenues." He then referred to a formula developed by the U.S. Bureau of Public Roads, which factors in the number of trains using a surface crossing, the number of vehicles tied up, fuel wasted by idling motors, and time lost to waiting drivers.

Vismore said, "I am confident that an accurate count over a period of just one week will prove that if we use the state's own figures, this planned construction will come nowhere close to meeting the standards required on this national formula. Bill Stokes (a member of the Planning Board and

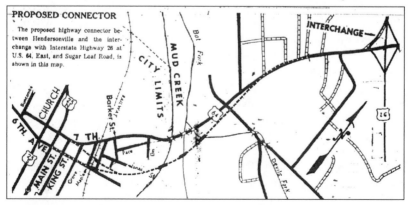

DOT map showing routing of proposed new connector from I-26.

director of the Water & Sewer Department) volunteered from his staff sufficient manpower to monitor the two crossings twenty-four hours a day for one week.

Everything went great for about five days; and suddenly, NO TRAINS. Someone had apparently passed the word to the railroad that "something was going on over in Hendersonville," so the railroad severely curtailed traffic between Asheville and Spartanburg; and the few trains that did run were scheduled to pass through Hendersonville between midnight and 5 a.m. Perhaps the word had leaked out that the Hendersonville Planning Board had employed an architect to do a sketch of actually lowering the railroad tracks so that simple surface bridges could guarantee passage over the trains. Next time you cross the railroad at 7th, notice that the 7th Avenue crossing is on top of a hill. We were going to provide an alternate solution that the tracks simply be lowered beneath the surface crossings. This may have sounded like a simple solution, but the highway folks just don't like to tangle with railroads. They almost always lose.

In fact, everybody thinks that all the new guard gates and lights at various railroad crossings have been installed by the railroad. Wrong! They're paid for by the Department of Transportation. We had gathered enough data during the first five days to document our argument. We could extrapolate our findings to cover a full week. We knew with these numbers we had a winner. With the help of professional planners, Hendersonville's case was thoroughly documented, and an appointment was made with Billy Rose (then administrator of the State Highway Commission) to permit Hendersonville to make its official presentation. Chief of Police Bill Powers served as escort for Mayor A.V. Edwards, City Councilman Melvin Hatch, planner Dan Vismore and myself.

That was the first time I was ever in the board room of the State Highway Building in Raleigh. In later years, when I saw the movie "Network," I was reminded of that experience. Billy Rose sat at one end of dual tables, which had twelve upholstered arm chairs on each side. Our little group sat at the other end. The presentation was made, and I could tell that when we presented the railroad crossing numbers Rose's entire attitude changed abruptly. We were told the state would re-examine the plan, and would be in touch with us, and we were dismissed.

The city was kept on hold for two years. On May 19, 1965, the State Highway Commission unveiled a totally new plan, which resulted in the connector as we know Four Seasons Boulevard today. There would be a new four-lane highway (elevated above flood plain level) and would cross the railroad on a bridge 22 feet above the roadbed of the railroad. Seventh Avenue would become one-way between Grove Street and its connection with 6th Avenue at Buncombe Street. Sixth Avenue would handle east-bound traffic to where both streets connected into a new four-lane highway at Harris Street and running on to I-26, exactly what you see today.

That plan had hardly been unveiled when property owners and merchants organized on 7th Avenue. In a letter, thirty-four business people advised the city of their active opposition, and demanded that the city go back to the original plan. The city mailed the letter to the Highway Commission. On August 6, W.F. Babcock (who had become administrator of the State Highway Commission) in a response to this letter from 7th Avenue business people, advised that the commission had studied and restudied the project and basically could find no reason to alter their position and would favor building the new boulevard.

Later in August, 14th Division Highway Commissioner Curtis Russ spoke to a joint meeting of City Council and the Planning & Zoning Board. He warned that if for any reason it now became necessary for this plan to go back for more study, "you will lose the priority which you now enjoy and I-26 could be in use for a number of years with no access from the interstate into town, except over existing and unimproved streets."

In that same meeting in 1965, Russ told of plans in the making for four-laning a new highway from Kings Mountain to Tryon—a road that was finally opened to traffic in 1992 (twenty-seven years later).

But the opposition continued to hammer away at Mayor Edwards and the City Council until March 10, 1966, when the city caved in and asked for the Highway Commission to do another study. The opposition had even brought people from a number of churches who were said to be opposed to the new Four Seasons Boulevard. City Council was told that the Grace Lutheran Church, the Catholic Church, the Presbyterian Church and the First United Methodist Church all opposed the new plan. I first called on the Rev. Walter Lee Lanier at the First United Methodist Church, who bristled visibly when I read from the newspaper that his church opposed the plan. "There is only one person who can speak for this church, and I am not opposed to the plan." I then called on Father Howard Lane, who said, "We are opposed to both plans. We would like to see a bypass built which would take all east-west traffic away from our school."

Shortly, I was appointed chairman of the Upper French Board Economic & Development Commission, and it was necessary to resign my position with the Planning Board. Frank Todd was appointed to replace me and was named chairman of the board. The day after it was announced that the city had reversed itself again and had asked the Highway Commission for still another study, Todd issued a statement saying that council had not con-sulted with him in any way, council had not even discussed the matter with the Planning Board; and he said, "Our board is not connected in any way with the action taken by City Council last night." The Chamber of Com-merce reaffirmed its solid support for the new boulevard. The Jaycees on March 16 passed a resolution urging the city to proceed with the boulevard.

When informed of the action of the City Council, Curtis Russ said, "If there are further delays on the Hendersonville project, the Highway

Commission will consider shifting funds set up for the Hendersonville project to one where local cooperation would be 100 percent."

By May 25, the 7th Avenue group was armed for bear. They were being led by L.B. Prince (himself a former chairman of the Highway Commission) who prepared a position paper for the group with blistering criticism of the Highway Commission. The paper accused the Chamber of Commerce with thoughtless meddling, making a feasible solution impossible.

Throughout the day, Mayor Al Edwards talked to a number of people, and it was obvious when the meeting opened that night the city had experienced a bellyful and had made the final decision. The mayor asked for and received a unanimous vote from City Council for approval of the new connector; and then advised the jam-packed crowd that the issue was ended.

The new road would cost (just in the city) $650,000; and normally the city would be expected to pay one half. But Commissioner Russ said because of the unusual circumstances involving the ralroad, the city would pay less than $100,000 and that could be paid for in installments.

While the state decreed that the totally new portion of Four Seasons Boulevard would have only "restricted" access where the new construction joined the old U.S. 64 at Linda Vista Drive, it would have grandfathered in free access from that point to the I-26 interchange. That is the reason that every business from Linda Vista on out the boulevard to the connector has entrance and exits onto this congested thoroughfare.

Speaking of congestion, remember: The state (in 1963, when it proposed the original widening of U.S. 64 and two-way traffic on 7th for access into the city from I-26) said that 9,400 vehicles per day were using U.S. 64 and 7th Avenue. The state projected that by the year 1980, 17,800 vehicles would be counted. By actual count in 1991, 30,000 vehicles per day were using Four Seasons Boulevard. In 1992 an extra lane was added from Dana Road intersection to the mall, and in that stretch of thoroughfare on a busy summer afternoon, 43,800 vehicles per day have been counted. At that Dana Road intersection (with the new lanes added in 1992), there are now seven lanes of traffic on the west side of that intersection.

A Bit of Retrospect and Trivia

In 1995-96 on several occasions because of high water, people on the east side of the county were able to get into Hendersonville on only one road—the elevated Four Seasons Boulevard. Every other road into the city from the northeast to the southeast had low-lying sections of roadway under water, including the busy U.S. 176/U.S. 25 intersection on the south end of town.

On one occasion, after having dinner at Kelsey's, we found the 176/25 intersection under water and quickly reflected on all the alternate roads from the east side into the city; and finally concluded that our only access would be to go to East Flat Rock, take I-26 to Four Seasons Boulevard and then into town, which we did.

Over the past 50 years, only the following new roads have been constructed in Henderson County:

1. I-26 through the county.

2. The I-26 connector (Four Seasons Boulevard).

3. Less than a mile from East High School to U.S. 176 to provide an alternate access from I-26 into the city.

4. A portion of N.C. 280 (the Brevard connector to the airport).

U.S. 25 North is now being improved, not just by widening but by enormous excavations around Stoney Mountain to straighten out the hazards that have always been at Newman's Curve. U.S. 64 East is to be widened from Uno (at North Henderson High School) to the four-lane boulevard at Ebenezer. A major item being pushed by the Chamber of Commerce's Highway & Roads Committee is for a new northern access interchange at Clear Creek, which would bring traffic from the north into the city along North Main Street, and would eliminate this traffic from the present congestion of Four Seasons Boulevard.

For the more than sixty years the N.C. Highway Commission has been in existence, in only eight of those years has a Henderson County man served as a board member or highway commissioner (as they used to be called). It is definitely a political appointment, but in the years and years the county voted Democratic, only two men served from Henderson County: L. Ben Prince and Harry Buchanan. In the GOP years, a short stint was served by A.J. Henderson and myself. And while the appointments always go to the other counties, Henderson County has the largest city in the 14th Division, more miles of highway than any other county by far, more people, and more unpaved miles of roads. Henderson County pays more taxes (income and sales) than any other county in the 14th Division.

A bit of trivia about your highways:

One standard traffic lane will carry 2,000 vehicles per hour traveling at 55 miles per hour. If it happens that 2,100 vehicles try to move on that same lane, traffic slows. If you add enough cars to that one traffic lane, then traffic comes to a total stop. You have a parking lot.

In the early days of Gov. James Martin, border counties all wanted the state to build welcome centers on all roads leading into the state through their area. The state agreed to build if the local county would staff the centers. In a couple of years, the counties came back and wanted the state to pay for staffing. At that point, the state agreed to staff only the welcome centers on an interstate highway and told the counties with other roads that they would have to furnish the staffing.

As these local areas began to battle for the money coming in for personal "vanity" license plates and from private contributions, Dottie Martin suggested to her husband (the governor), "Why don't we simply pledge all those monies to plant flowers along the highways for home folks and visitors to enjoy." So that's where the money came from for the many beautiful wildflowers you see along our N.C. interstate highways; and the program has won national awards repeatedly for innovative beautification of the nation's roads.

Wheels

Very few men leaving for military service in World War II had ever owned a car or truck. They had learned to drive in a brother's or buddy's car. As they were issued military vehicles and were shipped east and west around the world, they carried with them memories of the roads back home.

Stretches of those roads had been given sobriquets such as "the winding stairs" on U.S. 25 South; "dead man's curve" on U.S. 176; "drunkard's flats" on U.S. 74 East at Lake Lure; "the mile straight stretch" on U.S. 64 East at Edneyville; or "Newman's curve" on U.S. 25 North.

When the GI's returned, the two-lane roads were the same and the hazards had not been corrected. As their training had intensified in the military, these men had been issued jeeps, cargo trucks, recon vehicles, tracked weaponry units such as heavy artillery pieces and tanks. Young boys from the mountains and coves of Henderson County now commanded PT boats, LSTs, destroyers, and even heavier naval vessels.

When the war was finally over and the GIs were being handed their "ruptured duck insignia" along with membership in the 52/20 club. They suddenly found themselves rifted back to civilian life—now all they could think of was getting their own WHEELS!

It would be three years before Detroit could shift from military production lines to the production of family cars. Each automobile dealer made up his own waiting list; and it grew longer, and longer, and longer.

In the meantime, some of the lesser-known car makers had hit the ground running, and our family was lucky enough to own a brand spankin' new 1949 Nash "600." With a modern overdrive feature, the Nash people said you could get 600 miles to the tank of gas without stopping. It also had another great feature: the passenger's seat lowered and locked into the rear seat, forming a bed. It allowed drivers to alternate between resting and driving on long trips.

Prior to the war, all NASCAR or stock car racing was done on dirt tracks or at local fairgrounds. The cars raced on weekends. During the week, the owner-driver hauled white liquor or moonshine usually out of Wilkes County to Charlotte, Winston-Salem, or Raleigh. In every one of these moonshine families was a shade-tree mechanic who could figure out a way to get a little more power or better acceleration out of what the Detroit engineers had designed.

There were always good-natured arguments over who had the best car. So for fun, a bunch of them would gather on weekends and race each other on bets placed by their cohorts. Somebody figured out that the public would pay good money to witness these challenges, and before long, Buck Baker, Cotton Owens, Tim Flock, David Pearson, Lee and Richard Petty, Bobby Isaac, Cale Yarborough, Darrell Waltrip, and Bobby Allison all became household names to race fans. It even created a new industry of building these race cars; and Banjo Matthews gave up driving for the bigger bucks in manufacturing.

After the war, one of the sharpest race car promoters in the business, Bill France dreamed up the Grand National Circuit, which would race on paved tracks with races of 500 miles or more. To be entered, each car had to be a late model vehicle and abide by technical restrictions which would be updated every year. The first of these "super speedway" races was to be held in 1949 at a brand new track built at Darlington, S.C. for the Grand National Circuit. Even for these lengthy grand national races, most of the drivers were still sticking to Fords, Chevrolets, a few Pontiacs—though Buck Baker did enter the biggest Buick built that year. Some innovative soul had swallowed the Nash 600 hook, line and sinker, and was going to attempt to drive the Nash 600 the entire 500-mile race without making a pit stop.

In that we had just bought one of the 600s, I just had to go to that race and see "my car" run. I conned three friends into going along with me. To be sure we wouldn't miss any of the action, we left Hendersonville just after midnight and rolled into Darlington bright and early the next morning. We were shocked to discover there were no grandstands—no seats of any kind. In fact, there were just a few "Porta-Johns" and a few pipes sticking up out of the ground with spigots on them. The track was finished and paved—that's all! Though there were thousands of places to sit on the embankment around the track, all were occupied by millions of sand fleas.

The Grand National Race differs totally from the old short dirt track battles. There's tremendous excitement just before the race begins and perhaps the first ten laps. After that, watching a string of cars go round and round on a track is about as exciting as playing tennis without a net. By the time that first race had ended, the sun had crossed the yardarm and thousands of cars and passengers waited without hope of ever getting out of the field they were parked in, and then onto the road back home. It was not tailgating, but as Andy Griffith would say, "Buddy, let's have a little drank."

Covered with large, tender sun blisters, eaten alive by sand fleas, and a nervous wreck from dodging the wild driving of all the amateurs who had sought to emulate the race drivers all the way to Columbia, we finally rolled back in the yard, spent and exhausted from the only Grand National Race we would ever attend.

Oh! The Nash 600—after about 75 laps, the entire drive train fell from the car and it had to be towed off the track back to the pits, having run its first and only race ever on the Grand National Circuit.

Interstate highways

The years from 1945 to 1950 involved massive adjustment for the city and its services. The older servicemen who had left a job to go into military services were guaranteed their jobs back. But except for the construction of the Select Freezer Warehouse on Ray Street, there were virtually no other jobs available (except part-time "grunt" work). The 52/20 Club was devised by the U.S. government to provide $20 per week for 52 weeks to every veteran who would continue to look for work. This income (augmented by funds from family or friends) could finance a set of wheels for the returning vet, who argued that he'd have a better chance of finding a job if he could get back and forth to work. Even junkyards were scavenged for cars that could be made to run or for parts to make another car operate.

Traffic in the downtown became a bottleneck. Mayor Al Edwards appointed a Blue Ribbon Committee (chaired by Ben Prince) to study the traffic problem and bring forth recommended changes. The mayor also appointed Donald B. Keith and John Holly to head up a group trying to find more off-street parking. The Hendersonville Merchants' Association agreed to put up half the money (if the city would match it) to pay for a comprehensive study of the downtown area (or Central Business District). The city agreed. The downtown had always been the "cash cow" paying a major portion of the city taxes and virtually all the privilege license fees.

Almost no one here (and very few elsewhere in the country) realized that the "think tanks" in Washington were devising long-range plans which would change the face of America forever. Most economists agree that had it not been for World War II, this nation might still be under the doldrums of the Great Depression; and it was obvious to everyone in government that once the troops were sent home and the defense plants were closed, there would be an immediate return to the Great Depression.

Every American serviceman was impressed with Germany's four-lane superhighways called autobahns. This super-modern road system was conjured up by Fritz Todt, and was carried to completion by Albert Spear. The Keynesian economists in Washington were convinced that the national government would have to "prime the economic pump" and the program should be so huge and flexible that it could bolster the U.S. economy for generations to come.

Thus, in 1956 (during the Eisenhower administration), the Federal Highway Aid Pact was approved. It called for the U.S. government (in thirteen to fifteen years) to construct 41,000 miles of new four-lane highways connecting twenty-nine cities in the forty-eight contiguous states. The project would cost 40 TRILLION dollars. Lobbyists for the automakers, the cement companies, rubber tire manufacturers and the huge oil companies wielded sufficient power to admit to the Congress the total cost would likely exceed 50 TRILLION dollars. It was a cinch to sell. Everyone wants a new road to any and everywhere. Though the time frame of construction was set for fifteen years, the road (now forty-seven years later) is still being constructed through Madison County. The beauty of this basic foundation for the national economy was that every forty years, the roads would have to be rebuilt. Only during the last few years has there been any discussion of the reality that ultimately all the land will be covered by roads and parking lots, and nothing has been done for mass transit.

Battle to Save Downtown

As massive changes were taking place in small towns and big cities across America (as a result of the Interstate Highway Program), most towns felt their problems were totally unique. A lack of parking was universal and would become worse in every future year. In 1970, the city passed an ordinance that required any new business built in the city to provide defined off-street parking except: the Central Business District from 1st to 7th Avenue and bounded a block away by King and Church streets. The reason for the exception was obvious. Development within this area was already so intense such an ordinance was ludicrous.

The city gave approval for the establishment of a new Downtown Parking Corporation to be headed by Donald B. Keith. Not being an official part of city government, the new corporation could explore (without bureaucratic red tape) any area deemed appropriate for additional parking. Keith was successful in selling stock in this new corporation which could then purchase or lease property and hold it for the city to ultimately acquire with community development or other funds. With Keith as president and with the help of John Holley and other members of the Downtown Parking Commission Board, the group was successful in securing approval from the city to purchase an entire half-block area, bounded along 4th Avenue and running from Church to Washington streets. Two older hotels, the Ames (or Bowen or Hodgewell), along with the Kentucky Home, would be demolished for the new parking lot.

Donald B. Keith

Even with the successes so far achieved, a special CBD (Central Business District) study released in 1965 showed that while 3,036 new parking spaces had been added, at least 463 additional spaces were urgently needed between 2nd and 7th avenues. The 1965 study was completed with funds from the Urban Renewal

The only parking downtown in 1948 was "on street"; even the lot behind the Skyland Hotel was for private use. Almost no store attempted to provide parking for its customers.

Administration. The chief planner was Dan Vismore, with Alan Lang as design planner. The study also said:

"After prefacing remarks about the advantage of the city's wide Main Street, the broad sidewalks, the trees and shrubs downtown, the report said: WHILE THE CITY'S CBD OFFERS A GREAT MANY MORE DESIR-ABLE QUALITIES THAN OTHER TOWNS, THE MODERN DAY SHOPPING CENTER (AND MALL) POSES A SERIOUS THREAT TO THE FUTURE LIFE OF SUCH CITIES AS HENDERSONVILLE.

An earlier study of the downtown had been done by planners from Chapel Hill and naught had come from it. When the 1965 study was released, there had been no real development in the periphery around the downtown area, and business still boomed in spite of the fact that many of the property owners were absentee and not willing to re-invest any of their rental income for improving or even maintaining their buildings. The 1965 study gathered dust. In 1967, Hendersonville experienced its first competition from "the outside" when a new Rose's store served as an anchor of a new convenience shopping center on Hendersonville's south side.

As the years went by, nine vacancies occurred in the CBD. In 1972, it became obvious to the leaders of the "Save Downtown" effort that a new organization was needed whose only purpose was to work to revamp the Central Business District. A new Hendersonville Merchants' Association was formed, and it was interesting to note that while the primary objective of this group was to save the downtown area, of the thirteen charter members, seven had NO business interest of any sort in the CBD. If the entire town was to be successful, it was vital to save the core. One of the motions made to the city was introduced by Jim Taylor (manager of the Rose's store on the south side) and seconded by Bob Wilson at Economy Drug Store on 5th Avenue West.

The new Hendersonville Merchants' group was successful in persuading Cal Kuykendall to dispose of his own business and work full-time for the HMA. By this time, the HMA boasted as members 203 businesses in the greater Hendersonville area. To inspire merchant and landowner support, the city approved a request to invite the TVA Townlift Program for its cooperation. One of their main contributions was to persuade retired architects to redraw how the CBD should look, given an adequate facelift.

By 1974 the matter of Hendersonville's downtown had become urgent. In the past, sixty-one percent of city revenue had come from CBD ad valorem and license fees. In the countywide property valuation of 1974, value in real estate downtown was reduced by a drastic twenty percent; while value in other parts of the city and county had increased forty to fifty percent.

The 1965 CBD plan was inspired totally by a similar plan put to use in Grand Junction, Colorado. A group of twelve (including two city commissioners and the city attorney) flew to Grand Junction for an on-site inspection. This marked a turning point. Upon their return, the HMA decided that it was vital to have a "special tax district" established, now permitted under an act passed only the year before by the General Assembly. The first challenge was to sell merchants and property owners on the need for this tax. Hundreds of meetings were held, block by block, group by group, with a final meeting scheduled at City Hall, which attracted a standing-room only crowd. At the end of the presentation, a motion was made to approve an annual tax of three mils to be used to cover retirement of costs of improvements and maintenance of the CBD in the years to come. Only three votes were recorded as opposed to the proposed tax.

Mayor Boyce Whitmire had succeeded Al Edwards as head of the city, and he said, "All of this sounds fine and good, but the city has already invested hundreds of thousands of dollars helping the merchants downtown and we think it's time the merchants show their financial support by guaranteeing the repayment of whatever loan is needed. We will collect the CBD tax; but if for any reason the monies do not fulfill the obligations, it will be the merchants responsibility to guarantee the loan, and none of it would be paid by residents through their own taxes."

Thus began one of the weirdest campaigns ever held in this state. The HMA Board, aided by dozens of volunteers, canvassed businesses all over the county, asking them to sign a commitment to put up $1,000 of their own money to pay off any loan incurred by the CBD if not covered by the three mil tax. More than 250 businessmen signed the contingent liability note, and most of them had no business interest in the downtown: car dealers, lumber yards, farm-related industry. It is evidence of the affirmation of the love and devotion by all business people to "their downtown."

After Northwestern Bank had granted a credit line of $250,000, Mayor Boyce Whitmire appointed a special committee to oversee construction and be responsible for the expending of funds needed. Whitmire named Jody Barber as chairman, his wife (Mary Barber) as chairman of a special Beautification Committee. The Downtown Committee included Sam McGuirt of Duke Power; Donald B. Keith of Brunsons (who would continue to head the Parking Corp.); attorney Charles Waters, architect Emory Jackson, and myself. Cal Kuykendall and his secretary, Charlotte Buller, would provide staff. David Quinn, senior planner of the N.C. Department of Natural Resources and Community Development, would be consultant to the committee. Mayor Whitmire authorized William "Bill" Powers, who had just been promoted to manager of City Facilities, as overall superintendent; and Bill Lapsley, assistant to Bill Stokes at the water department as consultant on utilities. Also, Mayor Whitmire authorized Bill Powers to draw on the support of any and every city employee who could be "loaned" to him for work on the project. P.T. Green Builders also volunteered to provide equipment and/or staff (as available) and would be reimbursed only his cost. Dan Waddell and Bob Brummett volunteered (when needed) specialty heavy equipment. (One rail from the old Columbia Trolley Line that ran from Main down 1st Avenue to Lennox Park was unearthed during construction.) Because Frank Todd was a city official, rather than chance any sort of conflict of interest, he donated all the bricks needed for the project to a third party who, in turn, donated them to the city.

Cal Kuykendall

The CBD Committee met weekly from November 1974 until the completion of the project in 1977. Most of the meetings were held at the home of the Barbers in Laurel Park. From the time the committee would begin sipping soup or biting into sandwiches, talk would begin about the most current progress made and discussion of any problems encountered. Especially during the first year, members of the committee were roundly criticized by phone calls, letters to the editor, and general word of mouth. Teenagers didn't want an end to their constant cruising every night, some did not like the serpentine pattern of the street, which would slow traffic but was designed to make Main Street safer for pedestrians to cross. Cars could be parked diagonally (easier for older people than parallel parking) and yet could back out to leave without blocking traffic; but there were fewer spaces.

The spectacular flower show that goes on year 'round is the envy of every small town in the state. There are no store vacancies on Main Street and the diversity of the individual shop owners provides an adventure in shopping not found in malls that look the same whether in Las Vegas or Biltmore. There are now a half dozen fine restaurants for nighttime dining downtown. Even a number of two-story buildings have extensively remodeled the upper floor into beautiful apartments and condominiums.

The only feature the committee never got around to was to build our own local answer to the Hollywood Walk of Fame. On the sidewalk on Main Street near 6th Avenue (where the Barber family ran their stores for almost 100 years) should be installed the first two stars:

JODY BARBER   MARY BARBER

TRIVIA

Feb.	1946	City buys 250 parking meters for Main Street.
	1953	King and Church become one-way streets.
	1956	Efirds bought by Belks. Belks then closed all Efirds.
	1956	Federal Highway Act creating the Interstate System ap proved by Congress to cost 41 TRILLION dollars.
	1965	Central Business District Master Plan submitted to the city.
	1967	I-26 opened from S.C. line to Columbus, N.C.
	1967	Rose's, the first big non-downtown store, opens.
	1967	U.S. 25 from S.C. line opened to I-26 at Flat Rock.
	1968	I-40 to the Tennessee line opened.
	1968	I-26 opened to I-40. Named "Blue Star Memorial High way to honor the Men & Women Who Died in Service."
	1968	Belk opens enlarged store downtown.
	1970	Hendersonville Merchants' Association reorganized, Downtown Revitalization Committee named.
Dec.	1970	F.W. Woolworth closes after 43 years downtown. Northwestern Bank approves $250,000 credit line for work in t the Central Business District.
Oct.	1976	Last link of I-26 opened over Peter Guice Bridge to Columbus, N.C.
	1975	Metal license plates no longer issued annually; new plates every five years. Then later, no new plates, only stickers.
July	1974	Became legal to make a right turn on red.
	1992	Traffic lights synchronized in Hendersonville.

Two thousand acres of wildflowers planted along N.C. highways (paid for by personalized license plates; idea of Dottie Martin, wife of Gov. Jim Martin).

Dec. 7 1941 "The Bluebird," starring Shirley Temple, Spring Byington and Nigel Bruce was playing at the Carolina Theatre.

Penney's

For almost 70 years, Hendersonville has enjoyed a unique relationship with not only the J.C. Penney Company but with its managers and employees. The ribbon-cutting ceremony for their first store here took place on Aug. 1, 1929. That first store was located on the corner of 4th and Main, which has at one time or another also housed The Leader, Efird's, and Jack Schulman's Can-Do, Will-Do Store.

The first Penney's store manager was E.W. Ham, and he thus became the first manager of a "chain store" in Hendersonville. After just six years in Hendersonville, he was elected to president of the Chamber of Commerce. While serving in this high office, he was successful in having the hydrangea named as the official flower of the city—which proved almost as popular as the Susan B. Anthony coin. It was while he was manager, the Penney Co. elected to build a brand new building of their own at 422-24 North Main (now occupied by the Village Green Antiques). When the building was completed in 1939, Ham was promoted and transferred to a larger city, and Hugh Bowden was moved to Hendersonville as manager of the new store. He served here until his retirement and was succeeded by Bruce Needham. Hugh Bowden's wife, Geneva, took a strong and active role in every kind of community activity.

When Penney's opened that new building, the store featured not only a main floor level, but there was a complete basement of equal size filled with merchandise, and also a balcony. Every department had pneumatic tubes running directly to the cashier. The little canister would shoot like bullets through the tubes, be handled by the cashier, and then it shot back to the department from which it had come. Penney's was the first store in Hendersonville to open a complete toyland in the basement at Christmastime. I had never seen as many toys in my life. When the major department stores moved to the Blue Ridge Mall, Bruce Needham retired and Bill Reese assumed management when Penney's opened there.

The J.C. Penney Co. has always been a unique organization. Men who started at Penney's either retired at Penney's or became very successful merchants in their own right, such as Jim Pressley, who started at Penney's in Hendersonville and then was transferred to their Asheville store. He later opened his own highly successful J. Pressley Ltd. in Asheville.

The J.C. Penney Co. was the first major department store to build its own building in downtown Hendersonville. It operated at 422-24 North Main Street for more than 40 years before relocating to the blue Ridge Mall. The building is now occupied by Village Green Antiques.

Even in retirement, national executives of the Penney Co. still exhibit the same intense interest in the local Penney's store and in our community. Clint Thompson was senior marketing executive for J.C. Penney Co. in New York. Clint and Shirley retired to Hendersonville and Clint was one of the top five people in putting together the groundwork for the local multi-million dollar Community Foundation. He is also very active in Carolina Village. Penney's (in larger markets) created a new division that dealt exclusively with custom decorating. After being sales promotion manager, Charlie Logan headed up that division for Penney's. Charlie's interests, beyond the Shriners, knew no boundaries.

But there was one lady who was a fixture at Penney's until she retired a few years ago. She had the sweetest disposition I have ever known. Now, when

I identify her as Mrs. Oscar Milholen, I run the risk of antagonizing at least ten other long-term Penney's people who were personal friends–but Mrs. Milholen could remove warts by remote control. Quite a few people can rub warts and they disappear, but Mrs. Milholen (who lived across Chimney Rock Road from the old radio station) could remove warts and you didn't even have to be around.

Minding Their Businesses

Shortly after the child bride and I had exchanged vows, we set up housekeeping (as they used to say in the '40s) in what I had always called the Maxwell Apartments–though I notice official records list it as Jackson Apartments. It was owned and operated by Mrs. Bernice McAllister, who lived in one of the apartments. Before she would allow you to rent one of the units, she'd do a character investigation in more depth than that of a fraternal order.

We had one of the rear units, which consisted of a living room and kitchen. There was a Murphy bed that pulled down from the wall in the living room, and there was an adjacent closet which was just big enough for our son's crib when he was born in October 1948. The refrigerator in the kitchen had the motor on top, and the range had the oven on the same level as the burner units. Those were the golden years when I was young enough to run up and down the two flights of stairs to our apartment.

On the street level, Lawrence Orr and his wife ran Hendersonville's pioneer radio and TV center. To the left of the entrance to the apartments was where "B" and Betty Sims ran the B&B Jax Pax. After the war, Benjamin, the man everyone knows as "B" Sims, bought the grocery store and went into partnership with his brother-in-law, William V. Powers. Five years later, Bill Powers was appointed police chief and sold his interest back to "B."

Living there in the Maxwell (Jackson) Apartments and having the convenience of a mini-supermarket at the foot of the stairs was a dream because back then you couldn't afford a fully stocked pantry. You bought an item only when you needed it right then. If you were out of milk, it would mean running down two flights of stairs, buying a bottle (it was still sold in bottles back then), and then running back up the two flights of stairs.

I said "B" Sims' Jax Pax was a mini-supermarket because he stocked and sold any and everything you'd expect to find in one of the mega markets today, though in smaller quantities. "B's" produce counter was maybe ten feet long, and he had all the staple fruits and vegetables. After all, back then no one had ever heard of kiwi fruit, and the only time you expected to find oranges was around Christmas. "B" had a meat counter along with a cooler in the rear of the store. And naturally, he was the butcher. Nobody had ever heard of Walter, so "B" was the produce man, and most of all, he was bookkeeper and office manager. "B" ran credit accounts and he (like H.M. Flynn) will never tell you either the amount of money people beat him out of by not paying a grocery bill, and certainly would never mention their names.

Benjamin "B" Sims

I first encountered the word IPTAY at the Jax Pax. "B" was an ardent and resolute fan of Clemson, and I learned IPTAY was a contraction of some sort which meant you'd given money to Clemson. I knew there were some small schools like Duke, Wake Forest, and State outside of the great University of North Carolina. I was not as familiar with Clemson; but before or after any football weekend (which meant from Thursday to Tuesday) you knew the good-natured banter that was waiting for you about Death Valley and Clemson the minute you opened the door.

"B" and Betty were active in the Methodist Church. For years, as part of "B's" stewardship, he maintained the grounds around the church at no cost. He was a one-man sales blizzard for the Roy Johnson Bible Class, and they both have practiced their religion all their lives. For years, after he had closed the Jax Pax in 1976, you'd see "B" in other supermarkets loading buggy after buggy with groceries. He was still shopping for and delivering groceries to a dozen or so of the elderly ladies who had been his customers at the B&B, and he continued to be their groceryman at no charge, even when he was no longer in the business.

"B" and my older brother, Grady, went to school together and were lifelong friends. Every time I'd see Grady, sometime in the conversation he'd ask about B. I told Grady once that it would embarrass "B" if it should ever get back to him (being the macho man he is), but I said, "Grady, if you could ever describe a man as being a sweet person, it would be 'B' Sims."

Harkening back to the old country sermons about the pearly gates, I can sort of envision "B" sitting there with his little account pads of people who never paid their bills owed to him at the B&B Jax Pax, and assisting St. Peter on the character of those seeking admission. I can even envision an instance where "B" would study over a long unpaid account, and then flash that big grin and yell out, "Let him in. He's a good man." "B" never met a man he didn't love.

Becker's Bakery

For about 20 years, from the 1930s up to 1953, Hendersonville was Western North Carolina headquarters for Becker's Bakery, a very large family-owned baking company based in Spartanburg. Originally, the plant was located at the corner of 7th Avenue and Grove Street; and from this plant (every day) trucks would roll out, loaded with a variety of products from the Becker ovens bound for Brevard, Waynesville, Sylva, Bryson City, Murphy, and Cherokee. The Hendersonville Becker's plant served all of Western North Carolina.

The plant did not have to concern itself with selling their freshly baked products—Becker's was always in demand. It was an old-line baking family that dated back to the turn of the century. They were more concerned about safety. In fact, A.P. Cox (who was manager of Becker's here in 1941) sponsored a dinner meeting for all "inside" employees—that's the folks who actually worked inside the baking operation. This dinner meeting was for the express purpose of establishing a program to prevent accidents in the bakery. Two top officials even came up from Spartanburg to sit in on the meeting. A committee to develop a safety program was appointed: Glen Ward, Charles Wells, Haskel Buckner, Al Sumner, and James Brown. This committee would work with plant superintendent G.R. Fisher to establish safety guidelines for the plant. No accidents had occurred so far this year, and if no accidents occurred in the rest of 1941, another dinner would be given with a monetary imbursement.

I went to great lengths to talk about this safety meeting because obviously the plant was very healthy economically. In fact, they had built a brand new building at the corner of Church Street and Barnwell (now called Heritage Square and in which the Samovar Cafe is only one of many businesses). The Becker trucks kept rolling out of Hendersonville all over Western North Carolina.

Now there was an article I ran across in the *Times-News* (dated March 14, 1953) that said simply, "General Baking Firm Takes Over Becker Properties." The announcement said, "The General Baking Company acquired the Becker's property about two weeks ago. The Becker's plant is one of the largest in the Southeast."

I had many very good friends who were part of the Becker operation, including Norris Leopard, who had been with Becker's for seventeen years, seven of those in Hendersonville. Norris was promoted upstairs by General Baking. Then there was a local boy, Phil Thibodeau, who had been with Becker's sixteen years. Phil was promoted to supervise WNC Sales. But General Baking made the decision to do away with the Hendersonville operation altogether and service WNC from Spartanburg.

The big question in everyone's mind back in 1953 was why did the Becker family sell the plant to General Baking? Admittedly it is hearsay but

Becker's Bakery was located on the corner of Grove Street and Seventh Avenue in the 1940s.

the information came from my personal friends, who should have been in the know of everything that was going on in the Becker operation.

Here's the story I heard, hearsay though it is: As happens to so many family-owned businesses, the last of the Beckers (who knew baking) had either retired or passed away. The family began a search for an outside management professional, and the man they found turned out to be a real lulu.

He entered into a contract with the Becker family to manage and supervise the entire baking operation. He was to receive a substantial salary and the usual bonuses such a position deserves. An addenda to the contract, however, also made him totally responsible for cake sales, not just in the Becker area but anywhere in the United States. There were no provisions for profits on cake sales. It was out and out commission on the sale of cakes, whether the baker made or lost money selling them. You can anticipate what happened. Becker's suddenly started baking cakes and shipping them to St. Louis, Chicago, New Orleans ... all over the country. They were losing their shirts on every cake they sold, but this new manager was drawing his commission on the total sales of cakes.

By the time the family (in this family-owned business) discovered what had taken place, the business was cash poor and totally vulnerable, and the family had no choice but to sell. They were able to persuade one of the nation's top-quality firms to take over the Becker operation. The General Baking Company went through a re-engineering of the operation (that's what firms today call a downsizing to a lean, mean cadre). They went through this process, and found that with newer highways and better trucks, they could do the entire operation from the single plant in Spartanburg.

It would be a number of years later, but Hendersonville would experience exactly the same result when the original founders of the Coca Cola Bottling Co. of Asheville died, and incoming management quickly closed the Hendersonville Bottling Plant, which had been a part of the local scene for generations. I could add one chapter on this subject about the widow of the founder, who lived in Biltmore Forest. I appealed to her that if her husband was still alive, he would want the Hendersonville Plant to continue operations. She listened intently and said, "I may be old, but I can still pinch an ear or two." The closing was canceled until she died. After her death, within weeks, the plant was closed.

Cool places

Back in the early days of WHKP (in the '40s and '50s) one of the greatest places in all the world on a hot summer day was the Blue Bird. In fact, there were two Blue Birds back then. One was located at the corner of Second Avenue and Main, and the other was known as the Blue Bird Ice Cream Store and was part of the Hot Spot up the next block.

The Blue Bird at the corner of 2nd and Main, where Sinclair Office Supply operates today, was not only the manufacturing plant of the Blue Bird Ice Cream Company, but it was their flagship retail store. It was on March 13, 1940, when J.W. Carson (Julius Withrow Carson) bought out the ice cream manufacturing plant in Spartanburg and moved it to Hendersonville. It actually had started here in 1927 but then was immediately moved to Spartanburg. J.W. Carson moved with it, serving as vice president and general manager. Carson was a local boy, and he dreamed of the day when he could move the Blue Bird back to Hendersonville. The company (though its manufacturing plant was in Spartanburg) did operate the retail store at the corner of 2nd and Main here in Hendersonville. In 1940, Mr. Carson persuaded the owner (Mr. V.O. Garrison) to sell to him the manufacturing equipment and all other assets except the building. That was sold in a separate transaction to four buyers.

On March 15, 1940, all the equipment had been moved back to Hendersonville, and once again ice cream was being manufactured on Main Street. Mr. Carson also bought additional equipment which provided the capability of making popsicles, polar bars, and ice cream sandwiches. This was really a big deal back then because the value of the machinery and the dealer boxes was more than $50,000, a lot of money in 1940. The term "dealer boxes" referred to the individual freezers placed in stores around Western North Carolina in which Blue Bird products were kept for sale. Blue Bird would supply the box and fill it with ice cream products, and the merchant would profit from ice cream sales. At the Blue Bird (next to the Hot

Spot operated by Frank Edney), they carried every product made by the Blue Bird Company. Mr. Carson later persuaded Charles A. Allen to join the firm as general manager. For years, trucks would roll from 299 North Main Street, delivering ice cream products to stores all over Western North Carolina.

My only concern back then, as a very young man, was to accumulate enough money to walk under the bright awning at the Blue Bird and, standing beneath the gently rotating paddle fans in the immaculate confines of a real ice cream parlor, order a popsicle. Mr. Carson and Mr. Allen had dreamed up a gimmick of inserting not just a stick in the popsicles, but occasionally they'd slip in one that said "free." Of course, that meant you had another popsicle coming absolutely free.

Today, we have at least nine ice cream parlors in the area, including the famous "Miss Piggy's" just across from Broadcast House (which achieved national fame in 1997 through U.S. News' Vacation Supplement). Some of these are even air conditioned; but, as you recall the joys and delights of one's youth, nothing could ever be as wonderful as walking under that striped awning into "The Blue Bird." I believe Mr. Carson died in 1960. After the Blue Bird closed and the assets were liquidated, Charlie Allen then became associated with the Kalmia Dairy and Bert Browning, Jr.

Cream of the crop

Back in 1922, A. S. "Bert" Browning, Jr. went into the dairy business with a small dairy farm on Brevard Road. Five years later, after peddling his own milk on almost a door-to-door basis, he became manager-owner of the Kalmia Dairy. It was a very small operation, and in fact moved twice in the next three years before Bert bought the building on 4th Avenue East between Main and King streets and remodeled it into a dairy processing plant. The location was my first memory of Kalmia. Back then, you could take an empty lard bucket and have it filled with skim milk for only a dime, and that's before skim milk was popular. It was all the family could afford.

In 1950, Bert Browning went big time with the construction of one of the most modern dairy plants in the Southeast when it opened on the Asheville Highway across from Druid Hills. As part of this plant, there was included the Kalmia Dairy Bar. While local folks had eaten ice cream made on the premises of Carson's Blue Bird Ice Cream Plant, the Kalmia Dairy Bar also offered made-to-order sandwiches, including delicious pimento cheese, egg salad, bacon-lettuce-and-tomato, and hamburgers so juicy you were given extra large napkins to catch the "squeezins" when you bit into one. Banana splits, sundaes, sodas—and everything fresh, no cornstarch fillers used in anything. When it came to pies, "memorable" is the one word to describe the taste experience with a big hunk of fresh apple pie and a scoop of fresh Kalmia ice cream. Even today, the late Bert Browning would take no credit

This ad was in 1946 City Directory.

for the phenomenal success of the dairy bar. It was Mrs. Sara Browning and her full-time manager, Margaret Hyder).

The Kalmia Dairy Bar was a first for Hendersonville! In 1950, air conditioning was not commonplace everywhere, but you could drive out to the Kalmia Dairy Bar, step inside that cool oasis and be given a warm welcome by the staff of the prettiest and friendliest girls in town. It had all the ingredients that would make you want to come back again and again.

The Kalmia Dairy Bar operated from 1950 to 1957. One of the highlights of its history was when perhaps the most beautiful of all the staff members (Miss Carolyn Hyder, daughter of the manager) was selected as the North Carolina Apple Queen. She was later on was married to Senator George Smathers of Florida.

In 1957, in a major event for Hendersonville, Mrs. Huntington Jackson of Fletcher was instrumental in forming the Kalmia Dairy Cooperative which purchased the dairy (and, of course, the Dairy Bar) from the Brownings. In addition to Mrs. Jackson, other leaders in the co-op were Clayton Hodges, Zeb Cabe, Lee Pryor, Reid McConnell, and Tom Warren (who became the new president). The cooperative then hired Charles E. Denton of Hickory to be the general manager.

In the late 1960s, the dairy industry was experiencing enormous changes. Independent dairies were

Kalmia employee Carolyn Hyder was N.C. Apple Queen in 1962.

having difficulty in competing with the big conglomerates. The supermarkets had taken the bulk of the food businesses, and they did not want to negotiate individual contracts with small dairies. Kalmia was then merged into a much larger cooperative, Coble Dairies. Coble could handle all their products from another processing plant and the fate of the dairy was sealed.

Like F.W. Woolworth and McLellans, like the old Economy Drug Store and Freeze Pharmacy, and even Waldrops, Kalmia Dairy Bar provokes wonderful memories for people from 1950 to 1957, only seven years.

The type that didn't last

There was real excitement throughout the area when in April of 1951 an announcement was made that the Robotyper Corporation was moving not only its manufacturing plant but its entire operation to Hendersonville; and likely would employ more than 100 people when they reached full production. Prior to World War II, Robert Moore and George Carson invented a robot machine which would actually operate typewriters automatically. This was in Pittsburgh. They manufactured only a few of the workable machines until shortage of parts during the war forced them to suspend operations.

In 1946, Robert Moore set up a business in Detroit which he would call the Robotyper Corporation, and began manufacturing the machines. They operated on the same vacuum concept of the old player piano. The operator would use a cutter machine to type a master letter. Each of the custom holes in the roll of paper tape created a vacuum which caused a particular writer key to strike. Functions such as capital letters, tabs, even underlining could be achieved in a similar fashion. The operator could insert a "stop" in the roll at any place desired, so that personalization or specific numbers or individual products could be inserted on a customized basis in each letter or sheet typed. This process was long before any electronic specialist had even begun to conceive of transistors, chips and electronic activation of typewriters and computers.

Back in the '50s and early '60s this machine was a marvel. If you wanted to send 100 very personal letters to a select list (or for that matter, hundreds of letters), all the basic typing of the letter was done automatically by robot typewriters. A single operator could easily handle two electric typewriters typing at maximum speed, and would be required only to custom type the address, salutation and/or custom entries in the body of the letter. The single operator could also address the envelopes while the typewriters were automatically typing the text.

I remember when we installed a basic "letter shop" in one of our bedrooms, and the child bride in her spare time (and in time she forced to become "spare') ran this private, highly customized service.

Robotyper's plant was in what old timers called the Wetmur Motor Building at 125 Allen Street. After Robotyper closed, the building was acquired by the (then) County School Board and has been used for administrative and educational purposes ever since. An Open House was held at the Robotyper Plant on Saturday and Sunday, July 21-22, 1951. Of course, WHKP was on hand to cover the event with a live broadcast. Mayor A.V. Edwards cut ribbons, and thousands of Henderson County people "oohed and ahhed" at these robots and were fascinated with how they were made.

While my memory fails me on the names of many of the people involved with Robotyper when it came to Hendersonville, I certainly would recall our

Robotyper Inc.'s formal opening. Edney (with microphone) talks with Robert Moore. To Moore's left is Mayor A.V. Edwards; at right front is co-inventor George Carlson.

neighbors for twenty-five years, Pat and Etheleen Gallagher. D.C. Griffin, who was at one time plant manager of Robotyper, also served as president of the Hendersonville Country Club in 1958-59.

For the first four years, Robotyper operated as an independent company, with its own ownership, management, and sales operation located in Hendersonville. In 1955, the Royal Typewriter Company purchased an interest in Robotyper. In 1956, L.V. Oxley, a vice president of the company, announced that their production schedule would be increased to 100 units per month for the next three months; then would increase to 150; and in the last quarter, would be jumped to 175. Prior to being acquired by Royal-McBee, the Robotypers were sold in office supply and equipment stores, and most of the units were connected to IBM electric typewriters. At a meeting in January 1956, Royal wanted forty percent of the total production to go to Royal branch offices and distributors.

Our little letter shop in the back bedroom was one of the first to install the new Royal typewriters and immediately discovered a problem. When we switched from IBM to Royal machines, we began to experience glitches in production. If the robots ran at normal speed, the Royals would jam, but Royal remained confident of the marriage and hit peak employment of 120 in 1961.

However, the electronics industry was moving in such explosive development, the phrase "planned obsolescence" was coined. With new transistors, you were limited in reality only by your dreams, and the machine based upon the old player piano was doomed. In March 1965, Litton Industries merged with Robotyper's parent company, Royal-McBee, and two years later, the Hendersonville plant was closed. The manager at that time was Clarence Blythe, who would confirm only that "production was being maintained on a minimum basis," but from 1951-67, Robotyper provided much needed jobs for about 100 people.

Postmaster's post

An estimated 400 people watched the dedication and then visited the new post office building at 5th Avenue West on Oct. 30, 1966. E. Bob Quinn was postmaster at that time, and he would be the last postmaster receiving his appointment through political influence. After Quinn stepped down and died in 1971, postmasters have been assigned by the semi-private U.S. Postal Service.

Congressman Roy Taylor was responsible for getting more new post office buildings in the county that any other man. Virtually every neighborhood post office was granted funds for a new building during his tenure in Congress. And Roy thoroughly enjoyed being present at every dedication, always bringing a flag that had flown over the capitol building in Washington, D.C. to fly above the new post office. (By the way, there's a full-time crew that does nothing but hoist American flags above the capitol building, lets them hang for a few seconds, then lowers them, packages them appropriately and puts them in storage for ceremonial use by congressmen, senators and other governmental big wigs.)

In the earliest days, the postage was paid by the receiver, and it was up to the local postmaster to collect from those to whom mail was delivered.

Nobody really wanted to become a postmaster. The average pay was about $70 a year. Those who applied ran grocery stores, taverns, were millers, etc.–any type of business where traffic might be boosted by those coming to get their mail. There was one huge advantage discovered by the Rev. Samuel Edney, circuit rider for the Methodist Church. He learned that postmasters were given free franking of all their personal mail sent out. So, when the reverend applied and was granted a post office (which he called Edneyville), Samuel Edney could then keep in touch by mail with his far-flung parishioners and the service was at no charge to him.

At one time, Henderson County had thirty-seven post offices. The book is out of print, but copies are available at the library of "Postmarks" by Lenior Ray. It's the most exhaustive history of local mail service, I believe, ever compiled for any county in the country. In Lenoir's book, he provides the names of every postmaster from the first one, John Kimsey in 1841, to Bob Quinn, who was postmaster when the new post office opened on 5th Avenue West and when Lenoir finished writing his book.

Since WHKP went on the air in 1946, the following have served as postmasters in Hendersonville: Roy E. Johnson, C. Few, John Perry, Hugh Morrison, and Bob Quinn. Just prior to Quinn being given his permanent employment, the office operated under John C. Magness with the title of Foreman of the Mails. From 1946 to 1971, only two postmasters had permanent appointments: C. Few and Bob Quinn. The others were temporary.

Though Hendersonville welcomed the building of a new and larger post office in 1966, no one favored its location. It was moved from the downtown

The first modern post office in Hendersonville was completed in 1915. It is now used as the Federal Building.

area into (at that time) a residential section, generating heavy traffic between three schools, and offering only a single entrance and exit to a limited parking area.

In early years, the Hendersonville Post Office was located wherever the postmaster might be–in grocery stores, stationery stores. It was in 1911 when Congressman John Grant secured an appropriation to buy the Vernon Few property on the corner of 4th and Church for a new building to cost $25,000.

When I was doing the "Kermit Edney Weather Book" a number of years ago, I ran across an authority given by the Weather Service "for the weather flags to be flown in front of Vernon Few's Hardware Store." No one had the slightest recollection of Vernon Few's Hardware Store until I discovered (as explained in the preceding paragraph) where Congressman Grant was able to get approval to buy the property for $25,000–so that hardware store stood on the corner of 4th and Church, where the Federal Building now stands.

While there was a certain amount of puff in the local media about how marvelous the new post office was in 1966, the praise was nowhere near as outgoing as that given to the first post office when it opened at 4th and Church. The *French Broad Hustler* said, "The employees have so much room and so many facilities, they are about like a hen making a nest in a big pile of hay." After the new building was put into service in 1966, the old post office became the Federal Building and houses a variety of U.S. governmental offices.

Just in the last couple of years, a major change at the present post office greatly improved efficiency and made it far more accessible. A large and modern Carrier Service Building was constructed on Lakewood Drive, accessible from either Francis Road or Nix Road. All mail sorting is done at this facility and the carriers who used to battle for cramped spaces at the 5th Avenue building all now work out of this facility and the only postal employees in the downtown main office are involved with counter service or (as they say) "sticking" the mail into the hundreds of postal boxes in this new enlarged and modernized building.

As we said, Bob Quinn (who served from 1961 to roughly 1971) was the last political appointee as postmaster. Since then, managers (some with different titles from postmaster) came and went as assigned by the U.S. Postal Service, and I could not easily find any of their identities from 1971 to 1987. I talked with several old timers, and they said they had no idea what their names were. The present postmaster is Judy Depue. She's been postmaster here for about nine years.

Milroy Was Here

The other day, I was driving from Hendersonville into Dana and discovered when I reached Refuge Church, if you turn to the left, you're on Ridge Road; but a turn to the right puts you on Upward Road. All my life I'd thought of the road that "runs along the ridge" from Upward to Dana (and even beyond) as being "Ridge Road." Coming back into town, I traveled along what I now knew was Upward Road. As I crossed over the interstate highway and approached East Henderson High School, I simply bore to the left going directly to U.S. 176. This is a new road, and was conceived by the Chamber of Commerce Roads Committee to provide additional access to Hendersonville from I-26 without using Four Seasons Boulevard.

My thoughts drifted back to about ten years ago to a meeting that was held in the (then) board room of First Federal Savings and Loan. At that meeting was Gov. Jim Martin, Jim Meyers of the Department of Transportation, D.O.T. officials, members of the Chamber of Commerce Roads Committee and a few prominent Republicans from this area. The spokesperson was Phil Milroy, who was chairman of the Chamber of Commerce Roads & Highways Committee. That committee had come to the conclusion that with the explosive growth that had occurred along Four Seasons Boulevard, there was no hope of improving the bumper-to-bumper traffic on that "only" primary entrance into the city because of the enormous costs of acquiring expensive right-of-ways. Phil Milroy's committee had come to the conclusion that the only hope for traffic relief on the boulevard was additional access from I-26, a brand new entrance from the south along Upward Road, and a brand new entrance from the north at Clear Creek. Phil and his committee had done their homework. Their presentation to Gov. Martin was reinforced with maps, official traffic counts and estimates of cost, especially on the new section to be built from Upward Road to U.S. 176.

Gov. Martin listened to the entire presentation, fired off a half dozen questions to the (then) 14th Division board member, Jim Meyers, and then decided that funds could be made immediately available by borrowing from several projects that were experiencing delays in construction. This had to establish some sort of record of accomplishment. For your information, from the time the traffic signal at White Street and U.S. 25 was approved in 1992, it took four years to get it installed. Yet, Phil Milroy and the Chamber of Commerce Roads Committee was able to get a brand new road approved (that had never even been discussed by the D.O.T.) and get it constructed within eighteen months.

And, for your information, the "north" connector out North Main Street to Clear Creek and a brand new access to I-26 is still on schedule on the D.O.T.'s Transportation Improvement Priority.

Phil and Margaret Milroy had moved here (along with their four daughters) in January 1960. Phil was named manager of engineering at GE's Outdoor Lighting Dept. He succeeded "Chuck" Meloun, who was named as marketing manager. In 1966, Phil moved to the GE plant in Irmo, S.C. (which manufactured capacitors), where he was named general manager. In 1968 when Chuck Meloun was promoted to manager of GE's Power Distribution Division, Milroy was returned to Hendersonville to become general manager of the Outdoor Lighting Department.

In his business career, Phil Milroy had been general manager here only about three years before he announced an expansion program that would add one acre of factory structure to the GE plant. He said at the time, "This addition will give us added room for manufacturing space to allow for the production of new light systems designed and built here for worldwide markets. At that time, the plant's name was changed from "Outdoor Lighting Department" to "GE Lighting Systems."

Both Phil and Margaret Milroy were great believers in being active in the community. Just three years after he took over as general manager of the GE plant here, he accepted the presidency of the Hendersonville Chamber of Commerce.

He was a strong supporter of the United Way, civic activities and the Presbyterian Church. In his final years with GE, his job caused him to travel extensively all over the world; but always, when he returned, he was ready to jump right back into the community life of Hendersonville.

Phil was one of those recruited to be charter active in the new Community Foundation of Hendersonville. In those early years, the foundation had no staff. It operated with volunteer help from the members of the board. If you can, picture in your mind Milroy (this industrial "mover and shaker" at

GE) sitting alone in an office in the First Union Bank Building, just to answer the phone and do secretarial work. That gives you just an inkling of the total dedication Phil Milroy had for this community and for anything that would improve it. He chuckled to me one day and said, "You can't imagine how hard it is for me to have to write everything out in longhand when over all these years I dictated everything to my secretary in a fraction of the time I now spend.

Phil Milroy was one of twelve good reasons the Community Foundation became so successful and today manages $13 million dollars in assets, managed for the community by Priscilla Cantrell and her friendly staff.

And Margaret?? Margaret Milroy was named "Woman of the Year" by the VFW, and one of the top fifty leaders in the community over the past fifty years. You'd never know it by talking to her.

The One and Only Curly

I don't know why, but my name appears in the byline of a story in the *Times-News*, September 19, 1963, headlined "'Curly' Roper Recalls His 30 Years in Business Here." Elsewhere I did recall the most spectacular fires that have occurred in Hendersonville over the past fifty years, and one of them involved the blaze that destroyed the Hendersonville Lumber Company and heavily damaged Superior Laundry & Cleaners. At the time of the fire, the Ropers (Ernest, Elizabeth and Ernest, Jr.) were operating not only the main Superior Laundry plant but also two pickup offices downtown. The Ropers continued to operate their laundry and cleaning business, even as they rebuilt (after the fire) a brand new 8,000 square foot laundry building.

Ernest "Curly" Roper's roots in the laundry and dry cleaning business went way back to 1924 ... to when the firm was organized as the Hendersonville Laundry, Ice Fuel & Coal Company with C.R. Whitaker as manager. In that first plant there were *no* machines. Water had to be drawn from a well and carried into the building for the laundry operation. Everything was done by hand.

There was a brief change of ownership from 1923 to 1935 when belt-operated laundry tubs were installed. Curly Roper had first joined the firm at that time, and by 1936 he had become part-owner. In 1949 he bought out the Whitakers and became the sole owner.

In that story I did on Sept. 19, 1963, when the Ropers and Superior Laundry were preparing for a grand reopening), Curly told me his first job in the laundry business was a driver's helper on a Model T truck. They then acquired what Curly called a "silent starter" Dodge truck–that meant a truck you didn't have to crank.

In those earliest years, there was no such thing as cleaning solvent. It was pretty much gasoline; and Ernest said that even now and to this date,

Ernest "Curly" Roper goes along with a gag promotion for a Chamber of Commerce membership drive—heading into the darkness with a lantern to find new members.

something reminds you of that old gasoline odor. Incidentally, Curly established the Sanitone cleaning process in Henderson County.

I don't know at what age Ernest lost all his hair and became just "Curly," but he was another of the "boys who grew up here" and felt it was his solemn obligation to do anything and everything to help make Hendersonville a better place to live. He was president of the Chamber of Commerce in 1953, having worked his way through the chairs. He had already served as the fourth president of the N.C. Apple Festival. His term was in 1951, the year that Kathryn Hyatt Spritz of Waynesville was chosen Apple Queen. Curly was so used to checking and double-checking everything in Superior Laundry, he couldn't delegate committee assignments. He was always on the scene checking to be sure that everything was done and done right, even to delivering apples to the kiosks downtown.

Curly had served as master of Kedron Lodge AF&AM and had been named "Man of the Year" in 1957 by the Woodmen of the World. He was named chairman of a committee in the Chamber to raise money for the floodlights for Dietz Field, but as usual, he didn't form a committee. He raised virtually all the money by himself.

Back to that interview I did with him 33 years ago in 1963. He flashed an infectious smile at me and said, "Maybe you'd better not mention that I've been organist at the Elks Lodge for twenty-three years." I never heard Curly play the organ but he could mortally pound a piano. He played music by ear (using chords) and he could play anything from waltzes to out-'n-out hillbilly music. In fact, once in a great while, he'd sit in with Lon and "Sleepy" Brookshire and play with their string band. Lon played fiddle, Sleepy on rhythm guitar, and when Lon would yell "Down Yonder," Curly would flat out nail those piano keys to the keyboard!

He was the kind of guy everyone liked, and though not a Lion, anytime I was a guest of the Lion's Club, when Curly walked in there'd be shouts– "Did you bring your famous button crushing machine with you?"– again that little smile and he'd nod yes. The ribbing he took was unmerciful. One guy hit the floor and alleged he'd gotten a shirt back from Curly that started out with cast ceramic buttons and Curly's machine had pulverized them.

Roper was chairman of the Board of Ushers at his beloved First Baptist Church in 1963, and he was president of the Hendersonville Shrine Club. Ernest died at age 78 in 1985 and is buried next to his son, Ernest, Jr., in Shepherd Memorial Cemetery. Ernest, Jr. had died at age 45 from complications from an injury received in cross country motor biking. Curly's wife, Elizabeth, is still with us in 1997 to enjoy family and grandchildren of the one and only Curly Roper. She and Curly celebrated their golden wedding anniversary in 1977.

Seasons & Memories

You'd have to be a real old timer to remember taking the family on the annual Christmas tree hunt. Back when WHKP first signed on the air, we had only about a third of the population we have today. There were no massive residential developments or sprawling industrial operations. Once you left the city limits, you were in the country.

Jody Barber and I were laughing this past Christmas over our adventures in scavenging for the Christmas tree. To buy one back then was unthinkable. You normally looked for white pines because the balsams, cedars and other fir trees simply didn't grow naturally in this area. Jody and I laughed as we recalled how we'd spot a tree from the road, park and then run to the tree, only to find most of the branches missing on the back side; or, when you'd get up close, the branches would be so far apart that you'd never be able to fill the huge voids with decorations. We also recalled the paper rope garland—not tinsel, but green or red paper ropes—and an accordion-type bell that you'd open and hang from the light socket that hung in the middle of the room.

For a number of years about the only place in town where you could buy the perfect Canadian tree was at the VFW. They *were* gorgeous trees but in spite of being chemically treated for preservation, most of the trees were cut in Canada in early September for shipment. By the time Christmas was over, the tree had dropped most of its needles and would have been an embarrassment even for Charlie Brown.

My son Kerry can top any of the tree-shedding stores I ever heard. He and his family had worked all of one evening hanging the lights, putting up the ornaments, arranging the tinsel 'til all was perfection. The next morning when the family came downstairs, every needle had fallen from the tree during the night—every needle! This story I do remember because on the Christmas Eve broadcast we did each year with the grandchildren, his son (Kris) related the experience on the air in great detail, and then said his father had gone out and bought an artificial tree, which they were now using. Kris said, "Gramp, it's a fake. You can't believe it. We have a fake tree in our house."

Christmas tree production has become a major industry now in North Carolina. In 1996 I was chatting with Jerry Moody at the N.C. Ag Extension Service in Avery County, and he said they harvested a few trees as early as 1968. By the mid '80s, one grower had planted over a million trees. He estimated that there are at least twelve million trees in various stages of growth. If you'd like to enjoy Christmas in July, take a trip from Marion to Boone. Up around Newland, you'll see nothing but miles of specimen Christmas trees in various stages of growth.

Duke Power's downtown office display, back in the days when decorations didn't go up until after Thanksgiving.

> The holly bears a prickle,
> As sharp as any thorn,
> And Mary bore sweet Jesus Christ
> On Christmas Day in the morn ...

That's the last stanza of one of the old, old traditional carols, "The Holly and the Ivy."

In those early days here at WHKP (back in the '40s) most of the songs heard during the holidays were the sacred carols. We did have "White Christmas," which won the Oscar in 1942 in the movie "Holiday Inn." Some of the other pop songs that have been around for close to fifty years include "I'll Be Home for Christmas" (which was really big during World War II). Another was "You're All I Want for Christmas." Other songs included "Sleigh Ride," "The Christmas Song," and "Rudolph the Red Nosed Reindeer"—the song that gained more popularity in one season than any other pop Christmas song.

It would be years before the miniature Christmas lights would be developed and manufactured on a large scale. The miniatures operate in what is called a series circuit. They advertise "if one goes out, the rest keep on burnin'." What they don't tell you is that if a bulb drops out or is loose and does not have a good connection, the set will not burn at all. This is called "series" wiring, and all the earliest Christmas lights were manufactured to operate in series. If one didn't burn, you could cut the socket from the circuit and tie the wires back together and the set would burn again. However, this increased the voltage on all the other sockets, and if you'd done this sort of repair enough, when you plugged in the socket, the whole thing blew up in your face.

Southern Christmas for generations was more of a time for fireworks than even the 4th of July. I've heard many explanations. Folks lived so remotely they'd go outside and shoot shotguns to wish neighbors a Merry Christmas. If they had an anvil, they'd make as much noise as they could on it. They used to sell fireworks at Hoke's Store on Chimney Rock Road. There is a sheet metal shop in that building now between WHKP and the theaters. At Christmas, the store would be filled with fireworks in assortments, individual Roman candles or Skyrockets, or you could buy 'em by the box. Before the Space Age, *the* gift for a young boy was a cap buster and holster, along with a cowboy hat and gloves. In a neighborhood with lots of young boys, there was an almost constant chatter of cap busters being fired. Cherry bombs and the M-1 cracker were for the big boys. You could blow tin cans fifteen or twenty feet in the air.

I remember Christmas of 1962. We'd just built our first house in Laurel Park and my mother had spent Christmas Eve night with us. Bright and early we were up (as always) on Christmas morning and discovered that sleet and freezing rain had fallen during the night and had created a true winter wonderland all around the house. My mom was up with us, and even though she was 68 years old, she still loved Christmas as a little child. It was hard to tell who was most excited when I took the fireworks out on the front deck. Each time I'd fire a rocket or a Roman candle up over the ice-covered trees, the sparkling reflections of the brilliant colors was awesome and all Mom would say was "oooooh" and "ahhhhh."

Even my grandchildren grew up expecting their stockings to be filled with fireworks, and we continued to shoot them every Christmas until the new condos were built in front of us. The year the condo units were finished, we went right ahead with our annual Roman candle fight with my son, son-in-law, and three grandsons, having a time dodging the balls from the Roman candles—until we heard the sound of a siren. Through the dense smoky haze from where we'd been shooting the fireworks, you could faintly see the blinking blue lights coming up the driveway. With that, my cohorts (sons and grandsons) all broke for the house, leaving me standing alone in the smoke. The ground was covered with the paper litter of the expended shells we'd already run through. The entourage of the constabulary included police from the town and deputy sheriffs, one of whom said, "You been shootin' fireworks up here?"

Squinting to see him through the pyrotechnic haze and the ground layered with fireworks litter, I responded, "Yeah, the kids (who by then were all standing in the windows, laughing and pointing at old Gramps), the kids have fired a couple. We've always had fireworks at Christmas."

The police officer patiently answered, "Well, they're not legal now and we've had complaints. You better not shoot any more." I thanked them for their kindness, and though we still give all of the kids fireworks, I suggest they drive down to the South Carolina line to shoot them.

"B" as in Bull—"S" as in Sunshine

It was on a Christmas Eve night back in the late '50s when there was a knock at the door. When I opened it, there stood Walter B. Smith, carrying a doll actually bigger than our daughter Katina. Virtually everyone who lived in Henderson County from World War I through the early '60s knew "Walt" Smith. He was not just an individualist, nor just a character. He was not just an eccentric nor personage. He was born to be seen and heard. He would pin a huge corsage to the seat of his pants and walk down Main Street. He would pull a dog chain behind him—but no dog. The doll he had brought had been conned from some supermarket manager who had used it strictly for display purposes during the Christmas season. It had to be at least four feet tall, and it was impressive!

It was not uncommon for Walter to come to the house. When I was growing up, he would come to visit Dad, always timing his visit to be sure everyone had finished their meal because he knew Mom would always say, "Walter, sit down and eat supper. Whatever's there will be thrown away." After Dad died, Walter started making his visits to our house; and the child bride, like Mom, would insist that he have supper while he was there. In the years when he would visit Dad, I would go to bed whenever I was ready and had no idea how long Walter would stay. After Dad died he started coming to our house, and as he would rant and rave about the incompetence of the total population, I would doze, nodding occasionally, which was sufficient for Walt to keep his harangue going.

Back then, we had a little dog named Casper. Walter was never noted for sartorial splendor or even for the maintenance of the clothes he had. On this occasion, he had merely laid his hat on the floor next to his chair. As the evening wore on and on I was nodding off to sleep more and more. I finally jarred myself alert enough to say, "Walter, it's after midnight. I have to be at work in a few hours." No one knew how long Walter had worn that old felt hat, but the piquancy of the old sweatband was more aromatic that the little dog could stand. As Walter carried on his monologue, Casper had eaten the whole hat, except for the brim. Walter exploded, "That damn dog has eaten my hat!" Whereupon he picked up the brim, slapped it on his head and stormed out of the door.

Walter's greatest fame came from his telephone calls made to people in high places. His favorite routine was to walk into a very crowded restaurant,

Walter B. Smith

pick up the pay phone and say in a loud voice, "This is Walter B. Smith from Hendersonville, North Carolina, calling President Eisenhower on a very urgent matter. Would you get him for me at the White House, please?" No one really knew who he was talking to, but the place would get very quiet and whispers everywhere: "Walter is talking to the President."

While being a far cry from the President, he particularly loved to harass Billy Rose, who was administrator of the State Highway Commission. Most of those calls got through because I remember when the public hearing on locating I-26 through Henderson County was scheduled, Billy called me and said, "Kermit, if we have any outburst from Walter Smith during this hearing, we'll immediately adjourn the meeting. Is there any way you can reason with him to behave?" Down through the years, I have discovered there were two Walter Smiths. One that had to perform in public before any audience. The other (known to very few) was a private and highly intelligent man. I got hold of Walter and he gave me his word that he would cause no disruption of the hearing.

The hearing was to be held in the court room of the old Court House. Tables had been arranged down front to seat each member of the State Highway Commission and the department's top executives. At the exact time the hearing was to begin, the double doors to both aisles through the court room burst open, and Walter made an entrance to rival Ali Baba, without even uttering "Open Sesame." He was followed by a contingent of men, each bearing a box of Henderson County's fanciest apples, which were placed in front of each one of the dignitaries. Walter then gave a brief but almost poetic welcoming speech, bowed deeply and, followed by his cohorts, left the room. I looked at Billy Rose and winked. He just closed his eyes and shook his head. Later, Walter called a press conference and thanked William Dalton and Leon Stepp for the gift of the apples, and Bill Francis for the fancy boxes in which they were packed.

Back in the days of the big bands, whenever a name appeared in Hendersonville, sometime during the evening Walter would get the blessings of Bob Crosby, Hal Kemp, Johnny Long, or Jan Garber, and he would personally direct the band. When Jane Wyman and a group from Hollywood appeared to help promote the sale of war bonds, who found his way on stage to present an enormous corsage to Miss Wyman?? Walter B. Smith! He even presented a deed for a lot of his choice in Laurel Park to Jan Garber—at least he went through the act.

The North Carolina Apple Festival had always selected a beautiful young lady to serve as Apple Queen. In the early days of the event, they used to "elect" a King. It was more of a joke and petty money raiser than a serious competition. Anyone could be nominated for $1, and candidates' supporters would put the candidate's picture on jars and place the jars in stores throughout the community. In 1951, eleven candidates were nominated and votes were a penny apiece. Walter suddenly took the contest seriously and his jars kept being filled with pennies, likely provided by Walter. He finally edged out the popular Sheriff Bill McCall; and with his skill at gaining publicity, even had his picture run in the St. Petersburg *Evening Independent* captioned, "The new King of the North Carolina Apple Festival." (After his election, the King contest was discontinued.)

As to his skill in influencing press coverage, one warm spring night in 1964 Walter burst into our house and said, "I want you to call Dr. Bell right now and invite him to come over and see the apple trees in bloom." I knew at once that the "Dr. Bell" he was referring to was Ruth Bell's father, the father-in-law of Billy Graham.

"Walter, this is ridiculous. Dr. Bell doesn't need an invitation to drive over here and look at the apple blossoms." Walter argued, "But this distinguished man deserves a personal invitation." By ten p.m. it had become obvious that Walter was not going to leave the house 'til I made the call. So with trepidation, I dialed Dr. Bell's number. After I had made my spiel, I was stunned by the warm and friendly response. He said, "You can't imagine how relieved I am that you called, because Walter had told me earlier I would get an official invitation; and, knowing Walter, I knew the call would come. I was hoping I might get the call before midnight. Now I can go to bed."

On another occasion, he arrived in his usual blaze of enthusiasm, wanting me to get Carl Sandburg to go out and pose for a photograph with the Thomas Wolfe angel in Oakdale Cemetery. Walter said, "That old goat man (his way of referring to the great Sandburg) can wave his hand and get more publicity for this area than the Chamber of Commerce can get working all year long."

This time I was adamant. "No way, Walter! First of all, I'm not going to bother Sandburg about such trifles; and I'm not sure how he feels about Thomas Wolfe or whether he's ever even read any of Wolfe's works. This time Walter recognized that he had struck a raw nerve with me and left. Less than a week later, I picked up the morning paper and there on the front page of the feature section was a huge photo of Carl Sandburg standing admiring the Wolfe statue. I have no idea how Smith pulled that off.

When guests complained of strange noises in the old Ames Hotel, they discovered that Walter was slipping in the back door, going to the top floor where he had accumulated a huge quantity of newspapers which he used for cover. Every time he turned in bed, it sounded as if the *Times-News* presses were running.

At other times, he lived in a little pump house on the corner of Laurel Park Highway and Lake Drive. He had an old coal stove which not only smoked but backfired once in a while. It was not unusual to see Walter come downtown on a winter morning with only his white eyeballs shining through a soot-covered face. Walter rose from private to captain during World War I; he had a college engineering degree; he painted a picture for me (which was lost in our house fire); and I still have a copy of a hymn he wrote, "Harbor of His Love."

Head of the family

Around 1960, I purchased from Walter Smith and others all of the lots in Section A of the town of Laurel Park. "Are you sure you own these lots, Walter?" I asked.

"No doubt about it," he answered. "I just cut a dogwood tree and if no one threatens to sue me within a week, I know I own the property."

As we were closing the deal, attorney Ben Prince laughed when I questioned Walter's ownership. He said, "I have a deed on record that says any and all real estate which has been unsold in Laurel Park belongs to Walter B. Smith."

I finally found that unusual deed in 1996 in the Register of Deeds office. If you'd like to look it up, it's in Book 359, page 399. In this deed, attorney Arthur Shepherd is named by the court as commissioner of the estate of A.H. Smith (that's Walter's mother, Ann Hazeltine Smith) and the deed conveys to Walter 20 to 22 tracts of land in various subdivisions of the town of Laurel Park. It also deeds the mineral interests of the land in Mills River known as the old Boyleston Gold Mine. The deed conveys all park areas in Laurel Park and the abandoned canal and canal drive areas, plus—and get this—QUOTE: "Any and all real estate which remains unsold in the town of Laurel Park."

Attorney Kenneth Youngblood explained to me that Ben Prince could be very innovative; and through this deed, Shepherd was acting as agent of the court, and while the deed might even be fictional, it would become legal in seven years, affecting the future color of titles in all the land described. It worked because I know a number of those lots described in that deed are now covered by title insurance.

Walter B. Smith was one of eight children born to W.A. Smith and Ann Hazeltine Jordan. If there would be one—just one—person considered as having had more impact on Hendersonville than any other, it would have been Walt's father, W.A. Smith. He served not only as mayor, but resigned that job to become city attorney so that he could write the town charter. He was elected to the Legislature to get it passed in 1883.

Not only was he a brilliant attorney, he was a shrewd businessman. He started with 300 acres. Not content just with incorporating Hendersonville, he built the resort town of Laurel Park. There were really three corporations involved: Laurel Park Estates, Florida/Carolina Estates, and Rhododendron Estates. While the average entrepreneur years ago used to kite checks, deeds to land were kited and freely flowed among these three corporations to improve balance sheets as desired.

W.A. Smith built Rhododendron Lake, a skating rink, and a dance pavilion. He built a second lake and connected it by canal to the first one. Alongside the canal, he built a road still in use today known as Canal Drive. W.A. Smith built a counter-

W.A. Smith

balanced railway for scenic views at the summit of Mount Panorama. The first fairgrounds in the county were built by him. He was editor for a short period of time of a local newspaper, a partner in the famed Salola Inn on Sugarloaf Mountain, head of the first building and loan association, and president of one of the first banks. He built the famous "dummy line" railroad and a rock quarry. Two years before he died, he was presented (at an impressive banquet) a silver loving cup as "THE BEST LOVED CITIZEN."

As we said, W.A. Smith had eight children. There were three boys: W.A. Smith, Jr., who died in 1936; Hubert M. Smith, who was killed in 1918 in the last hours of World War I; and Walter B. Smith. There were five daughters: Lillie, the oldest, who never married; Annie, who married T.R. Watkins; Helen Grimes Smith, who married John Banta; Eva, who married the noted local architect Earl Stillwell; and Ruth, who married O.E. Hedge, a local Realtor who established a special fund in the Community Foundation in memory of his son Dick, who was missing in action in the Pacific Theater in World War II. The late William A. Smith, Jr. also had a son who was declared missing in World War II, Jack Smith, but he was later found to be OK. A large family, even by the standards of the early part of the century. A family whose father had provided all creature comforts for his estate and his children and who had, for his children, become perhaps the area's best known citizen.

Walter Smith was married and had two daughters, but he chose to live as a free spirit. Perhaps Walter couldn't get over the fact that in World War I he was a hero, had been gassed, had advanced from private to captain, and upon his return home, was ignored while the community mourned the death of his brother who was killed in the last 24 hours of fighting in 1918. Maybe it was jut too big a burden to be the only surviving son of his father, the great

W.A. Smith, the most outstanding person in the first 100 years of Hendersonville. When the candy tycoon Emil J. Brach died here in 1947, his widow became Walter's patron saint and befriended him the rest of his life.

In that he had a degree in engineering, Walter's dream was building a superhighway from the midwest to Charleston, S.C. He had even laid it out on a map in the '40s; and today, I-26 follows that route almost to the letter. In 1964, Walter came to my office and wanted assurance that he was going to live long enough to see "his highway" finished. It was obvious Walter was a sick man, but I joked with him, "Walter, you're going to live longer than I do." Then I stepped into another office and called his dear friend, Mayor Al Edwards, and told him of Walter's condition. In a few minutes the mayor arrived, picked Walter up and took him to the Veterans Hospital in Oteen, where he died—just before his beloved "Smith Highway" was finished.

The following is from his obituary, which I broadcast on WHKP on June 19, 1964: "Walter B. Smith was a dreamer of dreams from parkways to skyways—from huge parks to superhighways. The land boom of the '20s is long past. Laurel Park has closed its chapter on Jack Dempsey and the Fleetwood Hotel. The tingling thrill of the Dummy Line Railroad will be felt no more. The water in Crystal Springs is no longer fit to drink. Laurel Park is no longer a land of dreams—because now, at the end of this most colorful period in history, the Dreamer is dead. Walter B. Smith—"B" as in Bull, "S" as in Sunshine.

An Only Compliment

I received a call one morning, and immediately recognized the voice of a former teacher, Lucille Allen. "Kermit Edney," she said, "You are truly a remarkable person. I do believe that if you set your mind to it, you could do anything in God's creation." Caught off guard and stammering with embarrassment, I began to try to mutter when she interrupted and said, "You are responsible for this snow on 1st Avenue and that one block covered with newly fallen snow and no snow anywhere else in a hundred miles, I figured that some way, somehow, you had to be involved. It's beautiful, I am impressed, and I thank you."

Nancy Pryor McKinley, who was a key member of our sales and promotion staff then, and I had discussed what a feat we could achieve if we could absolutely forecast a snowfall and it absolutely would occur. We played around with the idea for some time, and she came up with the solution and she did all the work. We contracted with one of the big ski resorts to rent their snowblowing machines for one night of use in Hendersonville. All we had to have was a favorable temperature. With that we covered not just 1st Avenue West (for one block) with about six inches of snow, but also the south side of the Court House even had the windows glazed over as a southerly wind kept blowing our snow onto the Court House lawn and building. For safety, we placed bales of hay at the foot of the steep first block of 1st Avenue West to keep the sledders from sliding out into Church Street traffic.

We had forecast a 100 percent chance of snow would fall that night on First Avenue between Main and Church streets, and our forecast was 100 percent accurate.

Unfortunately, very few students will ever have the privilege of having a teacher by the name of Lucille Kirby Allen. She was a teacher in both public and private schools. She taught at Fassifern School for Girls, as well as Edneyville and Hendersonville High Schools. In addition to teaching, Lucille Allen had served as president of the Classroom Teachers of North Carolina Education Association. She had been a member of the board of the NCEA and in 1949 became president of the North Carolina Education Association. She served on the advisory council of the National Education Association. She also was western district representative on the NCEA Board for a three-year term. Lucille Allen served on the executive committee of the N.C. Democratic party and on the board of the YMCA.

Beyond the credentials, however, she was a dedicated educator who, long before her time, would (within her first month of a school year) determine which of her pupils would need (1) remedial help, (2) which could pass the classwork as expected, and (3) the few advanced students who could simply loaf and still make straight A's. She didn't need studies or tests or group analysis. She was able to recognize these characteristics in her students within a month of the start of a school year. She had infinite patience with the slow learners, but she was a demanding and stern taskmaster with the gifted students. She would give them extra assignments, demand more in

Lucille Kirby Allen

their homework, and she always challenged all of her students to think for themselves.

I remember when she was at Edneyville, she opened her senior English class one morning with a story she'd just heard about this friend of long standing who suffered from a heart condition. The lady had been dreaming that she was walking along the very edge of a cliff when inadvertently her foot slipped and she dreamed she was tumbling over the cliff. At the same time, the lady was too close to the edge of the bed, turned and rolled off the bed. The shock of the dream, plus the impact of the fall from the bed, caused her to have a heart attack and she died. Lucille Allen told this story, and after the class had "oohed and ahhed" over such a tragedy, she went on to the class study for the day. At the end of the class, she suddenly stopped and said, "I'm surprised that no one, not one person challenged me on the story I told you at the start of the class. You remember the story was about the woman dreaming of falling off a cliff, and then falling out of bed. The trauma of the two events caused a heart attack and she died." The class was absolutely quiet. Then she said, "Did your mind not question as to how anyone knew what this woman was dreaming if she died instantly when she rolled out of bed?" She then said, "The moral of that story: Always use your mind to weigh and challenge the information presented. Never, never accept hearsay as fact."

She hammered over and over again, "Education is not the retention of knowledge. It is the training that guides you into knowing where the answers are." In the gathering of information for the radio series, as I went from one reference book to another for memory refreshers, how often have I thought of Lucille Allen.

Lucille Allen was born in Petersburg, Ill., on Oct. 29, 1900. She was a graduate of McMurray College in Jacksonville, Ill., and earned a master's degree from Western Carolina. Her first teaching job was at the private Fassifern School in Hendersonville. It was only a short time before one Dr. Walter O. Allen took notice of this lovely lady, a lady of real class, and they were married after the usual courtship. At this time, the young ladies who were her students at Fassifern kept quizzing her on how it feels to fall in love. She finally described "being in love is having an itching sensation around the heart that you can't scratch."

The idyllic romance and marriage of Lucille Allen ended abruptly when Dr. Allen died at a very young age from a mastoid infection. Lucille became a widow at age forty with a child to raise. She applied for a job teaching at Edneyville and joined the faculty there, teaching English and dramatic arts. She would later transfer into the city school system and would continue teaching until 1966, when she retired after 26 years of service.

I felt toward Lucille Allen a bit like my son Kerry felt toward his football coach, the great Joe Hunt. Kerry confided in me during his fourth year playing for Joe, "Dad, I don't expect to hear Coach Hunt tell me I did anything good, but if he just smiles at me once before I graduate, I'll be happy." I felt the same toward Mrs. Allen. I always had an illusory dream that I might do something someday and do it well enough to merit her approbation.

In 1971, I thought I might have achieved that goal! The Hedrick-Rhodes Post of the VFW was celebrating its 25th anniversary, and the comrades had insisted that I make a speech in honor of that special occasion. The speech was to be broadcast. I followed all the rules which Mrs. Allen had pounded into my head—flawless research, check and double-check all facts, compose the manuscript, analyze the vocabulary used, could I substitute more definitive words, create more vivid description? I did all those things, and after having delivered the speech, I thought it had gone "pretty good."

About a week later, I bumped into Mrs. Allen at the B&B Jax Pax Store. I spoke to her; and when she smiled after returning my greeting, I said to myself, "This is it. At last, I'll get that long sought-after compliment." In her usual clipped voice, she said, "Kermit, the speech you made the other night to the VFW. "Yes mam," I answered (by now being hardly able to breathe with anticipation). "I noticed that you made three grammatical errors in that speech," and then she proceeded to spell them out.

I don't have any children in the public school system anymore, but I do have a granddaughter in public schools in Mauldin, S.C., and I often wonder: Do their teachers give them a hard time when they use lousy grammar? Does her teachers get upset when the students hang prepositions? Can my grandchildren diagram a sentence? Can they spell phonetically? Do they understand the free enterprise system? Can they read a balance sheet?

I gave my grandson Kyle (who is now a senior at the University of South Carolina) three books by Edwin Newman, including his volume "Will America Be the Death of English?" I told him, "Kyle, you don't have a teacher such as Lucille Allen who would make you want to speak correct English, but maybe these books will inspire you." First Union didn't award those crystal apples back in those years, but there were many Lucille Allens back then who deserved a hamper full.

Johnson Field

One of the most enjoyable days of my life was in the summer of 1985. An old friend had just celebrated his 90th birthday. He was still sharp as a tack and was sort of a self-appointed curator of one of the great treasures of this county, "The Johnson Farm," which is now a national historic site, and is operated by the Henderson County School System and Foundation.

I'm referring to Leander Johnson. I knew that Glenn and Dot Marlowe were sort of informally adopted by Leander and his brother, Vernon Johnson—and the love was mutual. Knowing this, I asked Dot if she might be able to persuade Leander to take the time to give us a personal tour of the farm. I planned in advance to record (without Leander's knowledge) our total visit that day, which must have run two hours.

Well, the weather was perfect and Leander was in great spirits. He had insisted on first showing us all the birthday cards that students from West High School had sent to him on his 90th birthday. He was living then in the tiny cottage down behind the main house, and he not only had the cards thumb-tacked everywhere, he even had them hanging on clotheslines across the room.

From the little house, we next toured the main building. He took the time to show to us and explain all the different kinds of wood, all of which had come

Jimmy Fain (center) talks with the Johnson brothers, Vernon (left) and Leander.

off the place. The bricks had been kilned right there on the farm. We then went to the newer building, which was built to handle the overflow of summer boarders who called the Johnson Farm their home when the weather got hot in the lowlands of the deep South.

We looked at the priceless memorabilia from North Carolina A&M (which is now N.C. State University)–his and Vernon's uniforms, school banners, memorabilia N.C. State University certainly covets today. Then to the barn where (over the past seven years after Vernon died) Leander had spent his entire time "straightening out the place" and arranging for viewing everything from the first radio ever to be heard in Henderson County to the old telephones (also the first phones ever to be seen here). He took special pleasure in asking me if I knew what this or that antique tool was and what it was used for, and of course I had no idea. He would then joyfully tell me what the tool was and how it was used. We came to his mama's saddle, or as they called them, "side saddles," for the ladies. Dot Marlowe was standing alongside as he told me about finally finding the "little saddle that had belonged to his half-brother Harvey." (All of the interview is contained in the "WHKP Sound Archives" in the Henderson County Public Library).

LEANDER: "We had a half-brother Harvey and this was his little saddle. It got lost, and last winter I was up here cleaning up this old building and found one way up on the top of that building next door, and it was exactly like this one, you see."

DOT: "Tell him about Harvey and what he did, Leander."

LEANDER: "Well, he was chief of engineers. He was second in command of the Coast Guard when it was a revenue cutter service, you see. He stayed there about forty years in Washington; and went everywhere with the Coast

Guard. He had a lot to do with building the Coast Guard to where it is today. That was our half-brother Harvey."

KERMIT: "Did he come back to visit often?"

LEANDER: "Well, yes, we'd see him all along. He'd come back here with his wife and his son. He's the one who helped us go through school. We wouldn't have gone to college if it hadn't been for him, you see."

Leander died Jan. 28, 1987. He and his brother Vernon not only gave land for the school–they left the entire Johnson Farm to the school system.

On the night of Sept. 27, 1967 (at the homecoming football game with West Henderson playing Erwin) then-assistant superintendent Glenn Marlowe, flanked by past presidents of the Booster Club over the years, announced that with the hearty concurrence of the County Board of Education, they were dedicating this field to Leander and Vernon Johnson, who never had any children of their own (and I'm quoting here) "but in truth have adopted every student who ever attended here."

I was still covering sports with Charley Renfrow back then, and we always looked forward to going to Johnson Field because Leander and Vernon would be there with cakes and cookies they had baked themselves, having been taught by the master of them all–their mother, Aunt Sallie Johnson.

Then to really add a bit of icing to their cake, not only did Leander and Vernon Johnson give their hearts and everything they owned to the schools of this county, but their half-brother Harvey, who had never seen any body of water bigger than the French Broad River, went on to become the #2 man and helped to build the U.S. Coast Guard into what it is today–Admiral Harvey F. Johnson.

Thomas Wolfe would be pleased that his father's "angel" stands vigil over the Johnson burial ground in Oakdale Cemetery.

Justus Field

If you're interested in a detailed chronology of the plan for consolidation and the establishment of both East Henderson and West Henderson High Schools, you can check Jimmy Fain's "A Partial History of Henderson County."

Most old timers (if you refer to the building of East High School) will say, "Oh, that's where the old fairgrounds used to be." But an all-important part of the property belonged to the Cleveland family of South Carolina and, similar to many other families, the Clevelands only bought property–they never sold it.

The superintendent back then, Mr. J.M. Foster, kept focusing on the urgent need of property for a new school building. Finally the Clevelands felt that it was their responsibility to help and the property was transferred to Henderson County. When the building was completed, there were then four high schools: the East and West High Schools, along with an improved Edneyville High School and Hendersonville High.

At the time East High was being completed, Ernest L. Justus was not only principal of Flat Rock High School but was also supervisor of the Flat Rock Administrative School District, which consisted of Flat Rock High, plus grammar schools at East Flat Rock, Tuxedo and Valley Hill. It was only natural that Justus be named as principal of the new East Henderson High School, which was now the largest school in the county.

Leonard Victor Huggins, who had been raised "out on the ridge," had gone to school with Ernest Justus. In Vic's book (which is now out of print), he concocts several tales using Ernest's real name in a couple of them, and calling him Ernest Huestis in another. Vic Huggins was head cheerleader of the University of North Carolina in the 1924-25 school year.

Vic made the Ram (Rameses) as the official mascot of UNC, and he also wrote the fight song ("Here Comes Carolina-lina"), which is still sung at every sporting event. Vic became so enamored with Chapel Hill and the university that he couldn't leave. He opened a hardware store on Franklin Street which was in business until 1991. Vic had an autograph party at Carolyn's Book Shop here in Hendersonville in 1982 to sell his book "Anecdotes," and in between broadcasts during that special occasion, he would fill me in with more experiences he and Ernest Justus had together growing up.

In 1960 (just before East Henderson High was opened), the great Frank L. FitzSimons joined Ernest Justus in a trip back over the old homeplace which had been in the Justus family for more than 175 years (at that time). Ernest Justus' grandfather (W.D. Justus) had at one time served as sheriff, and in 1868, he'd represented this county in the state Legislature. Mr. Fitz and Ernest Justus did find the little three-room house where Ernest's grandfather, W.D. Justus, and his wife, Nancy Pittillo Justus, had raised twenty-four children.

Ernest L. Justus

In Vol. III of "From the Banks of the Oklawaha," Mr. Fitz describes, in detail, the folks they met, the topics discussed on that day back in 1960. In closing that chapter, Fitz said, "To honor Professor Justus for his many years of dedicated service to several generations of the young people of our county, the football stadium had been named and will always be known as the E.L. Justus Stadium."

Almost ten years later, Ernest Justus was honored by his own student body as being the principal and educator with the longest record of service in the field of education in Henderson County. It was Feb. 5, 1969, when Ernest Justus (at the meeting of the student body) was presented with an oil portrait of himself to hang in the school library. The painting was done by Robert Gerstacker, and was presented to Mr. Justus by Troy Pace, president of the student body.

When Ernest Justus attended schools in this county, the only high school level of education was offered by the Fruitland Institute, from which he graduated. He then went on the University of North Carolina, and finally to Columbia University in New York for his master's degree in education.

You'll remember that earlier I told you when Boyce Whitmire became so involved in Elkdom and the State Senate, he called upon the same Ernest Justus to manage the Elks Camp for Boys in his absence.

Ernest L. Justus—a man who impacted the lives of thousands of young people in his long years of service to education in this county!

National Attention

Gamble Benedict would have been fifty-five years old Jan. 15, 1996, but when she came to Hendersonville in April 1960, she was barely 19 and in the company of a suave hairdresser by the name of Andre Porumbeanu, who was then 35–and whether or not divorced, a matter of conjecture.

Gamble Benedict (nicknamed "Gambi") was the granddaughter of Mrs. Henry Harper Benedict, and heir to the Remington Typewriter fortune. Earlier in 1960, "Gambi" had eloped with Porumbeanu to Paris. Her grandmother sicked her formidable law associates on her, and had Gambi returned to New York and declared a ward of the Girls' Term Court.

A second elopement–now get this, as you scan those yellow journal newspapers at the supermarket checkout–this elopement and subsequent marriage was totally financed by the prestigious *Life* magazine in return for an exclusive story on this romantic romp. As soon as it was discovered that she had eloped again, her grandmother had a warrant issued for her as a "wayward minor."

Late in the afternoon of April 6, 1960, "Gambi" and her thirty-five year-old Romanian lover appeared in Hendersonville at the Register of Deeds office in the Court House and applied for a marriage license. They had already been to Pardee Hospital for a physical and a blood test. The Register of Deeds back then was Marshall Watterson, and he became suspicious when he saw the two photographers from *Life* magazine and all their camera rigs standing alongside this 19-year-old girl and the 35-year-old man with brilliantine slicked-down hair. He asked for the girl's birth certificate, which was presented to him showing that she was born on Jan. 15, 1941. He said just looking at Andre Porumbeanu, you could tell he was way over the legal age. He said Porumbeanu had apparently anticipated questioned about being legally divorced from his first wife and produced a divorce decree

With his back to camera, Register of Deeds Marshall Watterson issues a marriage license to Andre Porumbeanu and Gambi Benedict. To left of clock is Ben Prince.

obtained in Juarez, Mexico. Marshall was still on the edge at these strange circumstances, so he called then-county attorney Arthur Redden, who in turn got an opinion from the N.C. Attorney General, who advised there was no legal reason the couple should not be wed.

With this information in hand, Marshall issued the marriage license. "Gambi" Benedict, along with 35-year-old Andre Porumbeanu, *Life* magazine photographer Norm Ritter, another reporter from *Life* and a few others were escorted to the hunting lodge of Arthur Redden in the Mills River section. The couple were married on the lawn of the hunting lodge by Justice of the Peace Fletcher Roberts. Witnesses included attorneys Arthur Redden and L.B. Prince, and Mack Aiken of Hendersonville. Marshall Watterson had also gone along with the group and was an observer of the wedding. It was reported that the millionaire heiress was married in a simple blue and white frock. Andre wore single-breasted two-button blue suit and a borrowed shirt several sizes too large for him.

The wedding took place on Wednesday afternoon, April 6, 1960. There were rumors everywhere that the couple was still at the Redden hunting lodge for the next couple of days. Vehement denials were issued because to fulfill Benedict and Porumbeanu's agreement with *Life* magazine, the photos had to be published by *Life* before any pictures could be released in any other element of the media. The couple alleged they had been driving 50 miles to a telephone from their hideaway to avoid being tracked down by the horde of reporters hunting them.

Shortly after *Life* had its field day with the pictures of the elopement that the magazine itself had financed, "Gambi" and Andre were discovered in a French Quarter motel in New Orleans. When questioned about "Gambi" being disinherited by her grandmother of the Remington fortune, she merely smiled. They also talked of Porumbeanu taking a job in Florida, though Marvin Hodas (a wealthy New York beauty shop owner for whom Porumbeanu had worked) had also advanced big bucks to help the couple on their honeymoon. Hodas said he planned to manufacture cosmetics,

DON UHRBROCK/Life Magazine © Time Inc.

Following the wedding ceremony a picture of the entire group was taken by Life *photographers on the lawn of the Redden Hunting Lodge, where the couple was married. From left: Mack Aiken, once chairman of the County Election Board; County Attorney Arthur J. Redden; Justice of the Peace Fletcher Roberts, Sr., who performed the ceremony; Gambi and Andre Porumbeanu; L. Ben Prince, prominent attorney; and Register of Deeds Marshall Watterson.*

taking advantage of the publicity around the couple, and Andre would represent him in Europe.

Immediately after the ceremony was completed, Gambi nearly collapsed in hysteria, alternately laughing and crying. It was reported that the couple kissed at least fifty times before leaving in a car. Obviously, their kisses back then were a lot shorter than you see on TV today, or they would have still been smooching at the end of their first week.

Now the bride's grandmother (when she was advised of the wedding) said, "I want nothing more to do with them or their escapades." Apparently she did not try to block the couple from traveling to Europe after the wedding. However, eighteen months later when Porumbeanu made his way from Europe via Canada and Bermuda to "tie up some loose ends" (including back alimony payments for his first wife), he apparently had forgotten about a court order issued by Judge Peter M. Horn of Brooklyn to stay away from the Benedict girl. He was immediately arrested, handcuffed, and taken before Judge Horn. In less than ten minutes, he was convicted and sentenced to thirty days in jail and a $250 fine. "If the fine is not paid in a matter of hours, it'll cost you another thirty days in jail," ruled Judge Horn. Porumbeanu complained that he was being made the sacrificial lamb. "This is the most reprehensible thing to happen to me," he said to reporters. "And further, please contact my wife and tell her not to worry."

Now, please remember we said that Gambi wore a plain blue and white frock and did not carry flowers or a Bible. She also did not carry a son that she had given birth to four days earlier. At the time of Porumbeanu's arrest in New York, United Press reported that Gambi (now twenty years old) was expecting her second child and was living in the French Riviera. The UPI story said, "The couple's first child, a boy, was born last April 2." That was four days before she and Andre appeared in the Register of Deeds office in Hendersonville seeking a marriage license.

As a final footnote, once again appears the great Walter B. Smith, a true character in every sense of the word. Walter sent a telegram four days after Porumbeanu had been arrested, offering him a beautiful building site in the North Carolina mountains. Walter B. said he offered them a choice of two or three beautiful building sites in Laurel Park, "where nobody will molest you." He would do this even if he had to cut down a dogwood tree to prove he owned the lot!

The King at Beaumont?

In doing the story of the Hendersonville County Rescue Squad, I mentioned that Ralph Jones had loaned to me not just scrapbooks with press clippings reporting activities of the squad's beginning and its earlier days; but that ultimately Ralph had given up clipping stories and just began saving entire newspapers that had articles concerning the Rescue SquaIn one of those papers loaned to me by Ralph (the *Times-News* dated Aug. 19, 1977) there was a bold headline: ELVIS TRIED TO BUY HOME IN HENDERSONVILLE.

Folks who lived in Hendersonville in 1977 will remember the wild enthusiasm among many in the area when the news broke that Elvis Presley was considering buying the Beaumont Estate on Kanuga Road and planned to move here. If I remember correctly, Jimmy Edney at Land O' Sky Realty had been in contact with Presley about Beaumont; and it seems to me that I remember it being said that Elvis had been here and toured the estate, both the house and grounds. The old ante-bellum estate had much more land than did his Graceland in Memphis (plus it was near a small town) and Elvis remembered the joys of being raised in a small town.

Beaumont, the Hendersonville home Elvis thought about buying.

In fact, he had been told that there were many famous people in Hendersonville, such as Carl Sandburg, Perry Como at Saluda and loads of millionaires. In fact, one person told him that at least 700 millionaires lived in Hendersonville, and once he had moved here, he would be able to lead an unfettered life and could come and go as he pleased.

Somebody (whether out of Graceland or from the local real estate office) leaked the news to the Memphis *Commercial-Appeal* newspaper, and they ran a story on it. As old Will Rogers said, "I only know what I read in the newspapers." Bob Freeman at Freeman's News Stand said everybody in town was trying to get a copy of that edition of the Memphis newspaper. He is quoted in the *Times-News* as saying, "I could have sold 200 copies if I could have gotten them flown in here."

Presley was quoted as saying he'd like to live where he could be just one of the boys. The idea of being able to get around without bodyguards and fans appealed to the singer. The deal, however, fell through. Though there were many locals who kept insisting, "Ah, it ain't dead yet. That Beaumont is a pretty place. I'll bet you he still will buy it." But apparently, when the hitches developed, he simply gave up on the deal. As Mead Parce (who wrote the feature for the *Times-News*) said in that article, "Presley remained at Graceland, a prisoner of his legend."

I said at the start, when I saw that story on the materials loaned to me by Ralph Jones, I felt a pang of embarrassment. For the first twenty years of the North Carolina Apple Festival, I served as emcee and produced the four "pay" events. A fifth one, the Coronation Ball, was added later. We had two elimination nights of folk music and clogging and square-dancing. Then the finals would be on Saturday night. While we'd usually fill the auditorium for the beauty pageant, it cost a lot to stage, with twenty-five to thirty contestants having to be housed and fed, and then the cost of prizes and trips for the queen—all to be paid for from the gate proceeds. The rest of the costs of the festival had to be paid from profits of the three-night folk music shows. In order to stimulate the attendance on the two preliminary nights, we'd try to book a celebrity who would help draw a crowd, people such as Red Foley, Clyde Moody, Red Sovine, Little Jimmie Dickens, Sonny James and George Hamilton IV. (All we paid George was $50 to do five shows for us—his first ever money made for a stage appearance.)

The embarrassment? I was dickering with agents over in Nashville about an inexpensive act we could book, and he suggested an unknown singer who had just dubbed a record on the Sun label that he thought would be a hit. He said we could get him for a couple hundred dollars. "What's the guy's name?" "Elvis Presley," the agent said.

"Never heard of him."

This was before Col. Tom Parker was fired by Eddy Arnold and took over the career of Elvis Presley. Arnold lost center stage and Parker made Elvis "the King." And I could have booked him for $200! A decision almost as brilliant as the Edsel, the "new" Coke, and the Susan B. Anthony dollar.

Ronald Reagan

In 1960, General Electric's Outdoor Lighting Department had been operating in Hendersonville for about four years. GE sponsored (at that time) a series of programs hosted by Ronald Reagan. As part of the sponsorship agreement, Reagan would make a certain number of visits to General Electric plants around the country as a goodwill gesture from GE to the people of communities in which GE had established operations.

In 1960, Ronald Reagan had not gotten involved in conservative politics, although before he married his second wife, Nancy Davis, in 1952, he would date Doris Day on occasion and she would complain, "All he wants to do is talk politics." But because he had not thrown his hat into the national political ring, he had not become the object of derision by leftists and the intellectual elite.

At the time Ronald Reagan came to Hendersonville, he had appeared with Bette Davis in 1939 in "Dark Victory"; in 1940 with Pat O'Brien and Claude Rains in "Knute Rockne"; in 1940 with Errol Flynn and Olivia deHavilland in "Santa Fe Trail"; in 1941 with Charles Coburn, Ann Sheridan, Robert Cummings, and Claude Rains in "King's Row"; and in 1942 it was "Desperate Journey" with Errol Flynn and Raymond Massey. In 1943, Reagan appeared with Irving Berlin, George Murphy (who was another object of academia's wrath), Kate Smith and George Tobias. Reagan would co-star with Barbara Stanwyck, Lee Marvin, Angie Dickinson, John Payne, Rhonda Fleming, Frank Lovejoy, and on and on.

And so it was with this impressive screen background that Ronald Reagan appeared in Hendersonville for the GE Outdoor Lighting Department. In the morning, he had appeared at a "meet and eat" gathering of community leaders, where he simply stood and in his inimitable, affable

way entertained these
people for more than an
hour. He was brought on
down to the studios of
WHKP on the banks of
the Oklawaha, where we
had promoted he'd be
available to answer any
questions posed to him by
any listener.

I referred to the impor-
tant films and celebrated
stars with whom Ronald
Reagan was associated
because, after he became
active and successful in
conservative politics, the

*Kermit Edney interviews Ronald Reagan,
who was in Hendersonville to promote
General Electric in 1960.*

"leftist" media always managed their usual derision by referring to his role
in "Bedtime for Bonzo." The interview I did that day with Ronald Reagan
was totally impromptu. Listeners were free to call and ask questions of him
on any subject. As the program progressed, the more impressed I was with
this man. He exuded warmth and friendliness, nothing rattled him and he
could glide from idle gossip about Hollywood to the manufacture of
generators by the General Electric Company. (That question had been
asked by Leander Johnson.)

At the time, Ronald Reagan was forty-nine years old; I was thirty-six. It
was by far the easiest and most delightful interview I ever did. Though he
probably said it countless times, it meant a lot to me when he turned as we
were leaving and said, "By the way, you have one of the greatest voices I've
ever heard on radio." A cassette containing the Reagan interview is part of
the WHKP "Sound Bit File," a part of the Henderson County Public
Library.

One of his great stories that day dealt with a cab driver who had driven
him from the airport into New York. He said as they approached their
destination, the cabbie said, "Hey, I know you. I've seen you on television."
As they pulled up to the curb, the cabbie was now shouting loud enough to
draw a crowd. "I watch you all the time. You're Ray Milland." So he said
he signed the cabbie's pad "Ray Milland."

It was from that visit with Ronald Reagan that I gravitated from
dormancy to activist in the Republican Party, and down through the years,
I have thoroughly enjoyed my friendships with Jesse Helms and Gov. Jim
Martin. It was a real pleasure to meet Bob Dole and discover how tall this
man from Kansas really is. Through these people, I got to know such
notables as Roosevelt Grier, and alas, a few of ignobility as well.

Roy Taylor was my friend, and I think it is worth noting that when he retired as the Democratic 11th District Congressman, the Asheville Civic Center was filled with longtime friends and supporters–but on the dais were two Republicans. I was the master of ceremonies and Jesse Helms was the featured speaker. We had both appeared at Roy's personal request.

The Cult Murders

The three murdered people, two men and a woman, had last been seen on Sunday, July 17, 1966. Their strangely mutilated bodies were discovered in a ten-foot triangle (feet together) in a clearing near Lake Summit almost a week later on Friday, July 22.

The victims were Vernon James Shipman, forty-three years old; Charles Glass, close to thirty-seven years old; and Louise Davis Shumate of Asheville, who was likely around sixty but looked forty-five.

It was Henderson County's first and only experience with a triple murder that could have been the work of a cult or cultist. No other murder of this magnitude, investigated by three police agencies over such an extended period of time, produced so little evidence of either how the killings occurred or the connection between the people involved. Thirty years later, there is still the hope that someone, just before they die, will confess to the details of this macabre activity about which the public knows no more today than the afternoon the bodies were discovered.

Charles Glass and Vernon Shipman were co-owners of the Tempo Music Shop on Main Street. Both had reputations for being homosexual. Glass was also known for compiling cheap pamphlets on voodoo and secrets of Satan. This was accepted to be more of a diversion for Glass than a source of revenue or a matter of serious pursuit.

The woman was a mystery from the beginning. No one ever was able to figure the connection of Shipman, Glass and the woman, Louise Shumate.

The chronology of activities on Sunday, July 17, 1966:

(1) Vernon Shipman talked with Charles Glass by telephone at about 2 p.m.

(2) At about 4:45 p.m., Shipman had talked to an unidentified person on the phone and made a dinner engagement for 5:30 p.m.

(3) At about 4:30 p.m., Louise Davis Shumate got into her four-year-old Ford Fairlane parked in front of her Ravencroft Apartment in Asheville and drove away.

(4) Later in the investigation, Sheriff Paul Hill alleged that he had learned that Vernon Shipman had made still another phone call from his home around 5:30 p.m. No identities were ever alleged and the call was never confirmed.

(5) A sighting was made of the three of them, plus one unidentified man, at 6 p.m. on Big Willow headed toward Little River Road. The sightings

were positive because both cars had to move very slowly to pass on the narrow road.

When the bodies were ultimately found, the clothing was the same as that they had been seen wearing that Sunday afternoon, except Shipman's coat, which was never found. Shipman was driving, Glass was in the right front seat, the woman was on the left rear seat, and the unknown man was in the right rear seat. He was wearing a shirt and tie, a dark sports coat and sunglasses. Nothing was seen or heard from any of the three until the bodies were found almost a week later.

When none showed for work Monday morning, Taylor Instrument (where the Shumate woman had worked) received no answer to phone calls, the company notified police she was missing. At 7:30 a.m. Monday morning, someone reported to the local Sheriff's Department that a Ford Fairlane had been abandoned and discovered on old N.C. 191 near the French Broad River. The sheriff determined that the car did belong to a Mrs. Shumate, but at the time word had not been distributed that she was missing.

Later on Monday, locals reported a car, identified as that of Shipman's, was found abandoned between the railroad tracks and Select Foods. By this time, all state police agencies had been notified of the disappearance of the three, and that two cars had been recovered.

Almost a week later (on Friday afternoon), Charles Hill of East Flat Rock and Larry Shipman (no relation) drove upon the most gruesome sight they'd ever seen, and raced back to town to report to police. The two had been carrying a load of rubbish to be disposed of in an area about a half mile off North Lake Summit Road, near the railroad and Lake Summit dam. When their truck had eased out into a clearing beneath Duke Power's major transmission lines, they saw the three bodies in a ten-foot semi-circle. Their heads had been smashed, and a part of a bumper jack had been forced up through the vaginal orifice of the Shumate woman.

Glass and Shipman were fully clothed. Shumate's skirt was pulled below her knees, and her blouse pulled from around her shoulders and placed under her back.

Although it was obvious that death in each case had come as a result of massive head injuries, an autopsy revealed that there were hundreds and hundreds of small wounds of similar depth as if made by nails partially driven through a board. Glass's self-winding watch had stopped at 1:50, though it did not reflect a.m. or p.m.

There was so much confusion and so many conflicting statements made by law officers, the SBI announced it would open a command post in the Mountain Air Cottages to establish coordination between law enforcement agencies, and would release any future information on developments in the case.

This grandiose move by the SBI turned out to be as worthless as a

Tinker's Dam. Sheriff Paul Hill announced within a few days that he had enlisted the help of Sheriff Clay of Buncombe County. Hill also said he had signed on the services of a private eye (Ed Stanton from Florida).

The conduct of the investigation turned into one of the great tragic comedies in local history. Whether the triple murder had anything to do with it or not, in the November election, all Republican candidates won handy re-election, except Republican Sheriff Paul Hill, who was stunningly upset by Democrat Jim Kilpatrick. But ultimately, these bizarre killings would come back to defeat Kilpatrick.

On Aug. 6, 1966, the SBI announced that agents Jim Maxey of Bryson City and Jack Peacock of Hickory were being transferred to Hendersonville to assist SBI supervisor P.R. Kitchen in this area, along with agents Gary Satterfield and Claude D. Davis. By this time, we now had five SBI crack agents working with more than 100 other police officers, and not a single new fact was uncovered from August 6 through Dec. 31, 1966.

I developed a close friendship with one of the younger SBI agents working on the case, who had only been a part of the SBI agency for a short time. He assured me that at first opportunity he would be leaving. He said he'd never seen as much incompetence and mass confusion in his life.

The editor of the (then) local weekly newspaper, *The Tribune*, (a man named John Sholar) tried to keep interest going in the investigation, running each and every week a rehash of the exact same information already covered. He did manage to sell the story as a feature to one of the "yellow journal" popular detective magazines.

My young SBI agent friend blamed over-eager, undertrained officers for virtually destroying all evidence at the crime scene before skilled investigators ever arrived. He said that the investigators were mistakenly trying to solve the killings as being the result of normal behavior. He felt strongly that whoever had been responsible for the crimes was a cultist and had not acted alone, and it was obvious that those involved were far more afraid of the cultist or organization than they were of the police.

He observed, "Take one of these migrant labor contractors. Some of them have several killings under their belt and have never been charged. Some of these migrant bosses will sell the workers (who are little more than slaves) illicit drugs or whiskey with a Bible on the table and a picture of Jesus on the wall. They look upon these workers as little more than animals. In many cases, these labor bosses feel morally superior. They don't commit the Saturday night-type sins—no carousing around or getting drunk or committing adultery. They're holier than thou, and to dispose of two homosexuals (and for some reason, that woman) in the macabre way that was done probably caused them to feel sanctified."

In defense of my young friend's theory, two different farm workers confessed to the killings in Florida, but when they were returned by the Sheriff's Department, it was found that neither of them had even been here at the time of the murders.

On another occasion, one person convinced Sheriff Kilpatrick he had personal knowledge of a peculiarity in the killings. The sheriff got a court order and had the bodies exhumed. There was no new evidence of any kind.

It's been thirty years now, and the chances are that the planner, mastermind and/or perpetrators of the most famous and bizarre murders ever committed in this county may now be in the eternal sizzling of "Gehenna." They were not the type to try to catch the spaceship riding out of here on the tail of the comet in 1997.

In a totally unrelated crime, Henderson County also has the notoriety of being the last county to have a man declared "an outlaw." A man by the name of Edward Thompson, Jr. had (through a burglary, robbery and kidnapping) started a crime spree that resulted in rapes and killings in both the Carolinas and Virginia. Law enforcement officers were frustrated by his continued ability to elude them. Chief of Police Bill Powers used an ancient statute in North Carolina and was successful in persuading the man to be declared as "an outlaw," which gives the right to any citizen to kill the man on sight. This information was widely publicized by the media, and Thompson was captured in less than forty-eight hours. That law has since been repealed.

The Mask Museum

There are only a few cities in the world that can boast of a Madame Toussaud Wax Museum, but I suppose Hendersonville is the only town for many miles around to have its own Mask Museum—a labor of love of Ellen Hobbs.

Looking back at the 1946 City Directory, I noticed that the General Insurance Agency was located across 4th Avenue from the Western Union Office. The directory shows that the manager of General Insurance was Homer C. Hobbs and his wife was Ellen C. Hobbs. I knew Homer real well. He was an avid golfer and active in varied civic activities. I knew who Ellen was, but only to speak to.

Ellen Hobbs, founder of the Mask Museum.

Ellen and Homer had their first son, Raymond, a year earlier than our son was born. Then their family was blessed with another son, David, born in 1953, a year after our daughter was born.

By 1970, Ellen had succeeded in persuading Hendersonville High School to formally establish an Art Department. She became the first director and held that post until she retired in 1985.

The Hobbs' first son, Raymond, took up flying at age 16. Ellen joined him in this pursuit, and ultimately Raymond acquired his own plane, which he and Ellen flew regularly.

Being devoted to arts, Ellen took a strong interest in masks and costumes used in native celebrations in countries around the world. This keen interest enticed her to visit countries and learn first-hand the history of the masks of each region, and she even learned how to make them. Her travels included Japan, China, Australia, Bali, New Guinea, Java, Mexico, England, Guatemala, Columbia, Peru, and Equador.

Ellen Hobbs made many purchases of masks and costumes during these foreign travels. As word circulated of this avocation, friends would donate to her individual masks, or even a small collection of masks they had made.

I drive 5th Avenue past the General Realty office on almost a daily basis, and when I first saw the sign "Mask Museum," my first reaction was, "If I were Homer, I don't believe I'd give up the real estate business." Then I learned the museum was NOT a business at all. Ellen Hobbs' intense love for her mask collection prompted her to share it with anyone who has an interest, and there is no admission charge at all.

I didn't know until recently that Ellen is an active member in the ATC–that's Alternative Transportation Committee–which seeks to promote sidewalks, bicycle paths and public transportation. It did not come as any surprise because for years I'd seen Ellen peddling her way around Hendersonville.

A friend of Ellen Hobbs sent me a picture of the Mahogany Lady, another great triumph of this unusual person. When I saw the envelope labeled "Mahogany Lady," I assumed it would be a small figurine of some sort inspired by one of her trips, perhaps to the Orient.

You can imagine my amazement when I opened the envelope and discovered a picture of a full life-size rocking horse. Ellen carved this rocking horse (life-size from mahogany) and it took over three years to accomplish this challenge. The mane and tail on the horse are made of hair that came from real horses.

I bumped into Ellen and Homer in the Harris-Teeter supermarket before Thanksgiving 1996, and I'm sure, had time permitted, we could have exchanged many wonderful memories because Ellen and Homer also are observing more than fifty years in business locally.

And Ellen is remembering a lifetime of service to the arts as a remarkable person who simply gravitated to flying and sailing or gliding as if she'd been born with wings. As she brought the many, many forms of art into the lives of young people (students at Hendersonville High School), she was also constantly expanding her skills and knowledge and talents to share even more with the next class to be enrolled.

If you'd like to visit the Mask Museum, it is open during business hours at 317 Fifth Avenue West. If you teach a class and would like to bring the whole class, or if you have an extra-curricula study group and would like to learn more about this fabulous collection, you might want to call Ellen for a personal guided tour.

Down through the years, I'd sort of lost track of Raymond, their oldest son. He's a Lear Jet pilot and scientist for Aeromet in Tulsa, Okla. The younger son, David, and his wife own and operate the Broadway Arts Building and the Green Door in Asheville.

355

Gifts of Nature

For more years that I can remember, every Easter Sunday I dutifully made my way from Hendersonville to Chimney Rock, and then up the mountain to the parking lot at the base of the rock where WHKP would originate the annual Easter Sunrise Service on our station, to be picked up and broadcast by other stations down through the years. Al Hope has now taken over where the old, old Good Morning Man left off.

To me the program was not only utterly beautiful in content but spectacular in setting with the sun rising to be reflected in the waters of Lake Lure far below. I sensed always a spirit of total cooperation between the people of Hickory Nut Gorge and the folks who operate Chimney Rock Park. The Easter program always included the pastors of the various church in the Gorge, none of whom did a full-fledged sermon but participated in the prayers and the story of Easter itself. Special music also helped draw thousands to Chimney Rock for this memorable experience.

When I was very young, the manager of the park was Norman Grieg, who was succeeded by Jay Freeman, but my contact over the past decade or so has been Mary Yeager-Gale, who handles a number of responsibilities in addition to public relations and marketing. Then a few years ago, I had the good fortune to meet Todd Morse, who now manages the Chimney Rock Park and is the son of Lu, the owner.

My first experience with the Morse family came when I discovered (in doing the "Kermit Edney Weather Book") that a man by the name of Dr. Lucius Morse was the cooperative weather observer in Hendersonville. He owned and operated the Duncraggan Inn from 1911 to 1913. Dr. Morse had started buying up property in the Chimney Rock area as early as 1902 from Jerome "Rome" Freeman (grandfather of Bob Freeman, Mr. Republican of Henderson County at Freeman's News Stand). Dr. Morse was one of the earliest dreamers and entrepreneurs in Western North Carolina. His early promotional material compared the climate of the Chimney Rock area as being equivalent to that of the French Riviera. He envisioned paved roads to the top of Chimney Rock, the building of a lake at the foot of the mountain, which would generate power for hotels and a growing residential community.

In 1913, he sold Duncraggan Inn and moved to be near his dream development. The late Clayton Drake of Hendersonville recalled working on the hydroelectric dam at Lake Lure when he was a young man. Lucius Morse had persuaded his brothers, Hiram and Asahel, to join in this visionary development, and the talents and financial resources of Asahel and Hiram came into play. The Morse family had gained wealth in publication of a financial newspaper in St. Louis, and had branched out over the years to encompass a variety of other businesses. At one time, Chimney Rock Park became involved in a public stock offering and owned more than 8,000 acres. After the 1929 crash and during the Great Depression, the Morse family was able to buy back total ownership of the Chimney Rock Company.

Lu Morse at Chimney Rock.

In 1949, the Morse family completed an engineering feat that was a marvel to the area and times. They had blasted back into the solid rock wall and installed an elevator that would carry passengers 258 feet straight up to the top of the precipice, where viewers could walk onto a level decking to the very base of the famed chimney.

In March 1970, a rumor swirled up and down Hickory Nut Gorge that Chimney Rock Park was to be sold. Norman Grieg was still the manager and answered all queries with "no comment." His face was as without expression as the face of the rock itself. As I visited that Wednesday morning in 1996 with the sole owner of the park, Lu Morse II, I asked what that was all about. "Oh," he said, "a potential buyer wandered in and offered an enormous sum of money for the park—the kind of money you can't ignore. When we investigated, he simply did not have the assets alleged, and we dropped any further contact."

Lu went on to say, "However, in 1974, we had a different situation. My Aunt Bea (Mrs. Edward Washburn), who was serving as chairman of the board, felt the corporation was not producing an adequate yield and the park should be sold. Lu said, "I was working in Boston at the time (living in Weston, Mass.) and happened to have a Realtor's license, so I suggested if we're going to offer it for sale, there's no better person than myself to handle the marketing challenges."

Lu had a friend named Steve Welch, a freelance copywriter eking out a living doing copy for a variety of agencies in Boston. Lu approached Steve and asked, "What would you charge to lay out an ad for me offering the sale of Chimney Rock Park?" Lu said Steve laughed and said, "Ah, I'll do it for nothing–unless you sell it, and then you have to buy me dinner." Lu said when Steve delivered the ad to him, he was so flabbergasted at the sheer genius of it, he bought an eighth-page ad in the Wall Street Journal, which was published Nov. 4, 1974. On that bright October morning in 1996, as we sipped coffee in the little house the Morse's call "The Lodge" (which sits in the final hairpin turn before you get to the parking lot), Lu said, "I have a copy of that ad around here some place. It was fantastic." I interrupted him, "Lu, I have excerpts from the ad," and started reading. The ad noted that the Morse family had owned the park since 1912. It was headlined "Chimney Rock Park at Lake Lure is for sale for a man with a dream and 3 million dollars."

"That's it," Lu said, "That's what caught your eye." The ad went on to say, "There are mountains here. Caves, grottoes, catacombs, cascades, forests, orchards, and a 75-mile view of the Blue Ridge Mountains from the top of Chimney Rock, that chauvinists claim is the most spectacular in the United States." Lu roared with laughter. "Isn't that fantastic?"

I read on: "Doubtless they exaggerate, more probably it is the second or third most spectacular. (Lu was still roaring with laughter.) Again I read on: "At any rate, millions of tourists have taken our elevator to the observatory–straight up through 258 feet of solid granite–for the view. Besides the vistas, what's there now is this: excellent roads, large parking areas, amusements, a moderately famous Sky Lounge, gift and souvenir shops, several picnic areas, a children's playground, splendidly maintained nature trails, rivers and waterfalls ... a plethora of timber and deer." (Lu interrupted, "Don't you

A.F. Baker's photo was used in ads for Chimney Rock for more than 100 years.

just love that 'a plethora of timber and deer'" and then he again roared with laughter.) I read on: "A 160-acre apple orchard that's about to come into its own, a modest but burgeoning annual profit and some of the most mind-warping potential on the continent. In all, some 865 acres of it. If you bought it, God only knows what you could do with it."

I stopped and asked, "Lu, did this ad produce any results?"

"Results?? Unbelievable! No buyers, maybe a nibble or two, but that ad was so unusual, it was picked up and carried as a feature by virtually every newspaper in the country. In fact, the *Boston Globe* had a field day just playing around with the copy in that ad."

"Well, obviously you didn't sell it," I volunteered.

"No," Lu answered, "but it sort of set the stage for me to buy out all the other members of the family and I became the sole owner of Chimney Rock Park in January 1975.

"My first concern was the safety of the park. All the improvements made in the late '70s and early '80s were to make the grounds and trails safer and more convenient. We replaced bridges and stairs, improved trails, added scenic view points, and hired Geoff Rausch (one of the most famous Environmental Planning & Design Engineers of Pennsylvania) to develop a master plan for the park and update that plan every five years. We created "the Meadows" to accommodate large groups of visitors, and most recently, relocated the main entrance gate from the highway to "the Meadows." Our business had grown so much over the years that cars would back up at the old entrance and block the highway. When the Sky Lounge burned in 1981, we rebuilt a much more complete and appropriate facility there at the base of the rock."

Lu said, "As the years went by, my son Todd and I realized that we had species of plants and wildlife living here in the park that confounded the experts. They simply didn't believe what we were telling them until they came to see for themselves. That's what Todd and I are now dedicated to do. With expert guidance, we will develop the park with the unique goals of developing sufficient revenue to make the company viable; and, at the same time, guarantee that the park shall forever retain its natural God-given habitat. Todd lives here. He is a part of the Hendersonville community ... Just between you and me, he does allow me to come and lend a hand during the spring blooming season and the fall coloring season. My job is to run the elevator and talk to our customers."

Or, as Uncle John Morris used to say when he ran the elevator in the old State Trust Building, "There's shore a lot of ups and downs in my business."

The Famed Saluda Grade

It would be difficult to find a true railroad buff in the country who has not heard of the famed Saluda grade, a winding 2.5-mile stretch of railroad that reaches from Church Street in Saluda to Melrose and the lower end of Pearson Falls Road. This is the steepest grade on any Class 1 railroad in the United States, averaging five percent, with a few limited sections running at 5.4 percent.

Considering that a modern rail coach is 100 feet long, on the Saluda grade, from the time you pass through one end of the coach to the other end, you'll be walking uphill five feet. Pearson Falls, by the way, was named for the man who designed the railroad up the mountain from Tryon to the crest of the grade.

In earlier years, there was always a "helper engine" on the siding at Melrose and the engine was ready at any time to either push or pull, or even to help hold back a train on the downgrade. There used to be two runaway cutoffs—one at the steep curve at the bottom of the Saluda straight stretch down to the Sand Cut, and another runaway cutoff was at Melrose Junction.

Coming down the mountain in the earlier days, trains could signal switchmen at Melrose by blowing their whistles to let them know that they were out of control. The train could then be diverted to the runaway tracks, which provided a ten percent grade to be climbed by the runaway (which would help it stop). Also, the runaway (or safety track) would shunt most of the runaway cars away from the main track. The Saluda Grade runs almost exactly parallel to Pearson Falls Road, steeply down the mountain from Saluda to Melrose. No longer do you have a helper engine at Melrose, and no longer are there switchmen to divert a runaway to the safety tracks. Every train is monitored electronically, and in the event the sensors detect excess speed, automatically the switches to the safety track are thrown.

The last wreck on the Saluda Grade occurred in 1971. A fifty-three-car coal train bound from Knoxville to Spartanburg was shunted to the safety track. All three diesel engines remained upright and stayed on the track as it raced up the 10 percent grade to a deadened sand pile. However, forty-seven cars (loaded with 3,290 tons of coal) jumped the track and accordioned in piles along the track and into the gorge. Six cars and the caboose at the very end of the train also remained upright and intact.

The spectacular wreck caused no injuries. It occurred on a Sunday in 1971 and a cause was never given. Traffic on the grade was blocked for almost twenty-four hours until wrecker trains with cranes arrived from Spartanburg and Asheville which could pick up the twisted cars and place them on a flatbed rail cars for transportation and disposal. Railroad crews quickly laid what they called a "shoo fly section" of temporary track around the wreckage so that traffic could be resumed on the Saluda Grade.

In spite of the dangers on the steep Saluda Grade, trainmen on the longer trains now plan "triplers." They break the train into three sections at either Melrose or Saluda; and then take each section up (or down) – reconnecting to continue their journey. While this process may take an hour and a half for a train crew, it takes three times longer to climb or descend the "loops" on Black Mountain where the grade is a measly two percent. Talk is always

Kermit Edney fulfilled a lifelong dream in 1992, braving the Saluda Grade on #611, "The Little Engine That Could."

present about simply closing the spectacular railbed from Haynes Station at Spartanburg to Hendersonville, and routing traffic over much longer distances to include the "loops" up Black Mountain. But as long as trainmen can maintain a record of safety with only one derailment in twenty-five years, Saluda may still experience some reprieve.

On Oct. 25, 1992, I experienced a lifelong dream. I rode in the engine of an excursion train from Haynes Station in Spartanburg to Asheville, observed the "tripling" done at Melrose where even this twenty-five-car passenger train with 870 passengers on board was broken into sections to climb the treacherous Saluda Grade. In addition to the Norfolk and Western 4-8-4 giant steam locomotive #611, we had three powerful SD diesels to assist in pulling power. At Melrose, the three diesels pulled all but five cars up ahead of the steam unit. No. 611 was pulling five larger passenger cars, and on the final link up the steepest part of the grade (1,000 feet from the Saluda crest) #611 spun out. The engine lost all traction and the wheels would just spin wildly with no pulling power. Every car had been assigned a trainman to operate the handbrakes; and the trainmaster (there in the cab where I was standing) announced on his radio, "Secure all handbrakes." Neither of the engineers could have been out of their thirties. The fireman, Scott Merrill of Edneyville, was in his twenties. None of them had ever seen the Saluda Grade before, let alone throttled a train up the mountain.

There was some discussion of radioing up to have three diesels come back down and help the train to the top. About two or three minutes went by. Then the older trainmaster calmly said, "I think we can make it. We'll just barely ease open the throttle, lay down sand, and release all the handbrakes. If it begins to move, don't touch that throttle. Let it develop its own speed from the least steam we can give it." It worked. As #611 began inching up the hill, you could sense a new confidence on the part of everyone. By the time we were pulling into Saluda, the engine was taking deep throaty barks and belching coal black smoke as the speed increased. One of the engineers simply laid down on that whistle. He made it blast, he made it roar, he made it moan— and the thousands of people lining the streets of Saluda were cheering like you've never seen. We had become the little engine that could!

I mentioned to the trainmaster (when we pulled into Biltmore Station) what a thrill it had been for me to be on that engine and that it was my fifth great desire—I had achieved all the others. He looked at me in a rather curious way and said, "I believe if I were you, I'd go home and make me another list."

Colony of Flat Rock

Back before World War II (and again just after the war) there was a gentleman who spent the summers at Flat Rock, and whose career was in broadcasting. In fact, he was vice president of CBS Radio. His name was Sam Pickard. I vaguely remember Mr. Pickard. His carriage, his manner of dress were exactly what you'd expect from an executive with the Columbia Broadcasting System. Sam Pickard had bought a number of pieces of real estate during his years in Hendersonville, and I ran across a story where he'd given a tract of land on Upward Road to Henderson County. This land would ultimately become what we knew as the fairgrounds.

Pickard was also a great lover of horses, especially the Tennessee Walking Horses, and he purchased and lived on the farm just this side of Kenmure. It is easily recognizable today with the Kentucky bluegrass-type fencing on the place. In fact, Mr. Pickard's son, Sam Jr., had served two years as co-manager of the famed Hendersonville Horse Show. The Pickards owned not only the Flat Rock summer home but also a home in New York and another in Miami Beach.

In 1944 (during World War II), Sam Pickard announced that they were selling their Miami Beach home, and would established their permanent home in Hendersonville. He also announced that he would seek a leave of absence from the CBS Network, and he and his wife, would enter full-time service for their country. He had served in World War I, and had earned a purple heart, being wounded in action. He said that while he was slightly over the age limit, he expected to get a waiver, which would allow him to go overseas. His wife would serve with the American Red Cross and would remain in the States because they still had a daughter at home. Their one son, Sam Jr., was already serving on Dwight Eisenhower staff in London.

As I continued to do research on this very colorful and dynamic person, whom I had met while working at Bob Freeman's News Stand, I ran across an agreement (in Deed Book 285 in the Register of Deeds office) that Sam Pickard had drawn up establishing covenants over some two square miles of property in what was called the Flat Rock "Colony." Parties of the first part were Sam Pickard and his wife. Parties of the second part were Reuben Robertson and his wife, the Robert Henrys, the D.E. Hugers, MacMillan E. King, Marion Brawley, Henry Laurens and his wife, Dorothea, and the Pickards.

The covenants agreed to for this two square mile section of the Flat Rock Colony were severe ... in fact, one could not even build a house or cottage in the area with less than six rooms. In this agreement, it stipulated, "the restrictions imposed shall constitute a covenant running with the title." Since discovering this unique agreement, I have queried two different attorneys about the strength and validity currently of this agreement establishing these covenants. As attorneys are want to do, each took a separate viewpoint. One argued that the agreement could be a nuisance in a property transfer. Another said that by signing of the agreement, the covenants would run with the title, and he said a smart lawyer could make very difficult any change that might be proposed by any future planning board.

What was most interesting to me (as an observer of the spirited election in 1996 establishing the "Village of Flat Rock") it was alleged that the incorporation of the village was for the express purpose of preserving the "Flat Rock way of life." Please note that in the Sam Pickard agreement it states "whereas the parties hereto are desirous of carrying out the intent of the original settlers in establishing a residential area which shall insure the tradition of the Flat Rock way of life." That was Oct. 31, 1947, fifty years before any of those involved in the last election had even heard of Flat Rock.

South Carolina Ties to Flat Rock

Sam Pickard was a friend for many years with William Joseph Urquehart, who was also a friend of Dr. Nick Fortescue and had trained Walking Horses for Fortescue. In 1949 when Sam Pickard retired, Mr. Urquehart bought the Pickard farm, including the large colonial home and two smaller houses. Mr. Urquehart later sold the two smaller houses and the training ring and land to Hugh Eudy and Sherwood Shipman. Eudy later sold a piece of the higher ground adjacent to Kenmore Golf Course to Don Howard.

Mr. Urquehart's daughter, Lucy Urquehart Fritz, is now head of a credit union here in town. The big house of Sam Pickard was later occupied by Mrs. Hamilton, an aunt of Dr. Nick Fortescue's wife. Mrs. Hamilton had operated at one time the famed Park Hill Inn. I understand the home was then sold to Newt Angier and later to the Kirtleys, who ran Allied Moving Vans.

Pickard retired to Crystal River, Fla., after completing his service with CBS during the "golden days of radio." The Pickard place at Flat Rock was known as "Green Lawn." It had been built by Arthur Huger, and it was sold later to Gov. Thomas Bennett of South Carolina who owned it from 1820 to 1822.

Now here's a bit of insight for us to share. In addition to Gov. Bennett, Gov. William Aiken of South Carolina also summered here at Highland Lake at

Rhett's Place. There was Gov. Burnet Maybank and his son (Lt. Gov. "Little Burnet") who had a home in the Maybank Drive area. Also I remember Strom Thurmon, who was the first governor elected to a four-year term in South Carolina! He frequented Freeman's News Stand whenever he was (or is) in the area. All these governors are from South Carolina. We also have one governor from Florida who lived here, Gov. Dave Scholtz, who built the house in which Nell Cantrell lives today.

In spite of the fact that Henderson County was chosen as either a home or summer place by at least four South Carolina and one Florida governor, the best any North Carolina governor has ever done for the area is maybe pass through here at high speed or come here to make a campaign speech. In fact, to the best of my knowledge, there are only two streets in this area named for a North Carolina governor—that would be Caswell, North Carolina's first governor after the royal governors, and Ehringhaus, named for Gov. Ehringhaus who served from 1933 to '37.

However, names of prominent South Carolinians? The Lowndes family lived here, and Rawling Lowndes was South Carolina governor in 1778-79. Sadie Patton (in her book) casually refers to the Lowndes place several times as Dulce far Niente, but she doesn't do us the favor of a translation. The only European language that includes the world "dulce" is Italian, and it means "sweet." "Dolce," as in La Dolce Vita, means the "good" life. We were discussing this among the old fogies at breakfast on a morning in May 1996, and Frank Ewbank says, "Print that out so that I can read it," which I did. That same afternoon, Frank left a message on the answering machine: "Dulce far Niente is Italian for 'sweet for doing nothing.'"

One of the major streets in the "village" or "colony" of Flat Rock is Rutledge Drive. There were two Rutledges who served as governor of South Carolina: John served two different terms and Edward from 1798 to 1800. Plus, there was an Archibald Rutledge who was poet laureate of South Carolina. There were Govs. Thomas and Charles Pinckney. The Pinckney name was familiar to Times-News readers and to patrons of the Flat Rock Playhouse during the '40s and early '50s because Elise Pinckney was their drama critic. There was a Gov. Henry Middleton, and we had our own Henry Middleton, who owned Piedmont Estate and whose nephew, Bevo,

The Flat Rock ante-bellum home, "Green Lawn," once owned by the Sam Pickard family.

was associated at one time with WHKP.

So the ties to this area, and especially to the low country of South Carolina, would be endless. Gov. Thomas Bennett lived at "Green Lawn" (the Sam Pickard home), and ownership of that place went to James Gordon, then through the Hugers, the Pickards, the Urqueharts, the Newt Angiers and even the Kirtleys.

But I did not give you the names of the current owners. One day in May 1996, I drove out to refresh my memory of the barns and fenced-in horse rinks. I even snapped a couple of pictures. The fences are no longer blue-grass country white—they're stained woodsy brown.

Rounding the drive at Green Lawn, now owned by Clark and Mary Hecker, this is the view that greets you.

Suddenly, from where I had parked my car, I could see the huge antebellum home that Sam Pickard once lived in. With a degree of apprehension, I drove up the typical Flat Rock winding driveway and was immediately greeted by a very friendly Roy Goetsch, who was one of several working on the mansion. He graciously gave me a few minutes of his time to step inside and see the total restoration that is going on. The place is now owned by Clark and Mary Hecker of St. Louis. Hecker comes from the famed Buster Brown shoe firm. This young couple is totally restoring the house back to the original condition when built by Arthur Huger. Window casements were being removed to permit installation of new weights and new suspension connections. Where a previous owner may have applied paint over stain, the paint was being removed and the original stain reapplied. It has twelve-foot ceilings downstairs, and ten-foot ceilings upstairs.

I have lived here seventy-one years and passed along the old Greenville Highway many times, but never had I noticed "Green Lawn" until the month of May 1996. When restored by the Heckers, it will be a true showplace for this county.

Planes, Trains & Automobiles

Railroad historians and the train buff elite loved to describe the make-up of passenger trains as the "consist." The Carolina Special, as an example, had a consist of a mail car, a baggage car, a diner, two or three day coaches and a couple of Pullmans. Once in a great while, a fancy observation car was added at the end. The consist of the "Toxaway Train" amounted to one car–half was a day coach, the other half was for baggage and mail.

The last passenger run (the sad remnants of the Toxaway Train) left Hendersonville on Dec. 5, 1941, running to Brevard, Rosman, Quebec, and Lake Toxaway. In announcing the discontinuance of this train, Southern agent J.W. Bailey said, "The demand for this service has declined to the point where it is unprofitable." He said, "The advent of the automobile and the construction of improved highways gradually removed passengers from the railway coaches." Those were Agent Bailey's exact words.

America's penchant for mobility, aided with unlimited lobbying funds from the cement, automobile, and rubber industries, has caused Americans to believe, "I'll build a house wherever I want to and the government will build a road to it." This is the only country in the world that follows this precedent. It has encouraged everybody in the family to have his or her own car. When Katherine and I were first married, we were responsible for only one vehicle. Now, we (our children and grandchildren) are glutting the highways and filling parking lots with eleven cars. While it is a marvelous convenience (this individual mobility), it took away the heart of short-haul railway and inter-city bus business. The airlines then served the death knell to the long-haul field, except for those who fear flying or those who simply love trains.

I happen to fall in the latter category. Going back to my very memorable first ride on a train from Hendersonville to Biltmore and back, I calculate that I have logged 33,310 miles on trains (during and since World War II) just in this country. That's not including several thousand miles on trains in England and Europe.

Even throughout the '40s and '50s, there were four trains daily through Hendersonville: Trains #27 and 28, the Carolina Special and Trains #9 and 10, the Skyland Special. The Carolina Special ran between Chicago and Cincinnati, and either Charleston or Jacksonville, depending on whether or not you changed trains in Columbia. The Skyland Special originated in Asheville and provided direct service to Jacksonville and St. Petersburg. In addition, there were the special "excursion trains" in the summer, bringing campers from the lowlands to the myriad of camps in the Hendersonville area.

During World War II, railroads provided the salvation to the country in transporting not only freight and war material, but also the 15 million servicemen and their families around the entire nation. As newer, faster cars were built to travel and new four and six-lane high-speed superhighways were finished, demand began dropping on all passenger trains.

After Southern dropped their Toxaway line, they next eliminated the Skyland Specials (Trains 9 and 10). That left only the Carolina Special with a Hendersonville stop. The railroads were regulated by the Utility Commissions in each state, so the railroads would use their significant political power in one state to get the portion of a train passing through that state discontinued. The North Carolina Utilities Commission in 1941 gave approval (in spite of wide protests) for Southern to discontinue all fourteen trains west of Asheville due to the so-called coal shortage.

After the Southern had rid itself of all passenger service (except the Carolina Special) in this area, their strategy was to get it discontinued in pieces, starting in Florida. For a while, the Special ran only to the Georgia line. Then Georgia gave in and the Special stopped at the South Carolina line. Finally, South Carolina gave their approval and the Carolina Special then ran only from Asheville to the South Carolina line (where it did its turnaround). That same strategy had been used by the Southern to eliminate service from Cincinnati south. The final life of the Carolina Special really went "from here to nowhere," and with proper bookkeeping manipulation of depreciation, share of overhead expense, etc., the Southern was able to prove that each trip cost them $444 and revenue for each trip averaged $32.19. The N.C. Utilities Commission, the last to give in to Southern's campaign, capitulated and the Carolina Special ran for the last time on Dec. 5, 1968.

While Amtrak still has problems (and there are some politicians who would do away with all passenger service in this country), one wonders what would happen in another national emergency; or in other situations when planes can't fly and cars find even expressways closed down.

Amtrak does still provide excellent service to Washington, D.C., New York and Boston (and likewise, south to Atlanta, Birmingham and New Orleans). Catch the Crescent in Greenville, S.C. at 10:55 p.m. You'll find your bed made in your own private bedroom. The following morning, you'll have breakfast as you pass through Charlottesville at 6:48 a.m., and you'll arrive rested and refreshed in the awesome Union Station in Washington at 9:28 a.m., with connections to the Metro or anyplace in the D.C. area. Traveling first class, your meals are free, and your car has been left in a protected storage area in Greenville, waiting for your return.

The North Carolina Department of Transportation does subsidize the operation of two trains each way daily between Charlotte and Raleigh, and the Legislature in 1997 appropriated the first monies toward extending the Amtrak service to Asheville. What a way to go to a football game in the Triangle area. You'd even get to see the famed geyser on Old Fort Mountain again!

No Trains, No Planes, Not Even a Bus

Very few people realize that Joel Wright (former football great and city councilman), a person I joshingly call "The Little Ole Oilman," was once a bus driver. A lot of people who knew and came in contact with Joe Wright (the city councilman) or Joe Wright (the civic leader) never knew his career as a bus driver. Charlie "Choo Choo" Justice remembers Joe when he drove buses. Charlie even rode with him on several runs. Joe didn't just drive a bus, he drove any bus his daddy told him to, because the Wright family owned the Smoky Mountain Trailways.

It was one of the many bus companies doing business in the highly competitive '40s and '50s when Buster Livingston's beautiful City Bus Terminal accommodated not only Smoky Mountain but also Carolina Scenic, Greyhound and Queen City Coach Line. the City Bus Terminal was located at the corner of 7th and Main (where NationBank's main building stands today). The giant buses would wheel in off 7th Avenue; and after handling passengers, baggage and express parcel service, would exit back into Main Street to continue their runs.

Oden Morris was not just the agent. Oden ran the terminal. He had been exposed to the schedules of all the bus lines so much, he didn't even refer to timetables. Without notes or prompting, he could give you the time you'd arrive in Birmingham or Cleveland or the price of the ticket.

"The bus station," as everyone called it, was busy 24 hours a day. Next door was the famous "Tracy's," a short-order cafe which never closed and was owned and operated by Tracy Oelkers, who had come here from Murphy. I went into military service with Tracy, and if ever you saw a man have trouble with basic training, it was Tracy, as told to you in an earlier chapter. He was the only man to receive the perfect assignment by the Army, according to his skills. After basic, Tracy ran a beer PX for the rest of the time he was in the service.

The bus business was still booming after World War II, and would continue to do so long after the passenger train business began to fade. Buses had more frequent schedules and traveled to more cities than did the trains. But again, the interstate highway system (four-laning of the primary highways of the nation) forced the bus lines to change. Instead of traveling from Spartanburg up U.S. 176 (through Inman, Gramling, Campobello, Landrum, Tryon, Saluda, Tuxedo, and East Flat Rock), to get an improved operating schedule they moved over to the interstates and simply bypassed the small towns. They saved time but they lost contact with the local business. Much the same as railroads, the local terminals became hangouts for loafers.

On our last Amtrak trip through Chicago, to solve the problem of loafers, dopeheads and bums from hanging around that great Chicago terminal, they simply removed all seats. There is (or was on our last trip through) not a seat in the Chicago train terminal.

Carolina merged with Queen City, which was purchased by Holiday Inn. In this area, the only service now is from a few Greyhounds-Trailways still running.

Talking about transportation, I certainly must include the City Bus Company, operated at one time or another by Ralph Young or John L. Loy. The buses operated by the City Bus Company were nothing at all similar to the huge vehicles you see today in metro areas. They were more like school buses, and as I remember, were painted white with a blue trim. In the years the company operated, they were simply vital because in the years during and just after WWII, cars were still not available to everyone. There were many who couldn't afford cars nor buy gas who were regular users of city buses. So Hendersonville had made the transition from the trolleys (which Mr. Fitz told you about) to a complete city bus service, which was operating here when WHKP first signed on the air, and now no longer exists.

In my freshman year at Chapel Hill, I had a driver's license but certainly no car. I learned I wasn't too good at "thumbing a ride." Once I had enough money for bus fare over to Durham but not enough for the return fare, so I figured I'd thumb my way back. BAD decision. I was ignored by every car and ended up walking the twelve miles back. An old Army friend, Bud Johnson, was a great thumber. He looked like the "All American Boy." He and I were thumbing from Fresno, Calif., to Los Angeles (his hometown) and caught a ride the minute we hit the highway. It was aboard a tanker truck. Back then there was a steep, winding highway from the San Juaoquin Valley into L.A. (which they called "the grapevine"). As we roared and careened down that mountain, the driver kept hanging on for dear life and whistling "Nearer My God to Thee." I gave up thumbing for good after that.

I do prefer trains, but trains had disappeared from Chapel Hill, I think, before I was born. So the best I could do was commute by bus; and in the days before the interstates, that was a long, long trip. To have as much time at home as possible, I'd catch the Queen City Bus to Bat Cave, then transfer to the Queen City bus headed for Charlotte. Another change there for Fayetteville and a final change to Chapel Hill. If on time (and you made your connections), it was a ten- to twelve-hour trip from here back to campus.

It was 1967 which marked the end of any sort of bus service from Hendersonville to Bat Cave. Queen City had petitioned the State Utilities Commission to discontinue bus service to Bat Cave, arguing that it was just as close to go from Hendersonville to Asheville and catch the same bus. The Chamber of Commerce objected, and at an earlier hearing, Queen City's petition had been denied and bus service continued. But on Nov. 24, 1967, the full Utilities Commission heard the Queen City petition, and Commissioner Thomas W. Elier (speaking for the whole commission) said that substantial evidence disclosed that the public convenience and necessity no longer justified the service and that to require the continuation of the service would result in undue and unreasonable burden on Queen City. The bus company was told that it could run their last bus from Hendersonville to Bat Cave on Nov. 30, 1967.

I couldn't argue with the decision. Even back in the '40s, I was one of the few people who ever rode the bus, and I imagine there were even fewer in 1967, but I felt for the people of the Gorge. We don't know how to appreciate bus service, the close proximity to airports and four-lane highways in Hendersonville. We take all those things for granted.

Back in the early '80s, I had persuaded the child bride that a great vacation for us would be an Amtrak package deal to New York that included accommodations at the Milford Plaza Hotel and also great seats at two Broadway shows. Other perks included sightseeing trips, a fruit basket and welcoming cocktails. I'm sure there are New Yorkers here now that remember the original name of the hotel that became Milford Plaza. It's the hotel just down from Sardi's Restaurant and in which the Stage Door Canteen operates.

The old hotel had been totally remodeled and a gorgeous new lobby had been completed. I immediately noticed that the place was loaded with airline pilots and stewardesses. For me, that's a good sign. They want something nice but at a reasonable price.

The Milford Plaza was within walking distance of eleven theaters, being located on 45th Street, a block off Broadway. We had walked up to the Trump Towers and visited the super-exclusive boutique shops on the various public access levels. In fact, it was our good fortune by sheer coincidence to bump into the Rev. George and Sylvia Robinson in the Trump Towers area. They were there for a special seminar.

The Amtrak package included an overnight sleeper from Greenville to New York on the Crescent Limited, three days at the Milford Plaza, the two Broadway shows and return by overnight sleeper to Greenville. We had done our typical tourist planning: "We want to be sure to see so and so, and such and such." One of the places we wanted to visit was Broadway Joe's, Joe Namath's emporium. There was a sheer outside chance that we might get to see Joe (and this was his heyday).

We noted on arrival that we were the only people in the lounge. The bartender sought to engage us in small talk. He learned we were from the mountains of North Carolina and quickly pointed out that his mother had retired to Highlands and inquired, "What's the best way to travel to Highlands?" The child bride and I did a couple of takes and then painfully explained to him that unless you have a car, there "ain't no way to get to Highlands." There are no planes (Asheville Airport is better than an hour and a thousand hairpin curves away). Obviously, no trains–there's not even a bus that goes to Highlands. Your only hope is to fly into the Asheville Airport and rent a car.

As I said, we take for granted the interstate at our back door. Amtrak train service is just forty minutes away in Greenville. Greyhound bus service in and out on a respectable schedule and the airport just fifteen minutes away. It's amazing how many towns in Western North Carolina do not enjoy the same access to the outside world.

E.R. on Wheels

The Thomas Shepherd Funeral Home and Stepp Funeral Home had been conscripted by the public into the ambulance business in the early days of motor cars. These two firms wee the only businesses in town that, with their hearses, had vehicles capable of carrying a prone human body. Thomas Shepherd was the prime carrier, and it became more and more of an expense to the funeral home to provide this public service.

People were less likely to pay a bill for ambulance service than one to H.M. Flynn for groceries the family had already eaten. Also, using the hearse as an ambulance required the coaches to move at high speeds, putting peak demand on performance. The service required someone to be available 24 hours a day. Usually, that "someone" was Hubert M. "Greasy" Barnett, who lived just across the street and in the same block as Shepherd Funeral Home.

In Greasy's era, we didn't have as many vehicles in town nor as many traffic signals as we have today, and caution was a word Greasy never learned. Running flat out, Greasy would (at extremely high speeds) weave in and out of a line of cars, and just to watch his skills would take your breath away. I don't ever remember him having an accident.

When the funeral homes began experiencing the necessity for very expensive liability insurance and were required to train ambulance employees as paramedics, the funeral homes simply notified the county that they would cease ambulance service effective Jan. 1, 1962. The Henderson County Commission, reacting to this notice, recognized that ambulance

*Hubert M.
"Greasy"
Barnett*

service had to be provided, but a legal opinion of the state's attorney general said the county did not have the authority to operate such a service. Regardless of this opinion, the county moved to buy two ambulances, hire four drivers and turn the service over to Pardee Hospital.

Pardee did not want the service. Its management was well aware of the money being lost on the service. Back then, ambulances were not the present day "emergency room on wheels." They were merely variations of large station wagons. The county's low bid purchased two brand new red Oldsmobiles and this county then hired (as drivers) John T. Wilkins of 5th Avenue and J.C. Moffitt of Horse Shoe. Further, they authorized a night shift radio operator, Clyde Jackson (former county wildlife protector), with all these men to be supervised by Sheriff Paul Hill.

At the same time, the City of Hendersonville had agreed to share in the service, so one of the two ambulances would be parked at City Hall, and "on duty" police officers of firemen (or volunteers) would operate that vehicle. The city ambulance would answer calls only in the city; the county ambulance only in the county. In fact, two phones were used: In the city for an ambulance, you called Oxford 3-4211; in the county, it was Oxford 2-2511. Fees for the service were to be added to the patient's hospital bill, even if transported only to the emergency room.

During the next decade, the North Carolina General Assembly passed legislation permitting counties to establish Emergency Medical Services. Henderson County immediately organized an E.M.S. and Tom Edmundson was named EMS director. In 1978, the EMS took a major step and purchased two fully-equipped ambulances, more like emergency rooms on wheels. The vehicles in 1978 were priced at $19,000, and another $10,000 was required to properly equip each vehicle. That was in 1978.

Each vehicle was equipped with four-channel radios, which permitted Emergency Medical Technicians to electronically transmit to emergency room doctors the patient's vital signs. The doctors, in turn, would advise the technician the proper medications/treatment for the patient. Life Paks were installed in the vehicles, which permitted the transmission of electrocardiograms and defibrillators. Edmondson placed into operation a program of training and qualifying each member of the team as EMTs.

As the years have gone by, a program of medical training has been ongoing in the various volunteer fire departments, and each fire department now has a para-medical team that responds to calls in their district, administering aid until the EMTs and their rolling emergency room arrive. With the state-of-the-art emergency room facilities at both local hospitals, with the trained Emergency Medical Technicians and modern ambulances, and with first assistance from paramedics with the volunteer fire departments, expert emergency health care is truly a matter of minutes from any home in Henderson County.

My hero, Greasy Barnett, who burned rubber for Shepherds Funeral Home all those years, wouldn't recognize the mass of men and equipment that now perform expertly in the procedures unknown to him as an employee at Shepherds Funeral Home.

To the Rescue

I experienced a "first" during the blizzard of 1993. Though I had a four-wheel drive vehicle, being semi-retired it was not necessary for me to make it to the radio station. And with our power out for only about twenty-four hours (compared to the extended outages experienced by some), we were prepared. We had a five-KW generator for heat, lights, and water pipe protection. We had fresh batteries in two radios, and our folks here at WHKP did a superb job of keeping the public informed.

Looking back on that week-long period when the power was out for thousands of people and travel was difficult, you heard very little of the Henderson County Rescue Squad. They were just going about their business as usual, seeing that nurses and medical personnel were transported to Pardee Hospital, checking on the elderly or disabled (who didn't want to leave home) were surviving. Squad members (without pay and on their own time) were getting fuel and food to those without, medicines were delivered, and even blood pressures and pulses were taken and reported to family doctors.

I thought of all the people I have known who have been active in the Rescue Squad, people such as David Bennett, Tom Edmundson, Arnold Heaton, Harvey Raines—and then I remembered that venerable old peddler of Cadillacs and Buicks and Pontiacs, one Ralph Jones. Now, Ralph is about seven years older than Shirley Temple, but he still is behind his sales desk at Boyd Pontiac-Cadillac, and I knew he was still active in the Rescue Squad.

Ralph has always been a very diffident person, and when I started questioning him about the Rescue Squad, he'd turn and look away and suggest, "Why don't you talk to David Bennett?" A few more questions and he responded, "Bill McClure can give you all the information you need." I had done a good deal of research even before I went to Ralph so I, at least, had plenty of questions to keep asking.

"It was organized with the VFW, wasn't it?" "Yeah," Ralph answered. "There were twenty-five of us who organized it, plus Police Chief Bill Powers, Fire Chief Ed Edney and Sheriff Paul Hill, as well as CAP Capt. Allen Foots as honorary members. Also, there were ten or fifteen community leaders we asked to be advisers." Ralph paused a minute and said, "It wasn't long 'til we

Ralph Jones, a senior and still-active member of the Henderson County Rescue Squad, next to one of a fleet of rescue vehicles.

changed the name to the Hendersonville Rescue Squad because there were quite a few people who wanted to join but were not members of the VFW, plus the city had offered us space in a city building to store our equipment."

"Name some of the men who were most active back in April 1957," I said. "Well, Ed Hunnicutt was our captain. I think we had five lieutenants: Jim Bartlett, Glenn Marlow, myself, Glenn Simpson and the late Buddy Richardson. Some of the sergeants were Bob Gillespie, Ron Stepp, Woodrow Bentley and later Bill McClure."

All of the sudden he said, "Here, let me get a copy of our current roster." He disappeared for a minute and then handed me a Xerox copy of the Henderson County Rescue Squad, January 1996, their call number, their job description, their pager number. I noticed the twelve officers, plus three squad members and three persons from the community made up the board. A separate category (consisting of some thirty-two people) were classified as full members; so, with the officers and current active members, it totaled around forty-four. In addition, there are eleven semi or inactive members plus four trainees listed.

"You first were the VFW Rescue Squad and then Hendersonville. When did you become Henderson County?" I asked.

"Oh, years and years ago. The city and the county (and the United Way) provide funding, which has changed very little down through the years. Not a person ever receives a nickel for the time they spend; and to help us buy new equipment, we receive donations from time to time."

"Ralph, do you have any idea of the number of calls or the hours of service performed?" He answered, "You come back tomorrow and I'll have all the material you need."

When I pulled up alongside of Ralph Jones' car, he opened the back door and handed over to me two huge scrapbooks and an enormous stack of newspapers.

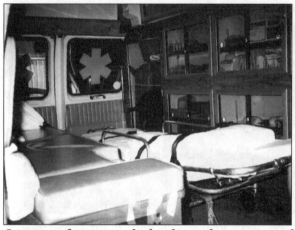

Interior of rescue vehicle shows how prepared squad is for life-threatening emergencies.

"This'll tell the story," he said, referring to the story of the Rescue Squad.

I spent that night going through the scrapbooks. In the beginning, Ralph had been very meticulous, clipping each picture and story and pasting them in an orderly fashion into scrapbook #1. I was able to quickly note that the first year the Rescue Squad operated, there were three drownings: one at Lake Summit, one at Laurel Park and one at a farm pond at Dana. I noticed also that at Christmas, a forty-seven-year-old man had suffered a heart attack in a tree while gathering mistletoe. He apparently had died instantly. The Rescue Squad was able to lower and remove his body from this very large tree.

It appears that the first really big snow that the Rescue Squad encountered was one in 1960 when the Squad answered fifty-seven so-called "mercy" calls. One of these was to bring out a very ill housewife on an arctic snow sled, and get her to Pardee Hospital. I used the phrase "mercy calls" because the Squad also routinely transports nurses and other medical personnel to and from Pardee Hospital. Those are not logged as calls at all, just services to the general public.

The Squad had operated maybe two years when a Florida man fell over the ninety-foot outcropping on World's Edge on Sugarloaf Mountain. They were able to get to him, using ropes, repelling over the side and then hoisting him back safely and transporting him to Pardee Hospital.

One lady tripped and fell over the edge of Jump Off Rock, and tumbled and bounced for 300 feet before being stopped by a tree. One tumble gave her a sheer drop of thirty feet, and Capt. Ed Hunnicutt said he was amazed that she had survived the ordeal with no greater injuries than she experienced.

The Rescue Squad dealt with its first flood in August 1961 and again with the giant flood that inundated WHKP in 1964. Folks wee rescued from cars stranded or washed away in the raging floodwaters. It was not mentioned in any of the scrapbooks, but I remember in the flood of 1964, there was no Four Seasons Boulevard. The only way you could get from the east side of the county (across the creek bottoms) was by boat, and one little mother-to-be was transported in a boat to Elm Street and 7th Avenue, where an ambulance waited on dry ground.

Then there were plane crashes. Their first was in 1963 when an aircraft crashed into the side of Sugarloaf Mountain. Their worst, by far, was the Piedmont Airlines disaster on July 20, 1967, where eighty-two people lost their lives. My son Kerry was a trainee of the squad then, and was assigned to the tutelage of the late H.D. MacAllister. The two of them (in the horror of those twenty-four hours) established a bond of friendship which became lifelong. In 1980, Herman Hawkins, David Bennett and H.D. MacAllister would receive twenty-year service awards.

The Rescue Squad, in those early years, also served as auxiliary policemen and they responded along with firemen to every major fire call: Winn-Dixie on 5th Avenue, Barber's Studio on Main, Hendersonville Supply & Coal, Hendersonville Lumber, and Superior Laundry.

By this time, I was deep into the second scrapbook, and Ralph Jones was not nearly as painstaking in Book II as he had been in Book I. Now the articles were just torn from the newspapers, and later, just the whole page was folded and inserted. By the 1970s, Ralph started just saving whole newspapers: *The Times-News*, the *Citizen*, the *Times*, the *Western Carolina Tribune*—even the monthly newsletters of the N.C. Rescue Squads. When I would start nodding as I gingerly opened up those faded and yellowed old publications, I would give it up for the night. But at 3 a.m. the next day (wide awake with my first coffee of the day) I'd be ready to begin again.

hen I finally worked my way through that huge stack, I noticed that by 1985, Ralph had even stopped saving newspapers. It was just too big of a job. Then I realized what a stupid question I had asked when I said, "Do you have any idea of the number of calls or the hours involved over the past forty years?"

Very few of the original twenty-five are still active, but down through the years, more than enough eager volunteers were always willing to become the "new Samaritans."

As St. Luke describes a Samaritan (Luke 10: 29-34): "But he, willing to justify himself said unto Jesus, 'and who is my neighbor?'

And Jesus answering said, 'A certain man went down from Jerusalem to Jericho, and fell among thieves, which stripped him of his raiment, and wounded him, and departed leaving him half dead. And by chance there came down a certain priest that way, and when he saw him, he passed by on the other side. And likewise a Levite, when he was at the place, came and looked at him, and passed by on the other side. But a certain Samaritan, as he journeyed, came where he was; and when he saw him he had compassion on him. And went to him, and bound up his wounds, pouring in oil and wine, and set him on his own beast, and brought him to an inn and took care of him.'"

The Henderson County Rescue Squad—good Samaritans for 40 years!

377

Healing Hands

T his chapter we're calling "The Girl Who Found a Face," and that's not a title we conjured up. It is the title of an article in the April 1970 issue of *Good Housekeeping* magazine. It concerns the birth of a child in December 1955 at the Curry Clinic in Chattanooga, Tenn.–little Debbie Fox. Once in every 180,000 births there occurs a congenital eye malformation called hypertelorism. That means the distance between the eyes is so great that the eyes are located on the side of the head. Once in every 700 live births, a cleft palate occurs. This child suffered both conditions, as well as a deformed right hand, several tight bands of tissue encircling the legs and thighs, and the left eye lacked a lid.

The baby was rushed to the Children's Hospital in Chattanooga, where Dr. Howard Barnwell (his family called him Brownlow, one of the leading plastic surgeons in the South) practiced medicine. Brownlow Barnwell assessed fifty-nine congenital anomalies of the skull, face, palate and extremities. Dr. Barnwell performed his first operation when the baby was three weeks old. After that, every few months little Debbie Fox would be taken by her parents (Edward and Sarah Fox) to Dr. Brownlow Barnwell, who would make another in a seemingly endless series of repairs. Slowly he rebuilt her palate, closing the hole that was larger than a 25 cent piece.

When Debbie was six, Dr. Barnwell was able to persuade the Hamilton County Board of Education into assigning a special ed teacher to her to start her on her school work. When the teacher, Mrs. Madeline Apple, first saw little Debbie Fox, she almost went into shock. For even after six years of constant surgery, she saw a little girl with blond hair who looked as if a firecracker had gone off in her face. Rather than give up, Mrs. Apple insisted on teaching Debbie, saying "There's something special about that child. In the meantime, Dr. Barnwell continued his surgery – by now having accumulated hundreds of photographs and plaster molds of the way he wanted Debbie to look, promising her she would be a pretty girl when she was sixteen.

In 1967, Dr. Barnwell had made a brief visit home for Christmas, and on his way back to Chattanooga, he was involved in a horrible traffic accident near Calhoun, Ga. Brownlow was killed and his son suffered massive injuries. The son gave up any thought of being able to practice medicine but went on to study law; and today, he practices his profession from a wheelchair.

But the "little girl who found a face," whose world was already tenuous, almost went into total collapse. For twelve years, Dr. Barnwell had pursued a goal and had shared his dream with Debbie. Her family, off the farm and of very meager means, had some help from Blue Cross with hospital bills for that twelve-year period, and Dr. Barnwell had either sent no bills or only token bills. The Foxes were ready to throw up their hands and relegate Debbie to a locked-up world where she would never be seen, but her teacher, Madge Apple— even without the beloved Brownlow Barnwell—still wanted to fulfill his dream. She located a plastic surgeon in Atlanta who agreed to continue the work. After this plastic surgeon had done his first operation, he suffered a heart attack and the work was placed "on hold" by his associate. The associate then contacted Dr. Milton Edgerton, chief of plastic surgery at Johns Hopkins in Baltimore, and he agreed to see Debbie.

Debbie was probed, poked, injected, photographed, questioned and totally researched by Dr. Edgerton's team of sixty-five physicians. She agreed to the very dangerous surgery of relocating her eyes

Dr. Brownlow Barnwell

fifty-five millimeters (almost two inches) closer together. The operation, which lasted from 7 o'clock in the morning until 10:30 that night, was a total success.

By her sixteenth birthday, Debbie's dream (given to her by Dr. Howard Brownlow Barnwell) had come true. There is a plaque in the City Hall of Chattanooga, Tenn., dedicated to this man who was born and raised on Grant Mountain Road, a few miles from Edneyville. The material I have used is from the June 1970 issue of *Good Housekeeping* magazine, and the July 1970 edition of *Reader's Digest.*

Brownlow was the sixth child of Edgar Brownlow Barnwell and his wife, Vertie Dalton Barnwell. Back in the days when land on Grant Mountain Road sold for fifty cents an acre, Mr. Barnwell raised $50 and bought 100 acres of rocky mountain land. He hewed the logs from which he made a log cabin, he and Vertie's first home. Altogether they had ten children, six sons and four lovely daughters.

Neither of the parents had any formal education as we know it today, but they knew the value of it. One of the daughters, Daisy Barnwell Jones, wrote a book back in 1985 (and revised it in 1986) titled "My First 80 Years." She wrote: "When Brownlow was in high school, our mother heard by way of the grapevine that he was not going to college. She confronted him with it and asked if he had said it. He answered, "Yes," and she replied, "If that is so, you might as well quit right now, get yourself a mule and start plowing. It's going to take you a long time to make a living."

That was the Brownlow Barnwell for whom the plaque was erected in Chattanooga.

A Remarkable Family

In addition to Brownlow, Edgar Brownlow and Vertie Dalton Barnwell had nine other children. Their first child was Daisy, who married Charles Jones. She graduated from Meredith College in Raleigh and from Johns Hopkins University and Hospital in Baltimore. She nursed dignitaries from a princess to the great baseball pitcher Walter Johnson. Her delightful book "My First 80 Years" is available in the Genealogy Room at the Henderson County Library, and there is also a copy in the Edneyville Branch Library.

Columbus Hershel Barnwell was the second child. He graduated from Wake Forest and from Northwestern University Medical School in Evanston, Ill. He was a urologist. His son, Franklin, is a professor of biology at the University of Minnesota. He had a daughter, who was an engineer.

Bertha Barnwell married Fredrich Karl Vielhauer after graduating from the Woman's College of Design and had a career in lithography.

Grady Glenn Barnwell attended UNC-Chapel Hill and Appalachian State University. He was selected as one of the first few national field executives for the Boy Scouts of America. His son, Glenn Jr., became an OB-GYN specialist, and his grandson is now a pathologist.

There was Paul Kermit Barnwell (I never knew his middle name was Kermit). Paul also graduated from Carolina with a degree in law. His offices were in what is now the First Union National Bank Building on Main Street. He had spent much time in his youth in the Court House watching the old-time lawyers practice cases, and he developed the bombastic style of the old timers. Even in the offices of a magistrate, you could hear Paul orate two floors down. He married Lavada Hoots and they had two daughters.

I have already told the story of the great Howard Brownlow Barnwell.

Then there was Clarence. When he was a small boy, he had fainting spells. Hershel took him to Chicago, where he was examined by medical experts but never diagnosed. He had learning difficulties the rest of his life, but was brilliant with tools and with his hands. He assisted Foy Hill in maintenance work at Edneyville School.

Edgar Dalton Barnwell had only one good eye and was told at Carolina at Chapel Hill that the study required to become a medical specialist as his brothers had done could ultimately destroy the vision in the one good eye. He graduated at UNC and studied dentistry at Emory University in Atlanta.

And then there was Ann. She planned to go into medicine, but at the time she was studying for a degree at UNC Women's College, she met and later married a Southern Baptist ministerial student, Darris Bingham, who made a career as an Air Force chaplain. They traveled in fifteen countries on every continent except the Arctic and Antarctica.

Edgar Brownlow and Vertie Barnwell (front center) with most of their children. On back row: Edgar Dalton, Ann and Barlow Brownlow. In middle row: Paul, Bertha, Ruth and Clarence. Front: Daisy, Edgar, Vertie and Glenn.

I knew Ann. She was valedictorian in the class one year ahead of me at Edneyville. I knew Clarence because he was always busy helping Foy Hill around the school. I knew Edgar, the dentist, because he was a classmate of my brother, the late Grady Edney. And I knew Paul, who was known to spend spare time in Smokey Levi's Barber Shop across 4th Avenue from his offices in the First Union National Bank Building.

In Daisy's book, her closing paragraph read: "At the auction to close the estate, a member of the family overheard two men (whom she did not know) sitting on a big rock, discussing the place. One said, 'Just look at this rocky place. How could anybody make a living on this place?' The other one, who seemed to know the family, said, 'I don't know but they made it. They are all college graduates—doctors, lawyers, dentists, nurses, teachers, etc.'"

This Is Your Life

The most often heard reaction about the special series of radio programs was "for a little town, you have certainly had more than your share of interesting people and unusual happenings." And I agree. Not every town in America has had a native son who was featured on TV's "This is Your Life," but Hendersonville did back in 1955. George Bond first came to Henderson County to summer camp when he was a young boy in 1926. When he completed his medical education, he returned to establish a practice in Bat Cave and throughout the Hickory Nut Gorge.

Back in about 1945 or '46, the old Bat Cave Elementary School building became available when the school was consolidated into the Edneyville High School (which is now North Henderson High School). Dr. Bond was deeply concerned that people in the remote areas like Gerton, Middle Fork, even Bat Cave and Chimney Rock, had to travel for at least fifteen or twenty minutes just to get to basic first-aid medical care. The people of Hickory Nut Gorge (and others around the county) pitched in and raised enough money to buy and refurbish the old Bat Cave school building. There's no way to even estimate the number of chicken dinners, rummage sales, bake sales and other activities that went on to create what was to become the Valley Clinic.

Dr. Bond was called to Naval Service in 1953 and was assigned to the Pacific Submarine Command in Hawaii. In the meantime, someone had contacted Ralph Edwards, who produced and announced the NBC program called "This is Your Life." Edwards became fascinated with the idea of this young man, George Bond, who had established a medical practice in the far rural reaches of this mountainous Western North Carolina county. He arranged with the Navy to

Dr. George Bond

fly (by now) Lt. Commander George Bond to California to act as a technical adviser on a naval training film. In the Ralph Edwards style, he traced how Bond had lost two friends who could not get to medical help in this remote location, and how Dr. Bond had resolved to return and establish a medical practice in his beloved mountains. "This is Your Life" covered Bond's return to Bat Cave, the raising of money for the clinic, and how (though called to the Navy in 1953) he planned to return to Bat Cave at the end of his tour of duty to resume his practice.

Appearing on the program were Mrs. Louise Bond, playing a major role as George's mother; Mrs. Doogie Connor of Bat Cave (his sister); Mrs. Mary Louise James Smythe of Balfour; his wife, Mrs. Marjorie Bond; and his four children, Gail, Judy, David and George, Jr. (who would himself later enter medical service by becoming a public health doctor). Two patients who credited Dr. Bond with saving their lives were also on the program, along with Mrs. Lonnie Hill and Mrs. Hedda Book of Lake Lure, who had helped build the hospital.

Now bear in mind, this was June 22, 1955. "This is Your Life" presented Valley Clinic with gifts from the sponsors of $2,000 in food and a brand new station wagon ambulance for use by the clinic.

Dr. Bond did return to Valley Clinic, but while he served his tour of duty in the Navy, he had been involved with research in the medical aspects of deep sea diving. His work in researching high-pressure effects on the human body as encountered in the submarine service preyed on his mind. So in 1957, at the urging of the U.S. Navy, he returned to duty at New London, Conn. In the meantime, he had recruited Dr. William Burch to take over his work at the Valley Clinic. On Nov. 22, 1957, he was cited for his work on high-pressure effects on the human body and also for his calmness in disarming a knife-wielding patient. Ten years later George Bond had achieved the rank of captain in the Navy and was chief administrator of the Navy's "Man-in-the-Sea" program.

The Navy made special arrangements to transport Capt. Bond to Chicago in May 1967 (though recovering from spinal surgery) where he was honored by the Geographic Society of Chicago. The society credited Bond with conceiving and directing experiments that have revealed the possibilities of extending man's horizon underwater in the new geographical frontier of the vast resources of the continental shelf still awaiting detailed exploration and utilization for the benefit of mankind.

Sealab I and Sealab II (the prolonged deep sea and surface decompression trials in the Pacific that developed from Genesis, which had been headed by Dr. George Bond) earned for him gold stars for his already earned Naval Commendation and Legion of Merit, the Navy's top peacetime awards.

Dr. Bond died young at age fifty-eight in 1973—a summer camper who moved with his family to Bat Cave, founded the Valley Clinic, and went on to become the world's greatest authority on the effects of compression on the human body. That was Dr. George Bond of Hendersonville and Bat Cave.

The Richard Petty of Country Doctors

Over the period of forty-seven years that Dr. J. Steve Brown practiced medicine in Hendersonville, he established a reputation of getting to his patient as quickly as possible even though exposing himself to danger beyond the call of duty—in his horse and buggy or in the new-fangled motor cars.

In the beginning, Dr. Steve Brown rode a horse to make house calls. Then he advanced to a horse and buggy, and it was in this period that he established a reputation for truly adventurous travel. He is said to have careened the buggy off into the Stepp Mill Pond. Continuing to respond to his patients'

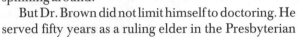

Dr. Brown's office hours: "9 to noon and as suits. "

ills with all the spirit of a Paul Revere, he finally graduated into the age of the horseless carriage, and that's when trouble really began.

My earliest memory of Dr. Brown is watching him climb into that huge Lincoln Town Car, back then built like a tank. It was always parked in front of his office at 428 North Church Street. He would rev the engine to maximum tach, and then just let the clutch pop out. With tires screaming, he would come roaring from the curb and head down Church Street. It was fortuitous that there was very little traffic on Church Street back then, because Dr. Brown neither looked up nor down the street. He fully expected everyone else to give him the right of way.

He led a miraculous life. There's no telling how many accidents he experienced in his various cars. I personally remember seeing one accident. He was headed south on Washington Street and started across 1st Avenue on a red light when a second car moved into the intersection. To avoid the second car, he sharply swerved to the left and rolled the car over in the front yard of the house where John Ross now maintains his yard and garden shop. I started to run toward the accident but suddenly saw the front door pushed open and out climbed Dr. Brown, who dusted himself off, gathered up his medical kit from the rear seat and walked hurriedly on down Washington Street. The wheels on the upper side of his overturned car were still spinning around!

Dr. Steve Brown

But Dr. Brown did not limit himself to doctoring. He served fifty years as a ruling elder in the Presbyterian Church. He was most active in the local, state and national medical societies. He joined the Kiwanis Club shortly after the club was organized and, on one occasion, to protect his perfect attendance record, the club merely recessed their regular meeting and reconvened the meeting in his hospital room, where he himself was recuperating.

In 1947, every civic club in town, the Medical Society and the directors of the old Patton Memorial Hospital nominated Dr. J. Steve Brown as the outstanding general practitioner in the entire nation.

Dr. Brown lived in an era when doctor bills were paid for in kind, if at all. His family always had plenty of chickens, meat, fruits and vegetables but very little money. What they did have was a rolltop desk full of memo books, ledgers, slips of paper, all silent testimony to the thousands and thousands of dollars that were owed to Dr. J.S. Brown. Many a credit agency would water their lips and make a big pitch to "let us help you, doctor, we can collect some of this money for you." "No thanks," he'd say. "When they can afford to, they'll pay it on their own."

On Friday, Dec. 26, the day after Christmas 1953, Dr. J. Steve Brown passed on to a better life. When Dr. Steve died, he was survived by a wife of fifty-seven years and five children: Dr. (Capt.) J.S. Brown, Jr., of the U.S. Navy; Ben Brown of Fayetteville; Mrs. Robert Campbell of Rowland; Mrs. Robert B. Cameron of High Point; and John L. Brown of Hendersonville.

At one time, Dr. Brown had mended a knee for me following an accident with a horse and wagon. At another time, he had tacked a quarantine sign on our house on First Avenue when I came down with the measles ... and after I was grown, we were often working together in Kiwanis Club.

As I would meet Dr. Steve (either coming or going from a Kiwanis meeting), he would always give that big laugh of his and say, "Oh, I know you by the shape of your head." He alleged that of 6,547 babies he had brought into this world, he could recognize every one of them by the shape of his or her head.

Many years after Dr. Brown had passed away, I needed my birth certificate for a passport. When I looked over the official copy handed to me at the Register of Deeds office, there was written: "Attending Physician: Dr. J.T. Egerton."

Dr. Egerton was the son of a Civil War surgeon. He had studied at the University of Maryland. Two months after his graduation (at age 21), he hung out his shingle on Main Street here in Hendersonville to start his practice. Dr. Egerton said that he had kept an accurate count of the number of babies he had delivered for the first forty years, and when the number topped 2,000, he quit counting. In March 1927 he was honored by the doctors of Western North Carolina for having served the area for more than fifty years.

Dr. Egerton's first wife was Martha Fletcher. That name may ring a bell for you because a young lady (Maria Beale Fletcher) was chosen as "Miss America" in 1962. Maria Beale's father, Charles Beale Fletcher, was a nephew of Dr. and Mrs. J.T. Egerton. After Martha Egerton died, Dr. Egerton married Miss Effie Burroughs of South Carolina. They had three daughters, one of whom married Dr. W. Redin Kirk, who had come to Hendersonville to operate a sanitarium for tuberculosis, which was located on Kanuga Street. When the old Patton Memorial Hospital opened on July 4, 1913, Dr. Redin Kirk was on the staff, along with Dr. Drafts, Dr. Dixon, Dr. W.B.W. Howe, Dr. Brown and Dr. J.T. Egerton.

In checking the medical staff at Patton Memorial when WHKP first signed on the air in 1946, there were: Dr. Joseph P. Bailey, Dr. James C. Billingsley, Dr. William E. Brackett, Dr. Gabe Croom, Dr. D.I.C.

Campbell King; Dr. Richard S. Major; Dr. Lester B. McDonald; Dr. Richard A. Porter; Dr. E. McQueen Salley; Dr. Robert C. Sample; Dr. Wallace Souther; Dr. Fred O. Trotter and Dr. Gustave Ulloth.

Prior to World War II, there were two Dr. J.S. Browns on the staff of Patton Memorial. Dr. J.S. Brown, Jr. left Hendersonville for service in the Navy and decided to make the Navy his career. At one time, he was commander of the Charleston Naval Hospital. At the time of his father's death, he was a U.S. Navy captain attached to Naval Headquarters in Philadelphia. Dr. J.S. Brown, Jr. was a brilliant surgeon. I experienced a ruptured appendix when I was a junior in high school and he did the surgery. Throughout my entire Army career in World War II, any time I would be subjected to a physical exam, the examining doctor would take one look at the tiny incision made by Dr. Brown Jr. and would call all the other medics to discuss "who did that surgery," all obviously impressed.

One of the truly great stories to come out of the old Patton Memorial Hospital was how Dr. J.S. Brown removed his own appendix (unassisted) by using mirrors. Apparently, he had not advised the staff of his intentions, and only when they heard his deep voice calling, "Nurse, nurse" did they discover what had happened. He had completed the surgery but could not complete the suturing.

Medicine, the Old-Fashioned Way

Dr. Fletcher Raiford could be best described as intransigent. As a doctor, he practiced medicine in the old-fashioned way. Both Kerry and Katina (our two children) had their health from infancy directed by Dr. Raiford. He had his strong convictions with no compromise.

He insisted on Baker's milk, which had to be boiled three hours before it could be fed to them. He was downright anti-aspirin. In fact, I was interviewing him on the air one morning in observance of Poison Prevention Week, and he suddenly said, "While I don't consider aspirin a poison, children shouldn't be given more than three or four in their entire childhood." Before I could say a word, he continued, "and certainly Co-Cola is not good for them." By this time I started talking louder than Raiford, afraid of what he might say next. (We heard from the Coca-Cola people in short order.)

Dr. Raiford was a Virginian, born in Sedley and graduated from the Medical College of Virginia. He spoke with a distinct and deliberate Southern drawl, but not the Virginia accent that uses such words as "potahtoes" and "toe-mah-toes." He came to Hendersonville to practice as a pediatrician in 1951. During his first two years here, any hospitalization of his patients would have been at the old Patton Memorial Hospital, until November 1953, when Pardee opened.

I knew that Fletcher Raiford was independent of purpose and was also a great outdoorsman—in the spring each year, I'd find where he'd left a bunch of ramps for me at the radio station which he'd gathered in his hikes back into the wilderness areas. In later years, I always gave them to Al Hope, because it takes a special constitution to eat and enjoy ramps, and some of the other concoctions that lowlanders can conjure up.

Even knowing that Dr. Raiford was an outdoorsman and enjoyed adventure, I was hardly prepared for a phone call from him several years ago. He said, in that Southern drawl, "Kermit, we want you to meet us up at Penrose Saturday morning at 7:30, and I suggest you wear a warm jacket."

After a long pause, I responded, "What am I going to do at Penrose?"

"Why, we're going to raft down the French Broad River to Marshall."

I said, "You're going to raft down the French Broad River—not me."

My response didn't faze him in the least. He continued to discuss the itinerary, approximate time we'd pass various places, where we'd stop to eat, while I kept trying to interrupt to insist that I was not going to be part of that trip. He talked right on. "It ought to be a real experience," he was saying when I finally virtually shouted into the telephone, "Dr. Raiford, I am NOT going to meet you at Penrose, I'm not going to be on a raft, I am not going down the French Broad River." His voice (still calm as he drawled), "You're making a terrible mistake. This will be the thrill of a lifetime." "Not my lifetime—just don't count me in." I think, by this time, he was ready to accept the fact that I was not going to be in this adventure he had planned.

I don't know how many trips he made on the French Broad and other rivers, but by 1973 he decided he was ready for the mighty Colorado River through the Grand Canyon. He persuaded more than twenty other "trippers" to shoot the rapids for 235 miles on a trip that would take ten days.

On Sept. 27, 1973, he, his daughter Harriett, and twenty-three others (including three river guides) entered the Colorado River fifteen river miles below the dam at Lee's Ferry. The party traveled the river in two rafts, one more than thirty feet long, the other consisting of three smaller craft lashed together (each of the two units powered by outboard motors).

After they had completed the 235-mile journey from Lee's Ferry to Diamond Creek, Arizona (taking them a total of ten days), Dr. Raiford had arranged for a small plane to take small groups back up the river to their starting point, flying low between the walls of the canyon so each could see below the waters they had just come down. The airplane ride back took only one hour.

One afternoon I was chatting with "B" Sims in the Jax Pax when Dr. Raiford came in. He explained that his wife was going on a visit out of town and that he'd be batchin' for several days. "B" Sims and I continued to talk as Raiford kept rummaging through the frozen food section, musing "Umm, that sounds good" or "Boy, that sure looks good." I said nothing. I couldn't believe this man who had cooked in the wilds, had communed with nature, was going to live off TV dinners 'til his wife got back. And apparently this was his first experience because he was selecting most of the meals on the basis of the picture on the carton. I never did get to ask him of the rude awakening that had come to him when he started eating those beautifully packaged frozen TV dinners.

Dr. Fletcher Raiford–truly one of a kind. He was an institution in Hendersonville from 1951 until he retired in 1988. It was certainly appropriate that the Pediatric Wing on the second floor at Pardee is named for him, and prominently displays a plaque in his honor along with a picture of the one and only Fletcher Raiford.

A "Nick" in Our Time

Dr. William N. "Nick" Fortescue was born in Hyde County down on the coast where the biggest town in the county was Swan Quarter. After graduating at Duke and interning in Boston, he moved to Hendersonville and established his practice in 1936 at the old Patton Memorial Hospital.

For many years (even though we had some sixteen to eighteen doctors in the area in the early '40s), there were only two surgeons: Fortescue and Dr. Lester McDonald. It became apparent to Nick Fortescue as the area grew that there would have to be a totally new site for the hospital to take the place of the old Patton Memorial. There was just no room to expand the old hospital which had been built in 1913.

Fortescue had been keeping his eye out for a totally new site. One day it dawned on him that the Oakley-Florida summer hotel had not operated for several seasons. It had been operated by my dad's Uncle Frank King (Albert Franklin Pierce King) and his wife (Sarah Bowden King). Most folks called her "Tid." Uncle Frank had bought the huge old wooden home from J.W. Wofford, and then added to it until it sprawled all across the top of the hill on Fleming Street between 7th and 8th Avenues. Fortescue, Dr. Fred Trotter and Dr. McQueen Salley got together and borrowed enough money to buy the old hotel, hoping that if they could get a new hospital built there, the assets of the old Patton Memorial would be transferred.

Dr. Nick Fortescue was the only doctor to serve as chief of staff at both Patton Memorial and Margaret Pardee Hospital.

While it would be 1953 before the new hospital would open, in the early '50s the board had hired a "professional" administrator to manage the transition from the old to the new hospital. This young man was anxious to prove to the board that he would put a stop to patients not paying their bills on time. Nobody back then had even heard of hospital insurance. Some patients would bring farm produce, eggs or milk or just put off paying their hospital bills. This young man was so adamant, arrogant and dictatorial about arranging for payment before admission, rumors abounded: "Another two

Dr. Nick Fortescue with his wife, Lottie, and their two children.

people died on the lawn over there at Pardee last night because they couldn't raise enough money to get in." This administrators truculence finally enraged the entire community. Pardee was the most hated place in town.

The board replaced this administrator with William E. Jamison, a highly decorated veteran officer of the African campaign during World War II. Jamison appealed for help from both Jim Fain (editor of the *Times-News*) and from WHKP. He was anxious to restore the goodwill and confidence that deservedly the old Patton Memorial Hospital had always enjoyed.

WHKP did 13 weeks of broadcasts explaining to the public how Pardee operated, why it cost more for a hospital room than a motel room, etc. The final broadcast was to feature a live broadcast from the operating room during surgery. Naturally, the surgeon was Dr. Nick Fortescue, the anesthesiologist was Dr. James Lutz, and the procedure was gall bladder surgery. Dr. Fred Trotter would work with me in the actual description of the surgery. Now the average person has an image in his mind of an operating room as a virtually sacred place. I was aware that Dr. Nick Fortescue used colorful language, with a few mild cuss words here and there. On that day, he used an abundance, PLUS someone in the operating room had a cold and coughed loudly during most of the surgery. In that everyone was masked, it didn't really hazard the proceedings at all, but again, hearing Dr. Trotter say, "He's now starting the incision" and in the meantime COUGH COUGH. Also, I didn't realize that every time the surgeon finished with an instrument, he would toss it into a metal container to be sterilized before future use, so it sounded a bit like the kitchen in Granny Waters' Boarding House. We simply couldn't use the tape. Dr. Trotter and I went to the station, and utilizing sound effects with Fred Trotter describing the procedure from memory, we faked the so-called "live" broadcast.

Nick Fortescue was named "Man of the Year" by the VFW in 1972, and if ever a choice met with unanimous approval, this selection did. He was cited for his lifetime of alleviating suffering of humanity, but also he encouraged his fellow men to seek the beauty in the wonders of the natural world. In the hopes that he could inspire the Department of Transportation to utilize native plants along the new I-26 being built, Nick Fortescue donated 9,000 azalea and rhododendron plants. He loved horses, especially Tennessee Walking horses.

The beloved Dr. J.S. Brown was widely known for having delivered 6,000 plus babies during his lifetime. No one has ever even tried to estimate the number of surgeries performed by Dr. Nick Fortescue.

When Nick Fortescue, Fred Trotter and McQueen Salley raised enough money to take possession of the old Oakley-Florida House, none would ever have dreamed of the multi-building health center covering several blocks in the Medical, Institutional and Cultural (MCI) District and a Pardee Hospital with something like 100 doctors offering state-of-the-art equipment and specialties only dreamed about in the days at Patton Memorial and in 1895 when the old "Flower Mission" became our first make-do hospital.

Helping Hands

In the years before 1953, Hendersonville (like so many other communities around the nation) had no United Fund nor United Way nor even a Community Chest. In January always came the most active of all the campaigns, the "March of Dimes" for polio. It would be a number of years before Jonas Salk would develop the miracle vaccine; but because of the popularity of Franklin D. Roosevelt, who suffered from polio, this campaign probably had more emotional support than others. After Salk developed the vaccine, the organization (to survive) changed emphasis to birth defects.

February: We had American Heart Month, and a campaign. The Boy Scouts also ran their campaign in February. In March it was the American Red Cross and the Girl Scouts. April was time for the Cancer Drive; Salvation Army Week occurred in May. The Lion's Club White Cane Drive was in October, and the local Lions Club ran a dime board on the corner of 4th and Main from Thanksgiving to Christmas to raise funds for all their benevolent programs. And, of course, the Salvation Army kettles came out on November 25th.

Virtually everyone in the business district was either "asking for" or "being asked for" contributions from early fall to late spring. Most organizations set their budget after the campaign, so each of the groups tried to raise as much money as possible. There were no goals, and if you happened to inherit the best workers in a given year, you'd raise far more than in previous years and other campaigns would come up short.

I remember being asked by Lloyd Biggerstaff of the Coca Cola Company and Forrest Gardiner of Advance Thread (both movers and shakers in the Boy Scouts) to head up their fund drive. Considering the value of the Coca Cola account, I was told by my bosses, "Do it."

I asked scout leaders, "What is your goal?"

"We have not set a goal. Raise as much as you can."

"Could I have a list of people who have supported the scouts in the past?"

"That's not necessary. We start fresh every year."

Truly, I was the blind leading the blind. I had no idea of how much any one person should give, or of how many people had ever given before.

I remember making a call on my friend, Mr. Frank FitzSimons Sr. He quickly responded, "I'll match whatever 'Foffy' Hunter gives." Hunter was second in the pecking order to president Bill Hodges. I got a flat turn down from "Foffy" – and as I glared at Mr. Fitz when leaving the old State Trust Company, he chuckled and said, "You can't imagine how much money I save just by saying I'll match Hunter." I will say that I found a way to really get to Hunter in a substantial way in one of the YMCA fund drives more than ten years later. By the way, my Boy Scout effort was successful only because of the tremendous generosity of Mr. Ashley Houston. He gave me $1,000, more than ten times that of any other giver!

I suppose that of all the fund raisers staged back then, the one dreaded most was the Lions Club Dime Board. They had this huge board erected at the corner of 4th and Main in front of the Westside Branch of the bank; and from about Thanksgiving to Christmas there was always at least two Lions working as pitchmen on the board. They were only after a dime, but a dime back then was worth more than a dollar today. If you passed that abominable board five times a day, you coughed up the dime or risked being belittled with shouts of "skinflint" or "tightwad." On occasions, I

Pleda Jackson (front) kicks off the infamous Lions Club Dime Board.

fully expected to be wrestled to the ground for that dime.

In those years, virtually all the money raised for any campaign came from downtown merchants and employees. In the industrial field, the plant managers simply refused to allow solicitors to go through the plants begging for money on the grounds of public safety. The retirement community had not yet developed here, and farmers were spread so far apart they were hard to solicit. The only exception was at Berkeley Mills where they ran a Plant Community Chest. They raised their own funds, and an employee committee decided how much the Berkeley Fund would give to the Red Cross, Boy Scouts, Girl Scouts and other charities, as well as fund their own benevolences within the Berkeley family. David Knotts, the current executive director of United Way, told me recently that it was only in the last few years that the Berkeley family discontinued its community chest, and key employees solicit directly for the United Way.

In August of 1953, a groundswell of support began to build for a once-a-year drive, and a slogan was born: "Give once and for all." By October 1, 1953, the united concept had been endorsed by virtually every organization: civic, social, military, and fraternal groups. The united concept movement was brought into the community in the summer of 1953. By August, we had signed agreements with the American Red Cross, the Boy Scouts, the Girl Scouts, and the Lions Club. We had agreements from all the major fund-raising groups except the polio group, the American Heart Association and the American Cancer Society. They (first of all) would not agree for any outside organization to tell them how much money they could raise in Hendersonville; and one or more would not permit any review or audit of how they'd spent the money from previous years.

I remember we offered to waive any rules for Polio if they would just not conduct another separate campaign. We offered to leave $10,000 on the Bowden Front Porch if they would not run a campaign. Mrs. Geneva Bowden (who was head of the local chapter) tried desperately to get agreement but the national and state organizations stood firm and refused to even consider becoming part of the United Way. The local chapters of the American Heart Association and the American Cancer Society simply withdrew from the national organizations and set up local chapters, with 100 percent of the money raised for them then being spent locally here in Hendersonville. In prior years, more than ninety percent of local funds were sent to national headquarters.

By October 1 (as a show of solidarity), a meeting was held in the Skyland Hotel by supporting groups of United. Attending were Commander Homer Hobbs of the American Legion; Exalted Rule W.F. Stokes of the Elks Lodge; Mrs. Joe Crowell of the Junior Woman's Club; president Dan Barber of the Kiwanis; secretary Hilary Neighbors of the Lions; B.M. Middleton of the Rotary Club; Mrs. Hamilton Coleman of the Women's Club; Commander Bill Powers of the VFW; and dozens of other citizens and owners of businesses and heads of local industrial plants. C.M. "Mike" Ogle was elected president; H.T. "Luke" Rindal was named executive director; and I was named general chairman of that first fund-raising campaign. We had hoped to do the campaign in the month of October, but it was not until early December that we could finally announce that we had raised $55,488.61 plus an oversubscription of 2.5 percent, or an extra $1,464.81.

I was chatting with David Knotts, executive director of the United Way in 1996. (Dave has been here about nine years.) He said that campaign chairman Spence Campbell has been challenged to raise $1,168,000 for the 1996-97 year.

But, as we said before when talking about the old Lions Club's dime board, a dime in 1953 would be worth a lot more than a dollar today. Remember, we were still on the silver standard in those pre-Lyndon Johnson days.

The United Way today supports almost forty different agency efforts. Some we raised money for back in 1953 are no longer in existence, but the stalwarts of 1953 that we raised funds for forty-three years ago are still supported by your support of United Way: the Red Cross, the Boy and Girl Scouts, the Salvation Army, the 4-H Clubs, and even the Childrens' Home Society and Florence Crittenton Home, plus the YMCA, which joined United Way the very first year it operated here.

It would be difficult to estimate the number of people who have served in various official capacities over these forty-three years, or those who simply went into the field to raise funds.

Ben Prince used to laughingly call this sort of work "laboring in the gentle vineyards of community service."

Only a dairy farmer would understand when I say, "We stripped every cow in the barn," and our cup finally did run over. But I learned from this exhausting experience: "If what you're pitching to your people is good and reasonable, and you're totally honest with them on everything; and if you work, and work, and then work some more, this county will always respond positively. As Grandpa Cal Edney used to say, "They come from good stock!"

Something Special

James H. McDuffie and his wife, Mary, found their way to Hendersonville because of the General Electric Outdoor Lighting Department. Jim was manager of Employee & Community Relations. Back in WWII, Jim had served in the 82nd Paratroops; and, along with wartime buddy Terry Sanford, had jumped on D Day into Normandy. It was that friendship with Gov. Sanford that helped McDuffie to persuade Gov. Sanford to come here for the annual dinner meeting of the Chamber of Commerce in 1961.

McDuffie was active in all phases of community life, but when he served as president of the Kiwanis Club in 1967, he launched a crusade for an activity to be sponsored by that club. Little did he realize it would grow into a community-wide commitment, too big for any civic club, in just a few short years. He dreamed up what was called the Sheltered Workshop, which trained and employed the physically and mentally handicapped. This project meant so much to him that rather than take a transfer with GE, he resigned to become a special agent with Prudential Insurance Co. in order to stay in Hendersonville.

The Sheltered Workshop began operations in a rented building off Haywood Road. Later, historian and philanthropist Sadie Patton gave property to the organization on the south side of Third Avenue West. The organization also acquired an area for a farm operation off Kanuga Road, made possible by a grant from the Cummings Foundation. In the first five years it operated, the Sheltered Workshop trained 325 people, with about 40 percent of those finding permanent jobs.

At the dedication of the first permanent facility on Third Avenue West and Ehringhaus Street, North Carolina Secretary of Human Resources David Flaherty complimented the community on this impressive forward-looking action and promised the General Assembly would take not of the achievements of this one community. By this time, the workshop was managed by a full-time director, Roger McDuffie (no relation to Jim). By 1976, Roger McDuffie announced grants from the N.C. Department of Vocational Education in the amount of $35,000. Much praise was heaped on the Sheltered Workshop by the United Way, Blue Ridge Community College, the Mental Health Organization, and the Department of Social Services. This strong support led to state recognition and funding.

The Sheltered Workshop began with one paid staff member and a handful of clients. At the end of the first ten years, it had grown to ninety clients, of which ten lived in a dormitory completed in 1977. It was at that time the organization also opened a downtown outlet store from which the products made in the plant would be sold. The store was operated by one of the workshop staff and one or two clients.

Much of the work performed is done under contract with local industries. One of the largest of these is General Electric Co. Sewing and quilting are subjects taught to clients—plus, there is a ceramics shop where clients learn to make vases, flower pots and other useful or decorative items. In the greenhouse, clients are taught to prepare soil, how to properly plant seeds and care for plants as they grow. Every activity at the workshop is designed to help handicapped people learn abilities to fit into gainful occupations.

While the organization was founded as the Hendersonville Kiwanis Club Sheltered Workshop, in 1974 the name was changed simply to the Henderson County Sheltered Workshop. The retail store we mentioned operated under the name "Something Special." The shop later moved to the corner of 7th and Church, and the later to Kanuga Road at the Nursery Garden Center. In 1990, though the official name remained the Sheltered Workshop, the organization started doing business as "Something Special."

Something Special started as a project of the Kiwanis Club in 1967.

Noel Watts joined the organization in 1974 and worked closely with Roger McDuffie. In 1989, Noel succeeded McDuffie as interim director and became executive director in 1990. Noel and his most active board of directors, including the late Ed Patterson, arranged for the sale of their property on 3rd Avenue to the Interfaith Assistance Ministry, and then purchased the manufacturing plant on U.S. 176 (Spartanburg Highway), which had been used as a furniture store operated by Spearman & Prim.

Something Special today has an annual budget of $1,943,045, fifty-seven employees and serves an average of 125 clients daily. Jim McDuffie died in 1985. One can't help but dream of seeing the reaction on his face if he were able to walk into his old Sheltered Workshop, the "Something Special" of today, and see what has happened to what was nothing but a personal dream of his thirty years ago back in 1967. Ed Patterson saw it before he died.

Miss Kate and the Taylor Maids

My memory of Kate Dotson is the same as remembering Sophie Tucker. When I sat down to do this piece, I thought, "Maybe I should check to see where Miss Kate is buried and that might give me a clue to her age." Kate Dotson was one of those people in my life who never changed. She looked exactly the same to me the first time I followed her direction of the Glee Club at Edneyville High School to the picture of her playing on stage the day WHKP signed on the air in 1946. She never changed; she always looked the same.

I ran through the index in the Genealogical Society's Directory of Cemeteries, and lo and behold, I couldn't find Kate Dotson's name. Then I remembered that when she ran her music studio upstairs at 224 North Main Street, her mother had lived with her, and Miss Kate had taken care of her mother until she died.

That's where the 1946 City Directory (which I had borrowed from Harold Huggins) was invaluable. I found, very easily, Miss Kate C. Dotson residing at 224 N. Main, and along with her, Maggie C. Dotson, obviously her mother and widow of William F. Dotson. Back to the directory of cemeteries: Listed was William F. Dotson, who was born in 1860 and died in 1923. There was Margaret C. Dotson, his widow, born in 1858 and died in 1953; and next to her, Miss Kate—except the tombstone lists her as Margaret Catherine Dotson (spelled with a C, the same as her mother). Miss Kate never married. She passed away in 1971.

Miss Kate had a husky, deep, throaty laugh, and she laughed often. Patience? Bless her heart, Miss Kate would have been an inspiration to Job. She either ignored or went along with the silliness of high school kids. She badgered and rehearsed them so much that (like Professor Harold Hill in Meredith Wilson's great Broadway musical) these kids, bedecked in their glee club robes, really believed they could sing, because Miss Kate made them believe it.

There was always an ebullience that came from Miss Kate. She literally bubbled with life and life was better with music. It was a mystery how she was able to support herself and her mother over those thirty years from the small fees she received for teaching piano or the very minor honorariums she might get from playing at civic clubs.

I have no idea of whether Miss Kate ever dated any one person occasionally or on a steady basis. I was just a young kid in her life and had no business to know. But Miss Kate was a matchmaker. She always clucked contentedly over the exploits of her most promising pupils; and occasionally she'd encouraged them to pair up, as she did with Gem Stepp Garren and Gerry Wilkie Shipman.

In her musical activities, she had run across Ray Taylor—in her own words, "one of the most talented young musicians" she'd ever met. Ray had planned to become a classical concert pianist and had studied for twenty-three years at the Philadelphia Conservatory, as well as Oberlin in Ohio. He became a specialist in harmony, counterpoint and composition. Ray studied for a year at Ecole Normale de la Musique in Paris, which I think is more difficult to say than just "The Paris Normal Music School." Then he was bitten by the theater bug.

When Ray Taylor returned to New York, he wrote musical revues, plus material for Jane Morgan, Julie Wilson, Robert Q. Lewis, and the famous Eartha Kitt song, "I Wanna Be Evil." Ray Taylor wrote that. After the Broadway "rat race," he came to Hendersonville for a bit of rest and relaxation, and to gain a new perspective. He found it through Kate Dotson.

It just so happened she'd given voice lessons to a couple of girls, Gem and Gerry. Gem S. Garren came from the J.H. Stepp family of Dana.

Kermit talks with Miss Kate Dotson.

Being a groceryman, cannery operator and entrepreneur, Stepp always simply said he had a half a dozen of girls and a quarter of a dozen boys. Another daughter, Lucille (the widow of Lenior Ray) worked at the old *Tribune* under Noah Hollowell and then retired from the *Times-News.* Lucille has told me how any time the family got together (mom, dad and the nine

Ray Taylor and the Taylor Maids, Gem Stepp Garren and Gerry Wilkie Shipman.

kids), they always loved to sing. So Gem Stepp (one of Lucille's sisters) had taken lessons from Miss Kate and had a beautiful voice.

Another of Miss Kate's favorites was Gerry Wilkie. She was one of a family of five (four sisters and one brother). Her father not only ran the old Green River Company Store, but was elected to be chairman of the Henderson County Commissioners. Later he was really active in church music and church building at the Mud Creek Baptist Church. It's the only church in the county that has built two brand new sanctuaries in the past thirty-nine years. So Gerry Wilkie's singing came about honest, also. Her husband was Sherwood Shipman, and his greatest thrill was to hear Gem and Gerry sing. Then Miss Kate added Ray Taylor and the group became The Taylor Maids.

The voice clips referred to are from an entire cassette of Bye Bye Blues songs dubbed by The Taylor Maids, now in the WHKP Sound Bites Section of the Henderson County Public Library.

Ray's extensive background in composition (complemented by his years on Broadway) gave to The Taylor Maids (Gem and Gerry) just what they needed: Special arrangements to complement each girl's voice and a flair for selecting attire which actually became costumes for the group. At their peak, they had six different matched outfits, including turquoise beaded gowns, and black-fringed shoulder frocks.

If needed, Gerry could belt a song like Sophie Tucker, but Gem preferred sweet songs and harmony. The three of them became hit sensations and performed together for some ten years. They did a show for Latin American buyers of GE products in Syracuse. They appeared at the old Ocean Forest Hotel in Myrtle Beach for the National Electric Contractors. They were featured at the N.C. Press Association Convention at Grove Park Inn.

No small part of the success of this local show business act was due to the fact (as one of them said) that they were such different individuals, they just got along well together. My memories of hearing Gem and Gerry, directed by Ray Taylor, was they were having fun and it was catching.

Forty years of YMCA

Forty years ago, in the spring and summer of 1957, several groups had come to me, as president of the Chamber of Commerce, and suggested that Hendersonville ought to have a YMCA, an organization founded in the U.S. in 1851. The Chamber of Commerce Board approved a feasibility study which would be conducted by George E. Simmons, interstate secretary of the YMCA of the Carolinas. The chamber also appointed a special YMCA committee, chaired by I.T. "Ollie" Olsen, and included as members: myself, Mrs. Alice Porter, Bob Whitmire Jr., W.W. Carpenter, Mrs. Sally Godehn, Dave Cooley, Boyce Whitmire, Sid Bakke, and Charlie "Choo Choo" Justice. Choo Choo's brother had been a dynamic figure in the YMCA in Canton for years.

On Oct. 5, 1957, Mr. Simmons advised the chamber that his report was ready and formal presentation was to be made by him to all interested persons at a meeting scheduled for the Skyland Ballroom. Mr. Bruce Drysdale had been ill and was confined to his home, and several members of the committee felt it vital that the report should be reviewed and input received from Mr. Drysdale before the public meeting was held. At his home, Mr. Drysdale proposed, and George Simmons agreed, that before anyone started talking about raising money for bricks and mortar, a YMCA program should be established in Hendersonville.

On Oct. 11, 1957, the YMCA survey presented by Mr. Simmons was approved, and the members in the chamber committee were asked to serve as a provisional board until a local charter could be obtained and corporate requirements fulfilled. Within six months, the charter was formalized, a new board was elected, and Boyce Whitmire became the first president of the YMCA. On May 30, he announced that Jack Cook, a native of Danville, Va., and at that time program director of the Spartanburg Y, had been hired as general secretary of the YMCA here.

Cook came here on July 15, 1958, and immediately started developing a YMCA program of activities, using a temporary headquarters office in a building located at the corner of 6th Avenue and Oakland Street. In 1959, Sid Bakke had been elected to succeed Boyce Whitmire, and the two of them negotiated the purchase of the Dr. J.S. Brown home at the corner of Oak Street and 6th Avenue West on Dec. 9. Bakke pointed out that property previously given to the Y by Roy and Myrtle Bennett, along with financial support from Forrest Withers, made the purchase of the Brown property possible and that it was large enough to serve the needs for some decades to come.

Nine years later, Oct. 14, 1967, a brand new YMCA building was opened in brief ceremonies. Don Godehn was chairman of the Building Committee and presided at the opening. He presented a symbolic key to the building to then General Secretary John Blackmore. The ribbon was cut by the children of board members.

The formal dedication of the $360,000 building took place in March 1968. Frank Todd was chairman of the Dedication Committee. I had the pleasure of serving as master of ceremonies. A high-powered program was scheduled which featured George Gullen (vice president of Wayne State University in Detroit), George W. Ivey (president of the Carolinas Council of YMCAs), with the featured speech given by the Rev. Calvin Thielman (research assistant to Billy Graham and pastor of the Presbyterian Church of Montreat).

Early general secretaries included Jack Cook, Ketchel Adams, Hendersonville's own Bob Elliott (former football star at the University of North Carolina), John Blackmore and Tom Hetrick of Durham. Gray Stallworth, after leaving Hendersonville a short time, was persuaded to return to become executive director. His leadership has produced an annual membership of 3,750 members, but with service to more than 10,000 individuals per year.

The "Y" has recently completed an 8,000 square foot addition, which provides for an expanded Wellness Center, a new Fitness Studio, and has freed the gymnasium for larger programs of the Y. A new Child Watch Center allows families with infants and pre-school children to use the Y and know that their children are being cared for. The Y's new Youth Center provides youth and teen-agers a place to meet and have fun in a safe, constructive environment. The Y has the only major indoor pool in the area, which is used not only for aquatic classes but sponsors a Water Fitness Program, the Hammerhead Youth Swim Team, as well as high school swim teams.

The YMCA–just a thought suggested at a PTA meeting by Alice Porter in 1957–now forty years later has over 3,750 members and serves 10,000 individuals in our community.

The Y provides recreational facilities and fitness equipment combined in an atmosphere of Christian charity. The first Y was formed in London, England in 1844 by George Williams, a dry goods store clerk who was knighted by Queen Victoria for his leadership in establishing this movement which then spread to seventy countries and territories.

Opportunity Knocks

Miss Grace Etheridge began to assume prominence in the community as early as 1960, when she started campaigning for a teacher-assigned art class at Hendersonville High School. She was able to persuade school authorities to authorize her to sponsor art classes after school hours in the lunch room with a certified art teacher in charge. The following year, Miss Etheridge was successful in persuading school authorities to hire a full-time art teacher and make it a part of the curriculum. She then focused her attention into establishing the Henderson County Arts League. She was one of the first members to serve on the Board of the Friends of the Library, and was very active in its early organization.

In the late 1950s, Pat Rothrock was director of Christian Education at the First United Methodist Church; and she and Grace Etheridge founded something called the Opportunity Group. It started with twenty-six members and its purpose was to utilize the energies of the ever-growing number of retired people here, giving them opportunities for meaningful activities. In just a couple of years, the group has doubled ... and doubled ... and doubled again until there was simply not enough room in the First United Methodist Church for their activities. On her own, Grace Etheridge purchased a large house at 819 Fleming St., renovated it and added two sections: One being for exchange where articles made by members were offered for sale, and the second an assembly room and well-equipped craft shop.

In 1965 the Opportunity Group numbered over 600. By this time, Miss Etheridge felt that by its growing membership, her faith in the project had been justified and she started proceeding to transfer ownership of the house to the Opportunity Group, and the transfer of ownership was completed in November 1965. Later, the group felt the need for greatly expanded facilities, and when the A&P supermarket closed on the Asheville Highway, the group disposed of the house on Fleming Street and acquired the huge A&P building and parking lot, which the Opportunity House occupies today.

Elsewhere in this book, I have written about one Phillip Kelley, who had written a book, "How to Grow Old Rebelliously." As Phil observed the intense activities going on at Opportunity House every day throughout the year, he became absolutely fascinated. Here were men who had been executives in some of the larger corporations in America, involved with their fingers and hands, creating and selling things with benefits to go to others. Phil Kelly then created the "Second Wind Hall of Fame." His marketing genius bore fruit with extensive articles published in a variety of monthly magazines. As the story of Opportunity House was spread across the land, groups of visitors started coming here to observe first-hand how it worked, and sought to determine if a counterpart might be started in their own community. The guest registers, even back in the '60s, show groups from as far away as Kansas coming to Opportunity House.

On May 9, 1996, I made a routine inquiry of Lucy Purkey, director of Opportunity House, and said, "Lucy, it doesn't have to be exact, but I'm doing a piece on the radio about Opportunity House, and I'm interested in the approximate number of members active today." With no hesitation, she answered, "Kermit, we have 1,988 active members today."

I laughed and said, "Lucy, do you think Pat Rothrock or Grace Etheridge would believe their dream could ever become so successful?"

Grace Baker Etheridge–a person who dreamed of a place where new retirees could find new friends, new areas to explore, new activities to try and (best of all) a place where one has very little time to become bored. In my stack of memorabilia at home, I still have a copy of the printed program distributed at her memorial service, May 28, 1993. In it is printed:

"The following quote was written by Grace and serves as a model for her life:

'Knowledge is life's greatest adventure. Serving is life's greatest privilege.'"

Grace Etheridge

Camping Country

"Indian Summer"–did you see the movie with Alan Arkin? It was made in 1993 and deals with the changes that have come about in the last few years which altered the very nature of summer camps. Thirty years ago, in 1966, it is estimated as many as 8,000 youngsters attended summer camps in Henderson County. The full camp season was normally eight weeks, though some camps broke the season into two separate sessions of four weeks each.

I had mentioned in an earlier chapter about the Evelyn Haynes family establishing Camp Minehaha back on Middle Fork. I had a nice letter from Bill and Jo Waggoner, who brought to my attention Dr. Seaton Smith at Camp Mishemoka at Bat Cave. I suppose Frank and Joe Bell ran some of the first camps here, opening in the early '20s Camp Green Grove, Camp Arrowhead and Camp Glen Arden. Also at Tuxedo were Camp Greystone, Camp Mondamin and Camp Wendy Wood.

In the heyday of camping, special trains would roll into the Hendersonville Southern depot, perhaps ten or twelve cars long, disgorge hundreds of youngsters with all their gear, to be picked up by buses and taken to their camps. I remember being at the depot on a couple of occasions when these trains would come in, and the excitement, the shouting, the general confusion during such arrivals was something to behold. And, when the trains would be parked on the siding, ready to load the youngsters for the return trip home, the atmosphere was totally opposite–quiet reigned. The campers knew that this one-time summer adventure was ending and would likely never happen to them again.

I mentioned the movie "Indian Summer," starring Alan Arkin, made in 1993. Arkin plays an older man who had spent his life operating a camp for youngsters. He had invited back for a limited stay perhaps a dozen of his favorite campers to share with them his decision to close the camp, and to enjoy with them the memories and happiness of the days that had been. It was a very poignant movie, and I recall that Arkin kept emphasizing that he'd gotten too old, he couldn't get kids excited about starting fires by rubbing rocks anymore.

And I thought ... maybe with TV, VCRs, the Internet, and the malls, camping as we remember it from the '40s and '50s and '60s was not the raison d'être it once was.

In the golden years, there was also Camp Pinnacle, Camp Ton-a-Wanda, Camp Blue Star, Camp Mountain Lake, Osceola Lake, Camp Pinewood and Camp Tekoa. There were religious camps operated by the Associate Reform Presbyterian Church, the Fruitland Baptist Conference Center, the Kanuga Conference Center, the Nazarene Camp, the Lutheridge Assembly and Camp Judea. Bill and Jo Waggoner started Camp Wendy Wood in 1957 and operated it with every success through 1984. They say, while you may not see the special trains coming and going anymore, there are still many camps in operation today. I'm quoting Bill Waggoner here: "I think that camping in our area is still alive and well."

Henderson County and Western North Carolina have no monopoly on summer camps. In fact, regarding the movie we referred to ("Indian Summer") the writer/director, Mike Bender, based the entire film on his own memories, and it was filmed at the actual Camp Tamakwa he attended in Canada.

As Bill and Jo Waggoner say, while camping is still alive and well in Western Carolina, the competition of electronic gimmickry, the lure of neon lights, four cars in every driveway, interstate highways to everywhere make it much more difficult to recruit youngsters and their families into committing for an eight-week summer session.

Years ago, it was estimated that camps provided a $3.5 million infusion into the local economy. It has been my experience

Frank and Joe Bell were among the first in the county to establish summer camp facilities.

down through the years (when I'm mingling in groups of strangers at conventions, seminars and area confabs), once you mention you're from Hendersonville, soon there'll be someone (now my age) come up and say, "I spent a summer in camp at Hendersonville."

Camping was not only a money producer, but a memory maker. If camping does not spark recognition, try this on for size: I was at a meeting in Montreal, and had tired of trying to explain where Hendersonville was located. I finally said simply, "I'm from a little town west of Charlotte and south of Asheville." The first time I tried that, this elderly woman spoke up and said, "And where is that from Tryon?"

The Music Man

Jim Stokes (Hendersonville High School Band Director) remembers the day vividly. Jim was in the band room at school when a handsome, distinguished man came in and said, "My name is Chan Harbour. I'm not a band director nor am I even a professional musician, but I think you and I should work together to organize a local symphony orchestra. Stokes, who had received many high honors for the bands he had directed, was not overly impressed with this conversation. Hendersonville had always been known to be frequented by folks who have grandiose ideas that they wanted to throw out to the world—and then walk away. However, Jim said he found out in a matter of weeks that Chan Harbour was "for real."

Chan had retired to Hendersonville in 1962 (nine years earlier) and had taken a strong and active role in organizations such as Opportunity House, where he was president for two years. He taught the Men's Bible Class at the First United Methodist Church and established the Philosophics Society in Hendersonville, as well as the Rainbow Round Table.

Chan, using his contacts within the community, began to ferret out people with professional music backgrounds, such as Joseph Falvo, Robert Barkley, Edward Schultz, and Marty Irving. Jim Stokes could see that with this nucleus of professional musicians, it would be within reason to round up enough former performers in high school bands to create (except for the string section) an actual symphony.

Jim said that Chan Harbour not only used his enthusiastic salesman-ship in recruiting musicians but others who would establish the framework of a marketing and performing organization. When it came time to acquire printed music for use in performing concerts, it was Chan Harbour who put up his own money. Stokes arranged for the symphony members to borrow, when needed, instruments from the Hendersonville Band Room—instruments you won't find in the average person's home, like the tuba.

By the holiday season in 1971, Hendersonville's first symphony orchestra was ready for its debut, and the concert was staged in the Hendersonville High School auditorium on the evening of Dec. 4, 1971. The reception was really an acclamation, nothing but rave reviews for the orchestra, the director, and everyone who had taken part in the effort.

The symphony had first rehearsed in the Fellowship Hall of the First Baptist Church, then later in the high school band room. With their fantastic success in the first concert, they decided to stage four concerts for the public each year. One of these would be especially for young people; and the orchestra would later sponsor "Strings in the Schools," a teaching program for would-be musicians. Ultimately, with the music program at Hendersonville High School in rapid growth and expansion (and the symphony ballooning as well), Jim Stokes said he had to give up the directorship of the symphony. He was succeeded by Ray Reid.

Stokes remembers the years that Virginia Tillotson was director of the symphony. He and Virginia had played together in the Hendersonville High School band. In later years, the symphony contracted with Peter Rickett, director of the Greenville Symphony Orchestra, to add the Hendersonville Symphony Orchestra to his directorial responsibilities. This introduced a new challenge for the amateur musicians in the Hendersonville orchestra. Mr. Rickett's schedule was so full that the local symphony would rehearse only three times prior to a concert. For a professional musician, this was not a challenge; but when certain of the amateur musicians could not deliver a polished performance in just three rehearsals, professional musicians were brought to Hendersonville and were paid for each performance. This practice is observed today by the symphony, with Robert Cranford as president and Manuel Alvarez as conductor and director. Mr. Alvarez is with the University of South Carolina. The costs for talent is included in the total budget, which is covered through their annual fund campaign.

An interesting spin-off occurred with the birth and growth of the symphony. Many of the musicians who had played together, either in high school or in the symphony or both, found a common interest in an extracurricular challenge in "The Community Band," which is still directed by Jim Stokes and numbers about sixty members. This band performs concerts for their own fun, and plays for special events.

Symphony orchestras don't march, but if they did, I can mentally picture Chan Harbour (now deceased) in the role of Professor J. Harold Hill, waving his mighty baton and leading that marvelous mass of music down the Main Street of the town he adopted and loved. Seventy-six trombones—with Chan Harbour leading the big parade.

Collecting History

I remember when my daughter, Katina, had hectored me into collecting the loose ends of a family history, which I had gathered over some fifty years, and began trying to put together something resembling a family tree. At that time, there was no Genealogical Society locally. There were many folks involved in genealogical efforts, but no central place where you could sit down with people with similar motives and share information and receive guidance on how to pursue such efforts. It was not until Dr. George and Evelyn Jones retired and returned in 1983 to Hendersonville that we had the instigators to put forth the efforts which led to a successful organization in 1985 with the formal incorporation of the Henderson County Genealogical & Historical Society.

Today the society is ensconced in space provided by the county in that beautiful historical three-story old First Citizens Bank building (long known as the State Trust Bank Building and later used for years as a tax office) at the corner of Main and 4th Avenue. The society distributes regular mailings to 700 members worldwide. It also maintains regular office hours, using volunteers to staff the phones, file new source material, and even sit down and tutor someone who has been "bitten" to discover their own roots.

After the incorporation of the society in 1985, George and Evelyn Jones (with the aid of Elsie Goephert and dozens of others) undertook the first major project: Volume I of Henderson County Heritage. So much material was left after the success of Volume I that Volume II was published a few years later. The two volumes not only document the early history of the schools, churches and other institutions of the county; but, even more important to those into genealogy, hundreds of family histories are presented and, in many cases, with family photos.

More recently, the society undertook a massive seven-year project of inventorying every public and private cemetery in the county. The society then published a comprehensive listing of everyone buried in Henderson

County, with easy directions on how to locate the cemetery and the individual graves of tens of thousands of people buried here. This publication has been used as the "how to" book by similar societies all over the state. The Journal (which is published regularly by the society) and the Cemetery Book prompted the Society of North Carolina Historians to honor Dr. George Jones with the "Historian of the Year-West Award."

At the time the new Court House and office facility was completed, Jones mounted a campaign to get an agreement from the county which would permanently establish the old Citizens Bank Building as permanent head-quarters for not only the Genealogical Society but for a new Henderson County Museum. The Gem and Mineral Museum will also be housed in this building. In addition to genealogical and historical activities and the substantial publishing efforts successfully carried on over the past ten years, the society and Dr. George Jones were designated the responsibility of arranging the Sesquicentennial Observance for Henderson County. Dr. Jones served as chairman of the local commission to commemorate the bicentennial of the U.S. Constitution and Bill of Rights, and was also appointed to the State Commission.

To mark the 50th anniversary of VE-VJ Days in Henderson County once again, Dr. Jones was asked to chair, plan and carry out the observance with participation from veterans organizations. These plans included highlighting by honoring surviving next of kin of every local service man who was killed in action in World War II. This impressive event took place at Dietz Field before a reverent and appreciative audience.

George has received the "Excellence in Community Service Award" from the National Society of the Daughters of the American Revolution. While he may be diminutive in physique, he is a giant in leadership, in dedication and is unswerving when a specific challenge is proffered.

He and Evelyn certainly were in the driving force of bringing to Henderson County one of the most active, most respected historical and genealogical chapters in the entire Southeast.

When Leadership Was Crucial

I first worked with James Pilgrim on Sunday afternoons back in 1947. His firm, Pilgrim Funeral Home, sponsored a live music program featuring spiritual songs, and was emceed by James himself. I was always impressed by his soft, pleasing voice; but the slogan he used for his business is as fresh in my mind today as the first time I heard James Pilgrim say, "It is better to know us and not need us, than to need us and not know us."

Pilgrim graduated from Stephens Lee High School in Asheville. It was a much bigger school than the local 6th Avenue High. After working with Thomas Shepherd Funeral Home through the late '30s, he decided to open

James Pilgrim

his own firm in 1941, serving the black community. He and his wife, Eva Robinson Pilgrim, were active within their community in the Star of Bethel Church and the Mud Creek Baptist Association. He was also given the signal honor of "National Mortician of the Year" by the National Funeral Directors and Morticians Association.

Sam Mills, on the other hand, grew up working as a shoemaker at English Brothers Shoe Shop on 4th Avenue West, across from what was then the post office. In those years, virtually everyone half-soled and reheeled shoes as long as they'd last. Sam Mills was not only a master craftsman but, in the many, many times our paths would cross, I noted he always had time for a smile as his greeting. Sam was born to Alex and Bertha Mills, but was raised by his grandparents (Jesse and Carolina Wheeler Mills). He not only graduated from the old 9th Avenue High School, he attended Harbison Agricultural School in Irmo, S.C.

When there were rumors in the community that the English family (Paul and his wife, Alice) had reached their senior years and were on the verge of selling the shoe shop, I said to Sam one day, "Why don't you raise the money and buy them out? There are loads of people who'd be willing to loan you the money or buy stock in your business." Still with that smile on his face, Sam said, "I'm not sure Hendersonville is quite ready for a black to own and operate a business in the downtown area." How wrong Sam was.

He ran for City Council in the '70s, and his childhood friend, James Pilgrim, served as his campaign manager. Sam Mills was not only the top vote-getter in 1977 and again in 1989—the council named him Mayor Pro Tem, an office he held until ill health forced him to resign in May 1993.

Sam was involved in virtually everything: Board of Directors at the YMCA; he was the first black Boy Scout leader in the county; he served on the N.C. Black Leadership Council; and was a member of the National Association for the Advancement of Colored People. He was on the A&B Committee of the United Way, and was an active member of the St. Paul Tabernacle AME Zion Church from 1922.

Those testy times when Hendersonville and other communities around the national were

Sam Mills

trying to feel their way to total integration saw both James Pilgrim and Sam Mills constantly calming the waters. Don Michalove (who was mayor at the time of Sam's resignation) expressed it most appropriately when he said, "Sam Mills was a peacekeeper, and aided in the smooth transition of integration in the city schools. He was the calming oil on troubled waters."

After James Pilgrim's death, John Marable, principal and educator, began to take an interest in politics in the black community, and when Sam Mills resigned from the City Council, Marable petitioned for the council to quickly appoint another black to assure representation. A black minister, the Rev. C.E. Rowe, was appointed prior to the November election. He was defeated by Diane Caldwell, a black woman from the Green Meadows area.

James Pilgrim's son, Army Col. James J. "Sonny" Pilgrim, has served as a dentist at Fort Bragg for a number of years, but each time he has tried to retire and return to run the family funeral business, the Army dangles all sorts of incentives to keep him on active duty for just a little while longer.

Sam and Mary Joyce Mills had no children of their own, but do have a niece, Marietta Ward of Hendersonville.

I am not as active now in either the black or white community, but being the optimist I am, I feel confident that among the young black people now ready to move into adult leadership, we will have in the future another James Pilgrim, a Rev. George Weaver, a Sam Mills, a John Marable, a Mary Mims or even a Bessie Horne. They will have mighty big shoes to fill.

The Venerable Ray Cantrell

In April 1997, I was having coffee with the Old Fogies Club, now meeting at Days Gone By, which used to be Justus Pharmacy, located at Main and Third Avenue as far back as 1882. Days Gone By is now more of a museum than a drug store, but they do serve delicious sandwiches, salads and all sorts of fountain treats, as well as complete breakfasts, including Belgian waffles. The owners are Kathy and Bill Danielson.

While not an Old Fogie, Ray Cantrell frequently stops by for a quick visit on his way to work at the Chamber of Commerce; and it dawned on me when Ray sat down at the table ... "Ray has been manager of our Chamber of Commerce longer than any other person."

When I checked my notes, I discovered that Ray first came to Hendersonville in February 1960–close to forty years at the helm of the second largest Chamber of Commerce in Western North Carolina.

In the more than seventy years the chamber has been active, there have been only seven paid managers, or executive secretaries. The chamber was formed out of the old Hendersonville Board of Trade in 1923 and F.S. Wetmur was the first president. Noah Hollowell served as volunteer secretary, drawing no salary. L.J. Penny was the first paid secretary. He was here only a short time up through 1933 and was succeeded by Mrs. Cathryn Wiseman in 1934, who served five years. W.C. Mitchum came here to succeed Mrs. Wiseman. He was from Marion and only stayed about a year. Fred Allen, Jr. (from Henderson, N.C.) served only two years from 1940-42. He was succeeded by P.M. "Pete" Camak, who came here in '42 and left in '52 to take a similar job in Wilmington, and that brought us to the second local person to hold the job, Dave Cooley, who served 1952-58. (The only other local person was Mrs. Wiseman.)

Dave was a dynamic individual and any successor was bound to live in Dave's shadow. That is exactly what happened to a young Bill Van Hoy, who served only one year.

Ray Cantrell

Ray Cantrell was chosen from a field of at least a dozen applicants. He was the manager, at the time, of the chamber in Ahoskie, N.C. When Cantrell joined the Chamber of Commerce here, his office was in the Skyland Hotel building.

Ten years later when the new Henderson County Public Library was completed on Washington Street, and the original library building was left vacant, negotiations were begun with the city for the chamber to take over that building which had been given by Capt. Marion Columbus Toms for library use only. There was a reverter clause in the event the facility was no longer needed for a library, but an agreement was reached with the Toms heirs and the Green Construction Company remodeled the building for the chamber, charging only outright costs.

In the nearly forty years that Ray Cantrell has served as manager, the chamber, in addition to being the only organization charged with recruiting new industrial plants or enhancement of existing plants, has for many years acted as a Merchants' Association. Until the Travel & Tourism Agency was created by the county, the chamber produced all the events of the N.C. Apple Festival. The chamber has functioned as a catalyst for community growth and improvement always in the thick of educational bond issues, property acquisitions for industrial relocations; and battling for adequate funding of roads, highways and utilities to serve this top growth area of North Carolina.

Ray has worked with twenty-five presidents of the chamber, all top business and industrial leaders. In his years of staging annual dinner meetings, he has been successful in securing as speakers both Gov. Terry Sanford and Gov. Jim Hunt, as well as former Gov. Bob Scott. Personalities who have been featured at the annual dinner meetings include Dr. Tom Haggai, humorist Chub Sewell, Joe Higgins (the National Safety Sheriff),

Dr. Kenneth McFarland (the dean of all professional after-dinner speakers and author of many "how to" books on public speaking), the late Harry Reasoner, Jim Lampley, Tom Wicker of the *New York Times* and twenty-four others.

In 1977, Ray Cantrell was honored by the Hendersonville Sertoma Club with the "Service to Mankind Award."

Ray has also served as a director of the North Carolina Industrial Developers Association; and he has been active in the chamber and trade groups across the state.

His wife, Priscilla, is no slouch, either. She is executive director of the 13 million dollar Community Foundation; and is chairman of the administrative board of the First United Methodist Church, the first woman ever to hold that position.

The Cantrells – they've made Hendersonville a better place to live and in which to retire.

A Little Name Dropping

Now, a bit of name dropping–famous entertainers, Hollywood stars, stars of the Broadway stage who have been in and out of Hendersonville over the past fifty years.

Ann Jeffries (whose full name was Ann Jeffries Carmichael) spent her summers in Hendersonville back in the early '40s. She was studying for a career in opera but instead found success on the silver screen. Altogether she played in thirteen movies, including "The Adventures of Topper" and a number of Wild Bill Elliott films. Her real claim to fame is that she gave Frank Sinatra his first film kiss. Ann Jeffries had many acquaintances and a few very close friends here whom she used to visit when vacationing.

In 1952, the Motion Picture Theatre Association to promote their 50th anniversary contracted with troupes to tour cities around the country. On November 12, what was billed as "Four Screen Personalities" appeared in Hendersonville in an Armistice Day program in the Hendersonville High School auditorium. The record shows that I emceed that show but I have not the faintest recollection of the program, which featured William Lundigan, who only appeared in six movies, including "The Fighting 69th." Also appearing with him was Douglas Morrow, who won an Oscar for screenwriting for the

Actress Ann Jeffries

"Stratton Story." I have never heard of Sally Mansfield or Kathleen Crowley, the other two stars.

One of the greatest laughs about so-called celebrities: Fred Reid, the manager of the Carolina Theater, called me and said, "I believe Jimmy Fain is totally illiterate." Jim was the editor of the *Times-News*. Fred said to me, "I called Jim to tell him that Terry Moore was in town and he asked me, 'What team does he play for?'"

There was a pause, and I said, "Fred, what team does he play for?"

"You're another idiot," Fred shouted into the phone. I learned that Terry Moore was a movie actress and she was visiting her mother out in Laurel Park, Mrs. Harry Schelba. Altogether, Terry made ten movies, including "Come Back Little Sheba," "Daddy Long Legs" and "Peyton Place."

The most prolific of all the screen stars ever to spend time in Hendersonville was the late Lee Marvin, who first appeared at the old Lake Summit Playhouse. Lee starred in more than thirty movies, including "Cat Ballou," "The Dirty Dozen" and "Paint Your Wagon." He returned to Flat Rock Playhouse on a number of occasions to renew old acquaintances. Producer Ernie Frankel, formerly of Hendersonville, loves to recall attending a Guild meeting in Hollywood when he heard a booming voice roll across the room ... "Robroy Farquhar." Ernie said he looked, and there was Lee Marvin grinning from ear to ear in all his glory.

We were running a sister radio station, WWIT in Canton, when Robert Mitchum, (who died in 1997) came here to film "Thunder Road." Many, many times I'd have to wait thirty or forty minutes on N.C. 280 near the river while they would film the ending of a moonshiner chase with a car plunging into the French Broad River. Mitchum was the big hit in the Apple Parade in 1957.

Lou Gallo was at the Flat Rock Playhouse in 1951 and again in 1954. He starred with Gregory Peck in "Pork Chop Hill" and with Susan Heyward in "I Want to Live."

Pat Hingle's family actually lived in Laurel Park, so when he took the lead role in "A Man for All Seasons" in 1974, he was able to stay with his mother, Mrs. Marvin Fincher. His daughter, Jody, was a second-year apprentice at the Playhouse that year.

Back in the days when WHKP was a Mutual Broadcasting affiliate, you heard the voice of Cedric Foster, one of the old line newscasters then—friend of Edward R. Murrow and H.V. Kaltenborn, both of whom had died in 1965, the year he visited Mrs. Marge Garrison on Rutledge Drive.

Shortly after the Gerber plant opened in Western North Carolina, Dave Cooley and I got the idea to call the company headquarters in Michigan and see if they would schedule for the Apple Festival a visit to Hendersonville by Bob Keeshan, Captain Kangaroo. Gerber sponsored the captain on the network. Gerber was delighted to oblige and Captain Kangaroo gave a performance to the largest crowd of kids in the history of Dietz Field. Gerber wouldn't allow us to charge admission, so we didn't make a penny.

Hildegarde and Billy Carter, the former president's brother, both came to Hendersonville in 1977. She had consigned a passel of jewelry to one of the art galleries to sell at auction, and she performed in the art gallery prior to each sale. Billy Carter came here for the Motorama and was a smashing hit.

Back in the '40s, a young lady came from the Pasadena Playhouse to Lake Summit. Her name was Janet Cole, and she asked only for room and board and $5 per week. The very next year, she hit the big time in the movies as Kim Hunter, playing in the "Planet of the Apes" series as well as in "A Streetcar Named Desire."

There was Don Dubbins, who after appearances at Flat Rock Playhouse, went on to "From Here to Eternity" and "The Caine Mutiny." Rosemary Prinz played on a major TV soap for more than a generation. Burt Reynolds brought Loni to his one-man show, and with him came Dom DeLouise and Charles Nelson Reilly.

June Havoc was a big hit on the Flat Rock stage. *Billy Carter* And one of the easiest, most laid-back interviews I ever did was with Andy Williams when he was at Brevard Music Camp.

Little Jimmie Dickens, Red Foley, Sonny James, Clyde Moody, Don Gibson, Billy Grammar, Ted Malone, the Statesmen and Blackwoods, Red Sovine—even Lulu Belle (of "Lulu Belle and Scotty" fame) who I served with on the WNC Tomorrow Board, bring back memories.

But memories get a little fuzzy after fifty years.

Flashbacks: Things You Never Forget

• Standing in the woods at Orr's Camp where in the tree directly over my head was an inferno of fire from the burning Piedmont 727 Jetliner, Flight #22, in which 78 people died in a crash with a smaller plane on July 19, 1967.

• Sitting in my Jeep alongside a wooded area in Germany, watching a tank battle between two of our 12th Armored's medium tanks in a battle against a heavily armored German Tiger tank. I tried to imagine the emotions of our GI tankers who were gearing frantically to keep their tank out of the line of fire of the Tiger's powerful 88 mm gun.

• On maneuvers in Abilene, Texas, watching Geza Horvath, a member of the Signal Company, stage a fight to the finish between a tarantula and a rattlesnake. The spider won. He carried cages of both tarantulas and rattlers in the back of his Jeep.

• Sitting in as a substitute officer at an Elks meeting and watching "Mr. Elkdom," Deacon Brad Hughes, suddenly slouch to the floor. Being totally inexperienced, I assumed this was part of the ceremony, only to discover that he had experienced a massive and fatal heart attack directly in front of me.

• In 1977, standing in water above my waist inside the radio station during a late season flood ... and less than two months later, watching our home burn to the ground on Christmas night.

• When I was in the sixth grade, watching Grandpa Edney's house burn; and, in a grove near the house, as each giant white pine would reach incendiary temperature and suddenly explode in a single blaze like a sky rocket.

• Seeing the emaciated humans–just skin and bones–as they were released by the 12th Armored Division from a concentration camp near Landsberg, Germany, as the medics kept shouting, "Don't feed them, they have to start eating again gradually."

• In the 1970s, after learning that a squadron the West German Air Force was based in Texas for training with the U.S. Air Force, I thought I had pulled off the coup of my life after getting agreement from the West German Ambassador to the United States that they would do a "flyover" of the Hendersonville area for the Apple Festival. Two hours later my elation was shattered by the Pentagon when I was told that the international agreement did not allow the planes to fly outside a 200-mile perimeter. I can still imagine seeing a squadron of jets with Iron Crosses on the wings doing a low-level flyover of Main Street.

• Playing golf, when the mercury topped out at 24 degrees, sculling a drive on #12, "the lake hole." The ball bounced on the ice all the way across the lake, hit a poplar tree that then stood on the dam, bounced backward all the way back across the lake and came to rest less than three feet from where I had hit it.

• When on a flight with Art Cooley to a convention in New Orleans, the flight aborted takeoff because someone forgot to secure the rear door. On the return trip, we aborted takeoff at New Orleans because another craft was crossing our runway for a landing. And finally, on landing in Atlanta, the plane blew one tire on landing and by the time we reached the end of the runway, had blown the other tire. A van came out and picked up the crew, leaving all the passengers standing on the tarmac, and advising us not to smoke because of the heavy diesel fumes at the end of the runway. Art was due the "White Knuckles Flying Award" for these experiences on a single trip.

• Bob Freeman's News Stand was the counterpart years ago to the Cigar Smokers Clubs of today. Gentlemen discussed law, politics and even occasionally placed friendly wagers. The longest ongoing annual wager was between UNC fan Lee Whitmire and Sid Powers of the University of Virginia. UVA had been through many winless seasons, and negotiations over the bet had been going on for weeks. Finally, Powers blurted out, "The only way I'll bet you is if you give me fifty points." Lee quickly envisioned the public relations value of such a ridiculous bet, and quickly answered, "You're on. You've got Virginia and fifty points." The wager was duly made and witnessed. That Saturday, Carolina beat Virginia 51 to 0, and Sid Powers didn't come back to the news stand for two weeks.

• Back when the radio station was located "on the banks of the Oklawaha," our traffic manager, Mary Ashe, came into my office and said, "Kermit, there's a man out front that has the strangest story I've ever heard. Maybe you'd better talk to him." As soon as I walked into the front office, I recognized Dr. George Saxmann, a highly respected chiropractor who lived at 1015 Maple Street. I had known who Dr. Saxmann was all of my life. And now in the very twilight of his life, he walked with the erectness of a West Point cadet. He ran up and down stairways; and even in his advanced years, he was the picture of health. "Good morning, Dr. Saxmann," I began (seeking to be as friendly as possible). At once he lashed out at me, "You're tearing the boards off my house. Your radio waves are causing the boards to warp and swell and physically pull the nails out

Sid Powers

of the wall. All night you keep me awake. I spend the next day driving the nails back into the wall." I'm listening intently, with the good sense to say nothing. Finally he stopped the harangue, and I said quietly, "Dr. Saxmann, this sounds like something that might happen with the high voltage of Duke Power lines." Quickly he fired back, "That was my first thought, but when I went to them, they sent me to you. They said this is the kind of things radio waves do." I finally persuaded him to check with the phone company.

• There used to be a Shell service station at 924 North Main Street which had been leased by one Lou Guesswein. Back then our business community was so small, we looked at every business as a prospect for advertising—even those seemingly hopeless. Guesswein fell into this category. He not only never bought any advertising, he never smiled. I nicknamed him "Happy Lou." During the flood of 1964, Lem Barnwell and I were standing waist deep in water in front of the radio station and noticed a car driven by Happy Lou start through the deeper water on old Highway 64 toward the bridges. I yelled, "Happy Lou, that road is closed. You can't make it through there." Paying no attention, he drove another twenty-five feet or so, and suddenly his car slid to the right and turned over in a ditch. Only the top part of the left doors were exposed. Lem and I waded out to the car and said, "You and your wife are going to have to get out of that car or you're going to drown." I explained that when Lem and I would pull open the door, the water would rush in—the two of them would have to hold their breath until we could drag them free. This time they cooperated and we got them back to dry land.

Just a few weeks later, Happy Lou was making a speech or leading the singing at the Senior Citizens Picnic sponsored by the Chamber of Commerce down at Frank Bell's camp. The Assembly Room is highlighted by a huge sunken fireplace where the campers can sit on the wall in front of the fire as their counselors tell scary stories. Happy Lou, as he performed, was walking back and forth right on the edge of the wall when suddenly he lost his footing and fell into the fireplace. Quickly I jumped to him, pulling him out of the fire and using my coat to beat out the flames. When things calmed down, I said to him, "Happy Lou, you've tested me with water and now flames. What do you now plan for an encore?" He never smiled, and never bought any advertising either.

It was tough to make a living back then.

The Baker-Barber Family

The early history of the Baker-Barber family has certainly been well documented down through the years in books and special editions of local publications. In fact, I have before me a copy of the *Times-News* dated May 2, 1959. What makes this particular story interesting reading is the following quote:

"He opened his photographic studio on the second floor of Shepherd's Store, now Drake's Store at the corner of Main Street and First Avenue, then the center of town."

I thought this was particularly interesting because when "The Brothers Three" were, with their dad, celebrating their 75th anniversary, "Skin" Drake's Store was still in operation–that was in 1959.

In fact, this newspaper feature had pictures of "Baker's" London Art Gallery in the building at 4th and Main, which was the second home of Barber's Studio, and finally, pictures of the buildings which used to stand at the corner of Main and 6th Avenue but are now gone, with First Citizens Bank currently occupying that space.

One has to wonder today how would Uncle Baker react to the mind-boggling innovative changes that have come to the field of photography. He had to renovate the old M.M. Shepherd building to include a skylight to provide adequate light for his work. Then the building he constructed on the corner of 4th and Main with a skylight was later made useless by having the light blocked by a taller building next door. His final building at the corner of 6th and Main had a bay window facing 6th Avenue so it could never be blocked again.

What A.F. Baker (of Tunbridge Wells, England) did for us, beginning on May 1, 1884, was establish an heirloom of photographs, action pictures, historical scenes and panoramas. It is A.F. Baker's picture of Chimney Rock (made more than a hundred years ago) that is still being used in promo material today.

My first recollection of Barber's was not from portraits or camera products–it was the Book Shop. When I was in the elementary grades, the state provided no textbooks. It was up to the student to procure his or her own. Thank God for Farry Barber. He not only sold new textbooks for those who

"The Brothers Three," plus Papa Barber: Jody (left), Farry Barber, A.F. "Unk" Jr., and Don.

could afford them, but he accepted used books in trade and these were then sold to those who couldn't afford new books.

The Barber family was an institution. Farry Barber (head of the clan) was a good businessman and a dedicated community servant. Farry Barber fathered A.F., Jr. ("Unk"), who ran Town Office Supply; and Don, who achieved fame over the entire state with his professional photography; and Jody (my age), who would run the camera and card shop.

When Jody and Louise Bailey joined forces to publish "The Pictorial History of Henderson County," this was a real adventure for me. I saw a picture of the Rev. N.B. Phillips baptizing congregates in Highland Lake. It brought back memories of the Rev. Phillips when he first came to the radio station to "Morning Devotions." He came in, sat down in a chair in a corner of the room. When I gave his introduction, he simply began talking with no concern for the microphone. I frantically waved for him to move over to the mike, but he totally ignored me. As a last resort, I raced from the control room into the studio and moved the mike in front of him. After the broadcast, he nonchalantly told me in the control room, "Young man, my job is to preach, yours is to broadcast. Let us never confuse these responsibilities again."

When looking through Jody and Louise Bailey's book, which is now in its second printing (and is again available at Mountain Lore Book Shop), I saw a picture of the Jan Garber Orchestra playing for the dedication of the city reservoir on Ewart's Hill. Jan played regularly at Laurel Park Pavilion–but to play for the opening of a reservoir?

Looking at the picture of the old Federal Building, the old post office at the corner of 4th and Church, can you imagine when this building was built in 1918, employees would come to work early to take a shower? (Very few homes back then had inside plumbing.)

In all the pictures Jody selected from the thousands in the Barber collection, there was one of the old Wilson Drug Store on 7th Avenue East where, at Christmas in 1941, I bought my first "Evening in Paris" cosmetics for someone special back then. You can't buy "Evening in Paris" anymore, nor will you identify that wonderfully distinctive smell of the old drug stores of days gone by, the odors fanned onto the street by the old-fashioned paddle wheel fans.

Maybe heaven will be strolling down a Main Street and wandering into a Woolworth's or McLellan's 5 and 10, or stopping in at Pattersons and jawing with Ed or Doris or Walter Drake about something other than an Arrow shirt or a Dobbs hat–or getting a penny mint at Dad Crosdale's fruit stand, hoping to win a huge nickel mint–or buying a popsicle at Carson's Ice Cream, hoping the stick says "Free."

All during 1996 (when I was doing the radio series "Where Fitz Left Off"), I'd have the pleasure of chatting with Jody at least once a week. I'd have a question about a family or business or place, and I'd call on Jody to help try to put a correct memory together. I always asked Jody to read through my scripts before they were broadcast to be sure I would not make any glaring errors–such as, being told by Jody that there was no Jump Off Mountain in Laurel Park–it is Echo Mountain.

And after the both of us had given up on locating where Vernon Few had his hardware store (after the turn of the century), we rejoiced discovering that when John Grant was congressman, he secured an appropriation to buy the Vernon Few property at the corner of 4th and Church for the new post office building. We finally knew where the Vernon Few Hardware Store had been located.

Had it not been for Jody's constant encouragement, I doubt whether or not I would have edited all those radio scripts into this book. The deep responsibility Jody feels toward maintaining the quality and integrity of the priceless Baker/Barber Photo Collection rubbed off on me to create a feeling that I had a responsibility to permanently record the contributions and exploits of the people you've been reading about in this book, who each carved their niche into making "our town" a place Thornton Wilder would have envied.

Thank you, Jody!

Appendix

The Appendix of this Book was inspired by an experience about the 2nd or 3rd of January, 1997. For the Radio Series, "Where Fitz Left Off", I was doing a chapter on Ray Cantrell, who had come to Hendersonville from Ahoskie, North Carolina to manage the Chamber of Commerce almost forty years ago. As I wrote about Ray, the memory of his wife Priscilla, and her extraordinary service to the community kept coming to mind.

While Ray was building industries, and jobs, and water systems, and schools, his wife Priscilla was building the Community Foundation to asset footings over $13 million dollars. And at the same time she had been elected as Head of the Board of Stewards at the First United Methodist Church.

I suddenly picked up the phone and called "our" church and a friendly and sweet voiced staff member answered the phone. I identified myself and said, "I'm doing a radio feature on the happenings and the people who made things happen here over the past fifty years. Am I correct that Priscilla Cantrell is the first women ever to head the Administrative Board of the Church?"

There was a pause, and I was advised, "Sir, I have only been here 6 months, and I've been here longer than anyone else in the office, and I don't even know if there is such a record."

This was a little salt in the wound I'd received at the Chamber of Commerce Office when I asked for a list of Past Presidents dating back to the beginning of the Chamber.

"Sir, our records only go back to 1965," I was told.

These two experiences goaded me into this appendix. Down through the years, we've had civic, veterans, fraternal, trade, social, health and a multiplicity of other organizations whose members have devoted endless hours to making "our town" THE favorite place for all of us today.

With the help of Oma Edney, who retired from G. E. but was part of the WHKP family in earlier years, we began the challenge of creating a permanent record of the leadership of all the Lions Clubs, the Woman's Clubs, the American Legions, and even United Ways and American Red Cross. We began with a list of such groups available in the chamber office, and then augmented it, and enlarged upon it as we continued to progress.

In the beginning, it was truly exciting to get responses from volunteer groups who had maintained complete and accurate records since 1917. In other cases, we did the research for them—as in the case of the Chamber of Commerce, which evolved from the old Board of Trade in 1923. We learned it was William Howard Taft in 1912 that really gave the beginning to Chambers of Commerce where he exhorted business groups "to united into a single Chamber of Commerce and speak with one voice for the free enterprise system of America."

There were many frustrations. Records had not been kept, or at least no records could be found. But calling on friends who may have had ties with some of these groups in the past, we were able to formalize at least a representation of the continuity of leadership back to the beginning.

In some cases, there were "gaps in the records" where neither the written word or memory could fill in all the blanks. If any of our readers feel they can help in making the records complete, local historians will be obligated to you!

LOCAL VOLUNTEER ORGANIZATIONS

1. AARP Chapter 8
2. AIR MUSEUM, Western North Carolina
3. AMERICAN ASSOCIATION OF UNIVERSITY WOMEN
4. AMERICAN LEGION, Hubert M. Smith Post #77
5. AMERICAN RED CROSS, Henderson County Chapter
6. AMERICAN SCANDINAVIAN FOUNDATION, Western Carolina Associates
7. APPLE COUNTRY ENGINE AND TRACTOR
8. APPLE FESTIVAL, North Carolina
9. ARTS LEAGUE OF HENDERSON COUNTY
10. AUDUBON SOCIETY, Elisha Mitchell Chapter
11. BELFRY PLAYERS
12. BIG BROTHERS/BIG SISTERS of Western North Carolina
13. BLUE RIDGE LITERACY COUNCIL, Inc.
14. BOYS AND GIRLS CLUB OF HENDERSONVILLE
15. BOY SCOUTS OF AMERICA, Daniel Boone Council
16. BUSINESS AND PROFESSIONAL WOMEN'S CLUB
17. CAMERA CLUB of Hendersonville
18. CAROLINA VILLAGE
19. CHAMBER OF COMMERCE of Greater Hendersonville
20. CHINA PAINTERS CLUB of Hendersonville
21. CIVIL AIR PATROL, Hendersonville Squadron
22. CIVITAN CLUB of Hendersonville
23. COIN CLUB of Hendersonville
24. COMMUNITY BAND of Hendersonville
25. COMMUNITY FOUNDATION of Henderson County
26. COMPUTER SOCIETY, Hendersonville Area
27. COUNTRY CLUB of Hendersonville
28. DAUGHTERS OF THE AMERICAN REVOLUTION, Joseph McDowell Chapter
29. DOES, Benevolent and Protective Order of
30. ECO (Environmental and Conservation Organization)
31. ELKS Lodge, Hendersonville #1616
32. FOUR SEASONS ARTS COUNCIL
33. FRIENDS OF THE LIBRARY
34. GARDEN CLUB of Hendersonville
35. GARDEN CLUB, Old Kanuga
36. GEM AND MINERAL SOCIETY, Henderson County

37. GENEALOGICAL AND HISTORICAL SOCIETY, Henderson County
38. GIRL SCOUTS
39. HENDERSONVILLE CHORALE
40. HOME BUILDERS ASSOCIATION of Hendersonville
41. HOSPICE, Four Seasons
42. INTERFAITH ASSISTANCE MINISTRY
43. JAYCEES of Hendersonville
44. JUNIOR WELFARE CLUB
45. JUNIOR WOMEN'S CLUB
46. KIWANIS CLUB of Hendersonville
47. KIWANIS CLUB, Golden Key
48. KIWANIS CLUB, Land o' Sky
49. KNIGHTS OF COLUMBUS
50. LA LECHE ASSOCIATION
51. LEAGUE OF WOMEN VOTERS
52. LIONS CLUB, of Hendersonville
53. LIONS CLUB, Daybreak
54. LIONS CLUB, Etowah
55. LIONS CLUB, Etowah Braille Service
56. LITTLE THEATRE of Hendersonville
57. MAINSTAY of Hendersonville
58. MERCHANT'S ASSOCIATION of Hendersonville
59. MINISTRY SEVEN RESCUE MISSION
60. MICHIGAN CLUB of Hendersonville
61. OPPORTUNITY HOUSE
62. ORGANISTS, American Guild of Hendersonville
63. PARDEE MEMORIAL HOSPITAL (Patton Memorial)
64. PILOT CLUB
65. POLITICAL - DEMOCRATIC PARTY of Henderson County
66. POLITICAL - REPUBLICAN PARTY of Henderson County
67. PROFESSIONAL SECRETARIES, Land of Sky Chapter
68. QUARTER OF A CENTURY WIRELESS ASSOCIATION, INC. (QCWC)
69. ROTARY CLUB of Hendersonville
70. SALVATION ARMY
71. SERTOMA CLUB
72. SIERRA CLUB
73. SONG O' SKY CHORUS
74. SOROPTIMIST CLUB
75. SQUARE DANCE CLUB, Southern Lights
76. SYMPHONY ORCHESTRA, of Hendersonville
77. TAR HEEL PIECEMAKERS (Quilting)
78. UNITED WAY of Henderson County
79. VETERANS OF FOREIGN WARS, Hedrick Rhodes Post #5206
80. VETERANS OF FOREIGN WARS, Auxiliary
81. WESTERN NORTH CAROLINA COMMUNITY ACTION (WCCA), Henderson and Transylvania Counties
82. WELCOME WAGON (Junior)
83. WOMAN'S CLUB of Hendersonville
84. WOMAN'S CLUB, Forrest
85. WOMAN'S CLUB, Possum Holler
86. Y.M.C.A. of Henderson County
87. WHKP/WKIT, past and present employees since 1946.

PRESIDENTS OF ORGANIZATIONS

AARP Chapter 8

1987	John O. Thompson
1988	Lloyd H. Steen
1989-90	Clyde J. Plexico
1991	John O. Thompson
1992	Elsie Richardson
1993	Richard W. Todd
1994-95	Donald L. Keefauver
1996	Ruth J. Hoots
1997	Lloyd H. Steen and Orma P. Vosseller

AIR MUSEUM, Western North Carolina

1989-91	Kenneth Stubbs
1992-93	William Schreier
1994-95	James Granere
1996-97	Dennis Dunlap

AMERICAN ASSOCIATION OF UNIVERSITY WOMEN

1978-79	Dorothy Jordan
1979-80	Harriet Smith
1980-81	Lois J. Doman
1981-83	Joy Drew Blazey
1983-84	Challice Weiss
1984-85	Anna Rockhill
1985-86	Florence Young
1986-87	Karyn Joyner
1987-88	Elizabeth Black
1988-89	Jane Knox
1989-90	Jane Halsted
1990-91	Audrey McLane
1991-93	Kathleen Ehlers
1993-94	Mary Congdon
1994-96	Kathleen Ehlers
1996-97	Gay Strong
1997-98	Mary Jo Pribble

AMERICAN LEGION,
Hubert M. Smith Post #77

1919-20	Wiltshire Griffith, Sr.
1921	Albert V. Edwards
1922	E.E. Latt
1923	R.L. Whitmire, Sr.
1924	Fred S. Justus
1925	James W. Duff
1926	Dr. W.E. Brackett
1927	J.B. Creech
1928-33	Unknown
1934	J.B. Creech
1935	Nathan Patla
1936	Paul W. English
1937	M.L. Walker
1938	J.H. Flanagan
1939	Sidney W. Powers
1940	C. Few
1941	C.J. Wile
1942	Roy E. Johnson
1943	Mingus Shipman
1944	Roy C. Bennett
1945	C.F. Stonecipher
1946	Thomas B. Freeman
1947	Keith Arledge
1948	Bob Amos
1949	John McLeod, Jr.
1950	George Wilkins
1951	B. Frank Crawford
1952	Unknown
1953	Homer C. Hobbs
1954	J.H. Henderson
1955	Kenneth Skaggs
1956	Charles L. Leslie
1957	Walter Crawford, Jr.
1958	Asa B. Hadden
1959	James W. Gilliam
1960	J.B. Creech
1961	Kenneth Ardron
1962	Carroll L. Lamb
1963-64	J.R. Miller
1965	Kenneth Ardron
1966	James S. Newman
1967-68	Willie B. Marshall
1969-70	Clyde B. Taylor
1971	B.W. Summey
1972	Nelson Young
1973	Grady Shealy
1974	Frankie W. Sitton
1975	James E. Baine
1976	Bruce D. Mowery, Sr.
1977-78	Dexter Thompson
1979	Walter Crawford, Jr.
1980	Morris J. Dale
1981-82	Travis L. Brown
1983	Morris J. Dale
1984	Thomas E. Nichols
1985	Morris J. Dale
1986-87	B. Frank Crawford
1988	R. Shuford Edmisten
1989-90	B. Frank Crawford
1991	Donald Rhodes
1992	Argie Taylor
1993-94	George Kehoe
1995-96	Leonard Moody
1997	Walter Penner
1998	Ernest "Skip" Boys, Jr.

AMERICAN RED CROSS Hendersonville
Chapter chartered August 6, 1917

1917-19	Dr. William Redin Kirk
1919	Dr. Albert Clayton Tebeau

Rechartered Henderson County Chapter
May 31, 1933

1950-53	E.E. McBride
1954-56	Dr. Clayton Vandiver
1956-57	Rev. Corley Lineberger
1957-58	Alston Broom
1961-62	Herman Heilig
1963-67	L.Y. Biggerstaff
1968-69	John Loren Brown
1969-72	Donald L. Barrow
1972-74	Clarence H. Schneider
1976-77	B.F. Sims
1977-79	Unknown
1980-81	Janet C. Bethea
1981-83	Henry Rockhill
1983-85	Earl D. Medlin
1985-86	Boyd Loveless
1987-89	Unknown
1990	Gary Sherrill
1990-93	Virginia Turner
1993-95	Ted Willsey
1995-96	Virginia Turner
1996-98	Steve Pennock

AMERICAN SCANDINAVIAN FOUNDATION,
Western Carolina Associates

1982-97	Eiler R. Cook

APPLE COUNTRY ENGINE
AND TRACTOR ASSOCIATION

1986-88	Perry Owensby
1989-91	Norman Lisenbee
1991-92	Jim Baity
1993-94	A.B. Wexler
1995-96	Robert Klefeker
1997	Furman Hoots

APPLE FESTIVAL North Carolina

1947-48	G.C. Richardson
1949	Truman Westmoreland
1950	William E. Dalton
1951	Ernest "Curly" Roper

1952	Dwight W. Bennett
1953	I.E. Johnson
1954	Fred Reid
1955	Kermit Edney
1956	J.T. Fain, Jr.
1957	Alston Broom
1958	P.T. Green
1959	Hardy Calwell, Jr.
1960	Don Gibson
1961	Jim Stephens
1962	Bob Quinn
1963	Jack Schubert
1964	Bill Robertson
1965	James Gibbs
1966	Bill Powers
1967	Joe E. Orr
1968	Frank L. FitzSimons
1969	Larry Feagin
1970	Joe Hamilton
1971	Mary Barber
1972	Volly Good
1973	Jim Kerterson
1974	Joe Crowell
1975	Hershel Buchanan
1976	Grace Gilliard
1977	Bill Powers
1978	Ron McAllister
1979	R.E. Harmon
1980	Jody Drake
1981	Don Jones
1982	Jake Justice
1983	R.D. Hodges
1984	Charlie Byrd
1985	Art Hazlett
1986	Pat Shepherd
1987	John Draughon
1988	John Shepherd
1989	Ruth Challand
1990	Carl Hill
1991	Grace Hay Brackett
1992	Helen Hauser
1993	Douglas V. Moon
1994	Melody Heltman
1995	George Jones
1996	Gary Sherrill
1997	David Nicholson
1998	Craig Fernside

ARTS LEAGUE OF HENDERSON COUNTY

1962	Grace Etheredge
1963	Meade Morris
1964	George Moyer
1965	Jan Ausing
1966	Paul Dry
1967-68	Mina Moessen
1969	John Halama
1970	Maynard Turner
1971	Robert Gerstacker

1972	Paul Sieber
1973	James Horton
1974	Joyce Blakely
1975	Frances McCall
1976	Paul Sieber
1977	Patrick Burke
1978	Andrew McBride
1979	John Gibson
1980	Peggy Horton
1981	Andrew McBride
1982-83	Karol Darling
1984	Evelyn Reed
1985	Patrick Burke
1986	John Gibson
1987	Bettye Paden
1988	Frank Ward
1989	Bettye Peden
1990-91	Barbara Enders
1992	Fran Turosak
1993-94	Sylvia Campbell
1995	Jane Franks
1996	Nancy Irving
1997	Geraldine Landriau
1998	Wil Irvine

AUDUBON SOCIETY, Elisha Mitchell Chapter

1987-90	Scott Parker
1990-91	Miles Tager
1991-95	Peggy Lasher
1995-	Janene Donovan

BELFREY PLAYERS

1988-90	Catherine Nicholson
1991-93	Hendryk S. Weeks
1994-95	Christine Folwell
1996	Sandra Jeffery
1997	Hendryk S. Weeks

BIG BROTHERS/BIG SISTERS
of Western North Carolina

1982-83	C. Lee Crisp
1983-84	James Cannon
1984-85	David Hiller
1986-87	J. D. Jackson

BIG BROTHERS/BIG SISTERS

1987-88	Grace Unruh
1988-89	Roger Gregg
1989-90	Tom McClellan
1990-91	Rob Geitner
1991-92	Steve Baldwin
1992-94	Keith Black
1994-95	Jean Frady
1995-97	Joe Brumit
1997-98	Stan Walker

BLUE RIDGE LITERACY COUNCIL, INC.

1978-81	Virginia Montgomery
1981-83	Betty Wilson
1983-85	Janet Snow
1985-87	James Breed
1987-82	Art Gobble
1992-95	Waleria Wysolovski
1995-96	David Bethea
1996-97	Evelyn Bowman

BOYS AND GIRLS CLUB OF HENDERSONVILLE

1993-96	Thomas Fazio
1997	Susan Fazio
1998	Roger Hill
1999	Jeff Miller

BOYS SCOUTS OF AMERICA,
Daniel Boone Council

This is a partial list of people who have been identified with scouting ranging from Scoutmasters to major financial supporters in Henderson County.

Einer Anderson
Lloyd Biggerstaff
Wilbert Brocconier
John Loren Brown
Bob Cheadle
Bob Cunningham
Grady and Graden Cunningham
Frank FitzSimons, Jr.
Edward Frost
M.E. Gambrell
Dan Gibson
Henry Graham
Don Henderson
Bill McGee
Bob Parrish
Cal Phipps
Frances Pless
Ted Reese
Luther Smith
Justin Smith
Emily Swaringen
Tommy Thompson
Edmond Walker
Clyde Whitlock
Minor Wilson

BUSINESS AND PROFESSIONAL WOMEN'S CLUB

1954-56	Lillian Rigby
1956-58	Marion T. Carroll
1958-59	Claris Russ
1959-60	Gladys Brown
1960-61	Jennie B. Edwards
1961-62	Ruth Last
1962-63	Mildred Reese
1963-64	Marie Brookshire

1964-65	Florence Barriers
1965-66	Virginia Arp
1966-67	Alva Orr
1967-68	Dorothy Meador
1968-70	Joan Murphy
1970-71	Lula Mae Briggs
1971-72	Laura McDonald
1972-73	Martha Nolan
1974-75	Nancy Porter
1975-76	Betsy Copolillo
1976-78	Rebecca Smith
1979-80	Betty McCallister
1980-81	Carolyn Rhodes
1981-82	Bette Crook
1982-83	Diane Masters
1983-84	Daisy Johnson
1984-86	Bessie Bright
1986-87	Daisy Johnson
1987-88	Sandra Walker
1988-89	Sue Ogle
1989-90	Mae Alexander
1990-91	Sherry King
1991-92	Casey Bragdon
1992-93	Nancy Laughter
1993-94	Dorothy Meador
1994-96	Faye Jackson-Henry
1996-97	Betty McCallister
1997-98	Angela Skerrett

CAMERA CLUB of Hendersonville
(Founded in 1972)

1979 & 2 other years	Joe Brant
1980 & 2 other years	Tom Hallowell
1981	Barbara Hallowell
Year not known	Don S.

Hoogstra

Year not known	Bob Shull
Year not known	Sam Bitner
Year not known	Charles

Bancise

1987	Dick Jacek
1988	Prentice Howe
1989-90	Peter Meyer
1991	Carlton Herman
1992-93	Marshall Ballentine
1994	Louis Garrard
1995	Charles (Bud) G. Rogers
1996	E.C. Franklin
1997	Ralph Workman

CAROLINA VILLAGE PAST PRESIDENTS:

Larry Butler, Founder
E.C. "Chuck" Snell
Robert Shull
Dan Gibson
R.E. Harmon
Clint Thompson
Jim Crafton

CHAMBER OF COMMERCE
of Greater Hendersonville

Year	Name
1922-23	F.S. Wetmur
1924	W.F. Penny
1925	Carroll P. Rogers
1926-28	Stanley Wright
1929-31	Bruce Drysdale
1931-34	Milo Strong
1935-36	E.W. Ham
1937	Thomas D. Clark
1938-39	Harry Buchanan
1940	W.B. Hodges
1941	C.M. Ogle
1942	James W. Duff
1943-44	L.Y. Biggerstaff
1945	J.D. Sloan
1946	Hugh Bowden
1947	G.C. Richardson
1948	E.A. Smythe, III
1949	J.T. Fain, Jr.
1950	W.A. Baxter
1951	L. Ben Prince
1952	Marvin Sutherland
1953	Ernest L. Roper
1954	I.E. Johnson
1955	B.M. Middleton
1956	Fred Reid
1957	Kermit Edney
1958	W.W. Martin, Jr.
1959	E.B. Quinn, Jr.
1960	Alston Broom
1961	Donald B. Keith
1962	Keith Arledge
1963	Kenneth Youngblood
1964	Bob Linder
1965	Dan Gibson
1966	Nick Semaschko
1967	James H. Gibbs
1968	Cecil Garrett
1969	Arthur V. Cooley
1970	Lawson Braswell
1971	Dr. Francis Buchanan
1972	Phillip R. Milroy
1973	William E. McGee
1974	P.T. Green, Jr.
1975	T.D. Hunter, III
1976	Thomas R. Shepherd
1977	W. Harley Stepp
1978	Duane McKibben
1979	William McKay
1980	William S. Prim
1981	Herb Young
1982	Frank FitzSimons, Jr.
1983	Dr. William Killian
1984	Sam McGuirt
1985	Henry Young
1986	Bob Ross
1987	Bill Stokes
1988-89	R.E. Harmon
1990	Dean Crisp
1991	H.L. "Jack" Ruth
1992	Tim Cosgrove
1993	Bob Ross
1994	David Reeves
1995	Bill Lapsley
1996	Albert Gooch
1997	Roger Hill

CHINA PAINTER'S CLUB OF HENDERSONVILLE

Year	Name
1973-75	Evelyn MacKintosh
1975-76	Betty Stanley
1976-78	Ruth Williams
1978-79	Betty Stanley
1979-81	Isabel Bruce
1981-83	Dot Blue
1983-85	Correne Langston
1985-86	Betty Stanley
1986-88	Alice McLennan
1988-90	Lydian Lawyer
1990-94	Betty Stanley
1994-95	Helga Ellis
1995-96	Betty Stanley
1996-98	Mary Meredith

CIVIL AIR PATROL, Hendersonville Squadron
COMMANDERS:

Year	Name
1955-66	Hugh A. Eudy
1956-58	Beverly M. Middleton
1958-64	Allen M. Foote
1964-69	John E. Laughter
1969-77	M. Prince Arnette
1977-78	Joseph Woodard
1978-81	Daniel P. Jones
1981-86	Ralph E. Brewer
1986-89	Edwin A. Connell
1989-93	William E. Davidson
1993-95	William E. Mendoza
1995-96	Edwin L. Wilson
1996-	Nicholas J. Genovese

CIVITAN CLUB of Hendersonville

Year	Name
1957	G. William Jordan (temp)
1957-59	Ray W. Ireland
1959-60	Tom Hart
1960-61	Rex D. Pearce
1961-62	Henry W. Newkirk
1962-63	Stanley G. Bachman
1963-64	William Van Tifflin
1964-65	Mead M. Morris
1965-66	Murray S. Moore
1966-67	Anson W. Devout
1967-68	Oliver L. Stevens
1968-70	J. Harold Worley
1970-71	William E. Hartman
1971-72	Harry E. Dexter
1972-73	Morris V. Boley

CIVITAN CLUB

1973-74	Harry Hurlburt
1974-75	W. Charles Snell
1975-76	John L. Clay
1976-77	William P. Ware
1977-78	R.E. Harmon
1978-79	James A. Smith
1979-80	Wayne K. Boulton
1980-81	Edward V. Luss
1981-82	Lisgar B. Eckardt
1982-83	Robert L. Piper
1983-84	Park D. Paxton
1984-85	Doley S. Bell
1985-86	J. Fred Walters
1986-87	Albert Reid
1987-88	Robert Mehrling
1988-89	Alfred W. Maner
1989-90	Robert W. Zura
1990-91	Donald F. Soula
1991-92	Richard Hood
1992-93	S. Clifton Pruett, Jr.
1993-94	Earl A. Elmquist
1994-95	John H. Bradke

COIN CLUB of Hendersonville

1963-64	Bill McEntire
1965	Harold E. McKinley
1966	Charles Leslie
1967	John Ford
	Tom Martin
	Harry Hoots
1979-85	Arthur Ericson
1986-87	Joseph W. Smolski, Jr.
1988	James M. Jones
1989-92	Joseph W. Smolski, Jr.
1993	Herschel C. Sutton
1994 to present	Joseph W. Smolski, Jr.

COMMUNITY BAND of Hendersonville

1991-94	Jerry Zink
1994-96	Hal Cook
1996-97	Hal Beam

COMMUNITY FOUNDATION
of Henderson County

1983-87	Kermit Edney
1988-89	Duane McKibben
1990-92	Hall Waddell
1993-94	Marcia Caserio
1995-96	R.E. Harmon
1997-98	Bob Sanford

COMPUTER SOCIETY, Hendersonville Area

1988	Tom Brevard
1989-90	Charles Gibbs
1991	Norman Morrison
1992	Rod Perry
1993	Jonathan H. Olds

1994-95	Tom Hooker
1996-97	David L. Strain

COUNTRY CLUB of Hendersonville

1933	Milo Strong
1934	Dr. J.G. Bennett
1935	C. Kirby Hoover
1936-38	Charles L. Grey
1939-40	W.B. Hodges
1941	James W. Duff
1942	P. Fred Sudduth
1943-45	James D. Sloan
1946	Phil M. Dietz
1947	R.L. Whitmire, Sr.
1948	Fred W. Streetman
1949-50	Clyde O. Arren
1951	E. Gus Thomas
1952	L.C. Longhurst
1953	L. Campbell Boyd
1954	Fred W. Streetman
1955	Clyde O. Arren
1956	William A. Gray
1957	Bleecker Morse
1958-59	D.C. Griffin
1960	A.F. Barber, Jr.
1961-62	R.L. Whitmire, Jr.
1963-64	John W. Holley, Sr.
1965-66	W.R. Royall, Jr.
1967-69	Kermit Edney
1970-71	Francis M. Coiner
1972-73	John Gregory
1974	I.T. Olsen
1975-76	Julius H. Purvis, Jr.
1977-78	C. Max Collins
1979-80	Joel W. Wright, Jr.
1981-82	Roderick Davis, Jr.
1983-84	Edward H. Sproat
1985-86	William E. Benoit
1987-88	William E. McGee
1989-90	T. Lee Osborne, Jr.
1991-92	William E. Penny
1993-94	Thomas R. Shepherd
1995-96	H.L. Ruth, Jr.
1997-	Dan Waddell

DAUGHTERS OF THE AMERICAN REVOLUTION, Joseph McDowell Chapter

1916-23	Miss Catherine Carson
1923-27	Mrs. Michael Schenck
1927-28	Mrs. C.R. McManaway
1928-31	Mrs. F.A. Ewbank
1931-35	Mrs. O. Meyer
1935-39	Mrs. R.P. Freeze
1939-42	Mrs. C.R. Whittaker
1942-45	Mrs. Mary C. Brinson
1945-46	Mrs. O. Meyer
1946-51	Mrs. R.F. Walters
1951-54	Mrs. Edward Bower

1954-57	Mrs. Forrest Gardener		1955-56	Homer C. Hobbs
1957-60	Mrs. Harold Chamison		1956-57	Richard S. Lee
1960-61	Mrs. Roe Remington		1957-58	William J. McShane
1961-62	Mrs. Harold Chamison		1958-59	William H. O'Cain
1962-63	Mrs. Paul P. Richmond		1959-60	Irvin T. Olsen
1963-65	Mrs. C.W. Shaffer		1960-61	John Frank McLeod, Jr.
1965-66	Mrs. Carl W. Hart		1961-62	J. Daniel Waddell
1966-69	Mrs. Ralph Harrington		1962-64	Monroe Redden, Jr.
1969-72	Mrs. Karl Nesslinger		1964-65	Robert C. Wilson
1972-74	Mrs. John C. Jeffers		1965-66	F. Richard Baker
1974-76	Mrs. R.A. Willer		1966-67	Ernest L. Roper, Jr.
1976-78	Mrs. Clint H. Holt		1967-68	Robert C. Brummett
1978-80	Mrs. C. Linwood Rhodes		1968-69	I.E. Johnson
1980-82	Mrs. Lucy G. Miller		1969-70	James E. Stephens
1982-84	Mrs. George H. Hembree		1970-71	Richard L. Davis
1984-86	Mrs. Wilbur W. Russell		1971-72	J. Fred Jackson
1986-88	Mrs. Oliver B. Glass		1972-73	Donald Michalove
1988-90	Miss Charlotte Carman		1973-74	John Frank McLeod, Jr.
1990-92	Mrs. Robert Applin		1974-77	C. Donald Justus
1992-94	Mrs. Gerald R. Lewman		1977-79	Russ Renauld
1994-96	Mrs. John F. Peavey		1979-82	Gordon C. Carpenter
1996-98	Mrs. Harold Chamison		1982-83	Clifford Laughter
			1983-84	Dennis H. Nix

DOES, BENEVOLENT AND PATRIOTIC ORDER OF No. 258

1993-94	Diane L. Grange
1995	Bette Case
1996	Sue Dale
1997	Alesia Clark

1984-85	Justin E. Etherton
1985-86	John Schnyder
1986-87	Billy M. Thompson, Jr.
1987-88	J. Frank McLeod, III
1988-89	F. Gordon Huntley
1989-90	John Boyd
1990-91	Charles S. Walrath, Jr.
1991-93	Richard LaGrange
1993-94	Tim Kelly
1994-95	Patrick E. Parkhill
1995-96	Ernest Wilson, III
1996-97	Lee Humphrey
1997	Raymond E. Snyder

ECO (Environmental and Conservation Organization)

1987-91	Mary Jo Padgett and David Malpass
1991-92	David Malpass
1993-94	Mary Jo Padgett
1994-96	Tom McCartney
1996-	Jeff Jennings

FOUR SEASONS ARTS COUNCIL

1982-83	Jim Thorndike
1983-86	Laura Davis
1986-88	Steve Webb
1988-90	Mary Jo Padgett
1990-91	Karyn Joyner
1991-92	Sam Neill
1992-93	Marilyn Bailey
1993-97	Elizabeth Black
1997-98	Nancy Bachaus

ELKS LODGE, Hendersonville #1616

1938-39	William D. Lohman
1939-40	Harry E. Buchanan
1940-41	Charles C. Oates
1941-42	Lawrence A. Blair
1942-43	J. Bratton Hughes
1943-44	Boyce A. Whitmire
1944-45	Albert W. Drake
1945-46	Arthur Shepherd
1946-47	James A. Smyth
1947-48	H. B. Bowden
1948-49	J. Steve Porter
1949-50	A.F. Barber, Jr.
1950-51	William W. Carpenter
1950-51	Leonard S. Morrow
1951-52	Raymond E. English
1952-53	Hugh R. Whisnant
1953-54	William F. Stokes
1954-55	Harry C. Williams

FRIENDS OF THE LIBRARY

1957	Ruth Chanon
1958	Ruth Chanon & Blanche Marsh
1959	General Ray W. Ireland
1960	Wilbur T. Smith
1961	Ralph Harrington
1962	Herbert E. Holt
1963	Rex D. Pearce
1964	William A. Hiles

FRIENDS OF THE LIBRARY, cont.

1965	W. Timothy Durrett
1966	Murray S. Moore
1967	William E. Hartman
1968	O.A. Ohmann
1969	Donald H. Sunderlin
1970-71	Clarence M. King
1972-73	Harry E. Hurlburt
1974-75	Raymond W. Heffron
1976	R. Douglas Esten
1977-78	Norman E. Olson
1979	Howard E. Gorton
1980-81	Betty Thomson
1982	Dorothy O'Hara
1983-84	Gertrude Badger
1985-86	Robert Mowery
1987-88	Larry Kenyon
1989-90	Elizabeth Black
1991-92	Frederic M. Krecker
1993-94	Blanche Coffey
1995	Wyn Hardy
	& Blanche Wayboer
1996-97	Maxine M. Krecker

GARDEN CLUB of Hendersonville

1960-61	Mrs. A.B. Chidester
1961-62	Mrs. W.A. Keith, Jr.
1962-63	Mrs. G.V. King
1963-64	Mrs. L.H. Hindsey
1964-65	Mrs. W.L. Butler
1965	Mrs. G.E. Martin
1965-67	Mrs. R.E. Williams
1967-69	Mrs. J.E. Barber
1969-71	Mrs. J.M. Ross
1971-73	Mrs. J.F. Runck
1973-75	Mrs. H.E. Dennison
1975-77	Mrs. C.L. Eigelbach
1977-78	Mrs. E.F. Briggs
1978-79	Mrs. A.L. Murray
1979-82	Mrs. G.A. Potter
1982-85	Mrs. E.F. Briggs
1985-87	Mrs. H. E. Brown
1987-89	Mrs. D.N. Hale
1989-91	Mrs. B. Loveless
1991-93	Mrs. C. Bogert
1993-95	Mrs. W. R. Christy
1995-97	Mrs. F. Bulman
1997-99	Mrs. E. Wilson

GARDEN CLUB, Old Kanuga

1974-75	Lillian Erlandsen
1975-76	Roberta Ashley
1976-77	Mary Hensel
1977-78	Judith Swanson
1978-79	Evelyn Reed
1979-80	Helen McKee
1980-81	Marilyn Wylie
1981-83	Margaret Foster

1983-85	Jeanne Grundies
1985-86	Mary Brodie
1986-88	Margaret Robinson
1988-89	Dottie Ritter
1989-90	Ruth Piland
1990-92	Gertrude Badger
1992-93	Virginia Cronkhite
1993-95	Mary Alice Freeman
1995-96	Mary Walters
1996-98	Margaret Robinson

GEM AND MINERAL SOCIETY, Henderson County

1978-79	Grant Kreinberg
1980-81	Margaret L. Johnson
1982-83	Harry Brooke
1984-85	Mary Conner
1986	Harry Brooke
1987	Harold J. Eadie
1988	Alice Simone
1989-90	Chuck Cochran
1991-92	Jack Bednarek
1993-94	Margaret Gilbert
1995-96	Gerald Kreussling
1997-	Lloyd Longacre

GENEALOGICAL AND HISTORICAL SOCIETY, Henderson County

1983-89	George A. Jones
1990-92	Elsie Drake Goepfert
1993-97	Evelyn Masden Jones

GIRL SCOUTS

A Regional Pisgah Girl Scout Council was responsible for supervising the activities of the many Girl Scout troops spread across Western North Carolina. Years ago, area leaders were called "Neighborhood Chairmen." Today they are known as "Service Unit Managers." The present Service Unit Managers is Mrs. Steve (Jean) Smith. Others active include:

Mrs. Robert Toubert
Mrs. William Lowry
Mrs. Charles Todd

In the past, the following were active:

Mrs. T.D. Clark
Mrs. Hugh Bowden
Mrs. Ivan Waller
Mrs. James Ward
Mrs. Melvin Lane

Pisgah Board Members have included:

Mrs. Phil Milroy
Mrs. L.L. Oyster
Mrs. H.T. "Luke" Rindal
Mrs. Jody Barber, who served as
    chairman (succeeded by
    Mrs. Billy Graham)

HENDERSONVILLE CHORALE

1974-75	Harold Allison
1976-77	Jack Gibson
1978-79	Pat Duvall
1980-81	Ken Gilbert
1982-83	Hollis Bert and Marge Little
1983-84	Don Stall
1985	Hall Halbedel
1986	Bill McKenny
1987	Paul Seaman
1987-88	D. Debaugh
1989 to present	Marion Tellefsen

HOMEBUILDER'S ASSOCIATION
of Hendersonville

1981	Donald Justus, Sr.
1982	Donald Justus, Jr.
1983	Ken W. Wilkie
1984	D.O. Thompson, Jr.
1985	Fred Mintz
1986	Jody Beal
1987	Ken R. Wilkie
1988	Chuck Cordray
1989	Ray Laney
1990	Ken Packard
1991	George Bond
1992	Evelyn Barker
1993	Ken W. Wilkie
1994	Ernie Ball
1995	Tom Beck
1996	Tedd Pearce
1997	Ken R. Wilkie

HOSPICE, Four Seasons

1980	Jean Moulthrop
1981-82	Richard Randolph
1983	Roger Congdon
1984-86	Howard Schoenfeldt
1987-88	Bettye Splittorff
1989	Alden Small
1990	Leslie Lucas
1991-92	Hank Young
1993-95	Lewis Lees
1996	Brad Rogers
1997	Jeff Ward

INTERFAITH ASSISTANCE MINISTRY

1983	Rev. Eugenia Dowdeswell
1984	Rev. Eugenia owdeswell and Margaret Milroy
1985-86	Margaret Milroy
1987	Donald Hoogstra
1988	Robert Ellis
1989-90	Rev. Eugenia Dowdeswell
1991	William Sanders
1992	William Sanders and Amanda Woodard
1993	Charles McCombs

1994	A. William Perry
1995	Rev. David Kelly
1996	Kenneth "Skip" Fendley
1997	Charles H. Tindal

JAYCEES of Hendersonville

In the early years of the Chamber of Commerce, there was an organization known as "Young Members of the Chamber" with their own officers, and agenda. In 1956, the nationally known JAYCEES formed a chapter in Hendersonville.

1956	Hesterly "Hess" Gibbs
1957	P.T. "Pete" Green
1958-59	Unknown
1960	Jim Stephens
1961	Hershel Buchanan
1962-64	Unknown
1965	Claude Drake
1966	Bob Murphy
1967	John Fox

JAYCEE Distinguished Service Award:

1955	Kermit Edney
1956	Dan Gibson

Other winners are unknown.
Active in the early years were:
J.B. Maxwell
Walter Bakes
Donald Griffin
Dr. Robert Vines
Sam Hunt
Monroe Redden, Jr.
J. Harold Worley
The JAYCEE organization was reactived in 1984.

1985-86	Brenda Sparks
1986-87	Mark Higdon
1987-88	Thomas F. Ramer
1988-89	Lorie Burgess
1989-90	Lawrence Pittman
1990-91	Rhonda J. Townsend
1991-92	David Christopher
1992-93	Victor Jennings and Thomas I. McCabe
1994-95	Karen Collins

JUNIOR WELFARE CLUB

1931-33	Mrs. E.A. Smyth, III
1933-35	Mrs. Frank Bell (Mrs. Herndon Alexander)
1935-37	Mrs. G.C. Richardson
1937-38	Mrs. W.B. Hodges
1938-40	Mrs. H.E. Buchanan
1940-42	Mrs. Gretchen Poole (Mrs. O. Y. Brownlee, Jr.)
1942-43	Mrs. William Freeze
1943-45	Mrs. D.I. C.King
1945-46	Mrs. James Smyth
1946-47	Mrs. Malcom Stonham
1947-49	Mrs. J.E. Barber

JUNIOR WELFARE CLUB

1949-50	Mrs. J. D. Sloan
1950-52	Mrs. Dubose McDowell
1952-54	Mrs. Martha Shepherd
1954-55	Mrs. R. A. Porter
1955-56	Mrs. Marriotte Stewart
1956-57	Mrs. William Brackett
1957-58	Mrs. O.W. Taylor
1958-60	Mrs. R.E. Brown
1960-62	Mrs. Wiltshire Griffith, Jr.
1962-63	Mrs. Charles Rouse
1963-65	Mrs. Charles Porter
1965-67	Mrs. William Francis, Jr.
1967-69	Mrs. Claude Beatty
1969-70	Mrs. Marion Ross
1970-72	Mrs. John Kievit
1972-74	Mrs. Robert Anderson
1974-76	Mrs. T.D. Hunter, III
1976-77	Mrs. Larry Blair
1977-78	Mrs. C.O. Williams
1978-79	Miss Lissa Wilkins
1979-80	Mrs. Sue Shetterly
1980-81	Mrs. Jeff Egolf
1981-82	Mrs. Deborah Kirkman
1982-83	Mrs. Steve Johnson
1983-84	Mrs. Dan Barber
1984-85	Mrs. Mike Jones
1985-86	Mrs. Jay Thorndike
1986-87	Mrs. Chip Gould
1987-88	Mrs. Ron Carland
1988-89	Mrs. Randy Terry
1989-90	Mrs. Turner Rouse
1990-92	Miss Karen Yagerhofer
1992-93	Mrs. Chuck Freeman
1993-94	Mrs. David Katz
1994-95	Mrs. Michael Thompson
1995-96	Mrs. Gary Faulkner
1996-97	Mrs. Danny Williams
1997-98	Mrs. Rutledge Livingston

JUNIOR WOMEN'S CLUB

Feb. 1939 - May 1939	Mrs. C.F. Kichline
May 1939 - Oct. 1941	Mrs. A.J. Redden
Oct. 1941 - Oct. 1942	Mrs. Ray Yeoman
Oct. 1942 - Oct. 1944	Mrs. F.V. Hunter
Oct. 1944 - Oct. 1945	Mrs. J.O. Bell
Oct. 1945 - Oct. 1946	Mrs. W.A. Baxter
Oct. 1946 - June 1948	Mrs. H.B. Bowden
June 1948 - Apr. 1949	Mrs. E.H. King
May 1949 - June 1949	Mrs. S.P. Garren
June 1949 -1950	Mrs. S.E. Owens,Jr.
June 1950 -1951	Mrs. J.G. Crowell
June 1951- 1952	Mrs. J.B. Kuykendall
June 1952- 1953	Mrs. J.M. Good, Jr.
June 1953-Sept. 1953	Mrs. Richard Engles
Sept.1983 - May 1954	Mrs. Gary Harthcock
June 1954 - May 1955	Mrs. William Waggoner
June 1955 - May 1956	Mrs. R.H. Lampley

June 1956 - May 1957	Mrs. Francis M. Coiner
June 1957 - May 1958	Mrs. William B. Wilson, Jr.
June 1958 - May 1959	Mrs. Zeb V. Kilpatrick, Jr.
June 1959 -Dec. 1960	Mrs. Robert L. Whitmire, Jr.
1961	Mrs. Aiken Pace
1962	Mrs. Jules Purvis
1963	Mrs. William Ponder
1964	Mrs. Claude Goswick, Jr.
1965	Mrs. Arthur Gebhardt
1966	Mrs. Harry Thorpe
1967	Mrs. John C. Kievit
1968	Mrs. G. Bruce Woods
1969	Mrs. Dan Gibson
Jan.- May 1970	Mrs. Curtis Bollar
June - Dec.1970	Mrs. Jimmy Hinson
1971	Mrs. Don Norman
1972	Mrs. James Crafton
1973	Mrs. Boyce Orr
1974	Mrs. Richard Fravel
1975	Mrs. James Coleman
1976	Mrs. Arthur Crocker
1977	Mrs. Arnold Sheldon
1978	Mrs. Joe Dixon
1979	Mrs. James Volk
1980	Mrs. Zorro Guice
1981	Mrs. Walter Ivkovich
1982	Mrs. Berend Van Der Meer
1983	Mrs. Robert Gussman
1984	Mrs. Frank McGlashan
1985	Ms. Linda Moxley
1986-87	Mrs. Alfredo Calvo
1988	Mrs. John Ogletree
1989	Mrs. Alan Ward
1990	Mrs. Carl Fisher
1991	Mrs. Sidney Williams
1992	Mrs. James Welter
1993	Mrs. Rod Carter
1994	Mrs. Gray Stallworth
1995	Mrs. Charles Mackin
1996	Mrs. James Horwitz
1997	Mrs. Michael Cooper

KIWANIS CLUB of Hendersonville

1921	J. Mack Rhodes
1922	William Kirk
1923	Stanley Wright
1924	P.L. Wright
1925	Bruce Drysdale
1926	J.C. Sales
1927	A.W. Honeycutt1
1928	I.C. Arledge
1929	Noah Hollowell
1930	J. Allen Rhodes
1931	Joseph Siever
1932	J.E. Shipman
1933	A.F. Barber, Sr.
1934	O.Y. Brownlee
1935	Thomas Franks

1936	C.M. Ogle		1995	Doug Dunlap
1937	F.M. Waters, Sr.		1996	Mike Orr
1938	J.G. Bennett		1997	Don Shoemaker
1939	George Flanagan			
1940	E.A. Smyth, III		**KIWANIS CLUB, Golden K**	
1941	T.D. Clark		1984-85	Earl Kelly
1942	Roy Bennett		1985-86	Les Gruol
1943	P.F. Sudduth		1986-87	Harvey Goehring, Jr.
1944	Edward Sutherland		1987-88	Lew Steinbach
1945	Bill Baxter		1988-89	Art Harrington
1946	J.D. Sloan		1989-90	Norm Morrison
1947	E.M. Boys		1990-91	Ted Willsey
1948	M.E. Gambell		1991-92	George McGregor
1949	John L. Brown		1992-93	Alex Briber
1950	Earl Dolbee		1993-94	Winfield McGrath
1951	Truman Westmoreland		1994-95	A. William Perry
1952	L.B. Prince		1995-96	Robert Bose
1953	Dan Barber, Jr.		1996-97	Bryce MacDonald
1954	Jimmy Fain			
1955	Kermit Edney		**KIWANIS CLUB, Land o' Sky**	
1956	F.O. Trotter		1975-76	Don Surles
1957	Buddy Richardson		1976-77	Hillary Collins
1958	Bob Whitmire, Jr.		1977-78	John Brookshire
1959	Glenn Nelson		1978-79	Charles Byrd
1960	Frank Hoyle, Jr.		1979-81	David Nicholson
1961	Hugh Lockaby		1981-82	Jeff Linder
1962	Dwight Bennett		1982-83	Malvern West
1963	Bill Lampley		1983-84	Bob Jesseau
1964	J. Loren Brown		1984-85	Craig Richardson
1965	Morris Kaplan		1985-86	Robert Thomas
1966	Buck Buchanan		1986-87	Rick Scronce
1967	Jim McDuffie		1987-88	Mark Morgan
1968	Bob Drake		1988-90	Russell Burrell
1969	W.D. Miller		1990-91	Trish Hughes
1970	O.B. Crowell		1991-92	Bob Jesseau
1971	Frank FitzSimons		1992-94	Dale Buehler
1972	Harley Blackwell		1994-96	John Woodman
1973	Bill Penny		1996-97	Cathy McKay
1974	Hardy Caldwell		1997-98	Bobbi Kornfeld
1975	Robert Fox			
1976	Harold McLaughlin			
1977	Norris Parker		**KNIGHTS OF COLUMBUS**	
1978	Laurie McKinna			
1979	Tom Ledbetter		1978	George Philipp
1980	Dick Baker		1979-80	Gene Schuler
1981	Art Brubaker		1980-81	Al Overgaard
1982	Bill Orr		1981-83	Jim Acker
1983	David Bethea		1983-84	Larry Carter
1984	Don Holder		1984-86	Ron Spanbauer
1985	Tom Wilson		1986-87	Henry Kovacs
1986	Tom Adcox		1987-88	Tony Gambone
1987	Chat Jones		1988-89	Mike Westlake
1988	Don Jones		**KNIGHTS OF COLUMBUS, cont.**	
1989	Richard Rhodes		1989-90	Tom Genaw
1990	Doug Moon		1990-92	Bill Carter
1991	J. Ray Bennett		1992-93	Chris Coleman
1992	J. Mac Drake		1993-94	Gene McFadden
1993	John Lampley		1994-96	Denis DeBan
1994	Billy Carden		1996 to Present Joel Carter	

LA LECHE ASSOCIATION
1980-82	Jan Garner
	and Mary Kevin Loper
1983-85	Teresa Knight
1985-88	Lorraine Norwood
1987-88	Susan Smith
1988-present	Mary Caroline Gaylord
1993-97	Kristi Combs
1995-present	Beth Ann Lehr

LEAGUE OF WOMEN VOTERS
1993-95	Marian Huffman
1995-97	Rebecca Sigmon
	and Marcie Grady

Others who served as president in the past:
Frances Sherman
Eleanor Cosgrove
Rita Hopkins
Margaret Milroy
Sally Godehn
Kathy Baluha
Crystal Smith
Renee Kumor
Barbara Volk
Mercedes Tocon
Linda Hawk Rodney
Marian Lowry
Grace Poli

LIONS CLUB of Hendersonville
1938-39	Lee Moose
1939-40	Everett Mitchell
1940-41	Roy Keith
1941-42	Don Barber
1942-43	Roy Cate
1943-44	Ben Brown
1944-45	Charlie Allen
1945-46	Boyce Whitmire
1946-47	Ralph Martin
1947-48	John Sinclair
1948-49	Norris Leopard
1949-50	Kenneth Skaggs
1950-51	Homer Hobbs
1951-52	Francis Drake
1952-53	Roy Johnson
1953-54	Robert Starnes
1954-55	Jody E. Barber
1955-56	John H. Todd
1956-57	Irvin T. Olson
1957-58	Earl D. Higdon
1958-59	Brownlow Merrill
1959-60	William S. Farrell
1960-61	Grover Peace
1961-62	Daniel C. Gibson
1962-63	Robert Linder
1963-64	William N. Ponder
1964-65	James C. Dishner
1965-66	Arthur Cooley
1966-67	Jim Lenz
1967-68	Ted Reese
1968-69	William E. McGee
1969-70	Joe E. Orr
1970-71	George Gretz
1971-72	Jim Mitchell
1972-73	Ed Walker
1973-74	Harry L. Horton
1974-75	Ron Swartzel
1975-76	J.L. Mashburn
1976-77	George Essig
1977-78	Hank Gregg
1978-79	Ray Farmer
1979-80	Ron McCallister
1980-81	Norman Mashburn
1981-82	Lee Thomas
1982-83	John Shepherd
1983-84	Bill Barnwell
1984-85	Jim Yarbrough
1985-86	Dr. W.A. Howe
1986-87	Frank Costerisan
1987-88	Steve Norwood
1988-89	Tommy Thompson
1989-90	David Blackley
1990-91	George Waechter
1991-92	Dick Bowen
1992-93	Verlon Pompey
1993-94	Steve Greene
1994-95	Phillip Walker
1995-96	Ray West
1996-97	Bob Hefner
1997-98	Sid Harbison

LIONS CLUB, Daybreak
1985-87	Steve Shepherd
1987-88	James L. Davis
1988-89	Gary Taylor
1989-90	Clarence Elliott
1990-91	John M. Shepherd
1991-92	Charles F. Byrd
1992-93	Dr. John Howard
1993-94	Robert Eklund
1994-95	John Frier
1995-96	Larry Van Der Vliet
1996-97	Tom Bullard
1997-98	Larry Pace, Sr.

LIONS CLUB, Etowah
1954-55	Claude Laughter
1955-56	Robert B. Childs
1956-57	Robert E. Greer
1957-58	Ray E. Parkinson
1958-59	Harry D. Woodson
1959-60	M.E. Allison
1960-61	Plato E. Reece
1961-62	Shelby N. Robinson
1962-63	H. Morgan
1963-64	Neil M. Greer
1964-65	Jesse H. Snyder
1965-66	John P. Ramsey
1966-67	Guy C. Morgan

1967-68	Gordon Hollingsworth
1968-69	Rankin R. Allison
1969-70	Grady L. Cox
1970-71	Charlie M. Morgan
1971-72	Donald A. Bradley
1972-73	Cecil R. Young
1973-74	Kenneth Calhoun
1974-75	Manley Johnson
1975-76	Charlie Morgan, Jr.
1976-77	Jerry G. Cox
1977-78	Charlie Morgan, Sr.
1978-79	Verne B. Crisp
1979-80	David Childers
1980-81	Richard W. Gardner
1981-82	Manley Johnson
1982-83	Ronald Davis
1983-84	Leon Lyda
1984-85	Virgle J. McClure
1985-86	Cecil Morgan
1986-87	Perry Davis
1987-88	Richard W. Gardner
1988-89	Rufus E. Pipes
1989-90	William S. Newsom, III
1990-91	Kenneth Raymond
1991-92	Plato Reece
1992-93	Jerry Cox
1993-94	D.C. Cantrell
1994-95	Virgle McClure
1995-96	Ed Toporzycki
1996-97	Neal Grissom

LIONS CLUB, Etowah Braille Service
No President - Chairman

1976	Gerry Warren

Other Active Leaders:
- Mrs. Gertrude Young
- Cecil Young
- Bill Maxwell
- Ron Davis
- David Childers
- Les Warren

LITTLE THEATRE of Hendersonville
A Little Theatre was first organized in Hendersonville in 1949. Robroy Farquhar was operating the Lake Summit Playhouse in the summer months, and agreed to direct winter performances of a Little Theatre. At the start of the second year, Farquhar accepted a generous offer in theatre work in Florida, and the plays in 1950 were directed by Ernie Frankel. (See an earlier chapter in this book).

1949-50	Jimmie Fain

Other active members were:
- Jo Kuykendall, Producer
- Lochran Saltz, Set Designer
- Mary Salley, Stage Manager
- Martha Shepherd, Prop Manager

When Ernie and Louise Frankel moved to California, the Little Theatre became inactive for a number of years.

1966-67	Ken Johnson
1967-68	Mrs. William Lampley
1968-69	Sam Story
1969-70	Jan Clausing
1970-71	R. Andrew Davis
1971-72	Hoyle Adams
1972-73	Ron Mathewson
1973-74	Marilyn Bovee
1974-75	Bill Hodge
1975-76	Vincent Colon
1976-77	Leo Muldoon
1977-78	Ellen Evans
1978-80	John Herman
1980-81	Agnes Kamerick
1981-82	Pat Christianson
1982-83	Jeannice Russell
1983-84	James Coleman
1984-86	Marilyn Speed
1986-88	Tom Asbury
1988-90	Jack Willis
1990-92	Len Raftree
1992-94	Marilyn Speed
1994-96	Beverly French
1996-98	Linda Brookes

MAINSTAY of Hendersonville

1985-88	Naoma Dean
1989-90	Renee Kumor
1991-92	Charlotte Buller
1993-94	Walter Wikstrom
1995-96	Deborah Kirkman
1997-98	Kaye Youngblood

MERCHANTS ASSOCIATION of Hendersonville
Prior to 1972, the Merchants Group was a Division of the Hendersonville Chamber of Commerce. The separate Association was formed to coordinate the Central Business District Transformation.

1972	D.B. Keith
1973	Kermit Edney
1974	Jody E. Barber
1975	James Taylor
1976	H.D. McAllister
1977	John Meadows
1978	D.B. Keith
1979	William McGee
1980	John Harris
1981	Hall Waddell
1982	Joyce McCrary
1983	David O. Roberts
1984	Garley Riggs
1985	Robbie Young
1986	Frosty Sinclair
1987	Bette Carter

MERCHANTS ASSOCIATION of Hendersonville Cont.

1988	Arthur Rubin
1989	Danny Williams
1990	John Boyd
1991	Don Holder
1992	Myra Wood
1993	William R. Reese
1994	Carolyn Swanner
1995-96	Doris Ecklund
1997	Vicki Brittain

MINISTRY SEVEN RESCUE MISSION directors

July 1982 - Feb. 1986	Mr. George Cox
Feb. 1986 - May 1986	Mrs. Anne Cox
May 1986 - Dec. 1987	Mr. Bradford Heil
Nov. 1987 - Jan. 1988	Mr. Kenzie Driggers
Jan. 1988 - Mar. 1988	Mr. Joe Boerman
Mar. 1988 - Sept.1989	Mr. Stanley Dixon
Sept. 1989 - Jan. 1990	Mr. Joe Boerman
Jan. 1990 - Feb. 1991	Mr. Kenzie Driggers
Feb. 1991 - Mar. 1991	Rev. John Hilbert
Mar. 1991 - June 1992	Rev. Jim Faust
June 1992 - Dec. 1995	Rev. Bill Valentine
Dec. 1995 - Present	Rev. Anthony McMinn

MICHIGAN CLUB of Hendersonville

1983-86	Rev. Floyd Porter
1986-87	Robert Miller
1987-89	Althea Brundza
1989-91	Inman "Duke" Burnham
1991-93	Peg Hunt
1993-95	Allen C. Smith
1995-	Thomas Hanson

OPPORTUNITY HOUSE

1958-59	Oscar Heffner
1959	Ralph Canfield
1960-61	Grace Etheridge
1962	Frances Riley
1963	Noah Hollowell
1964	Tim Durrett
1965	Lois Hartman
1966-67	Robert Yerkes
1968	Fred Siggelkow
1969	John Boyd
1970-71	Chan Harbour
1972	Robert Karlson
1973	Harold Reeve and Joseph Schatz
1974	John Liddie
1975	Irving Wade and Edward Luss
1976-77	Harold Carrick
1978-79	L. Hinderleiter
1980-81	Arthur Cree
1982-83	Fr. Nesserschmidt
1984	Harold Carrick
1985-86	Art Harrington

1987	George McGregor
1988	John Thompson
1989-90	Gladys Gableman
1991-92	Lew Steinbach
1993-94	Fred Krecker
1995-96	Bill Reed
1996-97	Alan Weess

ORGANISTS, American Guild of Hendersonville

1954-55	Joseph Privette
1955-57	Harold M. Frantz
1957-59	Walter M. Ball
1959-61	Clair F. Hardenstine
1961-64	May Jo Gray
1964-66	Paul H. Bates
1966-69	Mrs. William J. Peeke
1969-71	Lewis J. Fisher
1971-73	Dr. Nelson F. Adams
1973-75	Dr. Robert P. Keener
1975-76	Lawrence M. Skinner
1976-78	Dr. Schuyler Robinson
1978-80	Dr. Marilyn Keiser
1980-82	William H. Smyth
1982-84	Beverly A. Ward
1984-86	Stephen L. Allen
1986-88	Charlie W. Steele
1988-90	David L. Foster
1990-92	Beverly A. Ward
1992-93	Susan Hembree Wilson
1993-95	Robert E. Lamb
1995-97	Michael S. Brannon
1997-	Marilyn S. Munson

PARDEE MEMORIAL HOSPITAL (Patton Memorial)

1953-54	C.W. Cunningham
1954-58	Lloyd Biggerstaff
1958-63	George S. Johnston
1963-69	I.T. Olsen
1969-85	George F. Stowell
1985-87	Charles Waters
1987-89	Kermit Edney
1989-90	Charles Waters
1990-94	Don Holder
1994-96	Mary Ruth Smith
1996-	Mark White

PILOT CLUB

1967-68	Dot Payseur
1968-69	Mary Collins
1969-70	Lula Mae Briggs
1970-71	Carolyn Hawkins
1971-72	Margaret Staton
1972-73	Mary Lamb
1973-74	Evelyn Alexander
1974-75	Marie Muntley
1975-76	Sylvia Lee Waters
1976-77	Loretta Kilpatrick

1977-78	Carolyn Hawkins
1978-79	Beulah Chandler
1979-80	Sandra Fowler
1980-81	Cathy Henderson
1981-82	Peggy Mahaffey
1982	Trudy Bennett
1983	Margaret Staton
1983-84	Sandra Fowler
1984-85	Dixie Nix
1985-86	Cathy Henderson
1986-87	Loretta Kilpatrick
1987-88	Beulah Chandler
1988-89	Joni Wall
1989-90	Kay Duggnins
1990-91	Pat Sentell
1991-92	Doris Hammond
1992-93	Cathy Henderson
1993-94	Nancy Harrelson
1994-95	Beulah Chandler
1995-96	Sandy Fowler
1996-97	Inez Gasperson
1997-98	Carolyn Applin

DEMOCRATIC PARTY of Henderson County

1928-29	E.W. Ewbank
1930-45	Monroe M. Redden, Sr.
1946-51	L. Ben Prince
1952-55	Robert L. Whitmire, Jr.
1956-63	Arthur J. Redden
1964-67	Judge O.B. Crowell
1968-71	Robert Livingstone
1972-75	Harley Stepp
1976-77	Ed Groce
1978-81	Sam Neill
1982-83	Buddy Massagee, Jr.
1984-87	Mae Alexander
1988	Wick Haynes
1989-93	Jim Toms
1994-95	Kathleen Carland
1996-97	Jon Parce

REPUBLICAN PARTY of Henderson County

1928-29	Dr. W.R. Kirk
1930-31	Lawrence J. Pace
1932-33	Brownlow Jackson
1934-37	Frank Waldrop
1938-47	James J. Pace
1948-49	Lee Staton
1950-51	J. Willis Bayne
1952-53	C.W. Cunningham
1954-58	Richard C. Clark
1958-62	Robert R. Freeman
1962-67	Larry Justus
1967-71	W.B.W. Howe
1971-73	Tom Saltz
1973-74	Jim Mayfield
1974-75	Sophie Davis
1975-77	Fred Mason

1977-83	Harold Hill
1983-87	Vince Colan
1987-91	Jere Hyder
1991-95	Russell Burrell
1995-97	Kathy Willis
1997	Bobby Crisp

PROFESSIONAL SECRETARIES,
Land of Sky Chapter

1946-47	Constance Kidd
1947-48	Katherine Thompson
1948-49	Mary Lou Kirby
1949-50	Celeste Brookshier
1950-51	Cornelie Farrell
1951-52	Margaret Simmons
1952-65	Unknown
1966-68	Marie Eggert CPS
1968-70	Glorian Cordell
1970-72	Bernice C. Fowler
1972-74	Johnsie Waddell
1974-77	Glorian Cordell
1977-78	Shirley Dobbs CPS
1978-81	Bernice C. Fowler
1981-83	Martha Capps
1983-84	Carolyn Norvell
1984-86	Morna Moore
1986-88	Sandra Fowler CPS
1988-91	Bernice C. Fowler
1991-94	Linda Sledzewski CPS
1994-96	Mary Ann Carter CPS
1996-98	Carol Wolf CPS

QUARTER CENTURY WIRELESS ASSOCIA-
TION, INC. (QCWC)

1974-75	Harry Mills (K4HU)
1976	Doc Appleton (K4RR)
1977	John Wyman (K4HXZ)
1978	Bob David (W4YK)
1979	Bill Symons (K4YK)
1980	Tony Landry (W4MJG)
1981	John Frey (W3ESU)
1982	Hank Poole (K4MH)
1983	John McLane (K4FTB)
1984	Walt Steiges (W1HTL)
1985	Ed Cushing (W4GW)
1986	Bob Boaz (W1ACC)
1987	Duke Knief (W2YTO)
1988	Tom Kelly (K4IRD)
1989	Bob David (W4YK)
	Harold Johnson (W4ZCB)
1990	Harold Johnson (W4ZCB)
1991	Lee Cookman (K2ACE)
1992	Herm Fabert (W9FHW)
1993	Joe Gault (W4WZ)
1994	Charlie Jones (W1HVA)
	Walt Steiges (W4ZCB)
1995	Harold Johnson (W4ZCB)
1996	Harold Johnson (W4ZCB)
1997	Lloyd Kidwell (W1BHY)

ROTARY CLUB of Hendersonville

Year	Name
1927	D.C. Weeks
1928	J.R. Sandifer
1929	F.S. Justus
1930	M.W. Strong
1931	R.L. Whitmire
1932	A.V. Edward
1933	H.B. Kelly
1934	E. Ham
1935	W.O. Allen
1936	J.H. Flanagan
1937	A.S. Browning, Jr.
1938	J.P. Burke
1939	W.P. Andrews
1940	J.S. Porter
1941	J.C. Coston
1942	B.B. Massagee
1943	H.E. Katzenmoyer
1944	L.Y. Biggerstaff
1945	G.R. Fain
1946	H.B. Bowen
1947	F.L. FitzSimons, Sr.
1948	W.M. Shepherd
1949	H.R. Whisnant
1950	A.F. Barber, Jr.
1951	T.D. Hunter, Jr.
1952	F.S. Crumbley
1953	M.W. Walker
1954	F.W. Ewbank
1955	H.W. Heilig
1956	W.W. Martin, Jr.
1957	F.W. Steetman
1958	J.L. Moore
1959	C.W. Kuydendall
1960	K.E. Cosgrove
1961	J.E. Crowell
1962	E.B. Quinn, Jr.
1963	R.L. Gaffney
1964	N. Semashko, Jr.
1965	M.M. Goss
1966	W.E. Brackett
1967	H.A. Eudy
1968	S.C. Falvo
1969	E.L. Feagin, Jr.
1970	S.F. Padgett
1971	W.F. Stokes
1972	E.G. Harthcock
1973	H.D. Randall
1974	W.D. Killian
1975	W.T. Jobe
1976	A.M. Moreno
1977	W.D. Bacon
1978	H.G. Hutton
1979	J.W. Bartlett
1980	F.H. Niehoff, Jr.
1981	G.F. Bond
1982	H.C. Young
1983	W.F. Stokes
1984	R.R. Ross
1985	E.C. Brisley
1986	W.G. Lapsley
1987	R.D. Ward
1988	C.D. Crisp
1989	D.J. Godehn, Sr.
1990	A.S. Gooch, Jr.
1991	J.R. Crafton
1992	J.C. McCormick
1993	D.G. Cooper
1994	S.R. Johnson
1995	John Shiery
1996	Hoyle Adams
1997	Barry Edwards
1998	Brian Parsons

SALVATION ARMY

Years	Name
1965-67	Capt. and Mrs. Harry Foden
1967-74	Capt. and Mrs. Carl Tilley
1974-75	Capt. and Mrs. Charles Feld
1975-76	Capt. and Mrs. Leonard Whitaker
1976-80	Lt. and Mrs. Dalton Cunningham
1980-81	Maj. and Mrs. A. C. Sigmon
1981-83	Maj. and Mrs. Arnold Williford
1983-85	Lt. and Mrs. R. C. Fleeman
1985-88	Lt. and Mrs. Bruce Stefanik
1989-92	Capt. and Mrs. Mike Harmon
1992-96	Lt. and Mrs. Kenneth Morris
1996-	Capt. and Mrs. Siegfried Hackbarth

SERTOMA CLUB

Years	Name
1961-62	Thomas V. White
1962-63	Chris Goodwin
1963-64	James E. Stephens
1964-65	Gene Wilson
1965-66	Leonard Baker and Glen Melton
1966-67	Ted Bennel
1967-68	Thomas L. Lyda
1968-69	Ed Todd
1969-70	Edwin R. Groce
1970-71	Dan S. Jones
1971-72	Tom Grant
1972-73	Ed Todd
1973-74	Fred McLeod
1974-75	James A. Wortman
1975-76	Joseph P. Williams
1976-77	Donald C. Griffin
1977-78	J. B. Osteen
1978-79	Ed Deese
1979-80	James A. Wortman
1980-81	Mac Drake
1981-82	Ben Hall
1982-83	John Murdock
1983-84	Thomas L. Lyda
1984-85	Harry Rogers
1985-86	Grayson McCall
1986-88	Ed Deese
1988-91	John Murdock
1991-93	Norman J. Greig

1993-95	Richard Schuler
1995-98	Ed Deese

SIERRA CLUB

1990-97	Ken Woodward

SONG O' SKY CHORUS

1974-76	Mary Clark
1976-77	Lois Jobes
1977-79	Alice Greene
1979-80	Lois Jobes
1980-82	Ann Lawrance
1982-83	Janet Clevenger
1983-84	Lee Hines
1984-86	Betty Jean Parham
1986-87	Nancy Tyler
1987-88	Debbie Justice
1988-89	Ann Lawrance
1989-90	Astrid Johnson
1990-92	Ann Herman
1992-93	Margaret Tickle
1993-96	Ann Herman
1996-97	June Owen
1997-98	Ann Herman

SOROPTIMIST CLUB

1956-57	Nina Ruberstein
1957-58	Naomi Hartnett
1958-59	Alvine McCormick
1959-60	Vada B. Holland
1960-61	Myrtle J. Barnette
1961-63	Gladys Brown
1963-65	Bernice Cameron
1965-67	Camille Sentelle
1967-69	Lex McCarson
1969-70	Lucy Miller
1970-71	Charlotte Towers
1971-72	Grace Gaillard
1972-74	Margaret Schaffer
1974-76	Naomi Hartnett
1976-77	Margie Cantrell
1977-78	Kay Heyn
1978-79	Kay Heyn and Jennie McCullough
1979-81	Emily Davis
1981-82	Grace Hay
1982-84	Jane Mayson
1984-86	Grace Hay Brackett
1986-87	Jeanette Turner
1987-88	Jane Mayson
1988-90	Lynne Meyer
1990-92	Susanne Rollins
1992-94	Sharon Olin
1994-96	Kimberly Haddock
1996-98	Lynne Meyer

SQUARE DANCE CLUB, Southern Lights

1988-89	Robert Clagge
1989-90	Laurabeth "Rusty" Breeding

1990-91	Ken and Joanne Caraker
1991-92	Sam and Ginny Paine
1992-93	Tom and Sheila Wilson
1993-94	Jim and Mary Mabe
1994-95	Jim and Doris Tanquary
1995-96	Herman and Doris Miller
1996-97	Chuck and Mercedes Town
1997-98	Doug and Beryl Shaylor

SYMPHONY ORCHESTRA, of Hendersonville

1971-72	Chan Harbour
1972-74	Jim Stokes
1974-76	Raymond Reed
1976-78	Jack H. Freeman
1978-80	John E. McLeod, Jr.
1980-82	Lynn K. Neill
1982-84	Flora Lawson
1984-86	Martha H. Irving
1986-87	Lynn K. Neill
1987-91	Frank Byrd
1991-93	Rebecca Boswell
1993-96	William Humleker
1996-98	Robert L. Cranford

TARHEEL PIECEMAKERS (Quilting)

1982-83	Jeanette Ledbetter
1984-85	Peggy Genung
1986	Marilou Kimble
1987	Ruth Challand
1988	Ruth Young
1989-90	Penny Murray
1991	Jeanette Ledbetter
1992-93	Nancy Rogers
1994-95	Donna Edwards
1996	Ruth Challand/ Peggy Genung
1997	Peggy Genung

UNITED WAY of Henderson County

1953	H.T. Randall, Executive Director
	C.M. Ogle, Board President
	Kermit Edney, Campaign Chairman
1954	Kermit Edney, Executive Director
	Jody Barber, Campaign Chairman
1955	H.T. Randall and W.A. Baxter, Board Presidents
	W.W. Martin, Jr. Campaign Chairman
1956	H.T. Randall
1957	C.V. Peck
1958	James H. McDuffie, Board President

UNITED WAY of Henderson County Cont.

	Robert Starnes, Campaign Chairman
1959	W.F. Stokes, Board President
	John W. Holley, Campaign Chairman
1960	John F. McLeod, Jr., Board President
	Edward F. Sykes, Campaign Chairman
1961	Calvert C. Hunt, Board President
	James Dishner, Campaign Chairman
1962-63	Bruce Drysdale, Board President
	William A. Baxter, Campaign Chairman
1964	Frank L. Hoyle, Jr., Board President
	John Holley, Campaign Chairman

NO FURTHER INFORMATION WAS AVAILABLE FROM THE UNITED WAY OFFICE.

VETERANS OF FOREIGN WARS, Hedrick Rhodes Post #5206

Year	Name
1946-47	Robert Stepp
1947-48	John Shepherd
1948-49	Allen E. Brown
1949-50	William E. Jamison
1950-51	Raymond English
1951-52	Jack Duzenbury
1952-53	Edward Mottsman
1953-54	William V. Powers
1954-55	Jimmie W. Bartlett
1955-56	W.T. Justice
1956-57	D.W. Culp
1957-58	Ed Hunnicutt
1958-59	J.J. Patterson
1959-60	O. Raymond Latt
1960-61	Grady T. Carland
1961-62	Charles L. Ray
1962-63	Frank Coiner
1963-64	Hubert Harrelson
1964-65	Ray Parkinson
1966-67	Leonard A. Boyles
1967-68	Bill Prim
1968-69	J.B. Maxwell
1969-70	J.R. Miller
1970-71	J.R. Heatherly
1971-72	Travis Brown
1972-73	Edward C. Thomas
1973-74	Walter M. Burgess
1974-75	Rufus "Pooch" Pace
1975-76	Fred O. Brooks
1976-77	Jack Lancaster
1977-78	Allan G. Purvis
1978-79	J.R. Miller
1979-80	John L. Crozier
1980-81	Eldon T. Owen
1981-82	Gaden Garren, Jr.
1982-83	Joe Stempien
1983-84	Fred Goode
1984-85	Steve Hollingsworth
1985-86	George Kaltenbach
1986-87	Joe Stempien
1987-89	Ray Parkinson
1989-90	Walter Burgess
1990-91	Robert Wood
1991-92	Walter Burgess
1992-93	Everette Israel
1993-95	Ray Perkinson
1995-96	Donald Rhodes
1996-97	Argie Taylor
1997-98	Fred Ray Christopher

VETERANS OF FOREIGN WARS AUXILIARY

Year	Name
1946-47	Virginia Jamison
1947-48	Margaret Lane
1948-50	Ruth Franklin
1950-51	Ann Crouch
1951-52	Mary Ruth Wilson
1952-53	Margaret Rhodes
1953-54	Ruth Hendrix
1954-55	Wilsie Staton
1955-56	Margaret Hargrove
1956-57	Louise Burgin
1957-58	Viginia Gillespie
1958-59	Zoda Mae Hawkins
1959-60	Gertrude Lowe
1960-61	Dot Torres
1961-62	Virginia Gillespie
1962-63	Mary Israel
1963-64	Margaret Schaeffer
1964-65	Margaret Rogers
1965-67	Gertrude Lowe
1967-68	Daphne Waddell
1968-69	Mary Israel
1969-70	Cleo Blakely
1970-71	Mary Israel
1971-72	Dillie Staton
1972-73	Inez Norman
1973-74	Julie Bergwall
1974-75	Jean Pace
1975-76	Fannie Gaynor
1976-77	Dot Grasnick Viera
1977-78	Virginia Thompson
1978-79	Ruby Lancaster
1979-80	Louise Taylor
1980-81	Daisy Edmundson
1981-82	Marie Fox
1982-85	Dillie Staton
1985-86	Dorothy Elsner
1986-87	Grace Blackwell
1987-88	Shirley Brewer
1988-89	Jean Goode

1989-90	Edna Cox Allison
1990-91	Elsie Richardson
1991-92	Hazel Ballard
1992-93	Shirley Brewer
1993-94	Dorothea Branner
1994-96	Emma Freeman
1996-97	Ruth Hoots
1997-98	Hazel Ballard

WESTERN CAROLINA COMMUNITY ACTION, INC. (WCCA), Henderson and Transylvania Counties

1965-66	Keith A. Arledge
1966-67	Dr. Braxton Harris
1967-68	Hugh Randall
1968-69	Mel Everingham
1969-70	Doyle Smith
1970-71	William C. Allred
1971-72	Homer McCall
1972-73	H.M. Pullin, Jr.
1973-75	Harrison E. Tawney
1975-76	W. Roy Robertson
1976-77	Mary Vaughn Mitchell
1977-78	Donald E. McCall
1978-79	Mary Ellen Mazanec
1979-80	Sam Mills
1980-82	Jere Hyder
1982-83	Rev. G.R. West
1983-84	Walter Shepherd
1984-85	Betsy Copolillo
1985-86	Paul Welch
1986-89	John Marable
1989-90	Herbert Coolidge
1990-91	Herbert Coolidge and John Marable
1991-93	Doyle Smith
1993-95	John Marable
1995-96	William Hudson
1996-97	Dan McGraw and Tina Nicholson

WELCOME WAGON (Junior)

1980	Sandy Pfeiffer
1982	Terry Wallace
1983	Carol Patwin
1984	Brenda McCleerey
1985	Mary Ann Cotterill
1986	Ronda McCorkle
1987	Vicki Gusse
1988	Delores Kowalski
1989	Jennifer Lund
1990	Michele Sparks
1991	Carol Cecilia
1992	Diane Lapp
1993	Debbie Koenekoop
1994	Janet Elwell
1995	Kelly Spangler and Bennie Santisteven

1996	Bennie Santisteven
1997	Nancy Bockhaus

WELCOME WAGON (Senior)

1961	Miss Ruth Hillhouse
1962	Mrs. Meade Morris
1963	Mrs. Godfrey Jacobi
1964	Mrs. Clarence Schneider
1965	Mrs. George Griffin
1966	Mrs. Maurice Hegarty
1967	Mrs. Lawrence Coxe
1968	Mrs. William P. Jones
1969	Mrs. Robert Barkley & Mrs. Charles Woods
1970	Mrs. Willie Alguire
1971	Mr. Harry E. Hurlburt
1972	Mr. R Douglass Esten
1973	Mr. R. Steele Phillips
1974	Mr. Robert Piper
1975	Mr. Howard Gorton
1976	Mr. Arthur Brubaker
1977	Mr. Ralph Gregory
1978	Mr. Robert Koppenhoefer
1979	Mr. Richard Blackburn

WELCOME WAGON (Senior), cont.

1980	Mr. William Bawden
1981	Mr. Conner Gunn
1982	Mr. Richard Lungren
1983	Mr. Leonard Raftree
1984	Mr. James Robertson
1985	Mrs. Bess Patrick
1986	Mr. Robert Scherner
1987	Mrs. Gloria Jordan
1988	Mr. Ted Docherty
1989	Mrs. Marjorie Kistener
1990	Mr. William Charlesworth
1991	Mr. James Saum
1992	Mr. Win McGrath
1993	Mrs. Anita Hanson
1994	Mr. George Hursig
1995	Mr. Steve Messer
1996	Mr. Donald Giersch
1997	Mr. James Ballard

WOMAN'S CLUB of Hendersonville

1915-16	Mrs. E.W. Ewbank
1916-17	Mrs. Michael Schenke
1917-18	Mrs. E. W. Ewbank
1918-20	Mrs. B.M. Colt
1920-22	Mrs. R. Kirk
1922-24	Mrs. Frank Ewbank
1924-25	Mrs. C.E. Rogers
1925-26	Mrs. George Wing
1926-29	Mrs. J.A. Rhodes
1929-32	Mrs. O.A. Meyers
1932-36	Mrs. J.S. Forrest
1936-38	Mrs. Albert Durham

WOMAN'S CLUB of Hendersonville cont.

1938-40	Mrs. H.W. Fuller
1940-41	Mrs. Edmund J. Ford
1941-46	Mrs. J. S. Forrest
1946-48	Mrs. H. W. Fuller
1949-50	Mrs. H.G. Love
1950-52	Mrs. Pleda Jackson
1952-54	Mrs. Hamilton Coleman
1954-56	Mrs. Pleda Jackson
1956-58	Mrs. Wade Britt
1958-60	Mrs. S.M. Garren
1960-61	Mrs. Craig Baker
1961-62	Mrs. J.S. Forrest
1962-66	Mrs. Hugh Bowden
1966-67	Mrs. Charles Grimes
1967-68	Mrs. Margaret Harte
1968-70	Mrs. Guy Tart
1970-72	Mrs. Bert Cantrell
1972-74	Mrs. Lon Goodson
1974-76	Mrs. Sam Padgett
1976-78	Miss L. Sparrenberger
1978-80	Mrs. Guy Tart
1980-82	Mrs. Daniel C. Nelson
1982-84	Mrs. Charles Spencer
1984-86	Mrs. Stanley Kamerick
1986-88	Mrs. C.M. King
1988-90	Miss Margaret Mantel
1990-93	Mrs. Stanley Kamerick
1994-95	Miss Margaret Mantel
1995-96	Mrs. Kenneth Nagle
1996-97	Mrs. James Cannon

WOMAN'S CLUB, Forrest

1955	Mrs. Gary Harthcock
1956-57	Mrs. William C. Beck
1959	Mrs. W.W. Martin
1960	Mrs. Hoke McWorter
1961	Mrs. J.B. Crowell
1962	Mrs. Burns Schaeffer
1963	Mrs. Ray A. Slider
1964	Mrs. Earl Martin
1965	Mrs. Robert Drake
1966	Unknown
1967	Mrs. Paul Council
1968	Mrs. James Lenz
1969	Mrs. Robert Whitmire
1970	Mrs. W.H. Stewart
1971	Mrs. Reuel Davis, Jr.
1972	Mrs. Robert Drake
1973	Mrs. W.H. Stewart
1974	Mrs. Robert Dodge &
	Mrs. Sam Williams
1975	Mrs. C.F. Eralndson
1976	Mrs. Joseph Cowling
1977	Mrs. W.W. Martin
1978	Mrs. Paul Yavorsky
1979	Mrs. William Killian
1980	Mrs. Ernest Zelnick
1981	Mrs. R.E. Harmon
1982	Mrs. Henry Rockhill
1983	Mrs. Elliot Jaquith
1984	Mrs. Gary Carter
1985-86	Mrs. Elmer Buller
1987	Mrs. Vincent Rend
1988	Mrs. James Volk
1989-90	Mrs. G. Ray Cantrell
1991-92	Mrs. James Crafton
1993-94	Mrs. Alfredo Calvo
1995-96	Mrs. Larry Wing
1997-98	Mrs. Jerry Boy

WOMANS CLUB, Possum Holler

1960-97	Jo Waggoner

Y.M.C.A. of Henderson County

1958	Boyce Whitmire
1959	Sidney Bakke
1960-61	James Dishner
1962	Lowell Leonard
1963	Don Godehn
1964	Jack Leaver
1965	Bill Gaffney
1967-68	Al Gough
1969	Bob Linder
1970	Frank Ewbank
1971	Sam Padgett
1972-73	T.D. Hunter, III
1974	Fred Neihoff
1975	R.C. Richards
1976-77	Richard Fravel
1978	Bill Benoit
1979	Ernest Zelnick
1980	Jay Angel
1981-82	Dennis Honnold
1983	Frank Jackson
1984-86	Don Godehn
1987-88	Bob Ross
1989	Hank Young
1990-91	Ervin Bazzle
1992	Roger Hill
1993	Rob Cranford
1994	Frank Aaron
1995	David Sink
1996	Tom Novak

WHKP/WKIT, Past and present employees

Management

Bob Amos
Art Cooley
Kermit Edney
Ed Leach
Bevo Middleton

Sales

Paul Adams
Alan Bridgeman
Ken Burke
Sylvia Ducote
Bill Edmundson

Powers English
Jack Hammette
Reg Hill
Cathy Honeycutt
John Horton
Shawn Lee
Karen Levi
Bob Marlowe
Nancy Prior McKinley
Jim Odom
Robert Orr
Meg Penny
Jack Ramsey
Richard Rhodes
Jim Sawyer
Bob Smith
Bob Staton
Grover Stepp
Carolyn Swanner
Anela Swadowniski
Norma Williams

Public Affairs and News
Henry Condrey
Tippy Creswell
John Dozier
Larry Freeman
Jennie Irvin
Kim Kappler
Allen Reese
Emilie Swearingen
Gwen Thorburg

Engineering
Harold Brown
Mike Edney
Les Gratick
Cliff Inman
Norman Lyda
Dick Pierce
Henry Stewart
Orrin Waters

Maintenance
Eugene Justice
Samuel Haywood
Lamar Owens
Freda and Larry Hall

Personalities
Mary Barber
Jo Kuykendall
Bill Prim
Jean Banks

Traffic and Bookkeeping
Marilyn Bennett Aiken
Mary Barnette Ashe
Margaret Baldwin
Charlotte Bertran
Charlotte Bertran
Glenda Hill Carland
Marge Duncan

Kerry Edney
Oma D. Edney
Wanda Flavell
Don Gilmore
Mary Chaney Gilreath
Laura Green
Jean Mace Henderson
Pat Houck
Betty Rogers Lee
Elsie Levi
Jane Moorhead
Janet O'Neill
Boyce Orr
Villa H. Freeman
Florence Patterson
Sarah Pressley
Frances Freese
Henrietta Hensley Sain
Grace Flynn Smith
Susan Sullivan
Dottie Tebb
Norma Winters

Announcing
Al Adams
Jay Angel
David Bivens
Ken Blackwell
Doug Brooks
Dave Brown
Rita Case
Bill Christie
Tim Cochran
Walt Corbin
Tom Edgerton
Carroll Farmer
Doug Ferris
Ed Fisher
James Freeman
Allison Ford
Chuck Gaines
Ken Garland
Frank Hartley
Chuck Henry
Carver Hill
Chuck Hill
Al Hope
Jan Huggins
Jerry King
Frank Laurens
Halle Lentini
Bob Marlowe
Bob McGarrity
Baxter Morris
Chris Morris
Jim McCauley
O. M. Marty Morgan
Don Munson
Jimmy Northington
Rod Ollis

**WHKP/WKIT, Past and present
employees cont.**
- Taz Painter
- Myron Pace
- Rocky Phillips
- Irvin Price
- Allen Reese
- Red Reid
- Bill Reilly
- Charles Renfrow
- Chris Stoney
- John Taylor
- Richard Waters
- Allen Wentworth
- Cactus Pete Williams
- Lydia Wilson
- Rick Wilson

Index